XI
)

THE AUTOBIOGRAPHY
OF
AN UNKNOWN INDIAN

✳ ———————————————

The first book by the author was extremely well received when it was published by Macmillan & Co. in 1951 :

"This is an extraordinary book. It is written by a Hindu of East Bengal who has never been in Europe,* yet with a command of English that is not exceeded by Mr. Nehru himself . . . . No other Indian self-portrait can compare, for interest or challenge, with this product of a tortured and assertive spirit.

– *Glasgow Herald*

* He did visit England and France in 1955 and wrote a book titled 'A PASSAGE TO ENGLAND'.

——————————————— ✳

The Autobiography of
AN UNKNOWN INDIAN

By
NIRAD C. CHAUDHURI

*"En vieillissant on devient
plus fou et plus sage"*
LA ROCHEFOUCAULD

JAICO PUBLISHING HOUSE
Mumbai ● Delhi ● Bangalore
Calcutta ● Hyderabad ● Chennai

Complete and unabridged by arrangement with :
Macmillan & Co. Ltd.,
London

The Autobiography of
AN UNKNOWN INDIAN
ISBN 81-7224-287-5

Tenth Jaico Impression : 1994
Eleventh Jaico Impression : 1994
Twelfth Jaico Impression : 1996
Thirteenth Jaico Impression : 1997
Fourteenth Jaico Impression : 1998
Fifteenth Jaico Impression : 1998
Sixteenth Jaico Impression : 1999

Published by:
Ashwin J. Shah
Jaico Publishing House
121, Mahatma Gandhi Road
Mumbai - 400 001.

Printed by :
Paras Printing Press
123, Adhyaru Ind. Estate,
Sunmill Compound,
Lower Parel,
Mumbai 400 013.

TO THE MEMORY OF THE
BRITISH EMPIRE IN INDIA
WHICH CONFERRED SUBJECTHOOD ON US
BUT WITHHELD CITIZENSHIP;
TO WHICH YET
EVERY ONE OF US THREW OUT THE CHALLENGE :
"CIVIS BRITANNICUS SUM"
BECAUSE
ALL THAT WAS GOOD AND LIVING
WITHIN US
WAS MADE, SHAPED, AND QUICKENED
BY THE SAME BRITISH RULE

" Here lies the happy man who was an islet of sensibility surrounded by the cool sense of his wife, friends, and children. "

CONTENTS

PREFACE

THIS BOOK describes the conditions in which an Indian grew to manhood in the early decades of the century. His adventures in the world, where at the end of the narrative he is left more stranded than making his way, have to remain unrecorded for the present. But the argument of the whole life so far as it has been lived is stated here in its completeness. The story I want to tell is the story of the struggle of a civilization with a hostile environment, in which the destiny of British rule in India became necessarily involved. My main intention is thus historical, and since I have written the account with the utmost honesty and accuracy of which I am capable, the intention in my mind has become mingled with the aspiration that the book may be regarded as a contribution to contemporary history.

I do not think that any apologies are expected from me for the autobiographical form of the book or for the presence in it of a good deal of egoistic matter. A man persuades himself best, and best convinces others, by means of his own experiences. Also, the reader is entitled to information about the character and idiosyncrasies of a man who offers him unfamiliar points of view and interpretations, so that knowledge being relative he can make allowance for what is called the personal equation. Lastly, I want a declaration of faith for myself, because after passing the age of fifty I am faced with the compulsion to write off all the years I have lived and begin life anew. My friends say I am a failure; and I dare say they will now think I am trying to excuse that failure: I will not concede the point. These recollections of mine are in no sense *des memoires d'outre-tombe*. If anyone so chooses he may call them *memoires d'outre-Manche* in a figurative sense, in the sense that, retreating before the *panzers* of the enemy who has seized my past life, I have decided to put between him and me, between apparent defeat and acceptance of defeat, a narrow but uncrossable strip of salt water. The battle is not given up.

I have written the book with the conscious object of reaching the English-speaking world. One part of this world may still retain some curiosity about the combination of man and geography which has worn out the British Empire in India; the people of another part may not be wholly uninterested in a country which will provide them as likely as not with their most harassing future burden. For both these classes of readers, however, I feel I ought to provide two explanations which they are likely to need at the outset.

In the first place, my personal development has in no wise been typical of a modern Indian of the twentieth century. It is certainly exceptional, and may even be unique. But I do not believe that on this account the value of my narrative as historical testimony is impaired. Rather, the independence of environment which I have always been driven to assert by an irrepressible impulse within me has given me a preternatural sensitiveness to it. In relation to modern Indian society I am like an aeroplane in relation to the earth. It can never rise so high as to be able to sever the terrestrial connexion, but its flight helps it to obtain a better view of the lie of the land.

Secondly, an unstated reservation underlies the whole of the book. It is the reservation that there are exceptions to every generalization. In a country like India, so vast and so populous, the individuals who form the exceptions may well run into millions. But in spite of the weight of their numbers taken independently they are negligible when pitted against the hundreds of millions who constitute the norm. It truth, they are utterly ineffective, not only on account of their dispersion, but also for another reason. The exceptional individuals within the general body of a nation fall into two kinds. To the first kind belong those who possess to an intenser degree the dominant and active qualities of the general mass, and constitute the faster-moving van of that mass in its futureward progression, whatever that may lead to–growth or decline. Very few people seem to realize that nations stand in need of leadership in order to perish or to rot away no less than to rise and achieve greatness. The exceptional men who play this evil role are mostly plebeians puissant in speech, who with plausible words anaesthetize their fellows to the agony of death or drive them like Gadarene swine over a precipice after conjuring up a screen of black magic to hide the trap of death from the wretched herd. There have been too many of them in recent times, and there still are only too many of them at the head of affairs in some of the leading countries of the world, for any naming of them to be necessary.

Besides this kind of exceptional men, of whom we have not a few in India, there are those of another kind, who for good or evil constitute the national opposition. The exceptions to whose existence I wanted to draw attention in this preface are those belonging to the second order. To my thinking, they are exceptions for the good, but since they are contending against the prevailing current they have less power to influence events than even the good German or the good Japanese had in controlling the destiny of their countries. I respect them, but I see no reason to refer to their existence every time I speak of the general trends in my country.

In conclusion I have the usual acknowledgement to make. There are very few of them, and even those I have to make are only to catalytic agents in the production of the book. My two elder sons, aged fourteen and thirteen when I began the book, have always given me encouragement and suffered me to read out to them long passages from the manuscript even when they did not understand the greater part of what was being inflicted on them; my third son, grown from eight to ten during the time taken to write the book, has laid on me the heavy burden of making a success of it by building many of his own hopes on that eventuality; a young nephew of mine, who has been brought up in the same environment as I was in my boyhood, or at all events in as much of it as has survived the lapse of forty years, has given me invaluable help, whenever I wanted to check my early recollections, by placing his experiences at my disposal for confirming my own; a small number of friends to whom the manuscript was read in portions, in thoughtless recourse to the practice which Gibbon calls modest and yet I have found to be prompted by vanity at every stage, have expressed interest in what they had to hear but have not, like the author's handy witness and the publisher's tiresome nuisance, urged me to the venture of publication. I am indebted to my publishers and their printers for suggestions which have eliminated a number of the mistakes natural to an author whose English was not learnt from Englishmen or in any English-speaking country. I must also thank two friends who generously assisted me in preparing the typescript, but who wish to remain unnamed. For all this help I am deeply grateful.

I am indebted to the following for permission to use quotations in the text: The Clarendon Press, Oxford, for the lines from *The Testament of Beauty,* by Robert Bridges; the Institute of Sociology and Messrs. Chapman and Hall, Ltd., for the passage from an essay by Dr. S. D. Stirk in *The German Mind and Outlook;* and the translator and Messrs. John Lane, The Bodley Head Ltd., for the lines from the *Paradiso* in Mr. John D. Sinclair's version of *The Divine Comedy.*

To my wife also I have acknowledgements to make, but none of the usual kind. Although it is not good form to cling to one's wife in society, I have noticed that in the world of book production most authors advertise a loyal adhesion to theirs. I am prevented from following their example by the good sense of mine, who has maintained only an objective interest in the book. In our journey through life together she has steadfastly refused to be intimidated by outward good fortune and outward bad fortune. In the same way she has refused to take seriously my high-falutin moods–my winged exultations as well as my fits of gloom. Extending this calm philosophy of life to the process of turning out this book she has ignored equally my abject fears and my self-flattering exuberances. She has organised and sustained a balanced regime for me and kept me on an even keel amidst the many torments and not fewer inconveniences of presentday living. Those who know what it means in these days to provide a husband with good food and similar amenities of life, and how necessary and yet how impossible it is for a man to ride on an even keel in the contemporary world, will understand my gratitude to my wife.

Out of all this emerges the idea of an epitaph for me: "Here lies the happy man who was an islet of sensibility surrounded by the cool sense of his wife, friends, and children."

NIRAD C. CHAUDHURI

BOOK I

EARLY ENVIRONMENT

PREFATORY NOTE

SINCE it has been laid down as the basic principle of this book that environment shall have precedence over its product, I shall begin by describing three places--places which exerted the deepest influence on my boyhood, and form, so to say, the buried foundations of my later life. My first account will thus be of the little country town in which I was born and lived till my twelfth year; my second, of my ancestral village; and my third, of the village of my mother's folk. These three accounts will make up the first three chapters of this book; but as England, evoked by imagination and enjoyed emotionally, has been as great an influence on me as any of the three places sensibly experienced, I shall add a fourth chapter to complete the description of the early environment of my life. That chapter will contain a summary of my boyish notions about England.

The only additional information I need give in this introductory note is that not more than six miles as the crow flies separated my birthplace from my ancestral village, both of which were in the same district of East Bengal–Mymensingh; but that my mother's village was some forty miles away, in the next district and across the great river Meghna.

"Who doth ambition shun,.

"And loves to live i' the sun,

"Seeking the food he eats,

"And pleased with what he gets,

"Come hither, come hither, come hither :

"Here shall he see

"No enemy

"But winter and rough weather."

CHAPTER I

MY BIRTHPLACE

KISHORGANJ, my birthplace, I have called a country town, but this description, I am afraid, will call up wholly wrong associations. The place had nothing of the English country town about it, if I am to judge by the illustrations I have seen and the descriptions I have read, these being my only sources of knowledge about England, since I have never been there, nor in fact anywhere outside my own country. Kishorganj was only a normal specimen of its class—one among a score of collections of tin-and-mat huts or sheds, comprising courts, offices, schools, shops and residential dwellings, which British administration had raised up in the green and brown spaces of East Bengal. It had come into existence as a municipal township in the sixties of the last century and was, in the terminology of British local government in India, a subdivisional headquarters, which meant that it was an administrative unit next to the principal town of the district where the collector resided.

I shall presently have something to say of the moral quality of our urban existence. But to begin with, let me give some idea of its physical aspect. Had there been aeroplanes in our boyhood the town would have had the same appearance to our eyes, when looked at from a height, say, of five hundred feet, as a patch of white and brown mushrooms in the grass below must have to a little bird perched on a tree. The white corrugated iron roofs were indeed too hard for the surrounding landscape, but this unattractive material had in my childhood just begun to oust the thatch. The brown mat walls, however, matched with the trees and the soil. Altogether, the town did not mark too hard a blotch on the soft countryside. Besides, the huts were flimsy. They creaked at almost every wind, and one strong cyclone was enough to obliterate the distinction between country and town. I myself, arriving home one dark night from Calcutta after the great cyclone of 1919, had very great difficulty in finding the town among the fallen trees.

THE RIVER AND THE RAINS

The town had grown around and along a visible thread, a three-stranded thread, which was formed by a little river with two roads running along its two banks. We inherited the tradition that the river once had its day, but what we saw was only its impoverished old age. Except during rains, when it was full to the brim and shining across its whole breadth of some two hundred yards between one road-bound bank and another, it was an emaciated channel where the water never was more than waist-deep and in most places only knee-deep. But we loved the stream. To compare small things with great, it was our Nile. Our town was the gift of the river. We drank its water, although this water never allowed us to see the sides or the bottom of the tumbler unless fetched very early in the morning. We bathed in the river, paddled in it, and when we got dry after our bath we looked fairer than we really were with a coat of fine white sand. Sometimes we even glinted in the sun, thanks to the presence in the sand of minute specks of mica. The cows and elephants of the town also bathed in the river but, as a rule, only after we had had our turn and never alongside us. Often we ran after our cow when the servant took her down for a wash. We took up the water in our folded hands and, sniffing it, found it charged with the acrid smell of cattle. We also looked on with delight when the elephant of Joyka, a near neighbour of ours, waded majestically into the river and disported herself in it. She had a young companion, not her own calf though, who also came with her on occasions and had his bathe in the river.

If we loved the river where it permitted even those of us who did not swim to take inconceivable liberties with it, we worshipped it where it was deep, and there were such spots. Just as an old family fallen on poverty happens to keep a few pieces of valuable antique furniture, so our decayed river had, every two or three miles of its course, a large pool where the water was deep, dark, still, and cool. There was one such pool within the town about half a mile from our house, just behind the excise depot and the Government treasury. It was an oval expanse of water where we often went to bathe and swim. At our strokes the water broke into white streaks resembling crushed ice, and we could never dive deep enough to touch the bottom. Once we took a sounding. Even quite close to the bank the water was twenty feet or a little more. The place was the home of the big and fierce-looking but silvery *chital* fish which at times nibbled at us. We were told by our elders, I cannot say whether truthfully or with the sole object of keeping us out of mischief, that in the middle of the pool these creatures attacked human beings in shoals. On the far bank stood thick clumps of very tall bamboo with a border of scrub near the water, and almost exactly opposite our ghat a sandy lane opened out like a funnel. Down this path peasant women with earthen pitchers appeared off and on out of the dark jungle, walked into the water and bent over it, filling their gurgling vessels. We could always see the gurgling although we could not hear it. After they had filled their pitchers the peasant women went away.

Brick buildings were such rarities in our parts that one dilapidated pile to be seen from the ghat about half a mile to the west made a deep impression on us. It was a half-ruined mosque, standing on a terrace jutting well forward into the bed of the river. Its outlines always stood out against the sky, and against the sunset they were etched more distinctly still.

The contrast between the general poverty and the few surviving heirlooms of our river vanished for about four months every year. During the monsoon season it filled out, became swift, or at all events moving, and permitted navigation all the way through. After the first few showers the narrow watercourse would begin to gain on the low meadows and mud-flats on either side and reach out towards its old and higher permanent banks. Little by little the water rose and became muddy as well as full of life. The first crowd to hold revels in it were the frogs. We heard their croaking throughout the day and throughout the night. Then arrived the leeches, which frightened us not so much by sticking to our shins, arms and backs as by the threat, imagined by us, of creeping into the body cavities, of whose existence and vulnerability children seem to be so acutely and painfully conscious. At the next stage of the rise of the river came large parties of peasants from the hamlets surrounding the town. They came with bamboo fishing cages and small fishing nets fixed to bamboo poles slung on their arms. They had flat and wide-brimmed leaf hats on the head, but nothing beyond the thinnest of modesty clouts below the belt. They ran into the water with loud shouts, scattered into small parties, and plunged and shoved in search of fish. They came in this manner every day until the water became too deep for fishing by this method.

Last of all came the boats which were the sight of the season we loved best. Every year they came like migratory birds, in twos and threes for the first few days and then in larger numbers. Some chose to be moored in unsociable isolation, some even midstream, but the majority preferred the appointed mooring-places, and lay huddled together. When the boat traffic got into its stride these places looked like small planta- tions of bamboo shorn of leaf, for the usual method of making these boats fast was to tie them by the bows to the bamboo poles with which they were propelled, after driving the poles deep into the muddy bottom of the river. In most cases the boats also had oars and masts, but the first were folded away for use in really deep water, while the masts were laid flat on the mat-and-bamboo roofs, since in the wooded areas about our town there never was enough wind to make sailing possible. Punting was the normal method of propulsion of these boats. They were all country boats, having the outlines and general shape of the model boats found in the tombs of the Middle Kingdom of Egypt. But they could be classed by function like modern steamers and by power of propulsion like the ancient galleys. The tramps had no roof and carried poor people, market produce, or even fish, according to chance or expediency. The others stuck fastidiously to their line, the passenger boats to passengers and the cargo boats to cargoes, each being exclusive in its way. They were always kept spick-and-span, for, as the boatmen were in the habit of saying, "The fortunes of boat and wench alike depend on the make-up." Even the smell of burning paddy-husk which always hung about them (owing to the braziers being kept perpetually burning to feed the *hookah*) was clean and astringent. In respect of power the boats were graded according to the number of boatmen they had. The smallest had only one boatman and were called "single-handers". The next class with two men passed as "double-handers", and the largest boats used for passenger traffic were the "three-handers". Ordinarily we travelled in these. They were our triremes.

During the day the boats were a pretty and friendly sight. At night they became something more, mysterious. They themselves could be seen only as blurred masses, for their little kerosene lamps could never break up the nearly solid darkness around them, but the reflections of these lamps seemed to set the fringes of the river on fire. When the water was still, there appeared to be an illumination going on two or three feet below the surface of the water, and with breezes and ripples swaying ladders, spirals and festoons of amber-coloured light made their appearance. I was sorry to hear that thousands and thousands of these boats had been ruthlessly destroyed at the time of the Japanese invasion scare of 1942.

A less companionable vessel also visited us occasionally. One of the annual or biennial visitors was the budgerow of Mr. Stapleton, the Inspector of Schools. As the house-boat stood moored a little stand-offishly, we, the boys, gaped at it in wonder. It seemed to be a palace in comparison not only with the other boats but also with our houses. But in spite of its beautiful lines, its red, white and green paint, and its essentially aquatic presence it was not, now that I recall the picture after more than forty years, quite in keeping with the surroundings.

A more congruous pageant was provided for us on one day of August or September, on which took place the grand boat race of the year. Scores of racing boats came for the occasion. They were open, narrow, and long boats, brightly painted on the sides with red, yellow, blue, green, and white floral or geometrical patterns, and with tigers, leopards, peacocks or dolphin heads on the bows and sterns. The crews, varying between ten and thirty men, sat in two rows, oars in hand. These oars too were painted, but they were not fixed like ordinary oars to the sides of the boats. They were small and carried in hand by the men, who alternately struck the gunwales with them to beat time to their boat-song and plunged them into the water. We gazed bewitched at the boats as they darted past us one after another to the accompaniment of tremendous chorus, and we trembled with suspense when the fantastic *Ootar* boat, which looked more like a rainbow floating upside down in the water than a boat, came gliding with its apparent disequilibrium in the path of the shooting racers. We thought it would turn turtle and go down. But of course it did not.

We watched the race from land as it was not considered safe for small children to venture out in a boat for fear of collisions. Once, however, we went out in a boat, although not at Kishorganj but near our ancestral village, where the waters were broader. While the boats raced in the gleaming midstream we dawdled in the darker backwaters, looking on the race and at the same time luxuriously trailing our hands and feet in water. We not only stroked both the kinds of water lily, the red and the white, which were to be found on our side, but tore up their succulent stalks, which dripped cool threads of water. It is a strange and in some ways a most revealing experience for a terrestrial creature like man to get into intimate tactile relationship with the weeds and plants of water.

If the picture on the river during the rainy season at Kishorganj was the Deluge and the Ark made homely, gregarious and sociable, we were no less steeped in the spirit of water on land. Everything was wet to the marrow of the bone. Neither we nor our clothes were ever properly dry. When we were not slushy we were damp. The bark of the trees became so sodden that it seemed we could tear it up in handfuls like moss. We could not walk from the hut which was our bed-and living-room to the hut which was our kitchen and dining-room except on a line of bricks laid at intervals of about two feet or on a gangway made of bamboos, and the meals were more often than not held up by unseasonable showers. Little rills were running off the road cutting miniature ravines in its sides. Our servants were always wet, and their brown skins were always shining.

The tremendous drenching power of the rain was brought home to us by the dripping, coming and going of our father and of our visitors, but above all by the sight of the birds. The ludicrously pitiable appearance of the crows in the rainy season is so notorious that the phrase "bedraggled crow" has become the figurative synonym in the Bengali language for an untidy and dishevelled person. Apart from crows I once had a glimpse of drenched birds which has sunk ineffaceably into my memory because at the time it struck something like terror into my mind. A tall and slender betel-nut palm had been brought down by a rainstorm. Among its leaves was a nest and in the nest a pair of pied mynas, dead and stiff. Their feathers had been clotted by rain into hard and thorny quills and these quills stood up thorn-like on the ghastly white skin.

But one of the most attractive and engaging sights of the season was to be seen in the inner courtyard of our house, when there was a heavy downpour. The rain came down in what looked like closely packed formations of enormously long pencils of glass and hit the bare ground. At first the pencils only pitted the sandy soil, but as soon as some water had collected all around they began to bounce off the surface of water and pop up and down in the form of minuscule puppets. Every square inch of ground seemed to receive one of the little things, and our waterlogged yard was broken up into a pattern which was not only mobile but dizzy in motion. As we sat on the veranda, myriads of tiny watery marionettes, each with an expanding circlet of water at its feet, gave us such a dancing display as we had never dreamt of seeing in actual life. It often went on for the best part of an hour but had a trick of stopping suddenly. No magic wand could make elves vanish more quickly. The crystalline throng was brushed off even before the rustle of rain ceased in our ears.

Another curious sight of the season was a palmyra, fan-palm, or toddy-palm, as it is variously called, standing in water midway between the two permanent banks of the river, exactly in front of our house. These trees normally grow on high ground, and there were seven of them in a straight line on the western side of the front lawn of our house. There was also one on the low meadow before it which once was the bed of the river and in our time became flooded in the monsoon season. How the palm had grown in that situation was a mystery, for during its childhood it must have been totally submerged for three or four months every year for many years. But there was no doubt that it had survived the unnatural experience. In our childhood it was a full-grown tree, with the lower seven or eight feet of its shaft under water during the rainy months. The spectacle did not strike me as unusual until I had revolved it over in my mind a good many years later. As children we took the palm's presence in the water for granted as part and parcel of the landscape to which we were born.

THE PROCESS OF THE SEASONS

From all that has been written so far the reader must be forming the notion that ours was a water-sprite's existence. It was not, except for about four months in the year. A revolution took place between mid-October and mid-November, which was like passing from Shakespeare's sea dirge to Webster's land dirge. If, as Charles Lamb has said, the first was of the water watery, the second, as Lamb has equally said, was of the earth earthy. Generally, by the middle of October the water was going down and ugly grey mud-flats coming up. These took about two to three weeks to be covered again with grass. By that time the road before our house also had dried up, hardened, and decomposed again, completing the half-cycle from ankle-deep mud to ankle-deep dust. We held this soft deep dust in great affection. It offered not simply the childish delight of being able to make dust castles, but something more profound. We felt the same contempt for those who walked on this road in shoes, missing so much and so much, as Mrs. Cornford has recorded for the fat white woman who walked through the fields in gloves. The best part of the pleasure of walking was to feel one's bare feet sinking in the dust, just as the keenest edge of the joy of kicking, that activity so natural in children and so essential for them, was in raising dust as high as the head. One of the reasons why as boys we looked down upon and disliked the *other bank*, as we always called the half of the town on the southern bank of the river, was that its main road was metalled; of course not metalled in the proper sense but given a foundation of smashed bricks, with the only result (so far as we could see) that pieces of brick with sharp edges and corners were showing all over the road surface. Our bare feet, when not cut or bruised by them, became sore if we had to walk on that road. Our road on the contrary was so sensitive that we could always tell which way people had gone by looking at the footprints. There never was any time of the day and night when the road did not show footmarks. But they pointed differently at different times. At midday, after the great litigious crowd had gone towards the courts, the toes all pointed westward, and in the early morning eastward. In addition, in every section of the road coinciding with each house-front, there were one or more bigger depressions, showing where the pariah dog or dogs belonging or voluntarily attaching themselves to that particular house had slept the night before.

Another sign of the transition from the wet to the dry season was to be seen in the immense number of jute-stem stacks standing on every field and lawn. After the bark which yields the fibre had been stripped off, the stems of the jute plant were dried and put to a variety of uses. Consisting of a white pithlike substance and being light, brittle, and inflammable, they were used for lighting fire; and being tall and rigid at the same time they were made into screens, partitions and the like with a stiffening of bamboo. Every household bought the year's supply at the end of the wet season, but before being put away the stems were given a thorough airing and drying. So they stood everywhere in white stacks eight to ten feet high, spread out at the bottom and tied at the top, and bearing some resemblance to the wigwams of Red Indians. We made narrow doors into them by pushing away some of the stems and hid within, either in the course of hide-and-seek or for sheer mischief.

Generally we got punished for this, not by our parents though, but by a more appropriate agency. These stacks were full of hairy caterpillars, and more often than not we emerged out of them with blisters on the most sensitive parts of our bare bodies. These creatures were the plague of our lives almost throughout the year. We usually could spot the bigger and the more fiery ones, but the smaller greyish things passed unnoticed and caused us excruciating tortures. The only remedy we knew of was to smear ourselves with a mixture of mustard oil and slaked lime, which although frequently put on us was considered by us to be as bad as, if not worse than, the disease.

The ordinary ants did not give us much trouble except that by giving us swollen lips they almost always betrayed us to our mother when we had stolen sugar from the store-room. But there was one species of big and poisonous red ants living in trees which gave us a mortal fright whenever we saw them. A salutary respect for them prevented our keeping the magpie robin which was the best songster we had, because this bird had to be fed on the larvae of the dreaded red ant. Yet we saw them but occasionally. A more persistent nuisance were the centipedes. There were many species of them, some big, brown and poisonous, but these too were comparatively rare. The commonest was the small lacquer-red species which curled itself up into a tight ring as soon as touched. When it was in that state we could pull it to pieces more easily than straighten it out. These centipedes were so common that the very first riddle we were asked and learned was about them. It ran:

> "There's a creature red in tint,
> Struck like rupees at the mint;
> His shanks number ninety-nine:
> I trow on him you chaps dine."

At first we were totally baffled by this conundrum. But when once we were told its meaning we always gleefully shouted "Centipede, centipede", whenever the question was put to us. It was this vermin and not snakes which we feared most when we lay in the grass or hay or straw. The general belief was that they crept into the ears and finally made their way into the brain causing all kinds of mental disorders. "To have a centipede in the head" was the equivalent in our parts to saying that a person was crazy or had inexplicable fads and crotchets. The expression was used jocularly, but it must have had its source in a primitive conviction which even grown-up men could not wholly shake off and women and children certainly had not. Our ears were always examined for centipedes after we had rolled or lain for some time in grass.

Towards the middle of November we celebrated the formal passing of the wet season and the coming of the cold by lighting bonfires. For ourselves we wished good to come and evil to depart, and for the flies, mosquitoes and other insects the most humiliating discomfiture. Then we witnessed a succession of happenings which revealed to us the inexorable process of the seasons. First of all, the municipal workmen cleaned up the ditch which ran from one end of the town to the other separating all the houses from the road. This ditch had to be spanned in every case by a small bridge, made in some instances of brick but more generally of bamboo and beaten earth. The weeds which had grown in it during the rains were torn up and then the sides and the bottom scraped till the soft brown earth stood exposed. The drain, about three feet wide and only slightly less in depth, was never filthy, for it carried nothing but rain water. We always crept along it in our games, and after and annual cleaning it was our favourite resort.

A similar weeding was given to our grounds, as at this time large droves of swine were passing through the town in their journeys from their monsoon quarters to their winter quarters (we had no precise idea where they were), we requested the swineherds to bring their animals into our grounds and get them to dig up and destroy the bulbous arum plants which had grown so plentifully during the rains. We did not, however, allow the pigs to plough up our inner courtyard. This square of some forty feet by as many feet was entrusted to a special workman who tore up every blade of grass individually. It was *de rigueur* in every self-respecting house-hold to keep the inner yard free of grass. To have even short stubbles of green showing there was as improper among us as it is to wear two-day-old stubbles of beard in English society.

About the same time one or two women were requisi-tioned to recondition our earthen floors. All our huts were built on platforms of beaten earth, about three feet high, the tops of which, without any kind of additional covering, constituted our floors. These floors were rubbed every morning with fresh mud and water in order to keep them firm and clean, and the sides too were given the same treatment almost every day. But during the monsoon the sides could not receive the same attention, if any at all, and so, at the end of the rains, they became rough, peeled, and in extreme cases even pot-holed. Ordinarily the senior servant or even my mother did this daily smearing, for it called for considerable skill and practice if the whole place was not to be made utterly messy. But my mother could hardly be expected to carry out the extensive renovation and the senior servant was a busy man, having to see to cooking and the meals. Accordingly, professional "mud-smearers" were sent for and they saw the job neatly through for a few annas.

These floors of ours call for some explanation but certainly no apologies. Although in our childhood, so far as the houses of the gentlefolk were concerned, mud floors were to be found only in our district and in one or two adjacent ones, we were carrying on a venerable tradition once established all over Bengal and very solidly. In later life, I read an old Bengali tract written to promote the cause of "female education", which unconsciously provided a mud floor for a royal palace. The pamphlet was written and published in 1822 and has thus a just claim to be called a Bengali incunabulum. Its writer was concerned with citing instances of female literacy from ancient Bengali history and chose no less an example than that of the daughter-in-law of the famous king of Bengal, Vallala Sena, and wife of the last indepedent Hindu king of Bengal, Lakshmana Sena. Lakshmana Sena as heir apparent, the story ran, had been sent on some expedition by his father and separated from his wife, and one rainy day the love-lorn princess could repress her anguish no more. So, while smearing with water and mud the place where the king, her father-in-law, was to have his midday meal, she forgot herself completely and scratched a few lines of verse on the mud floor. The quatrain was in Sanskrit, but here is a rough translation:

"Rumbling cloud and rustling rain,
Peacock's call: the same thing say–
Lord of Love shall crown this day,
Or Lord of Death shall end the pain."

The princess forgot to rub out the lines, and when the king came in to dine he read the verses and immediately understood the situation. He sent for his son and united the unhappy pair.

That was decisive enough in its day to prove that the last Hindu queen of Bengal knew her three R's, but to me, when I read the passage, the most valuable point was the historical justification the polemist had provided in it for our mud floors. What old Bengali tradition considered good enough for the palace of Vallala Sena was good enough, if not too good, for us. Incidentally, I found many Bengali ladies, including my mother, given to the habit of scratching on the mud floor. I never saw my mother scratching any poetry but I often saw her drawing very fine little designs of florets, peacock heads, elephants, or horses on the mud floor with her nails or a bamboo pin, when she was abstracted either from vexation or some other mental preoccupation. We, the children, however, were never allowed to tamper with the floor, which, to tell the truth, if given a free hand, we would fain have dug up like the wolf in Webster's poem.

To conclude the story of the pigs, occasionally they and their men encamped on the low meadow before our house. I particularly remember one big camp, in which there were women and children as well as men and, of course, the pigs, and which was pitched so elaborately that it had bamboo screens all around it. I have no recollection why the party stayed in the town but I have a vague feeling that it remained for about a week and did some business with the sweepers of the town, who took this occasion to replenish their piggeries. Despite the severest warning against going anywhere near the unclean animals we felt the profoundest interest in the sucking-pigs which were carried in bamboo baskets and were perpetually squealing. We were always hanging about the camp, and when a particularly shrill chorus of squeals reached our ears we threw ourselves with desperation on the screen in order to peer and find out what was happening inside. The word went round that the sucking-pigs were being killed and roasted. Thus, even without knowing anything about Charles Lamb's Chinese boy or Mrs. Beeton's recipe for roasting sucking-pigs, we were taking the road which led to the first and through the first to the second.

There was another encamping we very much looked forward to seeing in the cold season, but which, throughout the years of my childhood spent at Kishorganj, I saw only twice.

It was the encampment of the gypsies. We looked upon them with fascination and fear not only because extra police were posted to keep an eye on their comings and goings, but even more because it was reported to us that they caught and ate the malodorous animal which was almost legendary with us and which in our dialect was given a name which indiscriminately meant the civet as well as the polecat. And one day I saw with my own eyes a gypsy coming in with a hairy animal, swinging it by a striped tail, and flinging the furry bundle on the ground before his tent.

There was another thing in the gypsy camp which perhaps we admired even more, certainly not less. It was the ass. Asses are not native to East Bengal, nor are they kept or used there as domestic animals, so we never had a sight of asses before the gypsies brought them to our town for the first time. They were a delight to child and adult alike, and no okapi even could cause greater sensation. Their braying was listened to with even greater pleasure, and we should not have been surprised if like the oryx of legend the asses had stood in mystical ecstasy before the rising sun and sneezed. I have read that when the Hyksos brought the horse in Egypt, the Egyptians, previously unfamiliar with that noble animal, gave it the name–Ass of the East. We were disposed to call the ass the Horse of the West.

Many years afterwards my friend Tridib Chaudhuri confirmed to me this fact of general ignorance of the ass in East Bengal with a most interesting anecdote. One day, when I casually mentioned to him that we in East Bengal had no asses, he immediately remarked that he had been given conclusive proof of that unfamiliarity when he was in Deoli detention camp in Rajputana as a political prisoner. That was the camp where, between 1932 and 1937, some hundreds of Bengali young men had been kept in detention without trial for suspected complicity in terrorist activities. The first day Tridib Chaudhuri arrived there some previously arrived fellow-prisoners, who were from East Bengal, told him that at night they could hear the roaring of the lions at Kotah, kept in the menagerie of the Maharao, a famous Rajput prince.

My friend was naturally surprised, for Kotah was fifty-four miles away. But his new friends promised to wake him up at night and make him hear the lions. A little after midnight the tired young man was shaken to wakefulness and his companions whispered: "There, listen!" Tridib Chaudhuri, whose home was in West Bengal, was stupefied at first, then he cried out, "Why, it's only an ass braying." For this remark, taken as an unseasonable flippancy, he got only icy looks to begin with; had he not been a newcomer things would have gone very much farther. But the next morning brought his vindication. While he was walking with his companions near the edge of the camp, which was on a hill, he saw down below the hut of a *dhobi* or washerman, with a number of asses grazing nearby. As good fortune would have it, just at the moment one of the animals began to bray, and the enigma of the Kotah lions was finally solved.

That reminds me of our general ignorance about animals. Anything with a feline look and dashes of yellow and black in it was, and still is, a tiger of some sort or other. With inexplicable perversity we persisted in calling the common hare found at Kishorganj "spotted deer". In the fine zoological gardens of Calcutta not the least part of the entertainment is provided by the visitors with their imaginative wealth of observations. Listening with appearance of unconcern, I have heard all kinds of names applied to the puma and the jaguar and all sorts of mythical attributes set down to the credit of the brown bear, the oran, and the hippopotamus. But the story which deserves to be classical is about a father and son and a zebra, and was told to me by another friend. The little boy was standing before the zebra enclosure and he asked his father what the animals were. The father replied that they were

African tigers. The boy, who apparently had more wits than he was born with, protested: "But, father, they look like horses." The father began to scold the boy, when my friend unable to bear it any longer, intervened: "Sir," he said, "why are you scolding the boy? You must be familiar with the shape of that animal, although it has not got exactly your coloration." The father got more angry still and moved away growling that he was not going to be insulted before his son.

Another outstanding experience of the cold season was a folk-ritual which was performed every day for one whole month from the middle of January to the middle of February. It was a ritual for little girls, but it was very elaborate and if one was to draw the fullest benefit out of it it had to be performed for twelve years in succession. Therefore the girls began quite early in life, even at the age of three or four, so that they might see a substantial portion through before they were married off. But of course one could not speak of standards of performance before they had done it for some six or seven years, because the designs which had to be executed required skill in drawing. About twelve feet square or even more of the inner courtyard had to be covered with figures of the sun and the moon, floral decorations of various sorts, and big circles which had to be truly drawn. The palette was similar to that used by the Cromagnon man–dull red, black, and white, with only a greater preponderance of white. The actual colouring material used was, however, simpler than those at the disposal of later palaeolithic society, namely, brick dust instead of red peroxide of iron, charcoal dust instead of pyrolusite, and rice powder for white. The girls took the powders in handfuls, closed their fist, and released the colours through the hole formed by the curled little finger, regulating the flow by tightening or loosening their grip. It was wonderful to see how quickly they filled up the space. The sun was a staring face about two feet in diameter, the moon slightly smaller. The first was laid out mainly in red and black, producing a fiery effect, while the moon was for the most part in rice powder which very successfully brought out its blanched appearance. The floral decorations were of course *motifs* on which Bengali women had practised no one knows for how many generations, and they came out as quickly and neatly as if they were being done from stencils.

Two girls of the house next to ours, whose parents we called uncle and aunt following Bengali custom, performed this ritual. At dawn they had their plunge in the cold river and came back singing and shivering. We, the boys, quickly collected twigs, dry leaves, bamboo scrapings, even a log or two, and made a fire for them. After they had got a little warm the girls set to work and it went on till about ten o'clock. The girls chanted hymns to the sun and the moon which could be called a crude and rudimentary version of the canticles of St. Francis. We could not go near or touch them because, being unbathed, we were unclean, but we did our best to make ourselves serviceable in every possible way.

This account of the process of the seasons at Kishorganj should now be closed. The campings and the rituals I have described were the rubrics of the year. Simultaneously, the ordinary text, though less colourful, was not unrolling itself less absorbingly. We were almost wild with excitement when the trees bought to supply the year's firewood arrived on the shoulders of men or on carts. The boles and the branches with leaves, buds, and even fruit were piled high on the wayside, on the riverside slope of the road, to dry. We climbed on them, heaved the whole green mass up and down, suddenly let go, and slid down to the ground. This lasted for about ten days, by which time the leaves withered and dropped off, and then the branches were cut up into logs.

After the firewood it was the turn of the year's supply of straw for our cows. Newly cut straw is lighter in colour, stiffer, and more hollow than dry straw. It is also sharp. After a bout of climbing and rolling on straw we had very fine invisible scratches all over the body, and these smarted when we entered water. That was why we were usually warned off the straw. But we did not rate too high the price which we had to pay for making free love to it at its most lovable age.

The oranges from the Khasi Hils, which are rather small in size besides being smooth, thin-skinned, and very sweet, were our regular winter visitors. They were quite plentiful at Kishorganj, and the cold season was for us a season marked by the flavour, fragrance, and colour of oranges. Those were previtamin days, when the eating of oranges was pleasure and not a duty. The colour of the oranges was taken up by the gorgeous borders of African marigold *(Tagetes crecta)* or *Gainda,* as we called them, which was the most common and in my childhood the only cold-season annual we had. By chance I and two of my brothers had bright orange-coloured overcoats, and we stood in the sun in these overcoats every morning eating orange. Perhaps I ought to explain here that from the bare skin of summer we passed to more adequate clothing in the winter.

As soon as the cold was passing off, our typical flowers began to come out. In addition to the marigold we cultivated another annual, the balsam, which, however, was a flower of the rainy season. In the meanwhile one glorious cycle of our prized blooms had come and gone. It was a remarkable thing that both the opening of the flowering seasons in the spring and its final closing in the late autumn were marked by the same two flowers, two of the most deliciously scented flowers we had. They were the Night-blooming Flower of Sadness *(Nyctanthes arbortristis),* called *Sewlee* in Bengali, and the *Champa (Michelia champaca).* Whiffs of their heavy scent came borne on every little breeze to us. Starting from the spring we had, in a steady stream, all the kinds of jasmine, also the so-called Cape Jasmine which was not a jasmine at all but our *Gandharaj (Gardenia florida)*, the China Box or *Kamini (Murraya exotica)*, the ravishing *Bakul (Mimusops elengi)* with its creamy green flowerets, and the exquisite Tuberose, *Rajanigandha* or *Gul-shabu (Polianthes tuberosa)*. All these flowers, with the exception of the *Bakul* whose colour I have mentioned and the *Champa* which was pale golden yellow were pure white, with scents which would be considered overpowering by many. The great floral attraction of the rainy season was the *Kadamva (Anthocephalus cadamva)*, which one could regard as the link between our white scented flowers and coloured unscented flowers. It had only a very mild fragrance and its spherical flowers could be easily plucked bare of the innumerable white stamens to expose the orange core. The tall and large-leaved tree which bears this flower is famous in legend as that under which Krishna used to play his flute on the banks of the Jumna.

Among coloured flowers we had, of course, the highly perfumed Bussora rose, and the scentless hibiscus–the red, the light pink, and the pendulous; also the *Hibiscus mutabilis*, which we did not look upon as a hibiscus at all but called "land lotus", the ixora, and the canna. Curiously enough, we never had oleanders. What passed as oleander or *Karavi* with us was a yellow, nectar-bearing, bell-shaped flower, to whose mildly poisonous fruit hysterical women bent on spiting their husbands by committing suicide sometimes had recourse. We, the children, loved all the flowers equally well. But our elders never thought much of any of the coloured flowers except the red hibiscus which was indispensable for worshipping the goddess Kali. Even the sweet-smelling Bussora rose was out of court because it was looked upon as an Islamic flower. China had got accepted at our hands, but neither Iran nor Araby.

It was an essential part of our education to be able to weave garlands of three kinds of flower–the jasmine, the Night-blooming Flower of Sadness, and the Bakul. We sat still with needlefuls of thread pricking our way through the fine stalks of all these minute flowers. But when this task of infinite patience was over, we put the garlands round our neck for a few minutes and then tore them and threw them away on the ground to be trampled under foot. Our floors and inner courtyard in the summer were almost always strewn with the loose end of garlands.

It was not by flowers alone that the seasons were marked for us at Kishorganj. There was another visitor both at the beginning and end of the cold weather, but mostly at the beginning, whom we did not like though we did not know him well. One day my father, who was the Vice-Chairman of the municipality, would come home and say, "There's cholera on the other bank." We felt vaguely anxious and, going out on the road, stared long and thoughtfully at the other bank. What we generally saw were very low strips of smoke and mist on the meadow across the stream. We came gradually to half-associate cholera with those banks of smoke and mist. But there was another thing with which we wholly associated it, that being one of the regular sights of the cholera season. Every evening a municipal workman passed along the road swinging a censer-like pot in which sulphur was burning. Thus sulphur dioxide became firmly united in our sensations with cholera. We did not, however, know cholera at close quarters until our baby sister had it. Even then we were not allowed to approach the sickroom, although we were very curious to see what cholera was like. I saw a case with my own eyes only in 1913 and then I undestood what cholera really was.

OUR HOUSE

Before passing on to consider the citizens of Kishorganj and their ways I shall give some description of our house as well as of some of the outstanding attractions of the town. When I speak of our house in this part of the autobiography I always mean the house in which our family lived from 1903 to 1909. Soon after he had come to Kishorganj to practise as a lawyer my father had bought a small house in which four of his eldest surviving children were born. He also built another house in later life. But the biggish house he built in 1903 and sold in 1910 was *The House* for us when we were boys. It is this house which I am going to describe now.

Although larger than the general run of houses in the town, it was typical of all of them. The land on which the house stood was about two acres, with a frontage of about sixty yards. The plot was thus a deep one and it was divided up into three portions: the front or outer house, the inner house, and the back, which was orchard, bamboo plantation and waste land, mostly overgrown with weed. The real nucleus of the house was the inner courtyard, kept, as I have already related, religiously clean of grass. But there was a coconut tree in one corner of it. The coconut is a rather rare palm in our district and so the tree in our inner yard was not cut down at the time of building the house as I saw some guavas being.

On the western side of the inner court was a big hut with an open veranda in front, an enclosed veranda at the back, and an attached shed serving as a pantry and storeroom to the north. This hut was the general living and sitting-room for the family and the women visitors (the men visitors, unless very near relations, were not admitted to the inner house), it was also the bedroom of our parents and for some years of us the elder boys as well. We called this hut the West Hut. On the northern side of the yard was the kitchen, and on the east what we called the East Hut as well as Vegetarian Hut. The latter curious name became attached to the hut because, besides being the general lumber-room for everything from wooden chests to firewood, it was also assigned to our aunts and other widowed relations when they came to visit us. Hindu widows, as must be well known, take only vegetarian food and that too only once a day.

One big jack-fruit tree overhung the West Hut, tall bamboos the kitchen, and one *Bel* or Bengal quince *(Aegle marmelos)* and one mango the Vegetarian Hut. Some space was left behind the huts and more at the corners, and this space was utilised for a flower garden on the western side and the kitchen garden on the eastern. Our outer house too had the flower garden on the western side and the kitchen garden in the east. The north-eastern corner of the inner house was set apart for garbage, which collected for one year before being removed. But it was thoroughly scavenged of all organic matter by sweepers far more efficient than any employed by the municipality. After dark, and more especially in the evening after our meal, a tremendous racket was always going on on the garbage heap, with the jackals as one team and our pariah dogs the other. It was a most unnatural quarrel, in which the jackals instead of howling snarled and laughed like hyaenas and the dogs howled. It also seemed as if another animal at times joined in. It was, so far as our senses were concerned, a great snuffler at garbage. For we never saw it, or rather saw it only once at dusk as a striped animal with a long tail. We assumed it to be the famous *tigeralia* (no relative of tigers but possibly one of the mustelids), about which our servants were always talking, and went for it with our father's muzzle-loader. But it gave us the slip. The whole of the inner house together with the structures--that is to say, the inner yard, the huts, the flower garden, the kitchen garden, and the garbage heap--was shut in and enclosed on all sides by a seven-foot-high screen of bomboo, mat, jute-plant stem, and partly, corrugated iron. It constituted a self-contained world and landscape of its own.

For some years these huts, the three I have mentioned, were the only ones we had in the inner house. In 1907 another was added at the south-eastern corner, and it was allotted to the three elder boys as school and bedroom combined. Strictly speaking, it was an amphibious hut, belonging to the outer house by virtue of its front door through which our tutors entered, and to the inner house on account of its back door by which we went in and out. There was a story behind its building, and it is this.

We used to read with our tutors on one side of our father's office, that is, the big hut in the outer house, where he had dealings with his clients. As we worked on our books and exercises certain expressions were continuously reaching our ears, to which, inattentive at first, we began gradually to devote considerable thought and reflection. There were, in the first place, cetain numbers which were always being repeated–Section 7, Section 10 and so on, rising to three hundred and something. Then came some sonorous and highly Sanskritized Bengali words–inelegant colloquialisms appeared to have been banned in that office, "What is your case?" asked my father or his clerk. To give the English equivalent of the answer given by the client, the reply was, "Abduction, sir." "What is yours?" "Homicide." "Yours?" "Assault." "What yours?" "Cattle-lifting." "And yours?" "Violation, sir." So it went on, and the most interesting thing was that whenever the last word was pronounced there invariably was a sad and prim young woman hanging about the back door of the office.

We began to take vivid interest in these proceedings, and what reinforced their appeal was that while these words were being uttered our father generally kept turning over the pages of the most gorgeous book he had. It was a thick volume, with a bright green back and vermilion sides, the edges of which too were coloured in three separate sections, yellow, red, and green. In later years we discovered that the yellow section contained the Indian Penal Code and the green section the Criminal Procedure Code. I forget what the red section contained.

We also discovered that there was a lot of difference between the implication of one word and another. The more sonorous they were the more money did they seem to mean for our father. Our father's clerk, an elderly, grave, bearded, and deeply religious Brahmin, nodded approval when some of the most resounding words were being uttered, as if saying: "That is the job for us," while he looked unenthusiastic or even contemptuous at others. In addition, we came to regard a crowded morning for our father as a good sign and felt depressed if the hut was not filling up with clients at the accustomed speed. My father, while busy with his clients, must have been observing us. One day we overheard him saying to our mother, "The boys must have a hut to themselves, they are taking too much notice." Almost the next day the builders arrived and set to work on our new hut.

One characteristic of these huts was that they were neater to look at from the outside than the inside. When built by the hereditary craftsmen who had specialized on them for generations, they were not crude. On the contrary, they were quite fine examples of folk art, particularly the walls which were elaborately worked over with geometrical designs in fine strips of bamboo and cane. But the interiors naturally were less finished, for all the posts, the framework, the joints, and the knots had to be there and were there, and these made the insides look rather like the seamy side of clothes. What furnishings and furniture there were in them did wholly remove the stark impression, although they contributed a certain fulness.

The traditional furniture of these huts consisted in the first place of two or three beds, which were so large and heavy that at least four men were needed to move each of them, and which had low railings running all around with the exception of a gap in the middle of one side, the railings serving to prevent sleeping children from rolling down on the floor and the gap as entrance for grown-ups. There was also at least one big wooden box rather like a Tudon or Jacobean chest, and a number of wicker baskets ranging in size from a casket to a receptacle big enough to hold a man. They were used to keep all articles of toilet and apparel, as also everything valuable enough to stand in need of padlocked security. For hanging clothes in daily wear there were hangers of cloth-covered bamboo and coloured rope, suspended from the beams. For the greater part of the year the family's whole stock of quilts and coverlids also hung in rolls from the beams.

In our childhood all except the beds were in full retreat before more modern contraptions. We found a large wooden chest and a number of wicker baskets in exile in the Vegetarian Hut and promptly made them the object of destructive exploration. English steel trunks were the rage of the day. The ladies were not happy unless they could add at least one a year, and my father would buy my mother two or even three. But I shall permit myself no cheap sneer at these trunks, for one of them bought before my birth is still giving service, although it has gone through countless journeys and survived one devastating earthquake which smashed nearly all its fellows. These trunks were arranged in a line along the wall on wooden benches and were chained, first, to each other and, lastly, to the iron safe, of which there usually was one for each well-to-do family. Among our trunks one black, one yellow, and another maroon, made a striking colour scheme for us. The iron safe was painted bright green. The rope hangers had in our time been wholly replaced by wooden clothes-horses.

This was the standard furniture to be found in every home as in ours. But our father was something of a pioneer and so he had added a table with one single drawer, a dressing-mirror, a glass-fronted cupboard, and two racks with open shelves. Of chairs, there used always to be two or three rustic, because locally made, models for the office hut of every house, where they hung from the wall with their back legs fixed between it and a bamboo rail. We also had two in our father's office, but they were placed on the ground. For the West Hut, however–and that was the innovation–my father had imported from Dacca two American (or at all events, so we believed them to be) bent-wood chairs, called "bentoo" or "lady" chairs by us, and these were hung from bamboo rails to be brought down only for very important visitors. To sit on chairs as a matter of regular habit would have been regarded at Kishorganj in those days as a conscious parading of wealth bordering on snobbery.

We flattened our noses to take stock of the contents of the glass-fronted cupboard. On the two top shelves were three wax dolls, three coloured-shell caskets, a green, wire-reinforced bottle with an egg inside, two blue China vases with floral decorations, six silver-plated spoons in a knitted case, and a few other knick-nacks. The next shelf was given over to clothes, and the next lower contained books. Among the books the most prominent for their size or brightness were the Holy Bible in Bengali, Annanadale's *English Dictionary*, Milton's poetical works, Cunningham's *History of the Sikhs,* two volumes of Burke's speeches on the impeachment of Warren Hastings, Shakespeare's *Julius Caesar* and *Othello*–the latter in the American Hudson edition, a few novels by Bankim Chandra Chatterji, and two volumes of the poetical works of the first modern Bengali poet, Michael Madhusudan Dutt. Apart from these books in the cupboard there were two additional volumes bound in leather which received very special consideration from my mother and were kept by her on

her table or at the bedside like a breviary. One of them was a
volume of sacred songs called *Songs of Brahma,* while the
other, entitled *Pearl Necklace of Song,* contained secular
songs as well as songs addressed to the gods and goddesses of
the Hindu pantheon who had no place in the first and monotheistic volume. My father's law books were, of course, kept
in his office. A row of glass and earthen jars stood on the lowest
shelf of the cupboard.

If these huts contained anything by way of pictures they
were usually very tawdry images of the Hindu gods and
goddesses. Here too my father was adventurous. On a pair of
stag antlers above the front door of the West Hut rested a
coloured reproduction of Raphael's "Madonna della Sedia."
On one of the wooden posts hung a young girl clasping a dove
to her breast. The name of the painter of this picture was never
told to us, as was done very carefully in the case of the first.
Perhaps the name was not on the print. It certainly was not by
Greuze, for it had neither the refinement nor the sentimentality
of that cloying master. The young woman was quite robust and
straightforward. The third picture was of the boy Christ sitting
with a lamb. It was equally nameless. There ware two more
pictures, very large and gilt-framed, hanging symmetrically on
two sides of the back door of the West Hut. They were
panoramic pictures of the Boer War, one depicting the battle
of Paardeberg, the other the triumphal entry into Pretoria.

As we paced up and down within the West Hut or
squatted on its floor, these things were always meeting our
eyes, and they seemed never to pall on us. The impression was
so thoroughly fixed that I have been able to resuscitate the
interior with everything in its place without the slightest effort
of memory after more than forty years. I think I should be able
to point out the exact shade of grey-blue of the two volumes
of Burke's speeches on a colour card even now. But strong as
the visual impression was, it did not remain visual alone. If

what we saw with our eyes, and what was stamped indelibly on our visual memory, was like the formed head of a comet, what we thought and imagined was like the comet's refulgent tail. I shall have more to say about this subject later.

The West Hut had still another distinction. It possessed a complete ceiling, which entirely hid the pavilion-type corrugated iron roof from our eyes. The ceiling was of mat, and, as we admired it lying on our backs on the mud floor, an inscription on the central tie-beam always received our attention. It gave the date of building of the hut and besides contained a name. We read out the name in a loud voice – "Abdul Mirdha". It was the name of a Mussalman, and it was there because the hut had been built originally for a Mussalman of that name who lived on the outskirts of the town. The story we heard was that he had given offence to a powerful and aristocratic landowner, and the landowner in his rage had ordered the hut to be pulled down by elephants. So Abdul Mirdha, with the object of saving both his money and his hut, had sold the structure to my father, who had it taken down and transplanted. The name of Abdul Mirdha always reminded us of the adventurous early life of the West Hut. I have forgotten to record that the West Hut was the *North* Hut in the original smaller house in which we lived till 1903, and that it was transplanted for the second time in that year and rebuilt on our new estate. The poor thing had to submit to yet another transplantation after 1910, and then it passed finally into the possession of a Mussalman, a worthy yeoman peasant of the name of Laloo Mian.

But however fascinating the ceiling might be during the day, at night it became our terror. It housed any number of rats, and as soon as the lights were extinguished a deafening clatter began overhead. It was the civets, the weasels, and the polecats chasing the rats. Awakened by the noise, and lying sleepless, I wished to God that the long night would end, and the ferocious creatures depart from this terrifying proximity. When the light of dawn twinkled like stars through the pinholes in the mat walls I felt relieved. Night by itself was gloomy within the West Hut. For although we had glass table lamps burning paraffin, with coloured glass shades, they were put away on shelves, and the usual source of light was the dim immemorial earthen lamp burning mustard oil on a thread-like wick. It was placed on a tall brass stand of traditional design and was a cheerful enough object by itself. But it did not have the strength to dispel the child's eternal fear of darkness.

A FAIR AND TWO FESTIVALS

The town of Kishorganj was divided into two nearly equal halves by the river. But we did not think equally well of both. Actually, we were openly contemptuous of the *other bank.* This was not egoism, a tribute of vanity to our own presence on *this bank,* but an indication of the age of our boyhood, which was vastly different from the spririt of the present or contemporary age. The bazaars and all the important shops were on the other bank, which meant that it had the formidable backing of economics. Yet we could afford to look down upon it on the strength of religious, cultural, political, and aesthetic considerations. The temple of the goddess Kali, the most important Muslim prayer hall in the town, the Idgah where the annual Id prayers were said, the prayer hall of the Brahmos or reformed monotheistic Hindus, were all on our bank. So were the schools, the cricket ground, the public library, the government dispensary, and the hospital. And so were the courts, the treasury, the police station, the post office, and the dak bungalow. Above all, we had not spoilt our river front. The road running along the river on our side had been kept as a sort of strand. But on the other bank there were, except for a small section, houses on the riparian side of the road. It goes to the credit of our crude childish aesthetic sense that we condemned this turning of the back on the river as a mark of stupidity, and the presence of sanitary conveniences of these houses on the river we loathed as an abomination.

Another fact which prejudiced us against the other bank was the location there of the prostitute quarters, which was a concentrated collection of some thirty or forty small huts, enclosed on all sides, like our inner house, by a high screen. Although the servants, the shopkeepers, and other small fry seemed to take much interest in this part of the town, we hated the very sight of the screen, and we hated still more the simpering women whom at times we saw sailing out from behind the barrier. We felt indignant when they invaded our bank on a certain day in the week in order to go to the police station to register themselves, or at all events to comply with some formality of which we had no very clear idea. One day I rather overdid the horror. Standing with a number of play-mates on the road I suddenly saw a group of these women coming. I at once put my hands over my eyes and then, not satisfied with that, ran into a hut to keep myself hidden until the group had passed by. We, the boys, whether brother, cousins or playfellows, never discussed these women amongst our-selves. Whatever intercommunication we had on this subject took place through the inaudible language of look and expres-sion. But my conduct on that day proved too much for the normal decorousness of my companions. They at first looked embarrassed, and then ragged me as Lakshman, the brother of Rama of the Hindu epic, the *Ramayana,* who is supposed never to have cast his eyes on the face, or any other part of the body except the feet, of his sister-in-law Sita, although he had to attend her constantly.

Certainly, we would never have set foot of our free will on the other bank had it not been for one or two things. The first of them was the Quarter-to-Four-Anna House. This name has no mystery behind it at all, because it derives from a very common method of designating landed estates in East Bengal. The Hindu law of inheritance does not recognize primogeniture, nor does it permit entail. So all landed estates are eventually split up. But the undivided glory of the most important or famous ones enjoys a fictitious continuity through the custom of particularizing each succession estate as such and such a fraction of the original undivided property. And since fractions are popularly given in Bengal as parts of a rupee, the smaller estates resulting from the fissions come to be called so-many-anna portions of such an estate. Supposing I am referring to an estate in a village well known as the seat of an old landed family, I shall immediately be asked, "Which wing– Six-anna or Ten-anna?" The house at Kishorganj I am speaking about belonged to a land-owner who had come to inherit a quarter-to-four-anna share, or fifteen-sixty-fourths, of a big estate founded late in the eighteenth century or early in the nineteenth, and therefore it had acquired the name of Quarter-to-Four-Anna House.

The first attraction of the house was a tank which supplied the clearest and coolest drinking water to be found in the town. The water of the pool which I have described was also cool and clear, but being connected to a flowing stream it came under suspicion as a possible carrier of cholera from villages up-stream. The water of the Quarter-to-Four-Anna House was safe besides being cool and clear, and for this reason it was in great demand in the cholera season.

But the house drew us children for something which was very much more important in our eyes than any question of water. In its grounds was held the annual car festival of Krishna and the fair which accompanied it. Those who have read about the car of Juggernaut should now shed all their inhibitions. We had not read English accounts of the car festival. Consequently no fear of being crushed by its inhuman progression troubled our imagination. On the contrary, it was an occasion of which we had the most fervid expectation, happiest experience, and tenderest retrospect. Of course, we were not allowed to go near the car when it was being drawn, but we were sent to the fair in charge of a servant and with a special allowance of money expressly to see the sights and buy toys.

And then, even if the whole generation of grown-ups had immolated themselves under the car, I do not think that would have made much difference to the enjoyment of us, the children. It was *the* fair for boys and girls, with dolls of many bewildering varieties, as good to smell as to see. There was an immense number of the famous Bengali doll which went under the name of the Spoilt Baby. It was either bright pink or flaming scarlet and it was given an ample middle to indicate that it had been spoilt by the most efficient method of accomplishing that end we knew of in Bengal. As soon as we had made our selection the potter-stall-keeper brushed it over with a quick-drying varnish and handed it to us, and we walked on looking at and smelling the doll alternately.

Besides the dolls there were many other kinds of clay figures—cows, hounds with collar and chain, cats with mice in their mouths, birds and even reptiles, and, of course, fruits and vegetables. In another fair too, held in the neighbourhood earlier in the year, clay figures constituted the *piece de resistance,* but those were brick-red terracotta of very primitive design, like the figurines which are being dug up on almost every archaeolgical site in India, things so simple and immemorial as to be timeless, witness rather of the residuary simplicity of every succeeding age than of the sophistication of any. The dolls and figures of the car festical were on the other hand very realistic in colour and modelling. They gave us infinite pleasure because, not having acquired the self-consciousness which is necessary for a conscious appreciation of the primitive, we wanted to be raised above our natural primitiveness. So we always proudly took home a cow or a hound or a cat in addition to the Spoilt Baby.

The car festival takes place in the monsoon season. On this account there always was a great contrast between the crowded and colourful scene on the ground and the brooding cloudy solitudes overhead. I do not remember that any fair I went to was ever spoilt by a real monsoon downpour, but occasionally the grave sadness of the sky descended on us in very light sunstreaked showers or haze-like drizzle. On its part, the earth sent up its jollity crashing high into the air in the form of a tremendous din made by the blare of hundreds of palm-leaf trumpets. This was the occasion for which these trumpets were specially made. They were made of palmyra and sometimes of coconut leaves. Every boy had one or two of them. They blew them all day long. At first the elders scolded, then they entreated, but the unheeding boys blew on until the trumpets themselves, unable to stand the energy of young lungs, un-coiled and reverted to their original and innocent state of pleated leaf. The festival had an ineffable quality very difficult to express in words. However humbly or crudely it was gone through, it still had that idyllic note which is perhaps felt at its intensest in the miniature paintings of the Kanga or Pahari Rajput school devoted to the Krishna cycle.

I now come to a thing by virtue of which the other bank scored decisively over us. This was the great fair of the Swing Festival of Krishna, held on the southern outskirts of the town. This fair did something more than simply redeem the other bank in our eyes; it drew us irresistibly. With us it also drew almost everybody within fifteen to twenty miles of us. It was held annually during September and October. To it came not only all the local traders, all the craftmen of eastern Mymensingh, but also big merchants from Dacca and Narayanganj. Our yearning for luxuries, for acquisition, for display, nursed through the year and repressed for lack of opportunity, waited to be satisfied at the fair. To it went a not inconsiderable portion of the savings of those who were thrifty nd nearly all of those who were not.

Although of the utmost economic and social importance for our parts, the fair had its pleasantest feature in this, that it was mostly an array of superfluities; that is to say, of things which were not considered essential by our Kishorganj standard of living. The very first row to our left on entering the fair was formed by the stalls of book-binders. Whenever we went to the fair we found them busy. All the year's new purchases of the Koran and all the year's worn and damaged copies of the Koran were brought there for binding and rebinding and silvertooling. The Maulvis brought their copies of the *Bustan* and *Gulistan,* the less literate brought their collection of novelettes. This row was patronized entirely by Mussalmans. The fair, though held on account of a Hindu festival, drew Hindus and Mussalmans alike.

Another whole row was given over to violins, all countrymade, and hanging from long lines of rope like game at the poulterer's. The most remarkable thing about this violins was that no two of them seemed to be of the same colour. If one was pale yellow, the next one was golden yellow, the third golden brown, and the neighbour of the third of the shade of burnt sienna. The row next to the violins belonged to harmoniums, either at the stage of assembly or at the more advanced stage of trial and tuning. Quite at the southern end of the fair, a long row was occupied by the *chamars,* men of the skin-and leather-dresser caste, engaged in making drums. They made every kind of drums, the Bengali equivalent of bass drums, the kettle-drum, the tom-tom, *tablas* and *bayas* (small side drums like the timpani, used to beat time as well as to maintain a sort of rudimentary harmony with instruments and voice), but, above all, the earthern *mridang* or two-sided tuned drum which was indispensable for singing the praise of Krishna and the song cycle of his love for Radha or, to be more accurate, Radha's love for him. Judging by the number of musical instruments, our part of the world might have been part of the musical spheres. Before I saw this immense accumulation of instruments of various kinds I had no idea that we were so crushingly musical.

There were, of course, utilitarian goods at the fair, but even as such they were not goods of workaday use. If there were clothes they were mostly of silk. If there were caps they were of embroidered velvet or fine muslin. There were chairs, tables, and cupboards. The fair was purveyor of luxuries for us, luxuries of two kinds–first, things which, as I have said, were luxuries by virtue of being superfluous to the living of the daily life, and, next, things which were luxuries only because they were unobtainable throughout the rest of the year. We literally thirsted for both, and fortunately got them cheap at the fair. We made no distinction, till the nationalist movement came, between the goods made in the factories of Great Britain and those made by our handicraftsmen. We still judged goods, neither by their provenance nor by their method of production, but by their usefulness or appeal to us–the buyers. We paid equal attention to hand-made and machine-made goods, but personally speaking I rather neglected one row of handicrafts which I would give much to see again. It was the row of our native cabinet makers who made the chests of which I have spoken, in the rich golden timber of the jack-fruit tree. In our pride of English steel trunks and English-type tables and chairs we disdained the chests which in my childhood were still being made for villagers. I could not make amends in later life because the craft had died out. There is only one other observation about the fair which I have to make. It made an impression of almost oppressive abundance on me. Growing up in a region which was adding to its population at a remarkable rate I had some evidence before my eyes of the fecundity of man as procreator, but I had no idea, until I saw and got dazed by the fair of the Swing Festival, that he was equally fecund as a maker.

Life at Kishoreganj was calm, regular, businesslike. For the elders it meant absorption in profession and earning money; for the young, in education and acquisition of knowledge. Colour and movement but rarely broke into it. I have described two occasions when they did, and I am going to describe one more. It was the Id festival of the Mussalmans, which, although Hindu boys ourselves, we looked forward to with the keenest expectation.

I am not speaking of the actual congregational prayers which took place on a large field at the eastern end of the town reserved as an Idgah, because I never went there, or rather went only once on the shoulder of a servant so early in my life that nothing has survived in my mind except the impression of a crowd larger than any I had seen before. What we waited for and watched with intense interest after arriving at conscious-ness was the march of the common folk to the field of prayer, the passage of the elephant procession of the Muslim zamindar family, a senior member of which acted as the leader of the prayers, and the return of the ordinary people as well as the elephants. These three movements of the whole performance had different qualities, but taken together they formed an atriculated whole of us.

Since the Id moves backwards round the year it had no particular association with season and weather as had every Hindu festival, and this was important because in our percep-tion it liberated the Id from all relationship with the earth and its animistic emanations, which is so strongly felt as a feature of Hindu pantheism. It made us feel that this Muslim was half a purely human activity and half the activity of something transcending both man and the earth altogether. From early in the morning Muslim family groups began to pass eastward along the road before our house–old men, young men, children, all walking intently in a fashion which seemed to suggest that they had the goal of their journey always visible before their eyes. I was quite familiar with the normal features and expression of these peasants. I always saw them in large numbers on the two weekly market days we had at Kishorganj, once when they went towards the bazaar with the heavy loads and again in the evening when they returned home chatting and hallooing. But the impression was quite different on the Id day. Not only were they washed, anointed, and dressed in white, they underwent a more fundamental transformation. Their whole face and mien changed. They had their countenance stamped with the visible marks of the state which Pater has called "inward tacitness of mind", and, curiously enough, this was reflected in the looks of the children as well. Although, in contrast to their elders, they were colourfully dressed, yet their faces were solemn. Children are solemn. Nevertheless, no one, not even those who have studied the baby Christs of high renaissance painting in Italy, could have formed an adequate idea of how solemn children could be unless they had also seen the little Mussalman boys I saw.

At about ten o'clock all who were going to the prayers on foot had nearly passed and the marching line was thinning. Then we looked out for the elephant procession. We expected it to emerge from behind the trees and houses of the other bank, to our front and slightly to the right, and after that to roll down the steep ramp-like path which led towards the river from the raised embankment which carried the road of the other bank. The party always crossed the river before our house, mounted up the slope to the dusty road, and passed out of sight with quick swinging strides.

We were quite familiar with elephants and their gait. During the dry season our friend, the elephant of Joyka, was picketed to the palmyra tree on the low meadow before our house, about which I have written before, and she was always swinging to and fro and side to side, as with her trunk she ripped open the banana trees placed before her as food and swallowed her large mouthfuls. There were, besides her, the elephant of Laundh, the elephant of Gangatia, the elephant of Goojaddia, the elephant of Talijanga, the elephant of Masua (the tallest elephant I have ever seen), and the grand tusker of Mahinand, frequently passing before our house. So it was not the elephants by themselves which stirred us. It was the combination of the elephants, their rich trappings, and the aristocratic riders all rolling and swinging together, which made the sight memorable. The elephants were carefully washed for the occasion and painted on the forehead with a mixture of oil and lampblack, and the edges of the leaf-like painted area, which had its broad end between the ears and the apex between the eyes, were picked out in vermilion. Thus on that day they had a polished concinnity which was no attraction of their daily appearance. Their harness on that day was equally out of the ordinary. The fringed silk caparison hung low on both sides, dangling in and out and forward and backward with the motion of the animals. The richly dressed Mussalman zamindars sat above, swaying incessantly to keep their balance and move in rhythm with their mounts. If the car festival was evocative of the spirit of the pictures of the Hill Rajput school, this scene could be compared to the elephant pageants in Mogul miniatures. As we looked on it we tried to make out how his gorgeous and rollicking vision was connected with the earlier vision we had seen of grave men in hundreds marching towards the prayer field. We knew they were indissolubly connected, yet on the surface it was difficult to see the connexion.

In the third movement, the return, everybody and everything relaxed. The men talked, the children talked, and the zamindars looked tired and languid. The old men, the young men, and the children, all marched back westward, walking very briskly and looking very happy as if they had had all their desires fulfilled.

CITIZENS AND CITIZENSHIP

The promised examination of the spirit of our urban existence is going to be the conclusion of the account of my birthplace. We were born and brought up in the town and so took its way of life as *the* way and had no perception of any quality in it. Of course, we paid visits to other places, our ancestral village and our mother's village, for instance, and even to Calcutta, but these excursions made us aware only of the peculiarity of these other places, and when we returned to Kishorganj we felt as if we had come back to our native element. It was only my subsequent stay of thirty-two years in Calcutta which made me truly aware of Kishorganj. The experience of this great city helped me to bring up certain feelings of ours about the town from the subconscious to the conscious level, and I summarize below the result of this archaeological excavation in the domain of civic psychology.

Certainly, we had a sense of the city and citizenship in a very specialized form. When we went to our ancestral village, Banagram, we found that everybody whom we regarded as an equal was a blood relation of ours. We also discovered that whenever we asked a person of lower social position to work for us we did not think of having to pay him, but ordered him about by virtue of some right which seemed inherently and eternally to belong to us. Both these things were totally absent at Kishorganj. Although even there, following custom, we called our neighbours uncles or aunts, we were also fully aware that this was a courteous fiction. What we really felt was neighbourliness, friendliness for people with whom we had to live. As regards the workers, we knew perfectly well that they had to be paid. We were very accurately posted in the wages account of our parents and knew that the domestic servants were paid three rupees a month and the workmen four annas a day. I suppose on this score our urban relationships could be called social as distinct from tribal, and economic as distinct from feudal.

That made a vast difference between our rural and urban life. But that was not all and certainly not the subtlest part of the distinction. At Kishorganj we felt that there was a tie which was not created by the mere friendliness of a number of people towards one another, nor by their having to pay one another, but by some cohesive power belonging to the town in the abstract and exerting its influence on everybody who came to live in it. This feeling owed nothing to the position of Kishorganj as a unit of local government. In fact, although the town was wholly the creation of administrative necessity, the administrative machine seemed to be altogether a stranger in it. The town had liberated itself from its administrative swaddling clothes. The town was the town in its own right, claimed loyalty in its own right, annd made people feel drawn to one another on account of their common membership of the town. The relationship created by the town was distinct from, and in advance of, social and economic relationships. It was also more rarefied. It must have been a feeling of this kind which lay at the root of the Greek loyalty to the *polis*. It created, and at the same time rested on, a new awareness, the political. Perhaps others would prefer to employ the word *civic* in this context. Here, however, I am making no distinction between the derivative of the Greek word and that of the Latin, although the first has travelled a longer way than the second.

But who were the citizens? Certainly not everybody who lived in the town. My father, being, as I have already mentioned, the Vice-Chairman of the municipality, was familiar with the statistics of the town. He told us that the population of the municipal limits of Kishorganj, which included three suburbs in addition to the town proper, was sixteen thousand. This figure surprised us very much, for we had no idea that there were so many of us. But the real point was that while my father was speaking of all the human beings in the town we were thinking only of the citizens, who according to our notions were a very much more restricted body.

We excluded people from the category of citizens without regard for their wealth or position, in the light of a criterion which perhaps was not any the less right because it was sub-rational. For example, there was an old, wealthy, and influential Muslim zamindar family which lived on the outskirts of the town and was very much respected as well as looked up to. The head of this family was a legendary figure to us. We longed for a sight of him, but in our time he had ceased to come out. We were told that he could be found awake only at night and slept all through the day. He had the reputation of being a poet and a master of the most classical and chaste form of the Bengali language. He had once come to a public meeting and begun his address with the Bengali equivalent of the following sentence: "All that my erudite predecessor has enunciated is comprehensibility and ratiocination." He had given his name to our public library. Although his real name was Diwan Alimdad Khan, he was affectionately known to us and to everybody else as the *Dulaha Sahib*, or the "Worshipful Bridegroom", from the fact that he was not the actual owner of the estate but the husband of the daughter and heiress of the previous zamindar. But he was also the scion of one of the oldest and most respected Muslim families of East Bengal, a descendant of one of the twelve chieftains of Bengal at the time of Akbar. Yet neither he nor the other members of the family were considered as citizens by us.

We equally excluded another zamindar, the descendant of an old mercantile and landowning family of weaver caste, although our town itself bore the name of his most distinguished forebear, Kishorimohan Paramanik, who lived in the late eighteenth or early nineteenth century. This zamindar too was a legend to us. All that we knew about him was that he lived in a very high two-storied house, built of brick in the degenerate late Indo-Islamic style, whose windows were always kept closed and which stood on extensive grounds by the road which led to the fair of the Swing Festival. He died when we were young. One day, very early in the morning, a messenger came to my father saying that the old Paramanik Babu was dead and permission was requested from the munciipality to cremate him on his own grounds instead of in the public burning yard. My father as Vice-Chairman issued the permission. A day or two later we went and had a look at the blackened and cinder-strewn place where old Paramanik had been burnt, and the next year we saw a tall mausoleum being built on that site.

The top range of the exclusions comprised also the landowners resident in the town. With equal rigidity we excluded all Government officials. These magisterial and judicial functionaries—the officials posted in the smaller towns formed a very homogeneous type—I found in later life to be with some exceptions both conceited and uncultured. But we had no such pronounced feeling when we were young. The parental class had to meet them, address them, keep them pleased in the interest of their profession, but they seemed never to cultivate these dignitaries. Only occasionally did they speak of the professional competence or the good manners of some and of the incompetence and bad manners of others. Perhaps they proceeded on the principle of giving to Caesar only that which belonged to him. In any case so far as citizenship was concerned, these officials were *in* the town but not *of* it.

At the lower extremity all servants, workmen, shopkeepers, traders, clerks, in fact all the hewers of wood and drawers of water were excluded. Thus what remained in the privileged group of full citizens were the lawyers, the doctors (excluding the official assistant surgeon who was an appendage of the magisterial body), the teachers, and a few accepted *metoikoi* who by their loyalty to the town had deserved well of it–in all, not much more than a hundred families, considerably less than the legendary and sinister two hundred which at one time were supposed to rule France and the three hundred "kings" who constituted the Roman Senate.

Although there was in Kishorganj a very strict notion of citizenship there was no corresponding idea of its burdens. Political or public affairs did not interest anybody deeply and we did not share the Athenian contempt for those who pursued their private avocations without paying attention to public affairs. On this score great change has come over India, for today we are always political, everywhere political, and wholly political. Even a little shopkeeper's itch to cheat his customer has become intertwined with a formidable body of political doctrine. Perhaps I could best illustrate the difference by drawing attention to the change that has come over the associations of the word "meeting", which I often heard in my childhood. In the last thirty years or so it has come to suggest a seething conglomeration of drawn faces worked upon by an oratory stupid and puissant, empty and gripping at the same time. But I had formed an idea which was utterly different. My father fulfilled some public duties both in the municipality and as a member of the school committee. On certain mornings he would suddenly dismiss his clients saying, " I have to go to a meeting". He used the English word "meeting" and not its Bengali equivalent. We felt very curious and made inquiries on our own and as a result came to form the idea that a meeting was the confabulation of some half a dozen elderly gentlemen round a big table where they transacted some urgent business and had done with it in about an hour. That was about all we knew about meetings and public duties. The nationalist movement, whose coming in 1905 I shall describe later, made a great difference, but I cannot say that, apart from making the citizens of Kishorganj excited, it made them very constructive or industrious politically. Thus a citizen's life at Kishorganj in our childhood was overwhelmingly the pursuit of personal prosperity. We had not yet become political animals but were not on that account outside Aristotle's definition of man, for I have learnt recently that what Aristotle really wrote in Greek was that man was an animal who lived in a *polis*. We not only did that, we were also fully aware of the fact.

But there was one compensation for the ignoble privacy of our lives. If our lot forbade our reading our history in the nation's eyes, at all events it tried to make up by giving us some amenity of manners. Within the body of citizens there was a remarkable feeling of equality. Being Hindu or Muslim, high caste or low caste, Brahmin or non-Brahmin made no difference. Being rich or comparatively poor made some, but not such as would make the poorer man feel invidiously treated. It was somewhat of a surprise to see a society given entirely over to the business of making money showing such good taste in respect of differences of wealth. Perhaps the approximate equality of the means of most of the families had something to do with it. But over against that explanation was to be set the fact that we were not snobbish to inferiors either, not even to the sweepers and menials. There was nothing which was looked upon and judged with greater disapproval than the parading of wealth and expectation of flattery or obsequiousness from men of lower position. An otherwise most respectable gentleman of the town became its laughing-stock by his too obvious pleasure at being addressed like a grandee by workmen and traders. Of course this equality did not extend to commensality. If we, who were Kayasths, asked Brahmins to dinner (which we did) we had to get the cooking and waiting done by Brahmins; if on the other hand we asked Muslims (as also we did) we had to engage Muslim cooks and waiters, for a Muslim of position too would no more eat at the hands of a Hindu than a Hindu would do at his. But this was a matter which concerned religion, which nobody expected to be mixed up with the manners and customs of social life.

Another striking feature of the small urban community was that when we were young there did not appear to be any old men in it. Not only was the town not tyrannized over by a gerontocracy, it did not even possess a real *geron*. I do not remember a single really old face among those whom I have described as citizens. This was partly explained by the fact that these people who had come to Kishorganj to pursue their vocations had in almost every case an ancestral village home, as we also had, and they had, when their parents were living, left them behind in unimpaired patriarchal glory. But this did not wholly account for the absence of aged men among those who were carrying on professions at Kishorganj. The explanation for this was that it was only at the very end of the nineteenth century that the members of the landed families, or what could be called our squirearchy, were being driven to adopt professions through the pressure of circumstances. Not that there were not at Kishorganj professional men of an earlier generation, but besides being small in number, they had all retreated in the early 'nineties in the face of the new generation of profession in English. The upshot of all this was that at Kishorganj in the first years of the twentieth century all the men appeared to be in the prime of life. I know my father's age in

1900 was thirty-three; the oldest among his co-citizens could hardly have been more than ten years older.

The consequence of the parental generation at Kishorganj being of nearly the same age, and a relatively low age at that, was that the rising generation too had no great range of age. It was comprised almost wholly by children. In this case too I cannot think of more than half a dozen young men who were at college, or learning a profession. Those of us who were not too young to be sent to school were only at school. This meant that Kishorganj society was composed of only two tiers of population—men of early middle age and children, without the two other intervening, complementary tiers—young men and old men. The character of daily life at Kishorganj was determined necessarily by this fact.

It was a routine of steady, unremitting and regular work for everybody, all round the year, except during the two yearly vacations. We generally walked straight from the bed to the schoolroom, and sometimes were even awakened in bed to the news of the arrival of our tutors. The elders went out for a short stroll on their wooden clogs and at times stood together under a lamp-post on the roadside, talking with large and expressive gesture of the arms. Even when we were free, it was not permissible for us to approach the group. On the other hand, if we had to pass it on our way to the grocer's or on some other errand, we were expected to keep our eyes modestly fixed on the dust of the road, while being subjected ourselves to the most searching stare. After this short distraction the elders returned home, took their station in the office hut, and began their consultations with the clients. By far the largest number of the citizens were lawyers. At about half-past ten we started for school and a little later the elders for the courts. We came back from school at about half-past four and had a round of games, and then, as darkness fell, settled down again to our books. The elders, who returned home generally at dusk, gave

themselves different occupations: some had more consultations, a few did nothing, others taught their children.

It has to be said to the credit of our elders that they took
the education of their sons no less seriously than their own
profession, sometimes even more seriously and with disastrous results for the health of the boys. The lads were spurred
on with all kinds of anecdotes, parables and advice. I contracted a lifelong dislike for a most estimable relative of mine
by being told that he was such a conscientious student that he
never used the mosquito net, lest left in peace by the mosquitoes might overindulge himself in sleep, and also that before
examinations he tied his legs with a rope to the beam so that,
not being able to lie flat and in comfort on his bed, he might be
cogitating his books in a state of half-wakefulness. That
perhaps was an extreme case of self-discipline. What the boys
were more usually asked to do was to sprinkle their face with
water as soon as they began to nod, which they did pretty
frequently, being hungry and dead tired after the whole day's
work. If the sprinkle of water did not prove effective they were
occasionally given some slaps. Of course, that did not happen
very often, but they were never left in peace to doze. But as
against that it must also be set down that a clever boy had every
prospect of being spoilt not only by his parents but also by the
neighbours; and this too must be added, that if the elders did
not spare the boys no more did they spare themselves. They had
read too well the maxim of the old Hindu aphorist that the wise
man is he who pursues wealth and learning as if he were
immortal and ever young.

This does not mean, however, that wilder winds did not
beat on us from the outside world. The seasons, the weather,
and the festivals blew some happy breezes, as must have been
apparent from this account. I have now to tell a different story,
which suggested to us that if nature was beautiful it could also

be red in tooth and claw. It was no fear of names and beasts of prey which troubled us. We had very few snakes, and the two kinds we normally saw were proverbially the most innocuous ones, the imbecility of one of them being bruited even in Sanskrit fables. As regards the great cats, we heard the story that before our birth a leopard had once strayed into the town and taken shelter at daybreak in the office-hut of one of the Muslim lawyers who lived in our street. At alarm being given, an armed constable was sent for from the treasury to deal with the animal. As he was reconnoitring through a window the leopard jumped out and made off, without harm to itself but with the constable's turban in its paw.

On another occasion, after our birth, there was a serious tiger scare among our servants. One evening our calf, let loose to graze, had not come back, and just as the presence of smoke is taken in Sanskrit logic to be the proof of the presence of fire, the failure of the calf to turn up after dark was taken by our servants to be a sure indication of the presence of tiger in the neighbourhood. To confirm their suspicions, just at that moment some loud and deep noises were heard, and the servants in panic rushed into the kitchen. When the hubbub reached the ears of my father he came out and listened. He had no difficulty in identifying the noise with the beating of the earthen drum used for singing the praise of Krishna, of which I have spoken above. The strayed calf also bellowed the news of his return. That was the last we ever heard of tigers or of tiger scares in our time at Kishorganj.

What we actually saw and heard about was neither ophidian nor feline violence, but human. We heard no end of stories about dacoities and murders and saw evidence of both with our own eyes. From time to time corpses of murdered men wrapped up in mat were being carried along the road before our house for post morterm to the morgue or, as we called it without euphemism, the "corpse-cutting hut". More frequently, blood-smeared men sat nonchalantly in the office hut of my father, whose practice was wholly criminal. They always came without bandage or dressing on their wounds, with the blood clotted and the gashes staring, because to interfere with the wounds before the Government assistant surgeon had certified them would have had the likelihood of prejudicing their case, and in that state they sometimes walked even twenty miles from their villages. On occasions we also saw blood-stained axes, *daos,* and sickles. When the last got stained, it meant that the quarrel was over cutting the grain. And, of course, we heard a lot about abductions, rape, robberies, riots, and arson, but very little or nothing at all about theft.

Our town too had its share of murders, which rather startled us, for we regarded it as an oasis of peace. One of my first memories is that of a murder only two doors away. I could not have been more than five years old at the time. I had been sleeping well into the morning and was awakened by loud voices repeating : Gaurikanta Ray has been decapitated." I sat up on the bed with an alarmed conviction that somebody had been killed quite close to me. As if to give substance to this idea, there was a large patch of dry blood on the white sheet within my reach. I rubbed my fingers over it and felt that portion of the sheet to be rougher and stiffer than the rest. Was it the blood of Gaurikanta Ray, I wondered. This was the second murder in the town we were hearing about in two successive years. The year before, Bhairav Chaudhuri of the other bank had been murdered in his bed together with his wife. There was another notable murder in the town a few years later, whose story I shall relate in another chapter.

The common folk expected to be killed or maimed in open brawls. The dread of the gentlefolk was about being killed in bed while asleep or assassinated when out after dark. The night was generally regarded as a time of extreme insecurity, and so far from sleeping in the open in the hot season, people did not even keep their windows open. A light was kept burning throughout the night. Every door and every window was barred and bolted, and the master of the house was expected to remain in a state of half wakefulness. He was reminded of this duty by the constable on the night watch. As they passed the houses in their beats in the course of their rounds, they stopped at intervals and sent forth the piercing yell: "O householder, wake up."

The precautions taken against murder by two of my father's friends who were staying with us when we were very young was the stock joke of the family. One afternoon, a stranger turned up from somewhere and begged for some food and shelter for the night. My mother, hearing of this from the servants, consented, as enjoined by the established tradition of hospitality. My father, when he returned home late in the evening, did not quite like it, but there was no question of the man being turned out since consent had once been given. The affair was liked still less by the friends of my father who were to undertake the more direct risk of sleeping with the man in the office-hut. The more they discussed him the more they recollected that he had red eyes, a downcast look, and a twitching mouth, all supposed to be the signs of a murderer.

At last what they decided to do in their desperation was to wind their knitted comforters round their necks in tight and thick folds so that, even if set upon, their throats might not be cut so quickly that they would not wake up before everything was finished and be unable to put up a last fight. The special solicitude about the neck was due to the fact that the classical method for killing a man in our parts was not to put a knife into him but to sever his neck. A village notorious for waylaying and killing those who passed by it at night was given the expressive name of *Galakata* or "neck-severer".

My father's friends lived to see another day. But the stranger had departed before daylight, which confirmed them in their theory that he was a murderer, although the others teased them for many days over their recourse to the comforter. But it was not all joke. Even as late as 1920, when I was at Kishorganj, I found an old couple who were my relatives, dividing the night into two watches and sitting up by turns. In the same year I too, perhaps unconsciously influenced by the tradition, went out for my evening walks with a hatchet under my shawl, and never felt ashamed of this act of stupidity. Rather, at the time, I felt reassured by it.

I never got the same first-hand, vivid, and personal impression of the avarice of man as I did of his violence. The lawyers at Kishorganj belonged to two groups. Those of the first group had higher academic and professional qualifications and were called *ukils* in Bengali, or pleaders in English. The other group was composed of what are called *muktears*, for which there is no English equivalent. Though there was nothing to prevent the pleaders from taking up all kinds of cases, at Kishorganj, by convention, they did not accept criminal cases, which were conducted wholly by *muktears*. My father was a *muktear* and therefore I saw plenty of criminal cases, but I did not have the same opportunity for observing civil cases.

It was in these cases that the middle-class could be best studied. If criminal litigation was the passion of the peasant the landowner's was civil litigation. These gentry seemed always to be in a state which signified their being cheated of lawful dues. When the frenzy came upon them nothing could prevent their ruining themselves by law-suits. If the lawyer himself, who at times was disgusted by the exhibition, tried to counsel moderation he was set down as a dunce and sometimes even worse, the recipient of bribes from the other side. But, as I have already said, I never got any real or full insight into the workings of this side of human nature except what, by being born into a landed family and marrying sisters and cousins into landed families, I came to learn by indirect observation.

The many-sided world which lay around us was, in one of its aspects, a world of murder, assault, robbery, arson, rape abduction; and, in another, a world of disputed inheritance, contested possession, misappropriation of money, betrayal of widows and minors, forged will, and purloined title-deeds. But there was consolation and security in the clear feeling which all of us had that these terrifying aspects of the world constituted only a thin layer between two more solid ones. The layer of simmering greed and violence which preyed on our peace of mind seemed to rest on a rock-like foundation of quite different composition never permeated or corrupted by it. We called this lower stratum religion and morality, things in which everybody believed and things to which in the last resort everybody returned. Overhead there appeared to be, coinciding with the sky, an immutable sphere of justice and order, brooding sleeplessly over what was happening below, and swooping down on it when certain limits were passed. Its arm seemed to be long and all-powerful, and it passed by different names among us. The common people still called it the Company, others Queen Victoria, and the educated the Government. The feeling, thus ever present, of there being a watching and protecting Government above us vanished at one stroke with the coming of the nationalist agitation in 1905. After that we thought of the Government, in so far as we thought of it in the abstract, as an agency of oppression and usurpation. None the less, although deprived of its subjective halo, the protective power survived for many more decades. Today everything is giving way. The thing overhead, once believed to be immutable, has blown up, and the primordial foundation of rock below, on which we thought we had our feet firmly planted, is rotting into dust.

CHAPTER II

MY ANCESTRAL VILLAGE

I HAVE already mentioned that the name of our ancestral village was Banagram. We paid at least one regular annual visit to the village, and that took place between the last week of September and last week of October, depending on the date of the great Bengali Hindu festival of Durga Puja or worship of the goddess Durga, wife of Siva. My father had a holiday of twelve days for this festival. Occasionally we went to Banagram to spend the Christmas holidays also, besides attending the weddings of our relatives when there were any.

THE CLAN AND BLOOD

Our grandparents had died before any of us were born. My father had no surviving brothers and no unmarried sisters. Therefore the relations who shared the same house with us at Banagram were all representatives of collateral lines. To use the Anglicized jargon of Hindu law, there were five "co-shares" of the house, constituting in reality five distinct families. The head of the first of these and titular head of the whole joint family was a first cousin of my father's, considerably older than he. The second family was headed by a son of another first cousin, or a nephew of my father by relationship. But this gentlman was at least ten years my father's senior. The third family was that of the stepbrother of the head of the second, a man younger than my father. The fourth had no male head. It comprised a lady, whom we called Aunt Sushila because she was a second cousin of my father, and her two children—a boy and a girl. She had the rare misfortune for a married Hindu woman of being deserted by her husband, although she was his only wife. Attached to her part of the house were two widows, whom we called the Grand-aunt of the Eastern Hut and the Grand-aunt of the Western Hut respectively. The fifth family was ours, and its special distinction was that while all the others were resident we were the absentee landlords.

Although this group of five families maintained the outward appearance of one joint family it really was not so, because after the death of the last representative of the old generation all the more important properties, or at all events such portions of them as had been left unsquandered by that extravagant and lazy generation, had been divided among the heirs. The homestead, too, had been allotted in clearly demarcated portions to each of the five families. But still certain parts of the outer house, and more particularly those used for sacerdotal purposes, and certain religious endowments of which we were the trustees, had remained joint. I am afraid all this is becoming very complicated, and, in fact, the division of property cannot be made clear without an elaborate family tree and an excursus on the Hindu law of inheritance. I would therefore omit further details. But there is one point which I ought to stress. Although connected by somewhat distant blood-relationships, and comprising in 1905 some thirty souls without counting the visiting relatives like the married daughters of the family and their children staying on a more or less semi-permanent footing, the tribal camp did have a genuine sense of kinship and gave a very pleasing exhibition of the fellow-feeling of its members.

All told, the periods of our stay at Banagram during the ten years from 1900 to 1909 could hardly have added up to six months. But the hold which our ancestral village had on us was not to be measured by the length of our direct contact with it. In the first place Banagram influenced us by contrast, by being totally different in appearance and spirit from Kishorganj, and, what was more, it was present with us even at Kishorganj.

This presence was not a thing which we the children alone felt. In fact, born and brought up at Kishorganj as most of the children of the town were, they would not have had the feeling at all had they not seen it in their elders and imbibed it from them. The ancestral village seemed always to be present in the minds of the grown-ups. Most of them had acquired extensive properties at Kishorganj. They had also acquired, as I have already described, some sense of citizenship. Yet I hardly remember one single adult who thought of his Kishorganj life as his whole life, who considered it in the light of anything but a sojourn, who appraised it as anything better than the utilitarian cutting edge or boring point of an immense shaft whose main body, fulcrum, and bearings rested elsewhere. In our perception of duration Kishorganj life was ever the fleeting present, and the past and the future belonged to the ancestral village. Our life offered no analogy to the life of an English gentleman of a bygone age, distributed between his town and his country house. The feeling which our elders had of the relative importance of their existence at Kishorganj and in their ancestral village cannot be described even by bringing in the parallel of the tree and its roots, of a house and its foundations, or of a bridge and its submerged piers, for in all these cases the buried parts exist for the superficial, or at all events are not more important. The immensely greater importance of the absent life was of the very essence of the matter in respect of our life at Kishorganj placed against our life in the ancestral village. We have to think of something like the stair or escalator heads of an underground railway existing solely to serve what lies below, in order to get a proper parallel of the ralationship I am speaking of.

This feeling was so strong that neither child nor adult at Kishorganj ever applied to his Kishorganj house the Bengali equivalent of the word *home*. The town house was only a *basha* (familiarized in a slightly different meaning by the Arakan campaign in the last war), a word which was conventionally rendered by us into English as *lodge*, while actually it conveyed the suggestion of temporary lodgings. Some of the families went further and gave material expression to their singleminded loyalty to the village home by calling their town house the *Lodge* of such and such a village. In addition, the distinction was preserved even in our use of English. In our English lessons and attempts at English conversation we replied "Banagram" when asked "Where do you *live*" and "Kishorganj" only when the question was put in the form, "Where do you *lodge*?" The example of the elders made the children think of themselves at Kishorganj as trailing clouds of glory come from the village which was their home. It was a remarkable tribute to the power of the old tradition that through it even the children's feeling for the place where they were born, in which they were steeped, and which seemed all in all to them, was swamped at times, and accompanied always, by the loyalty to the absent village.

As soon as we arrived at Banagram we became aware of blood, aware not only of its power to make us feel superior to other men, but also of its immeasurable capacity to bring men together. The demonstration was given in space as well as time. At Kishorganj we passed out of blood kinship as soon as we passed the bounds of our house. At Banagram we could never find a house or place where there was not at least one uncle, nephew or cousin. Furthermore, at five years old I was the uncle of half a dozen grown-ups and was addressed as such by them. At twelve I became the grand-uncle of a baby which was not so very far removed from me by filiation. Nothing disappointed me more in 1907 at the age of nine than not to have been permitted to go near a bride, in fact to have been turned out after having sneaked into the room in which she was, because her status in relation to mine was that of a daughter-in-law. I saw not only relatives but relatives two generations in advance of me.

The past generation was not physically in evidence in the same manner. As chance would have it, at Banagram, when we were young, nobody was left alive from the generation next above our parents. Or to be more accurate, only a few widows were surviving, but they did not belong to the older generation by virtue of their age; they belonged to it only because they had been the young wives of their very much older husbands. Despite this, the presence of the ancestors was quite masterfully felt. At Kishorganj our genealogy, like every other boy's, stopped at the father. The story ended with the assertion that Nirad Chaudhuri was the son of Upendra Narayan Chaudhuri. Not so at Banagram. There not only did we know, but we repeated as a catechism : "Nirad Chaudhuri is the son of Upendra Narayan Chaudhuri, who is the son of Krishna Narayan Chaudhuri, who was the son of Lakshmi Narayan Chaudhuri, who was the son of Kirti Narayan Chaudhuri, who was the son of Chandra Narayan Chaudhuri," and so on, to the fourteenth generation.

Not only was the descent in a straight line of Nirad Chaudhuri known, but also that of every collateral relative. We knew all about the brothers of Kirti Narayan and their descendants, the brothers of Lakshmi Narayan and their descendants, and the brothers of Krishna Narayan and their descendants. Knowing the exact lineage of every old man, every middle-aged man, every young man, every boy, every child, and every baby around us we saw the relationships so graphically worked out that the human beings whom we saw appeared to be no longer human beings but fruits hanging from the tiered and spreading branches of a tree.

The spirit of the old was inculcated into us through any number of anecdotes told to us by the matrons. We were told how my father went about naked when my senior-most aunt came into the family as a young bride and how he never wore anything but a few gold ornaments till he was about ten. We learned how artistic, generous, and patient my grandfather was. If he found one strip of bamboo out of the straight in a newly made mat wall he would have the whole thing pulled to pieces and rebuilt, and if he noticed even one twig of the tall climbing jasmine trailing untidily he would immediately send for the gardener and have it arranged properly. He also composed verse. We came to know further that he would put his signature to any document his relatives put before him without inquiring what commitments he was undertaking and that when abused from behind a screen by my hot-tempered and more practical grandmother for these acts of indiscreet magnanimity, he would still sit on his favourite low stool as if he were a statue.

We learned in addition that Kamal Narayan Chaudhuri was a little weak-headed; Aradhan Chaudhuri shiftless and extravagant, but that as long as the imperious and masterful Dharma Narayan was living nothing had gone wrong in the family. Two anecdotes of old Dharma Narayan impressed us deeply. One day his young son, who in our time was head of the family, wanted to say something to him. "Father," he began. Dharma Narayan paid no heed. "Father", repeated the boy. Still there was no reply. "Father," cried the boy for the third time. The limits of patience of the old man were reached and he thundered out: "Do not keep mumbling that word like the spawn of the rabble." We were told that from that day till the death of Dharma Narayan nobody heard the word "father" from his son. It should be borne in mind that even in our childhood it was not good form in the more orthodox families to address one's father except as "Sir". To descend to anything so familiar as the Bengali equivalent of papa or daddy, as became usual in later Bengali society, was of course inconceivable.

The other anecdote about Dharma Narayan showed and illustrated his faith in the dictum, *nobless oblige*. One day, when coming in to dine in the inner house, he noticed a young vegetable plant, a gourd or something of that sort, growing in one corner of the yard. "Who has planted that thing?" he asked. Everybody felt that something was wrong and tried to avoid responsibility. At last one of the daughters-in-law was mentioned, since she could not with propriety be taken notice of by the old man. He heard the name and ordered, "Pull it up. If I begin to grow vegetable in my house where will the peasants sell them?"

There were anecdotes about my ancestresses as well, and in them my own grandmother, another imperious personality, figured prominently. She had found a hoard of gold and silver coins in an earthen vessel buried under the ground just behind her hut. She believed that it had brought her ill-luck, for after that find all her babies are stillborn or died soon after birth. But she was able with this money to educate her son, my father, when, fallen on difficult days, my grandfather would simply shut his eyes and ears if asked to do anything. I saw quite a number of these gold and silver coins with my mother, to whom the old lady had left what was saved after the expenses of educating my father. They were very heavy and very finely worked, and certainly dated from the best days of Mogul rule.

One anecdote showed my grandmother's notoriously sharp tongue at its worst. After she had had her say at her husband from behind her screen one day she seemed to expect some reply, but my grandfather as usual maintained his silence. The old lady hissed, "I know when I speak no dog barks, but it runs after its masters when the relatives whistle." Another story illustrated her independence of spirit. She had been waiting in a village twelve miles away, where she had been on a visit, for arrangements to be made for her return, for palanquins and bearers to be sent from Banagram, but owing to some carelessness somewhere, which she laid at the door of her husband, nothing came. She waited for one or two days, and then with unheard-of audacity walked the whole day at dead of night with only one maidservant as escort. Everybody was aghast, but everybody admired her spirit and pluck.

She was an unforgiving and unrelenting woman and usually had the best of a quarrel, but a rival of her in the family, a grand-aunt of mine, scored involuntarily over her in death. They carried on a mortal feud with each other as long as they lived, calling each other the "High-nosed One" and the "Flat-nosed One", for my grandmother was high-featured and the other lady had an upturned nose. They threatened to spite each other even in death. In the end the flat-nosed lady won, and it happened in this wise. With us the period of mourning for a relation within seven degrees of consanguinity is one month, during which no fish or flesh or animal food of any kind can be taken. But after the performance, on the thirtieth day, of the ceremony of the *sradh* or oblations to the departed spirit, a grand banquet is held on the next or thirty-first day at which all the agnates are treated to fish, and this banquet is called the feast of touching the fish. Now, when my grandmother died, the other lady was ill and nearing her end, and, as it happened, she died on the very day of the feast of touching the fish of my grandmother. As two hundred guests were sitting down to dinner the news of the death arrived. With it another period of mourning and uncleanliness set in, and everything had to be thrown away.

I could go on giving similar anecdotes, but I believe those which I have already given are enough to show that the spirit of our ancestors, even if not the actual manes, was always about us at Banagram.

I have said that at Banagram we felt conscious of our birth. This is not wholly correct. For the blue blood of a Chaudhuri of Banagram was acknowledged as readily at Kishorganj and elsewhere as it was taken for granted at Banagram. We saw no occasion to emphasize or even refer to a thing which was so uncontested, and felt contemptuous only when a plebeian tried to trot out a claim to good birth by recounting the sort of anecdotes to which we thought we only had right. But we always had the tradition of good birth renovated and, if I may say so, springcleaned during our visits to the village, and that took place mainly through the discussion of the evil *mesalliance*. The five families of our common Banagram house were particularly proud of the fact that even among the Chaudhuris they were the only people who had never married, nor given in marriage, below them. Two stories used to be repeated to us. One of them concerned the second sister of my father, who was many years older than he but quite striking in appearance even when I saw her as a widow of advanced age. She was naturally much sought after, and a proposal for her came on behalf of one of the richest landlords on our side, who was rather inferior in birth. My grandfather, it was reported to us, only replied, "I would sooner cut her up and feed the fishes of the Brahmaputra with the pieces." The old gentlemen, or in any case the old matrons who related these tales, were given to expressing themselves in high-flown language when it was a question of blood. One of the bitterest pills my proud grandmother had to swallow in her quarrels with the flat-nosed lady was the taunt that her brother's daughter was married into a family of our village which was not comparable to ours.

The other story about the resourcefulness and pluck shown by the weak-headed Kamal Narayan when it came to the question of saving the honour of the clan. When a family, being equal to us in status, committed a particularly flagrant type of *messalliance*, even eating at their house was forbidden, and there was such a family in a village three or four miles away. One day Kamal Narayan had been taken on a boat excursion or, as the old gentlemen suspected, delibarately enticed away by some wily members of that family. He did not return after the dark, and the worst was feared. Everybody took as a certainty that young Kamal, unnerved by hunger and not protected by a strong mind, has compromised his family by taking food in that house. As hours passed the gloom deepened, but at last at about ten o'clock, out of the darkness of a rainy night, came the voice of Kamal Narayan uttering the Persian equivalent of the phrase: "*Adsum*, Kamal Narayan." He entered the hut in which the elders were in conclave and was found to be wet and dripping from head to foot. He said that he had indeed been trapped into a vile conspiracy but was not such a fool as to yield. His boat had been made fast to the ghat of that family, the boatmen ordered away, the oars removed, and he himself left to be starved into submission. But as soon as he had found himself alone and felt safe against recapture by the coming of darkness he had jumped into the marsh and half-swam and half-waded through it. The story was always told to us with the implied moral that if a nitwit like Kamal Narayan could do as much it was up to us to do better. Although Kamal Narayan had long been dead when we were being told his story, and although my aunt for whom my grandfather had rejected a wealthy match was a widow in not very easy circumstances, yet we felt our blood coursing with a more generous warmth at the stories and the effervescent pride of their narrators. The tradition had influenced even my mother. She was a woman of liberal and reformist views. None the less, even she would say with a toss of her chin, "I would never have my sons and daughter marry ..." and she listed a number of surnames with accents of crushing contempt. As fate would have it, both her eldest son and her second son (the writer of this autobiography) married young ladies whose maiden names were two of the surnames most despised by her.

The only family which we acknowledge as our equal, but which in point of fact was superior to us in blood, was that of the Dattas of Parasara *gotra*. They were an immense clan scattered over forty miles along the banks of the most important river of east Mymensingh, known as Kangsha in its upper reaches, Dhenu in the middle, and Ghorautra in its lower course. This clan, settled in the village of Tatior in the extreme north and Astagram in the extreme south and many more in between, had a fascination for us which we could never resist. We obtained any number of sons-in-law and daughters-in-law from that family. All the three sisters of my father were married into it, so has been one of my two sisters. I have long been out of direct touch with my district but I believe the selective aristocratic breeding is still going on.

But none of my three direct ancestors, my father, my grandfather, and my great-grandfather, had married into this clan. They had married outside the district. When in later years I was dabbling in evolutionary biology and trying to acquire a new conception of heredity in the place of that by which the Chaudhuris had for generations been guided, I took note of the "exogamous" marriage of my ancestors and connected it with two other facts which had come under my observation, namely, our cleverness at books and the comparative dullness of almost all the products of the Datta-Chaudhuri alliance. From this I immediately concluded that the intellectual incompetence of the half-Dattas-half-Chaudhuris must be due to close in-breeding.

This self-flattering conclusion served to wean me from the lure of the Datta clan and also to exorcise me of infatuation with the thing conventionally believed to be good blood. To this extent it did me good. I have, however, recently learnt that my genetics had all along been unsound. At a cattle show held in Delhi early in 1947 I saw the famous Shahiwal bull Ferozepur Diamond, his wife Mudini (one of the best milch cows of India), their daughter Pip, and another heifer called Pipy who was the daughter of Pip by her own father Diamond. As soon as I saw the genealogy of this family, my old theory of Datta-Chaudhuri cacogenics flashed into my mind and I wondered how the breeders of Pipy could have permitted this extremely close in-breeding. In my perplexity I consulted my friend, Dr. Bhattacharya, Officer-in-Charge of Animal Genetics to the Government of India, who had learnt his genetics at Edinburgh and Cambridge. He said that my notion about in-breeding was wrong and that in-breeding, even as close as between brother and sister, was not as axiomatically harmful as I had taken it to be. I was bound to accept his opinion, for these animal breeders know their business while the breeders of human beings do not, and I am now considering whether I should not revert to the ancestral practice and recruit my daughters-in-law from the Datta clan.

I hope the reader is not laughing at me for my crude biological heart-searchings. Nobody could be more conscious that they are crude. I have read just enough about heredity to know that there is no subject less foolproof. But biological superstitions, whether for or against in-breeding, when once imbibed die harder than even religious superstitions. With people who believe in blood, as for example, the Hindus, they scarcely die at all.

THE HOUSE AT BANAGRAM

The country round our village was more open than at Kishorganj, and as I loved open spaces the view should have pleased me very much. But when we went to Banagram on our short visits the human interest always pushed the landscape out of mind. Our house, which was called the New House, was originally built in the eighteenth century and rebuilt from time to time. When we were young it had wholly recovered from the shock of poverty it had got after the passing of the old generation. It had an air of prosperity and was built over a large area of land. Instead of the single inner yard of our house at Kishorganj there were four at Banagram. The outer yard was at least three times bigger than that at Kishorganj. The huts, though made of the same material, were very much bigger and more solidly built. There were four big huts in the outer house for lounging, one hall of worship, one long hut reserved for guests (not the visiting relatives of the family but passers-by who wanted a night's shelter and a meal), and a similar hut used by women as a gallery for looking on theatrical performances and the like. Sometimes even a big double-fly tent of the "Swiss cottage" type was set up to accommodate extra guests. There was a special yard for the family deity; that is to say, the deity in perpetual residence as distinct from the earthen images made *ad hoc* for the festivals and invested *ad hoc* with life by means of incantations. This resident deity of ours was a joint deity, a couple called by us Gopinath and Gopiniji, which names simply were one pair of variants of the many names of Krishna and Radha. There was, besides, the family Narayan, the sacred fossil shell, which we worshipped as a form of Vishnu. There was a special hut for these gods, a wooden car for the car festival, and a staff of officiating priests. There were three water tanks, one very big and of the type called in Bengal *dighi,* bigger in area than a football field; a bazaar on the banks of the *dighi,* which was our property; a middle-school on the far bank of the *dighi,* of which we were the patrons. The homestead proper was surrounded by the houses of the serfs, who gave us domestic service as a matter of hereditary obligation and had not yet (with a very small number of exceptions) been allowed to compound their obligation to give bodily service for rent. In short, though not very wealthy, we possessed all the secular and religious appurtenances of wealth.

With the exception of the four elders–my uncle, my father, the head of the second family whom we called Great Cousin, and his half-brother, called Golden Cousin by us–the other male grown-ups and young people alike lounged in the big hut at the north-eastern corner of the outer house. It was called the Hut under the Bakul, though the tree had vanished long since, and belonged by title to Great Cousin. It was used as a commonroom and was a very well-finished hut with painted woodwork and ornamented mat walls. Its great attraction was a little retiring-room, or rather cabin, at one corner, furnished with a carved fourposter bed. The main hall was occupied for the most part by an immense bed, spread with a white sheet and provided with cushions, pillows and bolsters. This was the place for every lazy fellow, and everybody was lazy. There always was a bunch of sprawlers throughout the morning, and the most assiduous were my brother and I. As we lay on our backs, a large giltframed picture invariably fixed our attention. It hung above the front door and was full of small but richly dressed figures. My brother climbed up a thick post by the side of the door to identify the figures for me. The subject was no other than the coronation of Edward VII. My brother repeated a number of names which made no difference whatsoever to me. But there were two of which both he and I took special notice as others do of their particular acquaintances recognized in the picture of a large and distinguished gathering. They were Archbishop Temple and Lord Rosebery. Archbishop Temple was, however, only the Archbishop of Canterbury to us, a dignitary who we believed had something to do with or was in some way related to Thomas a Becket. But Lord Rosebery was nothing but Lord Rosebery to us. I shall explain this cryptic statement later.

There was a second picture in the hut. It was of the Boer War. It showed a young man rising from a kneeling position with a rifle in his hand in the midst of wounded comrades.

There was no caption underneath the picture and we could not identify the man. He could not have been a British Regular, for he wore a slouched hat and a bandolier. He must have been a Boer or perhaps a man of the British Mounted Infantry. But, whatever he was, he drew my eyes and imagination like a magnet. I was almost bewitched by the moustached and light-eyed young man and contemplated him by the hour.

The great advantage of the Hut under the Bakul, or Great Cousin's Hut, as we the brothers called it privately, was that it enabled us to keep a lookout on all sides. Sitting in the large easy-chair or on one of the benches which stood on its front veranda, we could see two of the water tanks, including the big *dighi*, the bazaar, the school, the fields and the bamboo clumps beyond, and even the village of Gachihata, a mile or so away, where another branch of our clan lived. The appeal of the opposite side of the hut was far stronger. Through the doors and windows on that or western side, we could watch everything that was happening in the yard of the outer house, and it was a scene of ever-changing activity and interest during our visits.

On the northern side of the yard, which was quite close to us as we looked out of the window, was the worship hall, with its south front open, showing the goddess in all her splendour. Just before us was a pavilion formed by an awning fastened to tall poles–shafts of the slender betel palm, decorated some-what in the manner of maypoles but with mango twigs and coconuts instead of flowers. Within it sat the onlookers, who came to see the worship and sacrifice in the morning and the waving of lights in the evening. After the morning worship and sacrifice we went and squatted there, singing the praise of the goddess in a chorus with the grown-ups and the servants. Here also we had the mythological plays which did not require a stage but were performed in the open, with only an awning above and with the spectators seated all around the actors, who slowly turned round as they spoke, in order to show themselves equally to all.

The mythological plays were acted by professional parties and were elaborate affairs. The parts were half spoken and half sung, or, to be more accurate, after an episode in dialogue the chorus got up and sang one or two songs which summed up its leading idea and mood. Therefore these parties had, in addition to their full complement of actors (there were of course no actresses, boys taking the parts of women), also two choruses and one orchestra. One of the two choruses was made up of men and the other of boys. There was no mixing of voices or part singing. The men and the boys sang separately, and within each group the whole chorus sang in unison. The men normally sang in their natural voices but at times caused great amusement among the young by singing in a falsetto. The orchestra was composed of at least four violins, a number of small drums, and one or two harmoniums.

We always had these plays at the time of religious festivals and weddings, and at times also for their own sake. The repertory, though large, was almost exclusively drawn from either of the great epics, the *Ramayana* or the *Mahabharata*, and the stories were thus familiar to the audience. From this followed that the watching of the plays was even for young people like us not a passive gulping down of a story but an appraisal, in the light of a critical code which was never crude, of points of composition and acting, and, at times, even of doctrine. We, the children, preferred martial plays like the death of Karna and the last fight of Abhimanyu to the more didactic pieces or even pathetic pieces like the exile of Sita. To me personally no scene at these plays gave greater thrills than the last one of the death of Karna. After a vigorous fight with Arjuna (these fights at times resulted in the knocking off of one or two prisms from the chandeliers overhead) Karna found himself helpless through the curse of his teacher, and, face to face with death, gave out the triumphant shout: "It's only fate." I have that shout still in my ears as it was uttered by our star performer Kanto Babu.

This was not the only kind of plays we had, for at that time, amongst us, the European theatre too was at full blast. Amateur theatricals had become the rage in Bengal in the latter half of the nineteenth century, and we in the first years of the twentieth were bringing up the rear of that movement in distant East Bengal. A few years later these private stages passed out of fashion. Our house, the New House, and the Old House from which we had seceded in the eighteenth century and which was now in the occupation of the descendants of the brothers of Kirti Narayan, had between them an amateur theatrical party, complete with stage, scenes, wings, tackle, costumes, and orchestra. The speciality of the orchestra was that, besides the usual Indian instruments and the foreign violin, it also had the foreign clarinet. The playing of it, however, gave me a violent distaste for the instrument which was not overcome until I heard, first, the trio of the third movement of Mozart's symphony in E flat major, and then the clarinet quintets of Mozart and Brahms, on gramophone records. The leader of the theatrical party in our time was Cousin Girindra of the Old House.

The stage was set up on the side of the pavilion opposite to the hall of worship, so that people could use the pavilion to see the plays as well as the worship. The drop curtain, or "drop scene" as we always called it, using an English expression (all the theatrical terms used by us were English), showed a blue expanse of the sea with two highly coloured and nearly life-size winged figures. Nothing disclosed whether they were men, women, or beings above the distractions of sex. But we admired them as the guardian deities of the magic world behind.

It was just at this time that the Bengali theatre began to receive the historical and patriotic dramas written by D. L. Roy and Khirod Prasad Vidyavinod. When these came into the repertory of our village theatre they were most welcome. But our normal and usual fare was in an older style and manner. Among the plays we saw I particularly remember *Vilwamangal,* the story of the gay young man about town who loved a courtesan but at one stroke turned his back on her and the world alike.

The conversation took place in this way. One stormy night Vilwamangal went to visit his mistress, and finding the door closed climbed up into her room by means of what he took to be a thick cable hanging loose from her window. The courtesan was startled and asked him how he had come in. He took her to the window and pointed at the rope. But then he saw that what he had taken for a cable was a python, and this revelation of his infatuation killed all his love for the world and its lures. Just as I can recall the death of Karna, I can recall this scene also. I can see Cousin Girindra as Vilwamangal giving a start and stepping back from the window and from the young man who had taken the part of the courtesan. I also remember the very last scene showing Cousin Girindra wandering in the woods as a hermit.

THE CLIMAX OF THE YEAR

Life at Banagram always moved, as life at Kishorganj did not, towards a climax. It was not a feeling which we alone had by virtue of being visitors at the time of a festival. The natives had it equally, and they looked forward to the Durga Puja as the grand climax of the year, through which alone it could come full circle. Durga Puja is the greatest festival of the Bengali Hindu, of this there is no doubt, but it is difficult to say what it is besides. So many strands and layers of thought, beliefs and emotions have gone to its making that to try to come at its core as distinct from the superimposed layers, would be, in the hands of an amateur, about as fruitful as to try to lay bare the solid core of a cabbage. As we performed it there was in the ritual the idea of a daughter separated from her mother and rejoined to her only for three days in a very human sense and not in the more esoteric sense of Persephone coming back to Demeter, the idea of martial ritual held on the eve of a campaign, the idea of a goddess of the lower world demanding the blood of certain animals and conferring strength on her worshipper in return, and, along with it, the idea of the more sunny sacrifice of the Aryan peoples, shared alike by the Hindu, the Greek, and the Roman, which even a Christian Pater and a Christian Keats could partly understand and partly wonder at. Altogether, it is a medley which has a way of making simplified explanations look ridiculous. It would require the ingenuity, learning and patience of a Frazer or a Dumezil to unravel it. I certainly am not going to attempt any such thing. All that I shall do will be to describe the Durga Puja as I saw it at Banagram. I cannot even say whether the festival was exactly similar elsewhere, for I never saw it performed anywhere else.

The image of the goddess was pleasant enough despite her ten arms and ten different weapons in each of the hands, despite the grimacing lion on which she stood, and despite the villainous demon who kneeled at her feet in a defiant posture. All of these had resolved themselves iconographically into mere decorative adjuncts, bereft of realistic suggestion. The goddess had the beaten-gold complexion, slanting eyes, and the amygdaloid facial outline of the goddesses of northern Buddhism. Her eyes at times stared meaninglessly like those of the marionettes of puppet plays, but at times, I do not know how, they wore a look of peculiar benevolence. On her two sides were Lakshmi, the goddess of prosperity, and Saraswati, the goddess of learning, both of whom were of her type, except

that Saraswati, following convention, had a dead-white complexion. Next to Lakshmi and Saraswati and forming the
outermost wings of the group were the elephant-headed god
Ganes and the human Kartik on his peacock. Both the gods
were the sons of Durga. The elephant-headed one was the god
of success, while the other, supposed to be the general of the
Hindu pantheon, had become, as a result of successive soften-
ing touches at the hands of the potter, the very beau-ideal of
a Bengali dandy.

All the figures had draperies, Kartik and Ganes actual
dhotis and *chadars* of the Bengali gentleman, but the goddesses were dressed in tinsel, coloured pith, and gilding, laid on
clay. Behind the figure was a painted screen with a semi-
circular top resembling the tympanum above the door of a
gothic cathedral. This space was sometimes illustrated, but
more often only filled up with panels arranged in a geometrical
pattern, made of coloured paper pith, mica, and, again, tinsel.
But in spite of the cheapness of the material the effect was
never tawdry, particularly because we saw the whole thing
from a distance either in dim light or under a very brilliant and
transfiguring illumination. The lure of these romanticized
panels was so great that boys, and sometimes even grown-ups,
jumped into the tank to secure them after the goddess had been
ceremonially immersed in water, as she had to be. In their
heedless rivalry to secure the best portions they often got
entangled in the sinking framework and never came up again.
We the boys were particularly warned not to go after the panels
of tinsel. But sometimes we were given one of the ornaments
of the goddess or a small share of her salvaged weapons.

The festival lasted five days, of which the first, a day of the
sixth phase of the moon, was only the prologue, and the last
was the day of immersion and farewell, so that, of full and
regular worship, there were three days. The last or immersion
day was very important and had a special character of its own,
but before I go on to it I should describe the routine of the
regular worship, which was identical on all the three days,

although on account of the buffalo sacrifice the third day was the outstanding occasion in our house.

The day of regular worship began with a tune played by the Indian oboe to the accompaniment of a simple pipe and a timbrel, and with the taking out of the sacrificial goats for feeding on jack-fruit leaves by us the boys. These animals were our special charge. But we did not venture near the buffalo. In the early morning the priests carried on some preliminary worship in which we felt no interest, but at about ten o'clock the excitement mounted as the time of the sacrifice drew near.

The first signal for it was the arrival of the drummers, cymbal and gong beaters, and other musicians, all Mussalmans, who took their stand on one side of the pavilion. In the inner house there was hurry and bustle among the ladies, who were donning their best Benaras silk *saris* to see the sacrifice and make their offering. The servants, with an expert air, examined the long line of heavy scimitars hanging from brackets and took down one or two. And then, as the bells began to ring in the worship hall and heavy columns of incense-bearing smoke rose from it, they stepped briskly up to us and made their selection of goats. The animals seemed to have a foreboding of what was going to happen to them and began to bleat and resist, but they were dragged away to the tank to be bathed and decorated with garlands, and then dragged again towards the worship hall. Before the hall stood the sacrificial altar, no romantic thing, but a matter-of-fact wooden pillar, scooped out at the top and left with two branches on each side with two holes in them for a rod to pass through and make fast the necks of the goats.

The priest stood quietly, scimitar in hand. At a signal from him two of the servants caught hold of a goat, lifted it and put its neck between the branches of the wooden pillar and rapidly fixed it with the rod. As one of the servants took hold of the ears and horns of the goat and the other of its hind legs, and they together, pulling with all their strength in opposite directions, made its body taut, the animal set up a hideous bleating. But its hoarse blare was drowned by the beating of the drums, cymbals and gongs, and the frenzied shouts of the spectators: "To the pleasure and victory of Mother Durga!" In a flash the scimitar descended, the animal lay writhing on the ground, its legs stretching and bending, blood spurting out of the neck, the tongue in the severed head almost cut in two by the last snapping of the dying animal's jaws, and the eyes staring out of the head. The priest quickly laid aside the scimitar, kneeled down and took some spurting blood and the head in a platter and rushed to the goddess to put the offering at her feet. It went on like this, one goat followed another, till blood flowed in a trickle down the slope of the yard. We are told that this was nothing and that at Mathkhala, where we had some religious property and another *puja,* the blood actually ran into the tank.

The buffalo sacrifice was a grander affair. Not only were the scimitars examined more carefully for it, and the heaviest and the sharpest chosen, not only was a new wooden sacrificial frame of impressive size erected, but also a special priest arrived from Mathkhala. He was a very handsome and fair man, clean-shaven and stern of mien, and immensely powerful, although nearing sixty. No risks could be taken with the buffalo sacrifice, for if the scimitar stuck it meant ruin for the house: it signified that the goddess in her displeasure had refused the offering. Therefore on the day of the buffalo sacrifice particular alertness could be read on the face of everybody. All the members of the family, including my aged uncle and the other elders, were there. As the bathed and garlanded buffalo was made fast in a trice by three or four servants, my relatives fell on it, rubbing its neck with melted butter so as to make the skin soft. The scene was the same as at the goat sacrifice, but instead of the familiar priest there stood that singularly handsome old man, with the scimitar uplifted in a trembling hand. He waved it for a moment, and then brought it down like a guillotine on the neck of the animal.

The scene which followed seemed like an orgy even to us who were inured to these scenes. All the servants, all the spectators, all my relatives, old, middle-aged and young, fell on the convulsive and, as it seemed to us, mountainous carcass of the buffalo, smeared themselves and the others with its blood, kneaded the dust of the yard into a dough with blood, and pelted one another with the mixture. This went on for some fifteen minutes, while I looked on aghast and awestruck from the back door of the Hut under the Bakul. After this rampage the yard exhaled the mixed smell of blood, moist earth, decayed flowers, and incense for a whole day and even till the next day.

When about an hour after the sacrifice we sat down to chant the praise of the goddess in chorus the mood had miraculousely changed. My old uncle gave the word : "The world is pain ...", and we began gravely and slowly:

> "The world is pain,
> Its load all bearing past;
> Never pine I, never thirst,
> For its kingdom vain.
> "Rosy are her feet,
> A shelter free of fear;
> Death may whisper 'I am near';
> He and I shall smiling meet"

Then followed song after song, song of mortals to the Immortal, of the helpless and weak to the Strong, of the weary and heavyladen to the Comforter. There were even songs voicing perplexity at the destructive fury of the Great Mother. These songs could not with propriety be sung by men, not by any of the gods, because it was for the good and deliverance of both that the Great Mother was killing the demons. Accordingly, they were put into the mouth of the victims, that is, the demons. Terrified by the vision of a woman stalking the battlefield as the very death of the demons, they ask :

"Who is she, the Spouse so dread,
She that walks the field as death,
She that fights,
And swoops as death?"

Some of the wounded demons, groaning in pain and agony, say that she must be the Great Mother, for who else could be so irresistible? Others reply that this is impossible, since she is the mother of all and can never kill her children Then the chorus bursts forth :

"That the truth can never be,
Of all the worlds the mother is she,
A mother will not child destroy,
Her own flesh and creation's joy,
Yet the Killer's vision we see."

So we sang on, almost sharing the questionings and heart-searchings of the demons and perhaps also voicing our own after that bloody sacrifices, till the time for meal approached and dispersed us.

The evening which followed had no suggestion of what we had seen in the morning, nor what we had sung at midday. It was neither orgiastic nor devotional, but gay and heart-free, with lights blazing, a whole crowd laughing and jostling, and the wild music more self-abandoned and noisy than ever.

To our thinking the lights were the glory of Banagram and, in actual fact, they were sophisticated. For we had crystal-glass chandeliers, branched wall brackets, glass bells of different colours—clear, red, green, amber, some of which had lamps burning oil, other candles. The entire stock was kept carefully packed in hay and straw in a large carved wooden chest like the ones I have already spoken about. We sat round the servant who was in charge of the lamps, watched each fragile article being taken out, offered help which was normally refused, and begged a loose prism or two. After being wiped and cleaned the lamps were hung up in their proper place, mostly in the worship hall, but some in the pavilion. In addition, Japanese and Chinese lanterns of coloured paper were hung all around with brilliant and varied effect. It was under this light that the ritual of the waving of light took place.

This ritual was nothing more than the priest waving five brass lamps fixed to a branched bracket in the face of the gods and the goddesses. He held the lamp bracket in one hand and a bell in another and moved backward and forward and from side to side in a sort of subdued dance to the tune of the shrill music. The women, in shining silk as before and loaded with gold ornaments, stood at the sides like two rows of ballerinas, making on the whole a well-composed scene even when in motion. We, the boys, and the men stood in the pavilion, mostly chattering and looking on, but at times also sending up the shout: "Victory to the Great Goddess." The hubbub was deafening. The young men took advantage of this opportunity to have a good look at the young women, whom, unless they were close relatives of equal or inferior status, they had no means of seeing in the ordinary course. Not that there was much to be seen, for even there the young women had their faces covered up with the fringes of their *saris*. None the less the young men seemed to know them by their figures. They said, "Look, that slim one in the red *sari* is the wife of so and so"; and again, pointing to another, "That plump one in green is the wife of so and so." All this struck us as very clever and wonderful. The ritual lasted for about an hour.

I come now to the last phase of the festival, on which except for one feature the Bengali social tradition has deeply imprinted itself. There was no more pathetic event in the life of a Bengali mother than to have to part with her daughter after giving her away in marriage. After that, in one sense, she lived only in the hope of meeting her daughter again and looked forward to the day when the girl would be allowed to come back to her for a short stay. She kept thinking of her girl with an infatuation rivalling, if not surpassing, that of Madame de Sevigne for her cold and shrewish daughter.

The parting after these meetings, occasional as they were, was harrowing. Not only the mother and the daughter, not only the other women and girls of the family, but also all the visiting neighbours joined in a chorus of snuffling. The tradition was so well established that the newly married girl, whose only thought was to get back to her husband-lover, and the matron, who felt ever so worried to have been away from her well ordered household, kept up the wiping of the eyes until they were at least five miles beyond the parental village. It prejudiced the reputation of a woman, more especially of a young girl, if she remained dry-eyed on the occasions. Loud wails were heard among the women of the lower social classes who had no habit of emotional reserve, and I saw many *doolies* passing along the path before our Banagram house in which the wall had degenerated into hiccups owing to the jerks of the swinging vehicle. Even my mother, who belonged to the reformist school, never had her eyes quite dry after a parting from her mother until her side of the river Meghna became a bluish line on the horizon. This happened even when she had been twenty years married. One day, when she was nearing the er of a three months' visit to her mother and my father had come to take us back, I brought a stern rebuke upon myself for going up to her and observing cynically, "Now please go into the bedroom and have done with your blubbering."

If there are places in Bengal where the tradition still lives, as there must be, the tone in which I am writing of this subject will be resented as blasphemous, and I too must admit that in its essence it was moving and not ridiculous. Anyhow, the tradition had grafted itself on the Durga Puja. From one, and more especially from the women's, angle, the three days of regular worship were taken to be the three days which Durga had come to spend with her mother Menaka who was the wife of the mountain Himalaya, and the fourth day was the day of her departure. Indeed, on the afternoon of that day she departed bodily, for the image was taken out of the worship hall, carried in a procession to our big front tank, and thrown into it. But before the preparations for the procession began we had a short ceremony which showed that even in Bengal the memory had not wholly died out that this day was the day of the ceremonial opening of the campaigning season. This military character, in the form of the festival of Dussera, the day still retains in northern India.

All the male members of the family sat in a circle in the open, with trays full of ritualistic accessories round them as well as two heavy scimitars, glistening and, to us, fearsomely suggestive. The priest, the same man who had sacrificed the buffalo, came up, uttered many incantations, marked our forehead with vermilion and, last of all, touched our head with one of the scimitars. As he approached us we felt a little tremulous, not being wholly sure that the sacrificing habit would not get the better of him and he would not cut off our heads. This nervousness at times must have been betrayed by our faces, for the elders looked at us significantly and smiled reassurance. However, our anxiety did not last long, for the ceremony was always over in about half an hour, and we rushed towards the worship hall to see what progress the goddess had made towards the bottom of the tank.

By that time the high platform of the worship hall had been cut away to make a ramp for the goddess to come down. The women who were there, again in their silken clothes and with their last offerings, were as near crying as they could be. Slowly the heavy framework holding together all the gods and goddesses was raised from the floor by our servants, the elders just keeping in touch (literally) for form's sake, and a great heaving and hallooing began. Everybody gave directions and every direction was obeyed, so that the group of images instead of moving in one direction looked like being torn asunder by wild horses. It was a singular tribute to the solidity of the potter's work that the whole framework remained together and the divinities unhurt. We the boys were told that in this last tussle the little boys who went too near ran a greater chance of coming to harm than the gods. But willy-nilly, the throng and, with it, the images proceeded towards the tank. As the procession moved forward the women cried as if they were looking on a funeral procession going out of the house. The faces of the gods were kept turned towards the house, just as the heads of the dead are, for the divinities could never be allowed to turn their back on their worshippers. As the images went down with a crash into the water, everybody on the bank, and there were at times two hundred people there, fell to greeting one another, touching the feet of the elders and embracing all. This was the evening on which we expected to forgive every injury, bear no malice, and have love in our heart for all mankind.

It was at this moment that we the boys had a sudden inkling of a tragedy. We felt as if something we had been holding on to had given way and a void had been created within us. The long procession headed by my old uncle, in which we went to visit all our ancestral shrines, some of which lay in ruins on account of the great earthquake of 1897 with the idols still in place but exposed to the sky, was a very solemn procession. The return home after dark was sadder still. We could not bear to look at the worship hall, now empty and deprived of all its brilliant illumination, with only a little earthen lamp burning in it. We hurriedly went into the inner house, where the matrons were waiting with handfuls of grain and grass to bless us. To be near them was some comfort.

It was this denouement of the Puja that worked into the heart of the old Bengali poet and made him sing of the night before the farewell, the night of the ninth phase of the moon, as the last happy night and at the same time the night most heavily laden with the tense presentiment of sorrow. The sad refrain was put into the mouth of the mother of Durga, who piteously implored the night not to depart. I often heard my mother sing a song written by some humble and anonymous village poet, whose first line ran: "The night of the ninth phase of the moon, pray do not dawn!"

And the theme did not remain merely on the folk level. One of the most beautiful poems we have on it is a sonnet by the first modern Bengali poet, Michael Madhusudan Dutt. He became a Christian as a boy. He was more familiar with the European epics from Homer and Virgil to Tassa and Milton than even with the epics of his own language. His greatest achievement was the introduction of blank verse into Bengali. His next was the introduction of the sonnet. A set of one hundred sonnets, written when he was living in semi-starvation with his wife and children at Versailles, was the contribution of his suffering and his last contribution to Bengali literature. Their themes range from Valmiki and Dante to Hugo and Tennyson, from a ruined temple on a river in Bengal to the palace at Versailles. Among them is to be found the sonnet on the night before the farewell, which is not only one of the most beautiful in the whole collection, but also an unexpected renovation, through an exotic form, of the age-old Bengali theme. I give below an English rendering which I have tried to make as faithful as possible, subject only to the demands of the rigid sonnet form:

" 'Depart not with thy stars, O Night!
For a mother's life shall pass with thee;

The stern sun's rise shall signal be
For these eyes to lose their light.
A year's tears, drear and blind of sight,
As her coming's price were shed by me,
The glad days yet I count but three,
Thy starry braid shall fade to leave a blight.
Silver voice and lustrous lamps of gold,
Banishing darkness, thawing silence cold,
In my palaces light and music made;
But the ninth moon sinking leaves to me
Double gloom and parting's depthless sea'
–The Spouse of the Mountain sighing said."

In spite of the appeal of tradition in Banagram life and its apparent ease and independence, my father personally seemed never to feel quite at home in his ancestral village. He even disliked it positively, and this dislike was shared by my mother. They visited it as a matter of duty and form, in obedience to the universal habit of paying the ancestral village the homage it claimed, but when it came to the question of taking Banagram nearer to their life they felt all their inner revulsion. They went to Banagram thrice with the intention of settling there but came back every time.

My father never explained this latent dislike. But from my young days I heard him speak of the patriarchal type of family in a deprecating manner. Without bringing in any particular person, and least of all his father, he gave us the impression that the most serious vice of these families to his thinking was parental selfishness. One aspect of this selfishness was inequality in food. Although based on the idea "To every man according to his need and from every man according to his capacity", these families had utlimately sunk into the habit of giving least to those who needed most and taking least from those who had the greatest capacity to give. The women and children had to take their meals in the common kitchen and live on the plainest and the most monotonous diet, while the elders savoured no end of delicacies in their private rooms. The exact degree of softness or hardness of the boiled rice made such a difference of the peace and well-being of the persons responsible for the cooking, who were the women, that those who had to cook my grandfather's rice discovered a trick which ensured uniform satisfaction, and spared the ordeal consequent on dissatisfaction. They found that if they put the rice to the boil at the time of the ringing of the third bell at his late morning worship, the rice always turned out right for his midday meal. So they sat with the water boiling and the tray of rice in hand, waiting for the bell to ring. but in the common kitchen the rice at times required the jaws of the Heidelberg man for proper mastication.

The other aspect of this parental selfishness was a certain lack of the natural affections, rather reminding one of the observations of Marcus Aurelius and his tutor Fronto on the Roman patricians. Not that the children were not pampered and spoilt. Most often that, and not self-discipline, was the rule, but the end was accomplished partly through the agency of women and partly through the deliberate indifference of the elders. Tagore has written a poem addressed to the personified spirit of Bengal, in which he charges this fond mother with having shaped her seventy million children into Bengalis and not men. I shall give one instance of this process from the scores I can cite from my own experience. A boy is ill and he has been forbidden sweets by the physician, but he knows very well that he has only to keep up a howling for ten minutes for every tearful mother, aunt, sister or grandmother to be convinced of the monstrous cruelty of depriving him of sweets. Here comes one lady with a packet of sweets and the whispered injunction that it should be eaten up without the men coming to know of it. The men certainly came to know, but they chose the least troublesome way of turning a blind eye on the proceedings. In the case of real vices, like too early smoking or even taking to drugs or women, it was absolutely bad form for the elders to take notice, after perhaps giving one or two capricious preliminary thrashings, even if as much as that.

In the same general way as my father spoke of parental selfishness he also spoke of the influence and power of the old class of the servants, our serfs, who were always called uncles or brothers by courtesy. From his accounts some of them appeared to be as fond of power and as illtempered as the eunuchs of corrupt oriental courts. In my time, however, I saw nothing of this. On the contrary I found these hereditary servants very obliging and affectionate. But at that time they were passing through a stage of transition. They had got the idea of compounding their obligation to give bodily service for rent and setting up in business or farming on their own. They were loosening their old ties, and they did not feel, since they were no longer merging their existence in that of their masters, the old urge to satisfy their craving for power through the master's household. Thus they were left with their old affections and amenity of manners without the old imperiousness and jealousy. But in my father's time the traditional relationship was still unimpaired. He told us that the servant gave him a thwacking whenever they pleased, but he added too that they would have given their lives as readily. The old servants considered themselves the guardians of the boys in view of the absence of any direct interest of the elders in their children and the exclusive absorption of the women in cooking and other household work. It may also have been that they were the deputies of the elders in respect of the boys as in many other things, and acted only after consultations with them. Loyalty was the forte of these servants and love of power the foible. But although the weakness was very often atoned for by the virtue, my father perhaps preferred both, the forte as well as the foible, to be less overwhelming.

My mother's most vocal complaint against Banagram was over the general lack of freedom there and, more particularly, the illtreatment she received during her second confinement. She attributed the death of this baby of hers to asphyxiation by the smoke of a whole tree-bole which was kept burning in the small room without a door or window being left open. She also thought that her own health, which was delicate from childhood, had been ruined for the rest of her life by her sojourn at Banagram. Apart from this, my mother had the greatest dislike and distaste for the pettinesses, the little envies and meannesses, the little lies and dishonesties of which this patrician female society was capable. She hated, above all, the distrusts and suspicions of these women, which came to the surface at every crisis.

These were no ordinary suspicions and distrusts, but dark and terrifying emotions with their roots deep down in the primeval, subconscious being of these women. Of this, as a very young boy, I witnessed a demonstration which even at that age I thought revolting. One of my aunts had died and an old lady, who was her aunt and had taken care of her like a mother, was recounting her sorrows to my mother, who had gone to condole with her. I was sitting by my mother's side and listened to the whole recital. Between her lamentations and sobs the old lady related how one day she had found a packet full of human hair and pared nails under the pillow of my aunt, who was then bed-ridden. The old lady also said that on another day she had discovered that a snip had been cut off from my aunt's sari, and that on yet another occasion she had seen a root and something resembling raw meat in the food placed before my aunt and had removed them just in time to prevent her swallowing both. Throughout the conversation the old lady kept alluding to these means of bringing about the death of human beings by homoeopathic magic without realizing in the least, although she was a most gentle and considerate woman otherwise, that she was uttering the vilest slanders against the relatives amongst whom she was living. In her own unbearable sorrow she had forgotten everything but the impulse to create a feeling of resentment within her to dull the edge of that sorrow. As all weaklings do, she also was trying to create a living scapegoat to visit her feeble wrath against the irresistible.

I could say a good deal about the degradation of the old patriarchal Bengali life, of its repulsive degeneration in village and town alike. But here, as I think finally of my father's dislike for the home of his forebears, I do not consider that its sole cause lay in the things I have just mentioned. There must have been, there certainly was, a more fundamental cause, a still more elemental reason. My father was the abandoned son of the old order. He was educated by the money which his mother had found in the hidden hoard. With all the clan behind him he had gone to seek a livelihood at Kishorganj with only eight annas in his pocket. He must have felt that the bond had been finally snapped and he was not sorry. For he must also have felt, and here I seem to touch the heart of the matter and hit the hard core of truth, that to live at Banagram was to live only in the empty shell of the past. My father had the deepest possible conviction of the sanctity of the present and the future, and he hated Byzantinism in every form.

CHAPTER III

MY MOTHER'S VILLAGE

To PASS from Banagram to my mother's village, Kalikachchha or Kalikutch, was to pass into a world so different, so humble, so full of humility, and so self-effacing in bamboo and cane greenery, that it brought tears to one's eyes. The village was in the district of Tipperah, five miles from the steamer station of Ajabpur on the Meghna. There is now a railway bridge crossing the river just below this place, but in our time there was neither railway nor bridge. We had to come from Kishorganj either all the way in boat; or partly by boat and partly by steamer; or partly by road and partly by boat or steamer; or if we took a long detour, as sometimes we did, by horsedrawn carriage, rail, steamer, and palanquin—all combined. It will thus be seen that the choice of routes and means of transport to my mother's village was wide and complex. But whatever choice we made it made hardly any difference to the physical discomfort.

FIRST IMPRESSIONS

The country round Kalikutch (I shall use the shorter and humbler form) was open, but the village itself was thickly wooded, in places so thickly as to have the appearance of a tropical forest. It was only at Kalikutch on our side of east Bengal that I saw thick undergrowth at the foot of tall trees, climbers of all sorts and cane clinging to them, and bamboo, reed, and scrub all jumbled together. Sometimes through small gaps in the bushes we could see real wild cats *(Felis chaus)*, not merely the domestic cat become feral. These animals at times stared at us very gravely, at times dozed without paying us the

slightest heed, and at times also caterwauled. The least distance within which we considered it safe to approach them was
never less than one hundred yards. So after all there was not
much occasion for the cats to take us very seriously.

There were also patches of wood which were more open,
and through them we could see the sun rise or set with bizarre
effect, looking very big against the tree trunks which took the
appearance of dark and thick stripes on its body. Besides the
woods, there was almost everywhere about us some water-
way, marsh, pond, pool, or tank. The tanks were mostly, but
not in every case, in tolerable condition. That could not,
however, be said of the other domiciles of water. They were
all choked with weed and smelt of rotting vegetation. The
water of the little pond in which we washed our mouths after
meals was of the colour of lightly brewed tea without its
pleasant smell. The smell of the water was of the vegetation just
mentioned. The great attaraction of this pond were the moo-
rhens and waterhens, whose calls we always heard but whom
we rarely saw. Even when we saw them it was only a glimpse
of fluttering wings that we caught.

I shall now relate a curious change that came over me at
Kalikutch. It was only there that I did not have that fear of trees
and woods which was almost inborn in me. Hudson has spoken
of the animism of boys. My animism took the form of a
hyperaesthesia in the presence of trees. When I was in any thick
plantation without being able to see at least ten yards in front
of me I had a feeling that something was passing out of the trees
into me, and that sensation made me very uncomfortable. I had
not got rid of this morbidity even when I was fully grown up.
One bright and sunny morning in 1932 I was going up the path
which leads to the top of the peak above Shillong in the Khasi
Hills (altitude 6,441 feet). The peak itself is only a knoll some
one hundred or one hundred and fifty feet higher than the
cuntry immediately surrounding it, which is all open and rolling

downs. I was greatly enjoying myself, for as I have said I love open spaces and solitude, and that morning, on the wind-swept downs around me, very few men were to be seen and none at all felt as intruders.

But for about one hundred yards the path up which I was going skirted a clump of dark, gnarled, and more or less stunted Khasi oaks, which grew on the northern face of the knoll. The passage of this stretch cost me some effort. The place was one of the few surviving old sacred groves of the Khasis, and there were some menhirs and dolmens scattered about. But it was not these associations which troubled me. Having a taste for archaeology I went out expressly to see the menhirs and dolmens wherever they were to be found, and particularly at the village of Laitkor, about a thousand feet above Shillong, where there is a fine group. It was not these, but the trees of which I was afraid. And I breathed freely one when, reaching the open top, I recovered unobstructed vision and found everything stretched out to the horizon—the kind of landscape I have always liked.

There was before and below me the road to Cherapoonji and, branching off from it, the road to Mawphlang. There was the Laitlyngkot bridlepath. There was also the place where I thought would be Nongkhrem, famous for its Khasi dance, and the place further to my right where I placed Mawphlang with the beautiful gorge and rapids of the Bogapani. Turning round, and looking over the tops of the trees which a few minutes ago I had thought so sinister, I could see the bare ridge of Lum Dingei, the green and grassy Bhoi country, the dome-headed Sopet Bneng in the middle distance, and farther away the blue hills of Nongkhlaw. It was after sitting for a while on the top of the knoll and having a good look at the landscape and breathing the keen breeze that I recovered the composure which I had lost at the sight of the Khasi oaks. Since the feeling was so strong in me even when I was past thirty, it must have been embedded in my childish being pretty deeply. But the remarkable thing was that at Kalikutch I became completely free from it. I had no fear of trees, although we had very often to pass through wooded areas.

In all I visited Kalikutch six times, once in each of the following years: 1904, 1905, 1907, 1908; and twice in 1909. I left Kalikutch for the last time and for ever one New Year's Day 1910. My first coming to Kalikutch was wholly in harmony with the spirit of the place. It took place in March 1904, when I was six years and some months old. At sunset we had been dropped by a big two-decker river steamer on the sandy bank of the Meghna near the lonely and isolated station of Ajabpur. My father took us and the luggage to the bazaar, which was a little way off, and put us inside a very small and deserted hut, full of dust and reeking of goats, and himself went to look for palanquins and bearers. Just then a storm rose as is usual at this time of the year, and blew some mats and dust about us. But it did not last long, nor did it rain. Presently my father came back and said that though he could not find palanquins he had brought some *doolies*. We were put into them and the party started for Kalikutch. It was very dark and we were passing through open fields. We could see nothing. The bearers stepped unevenly, not only on account of the darkness but also because they had to walk over reaped ricefield left with stubble. With the bearers, the *doolies* also jolted violently, and the little smoking lamps swung from side to side, giving out even more smoke than they normally give. The only place which seemed to be lighted was the sky, which we saw as a vast blue-black, solid dome above us. The men occasionally talked, but the most constant sound was the barking of the pariah dogs–it was the long, trilled and nearly musical bark which they give forth after dark. The barkings seemed to come from all points of the horizon and from equal distances, so that we derived the impression that the dogs were standing in an immense cricle along the line where the sky met the earth. In this rhythmic monotony we fell asleep and woke up only next morning in broad daylight to find ourselves in a very humble hut. Our father had vanished. We went out and saw that although there were bare earthen platforms still standing, which gave evidence of there having been quite a number of big huts in this house at some former time, for the present there was only one other small hut besides the one we had slept in, and that was the kitchen. The place had the appearance of being an abandoned homestead.

The truth of the matter is that my mother's father had died in the late seventies, not only leaving his own widow, a young son, and two still younger daughters in straitened circumstances, but also other widows and minors who were dependent on him, in equal difficulties. To make matters worse, a great cyclone in the eighties had entirely destroyed the house. An aunt of my mother, a most pious and kind-hearted lady, was killed in this cyclone, being pinned under one of the wooden pillars. The whole famiy became, so to say, the charge of the neighbours, charge in respect of looking after and not of expense, for there were still some properties left, and the widows and the boys were determined to live humbly and struggle for better days to come on the income that was theirs instead of becoming dependents. While the boys had themselves educated at different towns through whatever facilities they could secure, an old Brahmin, the priest of the family, took upon himself the management of the properties and care of the girls and widows. I saw him every time I went to Kalikutch as a very benign-looking man, with a large vermilion mark on his forehead, but so wiry and vigorous as to give the impression of being a fencer. I also saw all the friends of the family in its difficult days, almost all peasants or men of humble station, all smiling, all ready to oblige, all treated with perfect equality by my grandmother and my mother, yet never presuming. At the beginning of the century the family had left its worst days behind. My mother's brother as well as her cousins were in Government service in Assam. But they had had no opportunity of coming back to their ancestral village and rebuilding the house. My old grandmother alone lived there, occasionally visited by her daughter (my mother) as also by the wife of her son and the grandchildren on that side. Her other daughter was dead, and the children of that daughter never visited Kalikutch. It was these circumstances of the family which were responsible for the neglect into which the homestead had fallen. Later, my uncle built a large house on the site.

The disappearance of my father calls for an explanation. He always left us either on the outskirts of the village or at Ajabpur, and on our return journey too picked us up at these points. A lady, distantly related to my mother, teased us about this. She said that my father was a thief, inasmuch as he had stolen a girl of the village, and he dared not show his face there for fear of getting a bastinado. This was a joke from the good old days of marriage by capture, but we did not relish it at all. Rather, we set down this aunt of ours as a very provoking and tiresome person. The real reason for my father's not coming was that in those days a son-in-law had to be entertained with considerable ceremony, and if he came for the first time to the village of his father-in-law even greater formalities were expected. Knowing my grandmother's circumstances, my father certainly wanted to spare her embarrassment. He came to Kalikutch for the first time in 1907, when my uncle was there with his whole family, when he had built new huts, and when two grand banquets were given, one by the host and the other by the guest.

Besides this there may have been another vaguely felt reason. Among us there was a tradition, not a wholly unhealthy one, of not becoming too familiar and intimate with the family of the father-in-law for fear of rousing uncalled-for jealousies between the family of the husband and the family of the wife. These patriarchal families were great sticklers for their rights, and no person was held up to greater ridicule than the so-called "domesticated son-in-law", or the man who had come over to his wife's parents and was living with them. This type was, and still is, quite common in Bengal, but familiarity has in no wise dulled the Bengali wit's keenness to be clever at his expense. The tradition of bidding defiance to the wife's family is also illustrated by a custom obtaining in West Bengal. There the mother-in-law immediately after the wedding asks the bridegroom to bleat like a sheep in token of submission to the bride, but a manly young fellow is expected to reply that he can roar but not baa. In all this we have perhaps a manifestation of the deep-seated antagonism of patriarchal society to the matriarchal.

Incidentally, it was at Kalikutch that I learned that a son-in-law could be actually bastinadoed. A buxom and pretty lass of one of the old tenants of my grandmother–a huge and fine old fellow he was, living just across the outer yard–had been married to a well-to-do young yeoman farmer from the other side of the village. After the marriage some misunderstanding had cropped up between the two families, and when once the girl came to visit her parents she was not allowed to go back to her husband. The poor thing suffered, but there was no help for it, because to betray the slightest emotion would have been to bring down on her head the jeers of the whole clan of brothers and cousins. As it happened, one day having some passing illness, she became a little indiscreet, and the next day the following song, composed by a cousin of hers who was not only a good singer but a composer as well, was on everybody's lips. I myself heard it many times without being allowed to join in the hilarious appreciation. Here it is:

"Hurry, sister, get some drug,
Die I wouldn't for a mug;
I so want to live.
But do believe,
Not to love that tramp;
O shame, O fie,
I would sooner die:
So, if I want a dose,
It's only a pose
To get him near
And kick the scamp."

The peasants at Kalikutch were generally witty, though often in the cynical vein. To finish the story–the young man could not remain passive. He was making his reconnaissances and was found one day hanging about not very far from the house of his father-in-law. He was immediately set upon by the brothers and cousins of the girl and given a good beating, which I personally at all events thought very cruel and inhuman.

A few days after our arrival a ceremonial welcome was given to my mother by a friend of hers, a young woman from a farmer's family in the neighbourhood. Then followed more welcomes from other women, so that there were in all four or five of these functions. Subsequently these affairs ceased to interest us, for they were repeated at every visit of my mother to Kalikutch, but when I saw them for the first time in 1904 I was greatly excited. These were not collective parties. Every woman came individually, accompanied by a small procession of other women and girls, who came only as spectators, not as participants. The woman who gave the welcome brought grass, grain, betel-leaf and betel-nut, vermilion, one or two coins, together with an egg, and stood before my mother. She touched my mother's forehead with the pleated bamboo tray in which these things had been brought. Afterwards, taking up the egg, she broke it softly on my mother's head, that is to say, just crushed the small end without making anything messy. Last of all, some vermilion was rubbed into the parting of my mother's hair. Occasionally, presents of clothes and sweets were also made. After the ceremony all the women and girls sat down in a circle and chatted.

Another ceremony was held soon after our arrival, possibly on the last day of the Bengali year, or the Bengali New Year's Day, and this was the first as well as the last pastoral ceremony I ever saw. All the cows, bulls, and oxen were washed and decorated for the occasion with paint, shell chains, and garlands of flowers, and made to go round and round in a wavy movement, which, on account of the flowing outlines of our humped cattle, was almost like a minuet. The animals retained their colour decoration for some days, and by virtue of it seemed to be lifted altogether out of the commonplace.

Our coming to Kalikutch meant absolute respite from books, whatever the elders might say, and vigorous assimilation into the soil, the vegetation and animal life. Therefore these stays too were in their way strenuous, and at the end of a tiring day we went to bed early and slept well. If any thought ever troubled us it was the thought of storms, for with that big river close by severe storms were frequent in the village, or rather they were always discussed and described with considerable earnestness. The story of the death of my mother's aunt and the imagined picture of her last struggles under the pillar which had pinned her down were always in our mind. We also noticed that, as distinct from Kishorganj and Banagram, the huts at Kalikutch had additional props and buttresses of bamboo to give them extra strength to withstand the storms. With these reminders it was not surprising that we were a little nervous. But we never had a real storm at Kalikutch except the cyclone of October 1909, which swept over the whole of lower Bengal and was less destructive than only the great cyclone of

September 1919. At Kalikutch, however, the cyclone of 1909 was not severe. While we read in the newspapers how the steamers of the I.G.N. and R.S.N. Companies on the Padma service had to pass through stupendous waves breaking over their decks, at Kalikutch we only saw torn and tattered clouds being blown and driven about in the sky and, below, the tall, bamboos getting a merciless belabouring for two days.

But we woke up at times at night, and in those short spells of wakefulness occasionally heard the deep siren of some steamer passing over the Meghna. This machine-made noise was perhaps the least dissonant sound we ever heard at Kalikutch. The siren seemed to be the voice of that gorgeous and noble river, speaking to men in the stillness of night. There was a touch of awe in it. But that was nothing compared with the uncanny associations of the thunderous peals called Barisal Guns, which boom along the northern coast of the Bay of Bengal.

One night we had a terrible fright, and that was during our first visit in 1904. We were suddenly awakened by shouts of "Fire!", and thought that our own thatched hut was ablaze. Rushing to the door we discovered that it was not our house which was on fire but another, a little way off. But our terror was not any the less on that account. A loud hubbub pierced by shrill screams was coming from the direction of the fire. I may as well explain here that in case of fire the behaviour enjoined by immemorial custom and ingrained habit was that the owner of the house should do nothing to help himself beyond madly rushing about, tearing his hair, and raving that he was ruined, and that his womenfolk should accompany him in the lament in the trouble. It was this noise mingled with the diapason of the helping neighbours' consultations which was coming across to us. The sky above the trees was red, and through the tree we could catch glimpses of leaping orange flames. But the immediate and the nearer danger for us lay in the sparks, which were coming borne on the wind, and which alighting on our thatch might set it on fire. The older peasants had gone off to help their neighbour, but they had left two boys to keep watch over our house. The boys jumped up as each spark came along and tried to keep track of its course. It was fire-watching on an entomological scale. In the end we came to no harm, and in the morning went to see the burnt-down house. What impressed us most were not the charred remains of the huts but the master of the house coming forward and showing to all the visitors molten lumps of silver which once were his rupees. Like most villagers he had hoarded them in the hollows of the bamboo posts, through slits made in them. It was quite impossible to get at them and take them out when the huts were on fire. So they had been melted by the heat and were lying among the ashes, to be sorrowfully picked up.

MEN AND IDEALS

My grandmother finished her single and simple widow's meal at about three o'clock in the afternoon. After that she usually sat down at the door of the hut, either telling us stories or watching us play, while chewing her daily piece of myrobalan. She had a high-pitched voice, but having lost many of her teeth was not very distinct in speech. Thus it happened that when she talked, and more especially when she scolded, there was just a suggestion of clucking. That, however, was not unbecoming in the old lady, for with us all around her, she had the air of a very experienced hen keeping an eye on her fluffy brood.

At this time, and also in the morning, her most frequent visitors were two women of the farmer class, called Pashani and Kali. I believe Pashani was a widow, but unlike a Hindu widow she chewed the *pan* or betel-leaf, and was always chewing it. I do not know how she managed about livelihood, for I never saw her doing any work. She was either visiting others or receiving visitors herself. Her hut was one of the cleanest and neatest places I have seen anywhere. It was in her hut that I saw for the first time the old Bengali coloured-rope hangers. She was considerably younger than my grandmother but older than my mother, and she was one of the best friends of the family.

The other woman, Kali, bore herself like an orthodox Hindu widow of good family. She was a tall, dark, plump, but flabbily built woman. She must have been quite a well-to-do person, for besides having a house which was very much better than that of my grandmother, she had had a tank dug with her own money before her house, which passed with us under the name of Sister Kali's tank. We used to bathe in it and drink its water till the big tank in my grandmother's house was re-excavated in 1907. Kali was rather peevish to look at, but that was only a superficial impression, for in reality she was a very witty person and was always spouting poetry. She immediately won our hearts by improvising the following verse on one of the commonest and most troublesome skin-diseases that we suffered from:

"There's only one joy for wretched man to snatch,

That's to get the dry itch, grimace and scratch."

We knew how true this was, for when we had that particular skin trouble we were not satisfied with merely scratching, rubbing and twisting our fingers and hands, we rushed on the heated glass chimney of the hurricane lantern and clasped it without feeling the least pain. On the contrary we felt the greatest relief.

Kali also satirized the cultivation of jute, for which the peasants had begun to give up growing paddy because jute brought in more ready money. Jute growing was becoming the means of getting rich quickly. Our Kali said:

"There's no farmer like Farmer Jute,
     For God or man he cares not a hoot."

The strongest point of Kali's improvisations was that she sang them out with expressive gestures of the hands and arms, like an operatic singer.

Here I must say a word about the love of music and musical facility of the common folk at Kalikutch. As a result of recent research my own district, Mymensingh, has acquired a great reputation for folk music and folk poetry. Many years ago, reviewing a work on Mymensingh folk songs issued by Calcutta University, the *Times Literary Supplement* called Mymensingh the marches of Bengal. Perhaps imagining as a corollary that we were the border barons, I felt very much flattered at the time. But even then, as soon as the heady fumes of self-adulation had been blown off, I felt that, compared with my mother's district, we had no right to appropriate the compliment. I never heard half as much folk poetry and folk music at Banagram and Kishorganj as I heard at Kalikutch. There the common folk—men, boys and girls alike, would burst into song at the least provocation. There were three boys of one of my grandmother's tenants, called Palah, Jalah, and Chhatrah, who were always coming to see us. As they had very good voices and were trained to sing we often asked them to give us something. Immediately they would sit down and begin:

"That's the river, there the ferry,
But I dread the crossing lone;
We will go in, Master, arm in arm,
And at His feet be thrown."

That was an idea very deeply rooted in the spiritual consciousness of these people. They took it that the religious preceptor whom they had chosen and followed in life had the salvation of their souls in his hand and could intercede with the Creator on their behalf. And, of course, being asked to sing before elders and more particularly before ladies, the boys could not think of singing a secular song.

This song was sung to us during our very first visit. When we revisited Kalikutch in 1908 we found that these boys had had a short sojourn with a *Yatra* party, having joined its chorus, and had learnt many new songs. When we asked them to sing some of them they gave us a song from one of the plays they had been acting. It was the old Bengali story of Kalaketu and Phullara, a king of the hunter tribe and his queen, who were devout worshippers of Durga but were put through great suffering as a trial of faith. The song was supposed to have been the speech of a messenger who had been sent down to earth to see how the hunter king and queen were taking it, but who on return made it a reproach against the goddess. This was the new song which the boys sang:

> "On earth, Goddess!
> I have been,
> And your mercy seen,
> And for men your boundless love !
> I have seen a woman moan,
> In hunger, thirst, and naked shame;
> Hunters vainly seeking game;
> Yet in tears begging, prone,
> Of a stony goddess love!"

This vein is not at all uncommon in Bengali devotion. Perhaps it is an inverted and rebellious form of the prayer "Give us this day our daily bread". One of the earliest songs my mother as a child had learned and sung without in the least understanding its meaning contained this implied reproach. Shortly after her father's death she and her elder sister were sitting under a tree in the outer house with their arms round each other and, as children often do, they began quite mechanically to sing the following song:

> "My star, Protectress!
> O'er horizon ne'er shone;
> By parents orphan left,

By men of wealth bereft;
An infant, drifting on a wreck,
On shoreless ocean thrown."

In the meanwhile the Brahmin priest had arrived and listened. He took the children in, wiping his own tears all the way.

I have no reason to think that the peasant at Kalikutch was fundamentally less quarrelsome, less violent, or less avaricious than the peasants of my own district, whose unsocial proclivities I have already described. One difference there was. The peasants we mixed with at Kalikutch were Hindus, while the peseants we saw at Kishorganj were Mussalmans, and the Hindu is less ready to resort to open violence than the Mussalman. But despite this difference in degree, there could not have been any basic difference. The real point seems to be that the Hindu peasant, besides being the particular worldly animal that he was, was also the carrier of a tradition of religious faith and morality which was Hindu spirituality reduced to its lowest and simplest, and which in addition was the heritage alike of the naive and the sophisticated. To a person of higher social rank the peasant would, out of a sense of propriety alone and with no intention to deceive, reveal only that part of his being which he thought was common ground between him and the other man. Thus we should be seeing only one part of his character and not all. That was what happened in our contacts with the Hindu peasant at Kalikutch. Later in life I came to see that the Mussalman peasant too had his own Islamic counterpart of this simple faith and morality. But since at Kishorganj I saw the Mussalman peasant mostly in connextion with my father's profession I never got an opportunity of discovering his other side. That I was capable of detecting the presence of the spiritual quality when I saw it, was made plain by the peculiar attraction that the march to the Id prayers held for me. At Banagram neither the one nor the other ever came to our knowledge, for we only met men of our own class.

But supposing it is permissible to abstract one part of the personality of the Kalikutch peasant, then the spirit of this rarefied part could be considered to be very truly summed up in these songs. They made articulate the spirit of a people meek and contented, without share in the kingdom of the earth, occasionally disposed to grumble at that fact but more often happy to forget it, judging everything that could not be won by the toil of their limbs as things lying within the gift of gods, praying for these boons, resigned withal to the inscrutable will of Providence.

I am trying to define my ideas on the subject because it was on the foundation of this very simple morality that my mother built up her later and much more complex morality derived from Brahmoism. Both were imbibed by me unconsciously through a large number of folk songs and more developed devotional songs which she was in the habit of singing or intoning, not only when she sat down with the express purpose of singing, but also when she worked. The morality which I learned in my boyhood was the morality of the liberal Hindu. I cannot make it comprehensible without bringing up by way of sample a portion of the deeper soil into which its roots reached down. However naive, and from the literary point of view however crude, these songs may appear to be, their spiritual and moral significance is out of all proportion to their worth as literature.

From what I have written so far about Kalikutch it might be imagined that it was a village fo peasants. It was not. On the contrary, it was well known as the home of gentlefolk noted for their birth, education, liberal ideas, and worldly position. There were many persons from the village who held high posts in the service of the Government, high, that is to say, by the scale of highness applicable to Indians in those days. Among the village's other titles to the world's respect, I might mention that two of the accused in the very first political bomb-manufacturing and bomb-throwing case in India were sons of this village; so also was one of the first Indians to go to Sandhurst and hold the King's Commission. Thus the village was able easily to make the best of both worlds–the nationalist Indian and the British Indian. In addition, its position in the old Bengali order was assured by its two highly respected Kayastha clans, the Dattas and the Nandis, the latter being my mother's folk. There were also a number of Brahmin families and some well-to-do traders.

Furthermore, just to the south of the village was the equally well-known, if not better-known, village of Sarail, which served to particularize Kalikutch as Sarail-Kalikutch, although we never heard of any other Kalikutch as we heard of Maishkura-Banagram as distinct from our Banagram which was Dhuldia or Gachihata-Banagram. This Sarail was the home of an old family of Muslim zamindars, who according to the old history related to us by our mother were given in their days of power and prosperity to having cow bones thrown into the temples or houses (I forget which) of a rival Hindu zamindar in the neighbourhood. Sarail was also famous, and most famous, for a breed of hounds intermediate in build between the Great Dane and the Grey-hound. These dogs were greatly prized throughout north-eastern Bengal.

But for many reasons we hardly saw anything of all this grandeur of the village. In the first place, the village was very large, comprising six or seven hamlets, each of which had quite a valid claim to be regarded as an independent village. Secondly, the persons in Government service were, like my uncles, absentees. Thirdly, the village was very much cut up by waterways, some of which could be crossed by arched bridges described by us as "elephant's back bridges", but the rest had to be negotiated by wading, accompanied by a gradual lifting of the *dhoti* until it became a small bundle on the head. Last of all, we were small boys not inclined to go roving unless there were strong attractions of fair or festival. One day I walked down to the village of Sarail with the hope of being able to see at least one pack of Sarail hounds and catch at least one glimpse of the cowbone-throwing zamindar. But I came back very disapppointed. I might use stronger language and say I was disgusted, for I saw nothing. That was the reason why we mostly kept to our side of the village and to the people who were about us.

There were frequent visitors, however, from two families–both of my mother's clan. Both these families were Brahmos, or monotheistic Hindus of the reformed sect. One of these lived in the house known as the Police Inspector's House, for that edifice of brick, in itself distinctive, was built by a police inspector of the name of Kali Nandi, an uncle of my mother's by blood relationship. But the police inspector was dead, and the head of the family in our time was his eldest son, whom we called Uncle Peary. Uncle Peary was an elderly man with a beard. When my mother stayed at Kalikutch he called almost every day to see her, since, besides being related to the family, he was also a great friend of my uncle. To us, however, Uncle Peary was a notable personality only by virtue of his being the master of Chilah, the magnificent fawn Sarail hound, and of his mate, Belle. Chilah was the embodiment to us of all that was dignified and stately in the animal kingdom, for he would never run about or take notice of anybody. He slowly walked in with his master, lay down at a short distance from his chair, and got up only when he said, "Chilah, let's go home." Belle was more sprightly. While Chilah never came to our house without his master, she would come by herself, off and on, on what looked like reconnoitring missions, go sniffing round the whole house, and then make off at top speed. She was jet-black. It was our ambition to have a pup of Chilah and Belle, and in the end I was presented with one.

The other family was altogether out of the ordinary, and was headed by a personality who would have been remarked in any society. His name was Mahendra Nandi, and by profession he was a physician. His professional reputation was such that people would come to be treated by him even from forty miles away. His grandfather was a notability of the district–Diwan Ramdulal Nandi, who was a minister of the Indian State of Tripura. His father, Ananda Babu, had embraced Brahmoism, but in later life had become the head of an esoteric sect. Mahendra Babu had inherited the religious leadeship of his father and, giving up the fine brick house left by his grandfather, was living near the grave of his father in very humble sheds, which had come to be known collectively as Under the Trees. This burial was another peculiarity of the family, for it is only among certain monastic establishments of the Vaishnavites or followers of Vishnu and certain esoteric sects that the custom of burial is found practised by the Hindus. Other Hindus are cremated. Mahendra Babu, when I first saw him, wore long hair and always went about barebodied, and in later life his hair became matted and coiled in the manner of Indian Sadhus. Thus, by virtue both of his secular and his spiritual vocation, he could be called a "medicine man".

But it was not what others had made of him but what he himself was that raised the man above his fellows. I often saw him when he came to visit my mother, and heard him calling her aunt in the most unaffected of voices–for by relationship my mother, although very much younger, was his aunt. He removed our awe of him in an instant by calling us cousins. I saw him in 1909 in Calcutta by the death-bed of his son, who had been an under-trial prisoner in the Maniktala Bomb Case, but had been let off and was dying of consumption. I saw the old man a few weeks later, the morning after the death of his son. At no time did I find him without his usual serenity. Yet his inner being was volcanic. It was swept, if I may say so, by a fiery typhoon, which was his patriotism. With him that overwhelming passion took a practical turn and did not assume, as was more usual with us, the demagogic form. He was spending all his fortune in setting up machinery and workshops in his house. Whenever we went there we found, to our intense interest and excitement, some machine or other working, for being rustics we had very little acquaintance with machines. He worked on the scale and principle of cottage industries and had set some of his sons to this work.

He lived in this manner without ever seeking or drawing the wider world's notice. But I was glad to see that after his death the famous Bengali nationalist orator and writer, Mr. Bepin Chandra Pal, described him as a Tolstoy-like character. I shall put on record my own curious feeling about him. As soon as I heard of Mahatma Gandhi and his characteristic activities soon after his return from South Africa, I involuntarily recalled Mahendra Babu. I cannot account for this association of ideas, since there was not in my mind any concrete notion of these two men being similar in views or activities. Perhaps what subconsciously influenced me was a perception that in both cases I was in the presence of characters whose strong idealism impelled them on the one hand to very clear and practical expedients, and on the other to ideas which were extremely elementary and yet, or perhaps on that very account, possessed of an immense power to bite and hold.

SHILLONG

Besides being what it was, Kalikutch had for us an insubstantial and exotic trailer. This was formed of our ideas and mental pictures of the Assam hill station of Shillong. There was no mystery at all behind this unexpected association of ideas. My mother's brother and his family, and a cousin of my mother with his family had been living at Shillong in the nineties, because they had taken up employment there. My grandmother, too, went and lived with her son for some years, and between 1895 and 1900 my mother visited Shillong thrice. The last time she went there was when I was two and a half years old. After that my uncle took up some work connected with the census of 1901 in a better-paid though temporary post, and having pleased his superior officer (I believe he was one Mr. Allen) was, when the census was over, permanently posted in the magisterial grade and became within a few years what in India is called a deputy magistrate or extra assistant commissioner. But this promotion involved my uncle's transfer from Shillong to the districts, and with that my grandmother's return to her village. My mother's cousin continued to live at Shillong and kept up the bond of the family with the town.

My mother never again visited Shillong after 1900, and I was too young to come away with any recollections of our stays there. But the place was as real and living to me as any place I had actually seen. From the descriptions given to me I could always visualize the town. To give one or two instances of the accuracy of my imaginative evocation: when after marrying into a family of Shillong I went to pay a visit to my father-in-law in 1932, I did not find the polo ground and the lake in any perceptible way different from my imagined picture of them, and the extraordinary thing was that I had in the meanwhile seen no photograph of the polo field and a very small and inadequate one of the lake.

I shall try to give an analysis of the ideas we formed about Shillong. It seemed to us to be a place of very much greater and more diversified natural beauty than any place we had seen. The long and difficult journey from Kishorganj or Banagram was described to us minutely: the successive stages of the journey by palanquin, steamer, boat, and *thapa* or the cane chair carried on their backs by the Khasis with the help of a strap passed round their foreheads; the steep ascent from Tharia Ghat to Cherapoonji; the careful picking of steps along, and sometimes across, the deep gorges of the southern Khasi Hills; the sudden feeling of having reached the end of a long journey on catching the first glimpse of the pines of Upper Shillong–all this, visualized through imagination and made as real as life, made the place appear more romantic still. My mother told me that when she was going to Shillong with me as a child two and a half years old I sat in the *thapa* looking solemnly on the fold on fold of the hills, sighed very sadly, and said, "How should we ever reach home!" To hear this incident repeated made me almost as wistful. Our idea of the beauty of Shillong was heightened by the information that all about it were plantations of sweet-smelling pines. We had the sensation of the fragrance in our nostrils because a few logs of the Khasi pine had been sent to us, and my mother burnt one or two pieces occasionally at Kishorganj.

Besides this, we came to know that at Shillong we could see not only grown-up Englishmen in flesh and blood, and at all times of the day, but also their doll-like babies, which sounded too good to be true. We also formed the notion that it was a place full of Gurkhas, as indeed it was, for it was the depot of two Gurkha regiments and always had two battalions of Gurkhas stationed there. My mother told us stories of the training of the Gurkhas, how they came down to the polo field with their mountain gun on their pack mules and before anybody could guess what they were about set it up, and how one day, while carrying out piqueting practice, a party of them trooped into my uncle's house and climbing the pear tree ate up all the pears.

As regards the Bengali population of Shillong, we formed two rather conflicting impressions. One was that the women were very much more free at Shillong than at any other place we knew of, and the other was that the men were very much less so. It appeared to us that the men at Shillong spent their days shut up in a room and working at their desks. The impression was right because most of the Bengalis at Shillong were clerks in government offices. It also seemed to us that Shillong was a place where monotheism prevailed over poly-theism and that in the face of the One-God or Brahma, as we called him following Brahmo theology, our familiar many-gods kept themselves very much in the background. This notion was due partly to the fact that my uncles–my mother's brother and cousins–had been strongly influenced by Brahmoism (in actual fact, one cousin had embraced Brahmoism, while the other cousin and the brother had not done so only in name), and partly to the fact that at Shillong nearly all the Bengalis affected liberal and reformist religious views. So, when we heard stories of Shillong life, we also heard a lot about going to the prayer hall on Sundays, and about prayers and sermons. One day, when my mother joined in the singing of a hymn, I took it in my head to get frightened and screamed so dreadfully and unappeasably that she was com-pelled to leave the prayer hall in deep mortification. But I was made to pay for my misbehaviour by being dragged over the stony road for about a third of a mile, receiving more than an occasional box and cuff on the way. This reminds me of another story told by my mother. The fashionable and Laodicean monotheism practised by the Bengali gentlemen of Shillong so annoyed a fervent and real monotheist that one day he resolved to go for the hypocrites who paid lip homage to Yahweh at Shillong and worshipped at high places in their villages. As he sat down to pray he slowly intoned: "O Brahma, O Lord! deal justly with them, they that worship you here but in their villages worship the image of Durga, and with an axe smite them on the head, smite them on the head, and smite them on the head."

All these notions of ours about Shillong, and the medley of images formed by the stories fo hills, trees, gorges, English babies, Gurkhas, pear trees, and prayer halls, came surging into our mind when at Kalikutch my grandmother said that she had got a letter from her son or her nephew or her daughter-in-law, or when she and my mother discussed old times. The evocation was so continuous that the idea of Shillong became the intangible fourth dimension of Kalikutch. Soon we saw something tangible, though short of the reality. In 1907 my uncle spent a few months in his village and at that time he showed us his collection of photographs of Shillong, taken by himself, for he was a good photographer. One day he took out two photographs and asked me to say whose they were. I saw that they were of the same man—a young man in a suit, with a beard and a whole head of curly hair parted in the middle—and looking at my uncle, who had both a beard and a good head of hair, I replied, "Yours, Uncle, when you were young." He was very amused and told me that they were my father's. I could not remember my father except as a shaven and bald man, and I had never seen him in a suit either. Therefore I was so very much struck by the two photographs that apart from other things they by themselves convinced me that Shillong was very different from Kishorganj. The other photographs of the sights and beauty spots of Shillong only served to deepen the original conviction.

But perhaps the strongest impression of the beauty of Shillong that I received was from my uncle's orchid collection. I believe at one time he had tried to set up as an exporter of orchids, but had given up the business and remained a simple collector. To collect orchids in the Khasi Hills in those days was not a very expensive hobby. But my uncle had to give up adding to his collection when he left Shillong. Shortly afterwards he sent us quite a number of plants which at Kishorganj we ruined through neglect and ignorance. Later, when he came to visit us himself, he brought two plants, and with his own hands he put one in a box and hung up the other on a tree. For one season–and one season only, because we did not know how to tend them–they bore flowers of dazzling splendour. The one in the box had a profusion of deep pink tulip-like flowers, which lasted for about a month, and the other on the tree bore one single flower, yellow and black like the skin of a leopard, with the similarity heightened by its downy texture.

My uncle's own collection, when he brought it down to Kalikutch, had dwindled to less than a quarter of its original size, but still it was not very small, and it was varied. He kept the plants under three mango trees. When they flowered the bloom was of such loveliness that, had I not seen it with my own eyes, I would not have believed that even the world of flowers was capable of giving birth to so much beauty and beauty of such duration. My uncle looked after each plant as if it were his child. It is still my dream to see, for I cannot hope to possess, a good collection of orchids. But I have not seen one other, whether at Shillong or elsewhere.

When there were no flowers it was a pleasure to go over the photographs of my uncle's orchid house at Shillong. In monochrome the flowers seemed to be possessed of an unearthly purity which they had substituted, not to their disadvantage, for the hues of their real existence. Not satisfied with this version of orchidian beauty we went for a different effect by looking at the negatives of these photographs. We took out the boxes which contained my uncle's negative plates and examined them carefully. The impression was disturbing. On those shadowy rectangles of glass we thought we had caught sight of the disembodied spirits of the orchids sighing for their lost colours. It was a queer and weird experience to pursue the image of the orchids from life into the negatives.

I sometimes wonder what would have happened if orchids had reached Europe along with roses and been as common. One consequence would certainly have been that some of the most splendid European poetry would not have been written. Waller would not have admonished, "Go, lovely rose!" nor Ronsard coaxed, *"Mignonne, allons voir si la rose ... "*, but beauties would have been spared a lot of tendentious parables; they would have been spared even larger quantities of special pleading on the part of poets. Compared to orchids in prefer- ence to roses, they would have gained confidence and not felt so very ephemeral and so relentlessly bound to fall off at the end of the day, *"feuille a feuille declose"*. Into the bargain, they would gave got some foretaste, even while living, of the floral immortality which was to be theirs among the fields of asphodel, while men, giving up poetry for gardening, would have been building greenhouses for them instead of strewing beds with rose leaves and graves with sprays of yew.

CHAPTER IV

ENGLAND

WHAT I have written about Shillong leads me naturally to speak of another intangible and exotic element in the ecology of our lives. To us it was absent and yet real, as Shillong was, but its power was immensely greater, for while our conception of Shillong soon reached the perimeter which bounded it, our idea of this other thing never struck against barriers from which it had to recoil. In the end this came to be very much like the sky above our head, without, however, the sky's frightening attribute of vast and eternal silence, for it was always speaking to us in a friendly language in the knowledge of which we were improving from day to day. Perhaps I need not formally proclaim that this was England as we defined and understood it, that is to say, with Scotland, Ireland, and Wales merged in it, and Europe conceived of as its corona.

The story of our preoccupation with England may justifiably give rise to scepticism. I have described the three places which constituted our boyhood's actual environment. If these descriptions have served their purpose, then with the sensation of that environment fresh in mind, one could question the presence in it, not only of any knowledge of England, but also of all means of knowledge. I too shall most readily admit that our means of knowing was as casual as our knowledge was extraordinarily uneven. If I may put it that way, the chiaroscuro of our knowledge of England was extremely sensational. It had intense highlights in certain places and deep unrelieved shadows in others, so that what we knew gripped us with immeasurably greater power than it would have done had we seen it in more diffused and, consequently, more realistic light. On the other hand, what we did not know was so dark that we could easily people the void with phantasms evoked out of our ignorance. In this chapter I shall give some specimens of both kinds, of what was thrown on our mind and what was thrown out by it.

FAMILIAR NAMES

I shall begin with our knowledge of English and European personalities. I cannot remember the time when I learned, just as I cannot remember any time when I did not know, the names of Queen Victoria, Prince Albert, Napoleon, Shakespeare, and Raphael. The next series comprising Milton, Burke, Warren Hastings, Wellington, King Edward VII, and Queen Alexandra is almost as nebulous in origin. Lord Roberts, Lord Kitchener, General Buller, Lord Methuen, Botha, and Cronje entered early, thanks to the Boer War. Next in order came Mr. Gladstone, Lord Rosebery, Martin Luther, Julius Caesar, and Osman Pasha (the defender of Plevna in the Russo-Turkish War of 1877-8)–these too belonging to the proto-memoric age. The beginnings of true memory in my case were marked by the names of Fox and Pitt, and Mirabeau, Robespierre, Danton, Marat, Junot (Napoleon's marshal), and also perhaps George Washington. On the literary side, in addition to the names of Shakespeare and Milton which we imbibed unconsciously, we came to know of Homer as soon as we began to read the *Ramayana* and the *Mahabharata,* which was fairly early.

Of course, these names were not just names to us. They possessed some meaning and much more of associations. These ideas and associations constituted what I may describe as the original capital of our intellectual and spiritual traffic with the West. As years went by the names acquired ever greater precision and ever greater significance for us, but the process never lost its incompleteness. It has not done so even to this day.

Queen Victoria we thought of as everybody else in England and India thought of her after the Diamond Jubilee, and about the Prince Consort our ideas were identical with those of the queen herself: he was the paragon of every virtue. But King Edward VII–he was already king before we had acquired the faculty of thinking–we regarded only as an elderly boy. The story we had heard that he was never taken seriously by his mother clung to our memory and prevented our acquiring till many years later even the popular notion of him as an astute diplomatist who had brought about the Anglo-French Entente. On the contrary, we thought of Queen Alexandra as a very gentle, gracious, and beautiful princess. Personally, I formed a notion that she had not been very well treated by the old queen. The origin of this idea is most curious to trace. Very early in life I had read an account in Bengali that soon after her marriage the princess had been distressed over the Prussian invasion of Schleswig and Holstein and had expected her mother-in-law to intervene on the side of Denmark, which of course the queen did not. Combining this detail with the general state of the mother-in-law-daughter-in-law relationship in Bengal, my child's mind entertained no doubt that the imperious old queen was something of what we in Bengal called a daughter-in-law baiting mother-in-law.

Coming to the literary and artistic group, the initial explanation I have to give is that although we had heard the story of King Lear from our mother and knew who it was by, our first notion of Shakespeare was of a man whose writings all grown-up persons were expected to discuss and, what was even more important, to recite. It did not take us long, however, to pass from the ranks of spectators to that of participants in the Shakespearean procession. By the time we had learnt a second story by Shakespeare–and that was the *Merchant of Venice*–we were almost ready ourselves to recite both the *Merchant of Venice* and *Julius Caesar*. Our familiarity with the name of Julius Caesar was only a byproduct of our knowledge of Shakespeare, and the first idea we formed of the great Roman was in the image of Mr. Rames Roy, a top-form boy of Kishorganj High School, who in a black English suit had taken the part of Caesar in a performance of Act III, Scene I, given by the senior students.

Of Homer we had a fuller but less correct notion. We were not so narrowly patriotic as to deny his claim to be the father of poetry, but we made him its joint father with Valmiki, the legendary author of the Sanskrit *Ramayana*. We knew the name and the story of the *Iliad* and regarded it as the Greek counterpart of our *Ramayana*. It was the obvious parallelism which deceived us. In both cases there was an abducted woman, Sita in the *Ramayana* and Helen in the *Iliad*. In both cases there were two rescuing brothers, Rama and Lakshmana in the Indian epic and Menelaus and Agamemnon in the Greek. In either case there was a magic car which could pass through the upper air. And, last of all, in both instances there was a long struggle round a fortified city before the woman could be recovered and brought back. All these similarities made us think of the spirit of the *Ramayana* and of the *Iliad* as comparable, and this misconception was natural because of the fact that we were told the outlines of the story from a Bengali version which gave no idea of the quality of the original.

Raphael's name we came to know as the painter of the picture above our front door, which we always called by its original Italian name of "Madonna della Sedia". We had taken over the word "Madonna" as equivalent of the mother of Jesus and never translated it into Bengali. "Raphael's Madonna" had passed into our language as a phrase of almost everyday use, the first part of which was inseparable from the second, for, strange to say, even educated people thought that Raphael was a painter of Madonnas and of nothing else and that all the extant Madonna pictures were by him. But we, even at that early age, were somewhat wiser. Certainly we also spoke of Raphael's Madonnas, of which we had seen a number of monochrome half-tone reproductions in a Bengali magazine. So far as I can remember, they seem to have been reproductions of the "Madonna della Granduca", "Madonna della Colonna", "Madonna in the Meadow", and one or two others, but we also knew that he had painted other kinds of pictures as well, because in the same magazines we had seen reproductions of his "Knight's Dream" and a self-portrait. This last we took as the final and decisive proof of Raphael's greatness, for we placed a painter's capacity to paint his own portrait on a par with a surgeon's capacity to operate on himself. We knew nothing, however, of the "Sistine Madonna" or of Raphael's great frescoes; nor did we know the name of any other painter either of Italy or of any other country. Raphael reigned supreme over us, but when after the theft of the "Mona Lisa" from the Louvre we for the first time learned the names of Leonardo and a few other Italians, we also picked up with that information the fashionable disparagement of Raphael.

Milton stood before us in solitary and somewhat awe-inspiring grandeur. His claims upon us were manifold. In the first place, he was the author of the bright volume in the glass-fronted cupboard. Secondly, he was the model of Michael Madhusudan Dutt. Thirdly, he was the writer of a most striking line which my father was fond of repeating and which ran as follows: "Better to reign in hell than serve in heaven." Lastly, it appeared he had something to do with the execution of Charles I, who had tried to deprive the English people of their liberties. The idea of Milton as a stern, unbending and powerful champion of liberty was confirmed in our mind by a picture of him we saw in an edition of Macaulay's essay on Milton, which was in the cupboard. It showed him as an old man, with long hair and a deeply lined face in severely simple puritanical clothes. We knew that the old poet was blind and this added a touch of compassion to our awe of him.

From our admiration of Milton to our admiration of Napoleon there must appear to be a long and difficult passage. We made it with the greatest ease and did not perceive any chasm. If any whole-hearted Bonapartists were to be found anywhere in the world at the end of the nineteenth century and the beginning of the twentieth they were to be found in Bengal. All educated Bengalis literally adored Napoleon and, not satisfied with mere worship, tried to understand his military campaigns. In one of the historical novels by our greatest novelist, Bankim Chandra Chatterji, a not very necessary allusion occurs to the Austerlitz campaign and to Wellington's Salamanca campaign. My father, without having any occasion at all to make a study of the life or the campaigns of Napoleon, had read one or two biographies and the memoirs of some of his marshals. I got from him quite a businesslike summary of the alternative theories of Napoleon's defeat at Waterloo, including the theory of his mental degeneration. Amidst all the wealth of Napoleonic literature it was quite a surprise to discover in one of our cupboards a torn copy of Sir Neil Campbell's *Napoleon at Fontainebleau and Elba*. In the public library of a small place like Kishorganj was to be found even the memoirs of Napoleon's valet, Constant.

As in France, so amongst us too, Louis Napoleon reaped the harvest of our Bonapartism. I made this discovery in the volume of secular songs entitled *Pearl Necklace of Song*, previously referred to. I found in it two songs devoted to the younger Bonaparte family, one purporting to be the speech of Napoleon III to General Wimpffen pointing out the futility of further resistance at Sedan, and the other the dying soliloquy of the Prince Imperial, mortally wounded in a skirmish in the Zulu War. I have forgotten the words of the soliloquy and only remember that it was addressed to his mother, Empress

Eugenie, and expressed the Prince's regret that he was dying so far away in a strange land without being able to see her face once again. But I have still got by heart the first two lines of the speech of Napoleon III and give below a French translation, because I find that I can reproduce the metre and the alliterativeness of the original better in that language than in English:

> "En vain, Wimpffen! vous voulez
> Livrer bataille dans Sedan!"

I would implore the reader not to set down the effect these lines produce on him solely to my inadequate French.

Thanks to this prevalence of Bonapartism amongst us we began to hear of Napoleon quite early in life, and the first picture of him that became fixed in my mind was that of a young artillery commander bending over his guns and laying them. For the siege of Toulon was the point at which my father began our Napoleoniad, initially skipping Corsica, Brienne, and the *Souper de Beaucaire*. I heard of Junot as part of the same story. I was told that during the siege Junot was engaged in writing near a battery and when a shell burst close to him and scattered some sand he coolly remarked that the sand was welcome as a blotter; and that that was the beginning of his friendship with Napoleon.

I have now to disclose a paradox. Although we regarded Napoleon almost as a god, and as invincible and unconquerable by straightforward methods of warfare, sometimes ascribing his defeat at Waterloo to the bribing of Grouchy, we still came to think of Wellington as the greatest general that ever lived. There are two possible theories on which I can explain this curious self-contradiction. Either we were thinking unconsciously of England only, which, while considering the outer world, we often did, totally forgetting the other European countries, or we were thinking of Napoleon and Wellington on quite different planes. That is to say, when we were thinking of Napoleon we had in mind only transcendental and supra-rational military genius, whereas we judged Wellington as the best rational and human general. It is a far-fetched explanation, and perhaps childish self-contradiction calls for no explanation at all.

From Wellington we made an easy descent to Lord Roberts, whom we regarded as the greatest living soldier, with only Lord Kitchener as a second. The Bullers, the Whites, and the Methuens, we sympathized with, but they were defeated generals. The prestige of Lord Roberts and Lord Kitchener with us was immense. Both were victors of the Boer War. In addition, Lord Roberts was the hero of the Afghan War and Lord Kitchener of Omdurman. Kitchener was Commander-in-Chief in India and Roberts in England, fitly dividing between them the military responsibility for the British Empire. With unspeakable disgust we heard from our father that the post of Commander-in Chief had been abolished in England and an Inspector-General installed in his place. Without knowing anything about Cardwell we were wholly Cardwellian in our military conceptions and thought of the military might of Great Britain as equally distributed between England and India. By the abolition of the post of Commander-in-Chief the English half was to our mind thoroughly disgraced, for a Commander-in-Chief was a man next only to the Viceroy, while an Inspector was only a police inspector and even the highest inspector was no higher than the Inspector of Schools.

The military glory of the two men, however, remained unaffected, and the two panoramic pictures of the Boer War in our West Hut always served to remind us of it. Every few days I asked my brother to climb on the trunks and read out to me the names of the regiments and officers provided in the key below. I listened mechanically to the names of the regiments, which conveyed very little to me, but as soon as my brother came to the commanders I pricked my ears. Standing in front of the Pretoria picture he would say: "General Roberts, General Kitchener, General Staff, General Staff, General Staff... " "All General Staff?" I would ask perplexed. "Yes," my brother would confirm. Then I would ask him to explain the other picture which was more exciting, for it showed the bend of the Modder River, the Boer laager formed by carts in the background, and, filling up the whole foreground, a long line of British guns, not simply flashing, but literally blazing away and bombarding the Boer positions. At the left-hand corner, on a small hillock, was a group of high officers on horseback. "Who are they?" I enquired of my brother. "General Kitchener," he replied. "And who else?" Again the reply was, "General Staff." It appeared to both of us that Staff was a very common surname among British generals.

The Boer War was very frequently in our thoughts and not less frequently on our lips. Its hold was reinforced by a magic lantern show with brightly coloured slides to which we went. We thought of the Boers as a heroic people and of their leaders, particularly of Cronje and Botha, as men of superhuman valour. Our reaction to the Boer War, as to every war in which England was involved, was curiously mixed. One-half of us automatically shared in the English triumph, while the other and the patriotic half wanted the enemies of England to win. When our patriotic half was in the ascendant, as it usually was after an English victory, we went so far as to believe that the victory had been won by bribing one of the opponent's generals. We were told that General French's successful dash to Kimberley was made possible by the treachery of a Boer commander who had been bribed. An Indian's faith in bribes is infinite and unshakable. Not only is bribing believed to be an infallible remedy for all workaday inconveniences–a belief justified by experience–it is also regarded as an equally effective means of managing high affairs of state, but in this instance without the same warranty. We heard that the English had won the Sikh War by bribing Lal Singh and Tej Singh. These suggestions are so commonplace that they have worked their way into history books. I, however, can cite an example which is far more striking and which has not received the publicity it deserves. During the late war it was believed by many Indians, and quite sincerely, that the help of the United States to begin with, and finally its participation, were secured by Mr. Churchill by bribing President Roosevelt.

Besides the Boer War we also heard of the Graeco-Turkish War, the Russo-Turkish War, and the Franco-Prussian War. All this knowledge was gained by us from a systematic enumeration given for our benefit of the more important European wars of the previous fifty years. It was in connexion with the Russo-Turkish War that we heard of Osman Pasha and of his heroic defence of Plevna. My father was something of a pro-Turk. After the Italian attack on Tripoli in 1911 he surprised us by making the observation, as we were seated at a meal discussing the latest news, that it was downright robbery. We were shocked by this exhibition of pro-Turkish partisanship, for we had in the meanwhile acquired a violent prejudice against Muslims and wanted them to get a licking everywhere. But at the time we first heard of Osman Pasha we had no such feeling and we thought of him as a very heroic man.

It is curious that the Russo-Japanese War was not followed by us from day to day, although it was fought when we were old enough to take notice of public affairs. Of course, we heard a good deal of the heroism of the Japanese, of the retreats of Kuropatkin, who came to be known to us as the "Retreating General", and also about Port Arthur. Our attention was drawn to the change that had come over the character of wars so that Marshal Oyama could now direct the Japanese armies from Tokyo. We heard too that the surrender of Port Arthur might have been due to the treachery of the Russian commander, General Stoessel–another instance of our nose for treachery–but we were conscious neither of the concrete military results nor of the far-reaching political significance of this war. But that holds good perhaps only for the conscious part of our being. There was not the least doubt that something had reached the subconscious. After the Japanese victory we felt an immense elation, a sort of reassurance in the face of Europeans, and an immense sense of gratitude and hero-worship for the Japanese.

I have still to explain our familiarity with the other twelve names: Luther, Burke, Fox, Pitt, Washington, Warren Hastings, Mirabeau, Danton, Marat, Robespierre, Gladstone, and Rosebery. But I cannot do so without going into a short digression about the religious and political ideas of our family. My father and mother believed in a form of Hinduism whose basis was furnished by a special interpretation of the historical evolution of the Hindu religion. According to this interpretation the history of Hinduism could be divided into three stages: a first age of pure faith, in essence monotheistic, with its foundations in the Vedas and the Upanishads; secondly, a phase of eclipse during the predominance of Buddhism; and thirdly, the later phase of gross and corrupt polytheism. The adherents of this school further held that all the grosser polytheistic accretions with which popular Hinduism was disfigured had crept in at the time of the revival of Hinduism after the decline of Buddhism in the seventh and eighth centuries of the Christian era, and that they were due primarily to the influence of Mahayana or polytheistic northern Buddhism and the Tantric cults. This degenerate form of Hinduism was given the name of Puranic Hinduism in order to distinguish it from the earlier and purer Upanishadic form of Hinduism. The reformists claimed that they were trying only to restore the original purity of the Hindu religion.

The very simplicity of the interpretation should serve to put historical students on their guard against it. But the reformers implicitly believed in it, and since they believed, their belief gave shape to and coloured their attitude to the other religious movements of the world; they failed to detect the true filiation of their theory, to see that it was only an echo and duplication of the theory of the Protestant Reformation. Although their claim to be restoring the pure faith of the Upanishads by ridding it of Puranic excrescences was certainly inspired by an unconscious absorption of the idea of the Protestants that they were reviving the pure faith of the Scriptures, the Apostles, and the early Fathers, the Hindu reformers looked upon Protestantism as the product of a parallel religious movement and were deeply sympathetic to it. They were correspondingly prejudiced against Romanism. As faithful followers of this school, we were little Hindu Protestants and No-Popery fanatics. Consequently we looked upon Luther as a reformer possessing as great importance and merit as our Rammohun Roy or Keshub Chunder Sen, and regarded the Pope as the European version, and a very magnified and therefore all the more condemnable version, of our worldly and luxurious *mohunts,* or heads of religious orders and monastic establishments.

With such views on religion our parents could not but be liberals in their social and political opinions, and from their casual talk rather than any deliberate instruction we imbibed the notion that European history was a series of struggles for freedom, as a result of which the ambit of a beneficent and fertilizing freedom had been enlarged in ever widening circles in the course of modern history. The more important and epochmaking of these struggles, to our thinking, were the Reformation, the Puritan Rebellion in England, the American War of Independence, and the French Revolution. The heroes of these movements were also our heroes, although about the heroes of Ninety-three our feelings were a little mixed. Not that we had much moral condemnation for them, for we thought it very exhilarating to be able to chop off heads as easily as Danton and Robespierre, incited by Marat, were reported to us to have done. But pondering over the guillotine's indiscrimination in its personal implication we were somewhat awed by it. Of mob violence too we were afraid. We had seen one highly realistic woodcut showing the head of Princesse de Lamballe carried aloft on a pike. The effect of this picture was, however, somewhat tempered by another woodcut printed in ultramarine blue depicting Theroigne de Mericourt on a prancing steed waving a sabre. The beginnings of the Revolution appeared to us as a more generous phase, free from excesses, and matinal in its promise, and of this phase we took Mirabeau to be the intrepid fighter as well as wise counsellor.

Towards Burke we felt nothing but whole-hearted reverence. We had heard that not only had he supported the American colonists but that he had also impeached Warren Hastings for his oppression of the Indian people. The two bulky grey-blue volumes of his impeachment speeches in the cupboard were in our eyes the impressively concrete evidence of his championship of the down-trodden. The names of Fox, Warren Hastings, Washington, and of the two Pitts were to us the names of actors in a very big, many-sided, and slowly unfolding drama, which in our conception of it was nevertheless very closely knit. We seemed never to have lost the sense of the underlying unity of the whole historical epoch beginning with the Seven Years' War and ending with Waterloo. The two Pitts constituted for us the visible symbol of this unity, although apart from this we also recognized their intrinsic greatness. In addition, we saw in them the marvel so rare in the sequence of human generations of a father and a son being equally great.

After all that has been said so far I need not make the explicit declaration that in our attitude towards current English politics we were unapologetic liberal partisans. In fact, we saw no reason for any apology. We had been told that English politics were run by two parties, but we hated the Conservatives, because we gave the same appellation to the orthodox Hindus whom we looked down upon as the upholders and adherents of superstition, by which we understood belief in ghosts, evil spirits, magic, witchcraft, and the like. We could think of no worse insult than to be called a Conservative, and with me this persisted up to the age of adolescence. When I was about seventeen I was having an argument one day with a cousin of my mother about the way to stage a play. We had staged it once before and I insisted that the second performance must be exactly like the first, while my uncle observed good-humouredly that it hardly mattered if there were small departures, particularly as we were going to give the repeat at very short notice. I still stuck to my point, and my obstinacy perhaps annoyed my uncle and he remarked in English, "You are very conservative." I felt hot and angry. I could not have felt more outraged if he had called me a liar. He understood my feelings and said with a reassuring smile, "Don't be so upset. Burke was a Conservative." I was astonished. Burke a Conservative! I had never heard of such a thing, never thought it possible. That remark became the starting point of a new understanding of Burke on my part.

From this it followed that we had a natural bias in favour of Liberal statesmen. Since we were carefully taught the names of the English Prime Ministers, it is quite impossible that we should not have been told the names of Lord Salisbury and Mr. Balfour, but I remembered nothing about them. Our idea was that Lord Rosebery was the last Prime Minister and the coming Prime Minister and we were passing through a sort of interregnum. Disraeli we had heard of, but thought of him only as a clever adventurer, not worthy to bear the shoes of his great rival, Mr. Gladstone. That was why we felt so interested in Lord Rosebery when we looked at the picture of the coronation of Edward VII at Banagram. But after the Liberal return in 1906 we seemed to have got very easily reconciled to Sir Henry Campbell-Bannerman, although we thought his a very funny name. I still remember the day we heard of his death at Kishorganj. My father had gone to the courts, but he came back at about twelve o'clock. I asked him why he had returned so early. He replied that Sir Henry Campbell-Bannerman, the Prime Minister was dead, and the courts had closed as a mark of respect. When I asked who was the new Prime Minister my father said, "Mr. Asquith." He did not explain that Mr. Asquith had been Prime Minister already for some days. That brought our knowledge of the English Liberal Prime Ministers up to date for the time being.

THE ENGLISH SCENE

However scrappy and simple our ideas of English life and society might have been, they could not exist at all without the accompaniment of some visual suggestion. Everything we read about the British Isles or in English evoked pictures of the external appearance of the country even when not avowedly descriptive. But we had plenty of verbal descriptions, and in addition to these we had pictures to go upon. Taken together, these gave us the impression of a country of great beauty of aspect, a country which possessed not only beautiful spots but also place-names which sounded beautiful. Isle of Wight, Osborne House, Windsor, Grasmere, Balmoral, Holyrood Palace, Arthur's Seat, Firth of Forth, Belfast were some of the names which attracted us. I seemed, speaking of my personal preferences, to like Osborne House and Holirood Palace best. Their beauty of appearance produced a vivid effect on me, and Holirood Palace especially gathered intensely romantic associations from the allusions to Marry Stuart, Darnely and

Bothwell contained in an article written by a Bengali student of Edinburgh University and published in a Bengali magazine.

Two coloured pictures seen in a school text-book printed in England made a profound impression on me. One of them wàs the picture of a cricket match, showing not only the batsman, the wicket-keeper, and some of the fielders, but also the pavilions in the background. Cricket was our favourite game; and in Bengal at that time it had not been ousted in public affection by football. Football also we played, but we regarded it as a game on a rather plebeian level, while there was not the least room for doubt about the refinement and aristocratic attributes of cricket. An extra reason which inclined us to cricket was that one of its early pioneers in Bengal was a man from our district, who came of a wealthy family whose seat was a village only six or seven miles from Banagram. His full name was Sarada Ranjan Roy, but he was known in Calcutta and all over Bengal as Professor S. Roy, for he was a university teacher and ultimately rose to be the Principal of his college. He taught mathematics, but was a greater Sanskrit scholar, and in the department of sport he was a keen angler and a competent cricketer. It was from the shop run by him in Calcutta that we got our sports goods.

Years later, when I was at college in Calcutta and staying in a hostel run by the Oxford Mission, Father Prior (a descendant of the poet Prior), who was in charge of us, asked me one day if I had ever played any games. He had noticed that it was very difficult to make me play even badminton without dragging me out by main force, and that was the reason for his question. "Yes," I replied, "I used to play cricket when I was a boy." "You call that cricket, do you?" observed Father Prior very justly. But whatever might have been the quality of our cricket there was no dross in our enthusiasm. Our school team, composed of the teachers and the boys, was not quite despicable. We had some good players, and all the accessories–

bats, balls, leg pads, gloves, stumps were by the English makers. Some of the more fashionable boys even went into flannels. But our show, proud as we were of it, seemed to be reduced to total drabness by the side of the cricket world revealed in that coloured picture. The game was transformed. It was cricket suffused with the colours of the rainbow.

The other picture was of a battleship which, so far as I can recall its outlines, seems to have been a ship of the 1895 *Majestic* class or might have been even of the 1901 *Formidable* class. Under this picture was the caption: "Hearts of Oak are our Ships, Hearts of Oak are our Men." The coloured illustration fascinated me not only because I had an inborn liking for ships, but also because it gave me an impression of the seas being an appanage and projection of England. I could never think of England, as I thought of Bengal and of India, as a stretch of land alone. Combined visions of land and sea were always fleeting through my mind and before my eyes whenever I tried to think of England. Of only one other country in the world did I ever think in that way when I was a boy, and that was ancient Greece.

This characteristic vision of the physical aspect of England as half land and half sea was confirmed in me by my reading of English poetry. The first piece of real English poetry which I heard was Colley Cibber's "O say what is that thing call'd light", read out to me by my brother from his text-book. But it was illustrated with a picture showing a blind Indian boy and therefore called up no associations of English life. English life proper struck me with the full force of its romance when about a year later I saw in my brother's new text-book a woodcut showing a high cliff, at its foot the sea, at the edge of the narrow beach a boat, near the boat a boy and a girl, and above and below the picture the following eight lines:

"Break, break, break,
On thy cold gray stones, O Sea!
And I would that my tongue could utter
The thoughts that arise in me.

"O well for the fisherman's boy,
That he shouts with his sister at play!
O well for the sailor lad,
That he sings in his boat on the bay!"

I did not understand half of it, but to me the lines distilled a yearning to which not even the magic casement of Keats about which I read three or four years later could stir me.

I had a serious grievance against my brother. He was always having more interesting text-books than I had, and that was due to the fact that in my time a change had come over the theory of teaching English to Indian boys. Formerly, Indian boys were being taught English mostly from text-books meant for use in England, or from the English classics. But when I was young the educational authorities had had a sudden inspiration that it was too much of a burden for young Indian boys to have to cope with English ideas in an English background in addition to having to master the intricacies of a foreign language. In pursuance of this theory our English text-books were being Indianized as the administration of India was Indianized later. Thus it happened that while my brother read things like:

"O Brignall banks are wild and fair,
And Greta woods are green..."

or,

"Why weep ye by the tide, ladie?
Why weep ye by the tide?
I'll wed ye to my youngest son,
And ye shall be his bride..."

and also read fine stories from books like Andrew Lang's *Animal Story Book* and Kipling's *Jungle Book*, I was being forced to repeat:

"The fox sat on the mat"
"The dog is in the well"
–and at the next higher stage to read about three Mussalmans
eating chilly and rice. I, however, tried to make amends by
reading all my brother's text-books two years in advance of
him, for in the school and by age he was two years my senior.
I am still unconvinced that inflicting "fat cats sitting on mats"
on little Indian boys is the best method of making them learn
English.

English poetry was to me and to my brother, even before
we could understand it fully, the most wonderful reading in the
world. We read the usual things, Wordsworth's "Lucy Gray",
"We are Seven", and "Daffodils", for example. We liked them,
but we were too young to understand all their subtlety. The
poem by Wordsworth which moved me most strongly at the
time was "Upon Westminster Bridge". As I read:

"Earth has not anything to show more fair......
This City now doth, like a garment, wear
The beauty of the morning; silent, bare,
Ships, towers, domes, theatres, and temples lie
Open unto the fields, and to the sky;
All bright and glittering in the smokeless air."

–the heavenly light of dawn with its purity and peace seemed
to descend on us.

There were two other poems which made an even greater
impression on us and they were placed one above the other in
Palgrave's *Children's Treasury,* which was one of my brother's
text-books. The first of them was Shakespeare's "Full fathom
five..." and the second Webster's "Call for the robin-redbreast
and the wren..." Again that juxta-position of land and sea. The
combination, as well as the contrast, was heightened in our
mind by Palgrave's note in which Lamb was quoted, which we

read very carefully without, however, taking in much beyond its general drift. But is was not necessary to understand more for the poems to set our imagination bestirring. What a magic country it was where the drowned were transformed into pearl and coral and where the robin and the wren covered the friendless bodies of unburied men with leaves and flowers, and the ant, the fieldmouse and the mole reared hillocks over them. Reading these lines of Webster, our hearts warmed up with a faith that could be described as the inverse of Rupert Brooke's. He was happy in the conviction that if he died in a distant land some part of that foreign soil would become for ever England. We had a feeling that if we died in England what would become for ever England would be a little foreign flesh, and with that faith there was happiness in perishing in an English glade, with the robin and the wren twittering overhead. But when we read the last two lines: "But keep the wolf far thence, that's foe to men, For with his nails he'll dig them up again," our boyish animalism got the better of us. Going on all fours on our earthen floor and stretching and spreading out our fingers as a cat stretches out and spreads its claws, we fell to scratching the ground.

If Webster's lines brought to us a very subtle realization of the quality of English land life, Campbell's "Ye Mariners of England" gave us a wholly straightforward initiation into the spirit of British maritime enterprise. We recited the simple lines, not with the half-perplexed, half-intuitive appreciation we had for the two poems by Shakespeare and Webster, but with great gusto and complete understanding. The climax of my own initiation into English seafaring life was reached when as a boy of eleven I read about the battle of Trafalgar and saw a coloured picture of Nelson standing on the deck of the *Victory* with Hardy. Nelson's signal kept ringing within me and I shouted out time and again, "England expects every man to do his duty" (that was the form in which I first learned the signal). On one of those days I was coming up from the river towards the road in front of our house, shouting at the top of my voice "England expects every man to do his duty", when I saw some gentlemen passing along the road on an elephant. The most elderly gentleman had the elephant stopped and, leaning out, asked me who I was. I replied that I was Upendra Babu's son. Then he asked me if I knew what those words were about. I said that they were Nelson's signal at Trafalgar. He seemed to be satisfied and went away on his elephant. I came to know later that he had spoken to my father about this meeting. It was my father who told me this.

THE ENGLISHMAN IN THE FLESH

It must on no account be imagined that in regard to English life and the English spirit we were always floating in the empyrean. In actual fact, we were as ready to walk on earth, and more often descend to the underworld, as to soar up to heaven. Our ideas of the Englishman in the flesh were very different from our ideas of his civilization. To be quite frank, our ignorance of the one remained quite unrelieved by our knowledge of the other, and it is this difference which I am now going to illustrate.

The normal reaction of the unsophisticated Indian villager in the face of an Englishman is headlong flight. I and my elder brother, as young boys, jumped into a roadside ditch. We did not do so, however, from any ignoble motive of self-preservation, but to save a precious cargo which we were carrying and which we believed to be in danger from the Englishman. The plain story is this. I and my brother had been sent to buy some bananas from the bazaar and were returning with a bunch when we saw an Englishman coming up the road from the opposite direction. I have no clear recollection who exactly he was, but he may have been Mr. Stapleton, the Inspector of Schools, whom I met with greater self-confidence some years later. As soon as we caught sight of him we hid ourselves in the ditch, because we had been told that Englishmen were as fond of bananas as any monkey could be and that they swooped on the fruit wherever and whenever they saw it. So we crouched in the ditch among the nettles until the Englishman had passed. This incident took place when my brother was only learning his English alphabet and when his sole source of knowledge about Englishmen was oral tradition. I was guided wholly by his example. Thus our behaviour on that occasion may be called behaviour appropriate to a state of innocence untinctured by any taste of the fruit of knowledge.

But this monkey analogy had deeper and less innocent antecedents. In our time it was trotted out rather jocosely. None the less I heard an old teacher of ours asserting it in the class with accents, not only of conviction, but of passion, and declaring that the English race were of a she-monkey by a demon born. The prevalent attitude towards Englishmen of our people was one of irrational and ineradicable cringing and equally irrational and unconquerable hatred. Grown-ups reserved the first for the Englishman present before them and the second for the absent Englishman. Our great moral and intellectual leaders of the nineteenth century were perfectly aware of this weakness in their parishioners and tried to cure them of it. Bankim Chandra Chatterji has written a satirical piece on Englishmen whose most sardonic and barbed point is reserved for his countrymen. A meeting of Englishmen is represented as a meeting of tigers, but the indigenes are shown as monkeys discreetly hiding themselves among the branches and leaves. When the tigers disperse, the monkeys swagger out and declare that they will now hold their meeting and abuse the tigers, and they do so. Finally, the meeting is closed with the observation from monkeys that after getting such a fusillade of bad language all the tigers must be dead in their lairs.

The remarkable similarity between the spirit of this satirical piece and the spirit of the passages about the *bandar log* in Kipling's story of Kaa's hunting has always intrigued me. Yet I can think of no explanation for it. Any possibility of borrowing on either side appears to be out of the question, for Bankim Chandra Chatterji died in the year in which *The Jungle Book* was published, and he had written the piece some years before his death, while Kipling could not have known anything about the Bengali skit since to my knowledge it has never been translated into English.

But the efforts of these manly and clear-sighted teachers of ours have been vain. The servility and malice ingrained in every fibre of our being which made us indulge in grotesque antics of alternating genuflexion and defiance before the Englishman persist to this day, and a most striking proof of this persistence was furnished by Mahatma Gandhi himself only one day before the announcement of the final British plan for transferring power to Indians, that is to say, on 2nd June 1947. After bestowing fulsome praise on Pandit Jawaharlal Nehru as the uncrowned king of India and emphasizing with what appeared like a licking of lips that he was a "Harrow boy", "Cambridge graduate", and "Barrister", Mahatma Gandhi went on to declare that "our future presidents will not be required to know English." The disappearance of the Englishman from the Indian political scene has not seen the end of this combination of servility and malice. Rather, as Mahatma Gandhi's pronouncement foreshadowed, the two-fold manifestation of homage and hatred has been transferred from the real to the imitation Englishman. I am thankful to my parents that they inculcated a saner outlook in their children and taught them, Indian gentlemen to be, to treat Englishmen as English gentlemen, no less, no more. But we could not help coming in contact with the debasing tradition.

The next time we saw Englishmen at close quarters was when Mr. Nathan, the Division Commissioner, arrived at Kishorganj with his wife. That was early in 1907. We had heard that he and his party were expected to arrive from the eastern side of the town at a particular time and waited for them to pass, perched on the top rail of the fence before our house. At last they drove past in a trap. The District Magistrate, who was accompanying Mr. and Mrs. Nathan, was for want of room seated on the footboard at the back, and this fact was later made the text of copious moralizing to us. That a District Magistrate could travel in a syce's seat was held up to us as an example of the Englishman's sense of discipline. But for the moment we were far more vividly interested in Mrs. Nathan, who gave us–the brothers–our first sight of an Englishwoman after we had become old enough to remember things. The resultant excitement was indescribable. We hardly talked about anything else but her blue eyes, her flaxen hair, her dress, and her hat for the whole day.

The next day the Commissioner was to distribute prizes to us in the school hall, and as both my brother and I were on the list of prize-winners we went to the prize-giving very neatly dressed and behaved with perfect propriety. As my brother went up solemnly to the Commissioner he clapped his hands and said, "A clever little boy!" And when I went up a short while after he remarked without knowing the relationship, "Here comes another little boy." But our later conduct was not on the same plane of impeccable decorum. As we had put on silk coats and shoes for the prize-giving we made up for the artificiality the next morning by showing ourselves to Mrs. Nathan in our unvarnished naturalness. While she was having her round of sight-seeing on foot, at least twenty scions of the best families of the town, bare-bodied, bare-footed, open-mouthed, round-eyed, and, at times, absent-mindedly chewing the ends of their *dhotis,* formed her train. It was, I believe, out of respect for her that the local officials did not chase us away. Her flaxen hair, blue eyes, high-heeled shoes, Edwardian skirt, plate-like hat, and the hat-pin running through the hat were all pointed at and discussed in undertones. It was many years before I had a second opportunity of seeing an Englishwoman at the same close range. But the thorough examination I had made at the very first opportunity carried me well through the barren intervening years.

Within a few months, however, something happened which gave me confidence in dealing with Englishmen. Mr. Stapleton had come to inspect our class and had asked the boy next to me, the best boy of our class and a particular friend of mine, to read a passage from our English text-book. The boy became a little nervous and began to trip and so I tried to help him in energetic whispers. Noticing this Mr. Stapleton asked me to read the passage, which I did passably, except that I could not pronounce the word "early" correctly. We always pronounced it as "ahrlee", and the more Mr. Stapleton said "airly" the farther I got away from the right pronunciation. Then, giving it up, he asked me who I was and how many brothers I had and a few similar simple questions. I answered in such tolerable English that that evening he sent his Bengali assistant to tell my father that he was very pleased with me. I was made much of and treated to some sweets, but from the next day a new torture began for me. My reputation as an English conversationalist got abroad and the senior boys took to asking me in English, "Where do you lodge?; "Who is your father?; "What is your name?" which from them were meaningless and irritating questions. But on the whole I felt confident, and when next year Mr. (later Sir Henry) Sharp, who was then the Director of Public Instruction in Bengal, came to inspect our school, I felt that I should be equal to the task if he asked me any questions. He did not. On that occasion the honours went to a senior student of the school, not for

English, though, but for drawing. This boy, whose name was Sashi Bagchi, had made a very good drawing of a tiger and this pleased the Director so much that he gave the boy some money to buy a colour-box with.

Speaking of the visits of these high officials to Kishorganj I am reminded of a fresh count of our ignorance of English ways. We knew something about the everyday clothes of Englishmen, but were completely uninstructed about their formal attire. Accordingly, on this score, we were given to making grotesque mistakes. Our drill-master, Mr. Hem Chakravarty, seemed to have picked up some knowledge of these matters and on inspection days he came correctly apparelled in morning dress. But we, as soon as we caught sight of him in that dress, felt like going into roaring fits of laughter and were restrained only by the fear of getting a thrashing, which we knew would surely follow as retribution. This mirth, I discovered, had reached higher quarters. One day my father said to me, "I hear your drill-master came dressed like a bandsman." That was the word, and in private we bagan to call our drill-master band-master. Poor dears! We did not know that the civilized world had already adjudged between us and our drill-master, and that while we believed that the joke was on him, it was really on us.

I have been furnished with very recent proof that this ignorance about the English morning dress and other formal costumes persists in my district even today. Early in the year 1947 a young nephew of mine (sister's son), who lived with his parents in a small town of east Mymensingh, came to visit us at Delhi. One day he was shown a picture of Mr. Churchill in the uniform of the Lord Warden and Admiral of the Cinque Ports (the picture which appeared in the *Illustrated London News* for 24th August 1946) and asked to say who it was. Without a moment's hesitation he replied, "A band-master,

Uncle." I could not help laughing out, because I had put him that question precisely with the object of testing whether our onetime ignorance was still surviving in Mymensingh. The little fellow was very much put out by my merriment and wanted to know the reason for it, and when I told him the story of our drill-master, instead of picking himself up, he appeared to fall into yet greater confusion. He did not like the idea of being held up as a vestigial specimen from the distant days of avuncular childhood.

I have now to tell the story of another and a more serious misconception, which is entwined with the central problem of our relationship with Englishmen, or, to be more exact, with all Europeans—the problem of colour. Their fair complexion was a matter of great curiosity and still greater perplexity with us, and we wanted to know why they were fair and we were dark. One theory was that we had been darkened by the sun whereas they had been bleached by the cold, both of us travelling in opposite directions from a golden or rather brownish mean. It is believed by some of our demonologists that the ghosts of cold countries are grey in complexion. So we argued that if pitch-black could become grey, brown could become pink. But one day a very close friend of mine told me a more sensational story. He was the son of a wealthy landowner who was also one of the leading lawyers of the town. All the sons of this gentleman bore different names of the god Siva. The eldest was called Lord of the Word, the second Trident-Holder, the third Primeval Lord, the fourth Master of Serpents, and so on. The third, Primeval Lord, was my friend. I regarded him as particularly well-informed about the wider world, because he often went to Calcutta and had an uncle there who was one of the foremost lawyers of the High Court.

Now, one day Primeval Lord told me in great confidence that all English babies were actually born dark, even as dark as we were, but that immediately after birth they were thrown into a tub filled with wine and it was the wine which bleached their skin white. Primeval Lord added that the English fathers sat by the tub holding in their hand the pronged instrument with which the English ate and watched if the babies were turning white within the expected time, and if they did not the fathers instantly thrust the pronged instrument down the throats of the babies and killed them. Primeval Lord did not improve on the story by pointing out its moral in so many words, but the hint was that if the English were fair they were so only because they were vicious. It was only through their alcoholism and cruelty that they got their fair complexion, while we were condemned to remain dark-skinned because we were not given to these vices.

I cannot say that I wholly believed the story, but pondered long over it. As was always the case when we received some particularly esoteric truth from our friends regarding the deep mysteries of life and death, I kept back this bit of information also from the elders and put it in an imperceptible mental drawer with a secret spring. There it ha lain all my life, and what interested me in later years was its affiliation with a general system of ideas, for this apparently crack-brained tale was only a freakish, and a very slightly freakish, product of an old and well-organized emotional predisposition amounting to a complex.

As I grew older I felt ever more intensely the implacable hatred of my countrymen for the fair complexion of Europeans. I shall give one or two instances. When I was a student of the higher school classes a university student whom I knew told me that another university student he knew had written in his examination paper of the "leprous white Englishwomen" and had been punished with rustication for that offence. The way the student narrated the story left no room for doubt that he considered the writing an act of great moral courage and the student who wrote it as a martyr to patriotism.

Again, in 1928, I was present at a social gathering of journalists in Calcutta, where a popular Hindi poet sang a patriotic song of his own composition in a stentorian voice to the accompaniment of the harmonium. The lines which called forth the most effusive appreciation contained the following idea: "One knee of Mother India is adorned by Tilak, the other by Das, but the White are spread all over her body as a disfiguring skin-disease."

It is possible to trace this skin-disease symbolism far back into history. In the latter part of the nineteenth century there was discovered a Sanskrit poem which purported to be an authentic contemporary biography of Prithviraj of the Chauhan clan, King of Ajmere, Delhi and the adjoining regions, whose defeat at the hands of Mu'izzud-din Muhammad bin Sam of Ghur (popularly known as Muhammad Ghuri) at the second battle of Taraori in 1192 finally established Muslim rule in India. There is no doubt that this work, which has only recently been published from the single manuscript known to exist, is contemporary. Internal evidence shows that it was substantially composed shortly before the final defeat of Prithviraj and was meant to celebrate his victory over Muhammad of Ghur at the first battle of Taraori in the winter of 1190-1. But the manuscript is incomplete and breaks off abruptly at the end of the twelfth canto. It is impossible to say whether the finished work contained more matter or whether the composition of the poem was interrupted by the defeat and death of Prithviraj. The prologue, which contains a lamentation over the Muslim occupation of Ajmere, suggests, however, that the poem was given the shape in which we have it after the Muslim victory. Now, this poem contains a description of the arrival of a Muslim envoy at the court of Prithviraj and of the physical appearance of this envoy, and in this account occurs the telltale aspersion that the envoy bore a paleness comparable to that given by the *unmentionable disease* (*avadya-roga-kalpam:* Canto X, verse 46).

Here then we have an emotional symbolism which dates from long before British rule, and which was only extended to the English rulers of India. What is the explanation? The obvious one is that it is an expression of the resentment of the autochthons against the colour prejudice or colour pride of their fair-complexioned foreign conquerors. This no doubt is partly true and needs no restatement at all. But what I want to say here is that there is another and a more fundamental element in this Hindu attitude which has not been noticed and which a Hindu would not disclose even if he were aware of it. It is this element, this locked-up secret, which I want to lay bare.

When not thinking of his foreign conquerors and taking up a self-pitying attitude in consequence, a Hindu is unsurpassed in his exaltation of colour and proneness to make a fetish of it. This comes out most blatantly in connexion with marriages, which certainly provide the most reliable test of the existence of colour feeling or colour prejudice among a people. An intense artificial selection in favour of fair complexion is going on throughout our country, and if we are not all as fair as the Nordics are it is certainly due to no fault of ours. I have seen many matrimonial advertisements laying down unreasonably un-Indian standards of complexion, and among them one, in one of the most important English dailies of Calcutta, asking for a bride of "Jewish complexion". At the time of the inspection of the girls for marriage their claim to fair complexion is scrutinized very rigorously. In West Bengal until recently it was not uncommon to rub apparently fair-looking girls with a wet towel to find out whether their complexion was natural or made up. On account of this insistence on fair complexion of the fathers of marriageable dark girls sometimes substituted a fairer sister at the time of the inspection, with dire results for the dark girl after marriage. I have heard of such cases and personally know of one which occurred in a house next to ours in Calcutta with all the scandal of detection at the time of the wedding.

The life of a dark marriageable girl in Bengal used to be one of unending private and public humiliation. Her mother would be perpetually reproaching her that she would never get married and remain an eternal millstone round her father's neck, and the prospective bridegroom's people coming to inspect her would be looking significantly at her. In this atmosphere of disgrace the dark girls hid themselves or kept in the background even when ordinary visitors came, while the fair ones strutted about like vain peacocks. This torture did not end even with marriage. The mother-in-law would give a scream if the bride on her arrival was found to be dark. When I accompanied my sister after her marriage to the village of her father-in-law a pack of rustic women who were going to have a look at her at first scrutinized me. "The brother of the bride," they said, "is dark", and went in with the greatest misgivings about the bride herself. Sometimes real tragedies happened. One of my uncles, a fair man himself, found after the wedding that his bride was dark and never saw her face again, and this aunt of mine was forced to live a widow's life. I shall give two more anecdotes from my personal experience.

In the late twenties I was requested by a friend of mine to accompany him for the inspection of a girl from whose father a proposal for marriage for him had been received. I am making repeated use of this word "inspection" deliberately, for the mission that is fulfilled on these occasions, the mission on which I also was being asked to go cannot be described as anything but a searching and exhaustive examination of all the data presented by the girl, among which the gynaecological are not included only because bare and elementary decencies stand in the way. The convention is that if the young man who is going to marry forms part of the inspecting delegation, as he sometimes but not invariably does, he is expected all the time to remain decorously silent but very indecorously staring at the girl, and have all his questions put through a confidant. In my life till now I have six times formed part of such delegations, thrice for three of my brothers and thrice for this single friend of mine.

Now it happened at this particular inspection that the girl (about four feet and a half in height and four stone in weight) was not actually dark, but she was very tanned and very freckled. My friend was glaring all the while and looking meaningly at me. The relations of the girls usually have keen eyes in these matters, and, as we were coming away, the father of the girl stepped up to us and said with a large gesture, "Gentlemen, if you have any doubts on the score of complexion I am ready to give you a guarantee that my daughter will become fifty percent fairer within three months of her marriage." We replied politely that we had no complaints to make on the score of complexion, but as soon as we were out of hearing my friend, who had been boiling with rage, burst out, "Oh, his guarantee! What should I do with the guarantee if she does not become fair once she is married off to me?" He went on harping on this grievance for some weeks, for he could not forgive the craftiness of a man who had tried to palm off a tanned girl on him with nothing better than his verbal guarantee.

The other anecdote concerns my own marriage. After it had been settled, an old friend of our family caught hold of me and gave me what he considered a timely and necessary warning. He said that after having given up Government service and turned myself into a poor and struggling journalist in the first instance, I was going to commit the second folly of marrying a dark girl. The consequence of this union, he continued, could only be that a number of girls would be born who would inherit the poverty of the father and the complexion of the mother and who, in consequence again, would be quite unmarriageable. After enunciating this proposition he asked me whether I had seriously considered this aspect of the matter. At first I felt inclined to be amused at the long view he was taking of the outcome of my marriage, but soon my anger at his impertinence overcame my sense of humour and I went up to my father to tell him that if that gentleman were asked to my wedding there would be another person away, and that would be myself. My father heard the story and was distressed. He fully sympathized with me but was embarrassed, for the family was under some obligation to this gentleman. At the moment I insisted on his exclusion, but in the end, not wishing to be unreasonably touchy kept quite. I maintained this self-restraint even when during the wedding I noticed the daughter of my well-wisher bustling about, and did not give a public exhibition of my annoyance. For this act of forbearance Providence has rewarded me by giving me only sons, all three of whom have, for boys, the passably brown complexion of teak and not the impossible brown of mahogany. Thus have I been released from worry over the colour bar to marriages.

This adoration of colour in the Hindu has a profound historical basis. The Hindu civilization was created by a people who were acutely conscious of their fair complexion in contrast to the dark skin of the autochthons, and their greatest preoccupation was how to maintain the pristine purity of the blood-stream which carried this colour. *Varna* or colour was the central principle round which Hindu society organized itself, and the orthodox Hindu scriptures know of no greater crime than miscegenation, or, as they call it, *Varna-sankara,* the mixing of colours. The *Gita* declares with burning and resounding conviction:

> "Samkaro narakayai 'va
> Kulaghnanam kulasya ca..."

(Chapter I, verse 42)

"Mixture (of caste) leads to naught but hell
For the destroyers of the family and for the family..."
(Edgerton's translation in the Harvard edition, 1944)

This faith in the sanctity of *Varna,* colour or caste endures and abides in Hindu society, and the fact–from the point of view of doctrine, the adventitious fact–that the inevitable intermixture with the indigenous element has made many Hindus dark-skinned, makes no difference to the hold and fascination of the ideal of colour. The Hindu regards himself as heir to the oldest conscious tradition of superior colour and as the carrier of the purest and most exclusive stream of blood which created that colour, by whose side the Nazi was a mere parvenu. When with this consciousness and pride he encounters a despised *Mlechchha,* an unclean foreigner, with a complexion fairer than his, his whole being is outraged. His deep-seated xenophobia is roused. He is intolerably humiliated, and in his unforgiving envy and hatred he seeks to obliterate the foreigner's superiority by casting on it the shame of the most loathsome disease which can afflict a man. The demented creature tries to console himself with the illusion that if in this world there is a foreigner fairer than he, it is only because that foreigner is a leper.

BOOK II

FIRST TWELVE YEARS

PREFATORY NOTE

MEN DO NOT become aware of the precise quality of their early years until late in life. Aksakov, Renan, Anatole France, Hudson, Tagore, all wrote their autobiographical master-pieces when they were advanced in years–in fact, advanced considerably into, and sometimes beyond, what Dante has called *il mezzo del cammin di nostra vita*. Like these great writers I too began to be reminiscent of my childhood when I had long passed my youth. But I am not, like them, calling up its memories and recording them either as things interesting in themselves or as a foil to my later life. It is not the aim of this book to create that kind of romantic interest or contrast. There is no room in it, since it is more of an exercise in descriptive ethnology than autobiography, for presenting childhood against the background of age, for presenting it as a submerged City of Ys or as the times when the intimations of immortality lay about us. If there is to be any vanished or vanishing Atlantis to speak of in this book, it should and would be all our life lived till yesterday. All that we have learnt, all that we have acquired, and all that we have prized is threatened with extinction. We do not know how the end will come, whether through a cataclysmic holocaust or slow, putrid decay. But regarding the eventual extinction there does not seem to be any uncertainty.

For us the irony of the situation lies in the fact that the very existence which has created the values whose passing I regret has also created the agencies which are destroying them. The catastrophe has unfolded inexorably from the environment I have described and the experience I am going to relate. There is a unity, an unbroken chain of cause and effect, running through the whole process, which if it has a fatalistic cast is fatalistic only in the sense that character is fate. We began the journey towards where we have arrived from what we did and experienced in our earliest years, which is only another way of saying that in this autobiography I shall have no phase of pure growth to set against a phase of unrelieved decay. In our existence growth and decay have been intermingled and parallel: we have seen life and death interlocked in an insepa-rable embrace; we have lived with mirth in funeral and with dirge in marriage. But the hour has come when life, if there has ever been any principle of life in us, must part company with its baleful mate and go its way. The marriage can no longer endure. Either we end it to be restored to cleanness, or it ends itself in a witches' sabbath.

At this stage all this will sound like a riddle, and a wordy riddle at that. But perhaps when the end of the story is reached this anticipatory leitmotiv will be recalled.

CHAPTER I

MY BIRTH, PARENTS, AND EARLY YEARS

I WAS BORN on Tuesday, Agrahayana 9, in the year 1304 of the Bengali era (which corresponds to 23rd November 1897), at 6 a.m. local time. I have no means of proving this date. I have no birth certificate in the Western fashion, and for reasons to be given presently no horoscope either in the Eastern fashion. The only document in the nature of a proof of age which I ever saw was an entry in my mother's handwriting on the fly-leaf of her notebook. But that notebook has been long lost.

Nevertheless I am quite positive about the date. It came to be instilled into me long before I saw the entry in the notebook, before any time of which I have memory. It did not enter a pre-formed mind. It was, like my father and mother, the brother just before and the brother just after me, one of the built-in fixtures of my consciousness.

NATAL CIRCUMSTANCES

There is a special reason for my emphasizing this trivial point. For I fall between two stools by virtue of this queer combination of extreme precision in respect of asserting, and total indefiniteness in regard to proving, the date of my birth. I belong neither to the populace nor to the patriciate. Among the former, it was quite impossible to come across precision in stating the age. An ordinary villager, asked the question, would give a figure with a wide margin of approximation. If pressed as to the actual date of birth, he would give what he considered to be the crushing retort: "Was I present at my birth?" As to the parents, the fathers most often lost count of the years, sometimes even of the children. The mothers were usually better posted, but they employed a relative chronological system. "My boy A," they would say, "began to toddle in the year of the earthquake"; or, "ceased going about naked in the year of the flood. Questioned about the dates of these events, the women would reply, "The earthquake took place when my B was in the belly"; or, "The flood occurred in the year in which the third girl was expected." The lives of those women were as featureless as the landscape of their country. They were punctuated only by the experiences of births when they were not marked by the slightly more memorable experiences of deaths. Thus the entire chronological system rested on the correlation of events inside and outside the body, and with its help all the children of the village were placed in a series like potsherds from an archaeological site. It was marvellous to see how this method enabled the women to keep an unerring grip on the age of the entire village population. But, of course, it was useless to outsiders.

If one had to state the theory of life of these people for them one could say that the only thing which mattered to them was the procession of the hungry generations. For both the great reaper and the small, it was enough to know that the crop was roughly contemporaneous. As to small individual differences, they were lost in the calculation of averages.

It was not so, however, with the wealthy and the aristocratic. They had sufficient consciousness of personality to be curious about their individual destinies. So they always tried to get glimpses into their future through the help of horoscopes, and since horoscopes cannot be made reliable without accurate information about the moment of birth, these upper-class families also kept exact records of the time and date of birth of their children.

Our family belonged to this upper stratum. Accordingly, there could be no question of any indefiniteness regarding the date and time of birth of us, the children. In fact, in the ordinary course, all of us would have had horoscopes. But, as I have already said, our parents had come under the influence of the Hindu monotheistic movement and were partly Deists and partly rationalists. Therefore they had no faith in horoscopes. Besides, apart from the question of principle, my father looked upon horoscopes as a nuisance from the practical point of view. The worries and complications horoscopes bring into life are almost endless to list. They draw a red herring across every personal problem–choice of profession, marriage, journeys, treatment in illness–and in truth disturb and upset every rational arrangement. For example, if a father has horoscopes of his sons and daughters, they have to be shown at the time of the marriage negotiations to the other party, and if by mischance the stars of the two young people do not agree the match is broken off. In cases where there is some special inducement to bring it about, private inquiries are set on foot regarding the possibility of astral incongruity and, if any is suspected to exist, forged horoscopes are presented. But this is not a very common practice. Normally, not a few otherwise desirable alliances founder on the rock of horoscopes.

The worst annoyance is caused, however, when the horoscope says that a certain person is in for accidental death at a specified age. Everybody, and more especially the women, is a-flutter long before the date. The priest, the astrologer, the mendicant *sadhu*, the *fakir*, the medicine-man—all have their innings and the time of their life. They give a long list of the articles which are indispensable for the magical ceremonies to be performed for averting the calamity, and, among them, intoxicating drugs have a not inconsiderable place. Of course, money also is expected to be bestowed in generous doles, and when not forthcoming from the generosity of the householder is extorted by blackmail.

In West Bengal a less expensive but more interesting device was resorted to for averting calamities foretold in horoscopes. It consisted in hanging a notice in bold letters at the gate of the house to the effect that a certain boy or girl of that house mentioned by name was destined to be killed by a fall from a tree, drowning, or some other accident (as mentioned in the horoscope) at the age of twelve, fourteen or any other age (equally specified in the horoscope). It was believed that giving the widest publicity to the impending calamity was the most effective means of averting it. The argument which formed the basis of this belief was subtle and somewhat like this: Evil spirits are always out to do harm to human beings, but they are, above everything else, mischievous and spiteful; so when they discover from the notice on the board that the householder has got reconciled to the idea of the death of his child, or else everybody has come to know of its possibility, they see no point in playing a stale prank which will not bring off a nasty surprise.

But in East Bengal, or at all events in east Mymensingh, this expedient was unknown and therefore the precaution my grandfather took was to avoid altogether the source of danger, which in his case fortunately was easy to do. His horoscope said, and I had it on the authority of my father, that he was destined to be eaten up by a crocodile, and consequently throughout his life he never entered water, never trusted himself anywhere near it, and never travelled in a boat. Nobody could induce him even to bathe in the family tank, although it was just across the courtyard, many miles away from any place where crocodiles could even be dreamt to exist, and enclosed on all sides by high embankments. All his life he took his bath on a stool in the veranda or in one corner of the courtyard with one pitcher of water. By this means he escaped the crocodile and died in his bed at eighty years old, having remained during the last three or four years of his life in a state of senile infantilism.

My father must have pondered over all these things when he set his face resolutely against horoscopes for his eight children. My mother was an uncompromising puritan to whom nothing was more revolting than superstition, within whose definition she included, first of all, belief in ghosts and, secondly, belief in astrology. She was such a reformist that after her marriage she had even refused to chew the betel-leaf, so ubiquitous in India, and as a mere girl of fourteen to eighteen had for five long years defied the jeers and importunities of the whole village. Therefore, she whole-heartedly approved my father's decision to have no horoscopes for us. At the same time, her methodical, puritanical cast of mind made her post us very accurately with regard to the dates of our birth. I have a feeling which I cannot call memory because it dates from too early a period of life, that she catechized us very early and very meticulously about our exact age. It was thus that I acquired that firm conviction about my age without ever having any document to support it.

Another circumstance connected with births in our family was that all of us were born without prenatal advertisement. We, the elder children, never got any inkling of the coming of our new brothers and sisters. Our parents never discussed these matters before us, and for all we knew they might have been dropped overnight by the proverbial stork. By a curious chance all of us, except one, were born either late at night or very early in the morning, and in any case we never saw our mother feeling uncomfortable or in pain.

This was not as common a state of affairs as many might be disposed to think, for among us these interesting conditions still form the subject of day-to-day and pretty thorough discussion. In 1917 the son of a first cousin of mine came to Calcutta to read at the university after passing his matriculation examination. When he came to visit us my mother asked him about his mother, and he replied in the most natural manner, "She is pregnant, and it's her seventh month." I, who was standing by, showed some discomposure at this answer but was instantly checked by a meaning look. Again, when I was at Banagram in 1923 on a short visit, the matrons were giving me, a young man of twenty-five, daily reports about the condition of almost all the young women of the village. I almost wondered if they took me for an obstetrician. My elder brother's wife, who had no children for the first ten years of her married life, was having interesting rumours circulated about herself every other year by the well-wishers of the family. In 1923, in Calcutta, I one day saw the six-year-old daughter of an advocate of Calcutta High Court jumping on her mother and snuggling against the right place holding a lisping and caressing conversation with what she called her coming brother inside.

Some years after my marriage, when we were living in Calcutta, my wife received a public and resounding query on this subject. A most esteemed friend of mine was living in a flat on the floor below us and across the inner courtyard, the distance between the two flats being about fifty feet. One day his wife, a most amiable lady, caught sight of my wife at the window and fancied that she (my wife) did not look quite well. (Incidentally, to say "You do not look well" is the most polite, friendly, and considerate remark that we can make on meeting an acquaintance, and one which will be appreciated by the person addressed with almost a lump in his throat. On the other hand to ignore his self-pity and assume that he is hale and hearty is to rival the heartless gruffness of the Gryphon is his attitude towards the Mock Turtle.) So the inquiring lady shouted, "O Dhruva's mother (that is the name of my eldest son), are you...?" She used the most colloquial expression for these conditions current in West Bengal, which is rather more shattering than the pure Sanskrit word used in my district.

These discussions were not, however, the whole of the matter. In my boyhood I often found that some of the other boys and girls could even say whether it was a brother or a sister they were expecting. They would observe: "My mother's nipples are purplish, she is going to have a boy"; or, "They are pinkish, she is going to have a girl". We were very much puzzled by these remarks, for so far from being able to observe the exact tint of the nipples of our mother we were not able even to see them. Having come under reforming influences, she not only wore a chemise under her *sari*, but very often also a petticoat and a blouse.

I have often reflected over the meaning of this unsophisticated garrulity and in frivolous moments have been disposed to conclude that just as our marriages have to be proved, not by legal documents or certificates, but by the collective testimony of the cognates and agnates who have to be present at the ceremony, so probably our legitimacy has to be proved by a continuous discussion of our foetal existence, the discussion being a counterpart of the putting up or calling of the banns in an English marriage, a challenge to all concerned to come forward and dispute the legitimacy if they possibly can. But that certainly is not the truth. In reality, behind this public discussion of the prenatal existence lies the Hindu view of life, which enjoins a number of purificatory rites or rites of a sacramental character at certain well-marked stages of life, beginning with conception and ending with the offering of the oblations after death. In former ages the purificatory rite for conception appears to have been performed as a matter of regular routine, but in our time I never saw any such regular performance. The ceremony had by that time come to be performed only after the first monthly course of a girl after her marriage and was euphemistically called the "second marriage". If at this juncture the husband happened to be away at college or at his place of work he usually received his summons through a vague but desperate telegram from his father-in-law. When a young man received a telegram soon after his marriage to come to the house of his father-in-law without any cogent reason being shown he had to endure a rain of ribaldry from his friends. The incantations for this ritual are largely of a magical character and the young man has to lay his hand on certain parts of his own body as well as the body of his wife in order to infuse the virtue of the incantations into them. The priest, however, manages this so discreetly that nobody has any suspicion of what he is really doing, more especially because in most cases there is complete ignorance of Sanskrit. This ceremony had to be gone through in the case of my first sister whose marriage took place in 1916. Her father-in-law and mother-in-law were aged people of the old school and they expected it. But after this solitary observance the ceremony was quietly dropped in our family, and I do not think it is performed anywhere now, except in very backward villages or in very orthodox families. There were also two or three additional but minor ceremonies for different stages of the foetal growth which may not have all disappeared.

One ceremony of a social character in any case survives. It is what is called the "wish ceremony". It is the custom for the other women of the family–mothers, mothers-in-law, elder sisters, and women standing in a relationship of seniority to the expectant girl–to treat her to milk pudding and presents of clothes shortly before her time. The most interesting performance of this ceremony that I ever saw was at Banagram in 1923, when an elderly aunt of mine was treated to milk pudding and new clothes by her married son. I had been invited to it along with a host of others. The sweets and presents were placed in the centre of the hut, but my aunt, suddenly feeling bashful, hid herself behind a screen. Two of the matrons went in search of her and, dragging her out, began to push and pull her towards the plate, encouraging her all the while by saying that for a mother to be so treated by her own son was a matter for pride. It was a little comical to look on the spectacle. My aunt was a woman of some stature and bulk, which was heightened by her condition, and the two encouraging ladies were very small, very wizened, and very fussy. So the whole scene suggested a liner being taken in by tugs. I must confess that the same ceremony, without the accompaniment of tugging, was performed in the case of all my sisters, all my sisters-in-law, and also *(mea culpa)* my wife. Even as late as 1943 it was gone through (again, *peccavi*) for the young wife of my fifth brother in my own house at Delhi. I do not want to prejudice anything I have to say in this book by making generalizations without adducing a sufficient volume of evidence to support them and thus laying myself open to the charge of making dogmatic assertions; so I draw no moral from what I have just admitted. But perhaps at the end of this autobiography I shall be permitted to say that *plus ca change,*

plus c'est la meme chose. The revolutionary thing in my
mother's case was that she did not have even this social
ceremony, except perhaps only once in so vague and veiled a
form that even now I am not sure what it exactly was. That is
why I contend that our being born without prenatal publicity
was no stale distinction.

A third peculiarity of our births was that we were all born
under the auspices of our father. I am not trying to be waggish,
but mean it literally. In Bengal it was not the custom, and in
most cases it is still not the custom, for a child, and particularly
the first child, to be born in the house of its father or of its
grandfather on the paternal side. The expectant mothers were
and are sent off to their fathers, so that the first children almost
always were born, and are still born, in their maternal grandparents' houses, the expenses of the maternity also being
always borne by the girl's father.

Everybody followed and follows this custom without
asking how and why it originated. But I believe the original
reason was that these child mothers felt too cribbed and
confined in the houses of their fathers-in-law. The code of
conduct for the daughters-in-law was too rigid and narrow for
them to be able to move about, speak, eat or sleep with any
degree of comfort. My mother, for instance, did not speak a
word to her mother-in-law for five whole years after her
marriage, nor could she uncover her face. She had to carry on
all her intercourse with the mistress of the house with the help
of only two movements of the head, the up-and-down positive
nod and the side-to-side negative shake. If she wanted anything she had to go without it until the other young girls of the
family discovered it and made representations to the old lady.
It was realized by the elders that such conditions could be very
irksome, even if not harmful, to a young expectant girl and she
was allowed to take advantage of the greater freedom of the
father's house, since no relaxation of the code for daughters-
in-law was conceivable as long as she remained under the roof
of her father-in-law.

Gradually, however, and subconsciously, an economic interpretation crept into the custom of sending away the girls to their paternal homes for *accouchement,* as has been the case with almost every kind of human activity since Marx wrote his treatise. The theory, as well as the practice, was more fully developed in West Bengal than in East Bengal, but in both parts it was assumed that having established his girl in a good family it was the duty of the father to give free service for a certain period. Under the same convention two extra responsibilities had to be borne by the girl's father: he was expected to get his daughter treated if she fell ill during the years immediately following her marriage and also to provide the everyday clothes of his daughter for at least two or three years. During this period it was considered the height of impropriety to expect the father-in-law to replenish the wardobe of his daughter-in-law, although he could and did give her costly presents of clothes and jewellery on ceremonial occasions. As to the young husband, he had no *locus standi* whatever except to sneak at night to his wife. Nobody took any account of him for any other purpose.

My father was an individualist and would have none of this dependence on the father-in-law. His first two children were born while his parents were living and when he had to submit to the old custom. But none of them survived. The eight of his remaining and surviving children were all born in his own house at Kishorganj and were born under his care. He was helped in this independence by the circumstance that before any of us eight was born all our grandparents except our mother's mother were dead, and this grandmother, too, lived too far away, besides being in not very easy circumstances, for my mother to be sent to her. This also has to be added that in many other families at Kishorganj children were born in the same way. But there was perhaps a difference in the spirit in which my father shouldered his responsibilities. Instead of maintaining an attitude of detached neutrality while the women managed the affair, he appeared to take everything quite actively on himself. Owing to this ready assumption of parental responsibility and certain other allied features, our family grew up as a true family–composed of the father, the mother, and the children–in which each element had its due share of importance and proper status.

This definitely was not the norm of the times. The common form of the family was the joint family, which was more like a tribal camp than a family. In these joint homes the family relations inevitably got mixed up. The father, the son, the son-in-law, the mother, the daughter, the daughter-in-law, were all having children at the same time. The uncles, the aunts, the cousins were doing the same thing, and the children called the elders and one another whatever they liked. The fathers were called brother, the grandfathers and brothers father, mothers daughter-in-law, grandmothers mother, uncles father, nephews brother, till there was indescribable confusion in the ideas of blood relationship and nobody could claim any exclusive right in a child.

I am doubtful whether Plato would have advocated the removal of children from the care of their parents and the extirpation of parental interest in the child if he had seen our system at work and in its results. We went very far towards not only his system but also the modern system of public creches. We almost succeeded in eliminating the influence of the mother and the father, in abolishing parental exclusiveness, and throwing the child on the lap of the community and its Nomos. But what a Nomos it was. It was not only not sifted by Socratic criticism and unilluminated by Platonic idealism, it was a Nomos about which even the Sophists did not bother one way or the other. It was the pure collectivism and the unchallenged Nomos of the gregarious ruminants.

My father's originality was that he built up a Bengali Hindu family of a different type. We never called our father brother, nor our mother daughter-in-law. It was a family in which every person knew his place and his function. In fact, the status of my mother was noticed by all our relatives and neighbours. The authority she wielded was considered to be a special characteristic of the little group of human beings comprised by Upendra Narayan Chaudhuri, his wife Sushila Sundari Chaudhurani, and their children.

MY FATHER

I want to give in this chapter character-sketches of my father and of my mother. But I know the pitfalls of the attempt. There are few things more unconvincing than a son's portrait of his parents. The varnish of filial piety, sometimes a very sickly varnish it can be, lies thickly on it and repels everybody but the children. Yet the most natural impulse in a son is to imitate the first and third sons and not the second son of Noah. Besides, it is implicit in the very nature of the relationship that large parts of a father's or a mother's character, personality, and life should remain as unknown country to the son and that he should shrink from probing into these parts with a reluctance which is somewhat akin to a healthy man's revulsion from incest. Therefore a son's delineation of his parents can be full and true only in so far as it describes the mutual relationship. A few successful biographies of fathers by sons which exist constitute, I believe, the exceptions which prove the rule.

For us in India these objections have even greater validity. Patriarchal society always prescribes and enforces the duty of filial piety, and one of the very first things a Hindu boy learns, or at all events used to learn, is and was the Sanskrit tag which declares: "Father is Heaven, Father is Morality, Father besides is the Highest Prayer, and if Father is pleased, pleased also are all the Gods." It is fairly common to find in the works of young

Indian scholars, and even in their theses for doctorate, the pious dedication in Sanskrit whose English equivalent is: "To my Father the God." Yet it is another confirmation of the strange duality of Indian life that in our country also is to be found some of the most implacable hostility towards parents, and more particularly towards fathers. One day with my own eyes I saw the spectacle of a grown-up son (a retired captain of the Indian Medical Service) flying with a cudgel at his decrepit father roaring: "I'll scatter your brains today, you bloody son of a bitch." I can also relate two stories which I heard soon after the deaths of the fathers in question.

In one case the son, he too an elderly person, nursed no friendly feeling towards his father because he suspected him of being more partial to his own son (the grandson, that is to say) and of entertaining the design of bequeathing the family property to the young man. So, when he learned the news of his father's death, he went into such rapturous antics of delight that the very servants implored him in the name of decency to restrain himself. In the other case one of two sons, again an elderly man, was alienated from his father for some supposed or real partiality to his younger brother, and so, when he got the news of his father's death from his brother, he wrote back: "*Your* father was the meanest person that ever lived on the face of the earth."

I do not think this hostility springs wholly from the fault of the fathers, although there are only too many of them whose lives are a long justification for the sons to feel glad when they are dead. This filial antagonism is often quite gratuitous and must be the complement of the filial piety extorted by patriarchal society. The sons, unable to assert any kind of freedom–moral, intellectual, or even economic–and too debilitated by custom to rise in revolt, pay back all the frustration in underhand malice and rancour. The artificial piety generates the unnatural toxin. Its equivalent in matriarchal society is perhaps uxorophobia.

Having warned myself against its risks, I think I can now attempt the portraiture of my parents. My father was born in 1867. I was born when he was thirty years old. Therefore I remember him as he was from about his thirty-fifth year to his death at the age of sixty-seven. I have no impression that he changed materially in character or outward appearance during all these years, although the softer side of his personality became rather more dominant after the death of my mother in 1924.

He was of middle height, judged by Bengali standards; that is to say, just under five feet six inches. But he had broad and square shoulders, a deep chest, and very muscular arms, so that he gave an impression of great physical strength besides actually possessing it. His body had none of those curves which in India are as much a part of masculine grace as of the feminine. More especially, seen in the profile, his figure presented neither the S-shaped nor the barrel-shaped outline, which are two of the commonest anatomical configurations to be found among us. In Calcutta I used to be regaled almost daily by the sight of a gentleman who in his middle parts presented a perfect sphere from whichever angle he was looked at. My father did not have this rotundity and, what was not less significant, despised obese people. He was very bony, his waist and hips were narrow, and thus there was a preponderance of nearly straight lines in his figure.

His face was high-featured. A domed forehead merging into the bald top, strongly marked ridges of the brows, a high and fleshy nose, and deep-set and rather small eyes gave an impression of sternness, which was further heightened by the thin and tightly closed-lips, the strong jaws, and a substantial and regular chin. But here appearances were deceptive. For my father, although never given to demonstrativeness or wearing his heart on his sleeve, was one of the gentlest and most affectionate of men. But neither this nor his great quickness of mind was apparent in his face, because it was not very mobile. The range of his face expressions was more limited than the range of his mind. In his old age he often sat still for hours on his bed, squatting and cross-legged. In that posture he bore a very striking resemblance to the famous statue of the scribe of the Old Kingdom of Egypt.

In dress he was simple to the point of being shabby. I never saw him in anything but the conventional Bengali dress, except that when going to the courts he put on a *chapkan* and trousers. But in that he was only obeying long-established custom. In the cold season he wrapped a shawl round himself, sometimes also put on an ordinary coat and sometimes even a chesterfield. But he was always giving away the more expensive articles of his clothing to us. He was a man who stood in need of very little personal service and even disliked too much attention of this kind from others. While my mother lived she looked to his personal needs. After her death he would rather be left to himself than made much of.

He was not given to criticizing or condemning others. He did not enjoy scandal even when it was of the most innocuous kind. I hardly ever heard him discuss his relations, friends, acquaintances, and neighbours. Only when there was some strong reason for anger or severity over somebody's conduct would he burst into a short contemptuous sentence, which gave us a greater sense of the guilty person's delinquency than any lecture could. But despite his capacity for moral indignation I do not think that morals were the central interest of his life. He left our moral and religious education to our mother, only giving us the impression that he was behind her in everything she said or did. When we wilfully went wrong this ultimate sanction came into play against us on application from my mother, and the form it took was whipping. In all I got two serious whippings from my father, and in both cases the reason was a serious moral lapse. Once I had concocted a false story against a schoolfellow in order to spite him. The other time I had defied home discipline and threatened to leave the house. In the ordinary course, paternal intervention had to be sought by my mother most frequently for preventing fratricidal strife. In spite of the blind devotion we normally showed to one another in boyhood, this was the most serious failing of us the boys. I particularly, being weaker than the two brothers on either side of me, was capable of biding my time with a slow and smouldering vindictiveness. One day my elder brother treated me highhandedly and, as it was no use trying to stand up to him, I lay low. But as chance would have it he got fever three or four days later and for about an hour or so both my father and mother were away from home. That was my opportunity. I walked into his room and gave him a cold-blooded beating. Of course the consequences of this action were very grave.

The thing my father was primarily interested in was education. He never tried to define his idea of a good education, but his casual remarks on this subject, his verdicts on men and things, and his emotional reactions to the different kinds of human activity, made it plain that what he understood by education was acquisition of knowledge, accompanied by and inseparable from the training and devolopment of all the mental faculties, and more especially the intellect. These two aspects of education were to him not only equally essential but, as he seemed to assume, automatically contributory to each other's growth. He not only felt that the one was useless without the other, he also felt that they were, like the twin gods of Aryan mythology, always present together and always to be worshipped together.

It was not with intellectual conviction alone that my father spoke of education. There was emotional fervour in his attitude, so that we got a sense that by educating ourselves we should be acquiring, not simply the means to do something else, not simply a key to other kinds of success, but some all-round and absolute goodness which was not mere skill but something desirable in itself. I am quite sure, if he had come upon it, my father could have read with delight and complete sympathy Rabelais' account of the education of Gargantua, and especially the description of little Eudemon in Book I. He had the same faith in *litterae humaniores* which made Rabelais attribute Eudemon's angelic looks and charming manners almost explicitly to his ablility, as a twelve-year-old French boy of the fifteenth century, to speak Latin like a Gracchus, Cicero, or Aemilius. I also think that my father was capable of writing the letter which Gargantua wrote to his son, and he did write many letters of the same general tenor: "The time of my boyhood was darksome, obscured with clouds of ignorance, and savouring a little of the infelicity and calamity of the Goths, who had, wherever they set footing, destroyed all good literature, which in my age hath by divine goodness been restored unto its former light and dignity, and that with such amendment and increase of the knowledge, that now hardly should I be admitted unto the first from of the little grammar-school boys; I say, I who in my youthful days was (and that justly) reputed the most learned of that age." I have a suspicion also that he would not have been wholly displeased if in our presence the other little Chaudhuris of Banagram had fallen to crying like a cow and become tongue-tied, as did little Gargantua after Eudemon's Latin discourse.

I shall never contend that in giving us an education which was the best he could think of and the best he could afford (which qualification is partly superfluous because he did many things which he could not well afford), he was disinterested in our worldly success and prosperity. On the contrary, as a result of this education, he certainly expected us to be better and earlier established in the world than others and the peculiar genius which we the brothers developed as we grew older for spoiling our worldly prospects was the sorrow of his age and its greatest disappointment. But what he had assumed was that worldly success would attend us as a corollary to our better education without being made its primary purpose. He was not disposed to treat education as the means to an end or as vocational training.

His faith was put to a severe test later in life and it may have been partly undermined, but I do not think, even when so far as he was concerned the last word had been said, he quite lost his faith. I rather believe that he attributed the ill-success of his ideal from the worldly point of view to our indolence or perversity which prevented us from putting our education to its best practical advantage. I, in particular, fell so headlong in love with the idea of being a scholar gypsy after reading Matthew Arnold's poem that this love marked its trail on all my subsequent worldly career. I may not regret it even now, but for a father to be reconciled to the penury of a son is a bitter ordeal.

This is anticipating a later experience of my life. For the moment my father had no qualms about his ideas on education and its value, and his tacit assumptions radiating through all manner of channels, mostly subconscious, made our passage through school and university, especially of us the first two boys, a journey endowed with the rare attribute of purposefulness and animation.

The educational system of British India has been accused of being only a machine for turning out clerks and officials. That certainly is true if we test the system by the use which was made of it in average instances and judge it by its average product. But it is not true if we take into account the intention of those who created the system. Their first mistake, however, was that they reproduced the outward forms of an educational system which existed in another country without enquiring whether the assumptions on which it rested there and the spirit by which it was animated in the country of its origin existed also in India. Their second mistake was that they introduced the system without making adequate, and for that matter any, provision for the conscious and continuous propagation of the assumptions, since they did not exist in India. Thus it happened that although there always were a select few who could supply the missing spark of animation from their private insight, some unusual and exceptional trait in the family tradition, or gift of grace, the many passed through the system quite mechanically or investing it with only that meaning which was most obvious to them. They used the system as a man who does not understand the nature and use of live ammunition uses a gun even when he has cartridges, that is to say, only as a cudgel. Although it is not fair to blame them for this, it is not fair either to blame a system or an instrument if one does not put it to its fullest possible use.

In our case, as I have described, an animating principle closely resembling, or at all events constituting a rudimentary version of, the original humanistic motive force of the system, was supplied through the influence of our father. This was noticed by our teachers also, for they were not all the mechanical drudges they are only too often taken to be. Whenever we met new teachers through promotion to an upper class or transfer to a new school, we were noticed by them as if we were the pupils they had been waiting for, pupils who came to school as live creatures and not as fossils, and their notice of us brought upon them the reproach of partiality and favouritism from the other boys. I should make it clear that we were not the sole recipients of grace, but that boys of similar outlook and spirit were coming to the educational institutions all over the country in a steady trickle. Nevertheless it still remains the fact that we belonged to the minority of live hundreds and not to the majority of dead thousands.

I wonder even now how and where my father picked up his ideas about education. Of course, I know their ultimate source and affiliations. I also know something about the specific system of ideas through which they found expression in nineteenth-century Bengal. About all this I shall have something to say in a later chapter. But I cannot trace the link between my father and the system of ideas in Bengal to which I have just referred. In regard to the reformed ideas on religion and morality to which our family subscribed, I can lay my hands on the persons and put my finger on the places through whom and which these ideas were transmitted to my parents, but in the case of my father's educational ideas I have no such information. On the contrary everything I know about the traditions of our clan makes me positive that from his family my father could under no circumstances have learnt to glorify education. In most well-to-do families education was despised as the last resource of the person who had no independent competence. The most natural remark for a doting grandmother or aunt to make was: "Why should my darling wear himself out with this silly reading and writing? He won't have to earn his livelihood like a poor man's son." At a later epoch this attitude was modified, but only in favour of education as a means of making money. In the first Bengali primer that most Bengali boys of my generation read occurred the famous couplet which was our first initiation into educational theory:

"The boy who for his studies cares,
In carriage and pair he surely fares."

As I read those lines I had the vision of a coach and pair standing before our house and myself stepping in with my Bengali primer under the arm. Even today, and even as an ideal, the notion of education as anything but the handmaid of money has not been widely accepted in India. The greater part of modern Indian scholarship consists only of theses for doctorate, and these formal gestures at the altar of learning are in fact only the crack of the whip (not taken overseriously even as that) to set the coach of career rolling. In such a society nobody thinks of going to a grammarian's funeral. In fact, it would be considered even more ridiculous than attending the funeral of an uncle, which the Bengali proverb regards as the preoccupation of the man who has no better occupation.

It is this tradition and background which made the appearance of a school of Bengali humanism in the nineteenth century a revolutionary phenomenon, and my father's distinction was that without coming into direct contact with this movement or being a highly educated man himself–his education was interrupted by family circumstances–he had almost intuitively imbibed the humanistic spirit, and tried to make it the spiritual heritage of his children.

The predominant form which this humanistic interest took in him was, typically enough, linguistic culture. He was careful and critical about the use of the Bengali language but still more curious and painstaking about English. The vocabulary of the English language, its syntax, its idioms, possessed a fascination for him which was self-sufficient. He started life with the dictionary of Annandale, went from Annandale to Chambers's *Twentieth Century Dictionary*, and when Fowler's *Concise Oxford Dictionary* came out he was an eager buyer. Looking into his copy I found it marked in many places, which indicated that he had not only consulted it for individual words, but gone through it as a whole, impelled by a purely verbal interest. From my childhood I saw him buying such well-known books as *Esop's Fables, Evenings at Home, Robinson Crusoe*, or Smiles' *Self-help*, going through them and marking them throughout in red and blue for his own use as well as for ours. He used one of the colours for new words and the other for idioms and interesting phrases and turns of expression.

At the age of eleven I went very carefully through the marked copy of *Evenings at Home,* and I count that reading among the most profitable of my life, for whatever may be thought of *Evenings at Home* as literature, it was both in diction and style and in subject-matter a log hewn from the native English woods, and for a foreign boy that was a most valuable quality. By adding to *Evenings at Home* Miss Mitford's *Our Village* two or three years later, I could claim that I was attuning myself very successfully to the spirit of the English language and English life. None of the classical children's books in English would have done the same thing for us. A masterpiece like *Alice in Wonderland* is quite inaccessible both in its ideas and its language to most Indian boys and to nearly as many adults. *Evenings at Home* and *Our Village* were both typically English, yet one of them had that touch of didacticism and the other that touch of sentimentality without which an Indian is very much puzzled about a book. So they could serve as a very good bridge between the Indian temperament and the English temperament.

After entrusting our English to the care of a tutor and finding that we were not making the kind of progress he wanted, my father took over the teaching himself and carried it on for about two years. He handed us over to a tutor once again only when he was satisfied that we had received a thorough grounding in the elements. These two years were the decisive years in my understanding of the fundamental principles of the English language. It is not the English vocabulary but the English construction which is the bugbear of Indian boys, and only too many never learn it at all. My father used to say that the first hurdle to take in English was to make a boy understand and thoroughly master the use and meaning of the verb *to have*. It may sound strange to Englishmen, Frenchmen, Germans, and other Europeans, but the fact is that neither Bengali nor, so far as I know, any other Indian language has a possessive verb. If I have to say "I have a book" in Bengali, the sentence will be equivalent syntactically to "A book exists of me". Therefore an Indian boy, when asked for the first time to write "I have a book", writes, "My book has." That was the point my father had in mind. The next two problems according to him were to teach the boys the use of the auxiliary verbs and the relative pronouns. He drilled us in both, and that very thoroughly. He would never permit us, as only too many teachers in India even now do with fatal results, to translate English passages into slipshod Bengali smacking of English, and Bengali passages into slipshod English smacking of Bengali. He made us place the sentences side by side and thoroughly analyse the differences in structure.

Just as he read dictionaries continuously when the mood for verbal investigation was on him, he also read books on English idioms and usage, especially those written for Indian students. But I never found him reading or even taking any interest in formal grammar. What attracted him was the living use of a language and not the study of linguistic forms. Of course, in this predilection he was helped by the fact that he was dealing with a modern and not a classical language. We, however, did not worry over these theoretical questions; we found his method of learning English much the pleasantest way, for not only were we spared the trouble and boredom of learning grammatical definitions but also we were daily showing our advantage over the other boys and showing to advantage in the class. On this score I had a brush with a teacher, when, at the age of twelve, I went to a new school. I had written a sentence in a certain way and not in another and the more usual way, and when he asked me the reason I replied that the other way did not *sound* right to me. He observed severely, and rather testily also, that how an English sentence sounded to me could not be taken as a criterion of its correctness, and I must produce something more authoritative. He was probably right, but at the time I thought him a very tiresome and perverse person, for I could see that even he had to admit that my sentence was correct. My other teachers were, however, content with the results and did not try to improve my methods.

Thus it happened that from my father I learned English without tears, although not without toil. But English was not the only thing in our education which he actively fostered. Although his own interest was centred round language and literature he had enough instinctive soundness in matters of education to give us equal encouragement and facilities in other subjects, so that we might discover our real aptitudes. It is one of the most extraordinary features of education in India that it is the parent or other guardian who most often chooses the subject of study for a student. A young man with no capacity for abstract thinking is made to read economics or philosophy, and another young man who cares only for literature is made to take up electrical engineering or medicine. The justification advanced is always some worldly advantage, fancied or real, most often fancied, and the person directly concerned almost always sighs as a lover and obeys as a son. This is the first command to "fall in" in that impressive or frightening drill (according to the temperament of the person who observes it) of square pegs in round holes which is so characteristic of modern Indian life. But my father, even from our earliest age, never dictated what subjects we should take up. He left the choice entirely to us, and, as a matter of fact, of his six sons only the two eldest went in for the so-called arts course. All the rest studied vocational subjects, medicine or engineering.

What my father did was to give us the means of learning anything from science to drawing and painting and then let us find out for ourselves what suited us best. The only extra effort he expected from us was that even though we became specialists in some subject we should not become mere technicians but acquire some ancillary qualification in the field of art which would lend grace to our life. He seemed to possess an unerring sense of the future, and of coming trends; and although he could not always carry through the projects conceived by him, or rather we did not complete the projects to which he initiated us, he was always forestalling others by at least ten years. I can illustrate this best by citing the example of our musical education. Today this subject, together with a kind of choreographic dancing, has become so well established in Bengali life that Terpsichore may now be fitly pictured as a female Orestes pursued by a million adolescent furies. The enthusiasm of these marriageable young persons makes at least ninety-eight per cent of Bengali homes unendurable at certain hours of the day and night, quite a substantial part of radio music unhearable, and not a negligible portion of gramophone records only fit to be broken up with the hammer. But in our childhood Hindu society, *our* society, looked upon a woman who sang as a *demimondaine,* and a man who sang as her parasite or patron. It was in that atmosphere that my father made us practise music as a regular subject of education. Of course, we had the tradition of devotional singing derived both from the Brahmo Samaj and Hindu worship, but while continuing these traditions my father also took a purely secular and aesthetic view of music and provided for us instruments and teachers which and who in that age were to be met with only in highly disreputable quarters.

While I am on the subject of my father's pioneering spirit, I had better complete the story by describing his enterprise in the material sphere. As Vice-Chairman of the municipality he used to get the catalogues of the large European shops in Calcutta. He regularly went through them for new ideas about house-keeping and promptly ordered anything which he thought would solve some pressing problem in our home. As the milk for the babies had to be warmed many times a day, and as it was very unhygienic, besides unsightly, to keep the brazier always burning, he first ordered a small paraffin stove and then a bigger one with an oven and every other accessory complete. Again, as it was a messy, and even with messiness an unsatisfactory, operation to trim our lamps with a pair of ordinary scissors, he obtained from Whiteaways, who had supplied the stoves, what we regarded as a wonderfully clever gadget in the shape of a pair of wick-scissors. He also adopted aluminium, showing considerable unorthodoxy and openness of mind, and was, I am quite sure, the first to introduce that metal in east Mymensingh. He had ordered a saucepan and a frying-pan, giving us only a vague hint, and when the two pearly white utensils arrived there was a tremendous sensation. We began by asking, "Is that a new kind of enamelled ware?" "No," replied my father, "it's a new kind of metal called aluminium." "Enamellum?" we queried. "No, aluminium," it was repeated. "Can they be put on fire?" "Yes, of course, that's what they are for." "Can they be scrubbed?" "No, not with tamarind and ashes, they have to be washed with soap." This catechism had to be repeated for every visitor.

When we reached the upper classes of the school course my father gave up teaching us, saying frankly that he did not consider himself equipped to do so. By that time we also had almost ceased to need tutors and coaching at home. At this point I think I ought to clear up the confusion I must have been causing to those who are not familiar with our educational system by my continuous references to home tutors and home teaching. The fact is that in India the schools are, so to say, merely examining bodies and the teachers employed by them hardly teach. Their main occupation is to set tasks for the pupils to learn and do at home, and put questions on these tasks the next day. Woe to the pupil who has not come with his lessons already learnt and exercises written out, or who asks too many questions of his teacher in the class. It is this apportionment of pedagogical responsibility between the home and the school which makes the education of boys in our country depend entirely on what they do or are made to do at home, and it is this state of affairs also which provides the well-known secondary source of income for Indian teachers known as "private tuition". In fairness to these teachers it must be said too that their salaries are such that they have, not infrequently, to take up as many as three or four private engagements in addition to their school work in order only to keep themselves barely above the starvation level. But the upshot invariably is that both the teachers and the education subsist only at that level.

After our father gave up teaching us we had two tutors to coach us at home. But very soon we ceased to be helplessly dependent on them. We were able to fend for ourselves not only without private tutors, but at times even without the assistance of the teachers at school. I have always very strongly maintained that a boy or girl who goes in for higher education and yet requires private coaching after the age of fourteen is not fit to receive that education.

We, however, were always trying to declare our independence of teachers, and our father whole-heartedly supported our efforts at yet greater independence. Our book allowance was not only liberal but lavish. While most of our school and college fellows hardly bought even the prescribed text-books and usually depended on what are called "notes" in India, we went beyond the text-books to the standard treatises on the subjects we were reading. As a student of the honours class in mathematics my elder brother bought any mathematical books he thought he wanted. It was from these books that in 1914 I first learned the names of Sir James Jeans and Professor Whitehead. When my brother brought home one day a book called *Theoretical Mechanics* by one Jeans, I asked him who the author was. He replied, "He is a very promising young mathematician and physicist." And when Professor Whitehead's *Science and the Modern World* came out, I, having in the meanwhile forgotten all about him, wondered if this very celebrated writer was the same Whitehead whose *Nature of Mathematics* I had seen my brother reading.

I was equally well provided. In order to prepare for the examination paper on the French Revolution I not only bought Sorel, Aulard, Madelin, the latest biography of Mirabeau by Paul Barthou, and other standard works, I was also on the point of ordering the entire collection of the *Acts of the Committee of Public Safety,* edited by Aulard, the corpus of documents on the convocation of the States-General in 1789 edited by Brette, and similar documentary collections, but was dissuaded only by my professor, who explained that for me to try to study the original documents at that stage would be to lose myself in a mass detail. None the less, for my post-graduate studies as a whole, I had a working library which was not equalled by those of many of my teachers.

After I had entered life my father's help was still made available to me, and in the pursuit of a hobby for which, since it was not a hobby to be ridden on the income I then, or at any time, had, I should have found the money or borne the consequences. I did bear the unpleasant consequences up to a certain point, but in the end my father always stepped in to save me. The hobby was bibliophily. I went in for Nonesuch editions, Bruce Rogers typography, French woodcuts on Japon vellum, and the like; schemed how I could buy the Kelmscott Chaucer, the 1734 Moliere, Durer engravings;

dreamt of the First Folio, the Mazarin Bible, and Padeloup bindings preferably with the armorial bearings of Marrie-Antoinette; talked about Mr. Pierpont Morgan as if he were only a fellow buyer of books and of the library of the Spencers at Althorp as if I would have bought it up if Mrs. John Rylands had not forestalled me; had designs on the Royal collection of drawings at Windsor; and, as a substitute, devoured the volumes of *Book Prices Current* and the catalogues issued by Quaritch, Sotheran and other second-hand book dealers. There would not have been much harm done had all my madness been restricted to this day-dreaming, but I also acted, and again and again this activity created situations in which I had to avoid walking along the book-sellers' street in Calcutta. When my avoidance of my creditors reached a point at which these gentlemen began to apply to my brothers, my father usually came down from Kishorganj and rescued me. To give one instance, he had to help me in the transaction over the Julian edition of Shelley and from that time he took a great fancy to those cream and green volumes. He would take out one and pass his hand over the smooth vellum back. I was almost ready to hope that he also would turn collector. Ultimately I had to dispose of the Julian Shelley in order to tide over one of my recurring monetary crises, and when my father noticed the absence of the volumes on my shelves he asked me where the Shelley was. He went on asking this question from time to time, and every time I put him off with gross prevari-cations. But I always felt that he did not quite believe me, although he never said anything.

To complete the account of my father's literary interests I should record that it was not only the more elementary books of linguistic interest that he read. He was ready to read anything that came to his hand. On going to pay him a visit at Kishorganj I was rather surprised once to find him reading *The Brothers Karamazov*. I found that he had read quite a number of books by Dostoevsky, who seemed to be a favourite with him. Tolstoy, of course, he enjoyed very much, and *War and Peace* he read more than once. He also borrowed my Jane Austen and read all her novels. I mention these books as those which I particularly noticed him reading.

Another mark of the catholicity of mind of my father was his awareness that every manifestation of life ultimately rested on physical foundations and that, unless they were soundly laid and constantly strengthened, there was no prospect of advancement in the so-called higher spheres. This may sound like making too much of a commonplace, but those who have any direct knowledge of the incredible shoddiness which permeates the upper-class Indian's outwardly sleek presence, of the flimsiness of the physical foundations of his life, of the appalling inattention to this prerequisite of moral, spiritual, and intellectual achievement, of the indiscipline in matters of food, sleep, and other physical necessities, will not think so. Developing the seed idea which my father's precept and practice implanted in me, I have come today to some very startling conclusions. Because I had got familiar with the idea that in the ultimate analysis moral qualities were not a matter of preaching but of vitality, I was able instantly to appreciate the wisdom of Ludendorff's ordering an inquiry into the protein ration of a German division whose fighting spirit was not up to the mark. I am convinced that if today moral energy is lacking in India the reason is largely physical. It amounts to no more than what a nervous system sapped constantly in strength and balance by lack of sleep and solitude can generate from a sustenance of starch unrelieved by anything but a liberal sprinkling of chilly. I am also convinced that by making a few but fundamental changes in our habits of food, sleep and exercise we can avoid a good deal of the evils of modern India, including the hysterical Hindu-Muslim antagonism which has succeeded in ruining our political life. I maintain that this idea is neither fad nor crotchet, and I am able always to prove it by pointing to the results I have achieved in my family by carrying out these reforms. I have only to add that within my experience I have hardly seen any consciousness of the problem.

My father had this consciousness. He also had the will-power to carry out the changes he thought necessary. Although he made some mistakes because the science of nutrition was not then what it is today, on the whole his instincts were right. He prescribed the kind of food we should take and the hours at which we should take it. He fixed our hours of study, our hours of sleep, our hours of exercise and play, our hours of other recreations. He never nagged us for taking it easy instead of reading at all hours of the day, as only too many parents do. What was even more remarkable, he never permitted us to read beyond the prescribed hours, and in no circumstances were we allowed to sit up at night in order to read for examinations. By this single quality of being regular and disciplined our family stood out among scores of others in which everybody ate whatever he liked, ate at any hour he liked, came in at any time he liked, went to bed at any time he liked, and generally made the life of the women of the household an unending stoker's job.

My father also bought for us any appliances for gymnastics or physical exercise we wanted. If in my youth and manhood I had not the strong constitution he desired for me it was because I neglected his advice and in matters of physical culture pursued the bad old tradition. My all too obvious failure on the physical plane was no less keen a sorrow for him than my ill-success in worldly advancement.

I come last to what I look upon as the most important and basic trait of my father's character, a mystery which I have not been wholly able to penetrate. This was his complete disregard of self, self not understood in the commonplace sense but in the higher connotation of personal achievement and acquisition of personality. That with the opinions he often expressed about parental selfishness, he should neglect himself for his children was not unexpected, but I am quite unable to explain how an individualist like him could be so utterly devoid of personal ambition. My difficulty is that I cannot correlate his unselfishness with any of the usual types of *Weltanschauung*. Thoughts of self are encouraged by a religious view of life, because it emphasizes our lone coming into the world and our lone exit from it and induces us to judge values in their relation to the individual voyager, the individual voyage, and the ultimate individual destiny. A purely secular view of life encourages individualism less, but as soon as there enters into it some perception of humanistic values individualism reasserts itself, although the man who orders his life in the light of humanism can normally discover and establish a most vital connexion between his individual growth and his racial and social function. In the case of my father, even to the end of his life, I was never able to discover what his religious views were. I fought shy of them and he also carefully avoided the subject.

But what I actually saw was this: he was totally indifferent to money, power, worldly position, fame, even in the form in which he could easily command them. This was all the more remarkable because he was a man with a very strong will. In fact, he was regarded as a very self-willed person by my mother, and she said that before her his own mother used to complain of the same fault. I did not see so much self-will, but I heard my father say a score of times that a man was nothing if he was not self-willed. He used that word of bad odour as a hyperbole to drive home his point among a people with whom will was the least part of character, but what he really meant was stamina, moral as well as physical. So I am not disposed to regard his unselfishness as a negative virtue, as a form of quietism; on the contrary, I think it was, albeit unconsciously, one of the most imperious and positive of urges, the kind of urge which makes a bird sit on her eggs and a hornbill even wall herself up and immure herself with her young. It was the impulse of self-realization taking the form of philoprogenitiveness, the individualistic urge transformed into and merging in the racial. My father was driven by a passion for creating a new type of human beings, a new breed, so that he might rise above his environment, have his revenge on it, not individually and episodically, but generically and for all time.

In old age, when he was disappointed in us in many ways, he made an attempt to reorganize his life round himself. But he failed completely. It was too late in the day for him to try pick up the egoistic thread from which he had cut loose in early manhood. He was always torn between his old habit and new desire, and it was the old habit which prevailed. Whether he lived at Navadwip or Benares he seemed always to hear calls from us, who were in Calcutta. The last call he thought he heard was from me. I had written to him to give him the news that I had not asked for help, nor even for advice. He wrote back saying that he was sorry to hear of my unemployment and would soon come down to Calcutta and try to do something for me. He was struck dead in his chair about an hour after writing that letter.

Many of my father's friends and relatives complained that he had spoilt us by giving us too much freedom and by giving us whatever we wanted. I do not think that they ever convinced him. He would hardly have understood their complaint. I heard him say time and again to my mother, to me, to my brothers that he would never try to influence our moral and religious opinions, that even in worldly matters, such as choice of profession and marriage, he would only give us advice and take no initiative unless we ourselves wanted him to. He could see his side of the task, not ours. If he is the only Bengali father I have seen who adhered consistently to this view of the father-

and-son relationship, it is because in a country where one finds only a wild desire for freedom without any respect for it, and without even the will to achieve it, he was a genuine liberal. To him freedom by itself was as important as the ends for which it is supposed to be desirable.

MY MOTHER

My father and mother were bound to each other by certain common principles and standards of conduct, but otherwise, in appearance, temperament, and outlook, they were the reverse or, if one chooses to say the same thing in a different way, the complement of each other. My mother was as slight and fragile as my father was robust, while her face was as responsive as my father's was impassive. It rippled to emotions as waters to the wind. It was quite out of the question for her to try to hide any feeling. We always saw at a glance whether she was angry or pleased and regulated our movements accordingly. Altogether, she was always vivid and highstrung, if not hectic and electrical. Even when she was young there were two deep vertical wrinkles between her eyebrows, which in normal cases would have signified a bent for thought. But my mother was not intellectual, although when she chose to be argumentative she could be devastatingly logical. Her natural propensity was intuitive, and those wrinkles were produced by the frequent fits of introspective brooding into which she fell.

She was not handsome, but no more was she plain. Her forehead was very well-shaped without being high, and the oval of her face was broad in its upper half but very quickly receding and tapering in the lower. Her eyes were large and liquid, her nose very regular and prominent, her lips well-cut but tending towards fullness in the lower one. The real weakness of the face was the chin, which though neatly shaped was not weighty enough for the upper part. Taken in their entirety, her features gave an impression of unsleeping alertness and inexhaustible animation. By nobody would that face have been called a face of simple and honest goodness alone. The openness, goodness, and generosity which were so obvious in that countenance were of an extremely restless, positive, and winged type.

But here again the appearances were deceptive, for her face did not show, hardly indicated even, the immense strength of her moral convictions. No one could have inferred from her face that she was capable of such fanaticism as she showed over questions of right and wrong. Even more than my father was she intolerant of demonstrativeness and the wearing of one's heart on one's sleeve. If we groaned too much in times of illness or expected to be made much of, we were quietly and firmly told to try to go to sleep instead of making things worse by complaining. Being a highstrung woman she was capable on occasions of turning panicky on some mishap happening to any of her children, but she restrained herself soon, and even in her worst panic she never went anywhere near the normal behaviour of Indian mothers on seeing accidents befalling their children. For example, if a one-year-old baby falls down from a height of, say, two feet, the first thing its mother would do would be to give out a hideous scream and begin to knock her head on the floor by way of mourning, on the assumption that the child was already dead and it was no use going to its help. My mother never gave such exhibitions. On the other hand, if we frightened her by giving a scream disproportionate to our injury the chances were that we should be getting some additional cuffing to redress the disproportion. No one who has not observed the behaviour of little children in India can have an adequate idea of the range of expansion of their mouths in self-pity and hope of external pity. The luxury of self-pity as well as of sympathy was severely rationed in our case. Yet no mother was capable of more businesslike attendance on her children in sickness.

The faults of character she disliked most were falsehood, dishonesty, moral cowardice, and meanness. A liar, a cheat, a coward, and a person "with the tiny heart of a minnow", as she put it, were the most contemptuous epithets we heard from her mouth. Not only did she condemn vice, she almost equally despised the tacit acceptance of an advantage. I shall give one or two instances. If she asked us to take a portion after dividing a sweet or some other dish, we always said, "Give us a piece yourself, mother," for we knew, if by any chance one of us took what appeared to be the biggest piece, she would look at him with a meaning smile or at times even angry contempt. Yet we could not always chasten ourselves to take the most patently small piece. So we thought we ran a better, or at all events an even, chance of getting what we wanted if we did not help ourselves.

Again, when in my school and college days I was staying in hostels and boarding houses, I found that there always was a crush at the first service of the dinner, because the dining-hall was nowhere large enough to accommodate all the inmates at the same time. In this situation many persons discreetly took care to be not very far from the dinning-room door without outwardly seeming to care about the dinner. I am putting the position at its most decorous, for I once stayed at a hostel in which the boarders who lived on the second floor came down the stairs in stealthy silence, carrying their shoes in hand for fear of warning the first-floor boarders of their descent towards the dining-room. Not to speak of the second type of management, my mother would have despised us if we had resorted even to the first. Her teaching saved me not only from manipulating my turn at dinners but also from pressing my claims in other walks. I have always assumed that it is not for me to lay down my turn;

if I wait for it there will certainly be the innate justice of society to offer me mine.

Another thing I learned from her was that good manners were a matter of fundamental decencies and not of external polish. If ever we whispered or laughed in the presence of visitors, and that even quite innocently, we were quietly called to order for the time being but afterwards more severely and seriously dealt with. The fault which my mother emphasized was not the mere lapse in manners but the meanness of behaving in a fashion which might wound the susceptibilities of those who had come to our house in friendliness. Bad manners, to her thinking, were a sin, not merely against a code of social behaviour, but against charity. As I grew older my mother had very often to remonstrate against my sharp and biting tongue. From quite an early age I displayed an unusual and unchildlike faculty for making barbed observations, whereas my mother was inclined to take the view of Pascal: *"Diseurs de bons mots, mauvais caractere."* I defended myself; and I knew I was taking the most plausible line of defence from her point of view when I replied "But mother, I never speak harshly of the underdog." The teaching of good manners from this line of approach and on this wider moral basis enabled me to grasp quickly the key of Emerson's essay on friendship when I read it for the first time, and also to see the truth of the saying attributed to Bismarck that a gentleman is never unintentionally rude.

My mother's honesty should be qualified by the adjective "fierce". I have to make this seemingly superfluous and astonishing statement because our female society even now does not think too severely of practising a little deception, particularly on the husband, in matters of money. In olden days it was given to shameless pilfering. The dames in that age actually sold their household stores on the sly and made money from those sales. Whatever I say about my mother's honesty has to be set against the tradition, and I think my mother had full right to the pride with which she used to relate the story of how her mother-in-law gave her the most practical certificate of character.

Some years after my mother's marriage my grandmother was going on a pilgrimage with her eldest daughter. She was anxious about her money, the money she had found in the buried hoard. She could not trust her husband with it, and she would trust nobody else, not even her son, who might be lured away from the path of rectitude by a siren of a daughter-in-law. So one day she came into the hut which was her bedroom and ordered out my mother, who was accompanying her. After about an hour my mother was given leave to return, and she found the floor newly smeared with mud and water. She had not the slightest difficulty in guessing what the mother and daughter had been about, nor much greater difficulty in finding out where under the floor they had buried the pot of treasure. But the old lady had no suspicion that her device had been understood.

She came back after nearly six months, and the day after she arrived she again ordered my mother out. My mother, who had slept in the room for the whole period of absence of her mother-in-law, went out smiling under her veil. After an hour she was sent for. She found the old lady and her daughter in great agitation and nearly the whole floor dug up. They had forgotten the place where they had hidden the treasure. There was no longer any room for pretence. So my grandmother asked my mother if she knew anything about the pot which had been buried under the floor. My mother nodded assent under her veil, and walking up to one of the posts pointed to its foot. The other two rushed to the spot, dug out the pot, and counted the money. The recovery of the treasure without the loss of a single gold or silver coin, even when my mother had located it, had a revolutionary effect on the old lady. From that day onward she never hesitated to keep her keys and even her money in my mother's care.

Let it be remembered too that losses of money trustfully deposited with a brother, uncle, or other relative are very common occurrences amongst us. Loss of sanity due to loss of money is also pretty common. At Kalikutch there was a madman, a frequent visitor at our grandmother's house, whose mental derangement had been brought about by the misappropriation of three thousand rupees by his brother. This again is a symptom of the strange duality of our lives. As darkness and light divide the course of time, and oblivion shares with memory a great part of our living existence, so do with us the world and the other world. For all that one hears about the spirituality of the people of India, while they are *in* the world they are also *of* the world, and the spell cannot be broken until it breaks itself. If in that unweaned state they are wounded in their love of the world, deprived of money which they regard as the world's highest and most precious gift to man, they are shocked almost as fatally as a dormouse awakened untimely from its hibernation. They go mad or die.

Reverting to the story of honesty and suspicions, I shall try to reinforce the moral by relating two experiences which befell me. In 1923–a year rich in experiences of rural life for me–being on a visit to Banagram, I had one day by way of a practical joke hidden the gold bangles of a baby, because the baby had been left alone with the utmost carelessness with those bangles on the veranda of one of the outer huts where strangers were constantly coming and going. When there was a hullabaloo for the bangles I restored them, warning those concerned against future carelessness of so risky a kind–for children are often murdered in India for the sake of their gold ornaments.

But afterwards I was taken to task for this in the most insulting manner by my father and mother, both of whom rated me as if I were a little boy or a servant. At first I could not catch the drift of their argument, but at last I realized that what my father was saying was that those people had actually suspected me of intending to appropriate the bangles and thought that I had given them up only when, on account of the hue and cry they had raised, it had become impossible for me to keep them on the quiet. I was aghast, and I asked, "But, father, are they really capable of thinking that I, who am now in the service of the Government of India and in not too bad a position, besides being a young man of some education, can steal a pair of trumpery bangles?" "Yes," replied my father with even greater displeasure, "you know nothing of village life." My humiliation was not lessened by the fact that in my hand was Bergson's *Creative Evolution,* which I had been reading at the time I hid the bangles. I was still reading it when my father spoke to me, but the argument about the inseparability of a theory of knowledge and a theory of life did not bring much comfort to a man smarting under the ignominy of the imputation of larceny.

The other experience occurred in 1927. An old lady related to me was passing through Calcutta and was staying for a day in my flat. With her also were her son and daughter-in-law. They had arrived in the evening, and as the old lady was tired I gave her one of my smaller rooms to rest in. Now, when the dinner was ready, I discovered that the dinner things had been left in the room in which she was, and going myself to fetch them I found the door barred from inside and nobody replying. I thought the old lady must be sleeping and, not wishing to disturb her, I gently raised the bar with a knife, opened the door, got the things, and shut the door behind me— all without awaking her. After we had had our dinner I again went in myself with her refreshments for, being a widow, she would take only fruit and a little milk, and standing by her bedside I said, "Madam, will you have your refreshment now?" She started up from her sleep and the first words she uttered were, "How did you get into this room?" I replied that the room could be opened from the outside. She stared at me in fright at this answer. She was not upset by the invasion of privacy of which I was guilty, for she had no notion of privacy and never had it at any time of her life. As a matter of fact, I was offering her the best of customary civilities by waiting on her myself, which I would not have done for a more modern person. But her thoughts were running along another track. Her real fear was disclosed by her subsequent action. She slowly got down from the bed, found her keys, opened her trunk, took out her purse, and there and then, and before me, counted all her money, including even the small change. Only when she found that her money was intact did she again look at me and speak to me. I was at first amazed, but fortunately retained my sense of humour even under that provocation. I cursed myself for coming to offer her personal service instead of sending to her my servant woman or her own daughter-in-law. But such a windfall of an opportunity did not come so often in my way that I could think of not taking full advantage of it, and so going back to my younger and more modern guests I told them the whole story with considerable gusto but complete objectivity.

These, then, are the antecedents which make the emphasis on my mother's honesty not insulting but necessary. The padlock and the key are in some ways the symbol of our existence. Wherever I go I find home life in the rigorous custody of padlocks and keys. You go on to the balcony and padlock your sitting-room, you go into the lavatory and padlock your bedroom, you go up to the roof for air and padlock your staircase door. In recent times I have also heard of highly educated modern young ladies counting every potato in the house before going out and re-counting them on return as a precaution against their theft by servants. I have heard too of mistresses who do not possess the courage to dismiss their thievish servants, but quietly search their belongings and salvage the stolen articles and thus win the battle of wits. It was the example of Father Prior of the Oxford Mission which first taught me that mankind could live without the protection and guarantee of padlocks. Since I saw him leaving everything about in open drawers in an open room I too gave up padlocks, and I have not been a loser.

As this narrative proceeds I shall have to recur to my mother's moral and religious ideas, and I dispense with a formal account here. But, as in the case of my father, here too I am confronted with a fundamental problem of personality. My mother was the opposite of my father in the sense that she was as egoistic as he was forgetful of self. But again, like my father's unselfishness, her egoism too was of an unhackneyed brand. There was nothing worldly in it. My mother's honesty was her covenant with the world, and just as she was not disposed to give to the world more than its due she did not expect from it more than a square deal. She cared as little for money, position, or power as did my father. But her expectations from life, as distinct from her expectations from the world, appeared to be limitless. They were all grasping emotional demands, made exclusively on her husband and children.

She expected from all her children what unfortunately was no child's to give, not because of any unfilial reluctance, but simply because it did not exist to be given. I, too, can say as Bridges does:

"Nor count I any scripture to be better inspired
with eternal wisdom or by insight of man
than the four words wherewith the sad penitent hymn
calleth aloud on Mary standing neath the cross:
EIA MATER, it saith, MATER FONS AMORIS"

But I agree equally with Bridges that this parential instinct, though it owns cousinship with breed, was born of selfhood; that a nursing mammal, since she must feel her suckling a piece of herself, will self-preserve and shelter it as herself; and that often hard to wean. My mother's elemental blunder was that she always wanted to feel her children as pieces of herself, and it was this which caused no end of unhappiness to all concerned. I was perhaps the one among her children who most resembled her in physical and mental traits, yet the misunderstanding too was the greatest between us. I could easily have behaved with ordinary consideration and courtesy, but I did not. I had two alternatives before me: I could be conventional, or I could give in to my mother. Both the alternatives irritated me equally. I say this without any intention of excusing myself, that the idea of regulating our relations merely by convention repelled me and provoked me evermore to show my contempt for convention; at the same time, I wanted my mother to understand that her idea of how a son should conduct himself was utterly impossible, and this demonstration gave rise to continual misunderstandings between us during the last eight years of her life. Fortunately there was no woman, a second woman, in the conflict. In the case of a mother-and-son conflict our people always say: "*Cherchez la femme.*" Mine at least was no prompted quarrel. I and my mother fought each other directly, on the plane of theory as well as on the plane of practice.

What my mother found wanting in my father I could never discover. To all appearance there was no more devoted and loyal husband to be met with anywhere; a husband who made no demands on his wife, on the contrary was ready to answer any and every demand from her. In actual fact, he seriously weakened his splendid constitution and went very near ruining his worldly career for her sake. Yet she was always complaining of his conduct towards her. She seemed to be like the person who did not know what he wanted and was not happy because he did not have it. Occasionally she told us that when we were grown up she would tell us why she was not happy and then we would understand. The obvious conviction and sincerity with which she said this made me feel very sad, and I wondered what the hidden tragedy of her life could be. She even promised to show me some letters. But she had no opportunity of explaining herself. Ordinarily, when she complained, I as a true son of hers tartly replied: "Mother, don't expect from life what it has not got to give"; or, "Mother, if you don't find happiness within yourself don't look for it elsewhere"; all of which only aggravated her sense of injury.

She was a woman with the conviction of a curse upon her life, and for a woman so singularly free from superstition this was a strange thing. She told me again and again that her mother-in-law had laid this curse on her by always repeating the same formula: "Have every kind of happiness but the happiness of the spirit." This, my mother said, had come true.

Here I touch upon one of the fundamental aberrations of Indian life–the mother-in-law-daughter-in-law relationship. Our young women, otherwise so demure and ready to efface themselves, gloat in unsubdued pride of flesh and pride of life on their power to snatch the son from the mother; and the desiccated old women, knowing and feeling in every fibre of their being what the inevitable turn of the wheel will bring, wave back defiant and derisive curses on their callow rivals. Some of the mothers speak out, others send up their secret thoughts to God, the unfailing Dispenser of Justice. And those accursed homes in which the mothers-in-law and daughters-in-law live together, only heaven knows why, are always smouldering from the fire of lovers' kisses and mothers' sighs. A stranger, not acclimatized to the immoral climate, but possessing keen sensibilities, can become physically aware of the glowing embers.

There was no reason why my mother should have allowed her life to be haunted by this unclean conflict, even assuming she had unpleasant experiences while living with her mother-in-law. She was married towards the end of 1887 at about the age of fourteen. Her mother-in-law died six and a half years later at the beginning of 1894. After this she remained for about a year longer at Banagram and then came away to Kishorganj. She was then a young woman of about twenty-two, with no children and with only her husband as the second member of the family. She had all her life before her and could have relived it in any way she liked. But she was endowed with a fatal facility for self-torture, and this capacity for self-torture was the cause, effect, and accompaniment, all rolled into one, of the calamitous malady from which she suffered all her life.

This was hysteria, a disease which at one time used to be quite common, almost fashionable, among Bengali women. But while others were able after a period of flirtation to get rid of it either through the coming of children, or assumption of household responsibilities, or some other change in the way of life, in my mother's case it became a psychologically well-organized, insane state running parallel to her normal life. My father once told me that all my mother's hysterical states were connected by a continuous pathological memory distinct from her ordinary memory, and that one coherent, though abnormal, complex of ideas lay behind them. I do not know whether that is admitted by clinical experts. But my father had observed my mother very closely and had, not only an uncanny insight into the workings of her hysterical mind, but also an uncanny control over her hysterical states. When she got a fit in my father's absence there was nothing to be done except to send for him. No one else could control her or reduce her to a state of quiescent torpor. Therefore, whenever she fell ill, and that happened very often, he had always to sit by her side either stroking her hair or her hand, neglecting everything else, including his clients and his cases. On those days my father's clerk would reply to the inquiries of the clients in the same impeccable Bengali which was usual with him: "I am sorry he cannot come today; there is a certain insuperable impediment."

How the disease had developed or what exactly was its aetiology I cannot say. My mother told me that she had her first fit at the age of three or four, when one day she had been frightened by a colossal naked image of the god Siva, which used to be made and worshipped annually in her village. That may have been the first shock which gave a jolt to her nervous system, but it could not have been the main cause of the ailment as I saw it, for that later state was always connected with my father. She never got it (except so far as I remember only in one instance) while living away from my father, as she occasionally did when she came down to Calcutta for our sake. On another occasion she told me that her fits had really begun at Banagram after the death of her second child and first son, as the result, as she thought, of the fumigation given to her and the child, about which I have already written.

But whatever the origin, this malady cast its dark shadow on the otherwise happy, sunny, and sane life of the family. During these fits the father, the mother, and the children were all in their different ways equally tragic figures. My father sat still with his eyes fixed on his wife as if she were dead but as if he had got a promise from some unknown Power that the life which had fled would come back after a period of whimsical truancy. My mother lay unconscious for the greater part of the time, but sometimes remained half and even fully awake with a wild, uncomprehending look in her eyes. Even when awake she could not express herself in clear language or with clear articulation; she only moaned or made gestures with her hand. I never saw her passing from her hysterical state back to her normal state, but my father told me that she suddenly recovered consciousness as if waking up from sleep, and he could tell whether she was normal by looking at her eyes. We, the children, ordinarily kept away from the sick-room as from a house of pestilence, but if we had ever to come into it we walked on tiptoe and spoke in low and tremulous whispers. My mother's case did not have, except in very infrequent instances, the sordid associations hysteria usually has, but it was terrible and intolerable. It enfeebled her from day to day and killed her before her time, and it undeservedly saddened my father's life and troubled ours. To me it has given a horror of disease which has made me incapable of nursing anybody even in ordinary illness.

EARLY YEARS

My earliest recollections are like everybody else's, points of light in a long dark tunnel, and to me as to all others in boyhood the unillumined voids were just as real as the luminous incidents. For children seem to retain a sense of the duration of their early years without being able to remember all the experiences which constitute that duration. One of the lighted points in my case was the murder of Gaurikanta Roy, of which I have already spoken. A second was its sequel, the buying of our new estate. After the murder the police sent up for trial three brothers of the washerman caste who lived next door to Roy. In later life I heard an unsavoury tale of there being something between the mother of these men and old Roy, and of the murder being a vindication of family honour. These stories are, however, so easily manufactured that it is quite impossible to find out what truth lies behind them. The brothers were defended by my father and were acquitted, but in disgust they decided to sell their house and move elsewhere. My father bought the whole estate, which became our house, for nine hundred rupees, a very moderate sum. The incident concerning myself which I am going to relate took place when the deed of transfer was being signed and the money paid.

The parties and the witnesses were in the office-hut, seated on the bed at its centre. The whole neighbourhood was hanging about, and the women were peeping through the holes in the mat walls. I had taken my station on something like a loft overlooking the bed. As currency notes were not liked in those days my father was making the payment in silver rupees. He took out a handful from a bag, tossed each coin from his thumb and forefinger, making it ring as a test of genuineness, and when ten coins were rung he placed them one on another in a neat pile on the bedsheet. I watched him with breathless interest, and maintained my self-control until about forty piles were laid. Then I set up a howl that all our money was being given away, and did not desist till I was carried out of the hut. Although I had to be removed for creating a disturbance, everybody was full of admiration for the cleverness of a child of five who had shown such precocious appreciation of money and such proper reluctance to part with it.

My continuous memory dates from 1904, which was a year of travels for us. In the early part of that year we went, first, to Mymensingh, the district town, and then to Kalikutch. In the first jouney we saw trains, and in the second steamers, for the first time. We had been told to be particularly careful when a train moved into the station, since it always made people on the platform to see if we did feel giddy. As a chance would have it, a train, not ours, was coming in, and three of us brothers sallied out on the platform to see if we did feel giddy. When the train steamed in we interlocked arm in arm and, swaying from side to side, giggled hysterically. Then we marched back into the waiting-room to tell our mother that we had really felt giddy. It was neither very childish nor so very backward on our part to have paid this physiological homage to a train in 1904, for when a railway line came for the first time to Kishorganj in

1916 there were boys of the matriculation class bowing down to locomotives as to gods. My first sight of steamers made quite a different impression. It still lingers in my memory like a painted nocturne. We were staying for the night in the waiting-rooms of the beautiful riverside station of Narayanganj and saw, moored out in the dark stream, looming very large and steeped in indescribable romance, two steamers, one of which was showing the green starboard light and the other the red port light.

Towards the end of the year *wanderlust* of a more ambitious kind seized us and sent us off to distant Calcutta, Deoghar, and Gaya. Of course, there was behind it that religious motive without which (or without the motive of medical treatment *in extremis*), a journey to Calcutta or any such fashionable place was regarded by our society as an unforgivable waste of money or another thing even worse—blatant display of it. In our case the religious motive was twofold. No dead Bengali Hindu is supposed to be finally admitted into the community of the manes until an oblation ceremony is performed for him or her on the banks of the Phalgu at Gaya. My father had not yet performed these ceremonies for his parents, and he wanted to discharge the duty. A different kind of religious debt had to be paid at Deoghar. After the death of her first two babies my mother grew a little anxious when my elder brother was expected. But a priest from Deoghar, where there is a well-known temple of Siva, had come on a wandering visit to Kishorganj and told my mother that this time a son would be born to her and he would live. He also gave her a large amulet to hang round the neck of the child and asked her to go to Deoghar and make an offering to Siva if his words came true. The promised offering was overdue, for my brother was nine. So off we went, taking Calcutta on our way back, partly because my mother had never seen the city and partly because it too had its religious attraction in its famous temple of Kali. I am not quite sure that the prestige of this temple was not the result of an attempt to legitimize the British capital of India. In any case, all upcountrymen who come to Kalighat, the suburb of Calcutta where the temple stands hail the goddess with the shout: *"Jay Ma Kali Kalkattawalee!"* (Victory to Mother Kali of Calcutta!) By the end of the nineteenth century the foreign Boxwallah and the divine Kalkattawalee had become wholly fused in our idea of the city.

But it is not of Calcutta, it is of the journey that I wish to speak here. It was made memorable by characteristic features of its own. In the first place, my mother had extracted a promise from my father that he would never make us travel in mail trains. She had heard that besides having a very small number of stops they halted only for a minute or two even when they stopped, and consequently, she thought, if we travelled by a mail train my father was sure to be left behind when he came to look after her in the women's compartment, for, of course, like all Indian women in those days, she also would be travelling in the zenana car. Secondly, she had made him give her the undertaking that he would never take us to Howrah, the western terminus of Calcutta, which, she had been told, was such a crowded place that there was not only an off chance but the certainty of the children being lost.

So, in fulfilment of these promises, my father had, first, to make the journey to Calcutta by the slowest and most uncomfortable trains, besides having to spend the night (which separated the starting time of the passenger train to Calcutta from that of the mail train) at Goalundo, a place then notorious all over East Bengal for its atrocious hotels, whose agents advertised the attractions of their establishments by shouting: "Good food and brick-built latrines!" And, next, my father had to de-train with us at a point twenty-seven miles north of Calcutta in order to cross the river Hooghly by the railway bridge near the town of the same name and catch the train for

Deoghar at Bandel. I believe, by the time he reached Bandel, my father's patience as well as honesty was quite exhausted, and there, without telling anybody, he put us in the Kalka express. My mother told us afterwards that as soon as she saw the train flashing past the smaller stations after leaving Bandel she realized what my father had done and feared the worst for us.

In actual fact, too, without her knowing it, something very near the worst feared by her had happened, for my father failed to reach our compartment after putting my mother in hers. When the train got into motion at Bandel without our father being with us the darkness of chaos descended on the face of the earth, and we sat stiff, like creatures turned to stone. A friend of my father's who was accompanying us tried to console us by saying that our father had certainly got into another compartment and would be rejoining us at Burdwan, the next stop, which was about forty miles away. He also gave us groundnuts to eat. Although that was the first time we had seen groundnuts we had no wish even to look at them, and we swallowed them only because we thought that otherwise our good friend would be hurt. I kept looking out of the window towards Bandel to see if a special engine was bringing our father up the second line. We neither spoke nor smiled till our father came back to us. At the time of the return journey, in order to prevent a similar misadventure, my father took the extremely unconventional step of making our mother travel in the same compartment with us. But he could not induce her to go to Howrah. So, in order to avoid that dangerous place, we took eighteen hours to cover a stage which by the direct route would have taken an hour and a half. In the end we returned to Kishorganj safe and sound.

Pets played a large part in my early life, and from my earliest years I was always keeping some bird or animal. I kept in turn, or together, grackles, ordinary mynahs, pigeons, parrots and cockatoos, as well as goldfish, goats, sheep and dogs. But the story I want particularly to tell here is of a ewe which I kept when I was about seven years old. The more I looked at the picture of the boy Christ in the West Hut the more I thought that there was nothing in the world which I wanted more than a lamb. Sheep, however, were not very common in our district, and a lamb could not be procured easily. My father had asked many people, and at last one day a young ewe was brought for me. She was not a lamb, but I took very kindly to her. I put aside my books, and was always to be found grazing her or sitting with her on the grass under a tree. The ewe on her part became so fond of me that she would begin to bleat piteously if I left her even for a few minutes. If I was at my meals and her bleating reached my ears I would leave off eating and rush back to her. I began to smell like a sheep.

At first everybody was full of admiration. They said I looked exactly like the boy Christ of the picture. Then they thought I might as well not neglect my lessons and be so casual about meals. At the next stage they complained that I was smelling of sheep and had too much sheep's wool on my body and clothes. Yet if the inevitable decision to get rid of the ewe was not taken it was because the school vacation was on, and while I was on the spot nobody could have taken away the ewe from before my eyes. Then something mysterious happened. The servants looked at the ewe with considerable interest and held a discussion. In the afternoon our old and purblind servant Dutiram, who carried about my baby sister and looked after the cows, said to me, "Brother, will you come along with me with the ewe? I am going to look for a ram for her."

My mother was sleeping, and I could not see any of my brothers. So I set out with Dutiram, leading the ewe by her rope. We knew that near the courts there were some very old, odoriferous, and hairy goats. I fancied I had seen a ram there.

Therefore we went first in that direction. We were disappointed. There was no sign of any ram at the place . Dutiram
reflected for a little while and then said, "There might be one
near the old police station. Let's go there." We walked that
way, a distance of just under a mile. We found no ram there
either. Then I suggested, "There always are sheep in the
bazaar, let's try there." "Yes," replied Dutiram, "we'll go to
the bazaar." So, crossing the river, we entered the bazaar and
saw a flock of some ten sheep resting under the small sheds
meant for the grocers on market days. "There!" we cried out
together, and strode briskly up to the sheds. "Now," asked
purblind Dutiram, "is there a ram among them?" "There must
be" I replied. "Then look," directed Dutiram, "my eyes are so
bad that I cannot see." I looked for a long while. "Which is the
ram?" asked Dutiram. I replied, "I cannot tell." "How can
you?" said Dutiram testily. "You have not looked underneath." I kneeled down and replied, "I do not quite know, but
they seem to be rams." "No," declared Dutiram finally, "I must
see for myself, but my eyes are so bad". Then kneeling down
he began to fumble between the hind legs of the sheep. "No,
it's a wether," he said of the first. He tried another and
remarked, "This too is a wether." In this manner he examined
every sheep, and when he had done with the last he rose up and
said sadly, "Brother, we are in for bad luck today."

But with this failure a new determination seemed to come
over the old man. "I'll find a ram today," he declared, "even if
I have to walk ten miles. There must be sheep in the villages.
Let us go south, out of the town." When in pursuance of this
decision we had gone some distance and reached the outskirts
of the town we met some peasants, who looked at me and my
companions in astonishment and asked where we were going
and what we were about. Dutiram related our errand and the
story of our failures, and appealed for help: "Brothers, can you

tell us where we may find a ram?" The peasants, who had listened to us very attentively, replied that there was a ram in a village about a mile away, but added that it was no use going because the ewe was barren and would bear no young. I did not believe it and was for going. But Dutiram appeared to be finally discouraged by this new information.

After another earnest discussion with the peasants he said, "Brother, let us go back today. You came away without telling anybody and they might be looking for you. If there is anything to be done I'll see about it another day." So we came back. My mother, when I reached home, was busy with some visitors. She did not ask me where I had been, nor did anybody else, and my wanderings in search of a ram passed unnoticed. But that night was one of the saddest of my life. I almost cried for the ewe, and kept on saying to myself that this could not have happened if God had made me a ram instead of a boy. I do not know what Dutiram did afterwards. The school re-opened within a few days, and finding me away for most of the time the ewe attached herself to the cow as her guardian. After two or three months, when they thought I was sufficiently weaned away, they took the ewe and sold her.

It would be quite wrong to pretend that our love for animals engendered within us nothing but affectionate inquisitiveness about them. I at all events developed some very macabre curiosities. I did not like the sacrificial bloodshed, but I was consumed by other un-Buddhistic or un-Vaishnava desires which by way of positive definition I might call Claude-Bernardian. I wanted to see the inside of living creatures. At first I satisfied myself by looking at pictures in a text-book of physiology. This, however, was not enough. The sight of the "corpse-cutting hut" into which we could not go evoked within us a most unholy passion to see the *disjecta membra* of human beings, and it found its very first impulsive expression in me in a manner which furnished decisive proof that children have a natural vein of cruelty in them.

There was a young man, a neighbour of ours, called Devendra, who was rather fond of me. I called him cousin and often went to him, for he told me stories and even played with me. After some time he got a very bad form of fever and wasted away from week to week. When I last saw him at the end of some months of illness and only a few days before his death, he smiled sadly at me, though he said nothing. I knew he was dying, for everybody was talking of its imminence. Then one night we got the news of his death. Some of our servants and certain others went to help in the cremation. The next morning I heard from one of them that Cousin Devendra's spleen had grown so large and hard that when the fire touched it the thing shot off the pyre and had to be picked up from a distance of some yards, put back in the fire, and kept in place with a pole. I began to tear my hair and gnash my teeth at the news and cursed myself for not having gone to the cremation and seen Cousin Devendra's spleen bounding away like a red football, and being picked up again.

Shortly afterwards I felt encouraged by the prospect of seeing the *disjecta membra* of another friend of ours, a servant of the name of Rohini, who worked in a house nearby. He was quite a handsome fellow and a decided dandy. Even when scrubbing cooking pots he had a pink vest on, and was never seen except in a fine, clean, and well-ironed dhoti. He wore a silver chain round his neck, and his curly hair dressed and parted in the style called Albert, from its supposed origin from the Prince Consort, was always a sight worth seeing. As he worked he sang only love songs, and his greatest favourite was a song by Tagore. Moreover, it was whispered that he was a man of extremely loose character, which whatever it meant to us made him appear in a very interesting light. He confirmed his reputation by being burnt to death in a house of ill fame. The means employed to kill him was so novel and original that we discussed it with as much wonder as in more recent times people have discussed the atom bomb. Rohini was not decapitated with a *dao* nor beaten into pulp with a bludgeon as everybody who died a normal violent death among us was. Somebody had put gunpowder under his mattress and set it on fire by means of a fuse.

Rohini was at first sent to the hospital, for he had not been killed outright. We heard at midday that he had died, and that after a postmortem his body would be released for cremation in the afternoon. That juncture we hoped to convert into our hour of opportunity. There was no other way to the cremation ground from the hospital except along the road in front of our house. So, in the hope of seeing the dismembered limbs of our friend Rohini, I, with a companion or two, stood waiting by the roadside. Our idea of an autopsy was that every limb was sawn off, the thorax opened, the organs taken out, and the skull cut in small pieces with a chisel. Thus what we expected to see was Rohini reduced to something like butcher's meat, and carried in large red chunks in an open basket. We were thoroughly disappointed, for we saw nothing beyond an ordinary funeral procession with the corpse wrapped up in the familiar roll of mating, from which not even a thin trickle of blood was oozing out.

From among the many recollections of my childhood I shall select for further inclusion in this book only one or two others connected with a second journey and our return home from it. Towards the end of 1906 my mother fell very seriously ill, and had one of her arms, nearly paralysed by rheumatism. My father nursed her himself for some time, but as it seemed the illness would be prolonged he asked his mother-in-law to come over from Kalikutch. She did, and with her this time came also her son, my uncle, with his family. He brought tiger and leopard skins for us from Assam, and also orchids. In addition, we the children got additional playmates in the two cousins, one a girl and the other a boy. The girl was about twelve and was already an exceptionally fine needlewoman. In spite of my mother's illness this winter was one of the happiest we spent at Kishorganj.

At the end of the cold season our visitors left, and one day, when we were still feeling lonely, my father suddenly announced that he was going to send all of us to Kalikutch for three months. My mother was then convalescing, and we naturally thought that we were going for the sake of a change of air for her and perhaps also to pay our uncle a return visit. I was told a little later that there was a political reason behind the journey, the kind of political reason with which we were to become only too familiar, or, to make no mystery about it, the Hindu-Muslim strife. My father did not, however, tell me the whole story of our removal to a place of safety till after many years. I shall discuss this background of our visit to Kalikutch in its proper place.

This time the journey to Kalikutch was planned in a complicated series of stages, each of which was traversed without mishap. One incident in this journey deserves mention because it had a strange sequel. As two of my brothers and I came upon the bank of the river at Dilalpur, there appeared before our eyes, through a wide gap in the long line of huts of the bazaar, a gloriously pastoral scene. Across the river was a small temporary hamlet such as the peasants in our parts build on the sandbanks of the big rivers. All the huts in it were thatched with bright gold-coloured straw; there was a corn rick of the same happy colour in every homestead; the river between us and the village was rippling to a light breeze and shining like cut-glass in the afternoon sun. The scene almost brought tears to my eyes from a sensation of peace. I now come to the inexplicable part of the experience. It lay utterly forgotten and dormant within me for thirty-five years, without being recalled even once. But that vision of the golden village across the river was brought back into my memory suddenly, at one stroke, one day in the terrible summer of defeats of 1940 by the tune of one of Haydn's quartets. How and why this happened I am totally unable to explain, because I can trace no perceptible link between the typical East Bengal scene and the snatch of a tune which was perhaps derived from a Croat folk melody.

We returned to Kishorganj after the break of the monsoons, and on the return journey an incident occurred at the steamer station of Ajabpur which showed my mother's independent temper. The steamers on this line were very irregular because they really plied on goods service and carried passengers only incidentally. Sometimes one had to wait for days before a steamer came along. When we arrived at Ajabpur we found that no steamer was expected till the next morning and decided to wait for it in the miserable little hut which was set apart as a waiting room. At night my baby brother began to cry irritated by mosquito bites. The main station was occupied by one of the inspectors of the company, an Englishman, who was touring the stations. He was disturbed by the crying and sent his servant to protest, which the man did many times and none too politely. My mother felt extremely humiliated and for the moment had to put up with the humiliation, but she vowed never again to travel in a steamer on that line, and she kept her vow.

On our return we found a great change at Kishorganj. In the place of the usual Bengali Deputy Magistrate an English Joint Magistrate of the I.C.S. had taken over the subdivision. His name was Mr. Stinton. The posting was perhaps due to the disturbed political conditions of the times. The agitation against the partition was at its height, and it was accompanied by a pronounced Hindu-Muslim tension. We discovered that

Mr. Stinton had already made a reputation in the town for astuteness. For the time being, however, we were interested not so much in his administrative activities as in a novel object he had brought into the town. One morning, as we were finishing our breakfast, a great shout rose from many mouths calling us instantly to the outer house. We left our meal and rushed out with unwashed hands, and found everybody looking down the road eastward. There was Mr. Stinton, about two hundred yards from us, learning over an object which looked like a bicycle but was very much heavier and more cumbrous. "Look at the motor-cycle," cried my father, and before he had finished, the motor-cycle with Mr. Stinton astride it began to roll roaring towards us and went past. We did not then actually sit down in the middle of the road with legs outstretched, muttering "Poop, poop", as did Mr. Toad of Toad Hall, but our state of mind was not very different. Of course, we could not follow up the excitement by buying a motor-cycle. That Toadian feat of imitation was reserved for the son of the worshipful Dulaha or Son-in-Law Sahib. He gave up his old and tried bicycle and went in for a motor-bike, so that very soon we had two of these self-advertising machines in the town.

I shall conclude this chapter with a methodological note. I have a feeling that I have been raising smiles by my seemingly airy references to the great movements of human thought in narrating the life story of such obscure persons as I am and my parents were. This critical amusement would be deserved if these references had been brought in with the object of shedding an artificial greatness on our existence. But there may be an alternative point of view. I do not think anyone will deny the connexion which even the humblest of us has with two of the most decisive movements in the evolution of the universe, namely, the emergence of life and the emergence of the warm-blooded animals. No one will feel quizzical if I claim to be the product of these two movements. In the same manner, our affiliction to the great movements of history ought to remain undisputed. In fact, I think the humbler we are the more completely are we made up of the material deposited by historical movements like the expansion of the peoples known as the Aryans; the rise of Buddhism, Christianity, and Islam; the Renaissance, the Reformation, and the French Revolution; the propagation of Liberalism, Socialism, and Communism. We are the sedimentary rocks formed out of these original igneous formations.

It is only the exceptional man, the genius and the creator, who brings something of his own which can be distinguished from the common legacy. But even in his case the novelty is not such that we cannot and should not trace back its filiation as a textual critic traces back the lineage of a new manuscript which gives him many interesting variant readings. As for the rest, we are as completely reducible to our constituent elements by means of quantitative and qualitative analysis as any material substance is, and if in the end we present something unanalysable that residuum is not more mysterious than the ultimate unanalysable of matter–motion.

Many years ago I read a small but weighty book by M. Julien Benda, in which I found him stressing the need for studying philosophical ideas as they exist in the collective consciousness, for writing a democratic history of ideas, for recognizing the high value of such studies. I agree with him. But I do not wholly share his contempt for the popularized great idea. I cannot go the whole way with him in thinking that the doctrines of philosophers, being adopted by the vulgar only to the extent that they satisfy their passions, are constantly deformed to satisfy these passions in still greater measure, and that it is the doctrines so deformed which constitute the history of ideas so far as ideas play a part in the lives of men in general and not in the lives of a few recluses. There may be some truth, in fact there is a considerable amount of truth, in this view of

M. Benda's when we consider thinkers like Kant or Nietzsche, to whom he expressly refers. It is, however, less true of the great historical movements in thought, morality and religion. These movements I am inclined to think, have as a necessary attribute of their greatness a certain element of simplicity which appears to be proof against distortion, so that even when common people–the *agrammatoi* and *idiotai* of the Bible– accept them they receive both the goodness and the badness which are inherent in the original movements. The recipients are not able to infuse their own badness into the legacy of a movement of this kind to the detriment of the good that was in it, nor can they introduce any goodness of their own to correct its badness; that is to say, until a new movement of equal power and greatness bursts on them, common folk remain in possession of the good of the movement of which they are the products together with its defects. Our existence, too, in that secluded and semi-primitive corner of the modern world bore all the stamps of its origins.

CHAPTER II

TORCH RACE OF THE INDIAN RENAISSANCE

I WANT TO DEVOTE this chapter to a consideration of the intellectual, religious, and moral ideas acquired by me up to the age of twelve. I attach great importance to this survey, although as actually written out it might be no better than an exhibition of samples.

All our ideas were the ideas propagated by the new cultural movement, mainly based on the formula of a synthesis of the values of the East and the West, which passes under the name of the Indian Renaissance. I am now of opinion that this comparison to the European cultural movement is not sound, but in early life I accepted it without question, as also did every other educated Indian. Our cultural movement began in the early part of the nineteenth century and reached its apogee in about one hundred years. Then it began to break up. If I were asked to specify when the signs of decay made their first appearance I should say in the years between 1916 and 1918. After the end of the First World War, and in the years immediately following, the change had become clearly perceptible.

Thus we were acquiring and assimilating a culture at that stage of its ripeness which just precedes decline. For this reason we who were born in the last quinquennium of the nineteenth century can claim to be the last of the Old Contemptibles, and I am fond of saying without wishing to be taken too literally that no one born after 1900 has any living, first-hand sense of that modern Indian culture which was built up by the great Bengali reformers from Rammohun Roy to Tagore, and which is now decaying. Accordingly, an examination of our ideas will give a more or less fair indication of the values created by this reforming movement.

Secondly, it will also disclose on a reduced scale the historical development of this culture. It was created in a series of waves of different composition: literary, humanistic, religious, ethical. The origins of the religious movement are contemporaneous with those of the literary, but in the actual process of unfolding it was not till the literary movement had attained its fullness that the religious reformation began to be felt as a force in the country. Thus the two movements, broadly speaking, recapitulated the connexion seen previously in history between the Renaissance and the Reformation in Europe; and the humanistic influences hung as pendants to the literary revival just as the ethical influences were the ancillaries of the religious reformation. By the beginning of the twentieth century, however, all the waves had merged together, so that we grew up in a subjective environment in which all the elements of modern Indian culture had nearly equal importance. But in our personal development and in our gradual absorption of this culture, we recapitulated national history as embryos are supposed to recapitulate the evolution of the species. We were initiated into the values stage by stage in the same order as they made their appearance in Bengali society, although the stages were gone through very rapidly and at times were even telescoped. We received, first, the literary and humanistic influences, then the religious and moral, till our culture, like the national, attained its three-dimensional fullness.

Thirdly, this analysis will show what this culture was like even when reduced to its simplest. I am not thinking here of the childish simplification to which we subjected it. Even if we had not been the youngsters we were, we could not make it very much more sophisticated. The whole community, child and adult alike, was rustic, primitive, naive. It was incapable of receiving any idea without diluting it and bringing it down to its own level. If, therefore, even after the unavoidable steppingdown our ideas are still found to retain some of the original civilized values, then I should be allowed to hold that despite the decline which has overtaken it today the new culture was not weak either in inspiration or in creative power.

BENGALI HUMANISM

The new literary and humanistic movement in Bengal began with the founding of the famous Hindu College in 1817, although its earliest creative achievements were not seen till about forty years later. The first students of the College took as enthusiastically to beef and drink as they took to Shakespeare. They jumped over the railings of the College to procure roast beef from an eating-house close by. In order to wean one of the most famous sons of the institution from this lure his father took the nearly desperate step of giving him a share of his own forbidden food and drink, which used to be brought to him every evening secretly in a trunk. Even in that orthodox age the taking of forbidden food was no crime in itself in Hindu society, if it could be done on the sly. The fault of the students was that they were giving a scandalous public exhibition.

Their iconoclasm did not stop at food and drink. One day one of these boys was taken to the famous temple of Kalighat and asked to bow down to the goddess Kali. He flatly refused, and when pressed by his father only raised his right hand and said in English, "Good morning, madam." The irate father fell on him and was on the point of giving him a beating when the other worshippers intervened with the argument that however serious the boy's offence the peace of the holy enclosure must not be disturbed. The father could only apologize to the others for the blasphemy of his son, and he cursed himself as the unfortunate father of a boy who wished good morning to the

Mother of All the Worlds, who was worshipped even by the great Trinity of Gods headed by Brahma.

But no great movement is carried on solely by its *enfants terribles*. It must have its serious apostles. The greatest exponent, and also the greatest martyr, of Bengali humanism was Michael Madhusudan Dutt, a great scholar and the first great poet of modern Bengal. The son of a wealthy and influential citizen of Calcutta, he left his family and worldly prosperity for ever behind to become a Christian, and such was the importance attached to his conversion by the missionaries who converted him that they hid him in Fort Willam, Calcutta, as a precaution against a raid and forcible rescue by the retainers of his father and his father's powerful friends. During Dutt's life, it was believed by many that he had become Christian from some ulterior motive, either with the object of marrying a Bengali Christian girl, the daughter of the most famous of the early Bengali Christians, or with the hope of being helped by the missionaries to go to England. Dutt himself never admitted this, and in his last moments made the declaration that he was a sincere Christian. But it is quite probable that the hope of being able to see the land for whose culture and literature he had such adoration was an important inducement in his conversion, and in no bad sense. From his early boyhood he felt that the mission of his life was to become a poet, and he wanted to prepare himself thoroughly for it. After paying cruelly for his choice in poverty and humiliation, he still felt that his wild heart was not tamed, and he wrote half in longing and half in dismay:

> "Of hope, the lure was great but small the gain;
> Still life seeks the dark-blue, boundless main;
> I know not how to stem that tide."

But in the end farewell had to be bidden to poetry, and he took it in his last sonnet, of which, too, I give an English rendering. In reading it one has to bear in mind the circumstances of his debut in Bengali literature. Dutt did not attempt Bengali poetry till late in life. He wanted to be a poet in English, and it was on a sudden impulse, combined with the need for Bengali plays felt by some of his wealthy, theatre-loving friends, that he turned his hand to the writing of drama and poetry in his mother tongue. The first three lines of the sestet allude to this fact.

FINIS

In oblivion's unfathom'd waters dark
I leave that worshipped, beloved image thine;
Tears welling up, blind these eyes of mine,
And flowing, drown the last live spark.

Now wilts the lotus, of evil fate the mark,
Whose fragrance drew me of a morning fine,
The world well lost! Ah, in its bitter brine
At day's end breezeless sinks the bark.

Fleeting vision! Her I knew not as a boy;
She in my manhood called me to her joy,
As loving mother straying child did guide.
From heaven wand'ring, exile now I seek,
One farewell favour beg with spirit meek–
Light up Bengal, India's jewel may she bide!

Although Michael Madhusudan Dutt did not begin to write Bengali poetry till he was past thirty, and although the period of his poetical activity covered hardly ten years, yet he created new epic and lyrical genres and achieved enough to make all subsequent Bengali poetry a derivative of his. In addition to his historical importance, the absolute value of his poetry is also generally undisputed; only his reputation, like that of every great writer, has had its ebbs as well as tides, its ups and downs; and his most modern Bengali critics have tried to be as clever at his expense as the modern detractors of Milton, about whom Mr. Logan Pearsall Smith has written so charming a book.

The significance of Dutt's life as the first Bengali humanist has, however, passed almost unnoticed. He died in 1873. At that time the tide of Brahmoism or Hindu monotheistic reform was flowing strongly. Deriving both the strong and weak points of its ethics from English Puritanism combined with the later Nonconformism, the movement approached Dutt's life didactically and treated it as a very valuable demonstration of the evils of improvidence. This condemnation naturally coloured the memoirs and even the standard biography written in the decades following Dutt's death. Subsequent research and curiosity have not accomplished much beyond laying a sentimental icing.

This is a great pity, for Dutt's life presents psychological and historical problems of great interest and subtlety. Besides, his personal career can be taken as a symbol of the entire history, not of Bengali humanism alone, but of the whole of Bengali culture. If he had lived twenty years longer he would have felt that the prayer in his last sonnet had been answered and that, although his hand had failed, others had lightened up Bengal and made her what he wished her to be–the jewel of India. But today the life and culture of Bengal have been overtaken by a blight as complete and sordid as that which put an end to his career. This degradation of Bengal is, of course, part of the larger process of the rebarbarization of the whole of India in the last twenty years, a story which is as sensational and as ominous for human civilization, but not as well known, as the story of the barbarization of Germany by the Nazis. But, somehow, one did not expect Bengal, with her record of cultural achievement in modern times, to follow in the wake of the rest of India to which she had given a new culture. In actual fact, the barbarization of Bengal has been even more complete than the barbarization of the rest of India.

The strength of the humanistic ideal remained unimpaired for about thirty years after the death of Michael Madhusudan Dutt, and in order to convey some feeling of what it was like after it had developed to its fullest point and been worked out as a programme of accomplishments for an idealized Bengali gentleman, I shall quote a passage from a famous Bengali novel published in 1877.

"A CULTURED BENGALI GENTLEMAN

[From *Rajani*, a novel by Bankim Chandra Chatterji, first published in book form in 1877. The narrator is the hero.]

"He did not disclose his business, nor could I ask him outright. So we discussed social reform and politics. I found him an accomplished conversationalist. His mind was culti-vated, his education complete, and his thought far-reaching. There being a pause in the conversation, he began to turn over *The Shakespeare Gallery* on my table. In the meanwhile, I had a good look at him. He was a most handsome man; fair, rather short but neither stout nor lean; his eyes large, hair fine, curly and carefully arranged; he was not over-dressed but was perfectly neat; a man with an exquisite conversational style and a beautiful voice. I could plainly see that he was a sophisticated person.

"Amarnath did not come to business even after the plates of *The Shakespeare Gallery* had been gone over, and began to discuss the pictures. His thesis was that it was an audacious conceit that tried to depict in a picture what was expressed in language and through action; such attempts could never be successful, nor were these pictures successful. He opened the picture of Desdemona and observed: 'You get her patience, sweetness and modesty, but where is her courage with the patience, and her pride of constancy with the modesty?' He pointed to the illustration of Juliet and said: 'You have here the figure of a beauty in the first flush of youth, but you miss youth's irrepressible restlessness.'

"Amarnath continued in this vein. From Shakespeare's heroines he came to Sakuntala, Sita, Kadamvari, Vasavadatta, Rukmini, and Satyabhama, and he analysed their characters. The discussion of ancient literature led in its turn to ancient historiography, out of which there emerged some incomparable exposition of the classical historians, Tacitus, Plutarch, Thucydides, and others. From the philosophy of history of these writers Amarnath came down to Comte and his *lois des trois etats,* which he endorsed. Comte brought in his interpreter Mill and then Huxley; Huxley brought in Owen and Darwin; and Darwin Buchner and Schopenhauer. Amarnath poured the most entrancing scholarship into my ears, and I became too engrossed to remember our business."

This passage is significant not because it came to be written by a man who probably had the most powerful intellect and the best intellectual equipment of any Indian in the nineteenth century, and who was the creator of Hindu nationalism and the writer of the *Vande Mataram* song, but because it embodied an ideal which even an ordinary educated Bengali felt compelled to pursue. The social compulsion was such that the volume of pretence sometimes exceeded the volume of real education, but on the whole it served a good purpose. It kept in check that display of ignorance, airy or arrogant according to the character and manners of the exhibitor, which today makes informed persons thoroughly ashamed of themselves in company.

Our introduction to Bengali humanism began very early in life, even before we had learnt to read. In a Bengali magazine subscribed to by my mother there had appeared in 1901 an illustration showing two Bengali girls in the late Victorian English dress. "Who are these girls?" we asked in some perplexity, for they, though dressed like English girls, did not look English. My mother explained that the older girl was Toru Dutt, the young poetess who was the only Indian whose English verse was recognized as poetry in England, and the other girl was her sister Aru. They were the daughters of Govinda Dutt of Rambagan and had died young, we were further told. In fact, the picture had been published as an illustration to a Bengali poem mourning their death. When we first saw the picture I could not read the poem or anything at all. But I felt very proud that a Bengali girl had secured a place in English literature. My brother also felt proud. So did our parents.

This was our introduction to Bengali humanism. Our acquaintance with it began with Dutt. When I was about nine years old I was one day asked by my father to learn by heart some passages from Dutt's well-known epic poem, *Meghanadvadha Kavya.* The story of the poem was familiar to us from the *Ramayana,* which all of us had read in the old Bengali version of Krittivasa. My father had given me the book a year or two before. But the versification of the *Meghanadvadha Kavya* was unfamiliar to us. Instead of being composed in *payar*, the traditional Bengali rhyming couplet in fourteen syllables with a caesura after the eighth, the *Meghanadvadha Kavya,* my father explained, was in unrhymed verse called blank verse, which Michael had copied from English. My father added that a Bengali who could not read Michael's blank verse properly could not be regarded as an educated or cultured person. In fact, in the decades following the publication of the poem, bridegrooms were challenged by their sisters-in-law to prove their culture by reading the *Meghanadvadha Kavya.* My father very carefully checked our tendency to stop at the end of the lines—a particularly important precaution because Michael had taken over as the foundation of his blank verse the fourteen-syllabled rhyming couplet, and we, finding the metre to be the same, unconsciously read blank

verse like couplets and made it sound incredibly grotesque. My
father showed us how to read this blank verse–exactly like
prose, with attention only to the sense and the punctuation; and
he said, if we did that, the rhythm would come out as a matter
of course. I did so, and after a little practice with my father,
began to recite the rolling verse paragraphs with complete
ease.

But while my father had given me certain selected passages which he thought suitable for me, I read through all the
nine cantos in my leisure time, sitting most of the time on a pile
of bamboos on the western side of the office-hut. This was an
introduction, not only to modern Bengali poetry, but to a far
bigger world lying behind it. It is impossible to read the
Meghanadvadha Kavya without being reminded both by its
own style and allusions, and even more by the remarks of its
commentators, of the whole past history of the epic form, both
"authentic" and "literary". The foreign names which we most
frequently came across were Homer and his *Iliad,* Virgil and
his *Aeneid,* Dante and his *Divine Comedy,* Tasso and his
Jerusalem Liberated, Milton and his *Paradise Lost.* We were
reminded that the entire eighth canto was modelled partly on
the *Aeneid* and partly on the *Inferno,* and it was precisely by
the eighth canto that I was held not only spell-bound, but
guiltily spell-bound. It describes an episode which does not
occur in the *Ramayana*–Rama's descent to hell. I was familiar
with the idea of a descent to the nether world of the dead, for
in the *Mahabharata* of Kasirama Das we had already read of
Yudhisthira's visit to the Hindu hell. But the eighth canto of the
Meghanadvadha created quite a different world in my imagination, a world which was entered by a dim and dread gateway,
over which was written in glowing letters:

> "This way pass the sinners to reach the Land
> Of Woe; to live in ever-during pain.
> All hope abandon, ye who enter here."

–a world where millions of creatures were swimming, struggling, and sinking in a lake of fire; where shadowy herds of human beings were driven like leaves before the wind; where women wan as the moon at daytime tore their hair in rage for the vain care they had bestowed on it in life; where beauties decked out in meretricious ornament entwined with men of god-like appearance, but suddenly turning from lascivious tenderness to frenzied hate, rent them with tooth and nail, till blood flowed and each couple rolled on the ground like maddened beasts locked in fight; where even the virtuous had such shadowy insubstantiality that one could pass through them as one passes through crepuscular darkness. A horrible world, it seemed to be, but as fascinating as forbidden fruit. And forbidden fruit it was, for I had been told not to read that and certain other cantos just yet.

It was not in his allusions, images, and episodes alone that Dutt was exotic, he gave us an impression of strangeness in the whole conception and working out of his poem. We regarded the war between Rama and Ravana, described in the *Ramayana*, as another round in the eternal struggle between right and wrong, good and evil. We took Rama as the champion of good and the Demon King Ravana as the champion of evil, and delighted in the episode of Hanumana the Monkey burning Lanka, the golden city of Ravana. But Dutt would be shocking and perplexing us by his all too manifest sympathy for the Demon King, by his glorification of the whole tribe of demons, and his sly attempts to show Rama and his monkey followers in a poor light. We were destined to get more shocks still. We heard a little later that he had actually written to a friend declaring openly that he did not care for "Rama and his rabble". We found an explanation for this oddity when we were somewhere older and came to see that this distortion by him of the traditional spirit of the *Ramayana* sprang from his entire poetic outlook and education. It was not that he had any innate sympathy for Ravana, as the Milton has been alleged to have for Satan; the sympathy was created for him by a literary association (a good instance of a literary man's imagination and morals being coloured by his reading). He had read Homer and was very fond of him, and it was the Homeric association which was making him represent a war which to us was a struggle between opposites and irreconcilables as a war between rivals and equals. When we were thinking of demons and of gods (for Rama was a god, and incarnation of Vishnu himself), Dutt was thinking of the Trojans and the Achaeans. Ravana was to him another Priam, Ravana's son Meghanad a second Hector, and Ravana's city, which to us was the citadel of Evil, was to Dutt a second Holy Troy. His predilection for Homer was so strong that he planned to write his last epic and *magnum opus* in Bengali on the death of Hector.

We received a valuable critical lesson from our perplexities over Dutt's treatment of the Ramayanic theme. Henceforward we never forgot that whenever a modern author was treating an old theme, and a traditional theme, he was likely to introduce something of his own or of his age, and we remained on the alert to find out what the new element was. This gave us such good practice that when in my higher secondary class I was asked to give a characterization of Tennyson's Oenone I wrote with a glib flourish: "Homer's heroine was made of sterner stuff. This pining young lady is essentially post-Renaissance"; which of course brought me marks.

From Dutt we learned another lesson, an immensely more valuable and characteristic lesson, a lesson characteristic not only of our humanism, but of all humanism. As in the case of Ronsard, Du Bellay, and Milton, so in Dutt's also, a consummate philological culture had brought back an assiduous student of foreign languages to his mother tongue. This ultimate return Dutt has described in a famous sonnet. But he stated his faith even more emphatically in a letter written in 1865 from Versailles to a friend of his boyhood. In this letter he advised his countrymen to speak in their own language when they wanted to speak to the world. He gave out the password: "Let those who feel that they have springs of fresh thought in them fly to their mother tongue." He assured the "gents who fancy that they are swarthy Macaulays and Carlyles and Thackerays" that "they are nothing of the sort". Although the advice was given in English Dutt was perfectly sincere and wrote from genuine conviction. His early poetry was written in English, but after once going over to Bengali he never came back to English for literary expression.

Bankim Chandra Chatterji, too, wrote his very first novel in English, but came over to Bengali permanently after that youthful misfire. It is curious that the only Indian to gain world-wide recognition through compositions of his own in English should be Tagore, who never in his early life thought of writing in English or attempted to do so, who even down to 1910, three years before he was awarded Nobel Prize for literature for his English version of the *Gitanjali,* was believed by most of his countrymen to be quite ignorant of that language, and who even after that had considerable difficulty in persuading the sceptics that the English version was by him and not by Yeats or Pearson or Andrews. We imbibed Dutt's teaching thoroughly and never thought of trying our hand at English for anything but livelihood. It was not a very easy decision to take, for our political status was always imposing bilinguality on us, and the lurking hope of making a literary reputation in the English-speaking world was a strong temptation. Why from this early conviction my thoughts finally turned to English has its own history.

After Dutt we took up Shakespeare. One day towards the end of 1907, my father was standing in the yard of the outer house with a book in his hand and, seeing me, asked me to come up, for, he said, he wanted me to learn something new and in English. When he gave me the book I found that it was *Julius Caesar*. He pointed to a place and directed me to read, and I began: "That you have wronged me doth appear in this ...". That was the first passage in Shakespeare that I learned by heart. My brother was given the part of Brutus, and between us we acted nearly the whole dialogue, which did not take us long to learn. The second dialogue we did together was Cassius's instigation of Brutus (Act 1, Scene 2). The next year we went on the school stage and acted one of the scenes with great spirit, I whipping out a dragger and crying :

> "Come, Antony, and young Octavius, come,
> Revenge yourselves alone on Cassius,
> For Cassius is aweary of the world..."

But, always reciting the part of Cassius, I got myself a bad reputation. I was small and thin, and some clever people began to remark when they saw me : "Yond Cassius has a lean and hungry look; he thinks too much : such men are dangerous... I wish he were fatter." And, as is proverbial, it was the enemy at home, my brother, who took the greatest and the most malicious delight in reminding me of the moral implication of my slight build in Julio-Shakespearean rhetoric.

I do not know if any other country or people in the world has ever made one author the epitome, test, and symbol of literary culture as we Bengalis did with Shakespeare in the nineteenth century. Homer may have been something like this to the Greeks, but that is too distant a parallel. It was a cult which we had made typically Bengali, although the deity was foreign. The Hindu religious tradition recognizes three equally legitimate modes of worshipping God : first, through knowledge; secondly, through action; and, lastly, through love. We thought we were pursuing the first path with Shakespeare. It was the glamour of litrary scholarship which made us look upon the barristers of Calcutta High Court as men to be placed far above any nobleman, magistrate, or merchant in the country, for we credited them with a Shakespearean erudition which probably even Sir Edmund Chambers or Professor Dover Wilson does not possess. But the idea we cherished that our Shakespearean worship was *jnanayoga,* or intellectual contemplation, was certainly an illusion. Schlarship was perhaps the least element in it. What we were really doing with him was to worship him in the third mode of Hindu religious culture–adoration. Even more than the Romantic critics about whom Sir Walter Raleigh used the words, we "busied ourselves ardently and curiously with Shakespeare's creatures", and satisfied our "feelings towards the creator by raising to him, from time to time, an impassioned hymn of praise". At times we went further. We cut him up, as also Sir Walter Raleigh has written, "into minute indigestible fragments and used him like a wedding cake, not to eat, but to dream upon." The celebrated first two teachers of Shakespeare in Bengal, Derozio and Captain Richardson, had done their work well.

Strange to say, my brother and I did not go on to lyrical poetry till we had completed our initiation into the epic and the dramatic. We knew a few odd pieces, of which Tennyson's "Break, Break, Break" was one, and a second was the first part of the last stanza of "To Althea from Prison", on the strength of which we came to think of Lovelace as a saintly puritan. But we never read any large quantity of lyrical poetry until, at the beginning of 1908, Palgrave's *Children's Treasury of Lyrical Poetry* was set as my brother's poetry text-book. This book was somewhat of an ordeal to our teachers, and more especially to Bankim Babu, who coached us in English at home. Their natural bent in the lyrical genre was towards the didactic. They could manage martial poetry almost equally well. So neither "Pet Lamb" not "Hohenlinden" gave them any trouble. Their troubles began with poems like "Where Shall the Lover

Rest?" Bankim Babu tried to make the transition smooth by breaking this new ground with Goldsmith's "Edwin and Angelina", whose edifying conclusion melted both him and us to the marrow. But he could not proceed beyond the first four lines of the anonymous "Gay Goshawk". He read in an undertone :

> "O well is me, my gay goshawk,
> That you can speak and flee;
> For you can carry a love-letter
> To my true love from me."

The amber-coloured glare of the hurricane lantern fell on the left side of Bankim Babu's face, throwing the shadow of his nose on the right half. After reading the lines, he turned his whole face away from the light till it was engulfed in total obscurity, and murmured bashfully and softy, "What poems they want the boys to learn!" He shut the book with a snap and would not teach us "Gay Goshawk". So we went no more a-roving into Palgrave's *Children's Treasury* with Bankim Babu. But we read the whole collection through by ourselves. None of the poems gave my brother and me greater amusement than those in the dialects, including two in Dorset dialect.

Besides English and Bengali literature, revived Sanskrit learning was another very important element in the humanism of modern India. But it was Sanskrit learning of the European Orientalists and their Indian disciples, not the hereditary learning of the priestly and pundit families. This distinction is very imporant, because it corresponds to the difference between the spirit of medieval Latin learning and the spirit of the classical learning of the Renaissance. In India, of course, there was no question of discovering an older language and a second literature lying behind Sanskrit as a truer and more powerful vehicle of the civilization sought to be revived, as Greek stood behind Latin in Europe, nor could any modern Indian writer say, as did Ronsard, that instead of imitating Latin authors and thus becoming the imitator of imitators, he would go back to Greek, the source of Latin literature. But the Indian could prefer the new Sanskrit learning to the old for the same kind of reason which prompted the Ranaissance scholar to prefer the new Latin learning to the old. The new Sanskrit learning gave to the modern Indian a view of Hindu antiquity which was historically truer and at the same time more intelligible. On the other hand, it was also more explosive, because it did nothing to soften the contrast between the modes of thought and mental attitudes of ancient Hindu India and those of the traditional, pre-British Hindu India of the late eighteenth century.

Neither my brother nor I imbibed anything of this Sanskrit element of our humanism at Kishorganj, because we did not learn Sanskrit there, nor did we have any contact with the existing English translations of Sanskrit texts. All that we did at Kishorganj was to assimilate as much of it as had percolated to a childish level through modern Bengali literature. But we became conscious of its existence, for we were being reminded of this new Sanskrit learning by the publication of scholarly articles even in the more popular magazines, in which we saw plenty of quotations in Sanskrit.

Of Islamic culture we knew nothing, although it was the spiritual and intellectual heritage of nearly half the population of Bengal and we in East Bengal came into intimate and daily contact with Muslims. In this we were true to the traditions of modern Indian culture as it was shaped by its creators in the nineteenth century. This culture was not exactly hostile to Islam, but it completely ignored the Muslims. I do not know of one great Bengali writer, religious reformer, or political leader after Rammohan Roy who had any first-hand knowledge of Islam as a whole or of any of its aspects. After the end of Muslim rule Hindu society had broken completely with Islam.

Here too my father showed some originality, which was all the more remarkable in that its motives were wholly disinterested. He once took it into his head to learn Persian himself, bought Sa'di's *Gulistan* and *Bustan* and a reading stand, and engaged a Maulvi. But on account of the demands of his profession he could not make any progress in his Persian studies. So he wanted my brother to learn Persian. But this project too had to be given up. My brother's ordinary school curriculum was already too heavy for him to be able to spare time for Persian. He could, of course, take up Persian as the alternative to Sanskrit, but that was not thought desirable for a Hindu boy.

Strange as it may seem, perhaps we knew more about Hellenic civilization than we did about Islamic. At Kishorganj my brother and I began our acquaintance with Hellenism at the point where modern Europe too began its acquaintance with Greek art, namely, with the Laocoon and Apollo Belvedere. Although Lessing was still an unknown name to us, we were highly impressed by the Laocoon group, as reproduced on a half-tone plate in a Bengali magazine. I did not begin to read about Greek myths and legends in English, apart from such rudimentary notions of the *Iliad* and the *Odyssey* as we had picked up, till I came to Calcutta, and for many years even after that I made no distinction between the Greek and the Roman forms of the gods of classical antiquity, calling Zeus Jupiter or Zeus, Hera Juno or Hera, and Artemis Diana or Artemis, just as it pleased me. But at Kishorganj I learned two Greek stories which have remained graven for ever in my memory. The first of them was the story of Demeter and Persephone and the second of Theseus and the Minotaur.

Characteristically enough, the first story came to us in the Latinized form, as the story of Ceres and Proserpine, and illustrated in the English academic-classic style of the late nineteenth century. A Bengali magazine to which my mother subscribed had published a reproduction of Lord Leighton's painting of Mercury bringing back Proserpine to her mother, and, together with it, a short explanation of the picture. My mother told us the story and showed the picture to us. After that we not only read the story by ourselves, but cut out the picture, and, mounting it on cardboard, hung it up on the wall of our school and bedroom. We immensely liked the story, but the visual impression and emotional associations which Lord Leighton's painting created had to be wholly revised when, later, I saw for the first time a reproduction of the famous Demeter of the British Museum. There was such a contrast between this Demeter and Leighton's Ceres that it took me some time to bridge the chasm.

But the Theseus story cost me no such subsequent unlearning, because the story was not illustrated and was told in a children's magazine in very simple and straightforward language. The deep impression that it made on me was due entirely to the intrinsic strength of the story, while its essentially Hellenic character evoked mental images of such consistency that I found my impressions of the figure and face of Theseus perfectly tallying with the figures and faces of the Athenian young men and of Theseus himself in the Elgin Marbles. The story carried me along in its tremendous sweep, but although it had so many points of absorbing interest, as, for example, the penetration into the labyrinth and the encounter with the Minotaur for excitement, and the abandonment of Ariadne for pathos, to me the most poignant part was the end. Whenever I think of the story it is the image of waiting Aegeus formed in my mind at the age of nine that comes back to me, and I have never been able to form an alternative image. It is as if a part of my brain had become a fragment of an Attic vase with a Hellenic design for ever burnt into it. I see the old king sitting on a jutting and overhanging rock at Cape Sunium, a black sail, and, with it, the prow of a galley rising above the horizon, and as soon as they appear I see a figure with two outstretched arms plunging headlong into the sea.

OUR RELIGION

When with the immaturity of undergraduate days I paraded my disbelief in religion I used to be told that the hot blood of youth did not remain for ever hot and I should soon come to heel. If I have not done so yet, I am at least ready to listen to a religious and moral discussion. But this is the last thing I can expect to hear in contemporary urban India. My attempts at raising steam on this subject in the course of conversation does not succeed even in stoking up a fire. Without becoming atheistic or agnostic or ceasing to be superstitious, modern Indians have ceased to be interested in religious and ethical problems. In India today religion in every form has become paganism, the faith of the *pagus* or the village.

This is one of the fundamental differences between the India of today and the India of fifty years ago. In the famous inaugural lecture of Lord Acton occurs the following statement: "The first of human concerts is religion, and it is the salient feature of the modern centuries. They are signalized as the scene of protestant developments." This is literally true of our nineteenth century. The religious controversies which began with the coming of Rammohun Roy to Calcutta in 1814 and the interest in religion which they aroused lasted till the end of the century. But although the beginnings of religious reform and humanism were coeval in Bengal, and the Brahmo Samaj, the institutional symbol of this reforming movement, was formally inaugurated in 1828 by Rammohun Roy himself, the religious movement which can properly be called Hindu Protestantism did not make its appearance till about 1860. But the two decades immediately following were a period of heroic activity. The Protestant movement within Hinduism brought about as its inevitable reaction a Hindu counter-reformation, and the forty years between 1860 and 1900 were vivified by the opposition between the Brahmo Samaj (the association of Hindu monotheists) and the Hindu revivalists.

This is not the place to recount the history of this religious conflict, but I feel I ought to give a few facts about the Hindu counter-reformation because its course and characteristics are less known than those of Brahmoism. Besides, I could hardly make the nature of the religious influences playing on us in early life intelligible without conveying some idea of the orthodox movement. The orthodox counterblast was simultaneous with the very first and tentative gropings of the reforming movement. Hinduism has an uncanny sense of what threatens it. No plausible assurances, no euphemism, no disguise can put its ever-alert instinct of self-preservation off its guard. No indirect approach can take it by surprise. Therefore, during British rule, Hinduism has fought tooth and nail even those measures of reform which a non-Hindu would consider as purely humanitarian, such as the abolition of infanticide and the burning of widows, the raising of the age of consent, the marriage of widows, and intercaste marriages. This being so, it was inconceivable that such a challenge to Hindu polytheism as Rammohun Roy was throwing out would go unanswered, or that the Hindu Argus would be disarmed in its suspicion by the plea that all that the reformers were preaching was warranted by the highest revealed scriptures of the Hindus.

I shall give an illustration of the quality of the Hindu counter-reformation at its earliest appearance. I can do so from a polemical tract written in Bengali expressly to confute Rammohun Roy, which was published in 1823, and has recently been edited and republished from the very rare original edition by my friend, Mr. Brajendranath Banerji. The writer of the book, a Brahmin pundit of the old school who was set to this task by a social rival of Rammohun, a wealthy landowner

of Calcutta, saw clearly that the method by which he could best
serve Hinduism and his patron was the *argumentum ad
hominem*. Therefore he addressed some questions to
Rammohun Roy with reference to the sins most commonly laid
at his door: for instance, giving up the beliefs of his own nation
and adopting those of foreigners, wearing the sacred thread
hypocritically, slaughtering goats to satisfy appetite, drinking
intoxicating liquors, having intercourse with Muslim women,
and purposeless cutting of the hair of the head. All these
charges are developed with an amazing and overpowering
array of orthodox Hindu learning, which provides the incidental revelation that the traditional Hindu way was a way strewn
with Sanskrit tags. The opponents of Rammohun remind me
of Rabelais' Sorbonnists. Here I shall quote in translation only
the passage about purposeless cutting of the hair in order to
show what Hindu learning and dialectic was capable of making
even of a point which to a man of these days would appear to
be very unpromising. The question was: "What should be
thought, in the light of the dicta of the *Kalikapurana,* the
Matsyapurana, and the *Manu Samhita,* of those persons who
indulge in purposeless cutting of the hair, drinking intoxicating
liquors, and intercourse with Muslim women?" Then begins an
exposition almost as edifying as that of Master Janotus de
Bragmardo making his speech for the recovery of the bells. It
should be explained that Muslim women were an obsession
with Hindus, whether unorthodox or orthodox. They were
supposed to be the best "Kissing carrion" because, as another
Bengali book of the same age (c. 1823) put it, "they ate pillau,
onions, and garlic."

*"Discourse on the
Sinfulness of Purposeless Cutting
of the Hair of the Head*

[Translated from the Bengali polemical tract, *Chastisement of the Heretic,* composed to confute Rammohun Roy and published in Calcutta in 1823.]

"This honourable gentleman, who has so much conceit of learning, should be aware that there are nine occasions for cutting the hair, namely, the seven beginning with Prayag, and, in addition, expiation and the tonsure ceremony. Cutting hair on any one of these occasions is called 'cutting of hair arising out of an occasion'. The use of the word 'purposeless' signifies prohibition of cutting of hair on any occasion exclusive of the above nine. For instance:

      " ' Prayag and other pilgrimage too;
      Of father, mother, and preceptor death;
      Conception and the drinking of Soma–
      Seven shavings are by Smritis enjoined.'

"That is to say, pilgrimage at Prayag [modern Allahabad], pilgrimage to other places, death of father, death of mother, death of preceptor, the conception ceremony, and the drinking of the juice of the Soma plant are the seven occasions on which the hair should be shaved, and this is laid down in *Manu Samhita* and other religious treatises. The cutting of hair for atonement and the tonsure ceremony is, of course, customary.

"It is the intention of the honourable Pseudo-Recipient of Truth to suggest that just as Prayag and pilgrimage, etc., can be occasions for hair-cutting so can be the motives of lessening the weight on the head and giving pleasure to Muslim women. Furthermore, he intends to say that just as the injunction ' In the Ganges and on the Field of the Sun' does not rule out the cutting of hair at Prayag and on other occasions, so it does not also rule out the cutting of hair for pleasing Muslim women and from similar motives.

"But this conclusion can never be valid, because no scripture lays down that the motive of pleasing Muslim women can be an occasion for cutting the hair. And if it were permissible to cut the hair for pleasing Muslim women, why should not also circumcision be permissible for the same reason?

"For although circumcision is prescribed for them only in venereal disease, yet it can be argued that an imperfection in the ancillary in the shape of Islamic injunctions has created in its train an imperfection in the principal. On the other hand, there can be fulfilment of the principal in the absence of the fulfilment of the ancillary. Some scholars prescribe in certain circumstances that no grass effigy is to be burnt in the case of a person burnt to death in a burning building, because the intention of the verbal root 'burn', which means reduction to ashes, has been fulfilled at first hand, and the imperfection in the ancillary in the shape of scriptural injunction does not inhibit it. In the same manner, in the case of circumcision, too, it may be the view of these scholars that when an operation on the prepuce is permitted in venereal disease, it is valid also more generally even in the absence of a specific injunction, because the intention of the verbal root 'operate' which means cutting off, is not barred...

"It is necessary to consider that purposeless cutting of the hair results in the absence of the top-knot, and, owing to the consequent incapacity to tie the top-knot, the daily worship of the top-knot-less person is rendered imperfect. For it has been laid down that religious duties should be performed with the top-knot tied. For instance, it occurs in the Smritis:

> " 'Top-knot by Gayatri tie
> From south-west to crown,
> Tie next the hair as a whole,
> And your rites begin.'

"That is to say, the performer of the rite should first tie his top-knot from the crown of the head to the south-west while uttering the Gayatri, next tie together all the hair, and then begin his ritual. Therefore, through the absence of the top-knot, the omission becomes equivalent to a great sin in the same manner as venial sins accumulating gradually surpass great sins, and ultimately it can prejudice Brahmanhood. The omission to ejaculate 'Live long' after a sneeze, to say 'Rise' after a fall, and to snap fingers after a yawn are not sins of the same order. How can purposeless cutting of the hair be then described as a trivial sin and how can a conventional expiation be prescribed for it?

"It is true that by the gift of gold venial sins are atoned for. But even though they who cut their hair without purpose do on occasions make gifts of gold, none the less it is no expiation of their sins, because if a sin is committed repeatedly there can be no cessation of that sin. We find a similar injunction in respect of bathing in the Ganges. For instance:

" 'He that commits repeated sins
Even the Ganges makes not pure.'

"If you argue that a householder is daily and repeatedly committing the sin of five slaughters, yet his sin is being cancelled by the performance of the five sacrifices and, accordingly, what bar can there be to the expiation of the repeated sin of purposeless cutting of the hair by repeated gifts of gold, the answer is this:

"The five slaughters consist in killing very small insects through the use of the fireplace, mortar and pestle, broom, the bamboo tray on which rice is separated from chaff, and the water pitcher. There is indeed destruction of very small insects in the use of these domestic contraptions and it can never be avoided. But there is in this slaughter neither the intention nor any effort to cause loss of life. Therefore this sin can be expiated by the five sacrifices comprised by the reading of the sacred scriptures, pouring of *ghee* into sacrificial fire, service of guests, libations, and common offering to all the deities. This is permitted by the scriptures, but how can any gift of gold expiate the sin of purposeless cutting of the hair, committed repeatedly and in pursuance of careful design?"

This was the stature of the Hindu counter-reformation as a baby–a hydrocephalic baby, ordinary and normal folk would take it to be. The most extraordinary part of this controversy was not that Rammohun Roy had to face this kind of opposition, but that he enjoyed fighting it on the same plane and often won. In meeting the pundits on their own ground he threw away not only any dialectical firearms he possessed but also the *armes blanches* and picked up an *assommoir,* with which he rushed upon his opponents. He wielded it in a lighter style, but it still remained an *assommoir,* and no one can expect to be left unscarred by polemics of this kind. When Victor Jacquemont, the young French scientist, met Rammohun in Calcutta at the full height of his powers and reputation he found the reformer's conversational style cramped by an excess of logical rigour.

Towards the end of the century the Hindu counter-reformation swung to the opposite pole of grotesqueness. From late Sanskrit scholasticism it passed to scientfic claptrap. Every Hindu custom and every Hindu taboo found its justification in some theory of elecricity and magnetism. At times even the science of bacteriology, new at the time, was invoked. It was proclaimed that if a Hindu kept a pigtail it was only as an electromagnetic coil; if he bathed in the Ganges it was because an unspecified European (for preference, German) scientist had demonstrated that Ganges water killed bacteria instantaneously; if he fasted at full and new moon it was only to countarect the gravitational forces of the sun and the moon; the Diwali illumination was supposed to be a collective lighting of fire for burning up the poisonous gases given off by the earth on that evening. In the end our good old legends and myths seemed like taking to their heels before the invasion of farads, ohms and amperes, protozoa and amoebae, and ethane, methane and other gases. In this instance, again, the most astounding thing was not that these antics should have made their appearance but that they should have been taken so literally and seriously as they were. Even so great an intellect as Bankim Chandra Chatterji was not wholly immune from the infection. Very discreet indications of his flirtation with the old dame trying to pass off as a *mondaine* are occasionally to be found in his writings. But he never resorted to this buffoonery in his explicit reinterpretation of Hinduism.

Had the Hindu counter-reformation been capable of only this, of nothing better than a polarity in its mumbo-jumbo, there would have been no place for it in a history of modern Indian culture. But Hinduism has never been so utterly bankrupt. It has an infinite capacity, almost incredible capacity, to survive and endure the outrages committed on it by its followers. In his celebrated reconstruction of the biblical episode of St. Paul's appearance before Gallio, Proconsul of Achaia, Anatole France makes one of the characters refer to the story of an outrage by a sacrilegious young man on the Aphrodite of Onidos, and then puts the following typically Anatole-Frankish observations in the narrator's mouth: "In the morning the priestesses of the temple found on the goddess the marks of the offence, and travellers say, since then, she retains an indelible stain on herself. One must admire both the audacity of the man and the forbearance of the immortal goddess." Hinduism does not possess the *venuste* of the marble divinities of antiquity, but it has a simple and roughhewn greatness derived from its Aryan creators. This part of it is capable of remaining uncontaminated and rising above the abominations which those who profess the Hindu religion have always been perpetrating on it. But this too has to be said, that there seems to lie within its cavernous foundations in India a clayey core, and within that core something irredeemably corrupt, which is in love with all the obscenities of which mankind is capable. The true autochthon of India has the one immutable role of wearing out, outraging and degrading everything great and good that comes into the country from abroad, and Hinduism, as we have known it during historical times, has always been an admixture of foreign goodness and indigenous debasement. Most often it is the debasement which remains ascendant, but at times, under the stimulus of some external influence, the latent greatness of Hinduism tries to reassert itself. In a majorty of cases it fails, but even when unsuccessful its voice is heard like the voice of one crying in the wilderness by those who have ears to hear.

This voice was heard in the preaching and writing of two Bengalis at the end of the nineteenth century under the impact on India of European culture. The first and the older of these men was Bankim Chandra Chatterji, a student of Comte and Mill, and the second was Swami Vivekananda, who was equally familiar with Western thought. The problem of culture was the main preoccupation of Chatterji; for he believed that the proper cultivation of all the faculties resulting in action and knowledge was the natural function of man. He thought that in none of the potential heads of developement was humanity fully developed, and he expressly stated that he looked upon even nineteenth-century Europe as an undeveloped state of human society. His life-long search was after the means of expanding and deepening culture.

Vivekananda, on the other hand, was more of a proselytizer than a theoretician. He revealed the inner urge of his being involuntarily in one of his minor speeches introducing another speaker at a meeting in Calcutta in 1898. Speaking in English, he said: "Let us remember that the civilization of the West has been drawn from the fountain of the Greeks, and that the great idea of Greek civilization is that of *expression*. In India we think—but unfortunately sometimes we think so deeply that there is no power left for expression. Gradually, therefore, it came to pass that our force of expression did not manifest itself before the world; and what is the result of that ? The result is this–we worked to hide everything we had. It began first with individuals as a faculty of hiding, and it ended by becoming a national habit of hiding–there is such a lack of power of expression with us that we are now considered a dead nation. Without expression how can we live ? The backbone of Western civilization is expansion and expression." So he called upon his hearers to go out to England and America, not as beggars but as teachers of religion. "The law of exchange," he declared, "must be applied to the best of our power." Of course, it is well known that Vivekananda practised what he preached.

As true conservatives, true to the established traditions of conservatism, both Chatterji and Vivekananda regarded religion as the central fact, the keystone of human activity and achievement, and both uncompromisingly rejected the idea of a purely secular culture. The dislike which Chatterji felt for the idea of a purely secular culture made him speak disparagingly of the ideal of culture propagated my Mathew Arnold, while Vivekananda was equally emphatic on the subject. "In other countries," he said, "a man may be political first, and then he may have a little religion, but here in India the first and the foremost duty of our lives is to be spiritual first, and then, if there is time, let other things come." As true conservatives, again, they looked to their own, their national, religion to furnish the basis of the religious culture they valued so much. On this assumption the two men between them offered a version of Hinduism to modern Indians which became a serious rival of the liberal doctrine offered by the Brahmo Samaj. These two schools wrestled for the soul of modern India, and there was hardly one modern Indian with any capacity for thinking who did not experience this struggle within himself. Even Tagore, a Hindu liberal if ever there was a Hindu liberal, felt drawn towards the new Hinduism, and his novel *Gora* is an exposition of this theme. By the time the nationalist agitation over the partition of Bengal had reached its climax (1907) Hindu conservatism may be said to have definitely won the battle. Politics made a powerful contribution to this victory.

The religious influences which I found at work in the formative years of my life at Kishorganj may be divided into five strands : first, the most elementary and elemental, belief in ghosts and spirits and animistic deities and the routine of magic and ritual organized round this belief; secondly, a polytheisn both anthropomorphic and pantheistic and on the whole sunny and benign; thirdly, the Brahmo monotheism; fourthly, the pseudo-scientific Hinduism; and, lastly, the Hindu revivalism preached by Bankim Chandra Chatterji and Vivekananda.

Of course, these strands did not constitute the whole of modern Hinduism. They did not include even all the aspects of Hinduism as it was practised in East Bengal. But they were the Hindu influences we directly felt, saw, and judged. Among them the first and the fourth we totally rejected and despised, the fifth and last we did not try to understand and assimilate till adolescence. Even then, with the exception of its ethical aspect, we never acquired any but an intellectual appreciation of it, but as between the second and the third I can hardly say which we followed more truly. We seemed to be equally at home in polytheism and monotheism and passed from one to the other without the slightest perception of any inconsistency.

Our beliefs about the future state were as heterogeneous, perhaps more–almost disparate. A Hindu is entitled to believe in any of the following four as his state after death : ghostly existence (assumed in normal circumstances to be a passing state), sojourn in heaven or hell, resumption of human life after a transmigration of the soul and its rebirth, and absorption in Brahma or the Ultimate Reality or Deity or whatever one calls it, for it is formless, attributeless, infinite, eternal. The first two states presuppose a continuation of personality, the other two do not, or, to be strictly accurate, the theory of rebirth assumes a continuation of personality but with no consciousness of the previous existence except in those very rare instances when a human being is believed to possess the recollections of his previous lives. But that is supposed to be the previlege of persons who spiritually are either very highly gifted or very highly developed through self-discipline.

We did not believe in ghosts or ghostly existence. In fact, our one and invariable criterion for dividing our companions into sheep and goats was to put them the question : "Do you believe in ghosts ?" If anybody said that he did, with us he was damned for ever. On the other hand, we also very often received the perplexed query : "Do you *not* believe in ghosts?" And when we said that we did not, we were set down in the same decided manner as impious heretics. But in spite of the universal belief in ghosts we never found any of our companions, or for that matter any of the credulous elders, capable of putting forward any coherent rationale of ghostly existence, and their only answer to our challenge was a sneering counter-challenge to pass under a certain notorious tree or by the burning-ghat at night. They knew for certain from their experience of the general cowardice they felt inside and saw outside themselves that this bluff of theirs would never be called.

There was, however, a boy, a classmate of mine and son of one of our teachers, who promised to show me a book which explained all about ghosts. I asked him to bring it and let me have a look at it, and the next day he brought a book called *The Mysteries of the Other Existence,* written by a man who came later to be known among half-educated Bengalis as "the philosophical novelist". I turned over a few pages, and even at that age (I was about ten then) felt contemptuous, for it contained nothing beyond the conventional abracadabra of demonology and some stale ghost stories.

The enigma of death had yet to be explained, and the formal answer which, following the Brahmo doctrine, we were taught to give was that our souls were reabsorbed in Brahma, and we did say it with an air of finality. But that was not the truth, for this colourless *post mortem* destiny did not appeal to us. It meant nothing at all. The view to which we felt drawn, in fact, accepted with cheerfulness and human affection, was the view enjoined by the doctrine of Karma, namely, that after death our souls were reborn in human form in some human household.

Another question we were given to asking our friends, acquaintances and companions, which also we regarded as a test question, was: "Do you believe in one God or many gods?" But in this case our reaction to the answers materially differed from our reaction to the answers to our question about ghosts. If anybody said that he believed solely in *many gods* we did not feel contemptuous, but only that he was a little benighted. On their part our polytheistic friends, when we asserted our faith in one God, did not feel outraged as they did at our denial of the existence of ghosts, but only thought that we were being narrow and bigoted like the Christians and the Muhammadans. For it is not natural in a Hindu to deny either one God or many gods. The only liberty that our orthodox friends would permit themselves was to be derisive of the repetition of the credo : "God is one and without a second." This was no expression of disrespect for the Islamic creed. A Hindu in those days had nothing but discreet consideration for Muslim susceptibilities. The contempt was only for the Brahmo creed which was adopted without any modification from the highest Hindu scriptures, believed by every Hindu to be revealed. Nothing evoked and even now evokes greater levity and flippancy among orthodox Hindus than the repetition of Upanishadic texts either in the original or in translation, and the famous passage of the *Brihadaranyaka Upanishad* which contains the sentence : "Lead us from Darkness to Light" is heard and burlesqued to the accompaniment of blasphemous laughter.

We were not, however, wholly truthful when we said that we believed only in one God. For in addition to the one God we believed also in the more important gods of the Hindu pantheon, although not in the minor ones, and, of course, never in the animistic horde. I have already said that we were conscious of no great gulf between monotheism and polytheism, and we stuck to this innate latitudinarianism in spite of what we said and in spite of the immense and almost fanatical efforts made by Brahmoism to make the two mutually exclusive. Perhaps this is a common attribute of all natural religions. When challenged to justify his polytheism even an uneducated Hindu will reply that the many gods are only particular manifestations of the one God, or that the gods in sensible form are only God or his attributes brought within the comprehension of ordinary intelligences. Bankim Chandra Chatterji makes a clear distinction between worshipping God in material form and believing God to have material form.

Although we never took the trouble of analysing and systemizing our beliefs till they reached the level of intellection, we were inclined to take the Hindu view of the inter-relation of monotheism and polytheism in preference to the Brahmo affirmation. The two were mixed up as inextricably in us as in Plato, Cicero, or Marcus Aurelius. Perhaps we had even an inkling of Plato's distinction between the one begetting God and a large number of begotten gods. Anyhow, I retained my faith in both until I lost my faith in both.

But I must admit that we never got any systematic religious instruction, nor–and that perhaps is the more important aspect of the matter–any religious drill. Even if anyone has a genuine religious bent it is neither fixed nor made fruitful without a regular routine of religious worship. Bankim Chandra Chatterji was one of the most assiduous preachers of religious culture; his conception of the perfection of faith was that it was the state in which all the human faculties, intellectual, aesthetic, and active, converged on God; and for the achievement of religious culture and attainment of faith he emphasized the need for strict regime, daily exercise, and regulation of the routine of living. Swami Vivekananda, if anything, went even further. In a speech delivered at Los Angeles in 1900 he said that once the ideal was chosen and the means determined we might almost let go the ideal because we could be sure that it would be there, when the means were perfected. He was speaking not only of the ethical but also of spiritual ideals. We never had this religious discipline, although in quite a large number of Hindu households, particularly scholarly and priestly Brahmin families, it was, and perhaps still is, very strictly practised. Therefore, I never developed a true religious and spiritual life.

Although I had no religious culture, I cannot say that I did not acquire a religious mood. This mood came to me through our regular routine of devotional singing, a routine which continued till nearly my eighteenth year. It must be known to many of my readers that the classical Indian melodies, which are fixed melodies and may even be called individual compositions in different modes, have certain times of the day assigned to them, to which alone they are supposed to be appropriate. Thus *Lalit* is considered to be suitable only for the morning, *Sarang* for midday, *Multan* for the afternoon, *Puravi* for the early evening, *Khambaj* and *Iman* for about the same hour, *Behag* for the night, so on and so forth. These associations are deprecated in these days, but they are still rigidly observed by the orthodox. Perhaps   this particular form of synaesthesia is not more illegitimate than the association of colour with key or pitch. If Scriabin, Schonberg, and even Bliss in England could toy, indeed more than toy, with the idea of there being some affinity between musical sounds and colours, our old *ustads* perhaps had as much right to their milder conceits. Anyhow, though being told of these associations, I have never been able wholly to discard their influence, and am a little startled if I hear *Puravi* in the morning or *Ramkeli* in the evening.

I have brought in this apparently irrelevant topic because by far the greater part of the devotional songs we heard and sang were set to these classical melodies, which meant that for us the words, the ideas, the tunes, the times of the day, and the moods came gradually to be fused together. Naturally, we did not have the same songs for the morning and the evening. They varied in their meaning, mood, and, of course, in their tunes. The morning songs were full of hope and cheer or, at all events, of serene faith. The evening songs breathed a nostalgia, almost pathological, for God who was our home, and proclaimed sometimes in exultation and sometimes in awe and fear, but always in abnegation, the transience and vanity of the world. Often in the early mornings, as the light of day was breaking fair, we were awakened from sleep by the treble voice of our mother singing in *Lalit,* with my father accompanying on an instrument :

> "O bright and happy Dawn !
> Whose hands have fashioned you,
> With the carmine of the baby sun
> Dyed your pearly hue ?"

At times she sang a graver, though comforting, song :

"O wake up, wake, who for God's love among you pine,
Whom the year has tried with broken hopes and empty heart -
The call is for you, the meek and deprived of the earth,
From the Father, who is yours, and everybody's, and mine."

While we sang these hymns, the idea of God became a
living thing with us, and as we chanted another well-known
hymn:

> "Eyes see you not, you are in every eye;
> Hearts know you not, hidden there you lie,"

we felt that God was indeed with us.

The evening melodies were generally sad, and there was
one song which we frequently sang or intoned at that hour. But
the deepest impression it made on me was on the occasion
when it was sung to us as we were ending the day on a long boat
journey. We were in the middle of one of those wide expanses
of water called *haors* in Mymensingh, which really are low
fields stretching for miles and miles in the dry season, but which
become flooded and look like immense lakes during the rains.
We were sailing through one of them and the sun was setting,
when in the sad and solemn *Puravi* melody these words broke
into our ears:

> "Now ends the day and life's sun sets,
> What keeps you waiting, O my soul ?"

Looking at the western sky I thought I was seeing my own
life setting and my maker face to face. The gentle accompanying murmur of the water under the keel sounded like the
unceasing music of the other world.

Another song was a particular favourite with me and I
often asked my mother to sing it. It was certainly a very unusual
song for a boy of six or seven to like. Some of its lines ran as
follows :

"What hast thou done by illusions drawn ?–strawed from
home to dark, deep woods; o'er foreign countries roamed.

Flees the time and dusk descends; across the sky the clouds
spread their veil; the body droops and falters in the march
with bleeding feet in thorns.

Pines the moaning heart for home, yet knows not where to
wend its way. 'Guide us, O guide,' cries the soul; but who
knows for whom rings that cry ?"

This song was sung as a recitative. Another song, which was about an equal favourite, was :

> "Say–'Lord, O Lord,' and let us turn for home;
> The daylight fades and evening falls;
> With fair ended, and played-out game,
> The inn turns dull, longs the heart for home."

I could go on multiplying these examples, for we sang literally scores and scores of songs. The repetition of the songs week after week, month after month, year after year, exerted a strong influence on my mind. My childlike faculty of wonder at the beauty of Nature became suffused with a very vivid awareness of another world, infinitely more happy, joyous, and serene than ours. In my boyhood I often lay on a mat in the courtyard of our house at Banagram looking at the sky through a pair of opera-glasses, professedly studying the stars but perhaps trying really to locate that unknown and unseen world, and I was filled with an unbearable homesickness mingled with awe.

Even to this day I have not been able to shake off this feeling, this conviction of the material world around me being insubstantial, although I have completely lost all religious conviction and also faith in the other world. Therefore I find myself at times in the curious position of being a denier of this world without having anything to put in its place. Though I have not the assurance of that duration which makes pyramids pillars of snow and all that's past a moment; though I have not the hope which makes one ready to be anything in the ecstasy of being ever, and as content with six foot as the moles of Adrianus; yet the earth seems to lie in ashes for me. And this happens to me not only in regard to the world which is of the world worldly, the world of far-stretched ambitions and madding vices, but even with the world which is made up of the wild loveliness of the face of the earth; of the grace of animal forms; of light raining down from the heavens– the light of the milky spray of the stars which illuminates only when universe is composed to rest by a vast darkness. The feeling seems to cut the ground from under my feet and throw me down from the only country I know into a dark abyss.

A NEW MORALITY

Our moral education was more thorough and systematic than our religious instruction. Brahamoism and revived Hinduism were both earnest, even fanatical, regarding questions of principle and conduct, although they derived their inspiration from different sources. Brahmo morality was based for the most part on Puritan Christianity, while the rival system sought to restore the specifically Hindu form of ascetism, partly in its domestic and partly in its monastic aspect. In point of time the Brahmo moral system preceded the new Hindu. The emergence of the latter may even be called the product of the propagation of the first. Brahmo ethical teaching had disclosed a real gap and serious weakness in the practice of popular Hinduism and created a new need. The Hindu Revivalist movement could not afford to ignore this demand and had to offer its alternative system. Even if it had not done so from conviction, from the conviction of the intrinsic importance of the subject, it would have had to do so at least to maintain its prestige, keep its hold, and put itself on a par with its rival. But revived Hinduism was as sincere and serious about morality and moral conduct as Brahmoism could claim to be. If anything, in later years, it showed itself to be the stricter and more active of the two.

The Brahmo Samaj began its moral crusade with a practical programme. It attacked four vices which it found to be very widespread in the society and the times in which it came into being. They were sensuality, drunkenness, dishonesty, and falsehood. In Bengali society, particularly among the middle class with which Brahmoism mainly concerned itself, none of the vices could be said to have reached criminal proportions, far less diabolic. Like most Hindu virtues, these Hindu vices too were the products of feebleness and passivity. Neither had behind it the driving force of good or evil. All the same, the tameness of the vices did not redeem them from being squalid. Euphuistic and euphemistic phrases like "devotion to the Venus of the marketplace", for instance, would ring utterly false when applied to the sensuality of an urban Hindu; and antonomasia which allusively evoked Lothario, Don Juan, Cassanova, and the like, would shed a wholly undeserved glamour on it. It was a sensuality which, in spite of its furtive sheepishness, advertised itself to the world by means of hang-dog looks and an irrepressible itch in unmentionable places. It filled one with nothing but choking disgust.

Similarly, the prevalent forms of dishonesty and false-hood inflicted no very great wrong on anybody, unless one was very weak and unprotected, as in most cases widows and minors were, or altogether a fool. The technique of these petty, though unending, series of lies and pilferings was so well-known to all, and so universally practised, that in the end the gains and losses in society as a whole cancelled out. It was a war of wits in accordance with one of the dicta of Marshal Maurice de Saxe, without any battle between the competing rascalities. "I am not in favour of battles," declared the marshal, "and I am convinced that a skilful general may wage war all his life without being driven to them. There is no method like this for reducing the enemy to absurdity and further your own interests. You must have frequent engagements and, so to say, melt your enemies away; after which he will have to go into hiding." These manoeuvres and skirmishes of dishonesty and mendacity were going on incessantly in our rural and urban life without raising much visible dust in either. Still, they could not flourish as they did without degrading the practitioners and besmirching the society in which they were carried on. These

sordid and banal vices overlay Hindu society like a coat of
slime.

Both Brahmoism and new Hinduism were determined not
to have any truck with these evils, and to cleanse out society
of them. Brahmoism was strict from a conviction that religion
and morality had equal and autonomous claims on us; new
Hinduism because it believed that moral discipline was an
indispensable preliminary to spiritual achievement. This difference of approach naturally resulted in divergent theories of
morality. Bankim Chandra Chatterji, for example, rather vehemently denied that the self-restraint preached by the *Gita* had
any affinity with "asceticism" or "puritanism", using both the
words in English because they had no exact Sanskrit or Bengali
equivalents. Yet even he, in his exegesis of the *Gita*, when
interpreting the verse: "The mentality of that man is stabilized
who withdraws his senses from the objects of sense as a
tortoise withdraws his limbs from all sides" (Chapter II, verse
58), quotes the following passage from Kant's *Metaphysics of
Ethics* by way of reinforcing his argument:

"All ethical gymnastic consists, therefore, simply in sub-
jugating the instincts and appetites of our physical system in
order that we remain their masters in any and all circumstances
hazardous to morality; a gymnastic exercise rendering the will
hardy and robust and which by the consciousness of regained
freedom makes the heart glad."

The fact of the matter is that despite theoretical differences both Brahmoism and new Hinduism were ascetical and
puritanical in practice.

In the light of their particular ethics, young and zealous
Brahmos vowed as sternly to eschew dance exhibitions because the *nautch* or dancing girls were persons of dubious
character, and the theatre because the actresses were *demi-
mondaines,* as they vowed to shun debauchery, falsehood, or

drunkenness. The spirit of Brahmo morality is perhaps best illustrated by an anecdote about Principal Heramba Chandra Maitra, a very notable Brahmo in his day. He, it is said, was one day walking down Cornwallis Street in Calcutta when a man asked him where the Star Theatre was. Annoyed by this query of unsavoury associations, Principal Maitra, it is reported, at first replied, "I don't know", and then, realizing that he had told a lie, ran back to the man and this time said to him: "I know but I won't tell." The anecdote is certainly apocryphal, but it is true in its spirit. Brahmoism would have been nothing if it were not equal to such undiscriminating and humourless intolerance of the things it condemned. Under the influence of Brahmo teaching I have not visited the Bengali stage even once in my whole life, nor even seen a Bengali play.

Of the puritanical rigour of new Hinduism I can give an example from my own experience. In our adolescence we became adherents of the school of Hindu asceticism and were particularly painstaking in our pursuit of one virtue–chastity. Now, in one of the books of practical morality from which we sought guidance, we found instructions for maintaining a *Book of Failings* in which some of the more serious youthful vices were to be set down in the form of a table, and the number of indulgences in these vices to be recorded every day, so that on the basis of these statistical data we could direct our moral energies in just proportions towards the various weak points in our character. Among other vices, there were included in this table "Sleeping in the Day" (described as a "libidinous dissipation"), and "Infatuation with Female Beauty". I did not maintain this book. Somehow I felt that it was not quite the thing. But my younger brother, being more immature, did. One day my mother chanced on the note-book, and going through it found it generously ticked under the head "Infatuation with Female Beauty". My brother was about thirteen or fourteen then–just the age to embark on that infatuated quest. But my mother brought no objectivity of mind to bear on the psycho-logical situation revealed, and tore up the book, warning my brother seriously against a repetition of such stupidity.

This ethical extremism in Brahmoism and new Hinduism was not all narrowness or lack of intelligence. It was almost deliberate, and had its basis in a thorough insight into the Indian character and its workings. There is nothing an Indian under-stands less in his unvarnished Indianness than the Greek notion of *sophrosyne,* which, to quote Sir Richard Livingstone, stands for selfcontrol, balance, sanity, and reasonableness; avoidance of extremes of action, speech, and thought; a rightness of mind which brings harmony into a personality or life. The Indian swings from pole to pole. If he is not one thing he can only be its opposite, and that was how, as a Bengali critic has remarked, a Hindu poet could easily and naturally pass on from the composition of an erotic century to the composition of an ascetic century.

Thus to ask an Indian to be balanced among a number of things, each good in its way, is to ask him, not to be effective in his varied loyalties, but to be futile in all of them. He has neither the vitality nor the will-power which springs from that vitality to observe proportion in his pursuits. He is and can be driven only by his impulses and emotions, fixed into impulsive and emotional habits, and these impulses and emotions cannot be checked in their natural course without bringing about, as a result of the check, an atrophy of the whole motive power of effort. Seeing this, our moral teachers decided in favour of the extreme which they cosidered preferable; or, perhaps, even without reasoning the matter out, they were almost instinc-tively drawn towards it. If the choice was to be between morality with some Pharisaism on the one hand and tolerance with libertinism on the othr, they thought, and certainly thought rightly, that the first was the more desirable alterna-tive.

Besides, they had to consider the appalling moral indifference and laxity around them. I am not insinuating that the moral conduct of the Hindus is worse than that of any other people who have suffered the same social and cultural degeneration and the same political servitude. That is not so, and Hinduism cannot justly be charged with having let down moral conduct. But it has safeguarded the operative part of morality through a method peculiar to itself. It has attacked not so much the impulse towards immorality as the physical capacity to commit it. For instance, it has kept its widows, whom it does not permit to remarry, on a diet of semi-starvation in order to preserve them from the urges of the flesh. It has discovered an intimate connexion between vice and animal protein, but has no inkling of the connexion between that organic product and the more positive virtues. Thus, sapping vitality with a good conscience, Hinduism has guaranteed a certain standard of moral conduct among its followers:

> *"Si le viol, le poison, le poignard, l'incendie,*
> *N'ont pas encor brode' de leurs plaisants dessins*
> *Le canevas banal de nos piteux destins,*
> *C'est que notre ame, helas! n'est pas assez hardie."*

But the same lack of vitality has also blunted moral consciousness and engendered a repulsive form of moral turpitude, exemplified most often by a timid avoidance of personal moral issues; and this turpitude, by reason of its persistence and obstinacy in individual cases, and, added to this, through the universal prevalence of these cases, has assumed a sort of cancerous malignancy for society as a whole.

The Brahmo movement fought not only the sordid immoralities it found practised by contemporary Hindu society, but even more resolutely this moral turpitude. In this it was inspired by Christian-European ethics, for in its essence Brahmoism was an application of Christianity to Hinduism as Sikhism was the application of Islam. The Hindu revivalist movement which sprang into existence as a counterblast to

Brahmoism approached morality from the specifically Hindu standpoint, and was not prepared to acknowledge any debt to Western Christianity, but there is no room for doubt that its conscience too was quickened by the example of Brahmoism and by the Christian leaven. Even the lowest estimate of the influence of the foreign element on new Hindu morality would rate it as a stimulant. But apart from the question of affiliation both Brahmoism and new Hinduism agreed in this, that they fostered with equal zeal the habit of remaining aware of moral problems. They not only never shirked any moral problem which faced them, whether it concerned public or private life, they often went out of their way to seek moral issues where an average practitioner of ethics could see none. Both these movements definitely favoured a course of moral gymnastics in order to develop a reserve of moral strength to be drawn upon in personal or national crises. The normal exercise of the moral faculties in order to lead a good life, they took for granted; and even this was a great revolution in the society to which Brahmoism and new Hinduism were preaching their message.

Thanks to these movements, I grew up in an atmosphere of moral awareness. Our family had adopted the Brahmo system, and naturally that system became the main influence and ingredient in our moral life. Later, at the adolescent stage, I made the acquaintance of new Hindu ethics and tried to assimilate many of its teachings. We were open to new moral influences, but at no time were we passive in our acceptance of any system. The mere fact that there were three distinct choices before us–the conventional Hindu, the new Hindu, and the Brahmo–forced criticism on us. We met adherents of all the three systems and heard well or ill of all of them. In my childhood and boyhood the rivalry and emulation among the three was pretty sharp, and, whatever the choice, it could not expect to escape rough handling at the hands of the followers of the rival schools. Each of the systems spoke a different language, and the whole vocabulary of the one was not intelligible to the others. In spite of that there always was an attempt at least to rebut criticism, if not fully to understand it.

As I have already said, this clash of systems would in itself have sufficed to check any trend towards stagnancy in our moral life. In addition, the duty enjoined on us as much by new Hinduism as by Brahmoism of reviewing our daily conduct in the light of the principles we held, fostered moral alertness. The early Brahmos were rather strict about keeping diaries. We also tried to keep them, but could never sustain the effort. Nevertheless, through the mere consciousness of our failure in this duty, we came to acquire the habit of mentally reviewing our conduct at the end of the day and partly spoiling our sleep through the gnawings of remorse. Perhaps it is needless to explain that the emphasis in these diaries was not on the observation of social life, but on moral judgements on oneself.

Conduct was a subject of explicit discussion, guidance, and correction with us. Therefore it could never be said of us, as it can be of the youth of my country today, that we received no moral training either at school or at home. And even if this direct moral training had not been given to us, we should have received an indirect initiation into moral values through the purely linguistic and literary education that we were getting at school. I have mentioned that the natural leaning of our teachers was towards the didactic. Over and above, we were asked to write any number of essays, both in Bengali and in English on such extremely un-Indian virtues as moral courage, perseverance, industry, self-help, and un-Indian conceptions like character, repentance, and conscience. In writing these compositions most of us certainly drew mechanically on a stock of conventional ideas set out in our books, but even those who did so could not help being influenced by the repetition of the same ideas day after day. The more intelligent boys made an honest effort to understand the ideas and write something from conviction.

There was yet another indirect means through which our moral consciousness was enlivened, and that was social gossip–the pretty thorough discussion of ourselves, our relations, and the neighbours and friends, in which we indulged. Even the scolding we got was a form of moral teaching, because one of the most important elements in it was furnished by comparisons to our disadvantage between ourselves and some neighbour's children or the children of our maternal kinsfolk. Married Bengali ladies in those days never employed the terms *mine* and *ours* in respect of anything belonging to the husband's clan, reserving the adjectives invariably for the belongings or products of their own parental clan, and they also showed a special affection for their brothers' or sisters' children. So Bengali children in their parental homes got quite used to the idea that they were intellectually and morally very inferior to their cousins by maternal relationship. The cousins on the paternal side, on the other hand, were supposed always to be setting bad examples, although at the same time, in some distant household to which they were connected through their mothers, they were being held up as paragons of virtue.

We received our share of these derogatory and humiliating comparisons. But neither the scolding we got nor the small talk with which our simple and rustic community was so murmurous was pure peevishness, pure malice, or pure triviality. It was, like the small talk in Jane Austen's novels, founded on a serene and stable system of morality, which knew its bearings very well and was not fuddled, which never trifled with moral issues and which had all its frivolity, mischief, smallness, in sum–all the malicious propensities in the right place. I do not think that we have really gained much by giving up this didactic garrulity. Since men, and more especially women, cannot live perpetually above the level of triviality, the prevalence of a moralizing tittle-tattle was certainly perferable to the prevalence of the new tittle-tattle which is about mere place and position with an undertone of envy running through it.

Last of all, even if all these expedients had failed us we should not have wholly lacked moral training, for we had one inexhaustible source of ethical inspiration. This was constituted by our epics, the *Ramayana* and the *Mahabharata,* which I began to read very early in life. No one can read these two grand works without becoming aware of the eternal conflict between good and evil, and with being warned that the price of virtue is eternal vigilance and effort. Although the epics are insistent that Right alone triumphs, they do not encourage faith in an easy victory for Right. We learned from them that it was Right and not Wrong which was at every turn in dire peril, and at every juncture in danger of being engulfed in ruin and defeat. We discovered that Right never won without infinite faith, toil, and courage. At the same time we were taught that the struggle always availeth. Since the Hindus as a rule are prone to throw up the sponge at the least opposition, both physically and morally, this was a most valuable lesson for us.

The moral preaching of Brahmoism and new Hinduism was not only justified, but also successful. Perhaps there never was any period in the last two hundred years of the history of the Hindu middle-class in which it showed greater probity in public and private affairs, attained greater happiness in family and personal life, saw greater fulfilment of cultural aspirations, and put forth greater creativeness in every field, than the fifty years between 1860 and 1910 dominated by the moral ideal: of Brahmo and new Hindu puritanism.

CHAPTER III

ENTER NATIONALISM

IT WAS IN October 1905 that we had our formal initiation into the nationalist movement. The previous year, after coming back from Calcutta, we had heard that Lord Curzon had been at Mymensingh and made a speech there, which our elders discussed with great vehemence and some amusement. It had something to do with the proposed partition of Bengal. In 1905 the partition came and with it the nationalist agitation. Our opposion to the division of Bengal was fierce.

The same class of Hindu Bengalis who opposed Lord Curzon's partition of Bengal have now themselves brought about a second partition of their country–a good illustration perhaps of the inconsistency which is inseparable from the method of arriving at political decisions by the assertion of collective whim. This politically incompetent and emotionally unstable class is having its post-partition heart-searchings. But these are caused less by any qualms that a mistake may have been committed in 1947 than by the difficulty of proving that the Bengali Hindu has been as right in 1947 as he was in 1905, for there is nothing he cares for more than his reputation for a superlative cleverness which, he thinks, makes everybody else look a blinking fool by his side. But at the time of the first partition we did not have this quandary before us, and the Press, that kept woman of Demos, egged us on against the partition as on the recent occasion it egged on packs of craven dotards and barbarized youngsters in favour of another partition. I still remember a cartoon in a Bengali newspaper in those far off anti-partition days which showed Lord Curzon sawing a live woman. I am living away from Bengal now and never see any Bengali newspapers. But I should think they must have been, with their normal crudity, representing Lord Mountabatten as a midwife attending the confinement of an elderly woman and holding up a promising little one-armed and one-legged baby to the world.

But I should not anticipate matters. For the moment I am concerned only with the first observance by us of the partition day, when a gentleman called at our house with a bundle of silk threads and my father asked us to have a bath in the river first and then in a state of cleanness tie the thread round our wrists as a token of the brotherhood of all Bengalis. We were to observe that day as a day of national mourning and fasting. We also put away all our clothes manufactured in England and put on *dhotis* made in the Indian mills, which at first were as coarse, heavy, and thick as sackcloth.

OUR POLITICAL IDEAS

I was, however, too young at the time to have an understanding of the intellectual content of the new nationalism. But I did share the twin sentiment which with the boys of my generation was the nearest approach to a political concept. We had already acquired a genuine passion for personal freedom, and any suggestion that we could not hold whatever political, religious, or moral convictions our conscience prompted us to adopt, or that we could not give free expression to them, would have been resented even by the boys that we were as a monstrous tyranny. With this feeling for freedom and impatience of outside compulsion went a very idealistic and fervent republicanism. We unquestioningly assumed that there was some inherent virtue in the romoval of an absolute monarch, or even in a partial reduction of his powers. Harmodius and Aristogeiton and Lucius Junius Brutus were as much our heroes as the heroes of the Athenians and Romans. In fact, Greek and Roman republicanism had cast its spell as decisively on us as on the makers of the French Revolution, and under its influence we seemed always to feel on our shoulders the weight of an unseen toga. In the actual unfolding of contemporary history it made us read with delight and high hopes the news of the political revolutions of our youthful days–the Russian Revolution of 1905, the Young Turk Revolution of 1909, and the Chinese Revolution of 1911. We invariably identified political freedom with two things: the absence of an absolute monarch and the presence of an assembly of representatives of the people. But we never worked out the relationship between these representatives and the general mass of the population of a country.

Certain modern personalities and movements contributed powerfully to our political consciousness, of which there were two clearly discernible facets. The first and rational facet was indoctrinated by Burke and Mill, but shaped in its practical expression by the liberalism of Gladstone and Lincoln. The second facet was purely emotional, and its inspiration was furnished by Rousseau and Mazzini besides the Ancients. The methods of political action were suggested by the leaders of the American Revolution, the Italian Risorgimento–particularly Garibaldi–and the Irish Nationalists. The entire course of English constitutional history and, more especially, the turmoils of the seventeenth century, together with the American, French, Italian, and Irish movements were freely drawn upon for precedents and also for operational hints. Of course, it was some time before we the boys could mix our political physic ourselves. For the time being it was dispensed to us by the grown-ups. But eclectic as they and we were, the German nationalism of the nineteenth century, curiously enough, did not influence us. This appears surprising in view of the close resemblance to Nazism that Indian nationalism came to bear later, but it is also perfectly intelligible, because the German nationalist movement of the nineteenth century was not like the nationalism of Italy or of Ireland, the nationalism of a subject people. The other fact that we were not influenced by the nationalism of the Balkan people appears stranger, and is only to be accounted for by our ignorance of it. For when in later life I read Professor Seton-Watson's works and also Miss Rebecca West's *Black Lamb and Grey Falcon* I found the nationalist emotions and impulses described in these books to be very similar to those we felt between 1908 and 1919.

We went no further in comprehending the intellectual content of the nationalist movement. But we were swept by its emotional fervour. The first element in this emotion was an intense, almost religious, hopefulness. We believed in the second advent of our country and nation with a firmness of conviction which nothing could shake. We knew that our present condition was pitiable: we were poor, subjugated and oppressed, and even degenerate in certain respects; but we were great once and should be even greater in the future. This amazing faith, running counter to all the known facts of history which go to prove that a nation overtaken by decline after once creating a great civilization never rises again, was to us justified by itself and needed no evidence of validity external to itself. If at all any proofs were needed, we could point to the fact that while every other ancient nation which had created a civiliza- tion–the Egyptians, Chaldeans, the ancient Greeks, the Ro- mans–had disappeared, we, the Hindus, had survived; this could only mean that we were a chosen people who were destined, or rather ordained, to have a future more glorious than even their past.

The faith was fixed in our mind by a large number of patriotic songs whose single theme was that our country would be great again. When I was a boy I was once told that the regimental band was the most important part of a regiment, for the men fought only as long as the band urged them on to fight with music and as soon as the music ceased the fighting spirit of the men also disappeared. I was further told that for this reason the enemy always tried to pick off the bandsmen first. If not true of soldiers, that was certainly true of us, for I am quite sure that all our patriotic fevour would have vanished but for the songs. St. Paul declared that without charity he was as sounding brass or a tinkling cymbal; we should have been without charity even for our mother country without the sounding brass and tinkling cymbal.

To begin with, however, we had wood-winds rather than a brass band. When the anti-partition agitation began there were no ready-made songs embodying the sense of grievance created by Lord Curzon's administrative measure, and no songs crackling with the anger of the hour. We had to fall back on the patriotic songs composed in the preceding era, many of which were by Tagore and breathed a lyrical love for our country, both India and Bengal. This patriotic lyricism was the second note in the emotion we felt at the coming of the nationalist agitation, and its poignancy lay in the continuous evocation of the beauties of nature: the waters, the green grass, and the golden cornfields of Bengal, the fragrance of the mango blossom in the spring; while on a grander level we had the snows of the Himalayas and the waves of the Indian Ocean. Even now I cannot read the words of these songs, far less whistle the tunes, without instantly bringing back to my ears and eyes all the sounds from the soft rumble of the rain on our corrugated-iron roofs to the bamboo pipe of the cowherds, and all the sights from the sails of the boats on our great rivers to the spreading banian tree–the sounds and sights which embody for me the idea of Bengal.

An eagerness to serve and sacrifice ourselves was the third element in our patriotic emotion. Henceforward, we thought, we had no right to live any other life but a dedicated life. Our country was waiting for us to rescue and redeem her. She could be only what our faith and effort would make her.

The sense of the demand made on us by our country was so real that it seemed as if actual calls of distress from some living person were reaching us, and we felt guilty if we could not show some activity at every hour of the day which could be interpreted as the service, direct or indirect, of our country. It was living with an all consuming intensity; but even with that strain it was delightful; if I were to say,

"Bliss was it in that dawn to be alive
But to be young was very heaven!"

—that would not be mere, and rather threadbare, rhetoric.

Gradually, however, as the agitation became more intense and heated, other feelings began to take possession of us. Our messianic faith in the future of our country was filled out with a definitely Hindu content; to our lyrical love for our country was added a fierce hatred of the English; the spirit of self-sacrifice and dedication found its natural, but always fatal, complement of fanaticism. When in later life I read Sir Valentine Chirol's *Indian Unrest*—we had been taught to hate him and his book equally well—and compared what he had written with my own recollections, I found that he had been wholly correct in his estimate of the Swadeshi movement, in representing it as being essentially a movement of Hindu revival. It was not the liberal political thought of the organizers of the Indian National Congress, but the Hindu revivalism of the last quarter of the nineteenth century—a movement which previously had been almost wholly confined to the field of religion—which was the driving force behind the antipartition agitation of 1905 and subsequent years. This movement was bound sooner or later to clash with liberalism, and the clash which occurred at Surat in 1907 was only superficially a quarrel between the Moderates and the Extremists; in essence it was the manifestation of the irreconcilability of liberal nationalism and Hindu nationalism.

In demagogic politics the less extreme never has any chance against the more extreme. There is a Gresham's Law as much in politics as in economics, and therefore the liberal form of nationalism began to lose not only support but also reputation. We always turned up our noses at the mere mention of the Moderates, and even before we had begun to air our contempt for them a complete transformation had come over our spirit. We found the older patriotic songs very tame and uninspiring. They seemed to contain very namby-pamby sentiments. Inevitably, new songs began to make their appearance to cater for the new spirit. It is significant that one of the new songs, and one of the most popular, was composed by a journalist of the orthodox Hindu school, a man who had once been sentenced to imprisonment for a most dishonourable libel on the wife of a distinguished Brahmo. Some of the lines of this song were:

> "If I should die,
> By our Mother, let me die,
> Fighting for my land.
> The cops in blue and red
> A little blood may shed;
> The more our blood shall flow,
> The stronger should we grow;
> Bogey's had his day,
> To him we will not pay
> The tribute of a pie.
> Even if I die,
> By our Mother, I shall die
> Fighting for my land."

We were highly taken with this song, and we thought it very much better than the Tagore songs we formerly used to sing. On the second or the third anniversary day of the partition we were going round the town singing patriotic songs, and when we came near the Government treasury we stopped at a distance of about fifty feet from the armed sentry, singing with the greatest imaginable gusto: "The cops in blue and red..." We snapped our fingers at him and yelled and danced in cannibalic exultation, with the poor fellow looking on helplessly, perhaps all the time feeling more and more guilty of his unpatriotic employment.

A year or two later we went further and adopted an even more uncompromising Hindu song, one stanza of which called on the goddess Kali to come to our aid. We sang:

> "O Great Mother, now descend
> With your looks that horror shed;
> Also all your witches send,
> Who the burning-ghat do tread."

Her help was asked of course to drive out the English. My brothers and I often sang the song, because it was a great favourite. I still remember the evening when my elder brother and I, having been sent to do some shopping, went along singing this ultra-Hindu song at the top of our voices, singing it even more lustily when we were before the police-station and the Kali temple, both of which were on the main road adjacent to each other. Two clear young voices sent the terrible invocation ringing through the stillness of the evening. It was dark, and the street was very poorly lighted, so nobody could identify us.

Not less significant as an indication of the change that was coming over us was the fact that after a little while we ceased, when we playfully charged one another, to give our childish and unmeaning yells. We rushed on our momentary enemies, sometimes with awful seriousness and sometimes by way of horseplay, repeating the Maratha war-cry–"*Hara, Hara, Mahadeo!*" Perhaps equally significant was the adoption in our family of the *Basumati,* the organ of orthodox Hinduism, as our daily newspaper, instead of the *Sanjivani,* which was liberal, although the Brahmo editor of the *Sanjivani* was one of the famous nine to be deported under the notorious Regulation III of 1818.

One destructive form of patriotism, however, we avoided in our family. There were only too many who did not feel that they had made their final choice for nationalism, and burnt their boats behind them, until they had also literally burnt their clothes of English manufacture. Neither my father nor my mother saw any sense in the demonstrative exuberance. They put away our old clothes and made us put on Indian clothes, and they also used nothing but Indian clothes. Even so, the patriotic fury touched my mother once, illustrating the extreme emotional instability which the nationalist agitation had generated in us. The result was the unnecessary destruction of a poor glass water jug in 1909, after it had survived the emotional storms of the first four years of the Swadeshi movement. My mother was coming from Kalikutch to Banagram, and she was travelling in a palanquin for a part of the way. When not very far from our village she felt thirsty and asked for some water. The water was brought to her in the glass jug. Suddenly she took a violent dislike to the vessel as a foreign article, and told my brother–the brother next to me who was called madcap and who was always ready for feats of this kind–to break it. The boy was overjoyed and smashed the jug against a tree.

HINDU-MUSLIM ENMITY

I can throw a collateral beam on the character of our nationalism by describing what we felt about the Muslims. When I see the gigantic catastrophe of Hindu-Muslim discord of these days I am not surprised, because we as children held the tiny mustard seed in our hands and sowed it very diligently. In fact, this conflict was implicit in the very unfolding of our history, and could hardly be avoided. Heaven preserve me from the dishonesty, so general among Indians, of attributing this conflict to British rule, however much the foreign rulers might have profited by it. Indeed they would have been excusable only as gods, and not as man the political animal, had they made no use of the weapon so assiduously manufactured by us, and by us also put into their hands. But even then they did not make use of it to the extent they might easily have done. This, I know, is a very controversial thesis, but I think it can be easily proved if we do not turn a blind eye to the facts of our history.

When we were very young, that is to say when the Swadeshi movement had not coloured our attitude to the Muslims, we presented four distinct aspects in our attitude towards them as it was shaped by tradition. In the first place, we felt a retrospective hostility towards the Muslims for their one-time domination of us, the Hindus; secondly, on the plane of thought we were utterly indifferent to the Muslims as an element in contemporary society; thirdly, we had friendliness for the Muslims of our own economic and social status with whom we came into personal contact; our fourth feeling was mixed concern and contempt for the Muslim peasant, whom we saw in the same light as we saw our low-caste Hindu tenants, or, in other words, as our live-stock. Of these four modes of feeling the first was very positive and well-organized intellectually; the rest were mere habits, not possessing very deep roots.

Nothing was more natural for us than to feel about the Muslims in the way we did. Even before we could read we had been told that the Muslims had once ruled and oppressed us, that they had spread their religion in India with the Koran in one hand and the sword in the other, that the Muslim rulers had abducted our women, destroyed our temples, polluted our sacred places. As we grew older we read about the wars of the Rajputs, the Marathas, and the Sikhs against the Muslims, and of the intolerance and oppressions of Aurangzib. In nine-teenth-century Bengali literature the Muslims were always referred to under the contemptuous epithet of Yavana. The historical romances of Bankim Chandra Chatterji and Ramesh Chandra Dutt glorified Hindu rebellion against Muslim rule and showed the Muslims in a correspondingly poor light. Chatterji was positively and fiercely anti-Muslim. We were eager readers of these romances and we readily absorbed their spirit.

Our attitude to the Muslims whom we saw around us was also influenced, if not by the positive utterances, at all events by the silences, of our nineteenth-century writers. In them the hatred of the Muslim was the hatred of the Muslim in history. It operated, as I have said, retrospectively. Of Muslims as contemporaries they were almost totally oblivious; and when they were not forgetful they were indifferent. British rule in itself was a factor which discouraged the cultivation of Islamic culture and sympathies by the Hindus, and to British rule was added the far stronger influence of the discovery of the ancient Indian civilization. The very first result of this renaissance was a progressive de-Islamization of the Hindus of India and a corresponding revival of Hindu traditions. Throughout the nineteenth century the culture of the Hindus of India was taken back to its ancient Sanskritic foundations. The only non-Hindu influences which it recognized and tried to assimilate were European. All the thinkers and reformers of modern India from Rammohun Roy to Rabindra Nath Tagore based their life-work on the formula of a synthesis, by which they understood a synthesis of Hindu and European currents. Islamic trends and traditions did not touch even the arc of their consciousness.

Thus the new Indian culture of the nineteenth century built a perimeter of its own and put specifically Muslim influences and aspirations beyond the pale. In relation to it the Muslims stood outside as an external proletariat, and if the Muslims wanted to come into its world they could come only after giving up all their Islamic values and traditions. The modern Hindu did indeed send many invitations to the Muslims:

"Will you, won't you, will you, won't you, will you join
the dance?"

Will you, won't you, will you, won't you, won't you
join the dance?"

The modern Hindu also felt very aggrieved when the Muslim did not show any alacrity to accept their invitations. But the Muslim was perfectly clear-sighted and sensible:

"Said he thanked the whiting kindly, but he would
not join the dance.

Would not, could not, would not, could not, would
not join the dance."

When the Muslims were invited to join the Congress on its very inception their leaders very politely but firmly declined, and one of them said shrewdly that the Muslims, "tied to the wheels of the Juggernaut of majority, would be in the end crushed out of all semblance of nationality." The so-called two-nation theory was formulated long before Mr. Jinnah or the Muslim League; in truth, it was not a theory at all; it was a fact of history. Everybody knew this as early as the turn of the century. Even as children we knew it from before the Swadeshi movement.

The nationalist movement brought about an accentuation of the difference. Theoretically it preached Hindu-Muslim unity. We sang quite a number of songs which taught us that the Hindu and the Muslim were brothers. But against that unconvincing preaching was to be set the definite inculcation of an anti-Muslim doctrine, which took two forms. In one of its aspects it was a further perfection of the historical enmity. Nationalism cannot flourish in the abstract: Indian nationalism had to be correlated to the facts of the political history of India;

and in bringing about this necessary correlation the Hindu nationalists showed themselves to be highly selective. Even the theoretician of the Swadeshi movement, Bepin Chandra Pal, wrote: "If the Moslem leaders tried to wipe out the memories of the Sikhs and the Mahrattas, the Hindu nationalist leaders sought to revive them. It was no doubt a supreme psychological need of nationalist propaganda; and so far as these memories were revived to recreate the self-confidence of a people suffering from a state of hopeless and listless inertia, they did only good and no harm." But even Pal had to admit: "It gradually awoke, at least in a section of the nationalists, the foolish and suicidal ambition of once more re-establishing either a single Hindu state or a confederacy of Hindu states in India.

The other and the more dangerous form of the aggravation of Hindu-Muslim antagonism by the Swadeshi movement was that this hostility was now brought down from the historical to the contemporary plane, and converted from a retrospective hatred to a current hatred. For this the Muslims were as responsible as the Hindus, although, as I see it, they could hardly have acted otherwise than they did without abandoning their group consciousness as Muslims. With the prospect of a transfer of political power from British to Indian hands the old Hindu-Muslim political rivalry was bound to be resuscitated. It was; and to begin with, the Muslims showed themselves as the allies of the British and opponents of the nationalists. It was in two districts adjacent to my own that this new form of antagonism first made its appearance. My early memories are crowded with the incidents of this clash and the conversations arising out of it. The Muslim League was formed at Dacca, and one of the earliest Hindu-Muslim clashes with a purely political complexion took place in the chief town of my mother's district, Comilla.

I shall cease geaneralizing at this point and relate some of the experiences of my boyhood. When living in Calcutta, as I have done for the greater part of my life, I hardly met any Muslims and became intimate with none. There I found an arrogant contempt for the Muslims and a deep-seated hostility towards them, which could have been produced only by a complete insulation of the two communities and absence of personal relations between their members. This inhuman antagonism could not exist in East Bengal, where, owing to the number of the Muslims and also to the fact they were Bengali-speaking, the economic and social life of the two communities was interwoven. Even when there was no unity of moral and religious outlook, as for the most part there was not, the mere physical contiguity could not be avoided; and when one has to meet another person at all times of the day on personal business, it is very difficult to visit on him the wrath generated by the supposed historical injuries inflicted by his community. The most serious and tragic aspect of the Hindu-Muslim discord in India today is the creation of a rancorous hatred which one can feel only for an abstract entity, or only for the foe who is of one's household, to the relations between man and man, neighbour and neighbour, friend and friend, playfellow and playfellow, fellowworker and fellowworker, when they happen to be of rival faiths. We began without this hatred. There was a number of Muslim lawyers in our street, whom we respected as much as any other colleague of my father. With their sons and nephews we were as friendly as with the children of our Hindu neighbours, and two boys, Akhtar and Karim, were my particular friends. A very large number of our school-fellows were Muslim, and in the whole school there were at least as many Muslim boys as Hindu. We worked, talked, and played with them quite naturally. We never associated them with the abstract entity labelled Muslim, existing in our historical consciousness, for which we had such hatred, and it never occurred to us that anything could happen which could make us modify our behaviour towards our Muslim neighbours in the light of collective emotions generated by collective rivalries.

But the change inevitably came, and came very early. It was from the end of 1906 that we became conscious of a new kind of hatred for the Muslims, which sprang out of the present and showed signs of poisoning our personal relations with our personal Muslim neighbours and school-fellows. If the sprouting enmity did not go to the length of inducing us to give up all intercourse with them, it made us at all events treat them with a marked decline of cordiality. We began to hear angry comment in the mouths of the elders that the Muslims were coming out quite openly in favour of partition and on the side of the English. Nawab Salimullah of Dacca, the protagonist of the Muslim League and new Muslim politics, became our particular *bete noire*–and we contemptuously called him "The One-eyed". We also noticed that our Muslim school-fellows were beginning to air the fact of their being Muslims rather more consciously than before and with a touch of assertiveness. Its first expression in our school was the protest of the Muslim students against acting certain scenes from a Bengali drama on the school anniversary day. We had always acted these scenes and saw no justification for the protest, but the Muslim boys said that the speeches were offensive to Muslim feeling, which of course they were, because no Bengali historical play written by a Hindu is complimentary to the former Muslim rulers of the country. The school authorities stopped the anniversary celebrations altogether, and we waited long in the hope of their revising their decision. But they did not, and we came back home almost in tears, leaving all the decorations of the hall, over which we had spent so much labour, as if the performance were to take place in the evening.

At about the same time we heard of the rioting in the town of Comilla, occasioned by the visit of the Nawab of Dacca. The conversation of the elders gave us the impression that although the troubles had been provoked and started by the Muslims, they and more particularly their Nawab, had not come out of the affair with flying colours. The elders related with contemptuous amusement that as soon as a gun had been fired at the Nawab from a Hindu house, he had run for dear life to Dacca. That was our version of the events, and we, the children, discussed with glee the flight and loss of face of Salimullah the One-eyed.

But the next Hindu-Muslim episode gave us a sense of frustration. Late in the spring of 1907, at the time of the Hindu festival of Vasanti Puja, the image of the goddess Durga was desecrated; in fact, broken to pieces by a Muslim mob at Jamalpur, one of the subdivisional headquarters of Mymensingh district. We were furious, and we heard with still greater fury that the magistrate of Mymensingh, Mr. Clarke, had prevented the volunteers of the Suhrid and Sadhana Samitis from going to Jamalpur to help the Hindus there. Had they been allowed to go, we felt certain they would have taught the Muslims a lesson which they would not have soon forgotten. It appeared that the Muslims were doing for the British the dirty work of suppressing the nationalist movement by terrorizing the Hindus in general, and we could not get at them on account of their powerful protectors. Mr. Clarke, the magistrate, was already very unpopular with us as a violent opponent of the Swadeshi movement. He used to fly into a rage, and the most undignified rage, at the mere cry of *Vande Mataram,* and mischievous little boys let go no opportunity of annoying him and watching the fun by shouting *Vande Mataram* from behind walls and hedges when they saw him passing. After the Jamalpur affair both he and the Muslims became even more unpopular with us.

It was just after this incident that we heard Kishorganj people talking with some excitement and panic of the possibility of the coming of Nawab Nawab Ali Chaudhuri, a well-known Muslim zamindar, to our town. Though not hated as much as the Nawab of Dacca, he too was suspect in our eyes, and people felt that if he came to the town serious trouble would follow. My mother and we, the children, were then getting ready to go away to Kalikutch, and we did not pay much attention to the rumours, nor did it strike us, as I have already said, that the possibility of a Hindu-Muslim riot in the town had anything to do with our going. At Kalikutch people surprised us by asking whether we had come away on account of the likelihood of trouble at Kishorganj. We pooh-poohed the idea, but when we came back to Kishorganj we were told very definitely by our school-fellows that my father had sent us away to be out of harm's way, should anything have happened at Kishorganj. But, actually, Nawab Nawab Ali Chaudhuri had not come. Most probably he had been advised not to, in view of the Hindu-Muslim tension throughout the district. The year 1907 was a year of very bad feelings between Hindu and Muslim. At Kalikutch we heard ceaseless talk about the possibility of attacks on us by the Muslims, and at Kishorganj, too, these rumours were persistent. Even friends, when they belonged to the rival communities, kept discreetly aloof for the time being. The Nawab came to Kishorganj a year later and was given a tremendous reception by the Muslims. The high feeling had by that time subsided, and there was no incident. On the contrary, we rather admired the Muslim procession and thought they were making quite a good show of it. This was all the more of a surprise because the Muslims were not as practised in public demonstrations as we Hindus were.

Many years afterwards my father told me the whole story of our going away to Kalikutch. It was indeed due partly to the expectation of Hindu-Muslim trouble. In recent years, whereever Hindu-Muslim rioting took place in Bengal over large tracts of the countryside, the men were seen to run away leaving their women folk and children behind. But in our childhood this was not considered to be quite creditable on the part of the men, and my father particularly was a believer in the English method of putting women and children out of the way when he wanted to fight. He told me that very thorough preparations had been made by the Hindus to meet possible Muslim attacks. Trunkfuls of pistols and ammunition had been passed from house to house; swords, spears, and even bows and arrows had been collected in large quantities. Every Hindu house would have been defended by men practised in arms, and blood would have flowed had there been a clash. At the same time, my father also told me that he had got the Muslim version from a close friend of his, who was a notable Muslim gentleman from the village of Baulai, near Kishorganj. This friend told him some months afterwards, when they could exchange notes, that, all along, the Muslims of Kishorganj on their part had been anticipating Hindu attacks on themselves in retaliation for what had happened at Jamalpur and had made their defensive preparations. To fear the worst and be prepared for it is always a very dangerous game, and when during the recent riots in Delhi in 1947 I heard the Hindu chatter that the Muslims had made extensive preparations for attacking the Hindus, I naturally recalled the story of the Hindu preparations and Muslim counter-preparations, or, if one wants to have it put differently, of the Muslim preparations and Hindu counter-preparations at Kishorganj in 1907 in the now forgotten epoch of the Swadeshi movement, and I thought that there was no new thing under the sun.

Although open clashes were avoided, the year left a permanent legacy of estrangement. A cold dislike for the Muslim settled down in our hearts, putting an end to all real intimacy of relationship. Curiously enough, with us, the boys of Kishorganj, it found visible expression in the division of our class into two sections, one composed purely of Hindus and the other of Muslims. We never came to know all the circumstances of this division. Whether or not the Muslim boys had also expressed unwillingness to sit with us, for some time past we, the Hindu boys, had been clamouring that we did not want to sit with the Muslim boys because they smelt of onions. The authorities of the school may have heard of this. It is also possible that they acted on their own initiative. A third possibility is that they received instructions from the Inspector of Schools. In any case, they carried out a change of deep significance. Compartmentization by communities came into our education before it was introduced into our politics. Nobody seemed to be sorry. On the other hand we were as pleased with the division as were quite a respectable number of high-placed and low-placed imbeciles at the division of India in 1947.

POLITICAL INCIDENTS

We were soon to receive a demonstration of Mr. Stinton's political ability. Noticing the interest of the school students in cricket he suggested a cricket match and offered to present a cup himself. I no longer remember who the sides were, but for some days the game was played with great enthusiasm, before quite a large gathering of spectators. Then on the last day a very unexpected thing happened, about which I heard first from my playfellows and then from the grown-ups, because I was accidently absent from the cricket field on that day. The news was very exciting. Some boys of the topmost class had refused to play, alleging as their ground the discovery that the cup which had at last been brought to the field was of English make. Whether the inspiration came from the boys or from higher up I do not know, but I am inclined to the latter hypothesis. However that may be, on account of this exhibition of indiscipline the recalcitrant boys were threatened with expulsion. At this point my father came out on the side of the boys. A meeting of the guardians was called and it was decided that unless the boys were taken back all the guardians would withdraw their wards from the school. The headmaster, probably instigated or supported by the magistrate, stood firm, and as a consequence most of the boys, including ourselves, left the school. Only the sons of the Government servants and of some others whom we stigmatized as "very loyal" remained behind, and they were duly abused as the sons of slaves.

A tussle between the citizens and the magistrate followed. Mr. Stinton sent for the guardians in batches and tried both cajolery and threats on them. At length most of the guardians yielded, pleading the excuse that Mr. Stinton had threatened to bring Gurkhas into the town. The breaking up of the Barisal political conference in 1906 was fresh in people's minds, and the Gurkhas had become a formidable bogey to child and grown-up alike. The Kishorganj guardians declared that they had yielded to the magistrate only to spare the town molestation at the hands of the Gurkhas. Mr. Stinton won, and my father, smarting from a feeling of being let down by the others, did not send us back to school. He said that he would decide what to do with us after the summer vacation, and as the summer vacation was not very far off the interruption of our studies was not very serious. In the meanwhile my father sent for the prospectuses, handbooks, and calendars of the National Council of Education which had been established in Calcutta with the object of introducing throughout Bengal a system of education parallel to that of the Government, and studied them very carefully. His thoughts turned towards developing the newly established national school in the town.

All this happened in the early part of 1908. The summer of this year was very interesting to us politically. It saw an event which I may call one of the most memorable of my early years, and that was the district political conference held at **Kishorganj** in late March or early April. This conference showed us, who were living in backwaters, the true form of the political agitation which was then sweeping over Bengal, and for a few days we experienced an intensity in emotion and action that we had never experienced before. This exciting interlude in our placid life was heralded by an incident very small in itself but very explosive emotionally.

One day, as I was going out of the inner house, I saw my father coming in clicking something in his hand. "What is it, father?" I asked. "Come with me." he replied, "I am going to show it to your mother and to you all." I ran after him into the West Hut, where, meeting my mother, he said, "Look at this thing." "A revolver?" asked my mother. "A revolver?" echoed all of us. Was it the thing we had heard about and dreamt about for such a long time? It was on this romanticizing of the revolver, on the investment of it with limitless potencies for political agitation, and on the thought of it as the Aladdin's lamp of freedom, that the entire revolutionary and terrorist movement in Bengal rested. After showing us how the weapon was opened, loaded, and fired, and letting us click it by turns my father went back to his office and handed it back to the person who had brought it. He was a man whom we knew very well, for he was distantly related to us, and although nearly as old as my father was by relationship his grandson and, consequently, our nephew. He and his brothers were the owners of our friend, the elephant of Joyka. We called him Nephew Rajendra and thought very highly of him, for he was a most vivacious and jovial person.

About three months later I had another meeting with a revolver, this time a fairly big six-chambered weapon. Perhaps I need not explain that all these were unlicensed and smuggled revolvers. It was very difficult to get a licence for a revolver, and for people who were politically suspect, as my father was at the time, it was quite out of the question to be allowed to have a revolver. Even the licence which my father had for a mere muzzle-loader was cancelled and the weapon of which we used to be so fond was confiscated about this time. Besides, there would have been no romance at all if the weapons were licensed.

One day, as I was playing in the house of a neighbour, my younger brother, the same naughty madcap about whom I have spoken, came up to me and, taking me aside, said, "Golden Brother"–in our district the second elder brother used to be called by that appellation–"there is a Gurkha *kukri* on the top of the cupboard in the West Hut." "Nonsense," I replied, "how could a Gurkha *kukri* get there?" "Come and see," he replied. "I and Nabani have seen it with our own eyes." The boy called Nabani, a faithful friend of my brother and a most devoted follower of mine, confirmed the testimony. So we ran back to our house and went into the West Hut. There was nobody in it and I, drawing a stool and standing on it peeped over the cornice of the cupboard. There indeed was something like the handle of a *kukri*, but the rest of the object was hidden under some sheets of paper. I pulled and out came a big and very heavy fully loaded revolver.

Gripping the handle I carried it to my mother, who was in the kitchen busy cooking. "What is it you have got in your hand?" She asked, and taking it from my hand added, "It's a revolver, and loaded. Take it back to the West Hut, I'm coming." We took it back, but instead of leaving it alone we sat down round it, and began to tug at its parts. Fortunately the weapon was jammed by rust, otherwise something would surely have happened. While we were engaged in this pastime, my father came in and, very much surprised, asked us where we had got the revolver. We said that we had got it on the top of the cupboard. He appeared to be puzzled and said more to himself than to us, "I thought I had hidden it in the haystack.

Anyhow, give it to me." He tried to open the revolver and take out the cartridges, but seeing how it was jammed observed, "It's no use. I must send for Girindra. In the meanwhile put it in the kerosene tin." We dropped it in the tin for the time being.

Girindra, to whom my father had referred, was the same Cousin Girindra of ours who was the leader of the theatre party of Banagram. We came to know only after this affair of the revolver that, besides playing musical instruments and taking the part of Vilwamangal, he had another side to his character. He arrived in a day or two, and to our grateful satisfaction allowed us to sit by and help him while he stripped and cleaned the revolver in our hut, that is to say, the combined bed and schoolroom in which we studied and slept. Henceforward, for some weeks, the floor of that hut was hallowed ground to us.

Some time afterwards I heard from a common relative of us and Cousin Girindra the story of his cool nerves. Cousin Girindra was coming from Calcutta, and had been entrusted with the mission of smuggling a revolver. He had simply put it in his trunk, not expecting any trouble. But when he was on board the steamer between Goalundo and Narayanganj some police officers who had been searching the luggage of certain other passengers came up to him and said that they would search his trunk. Repressing his real feelings Cousin Girindra jumped up with alacrity and showed the utmost readiness to oblige the police officers. He took out one article of clothing after another and shaking them out laid them aside. The revolver was midway in the trunk and under a thick Turkish towel. Cousin Girindra lifted the towel and along with the towel the revolver, gripping the ring of the butt between his thumb and forefinger. He even asked the police officers if they thought there was a revolver in the towel. They shrugged their shoulders, and, looking very casually into the rest of the luggage, left him. I know the police had not then acquired that experience in their dealings with the terrorists which they acquired later, and were easily misled, but that does not take away from him the credit which Cousin Girindra was justly entitled to. He died, untimely and young, of consumption.

The pistol cult which the nationalist revolutionaries of Bengal developed would have continued in my case also, as it did in the case of most young Bengalis, had it not been for the accidental opportunity I had three and a half years later to learn a good deal about the real weapons of warfare. I picked up information, not only about the army rifles of almost every nation –the Lee-Engield, Lebel, Mauser, Springfield, Arisaka– but also about the newest field guns, medium guns, heavy guns, and siege howitzers, as well as naval guns of almost every great power. This knowledge, though it was nothing better than book knowledge, saved me from the worship of the pistol and gave me an unqualified contempt for so dubious a weapon as the revolver. The contempt grew as years passed, and when in the late twenties I heard of Mr. Subhas Chandra Bose being presented with a silver model of a pistol by some of his admirers I felt disgusted.

The political conference at Kishorganj took place between my two visions of the revolver. One morning, while I was talking with my father, Nephew Rajendra came up and told him that he had had a strange dream the previous night. Mother Bengal or Mother Durga (he made no clear distinction between the two) had appeared to him and told him to hold a patriotic demonstration in the town. How about a political conference? he suggested, after telling his story. My father thought it a rather good idea and said that they should consult others. In the next few days we heard that the district political conference was going to be definitely held at Kishorganj. It was decided that Babu Sasi Kumar Chaudhuri, a pleader of the town and an elder cousin of my father, was to be the chairman of the reception committee and Babu Anathbandhu Guha, one

of the leading lawyers of Mymensingh, the president. Some
lions had also been roped in from Calcutta, and among them
there was no less a person than Aurobindo Ghose (later Shri
Aurobindo of Pondicherry). My father chose to become the
quartermaster-general and made himself responsible for housing, feeding, and looking after the guests. My elder brother and
I enrolled ourselves in the volunteer corps.

The pavilion was to be on the meadow before our house,
the delegates were to be accommodated in the national school,
and the lions from Calcutta were to be the guests of the father
of my friend, Primeval Lord. The work on the pavilion, the
gates, the kitchen, and dining-sheds proceeded apace. The
stores were put in our school-bedroom. As the date of the
conference approached we worked ourselves up to a state of
restless excitement. My first posting was in the hut of the
delegates from Netrakona, a subdivision of our district (like
Kishorganj) but so rustic that even we regarded Netrakona
people as barbarians. The delegates on whom I had to wait not
only smoked the hookah nearly all day long but exuded the
smell of country tobacco through their pores when they did
not. They made me fill the hookah all the time, and after doing
it I felt so sick each time that I went to my father and begged
him to have me transferred elsewhere. My father put me on
sentry duty before the store-room. My elder brother had been
posted with the Jamalpur delegates, who were a nicer lot.

On the morning the conference was to open I was standing
before the hut of my delegates who had left, when I heard,
coming from the direction of our headquarters, a bugle call
somewhat resembling a reveille. We had been told that at that
call every one of us was to fall in before our headquarters
wherever we were. All of us began to run, and by the time I had
fallen in I was quite breathless. "What was it?" I asked the boy
next to me. He replied that he did not know but that something
must be up. Then, looking by chance towards the other bank

and the dusty road, I saw something which startled me. A platoon of men, formed in fours, were marching steadily towards the pavilion, raising clouds of dust with their rapid, heavy tramp. I also heard somebody saying that he had seen files of men in khaki crossing the western bridge. I concluded at once that the Gurkhas had arrived and were coming to break up our conference and we were being mustered to resist them. We had only our bare hands! My heart pounded away, and before I could collect my thoughts the order came: "Quick march", and in a second our column was on the move. I was borne along and kept repeating to myself that, after all, I was going to give my life for my country. We reached the conference ground before the hypothetical Gurkhas and were formed on two sides of the path leading from the main gate to the pavilion. My agitation was not lessened by the sudden glimpse I then caught of a body of men in khaki, with something on the shoulder at the slope, coming in our direction across the meadow in front of us and in a column parallel to that marching along the road. We could even hear the sharp orders of the tall khaki-clad officers who marched by their side. To my surprise, however, there appeared at the gateway, not Gurkhas, but a group of Bengali gentlemen–our president and his companions, and behind them a very smart column of volunteers in khaki giving the salutation *"Vande Mataram." "Vande Mataram!"* we shouted back. They were only the volunteers from the Sadhana Samiti, a physical culture club of Mymensingh town, who had marched all night from the railway station sixteen miles away and reached Kishorganj just in time to be present at the opening of the conference. The other column was formed by the volunteers from the rival club of Suhrid Samiti.

On the afternoon of the second day I was let off from duty to go and see the conference and hear the speakers. I heard Mr. Suresh Chandra Samajpati of Calcutta speak. He was the grandson of the famous reformer, educationist, scholar and philanthropist of nineteenth-century Bengal, Pandit Iswara Chandra Vidyasagar, and was a literary man, critic, and editor himself. Besides him, Raja Subodh Chandra Mallik, who had been given this title by his appreciative co-citizens (not by the Government) for his munificent gift to the National Council of Education, and Pandit Satyavrata Samasrami, a Vedic scholar, had also come from Calcutta. Mr. Aurobindo Ghose had sent word that he had been kept back by some urgent business but would try to come later. He was expected on the fourth day and did come on that morning, but before that a catastrophe had overtaken the pavilion.

On the afternoon of the third day a tremendous thunder-storm–these are quite common at this time of the year–blew away the greater part of the tent. As I stood on duty before the storeroom I saw the storm strike the pavilion and blow away one portion of the awning at the first gust. There was a wild scene following this. The older volunteers, including the volunteers from Mymensingh, rushed into the pavilion and did their best to save it; and they did save it, but it was no longer its old spick-and-span and decorated self. When I went into it the next morning to hear Mr. Aurobindo Ghose it was a sadly untidy place. But we thought ample amends had been made to us by the coming of so great a man as Mr. Aurobindo Ghose. He spoke in English, because having been educated wholly in England he could speak no Bengali at all when he came back to his country, and when he came to Kishorganj he had learnt just enough to carry on a simple conversation.

On the afternoon of the same day we were shown a display of military drill and swordsmanship by the volunteers from Mymensingh. It was a spectacle which seized me with immense power. How that display influenced me and how it left a permanent mark on my conception of political action and agitation I shall relate now.

THE PROBLEM OF POLITICAL ACTION

Before doing so it is necessary, however, to recapitulate the antecedents. The problem of political action exercised us from the very beginning. The meetings, processions, demonstrations, and the boycott were good enough as the means of expressing our discontent, but even as children we felt that they were not to be identified with true political action and could not by themselves bring us liberation from foreign domination. At best they offered us openings for suffering for our cause, and we were prepared to suffer because we knew unless we went through suffering we could develop neither will nor character. Nonetheless, we almost instinctively felt that the most effective kind of effort could not come unless we were given a method containing the possibility of going over to the offensive, wresting the initiative from the English. This, in the ultimate analysis, we could think of as nothing but armed rebellion. From the outset we judged all political action by the criterion of insurrection. We took it as an axiom that only military power, actual or potential, could drive out the English. This idea obtained a lodgment not only in the minds of us, the young, but, fantastic as it may sound, in those of our elders as well. I can cite a casual remark of my mother to illustrate this point. One day a school-fellow of mine and I had a great argument whether we should or should not be able to keep our independence if we won it. We carried the dispute to my mother. She heard us and then made a very brief remark, "If you are able to win your independence from the English by driving them out of the country, you will also be able to keep it." I was not more than ten years old when my mother told me this. But her remark made a deep impression on me. Of course, at the time, neither we nor our parents could conceive of a situation in which, in less than fifty years, the English power in India would come to an end of its own inanition without our acquiring in the process of extorting our independence that strength which would be adequate to preserve it. We never thought we could secure independence, or even gain it, without military power, and therefore military power was to us the key to the political problem. All our thoughts and efforts converged on the task, however small to begin with, of creating military power.

The first step towards this end was to set up physical-culture clubs. These became a feature of the nationalist agitation of 1905. They were not pure and simple institutions of physical culture, but were, like the Prussian gymnastic clubs organized by the poet Jahn before the war of liberation against Napoleon, institutions for giving training in patriotism, collective discipline and the ethics of nationalism, with the ultimate object of raising a national army to overthrow British rule. There were two such clubs at Kalikutch, one of them conducted by Mahendra Babu and the other run by a young gentleman of the same clan whose name was Rasik Nandi. His associate and right-hand man was the husband of my Aunt Sushila of Banagram, the same man who had abandoned her and his two children. His name was Prakash Chaudhuri. Neither of the men had any education, and therefore their club was on a lower ideological plane compared with Mahendra Babu's. But they had enthusiasm.

We frequented their club, not Mahendra Babu's. Almost every afternoon for some weeks we went there as the tomtoms began to beat, and watched the display. The greatest emphasis was placed on fencing with singlesticks. Rasik Nandi and Prakash Chaudhuri led like the most important couple at a ball. In this case the partners stood facing each other from the opposite ends of the lawn, their *dhotis* tucked high, the stick in right hand, and the cane buckler in the left. They glared at each other and gave the traditional war cry of the Bengal dacoit and fighter– "*ha re re re re-e-e-e-e-e-e*.!" In actual fact the first teachers in these physical-culture clubs were the hereditary Mussalman retainers who were kept by the zamindars in their employ to do all their violent work and had the craft handed down from father to son.

After the opening shout the fighters began to advance towards each other, making figures on the ground which were as elaborate and complicated as those of a dance. As they closed up there commenced a tense struggle in which each tried to hit the other, and the field rang with the raps of sticks on bucklers. But as soon as one of the men thought he had had enough he relaxed his grimace and began to fall back, making the same complex figures and fighting back against the vigorous pursuit of his opponent.

The excitement spread to us, and soon we began to practise on our own. Our teacher was an old but immensely powerful fisherman, Golak by name, who was also in the habit of holding forth on the motive behind all this practice as he understood that motive. "Don't worry," he assured us almost every day, "if the Mussalmans come we'll fight like this." Golak made long bamboo spears for us and put us through the practice of thrusting and counter-thrusting with them. One day while practising I wounded my sister, and after that we were forbidden to handle spears. But the stick practice was kept up.

The military cast of my political thought was hardened by the drills and physical exercises I went through, by the inculcation in all of us of the habit of implicit obedience to our leaders, and the preaching of an impossible ideal of discipline. But there could not be, of course, any open preparation for military action, not even talk about it. Thus from the very beginning our military thought fell under the shadow of conspiratorial methods. I discovered later that from the outset many of the organizers of the secret conspiratorial societies had contemplated a quite different method of political action–assassination, in imitation of the Russian revolutionists. But for a long time I did not realize this, and when at last I perceived in what direction the revolutionary movement was going I lost much of my sympathy for it. But that is a later story. At the beginning even the outrages on individuals–the attempt to blow up the train of the Lieutenant-Governor of Bengal, the murder of Mr. Allen at Goalundo, the explosion at Muzzafarpore of a bomb which was meant for Mr. Kingsford, the judge, but succeeded only in killing two English women, all examples of that side of the conspiratorial method which relies on the assassination of officials and terrorization of the governing class–were interpreted by me as experiments in insurrection. I even glorified the dacoity of Barha, the first, and still the most sensational political dacoity in Bengal.

In the light of these early feelings the men of the Maniktallah Bomb Case, who were the organizers of the Muzzafarpore outrage, became our heroes instantly. They were all arrested in May 1908, and in the weeks following my brother and I were almost always engaged in manufacturing make-believe bombs of coconut shell with charcoal, kerosine, and other combustible substances inside them. One day a friend of my father saw us at work and remarked to him that quite a new mood was coming over the country, so that even small boys, instead of being frightened by the arrests, had been prompted by the account of the activities of the Maniktallah conspirators to imitate them. But even then I could not make a hero of Praphulla Chaki, one of the young men who had killed the Kennedys and had escaped arrest only by committing suicide. Nor could I share the apotheosis of Khudiram Bose, the other young man responsible for the Muzzafarpore outrage. I felt that there was something repelling in the glorification of mere murder. Pictures showing the dead body of Praphulla Chaki tied to a frame and portraits of Khudiram Bose were circulating in large numbers at the time. I never could bear to look at them, far less take them home and keep them religiously in our boxes. As the revolutionary movement tended more and more towards the method of murder and robbery I began to feel an emotional revulsion from it. In this my mother's attitude influenced me very strongly. From the very beginning she came out very decidedly against murder and dacoity. She refused to concede that the end justified the means. Her mind never succumbed to the casuistry which became all too prevalent amongst us.

In spite of the utter impracticability of the military method my mind remained permanently militarized in regard to politics. In other words, it remained wedded to a vision. War to me always was, and with qualifications still is, the ultimate and supreme resource of policy. This bent was confirmed in me by the spectacle of military drill and military smartness presented by the volunteers of the Sadhana and Suhrid Samitis at the time of the political conference at Kishorganj. After the conference I was always drilling my brothers, and one day our nephew Rajendra, seeing me doing this and observing how faithfully I was copying the drill of the volunteers, made me the captain of a small team, in which there were not only my brothers, but also all the boys of our side of the town. He told them that I was their captain, and would drill them every day, and that they were to obey me implicitly. It speaks volumes for the sense of discipline that was coming over that very indisciplined people, the Bengalis, under the stimulus and influence of the Swadeshi movement, that even boys who were older than I or considerably stronger never demurred to my orders. It was almost like the young and slight Napoleon cowing down the Massenas and Augereaus.

I drilled the boys throughout the summer, sometimes making them go down to the edge of the river and lie down in the mud. We built a small redoubt behind our study and bedroom in two floors, and stored in it not only mud shells but also bamboo and wooden spears, which in the hands of small and irresponsible boys could easily prove lethal; and one day an incident did happen that led to the demolition of the structure and confiscation of the arms. As I was leading a storming party after bombarding the fort, the garrison, which had had to endure a shower of lumps of earth for some time, went for the attackers with their spears. One of these, in the hands of my fiery younger brother, hit the head of one of the boys on my side and made a flesh wound. We were terribly frightened, and my mother hearing of it came running and bandaged the boy's head. After that she ordered the immediate destruction of the redoubt.

The permanent result in me of this early initiation in military ways was the development of a taste for the study of military history and art of warfare, which enabled me at a considerably later period of my life to earn my living as a commentator on the operations of the Second World War. But something was absorbed also by my moral being. I could and can never think of any collective action, and more especially political action, except as the calm and resolute action of formed bodies of men. The vision of valiant warriors in uniform marching under the complete control of their leaders, who can urge or check them by a sign of the hand, keeps rising before my eyes. For this reason the course of political agitation in India has been one of the greatest mortifications of my life. I have been compelled to look on spectacles of simian gesticulation and chatter by ragged and wild mobs and read or hear them glorified as rebellion or revolution. Even when my heart was wholly in the nationalist movement I could never endure that sight, nor tolerate that misrepresentation.

THE NATIONAL SCHOOL

The summer vacation was coming to a close. With the new term at hand the question of what to do with us became urgent. My father decided to send us to the national school, and had us admitted there at the end of June. We found the atmosphere rather different from that at the high school, both for the better and for the worse. I shall recount the good points first. We had in the national school a greater sense of duty to the country and society and greater readiness to serve the community. While in the high school we never thought that we owed anything to the school or that the school stood in need of anything from us except the fees, in the national school we assumed as a matter of course that the school would be exactly what our powers and devotion could make it. Therefore, we never hesitated to give even bodily service to the school. For instance, our assistant headmaster and the senior boys brought the wooden posts for the national school building from two miles away, carrying them on their own shoulders. Of course this is exactly the way in which the awakening of political consciousness among a people used to autocracy reacts on the individual. As Tocqueville has said, despotism immures its subjects in private life.

Secondly, there was immensely greater emphasis on the value of physical culture. We had not only to go through the usual physical drill, but had to learn military drill and undergo a regular course of gymnastics. Thirdly, greater stress was placed on science. It was in the national school, poor as it was, that I first saw some apparatus for teaching the elementary principles of physics. At a small exhibition which was held in the school shortly after our admission simple scientific contraptions formed a section. They were rather crude, but, even so, what we saw in the national school was better than the purely book and exercise-book work in our old school. Fourthly, the necessity of handwork was recognized, and there were carpentry and pottery shops attached to the school. Last of all, our new headmaster, although no educationalist, was a fair orator in the national style, and he succeeded in bringing into our consciousness a clear though rudimentary sense of public life and political agitation.

Now I have to take the other side. Inasmuch as these schools were yet very experimental, and nobody really expected them to succeed and replace the Government's educational system, they had the greatest difficulty in attracting the most promising boys who would have been able to take greater advantage and make greater success of the new type of education that was being offered. The schools and their curricula both suffered from their not being utilized by boys of above average ability. If it was a feature of the official system of education that the boys were in many cases better than the system, in the national school the system never had a fair chance at the hands of the pupils. It was mostly students of second-rate intelligence from the less well-to-do and less educated families that they obtained. The Indian middle-class intelligentsia is too worldly wise to be swept off its feet even by the rabid nationalism which is the staple of its recreational mood. I have never yet met a member of this class who does not possess an uncanny sense of which side of the toast is buttered. Nationalism in those days did not have any butter, or, for that matter, even any margarine, to coat itself with. So the national schools could not get the proper human material, and, since a system is only worth as much as the men who work it, the experiment failed.

Throughout my life I have observed the operation of this curious natural selection, not only in our educational system but in the whole range of our political and cultural life. After it had once made its appearance, it speedily brought about a divorce of character from intelligence. The brighter boys, going in naturally for the coveted prizes of Indian life like government service, or as the second best for the professions, drifted towards leading purely private lives, because they dared not spoil their worldly prospects by participation in public affairs frowned upon by the Government, or, if they themselves dared, their parents dragged them back. On the other hand, with rare exceptions, political activity and agitation became the business of an insufficiently educated, insuffciently intelligent, and insuffciently cultured, though serious and earnest-minded, class, and this gradually brought down the standard of political life till it seemed to have become the monopoly of pig-headed fools or faddists. The Indian middle-class became separated into two distinct wings.

I have always taken great pleasure in observing the behaviour of these two classes, and have felt tempted to call them, not sheep and goats, but the sons of Belial and the sons of Moloch. It has been given to me to know the moral characteristics of both intimately. In respect of livelihood my existence has been amphibious. I have been as much in the service of the British Government in India as in the employ of the most extreme nationalist journalists and politicians. This experience and the knowledge gained from it have generated within me a mood which is able to enjoy with the most malicious delight the spectacle which has become so common in India today: the spectacle of the sons of Belial, including the arch-Belialids of the former Imperial Secretariat of the Government of India, cringing to the sons of Moloch whom they despised and jeered at till yesterday. This is the only comedy in the heart-rending tragedy of India today. The sons of Moloch are overjoyed at this victory of theirs over the sons of Belial and are reciting their *Nunc dimittis*. May a merciful Providence grant their prayer, for disillusionment awaits them. If they live a little longer they will find that it is not they, the sons of Moloch, who have won in the end, but the sons of Belial. The suppleness of the Belialids is invincible:

> "*Je vais, je viens, je glisse, plonge,*
> *Je disparais dans un coeur pur!*

Je disparais dans un coeur pur!
Fut-il jamais de sein si dur
Qu' on n'y puisse loger un songe?
Qui que tu sois, ne suis-je point
cette complaisance qui poind
Dans ton ame, lorsqu'elle s'aime?
Je suis au fond de sa faveur
Cette inimitable saveur
Que tu ne trouves qu'a toi-meme!"

Le Serpent, Paul Valery.

POSTSCRIPT TO BOOK II

WE LEAVE KISHORGANJ

I SHALL conclude this part of my book with an account of how we came to leave Kishorganj in 1910. My father broke all his links with the place by giving up his profession and selling his properties against the remonstrances of his friends. His intention was to go away for ever and never return. We were not old enough to be wholly taken into confidence by our parents, and were given only a very general idea of their plans for the future, but we knew the external circumstances very well. They had that air of mysterious fatality which my mother's highstrung temperament seemed always to draw upon the family.

My mother for some inexplicable reason had never taken kindly to our new house, and in the spring of 1909 her aversion to it reached its highest point. One day, early in the afternoon, I was playing in the house of a neighbour, when three or four of my usual playmates, both boys and girls, came running to tell me that a woman had tried to cut down my mother with a sword, but in the end had gone away only uttering some imprecations, and that my mother was now taken with a fainting fit. I with the other children ran back at top speed to

the house to find my mother, not actually senseless, but in a
state of collapse. She was lying on a mat on the floor and was
agitated, excited, and trembling all over. She could give no
coherent account whatever of what she had seen, nor could any
of the children who professed to have seen the incident give me
any coherent report. One of them, a girl, told me that she had
seen a huge woman like the goddess Kali threatening my
mother with a scimitar, standing at the doorway. She added
further that she had heard the woman saying that she had come
to kill my mother. But the child could not say who the woman
was and was not even sure that she was a real woman and no
apparition. As soon as they heard the commotion the servants
had rushed in from the outer house, and seeing my mother's
condition one of them had run off to the courts to fetch my
father. Within a minute or two of our coming my father also
arrived and asked us not to be afraid and to go away. After that
nobody talked about the incident. We instinctively avoided it.
Years later, when we were grown up, my mother referred to
it once or twice very vaguely, but was always agitated by the
mere recollection of it and could never call up strength to relate
her experience. Once she actually began before one of my
sisters, saying that she had seen a thing so horrible that she had
never been able to forget it, but going only as far as that point
she broke off and postponed her narration for another time.
She never returned to the subject.

From this unexplained and enigmatic incident unfolded
the circumstances which led to our leaving Kishorganj about
a year later. For some days my mother was very wild. One
afternoon she was missing from the West Hut during a short
absence of my father, and after looking for her everywhere he
found her sitting under a tree at the edge of the wasteland
behind our house. From that day she became wholly bedridden,
and when she recovered from her hysteria she showed symptoms of another serious disease. After consulting the local

doctors, my father took her, and with her us also, to Mymensingh town. The doctors there feared cancer and advised immediate treatment in Calcutta. My father at first thought of leaving us, the children, behind at Banagram in the charge of our aunt, but as my mother did not like the idea of leaving us behind, probably not being sure of herself, we also went to Calcutta. The Calcutta doctors ridiculed the idea of cancer, but in any case it was a very troublesome illness which compelled us to stay in Calcutta for three months. During these months doctors and nurses were always coming and going, and the house was full of the smell of medicines. This experience added to my already strong dislike of disease a stronger dislike, amounting to intolerance, of the smell of most medicines, and more particularly disinfectants.

During this stay in Calcutta one of our frequent visitors was a friend of my father's who came from a village near Banagram but was carrying on business in Calcutta as the owner of a small printing press. My father often discussed prospects of business with him. One day my brother and I were asked rather casually how we should like the idea of settling down in Calcutta. We immediately inferred that there was more in it than we were told, and joyfully declared that we should like it very much indeed. The prospect of coming away from a small and rustic place like Kishorganj to live in Calcutta seemed to open out endless vistas of ambition before us. My father took care to explain, however, that as yet he had decided nothing.

But he must already have made up his mind that he was no longer going to let my mother go back to Kishorganj. In October he took all of us to Kalikutch and, leaving us there, himself went to Kishorganj. A month later he returned to take us to Kishorganj to appear at our annual examination, so that we might not lose a year at school. His plans had not been finally settled, and for some time still he wanted to keep my mother at Kalikutch. But there followed another fatality, this time in the family of my uncle, which compelled my father to hasten the departure from Kishorganj. The marriage of my uncle's daughter–the same cousin whom I have mentioned as an exceptionally fine needlewoman–had taken place when we the boys were at Kishorganj for our examination. The wedding was a very grand affair, and my father had gone down to Kalikutch to be present at it. Some days before the wedding there was an attempt at theft in my uncle's house, and although the thief was foiled and had run away, in the darkness and confusion my aunt fell down and broke a rib. This mishap was afterwards cited as an unlucky omen, but for the moment nobody was perturbed by it, and the wedding went off splendidly. Within a month, however, a most unfortunate calamity happened. The young man to whom my cousin was married died and she was left a widow at the age of fourteen. My uncle, who, in spite of being a man, was as highstrung as his sister, was not only shocked but began to feel irritated at the mere presence of my mother and the others of our family, because my father had proposed the match and been largely instrumental in bringing it about. My father, who had gone to Kalikutch to condole with his brother-in-law, brought away my mother as soon as he perceived the state of my uncle's mind. He did not think it desirable to bring back my mother to the old house at Kishorganj, for which she had contracted such dislike, and so he took her and the younger children to Banagram. He decided to leave Kishorganj immediately, to go for the present to Banagram, and then think out at leisure what to do next. There was no difficulty in selling off the properties at a good price. All the transactions were completed by the end of January 1910, and we got ready to leave our birthplace by the beginning of February.

All the movables were sent away by bullock cart, and one afternoon we–our father, the three elder boys, a servant, and my dog Carlo–stepped into a carriage and rolled away out of the town by the road to the south. Two hours later we reached a bazaar three and a half miles from Banagram, and as the rest of the road was unsuited for wheeled traffic, we got down and walked to our village. We reached it as darkness was falling. Although I was coming to the village of all my known ancestors, where the Chaudhuris had lived for no one knew how many hundreds of years, I felt as if I had left home to trudge for ever along a public road. At night I heard that Carlo had refused food. The real reason was that he had not been given his accustomed quota of fish. But I was inclined to think that he also was feeling like me.

BOOK III

EDUCATION

PREFATORY NOTE

I LIVED continuously in Calcutta from June 1910 to March 1942. My father's business ventures there did not succeed. He went back to Kishorganj in 1913 to resume his practice, and did better than before. My mother and the younger children accompanied him, but my elder brother and I remained behind. During our school and college days we regularly went to Kishorganj twice a year to spend the vacations with the family, except when my mother came down to Calcutta and stayed with us. In 1921 I took up employment, and in the next few years visited my parents only occasionally. I came away from Kishorganj for the last time on 14 November 1927, and have not seen my birthplace and my district again.

If only a small part of my later life was spent at Kishorganj, other places besides Calcutta had even less. My excursions to holiday resorts by the sea or in the hills were very infrequent. In all, of the thirty-two years between 1910 and 1942, not more than three and a half were spent by me outside Calcutta, counting all absences. Thus, by the criterion of domicile, Calcutta can claim me as her own, and to belong to Calcutta is not to be just anybody. It was the City of Palaces, the Second City of the British Empire, the birthplace and centre of modern Indian culture, and a very impressive place in its looks and spirit. After the outbreak of the war of 1914-18 a prominent English (or he may have been Scotch) businessman of Calcutta hit off what every Calcutta man felt, by subscribing himself in a letter to the Press as "A Citizen of No Mean City".

There was a time when I attributed everything I had learnt and acquired to Calcutta, and thought I should never be able to live anywhere else. But after some twenty years of residence in it the city began to lose its hold on me. Today I can appraise with some objectivity what I owe to it, and I find that while I have learnt a good deal in Calcutta I have learnt hardly anything from it. I shall set down my debts to the city *seriatim:* In it I learned to speak the standard Bengali, yet I never gave up my dialect; in appearance and manners I was a semi-savage when I came to Calcutta, the city polished off the rough edges but could not break the rustic core, nor remove for many a day, if ever, the awkward shyness I was born with and the greater awkwardness springing from my consciousness of my shyness; Calcutta made me dependent on urban sanitation and other urban amenities, still it could not reconcile me to city life; that forbidding loneliness which only crowded city streets possess developed in me the habit of abstracted musing in which I often remain unconscious how many miles and by which roads I have walked, but this gregariousness without sociability has also engendered in me a violent dislike for crowds which makes me trudge miles rather than get into a bus or tram-car unless I am pressed for time; I learned much from the libraries, museums, gardens, and parks of Calcutta and even from its shabbiest buildings and streets, none the less I remained wholly unaffected by the surge of its daily life; the city as an abstract entity engrossed me, as a reality it was intolerably irksome.

A few particulars selected at random will illustrate better than any general statement what a stranger to Calcutta I was in Calcutta. I did not set my eyes on Tagore till 1927, and though belonging then and afterwards to a literary clique of active Tagorites, never had with him more than one single, very brief, and formal conversation. I was fond of literature and cherished literary ambitions, but shunned the society of writers until I was almost dragged to literary circles by one of my former teachers who was a well-known poet. I took deep interest in politics, but not only avoided ordinary public meeting but also did not care to attend any of the three important sessions of the Indian National Congress which were held in Calcutta in my time. They were the 1917 session, the special session of 1920, and the very garish session of 1928, at which, as a college girl, my wife was a volunteer. Speaking of political personalities, I saw Surendranath Bannerjea only once, and even that was a fleeting glimpse in the entrance hall of Ripon College; I never heard his oratory. I went to a public meeting one day to hear Gokhale, but was nearly trampled to death and had to come away. C.R.Das, I just fancy to have seen once getting down from a car. For many years Mr. Subhas Chandra Bose remained a total stranger to my eyes. I was in the bad books of the police as a follower of his, but, actually, I met neither him nor his elder brother, Mr. Sarat Chandra Bose before 1937, when I became the elder Bose's secretary. My first sight of Mahatma Gandhi dates as late as 1934 or 1935, and that too was a blurred vision, for he was passing in a car along the road in front of my house. I did not see him in repose till 1937, but did not even then care to attend any of his prayer meetings, which were being held daily on the roof of the house I was working in. I saw Pandit Jawaharlal Nehru for the first time only in 1931. I was taken to him by a friend who was known to him, and I summoned courage to appear personally before him only on the strength of the reputation I had then made by publishing some articles on military subjects and the self-confidence I had acquired thereby. But though urged by my friend to keep up the acquaintance, I dropped it so completely that Pandit Nehru did not even recognize me when, six years later, he saw me at the house of Mr. Sarat Chandra Bose, and I too did not thrust myself on him, although I could easily find an excuse, in as much as the Congress had in the meanwhile published an essay by me on the Indianization of the army.

The cultivation of important people did not come naturally to me. My life was the hermit-crab's life. Yet I noticed one extraordinary thing. Whenever through circumstances not of my own choosing I was brought into direct personal contact with public men and movements, political or literary, I discovered that the ideas I had formed of these men and movements from reading and distant contemplation were not wrong and that I needed only one or two direct contacts, and even then nothing more than a grazing or skimming contact, to acquire a very vivid sense of their quality. Perhaps the process of detachment from environment which began with my coming to Calcutta sharpened my perceptive faculties; I understood the life around me better, not from love, which everybody acknowledges to be a great teacher, but from estrangement, to which nobody has attributed the power of reinforcing insight; my knowledge is comparable to the snail's gained through his tender horns and guarded jealously within his shelly cave.

The simple truth is that after I had left Kishorganj the relation between me and the environment in which I lived underwent a revolution. Kishorganj, Banagram, and Kalikutch are interwoven with my being; so is the England of my imagination; they formed and shaped me; but when once torn up from my natural habitat I became liberated from the habitat altogether; my environment and I began to fall apart; and in the end the environment became wholly external, a thing to feel, observe, and measure, and a thing to act and react on, but never to absorb or be absorbed in. It is said that to be once bitten is to be twice shy, I suppose to be once *deracine* is to be for ever on the road.

Thus it happens that today my zoological status has altered. From being the most firmly rooted and stationary thing a man can be, the nearest human approach to vegetation–the offspring of a rural land-owning line–I have become what is perhaps the most unsettled product of modern urban life, a journalist, who is as ready as his paper to circulate everywhere for a penny and bear gladly on his back any advertisements he is paid for. Even if I had not taken to journalism I could not have helped becoming a nomad of the industrial age, wandering from pasture to pasture, not of grass, but of employment.

This change of status has necessarily brought in its wake a complete transformation in my feelings for the environment. A true rustic can never separate himself from his surroundings, and is hardly even conscious of them. I am ever aware of mine as an intolerable pressure. Sometimes the burden is static, like the burden of the old Titan, Atlas; at other times I have for it the same kind of feeling as, endowing the aeroplane with consciousness, I imagine it to have for what is popularly believed to be its home element, but through which it really has to drag its heavier-than-air body with infinite strain. I know what it means to be never able to forget that strain–to be perpetually remembering that as soon as that colossal horse-power and those thousands of revolutions per minute have ceased to shake and tear one's being, one would plunge headlong and crash. Since the environment is felt by me as a dynamic burden, I should not be surprised to hear from the aeroplane a confession that in spite of being the proudest of modern beauties it feels thoroughly unhappy comparing itself with its out-of-date rival on the sea–the last of the windjammers which used to bring grain from Australia to Europe. There is a world of difference between being buoyed up by one's environment, so as to be able to glide naturally on it, and having to beat it until it unwillingly generates the force to keep one afloat.

CHAPTER I

CALCUTTA

CALCUTTA GREW enormously during the thirty-two years I lived in it, and became amorphous. Since 1942 it has received hundreds of thousands of additional immigrants and, according to old residents, is no longer recognizable as its familiar self. I have not seen Calcutta after this recent adulteration, but even in 1910 it was not one city. In certain of its quarters a man could easily fancy that he was in China. Other parts looked like *mohallas* torn out of the cities of upper India, and, in fact, till recently Calcutta had the largest Hindi-speaking population of any city in India. Along the Chowringhee and south of Park Street the city had an appearance which probably was not materially different from that of the European adjuncts of Chinese, Malay, or Egyptian ports, but even here it did not exhale mere commerce, club life, sport, and turf. Those who were historically conscious could sense these parts of Calcutta to be very perceptibly breathing the spirit of the builders of the British Empire in India. The rest of the city was purely Bengali.

Between the European and the Bengali parts, however, there always was a Eurasian and Muhammadan belt, very characteristic in appearance and still more so in smell. One of the typical sights of these quarters were the butcher's shops with beef hanging from iron hooks in huge carcasses, very much bigger than the goat carcasses to whose size we the Bengali Hindus were more used. These wayside stalls were redolent of lard, and were frequented by pariah or mongrel dogs of far stronger build and fiercer looks than the dogs of the Hindu parts of the city. These animals always reminded me of the dogs in the butcher's shops of the *Arabian Nights*. All the components of Calcutta had personality and character, but the foreign elements seemed to be even more particularly asser- tive. In spite of the numerical preponderance of Bengalis the city was, and perhaps still is, an international concession, once flourishing but now moribund, on the mud flats of deltaic Bengal.

Even when we first came to it Calcutta was vast. At the same time it was very close-knit and compact. It was not broken in relief like Rome with its Seven Hills, nor scattered in space like Delhi with its seven historic sites. That did not mean, however, that from a height the city had a smooth appearance. Looked at from the top of the Ochterlony Monument, or even from the roof of a high private house, the house-tops of Calcutta seemed in their crowded and untidy rows to bid the most solid and the ugliest imaginable defiance to the sky. They made a deep impression on me when I contemplated them with the newly acquired sense of being a citizen, immediately after our arrival in 1910. Our house, which was in the Bowbazar quarter, was a four-storied building, and as we went up to its roof an amazing confusion met our eyes. There was an immense expanse of house-tops fading away on all sides into the smoky horizon, but no two house-tops were alike in shape, height, colour or arrangement. If one had a parapet, another had a wooden or iron railing, and a third nothing. The levels were nowhere uniform, nor even rising or falling in any discernible pattern of tiers, banks, or terraces. Another extraordinary thing we noticed was that the roofs seemed to be the favourite dumping ground for lumber and waste of all kinds, from broken furniture to smashed earthenware and pieces of torn canvas or sack. The irregular upper surface of Calcutta was made more jagged still by the edges and points of this junk.

The only place where the skyline appeared to suggest architecture was the extreme west. There we could see in one ample curve the tops of the well-known public buildings of the Esplanade and Dalhousie Square. The line began with the cupolas, small and big, of the new building of Whiteaways and ran through the tower of the High Court, the flat dome of the Government House, the square tower of the old Central Telegraph Office, the high dome of the General Post Office, the leads of Writers' Buildings and the statues on its cornices, to the steeple of the Church of St. Andrew. The scene gave the impression of an ugly sea of tossing brickwork contained along a clearly marked line by an architectural breakwater. If the view of Calcutta from above was ever softened it was only by its own appalling domestic smoke and the not very much more pleasant mist rising from the river to the west and the marshes to the east.

But three special features of the top face of Calcutta must also be mentioned, not only because they somewhat redeemed the squalid general effect, but also because they could not have been missed by anybody looking at Calcutta from an elevated point in the years following 1910. They were, first, chimneys and church spires. Two of each could be very prominently seen from the roof of our house. To the south-east rose the very tall chimney of the sewage pumping station at the Entally end of Dhurrumtollah Street, and the other was the ornamental chimney of the municipal waterworks on Wellington Square. Both the chimneys have now disappeared. The church spire nearest to us was that of the Roman Catholic church at Bowbazar-Sealdah corner, but we could see the taller spire of the church on Wellesley Square almost equally distinctly. In Calcutta of those days no temple or mosque rose into the air. If any bells rang they were church bells. The people of Calcutta were so used to church spires that they gave the distinctive name of Bald Church to a steepleless church in our locality. In

my time the church had disappeared, but it had bequeathed its
name to the quarter. The second landmark in the Calcutta sky
was the group of five cranes on the site of the Victoria
Memorial, then in the course of construction. These impressive architectural ancillaries were not less decorative and
monumental than architecture itself, and for many years these
magnificently arranged objects, imprinted as they were on the
southern sky of Calcutta, created the illusion of a vast
Brangwyn etching overhanging the city or some colossal ghost
ship working its derricks in the upper air. When with the
completion of the building the cranes disappeared, with them
also disappeared one of the most vivid and poetic associations
of my first years in Calcutta.

The third feature we noticed has also become rare, if it has
not disappeared altogether. Every thousand yards square or so
of the top face of Calcutta had a bamboo mast bearing on its
head a bird-table, consisting only of a trellised frame, for
pigeons to sit on. At the foot of the mast crouched a watchful
man with an upturned face; he held a long and thin stick in his
hand and from time to time prodded the birds with it. The birds
at first tried to avoid the stick by changing places; then one or
two began unwillingly and lazily to ascend with laboriously
flapping wings; but as soon as three or four had gone up the
whole flock rose with a whirr and began to fly to and fro over
an orbit of about a quarter of a mile, keeping the trellis at the
centre. They flew in one direction to begin with, and then took
a complete right-about turn towards the other direction. At the
turning points they wholly melted away in the atmosphere, but
as soon as they had taken their turn flashed back into vision like
silvery scales on the blue-grey sky. After about half-a-dozen
turns in this fashion they came back to their frame and began
to drop by twos and threes on it, and with a little jostling and
elbowing settled down for the time being, to be prodded up
again after a while by their keeper. Eight, ten, or even a dozen

flocks were seen flying at the same time, and they gave a feathery and shot effect to the Calcutta sky. This sky was never gorgeous, but it had at times a pearly tenderness, and to this softness the flying birds added not only a suggestion of the pastel shades of the pigeon's throat, but also a turtledove sensibility. The contrast of such a sky with what lay spread out below was very marked. It seemed as if a crowd of misbehaved and naughty children were showing their tongues and behinds to a mother with the face of Michelangelo's Night.

Within a few days of my coming to Calcutta I learned with astonishment from my new school-fellows that the pigeons, and, even more so, their keepers were held in the worst possible disrepute by the human beings of the city. I casually mentioned to some of my school-fellows that I used to keep pigeons at Kishorganj. They looked with scandalized incredulity at me, because I had already given proof in the class that I was clever at books, and in my general behaviour, too, there was nothing to suggest a keeper of pigeons to these Calcutta boys : I showed no obvious signs of the moral degeneration which pigeons were supposed in Calcutta to bring on mankind. Fortunately, the boys took my former pigeon-keeping as the oddity of an East Bengal boy and did not report to the teachers. In the case of a Calcutta boy a cry would have arisen : "Sir, this boy flies pigeon," and at that cry the cane would have descended mercilessly on my back.

On the ground Calcutta presented a very impressive facade. But it was a facade which looked inwards, like the amphitheatre on the arena. The arena was formed by the famous Maidan or, as it is called in Bengali, the Field of the Fort, and the city stood in a rough arc round it like the inner face of the Coliseum. The parallel is not as correct for the two wings of the facade of Calcutta as it is for the eastern or Chowringhee section, for both the wings–the first from Hastings to St. Paul's Cathedral and the second from Esplanade corner to Outram Ghat–were leafy. To the north, the Government House was all but hidden by the trees which stood trunk to trunk along the low white balustrade which formed its outer boundary wall, and towards the river the long line of the beautiful *polyalthia longifolia* of the Eden Gardens hid the High Court and the Town Hall even more effectively. Only through the funnel-like opening of the road called Government Place West could a glimpse of the Treasury Buildings be caught. At this entrance a formidable group of statuary stood on guard. Queen Victoria, Lawrence, Hardinge, Canning in greenish bronze reminded everybody in 1910, even if the unobtrusive Government House modelled on Kedleston Hall did not, that he was very near the heart of the British Empire in India. To the south of the Maidan there was a similar line of trees along Lower Circular Road, and although there was not in that quarter the same reminder of British power in India as there was to the north, there was at least a reminder of British sickness, both civil and military. For one set of the buildings which could be seen through the trees constituted the British Military Hospital and the other the Presidency General Hospital. The first was reserved for British soldiers and the second for British civilians.

Although the wings of the facade of Calcutta were leafy, the brickwork on the eastern side was long, high, and solid enough to obliterate all sylvan atmosphere. This front would not have stood the scrutiny, building by building, of an architectural designer, but, seen from the distance and as a whole, it was not unimpressive. The skyline, though not absolutely uniform, was not unbalanced by any pronounced irregularity. I once saw the Chowringhee from the River Hooghly when going to the Botanical Gardens at Sibpur in one of the Port Commissioners' ferry service steamers, and the familiar line of buildings beginning with the Army and Navy

Stores and ending in Whiteaways was estranged to my eyes by the beauty shed on it by the distance.

The central point in this facade of Calcutta was certainly the high pile of the Indian Museum, rather dull-looking from the outside but always enlivened by the thought of what it contained within. There was no place in Calcutta, unless it was the zoological gardens of Alipur, of which I was more fond. The huge galleries, each at least one hundred feet long, forty feet wide, and as many high, were always reeking of the sweating upcountry men who visited the museum as a matter of duty and trudged through the galleries as solemnly and steadily as my Kishorganj peasants marching to the field of Id prayers. They never stopped before anything unless they saw some visitor taking particular interest in one or other of the exhibits or comparing something in a book with the objects. Then they crowded round that visitor and asphyxiated him with their body odour. It was, however, impossible to get angry with them. They were as natural and primitive as the exhibits, though not as monumental. In the entrance hall were the bull and lion capitals of the pillars of Asoka, in the hall to the right were the highly ornamental red sandstone railings of the Bharhut Stupa, and in the hall to the left the Siwalik fossils together with the skeletons of the huge Hasti Ganesa or *Elephas Antiquus Namadicus Falc.* of the Nerbudda valley. It could be said that in these galleries of the Indian Museum were represented all the previous empires in India from that of the gigantic prehistoric elephants to that of Asoka the Buddhist and Samudragupta the Vishnuite.

Facing the Indian Museum across the Maidan stood Fort William, equally silent from the outside but busy and humming like a beehive within with sun-helmeted British soldiers. It was impossible for any person endowed with the consciousness of history to overlook the correlation of the museum with the fort. It was as if those who were living for the time being in Fort William were saying to those who had been housed for all time in the Indian Museum– "Hail, dead emperors, emperors about to die salute ye!" In 1911, unknown to all of us, the shadow of death had already fallen. I still remember my father reading with his friends the news of the transfer of the capital to Delhi. *The Statesman* of Calcutta was furious, but was thinking more of the past than of the future and was not inspired to prophecies like Cassandra. We, the Bengalis, were, but not in the spirit of Cassandra. We were flippant. One of my father's friends dryly said, "They are going to Delhi, the graveyard of empires, to be buried there." Everybody present laughed, but none of us on that day imagined that although the burial was the object of our most fervent hopes it was only thirty-six years away.

Only one section of the facade of Calcutta had depth, and that was the section between Park Street and Lower Circular Road. The interior here was like the front, only quieter and more spacious. To walk down Middleton Street, Harrington Street, and Theatre Road was to walk into an area of large, still houses standing in their own grounds planted with *lagerstroemia indica,* canna, and ixora, and of wide silent streets shaded by *gul mohurs,* and cassias, and an occasional *lagerstroemia flos-reginae.* All these flowering trees and shrubs blossomed from April to September, making a gorgeous blaze of colours– scarlet, vermilion, pink, purple, lilac, blue, white, and golden yellow, in the midst of which the houses looked dull and ordinary. They did not, however, jar with any obtrusive ugliness. The majority were impressive by reason of their size and solidity, although not by their architecture. But a few had style. They were old buildings in the modified Georgian manner of the East India Company. Here too, as in the facade, it was the effect as a whole and not the details which consti-tuted the attraction, and in this attraction space and silence were the principal elements. The whole area was very much like the old cemetery at its centre, where Landor's Rose Aylmer lies buried.

> "Ah, what avails the sceptred race!
> Ah, what the form divine!
> What every virtue, every grace!
> Rose Aylmer, all were thine.
>
> Rose Aylmer, whom these wakeful eyes
> May weep, but never see,
> A night of memories and sight
> I consecrate to thee."

The inhabitants of the locality prized the silence greatly, and they wrote angry letters to the newspapers against the tooting of horns by taxis prowling for fares at night.

For us Bengalis one street of the area came to acquire a dreaded notoriety. It was Elysium Row. This was an inviting name, to which the great Bengali barrister, Sir S.P.Sinha, the first Indian member of the Viceroy's Executive Council, and later to become Under-Secretary of State for India and the first Indian peer and Governor of an Indian province, who lived in the street, added greater lure. But the pleasantness of the name and the pride evoked by the association with Sinha were wholly smothered for us by the fear inspired by Number Fourteen, the headquarters of the Special Branch or the political police. There were few Bengali young men with any stuff in them who did not have dossiers in Number Fourteen, and many had to go there in person, to be questioned, or to be tortured, or to be sent off to a detention camp. After the passing of the Defence of India Act of 1915 we began to think of Elysium Row more in connexion with the police than with Sinha. To have been in Elysium Row came to be regarded as equivalent to being branded on the forehead or having a ribbon on the chest, according to the standpoint or courage of the dragooned visitor. My younger brother as a young man of eighteen was taken there, questioned by third degree methods, and then photographed in full face and in profile for future identi-fication. That did not, however, prevent his identity being mixed up in the mind of the police with quite a different person's, and this confusion caused no small amount of harassment to my brother. I did not have to go there at any time of my life, but at a late stage I had a dossier. In my school and college days I did not come in the way of the political police nor did they come in my way, and I never walked through Elysium Row. Therefore the spaciousness, the silence, and the flowers remained my only impressions of this part of Calcutta.

The rest of the Chowringhee facade was only skin-deep, and the hinterland was a strange world whose strangeness was not felt by us only because everybody took it for granted. Russa Road at the southern end of Chowringhee led into the old and respectable Bengali quarter of Bhowanipore, best known for its lawyers, and through Bhowanipore to the less wealthy but more religious quarter of Kalighat; Bentinck Street at the opposite end was famous for its Chinese shoemakers; Dhurrumtollah, which was at the same end, was itself a street of shops, bazaars and Eurasians, but it was also the ingress to the main Bengali parts of the city. An observer could stand at the Chowringhee ends of Dhurrumtollah and Russa Road and watch men coming out between nine and ten in the morning and going in between five and six in the afternoon like ants out of and into their holes. The Bengali parts of Calcutta, both north and south, sent them out in the morning for office work and sucked them back in the evening. These were the men to whom Calcutta belonged by birthright. They loved Calcutta as nobody else did. They lived in it like deep-sea fauna in the depths of the sea. Most of them would have preferred death to being removed from Calcutta.

Their Calcutta, which was also my Calcutta for thirty-two years, was an immense maze of brickwork cut up by streets and lanes. It was not labyrinthine like the Indian quarters of the

cities of northern India, and it did not bring on that claustro-
phobia which impels newcomers to those cities to rush out into
open spaces in order to breathe easily. Nor did it have that
putrid squalor which makes the inhabitants of the same upper-
Indian cities feel like living in the intestines of the Leviathan.
Also, there was not that accumulated dust, to try to remove
which was equivalent to raising only more dust. All these
unlovely features of urban life in upper India, our part of
Calcutta did not possess, but there was no limit to its architectural meanness. Walking along the ever-lengthening streets
and lanes of these quarters one expected at every turn and step
to come upon some spot of handsomeness and repose, for
instance, a fine building, a spacious square, a wide vista, or at
least a colourful bazaar. These expectations were never
fulfilled. The more one trudged, the more one felt like swallowing an endless tape of shabbiness.

On account of this all-pervasive inelegance even the wider
streets gave no impression of being straight, although they
were straight in layout. The awry fronts on either side, taken
with the erratic skyline and the unfinished surfaces, checked
the growth of any impression of symmetry and harmony. Three
or four times every hundred yards the skyline would be falling
down abruptly from sixty to ten feet and changing its outline
from that of the straight parapet of a flat-roofed brick house to
that of the sloping roof of a mud-walled and tiled *bustee*. For
the same distance the street front would be presenting three or
four incongruous patches : a gaping shed, a solidly built wall
pierced by small windows, an unglazed shop window or,
rather, a mere opening, and a house with venetian blinds. There
was not a single inviting front-door anywhere. The Bengalis
of Calcutta seemed to have a particular aversion to attractive
entrances. One of the two entrances to a particular house I
knew had a new door. But it had its attractiveness, which in
truth was no more than that of newness, reduced if not wholly

suppressed by an infelicitous attempt on the part of the owner at being helpful to his visitors. What welcome the door offered was rendered unwelcome for persons with a sensitive verbal taste by a signboard bearing in English the inscription: "Female Entrance." Even where the interiors were luxurious the front door was made to disguise the fact as completely as possible. This particular aspect of the architectural dowdiness had its counterpart in the insensitiveness often displayed in Calcutta in the naming of persons. "Demon", "Goblin", "Owl", "Idiot", "Tuppence", "Snub-nosed", were quite common names for men and women there. In fact, through a whimsical affectation of Calcutta ways my eldest son came to acquire, to the great disgust and indignation of my father, the nickname of "Imbecile". Of course, these names never bore any relation to the appearance or abilities of the persons so named. When upon the announcement of such names you would expect the emergence of a corresponding physiognomy, a very handsome man indeed might step into your room. In regard to names the trick was meant to avert the Evil Eye or befool evil spirits, but I am unable to account for its extension to the design of front-doors, unless it happens to be a legacy from the days of Muslim rule when rich people did not care to give any outward expression to their affluence for fear of attracting the attentions of the tax-farmer.

To this morphological dinginess the Bengali parts of Calcutta added the ebbs and flows of a functional dinginess: the first daily, the second seasonal, and the third yearly. The Bengalis wash (i.e. rinse in plain unsoaped water) their cotton *dhotis* and *saris* at home every day, and the Bengalis of Calcutta are even more fond of this daily washing than other Bengalis. Actually, the afternoon toilet of Calcutta women passes under the name of "washing" in thoroughbred circles. Thus, at least twice a day, and sometimes more often, an immense amount of washing has to be hung up to dry. The front veranda, if there is any, or the roof is the place reserved for this purpose. In some houses there are a number of clotheslines, in others the *dhotis* and *saris* are simply let down from the parapet or railing with the top ends tied to a pillar or rail. When wet they hang heavy and straight, dripping water on the footpath below, and when dry they flutter and twirl in the wind. As each piece is at least fifteen feet in length and forty-four inches in width, the houses when the washing is drying have the appearance of being draped in dirty linen. In addition, there always are subsidiary lines carrying the children's shirts, frocks, vests and drawers, and the napkins and sheets of the very large number of babies that there always are in these houses, and on most occasions the exhibition of cotton garments is reinforced by bedclothes–mattresses and quilts, large and small, wetted by the children and the babies.

The gathering up of these articles in the afternoon is almost a ritual, like the hauling down of flags on warships in the evening. Except in the houses of the rich this is in the hands of the girls of the family. In the afternoon two or three comely persons appear on the veranda or roof, as the case may be, advance to the railing or parapet, and, leaning on the one or the other, carry out a composed survey of what is going on below. If anything particularly interests them they rest their chins on the rail or wall and contemplate it with wide open, round, solemn eyes. There never is any mobility or change in their expression, but suddenly a face is tossed up and an electric glance flashed towards the window across the street, where the presence of a lurking admirer is suspected. But this ripple passes away as soon as it makes its appearance. The face relapses into the usual immobile placidity, and the girls go on gathering up or pulling down the *dhotis* and *saris,* normally in a very unconcerned manner, but sometimes screwing a puckered mouth in undoing the knots. They move up and down, piling up the clothes on one of their shoulders or arms, and when at last they walk away they look like huge washerwomen.

Another source of untidiness in our parts of Calcutta was the inexplicable but at the same time the most complete non-co-operation between the domestic servants and the municipal sweepers. In Calcutta of olden days the municipal sanitary service was not haphazard as it has grown recently. The streets were regularly watered, swept, and even scrubbed. But while the street-cleaning ended by about six o'clock in the morning and three in the afternoon, the kitchen-maids would begin to deposit the offscourings exactly at quarter-past six and quarter-past three. Nothing seemed capable of making either party modify its hours. So little piles of waste food, ashes, and vegetable scraps and peelings lay in individualistic autonomy near the kerb from one sweeping-time to another sweeping-time. During this interval, however, the refuse deposit was respected like an archaeological deposit, and was never trampled on or kicked about. All Bengali Hindus are very particular about left-over food, which they consider to be very unclean; therefore they never go anywhere near it. A small boy I knew used to take the most intelligent conceivable advantage of this prejudice in order to escape punishment for his naughtiness. He would make straight for the garbage heap before his house and stand on it. Then there was nothing else to be done but for his elder sister to throw away all her clothing, go up to him, retrieve him, and, dragging him inside, give him a scrubbing under the tap and have an untimely bath herself. The prejudice did not, however, extend to fruit rinds. They were thrown indiscriminately on the footpaths to be trampled on by all and sundry. To slip on a mango or banana skin and have a sprained ankle was a very common mishap in Calcutta.

The contribution of the seasons has now to be considered. It was in Calcutta that I learned for the first time that the seasons could uglify no less than beautify. At Kishorganj, Banagram and Kalikutch every season added something to the attraction of the world around us. The summer sun, hot as it was, shed more happiness than discomfort, for besides being white and clear it had a life-giving quality. This, we used to say, is the sun to ripen the mango, the jack-fruit, and the melon, and it did ripen not only the fruits but also the earth, which became seasoned and mellow like an old violin. To this heat there was an extraordinarily harmonious accompaniment of sound, a sound so intense and energetic and yet so mild and musical, that one could imagine its having been produced by the revolving top that our earth is. It was the crickets which converted the earth into a humming top. They began at about ten o'clock in the morning, just as the earth and the trees also began to feel warm to the touch. They constituted the Grasshopper's Green Herbarian Band. We hardly ever saw the brown little creatures, but we could call up before our eyes an immense string orchestra madly scraping, bowing and fingering, swaying and stretching. The *Yatra* parties had made us quite familiar with the movements of violinists. This rilloby-rilloby rilloby-rill went on till about five in the afternoon and then suddenly ceased. As dusk fell, there began the gorgeous outings of the fireflies in clustered nebulae of phosphorescent light in the midst of the darkened foliage.

These were my summer associations in the country, but on coming to Calcutta I saw that the summer heat could only produce stench more quickly, and make the streets even more messy than they normally were. They would now be strewn with empty coconut shells, whose milk is the favourite summer drink. The only thing which in our parts of Calcutta redeemed the summer was the cool evening breeze from the south and the sea. Without this breeze, I believe, the *embonpoint* of all denizens of Calcutta, who in their inordinate fondness for *ghee*, sweets and starchy foods take immense quantities of them daily, would have rotted away in sleep and the bodies begun to emit stench like the tight carcasses of dead bullocks. It may have been some instinctive fear of this kind which made all wealthy citizens of Calcutta keep the electric fan on all through the night.

The winter was not pleasanter. The temperature never went down low enough to make the cold bracing, but it became just cold enough to make people catch cold. There was grime everywhere, and, in addition, an accumulation of dust which, if it was not as overwhelming in quantity as the dust of upper-Indian cities, was worse in quality, for it was a dishonest half-breed between honest coal and honest earth. The winter mornings in the city were never refreshed for me by the dew I was accustomed to in the country, where to walk through the grass at dawn was to crush a mass of diamonds. The only evidence of dew that I saw in Calcutta was the damp surface of the footpaths. But the worst thing was the smoke and the combination of smoke and mist in the evenings. At Kishorganj the mist hung over the landscape exactly like a veil of fine muslin. In Calcutta both the smoke and the mist spited each other. The mist would not allow the smoke to go up, and the smoke would mix itself up with the mist as it came down. We could never determine how much of the dark mixture we saw all around us was mist and how much smoke, but it was so thick that we could fancy beating it up with a stick. In any case, we were suffocated, and the gas-lamps in the streets looked reddish yellow. It was only on those rare evenings when a strong cold wind blew from the north that the atmosphere was swept clean of this dirt and the street lamps in their long lines took on the appearance of an endless and wavy festoon of soft greenish light. But in these evenings no true son of Calcutta came out willingly into the streets. He stood in mortal fear of catching pneumonia. He preferred to die of consumption in his dovecote.

But drab as the summer and winter were in Calcutta, in order to measure the full power for uglification of the seasons it was necessary to live through the rains. I have already described the rainy season at Kishorganj, but I might recall one or two impressions to bring home the contrast which Calcutta presented. The sheet-like downpour at Kishorganj had the quality of crystal, drizzle was opaline, and both were set off by a shining green. The clouds varied from the deepest collyrium blue to soft pearly shades, and apart from this infinite gradution from dark to white they burnt in piled-up masses of gold, orange and red, or blushed in equally immense masses of pink, at sunrise and sunset. On moonlit nights, if the sky was lightly clouded, a ring with rainbow colours appeared round the moon; if there were those beautifully diapered cirro-cumulus clouds, their rippling outlines would be edged with amber. I never saw any of these things in Calcutta. The buildings hid the lower sky, and all the finer shades of the portions overhead were blotted out by the smoke and the lights of the city. For most of the time we could see only an unbroken shroud of grey.

The grey on the ground was worse. In Calcutta of those days tarmacadam was reserved for the so-called European quarters, and we, the Bengalis, had only rubble and earth on our streets. This mass decomposed during the rains, became thin and watery enough to be capable of being splashed head-high, but even in that diluted state lost none of its stickiness. This mud, as it lay on the flagstones of the footpaths, converted them into grindstones for our shoes. Thus it happened that those of us who could not go about in carriages were always down at heel and bespattered on the back during this season. Those who went about in carriages spared themselves but made the lot of the pedestrians harder. Fortunately, nobody minded anybody else's appearance, since it was taken to be the normal aspect of mankind during the rains. As for the houses, they looked worse. There were very few of them which did not wear a thoroughly bedraggled and miserable air. The trees, though washed of the dust which normally lay thick on them, did not look bright or refreshed. At Kishorganj, even after a violent gale, they looked as if they had had only a bit of wild horseplay, but in Calcutta they appeared as if they had undergone a ducking.

Sometimes the rains were so heavy that instead of the usual mud we had floods in the streets. The sewers of Calcutta were never equal to coping with the rains. The difference between their highest capacity and the demand made on them during the rains could be stated only in astronomical figures of cu.-sec.-s. I had once to go into the subject, but have forgotten all about it except the esoteric abbreviation I have used. The tangible fact was that after even a moderate shower certain streets and crossings were inevitably flooded, and heavy showers converted them literally into canals and ponds. I have seen collapsible boats brought out in the streets. People who piqued themselves on their wit used to say that such and such a street in Calcutta was flooded if a dog raised its hind leg. The water was of the dirtiest shade of brown, with all the floatable elements in the garbage afloat, and all the soluble elements in solution. It was knee-deep at certain places, at others even deeper. Some carriages and motor cars would be ploughing their way through it, leaving swirling wakes and backwashes behind, but the trams would be completely held up. The anxious inspectors would be wading about, with their trousers tucked half-way up the thigh, taking soundings with their own lower limbs. The sweepers stood at attention at regular intervals like statues, each at his manhole after having opened it to let the water pass down into the sewers quickly. Even then the water did not subside for three or four hours. Sometimes even a whole day or night was required. It was being Venice with a vengeance.

Tagore began a famous political speech of his with a reference in his characteristic style to these immemorial floods. "No sooner has the smallest pluvious wind blown," he declared, "than the floods rage from our lane to our main street, the wayfarer's pair of footgear is borne aloft over the head like his umbrella, and at least the denizens of this lane are seen to be no better adapted to life than the amphibians–these are the things I have been observing from our veranda year after year from my childhood till my hair has grown grey." Tagore attributed it half to foreign rule and half to the fatalistic resignation to evil and authority of his countrymen. His countrymen attributed it wholly to foreign rule. The Calcutta Corporation attributed it to a number of causes which it was difficult to understand without a considerable knowledge of irrigation and sanitary engineering combined. But whosoever's the fault, the fact indeed was that those of us who cared for our shoes did wade through the streets with the precious pair in hand. I did so on a few occasions, but the universal spectacle of men going about shoes-in-hand sometimes drove me to attempts at originality. I tried to walk in my shoes. It was worse still. There was more unpleasantness in having them on, for the water was clammy enough by itself, and to have equally clammy leather round the feet, and to feel and hear the water in the shoes squirting in and out noisily at every step were sensations even more unbearable. So our wading shoes-in-hand was not wholly parsimony, it had in it an aesthetic impulse as well.

Last of all I must refer to the yearly accumulation of shabbiness. The house-owners in Calcutta had no notion of maintenance, and even though the preservation of their own property was involved in it considered expenditure on such things as annual repairs and painting utter waste. It would be only after a sustained campaign of complaints and dunning on the part of the tenants that they would send a workman or two to give the house a coat of dirty whitewash inside and a dirty coat of paint outside. Thus the general run of houses in Calcutta, even at their best, looked as if the sharp edge of their cleanly appearance had been rubbed off. This dinginess accumulated from year to year till the general effect became one of mottled grey.

To go out of the city into the suburbs or the countryside did not offer better prospects or aspects. The immediate outskirts of the city were squalid and congested beyond description. They were full of mean and insanitary sheds and *bustees,* built wall to wall, and separated only by dusty roads when not by narrow and evil-smelling lanes. All the bigger roads had open drains on both sides, running with coal-black sewage, and this drain had to be crossed and recrossed every time when one wanted to go into or come out of a house or a shop. None but the inhabitants of these localities could go about in them without handkerchiefs to the nose.

Little relief awaited me even when I broke my way through the suburbs, for the countryside just around Calcutta, though open, seemed to have been poisoned to death. It lay like a mangy bandicoot bitten by a snake. The trees did not thrive there, the grass had a burnt-up look, the cottages were exact replicas of the suburban *bustees*. These parts brought desolation into one's heart.

The next ring was chlorosis-stricken. Here too the trees did not flourish. They were pallid. The houses, both brick-built and thatched, wore a deserted appearance. It was not till one had moved twenty-five miles away that the earth seemed to be its old self. I noticed these concentric rings of different atmospheres and effects whenever I had to come to Calcutta by train.

So, ultimately, one had to work one's way back towards the Chowringhee front in search of repose and order. As long as I lived in Calcutta, I kept up the habit of walking down to the Maidan as far as the Victoria Memorial, or to the Eden Gardens and the riverside between Outram and Prinsep's Ghat. But my yearning for fine architecture was never destined to be satisfied. Domestic architecture was, of course, inconceivable but even the public buildings I scrutinized in vain. Some of them were presentable, some even imposing and handsome to my unformed taste in architecture. But I soon learned that they were all imitations. The High Court was a copy of the Cloth Hall of Ypres, the Government House of Kedleston Hall; Writers' Buildings and the Revenue Office were passable imitations of the style of the French Renaissance; certain other buildings were pseudo-Greek–Doric, Ionic, or Corinthian. The Cathedral, which had a western window of stained glass after designs by Burne-Jones, was in very pinchbeck Gothic. The Military Secretariat built for Kitchener, although ambitious, was so devoid of true character that in the medallions on its facade the heads of Venus could hardly be distinguished from those of Mars. Nowhere was there anything authentic or original. Only in 1921 did Calcutta get a genuine specimen of architecture in the Victoria Memorial. It has faults of design, but still it is the only thing to redeem the City of Palaces architecturally. Yet it is extraordinary to relate that the Bengali citizens of Calcutta, who are totally unconscious how many of their pre-existent public buildings are imitations, regard the Victoria Memorial as such. They think that it is an unsuccessful imitation of the Taj Mahal. Let alone Emerson, the designer of the memorial, even if Brunelleschi, Bramante, Michelangelo and Wren had appeared in person and sworn otherwise, they would not have convinced these scoffers.

CHAPTER II

EXPERIENCES OF ADOLESCENCE

WE LEFT Kishorganj in February 1910, and went to Calcutta at the beginning of July. Within the four intervening months occurred one of the unhappiest experiences of my life and one of the happiest. The unhappy experience was a stay of about two months at Mymensingh, the district town, where my elder brother and I were sent provisionally to school while my father was making his final arrangements to settle down in Calcutta. My sufferings at Mymensingh were due to quite a number of causes, of which the following three were the ones most acutely felt. In the first place, I had never before been away from home, and the crowded and insanitary hostel in which I was lodged was not the place to reconcile me to the novel experience of being absent from home. Secondly, like all country towns in India, Mymensingh had all the worst features of town life–congestion, open drains full of filth, squalid streets and bazaars, flies and mosquitoes–unaccompanied by any of the amenities of big cities, of which I had gained some idea during my stay in Calcutta the previous year. Thirdly, my school fellows quizzed me. Although, with my experience of Calcutta, I thought nothing of their townsmen's airs the Mymensingh boys treated me as if I were a boor from some backward village. They teased me for my accent, which certainly was better than theirs, for their idea of smart speech did not go beyond an affectation of the accent of the city of Dacca, an accent notorious as the most uncultured and atrocious in all Bengal, whereas I could speak with a suggestion at least of the standard Calcutta accent. These boys behaved towards me with a superciliousness which I did not meet with even in Calcutta boys when only a few weeks later I went among them.

Altogether, I was always low in spirits and sick in body. I could not eat properly, and every day at mealtimes the Brahmin cook, who invariably is also the waiter with us, had his stock joke for me: "When you come back next term, come with a sack tied to your tummy." There were, however, one or two things which consoled me for this misery. The first of them was the riverside, for Mymensingh was on the old channel of the Brahmaputra. Broad stretches of water were always a delight to me, and the Brahmaputra at Mymensingh, though neither broad nor deep in its existing channel, particularly in the summer, had something of its old majesty clinging to it on account of its partly dry, wide old bed, and immense sand-banks. Besides, looking across the river and over the line of trees on the other bank which appeared like a shallow border of deep greenish blue to the sky, I could always see the lighter silhouette of the Garo Hills. Day after day I went to the riverside and contemplated the hills until their outlines became engraved on my mind.

The next thing to comfort me was the engine shed and yard of the railway station. A distant relation of mine, who was a student of engineering, had explained to me the mechanism of locomotives, and I went to the yard to verify what he had told me. I examined whichever of the shunting engines happened to be not working, and got the functions of the throttle and the other controls, the boiler, the cylinder, the driving rod and similar prominent features clear in my head. But for two or three years yet I did not fully understand the working of the eccentric and the reversing gear.

There was also another place which was a favourite resort with me, and this too possessed a mechanical attraction. It was a shorthand and typing school just in front of my hostel. In accordance with the peculiar convention among schools of stenography in India it was called "The Fonetik Skool". There were three machines in it, and the proprietor and teacher allowed me to tap away at them out of school hours. He was also given to the practice of palmistry and, studying my palm, would prophesy a great future for me. I was quite ready to believe these forecasts.

At last one day I thought the promise of release from Mymensingh had definitely come. The summer vacation was approaching. It would in any case have brought a respite from the hated town, but I was worried by the fear that I might have to come back to it. What I saw on that happy day assured me that I should not have to. Four cousins of my father owned in common a big departmental store in the town, and the store had a cycle department attached to it. In this part of the shop one day I saw some new lamps, saddles, and other accessories. The lamps were not the usual Lucas things we were familiar with. A son of one of the cousins, who was in charge of the department, came up smiling and, tapping one of the lamps with his forefinger, asked me, "Do you know where these have come from?" I had no idea, but he thrilled me by giving me the information that they had come from my father's new cycle shop in Calcutta. We knew that our father was in Calcutta and had received a vague hint that he had gone there to set up some sort of business, but neither my brother nor I had any notion that the matter had progressed so far. We now felt that it would not be long before we also started for the great city.

In the middle of May we went back to Banagram, where besides being rejoined to Carlo, my dog, I found a new attraction in the shape of a charitable dispensary, just established with the help of a gift from a wealthy neighbour of ours, Ananda Roy by name, who later also endowed a school in the village. But the most memorable experience for me in this stay at Banagram was the sight of Halley's Comet, the happy experience I have alluded to. At Mymensingh we had tried to observe it, but the comet was still far away and it was appearing after midnight, a most inconvenient hour for us. One night, however, we tried to see it through the college telescope, which was a two- or two-and-a-half-inch refractor on ordinary tripod mountings. The man who was giving the demonstration was not very skilful in his handling of the instrument, and therefore as soon as the faint object was being focused it was passing out of the field. Thus not even a dim or flitting vision of Halley's Comet served to redeem the bleakness of my stay at Mymensingh. At Banagram also, for some days, we could not see the comet. But one day it suddenly appeared in the evening in the western sky and continued to do so, remaining in view for quite a long time. It was a glorious sight, putting even the Milky Way into the shade. Evening after evening, I sat on a mat in the inner courtyard of our house gazing at it with bewitched admiration. Among us, as in the West, a comet is regarded as an omen of evil by the superstitious. But for me Halley's Comet had no such suggestion. I was engrossed only with its refulgent beauty. It rose lower and lower, till at last, one evening, it disappeared behind the tall bamboo clumps at the back of the house. I tell my children that they will see the beautiful thing in 1986, but not, as I did, with the wondering eyes of boyhood.

The monsoon was upon us before we left Banagram for Calcutta, and we started on the journey one drizzly morning. Our father had written that he would not be able to come to the village, but would pick us up at the railway station of Kaoraid, nearly thirty miles away. It was not an easy place to get to. The journey had to be broken into two stages: the first on land to our old estate at Mathkhala, twelve miles distant; the second over a river for the rest of the way. It was decided that my mother and the younger children should go by palanquin and we, the three elder boys, walk. The parting with Carlo caused me some sorrow. It had been understood from the very beginning that the dog was to be left behind, yet I am sure at the last moment I would have insisted on bringing him away with us. But the poor animal fell ill. So I had to say goodbye to him, and he was given to an old tenant of ours, who promised to take good care of him. I never saw Carlo again, for before we returned to Banagram two and a half years later he died.

We reached Kaoraid early in the morning before it was light, and found our father waiting by the riverside. We, the older boys, jumped ashore and started towards the station, which was about a quarter of a mile away, in the company of an old servant who had come with us from Banagram as escort. We had not gone more than half the way when, across the railway track and among the bushes which were looming very large in the dark, we heard a sound which was like the sound of timber being sawn. Our old servant gave me a nudge and whispered, "That's Great Father roaring!" It was, of course, a leopard, but common people in our parts never mentioned a beast of prey or a snake by its name at night. Formerly, this station was badly infested with tigers and leopards, for it was on the outskirts of the well-known forest of Bhawal. We had heard stories of passengers being pounced upon by the animals when coming up from the river or going down to it after dark.

The anticipation of new life transfigured this journey of ours, although the river Padma at this season needed no adventitious aid. It was gorgeous in itself, swift-moving, wide as the sea, and ochre-coloured with the rich silt it had laden itself with in its thousand-mile journey from the hills to the plains of lower Bengal. After reaching Calcutta I wrote a longish essay on the journey, charged I believe with all the excitement of the occasion. Since it was sent for from time to time by my father or mother I came to form the notion that I had made a good job of it. The morning after the steamer journey over the Padma our train steamed into Sealdah

Station. All around us was the grey smoke and haze of the great city, and the streets were darkened by the usual morning shadows. But for us it was an illuminated, a red letter day. We had come to Calcutta to live in it.

There was rather farcical prelude to our entry into our new house in Calcutta. All of us together with the heavy luggage, had been loaded into two hackney carriages; in one were we, the elder boys, and two of the younger children, in charge of a grown-up cousin; our parents and the other children were in the second carriage. Our cab started off before the other and did not wait to be overtaken. It had been told to go to Serpentine Lane, which was not very far from the station, but the cabman apparently had his own idea of where the lane was, and so instead of entering the lane from Lower Circular Road, he rattled on up Bowbazar Street. After the detection of his mistake and some hallooing on the part of our cousin, he turned into the first lane to his left, and stopping before almost every other house asked, "Is this the house?" At each question, our cousin put his head out through the window and scanned the house from the roof to the door-step, and a whole troupe of girls, young women, and elderly women either appeared at the door with an astonished air, or leaned in curiosity over the railing of the first-floor veranda, and shouted, "No, No." It was only after some floundering in this fashion that we got into the right lane and arrived at the door of our house. I learned afterwards that the lane in which we had searched for our house in vain was one of the second-rate disreputable quarters of the city. It must have been our unmistakably rustic appearance no less than our too obvious familial status which had made these women of the town reject us so vehemently.

For the moment, however, we knew nothing of the matter, nor thought of it. As soon as the carriage stopped at the door of our house we ran in, ran up, ran down, and ran up again, making a complete survey of all the four floors. The two main rooms on the second floor pleased us immensely. One of them was paved with black and white marble, the other had mosaic of coloured stones. The windows were provided with venetian blinds outside and frosted panes inside, while the fanlights had pieces of blue and red glass in alternating panels. These two rooms had a western aspect, and therefore in the evenings, as the rays of the setting sun poured in, there was in them a play of finely diapered light on marble and mosaic, with patches of coloured light on the walls.

It took us less than a week to settle down, and then we were admitted to school. My father had in mind at first one of the two leading schools in Calcutta, The Hindu School or Hare School, but a friend of his, an old resident, advised him to send us to a smaller school to begin with, because he thought we might not be able to hold our own against the boys of the bigger schools, who came from the best or, rather, the wealthiest families of Calcutta and were as a rule very turbulent and indisciplined. So we went to a smaller school near our house, which was a proprietary institution. The idea was to transfer us from this school at the end of a year or so, after we had got used to Calcutta life. But once admitted to the smaller school we could not come away, for the proprietor would not even hear of our doing so. He wrote extremely ingratiating letters to our father and persuaded him to keep us in his school. Thus both my brother and I appeared at our matriculation examination from this school.

Our new scholastic atmosphere was utterly different from the old. For one thing, we were cooped up in small rooms and missed the spaciousness which, in spite of the absence of impressive buildings, had been an integral feature of our school life at Kishorganj. But even more than spaciousness did we miss discipline. There were greater external restrictions. Door-keepers stood at the gates, making French leave a risky affair. The gates were inexorably locked during the midday recess.

Yet not a single boy would remain at his place in the class if during a lesson a band struck up in the street. When the teacher entered the class the boys rose in the most casual manner, some even remained seated whereas at Kishorganj the monitor got up and gave a formal command to salute, and the whole class rose as one man, saluted smartly, and would not sit down again until the teacher had said "Sit down". There was also a distressing lack of respect for the teachers. At Kishorganj we looked upon them as if they belonged to a sacerdotal order. But the Calcutta boy prided himself on his capacity to quiz and tease his teachers and play all kinds of mischievous pranks and practical jokes on them, so that it was impossible for anybody but a violently forceful personality to maintain order in the class. At home the Calcutta boy, with an aggressive conscious-ness of his superior social and economic position, treated his tutor as his fag, a man who was expected to do his home exercises for him and actually did them, and, strange to say, the guardian seemed to share this view. We were scandalized by all this, and shocked when a particularly irreverent boy went to the length of doling out some smutty tittle-tattle about a teacher. I do not know how we should have fared had we been admitted to one of the bigger schools, but in the school to which we went both my brother and I were able to impose our idea of decorous conduct on the other boys. We showed a sort of untamed puritanical ferocity which earned us the consider-ation of the normal boys and the fear of the vicious ones, of which, truth to say, there were very few in the school. It was from the wealthy families that the intractable boys mostly came, and our proprietor's clientele, with a small number of exceptions, was not rich.

Whether it was due to our going to a second-rate school or not, our school life in Calcutta in one sense, was a disappointment, for we saw nothing of that precocious intel-lectual brilliance of the youth of Calcutta of which we had heard so much. We had learnt to think of the Calcutta schoolboy as they thought of the Normaliens in France. His knowledge of English, more especially, was a legend with us. His general knowledge and argumentative powers were believed to be almost commensurate. None of these fabled things were apparent to us. Neither my brother nor I saw any reason to feel inferior before a Calcutta schoolboy, or, for that matter, even to emulate him. In fact, if English was to be the test, we wrote and spoke the language better than most of our schoolfellows.

In another sense, however, we stepped into a more lively and generous literary atmosphere in Calcutta. This had nothing to do with our school life, but resulted from the wider literary life of Calcutta. The city was the centre of the literary, as of every other, activity in our cultural and political life, and in those days it had a very lively literary society. We did not, indeed, go into this society, but its tidings were brought to us by an uncle who was a university student. This uncle was a distant cousin of our mother and came to live with us after our arrival in Calcutta. He was not a very good student in the usual meaning of the phrase, for he got plucked in his B.A. examination twice, but he was a young man with genuine literary enthusiasm and real taste. He was a regular buyer of books even on his modest allowance, and had already formed a fair collection of English classics in the Everyman's Library and Nelson's sixpenny series, while his Bengali books comprised nearly the whole of our contemporary literature. It was by looking at the titles of his English books that I learned the names of Jane Austen, Charlotte Bronte, and George Eliot as the greatest women writers in English literature. My brother gave me the additional information that they were novelists of a new kind– "psychological novelists", which sounded very impressive. Where and how he had picked up that idea I cannot say, but he did give the explanation, "Look at the titles–*Pride and Prejudice, Sense and Sensibility.*"

While my uncle's English books were kept on open shelves, the Bengali volumes snuggled in the privacy of a wicker basket, guarded both against "pinching", the common fate of all things printed among us, and unauthorized reading by young people. Bengali parents considered juvenile addiction to fiction as the equivalent of juvenile addiction to smoking. But the unlocked basket served only to relieve the conscience and not to prevent our corruption. What I did was to take out one book at a time and read it sitting on a windowsill while my uncle was out. If by any chance Uncle Anukul–his full name was Anukul Roy–came home unexpectedly I just sat on the book and pretended to watch the street, and when he had gone for tea quietly replaced it in its box. It was thus that I read, among other things, all the novels by Tagore and all the plays of D. L. Roy. But certainly I did not succeed in deceiving my uncle. He noticed the traces of rummaging among his books and suspected me, although he never flatly accused me.

This may have contributed to a certain dislike for me which I noticed in my uncle. In addition, I was perhaps repelling him by that queer alternation of extreme shyness and extreme pertness which characterized my behaviour as a boy. There never grew up between him and me that sympathy which was so obvious between him and my brother. I was hurt by this contrast, for this uncle continued to exercise a strong influence on me for many years.

Shortly afterwards a second personal influence entered my life. It was that of a teacher. Our headmaster one day entered the class with an almost boyish young man by his side and introduced him as our new teacher of English. He was very dark, but possessed of decidedly handsome features, his eyes particularly being very fine. Though short and plump, he was not so much so as to repel me with a suggestion of corpulence. He provoked notice and criticism by being dressed in a navy-blue striped suit instead of in *dhoti* and shirt. He drew on himself greater criticism by introducing an unwonted fervour into his teaching of poetry. It was reported that he moved in literary circles and even contributed to magazines. The general opinion of his pupils was that he was no good, for literary enthusiasm was considered bad form in teaching and useless, if not worse, for examinations. One day some boys wrote *ass* in reverse with chalk on the back of his chair, and the word imprinted itself right and distinct on the blue-black coat. The offence was discovered and the culprits punished, but only too many thought that the practical joke had not been undeserved. He particularly scandalized one of my best friends in the school, a boy Gangadhar by name, by teaching us the "Ode to a Nightingale". Gangadhar indicted our new teacher as a champion of booze, on the strength of the famous stanza on the blushful Hippocrene. For my brother and me, however, this teacher completed what my father and Uncle Anukul had begun. He not only communicated to us his love of literature but also taught us to be exacting in writing the two languages we used. I remember him as something more than one of my teachers, for as Mr. Mohitlal Mazumdar, the distinguished contemporary poet and critic, he exerted a very strong and beneficial influence on my later life. He introduced me to the literary society of Calcutta and made a writer of me almost by main force.

Here I had better have done with Gangadhar, who was the only schoolfellow I met again in after years. Gangadhar was a stern puritan. He was as severe with Bankim Chandra Chatterji as he had been with Mr. Mazumdar. Of one of Chatterji's most famous novels, Gangadhar declared, "The book has indeed a moral, but in places the pages are flooded with eroticism." The flood was one solitary scene of kissing within wedlock.

Gangadhar shared the prevalent dislike for any mention of kissing which at times made our novelists interpolate half-serious, half-facetious apologies after references to kissing in their books. Some even totally refrained from describing that indelicate act. One of our greatest novelists, who was looked upon as an iconoclast in matters of morality because he preached the saintliness of fallen women and spent a not inconsiderable part of his life in their company, even boasted that his pen always shrank back from the word "kiss". Perhaps that accounts for the surprising absence of convincing novels of love in my mother tongue, for if, as a French aphorist has said, love without letters is like a bed without pillows, love without kisses must be colder than even a bare iron bed in an unwarmed hospital ward unattended by nurses.

I lost sight of Gangadhar for many years. But he suddenly came back to my notice for a short while in 1927 as a solicitor's clerk. Mahatma Gandhi's teaching, he said then, had brought about a revolution in his outlook on life and way of living. Upon my asking what it was, he replied in the mixture of Bengali and English (italicized) in which he normally spoke, *"My dear,* the world is given to two opposed things–*sociality and naturality.* In the cities you have only *sociality,* but *naturality* still exists in the villages. I live in my village, my wife spins, and we are happy." I saw no Adam before me delving in apparel of Eve's spinning, nor an Augustus in Livia's handi-work. Gangadhar was only a Bengali clerk in a *dhoti* and threadbare coat of English cut, but he was, and always remained, a chip of the old block, a son or our venerable but incorrigibly unsophisticated Mother India.

I shall bring my narrative to the end of 1910 by referring to two incidents which, although unrelated to my current activities, were the first knots on two long, continuous, and coherent strands of my subsequent experiences. One of them was the first Hindu-Muslim riot I saw in Calcutta, the other was the visit of a German warship. One day I had gone to our tailor to take the delivery of some warm clothes, and while waiting in his shop, which was on Bowbazar Street, I saw a platoon of British soldiers marching down the road. They were in khaki shorts and grey flannel shirts, and carried their full kit. It was the first time I had seen British soldiers in their tropical service dress, and I wondered why they were out. I soon came to learn that a Hindu-Muslim riot had broken out in the Burrabazar area. It lasted for a day or two and resulted in some sensational looting. We saw nothing of the actual fighting, but we hugely enjoyed reading and talking about it. Our enjoyment was all the more unqualified because behind this rioting we did not feel the presence of that organized and doctrinaire hatred which we had perceived distinctly as the background of the Hindu-Muslim rioting of 1906 and 1907 in East Bengal. The Calcutta riot of 1910 was the outcome of sheer hooliganism, a clean thing compared with what was to come afterwards, and thus it was great fun.

I cannot recollect now whether it was in the German warship that the German Crown Prince came to Calcutta, but in any case the visits of both coincided. The vessel was the light cruiser *Leipzig,* whose gleaming shape I recalled on reading the news of the battle of the Falkland Islands in 1914. One morning in the school a boy who lived on the other bank of the river gave us the news of the arrival of the ship, the "man-of-war" as he and we called it, for we still employed this time-honoured word to designate a warship, just as we used the word "cannon" to designate a gun. The previous night, the boy said, he had seen a white ship with tall masts coming in with powerful searchlights playing. It was announced that the public would be allowed to see the ship, and our headmaster gave us a letter of introduction to the captain. We, the three brothers, did not, however, accompany the school party, but went by ourselves in charge of a grown-up relative.

As we came on the river we noticed, lying moored near the Eden Gardens, a striking white vessel utterly different in appearance from the familiar merchant ships. As we had seen a greater number of pictures of the old wooden ships of the line than of modern warships, we cried out as soon as we caught sight of the portholes, "How many guns!" But we promptly corrected ourselves, noticing the real guns on the deck and at the sites. There was an immense crowd of Indians creating a scene of wild commotion. The Indian constables under their English sergeants were moving about, making their only contribution towards keeping order by using their batons, whips, and *lathis* freely. Without being intimidated by this beating the crowd was trying to make its way towards the ship. A party of German sailors under an elderly petty officer with a pointed beard of the French type were standing before the gangway to regulate the flow of the visitors. The rest of the sailors were looking on from the deck, some smiling and some wearing an astonished air. As the hour fixed for Indians to go on board had not arrived and only Europeans were being allowed to do so, the petty officer was imitating the English sergeants and lashing out with a whip at every Indian who approached him. One Indian, however, slipped past him, and ran towards the ship. He was quickly overtaken, caught by the scruff of the neck and dragged back, to the accompaniment of a truly Homeric laughter from the ship and the bank. All at once, upon the signal being given for Indians to go up, the whole crowd made a rush and, sweeping everything before it, reached the gangway, which gave way. A crash, followed by a wild yell, was heard, and we, the brothers, together with our relative, ran for dear life, shouting; "They will now fire the guns." We did not stop until we were well behind the High Court and, to our thinking, safe.

I have seen this spectacle repeated year after year, on the occasion of every visit of the ships of the East Indies Squadron.

These visits gave occasion for a display of racial discrimination which was not surpassed even in all the squalid history of Indo-British personal relations. The arrogance and absence of consideration shown by one side was matched only by the indiscipline and lack of self-respect shown by the other. I often wanted to go on board these ships. More particularly did I want to see the *Southampton* when it came to Calcutta, because I had a romantic feeling for this ship for its part in the battle of Jutland. But I was deterred almost every time by the fear of intolerable humiliation, and if I found myself on three ships, the *Norfolk,* the *Emerald,* and another very old ship which came to Calcutta in 1919 (whose name I have forgotten), it was only through being swept aboard by the crowds behind me and not through my own volition or locomotion.

These experiences turned my stomach. In 1919, more especially, I was indescribably disgusted. On the bank I saw a private of the Marines being literally knocked about by the crowds while on sentry duty. Yet the man was showing an amazing patience. I saw him struggling for something like two hours with the crowds which were surging round him, without thinking of clubbing anybody with his rifle. For all I know the man's torture might have continued longer. Another reason for disgust was provided on the ship. As I was going over it with my younger brother an elderly person suddenly came forward and greeted him. After the man had moved away my brother told me that he belonged to the Intelligence Branch. This brother of mine, being a police suspect, knew some of them. These agents had come on the ship to see if any visitor was taking more than an ignorant interest in the vessel. If he did he was sure to be somebody interested also in overthrowing British rule in India. The Intelligence Branch was not at its most intelligent even in this, for in those days its officers used to take away Tolstoy's *War and Peace* if they found the book at any place they searched. They also seized Jethro Brown's

Underlying Principles of Modern Legislation, which was one of the text-books of jurisprudence in Calcutta University, because its first chapter was entitled "The Challenge of Anarchy". The presence of the political police on the ship gave me a momentary feeling of sickness. It was only my great and almost inborn love for warships which prevented my acquiring an unconquerable dislike for them from the recurrent association of national and personal degradation with their image.

As a pendant to the account of my first sight of a warship I shall add a mention of my first sight of an aeroplane, which also occurred at the end of 1910. I have forgotten who it was that came to Calcutta in that year, and have only a very faint recollection of a machine of the Farman type. The flight left no deep impression on me, comparable to that made by the warship. When we went down to the Maidan and saw the queer-looking machine standing on the racecourse, we hardly expected it to rise from the ground, and when it did rise and fly, that was taken in the light of a freak. The aeroplane had not yet had its innings.

At the beginning of 1911 we shifted from Calcutta to Ballygunje, not the upstart and overcrowded suburb of today, nor the expensive and fashionable suburb of those days, but a semi-rural lower middle-class suburb near the railway station which disappeared in the 'twenties. The reason for the move was my father's health. He had fallen seriously ill at the end of 1910 and had to undergo an operation. For his convalescence the doctors recommended quiet and air, and Ballygunje was suggested by an assistant in my father's business who came from the place. Our new house was quite roomy inside, and open all around. In its grounds there were two tanks, in which we could bathe or swim, and there was also plenty of land for playing about. The house was not quiet though. The railway station on one side and a mill for grinding brick-dust on another generated noise, but they saved us, the boys, from boredom.

In them I could pursue my investigation of steam engines, and at the station, besides completing my knowledge of locomotives, I learned all about signals, the block system, and control of train movements. The owner of the house and of the mill was the richest landlord of the locality. About his wealth it was, however, rumoured that it had originated in a fraud on an insurance company. He had pretended to be dead and obtained payment on a life policy. He had indeed been jailed for it, but while the imprisonment came to an end the money remained. This placid calculation lies behind most of the embezzlements which are so common among us. But when I saw the gentleman in 1911 he looked quite venerable and did not even remotely suggest a crook. The local people also did not like to remember his past, far less throw it in his teeth.

The first project I undertook in the new house was to build a model of the *Leipzig,* and my younger brother, who was good at handwork, served as my shipwright. We had, however, no drawings of warships with us, nor any accurate recollection of the plan of the cruiser. Therefore our progress was slow. But in the end something like a hulk was floated in the tank by the side of the house. At the same time, with ample space going and quite a large number of bushes and brick-mounds all about us, I naturally reverted to my military exercises, and two of the ambitious manoeuvres I held were a rehearsal of the Abor expedition which was going to Assam that year, and an enacting of the defence of Malta by the Knights of St. John.

Gardening followed presently. Its inspiration came from the house next to ours, which stood in the same grounds. This house received new tenants about the middle of the year, and their coming provided a sensation, if not a scandal, for the locality, for not only was the young man who had taken the house "England-returned", he had also an English wife, whom he had married in spite of the existence of a previous marriage with a Bengali Hindu girl. In fact, the expenses of the young man's stay in England had been borne by the father of the first wife, and if the desertion of his daughter was the only repayment the accommodating father-in-law got, he was not the only father-in-law in Bengal to be so recompensed. The father cohort in Bengal brought these misadventures upon themselves through their peculiar habit of trying to guarantee the good behaviour of their sons during their sojourn abroad by marrying them to minor girls just before their departure and packing them off as soon as this marital insurance policy had been taken out, without even giving the young men time to become properly acquainted with their wives. Our neighbour showed himself to be eclectic. A few weeks after his coming, his English wife, who was expectant, left for home, and instead of living the life of a grass-widower, he immediately brought over his Bengali wife, who became very friendly with us, and to whom all our silent sympathy went. The next year the Englishwoman came back with a baby, and the husband went to live with her in another house about a mile away, keeping the Bengali wife in the old house and also visiting her occasionally.

While living with his Bengali wife, he had with him also his elder brother and this brother's family. This man had squandered all his money in drink and was a confirmed drunkard. So his younger brother had to keep him and his family. Even then he occasionally ran away to Calcutta and came back dead drunk. One night, when he had returned in that state and was abusing his wife in filthy–language for not opening the door quickly enough for him, she refused to open it at all. Then he began to howl like a jackal, and when even that did not produce any effect, he roared out, "Then be a widow for ever", and jumped into the tank. The wife gave a scream and called her brother-in-law to come and save her husband from drowning, and the old man was hauled out of the water in a half-choked condition.

He was given to boasting to me about his grand old life. In his hoarse drunkard's voice he told me stories of his big house, his carriages, his servants, and his dogs. He was especially fond of telling the story of a bulldog he had, which, he said, was so vicious that nobody but its keeper, a sweeper, could go near it. The story was this: one day the dog, being loose, turned on one of his daughters, who was then a toddler; the girl was held by the throat in the dog's teeth and was screaming frightfully; at first he thought of going to her help but while he was hesitating how to do it his wife dragged him into a room and bolted the door, saying, "Don't throw good money after bad"; at last the sweeper heard the child's cries and came running to rescue her. I later saw the girl and the scars round her throat. Even at that age I listened to this narration with a cynical curling of the lips. My father curled them even more decidedly when I went and, in full consciousness of its enormity, told the story to him. "I wonder he did not feel ashamed to tell that story to others," was his comment.

But the man was redeemed by his love of flowers. When he first boasted about his pinks, asters, and phloxes I thought he was being the bragging fellow he always was, but he gave a demonstration of his gardening in the cold season. Even in the restricted space given to him, and the worst of soils, he made his borders a lovely sight. He had given me a good foreign variety of marigold, which also came to have a very attractive bloom. But I was jealous of his more choice flowers, which, of course, I could not have grown. I became more and more angry and envious as his beds looked more and more gorgeous, and one day that ancient malice to which I was heir got the better of me. I went up stealthily to one of the beds when no one was about and tore up a fine pink. In the afternoon when I was in my garden I saw the old man discovering the mischief. He went pale, and such a look came on his face as made me feel an unspeakable skunk. I suppressed the whole mean episode even from my brothers, and if any of my parents had come to know of it I should, of course, have received the severest whipping of my life.

Towards the end of 1911 my father subscribed to an advanced literary magazine for us. It was edited by a man whom we regarded as the leading critic in Bengal. He was, however, a writer of the orthodox school, and, in order to balance his opinions, my father a little later added to our repertory the leading liberal magazine. At the same time the ban on novel reading was lifted, and we joyfully took advantage of this freedom to read openly a fair number of Bengali and English novels. The avowed purpose of all this reading, and more especially of the reading of the English novels, was, however, mastery of language, and the amorous themes were assumed to be nonexistent. In our family that section of a collection of Tagore's songs which contained the love songs written by him was always referred to as "miscellaneous", and, stranger still, it was so subtitled in actual print.

From reading, our thoughts naturally turned to author-ship, and, as usual, it was my elder brother who took the lead. He wrote a short story and very shyly showed it to me. But his diffidence did not disarm the critic in me. I thought here was my chance to imitate our eminent critic, who was at his most ferocious with new and young writers. I hung up my brother's manuscript at the end of a pole and fastened over it a cardboard placard bearing the inscription "Guy de Maupassant" in large letters. Carrying this pole aloft like a standard, I took out a procession headed by me and formed by my uncomprehending younger brothers. All the while we kept on chanting very gravely, "Guy-i-i-i-i de-e-e Maupa-a-a-a-a-ssan-an-an-an-an...." My brother was so abashed by these proceedings that he did not even think of turning the tables on me by appealing to my mother. He threw up the sponge altogether. I have a recollection, however, that my mother, coming to know of my misdeed, did give me a sound scolding.

The greatest public event of 1911 in India was the Delhi Durbar, but for me the most memorable experience was my first acquaintance with the *Encyclopaedia Britannica* in its newly published eleventh edition. At Kishorganj we had learnt that the biggest English dictionary was the Webster, and whenever anyone there wanted to emphasize the size and weight of a book he said, "As big as Webster". Even then a rumour had reached us of the existence of a still bigger dictionary whose name we heard as *Anti-cyclopaedia Britannica*. This mistake was a tribute to the nationalist movement which had taught us to be *anti* most things rather than *pro* anything and also to assume an inherent virtue in being *anti* something or other. On coming to Calcutta, however, we were enlightened as to the correct title and true character of the work. We even caught a glimpse of a set of the tenth edition under the double protection of a locked cupboard and a locked room in our school. But our real introduction to the *Encyclopaedia* took place in October 1911, when a cousin of mine who was an advocate of the High Court and who had bought the eleventh edition just after its publication, left the set in our house for two months, during which he was out of town on account of the annual vacation. We were not expected to take the volumes out of their packing-cases, but we did, although with a bad conscience, and, to begin with, a delicious fragrance gave us notice of the unusual greatness of the work. The appearance of the volumes made a still greater impression. Opening one I murmured, "How beautifully smooth and white the paper is, yet how thin!" My cousin had bought the India paper edition in a semilimp binding of dark green sheepskin, with the arms of the colleges of Cambridge stamped on the sides. For some time we could take in nothing but an idea of the material appearance of the work.

Then we tried to find out what it contained. As chance would have it, the first article to fix my attention was that on dogs. "What lovely pictures and what lovely dogs," I cried. The previously unheard-of breeds to which I lost my heart at first sight were the Great Dane, the Dalmatian, and, above all, the Borzoi. It took me a number of days to work off the excitement over the dogs and take stock of the rest of the work. When I had done that, four articles came finally to keep me engaged on them throughout the time the set remained with us. They were the articles on artillery, ordnance, ships and ship-building. As I looked over the plates and diagrams of the warships, I thought if I had seen these six months ago I should not have gone wrong over the building of the model of the *Leipzig*. Of all the names of warships given in the article those which struck me most were, curious to relate, the Norwegian *Norge* (to go down with glory at Narvik in the last war) and the Brazilian *Minas Geraes* (perhaps still afloat), although even the *Dreadnought*, the *Invincible* and the *Inflexible* were illustrated.

The articles on artillery and ordnance were a genuine revelation. I had already seen some live artillery, but they were fixed-cradle breech-loaders which in those days used to be drawn in the Indian Army by magnificent white bullocks. So the very first impression the plates in the *Encyclopaedia* made on me was of a very high degree of mechanical complexity. "Why, they are like machines," I thought. I was puzzled by the mysterious abbreviations 18-pr. and Q.F. in the caption under the British field-guns. I was more puzzled by the buffer. "Are they double-barrelled or is that only a telescope?" I asked myself. It was not long, however, before I cleared up all these mysteries. I was particularly impressed by the Krupp siege-guns, the 11.2-inch howitzer and 8.26-inch mortar, and almost entranced by the look of the 3.4-inch Krupp automatic gun. The big howitzer was shown on its fixed mountings under a huge shield which reminded me of the testudo of the Romans, and not on the field mountings on which it was used later. Another picture whose charm sank permanently in my mind illustrated the article on artillery, and showed the men of the R.H.A. in their busbies firing their thirteen-pounders. The sight of these pictures was the beginning for me of a study of artillery technique which lasted many years. I shall relate later the extraordinary story of my preoccupation with the breech-mechanism of guns.

My father's business was not flourishing. The cycle shop had been badly neglected during his illness and had to be wound up. He tried other ventures, but apparently these, too, were not successful. Neither he nor my mother ever communicated their anxieties to us, but even so we could feel the presence of a cold shadow. There were two alternatives before my father: he could either stick to his guns and remain in Calcutta, or go back to his village. At first he inclined towards the first or the more desperate course, and went to Banagram to collect money to buy the house we were living in at Ballygunje, not the first house but a second and smaller one to which for economy's sake we had moved in the summer of 1912. But at the end of the year my mother had a severe attack of malaria, which we thought she had contracted from the marsh at the back of the house. My elder brother also had attacks, which, though not so serious as my mother's, continued longer, in fact recurred off and on for nearly two years. So it was decided that we should go back to Banagram, and we did so in December. Thus, just as one illness had brought us to Ballygunje, another took us out of it.

For about six months the family remained at Banagram, and my father was not able to decide what to do. He could, of course, remain at Banagram and live on his property, but the old standard of living could not be maintained on his income from it, and perhaps the expenses of his children's education could not be met at all. Therefore, when we were at home for the summer vacation of 1913, he one day called my brother and me and asked us what we thought of his going back to his old practice at Kishorganj. It seemed as if his consultations with my mother had not been decisive. She was a woman who attached a good deal of importance to prestige, and having once come away from Kishorganj she did not like the idea of going back like the prodigal son. My brother and I declared even more decidedly for prestige, and did not flinch even when our father said that his not going back to Kishorganj might mean our having to complete our education by means of our own earnings. But my father was not the man to shift his own burden to other and weaker shoulders, and he took a decision which was consistent with his manly nature. He went back to Kishorganj. As it happened, Kishorganj did receive him back like the prodigal son. We regained our prosperity.

CHAPTER III

CITIZEN-STUDENT

WITH THE departure of the family from Calcutta I began to live, while still a schoolboy, the distinctive life of a university student in Bengal. These students lived in all kinds of places—college hostels, hostels run by the missionaries, boarding-houses recognized by the university and in some cases unrecognized, and also their own homes or the houses of relatives. But wherever they lived they conformed to a common type, the citizen-student, for in their existence politics, both open and secret, studies, gadding about, and interminable talk formed almost equal ingredients. There was, however, practically nothing of sport.

I had my first taste of this life in what among us were called "messes". These were really boarding-houses run by the inmates themselves, and their popularity with the students from East Bengal had made this chummage a feature of the educational life of Calcutta. At the end of 1912 my brother and I were sent to one of these places and found ourselves confronted, not only with a new academic landscape, but also a new awareness of our home district. Although these messes were students' institutions, the real bond of unity among their inmates was not studentship but provenance. As a rule only students coming from one district or one of its parts lived together, and if by any chance a mess became cosmo-parochial trouble could be anticipated. For instance, the mess to which we went had a membership of about twenty, divided almost evenly between Mymensingh and Tipperah, and in it not only had the districts come to be segregated on two floors but they were also keeping up a vivacious competition in mutual fault-finding.

Thus the messes could be regarded as little colonies in Calcutta of the different districts of East Bengal. The inmates frequently were old acquaintances, further divisible into smaller groups of actual relatives, and even when a young man was personally a stranger his family was sure to be known to the others by report. We, for example, were formally in charge of Uncle Anukul, but were directly looked after by other young men who had known our family for years. Accordingly, there was no relaxation, even in the incohesive society of Calcutta, of the social control operating at home, and despite the absence of all authoritarian supervision the sowing of wild oats was very successfully kept in check. But, on the other hand, the cultivation of any cultural wheat was also made difficult. These young men from the villages and small towns of East Bengal saw hardly anything of the larger life of the city, did not acquire its ways, and only in very rare instances even learned to speak the standard Bengali. In fact, the shedding of provincialism was considered "unpatriotic", and Calcutta speech and Calcutta cuisine were the two things most emphatically frowned upon. Thus it happened that even after a stay of years in the city the young men went back the same rough diamonds they had been, and were not thought any the worse of on this account. By refusing to accept from the great city anything but a diploma of some kind to earn a living they tried to show that they had not been corrupted by the seductions of Babylon.

Life in these messes was hard, drab, and devoid of repose. They were always overcrowded and often dirty. Usually three to four students lived, studied, and slept in one room. There were no fixed hours for anybody or any particular activity. So while one slept the others might be entertaining friends, or the study of one young man might be accompanied by the snoring of a second, the singing of a third, and the gymnastics of a fourth. Thus, for quite good reasons, among the students, the word "room-mate" became an expression of crucial significance. But in my whole experience of mess life I was never able to discover the limits of the marvellous forbearance I saw all around me towards all the vagaries of human nature.

The tolerance of material ugliness was even more wonderful. Nobody objected to any object on the score of its looks. The ugliness of our mess furniture had to be seen to be believed possible. It came from the hands of the same carpenters who made the hideous *charpoys* used for carrying our dead to the burning-ghat. Nor was the board better. The food was always poor in quality, and sometimes even insufficient in quantity. On the last day of the month the manager tried to make amends in a feast, but in spite of its degeneration into something like an orgy it provided no counterpoise to the daily deprivation. So the students resorted to the more effective method of making good by gluttonous extravagance (based on credit) in the sweetmeat shops and restaurants. I remember having once, while walking only the short distance between College Square and Mirzapore Square, stepped into almost all the wayside eating-places and eaten five times in the space of about an hour and a half. Although this feat was not wholly typical, it was by no means very much out of the ordinary either.

After living for some time in these messes the young men became casual in their daily habits, and, surely, nobody could blame them for it. If they did not also become wholly Bohemian, it was only on account of the ballast furnished by the examinations. On the other hand, if they were not driven to jaded stupidity, that was due to their interest in politics and public affairs. In my case a change was provided by a stay of two years in the hostel of the Oxford Mission, and also by home life. The missionary hostel did not change the basic quality of our student life, but there was in it more space, quiet, order, and regularity, all contributing a slightly different flavour. I cannot say, however, that these refinements were appreciated by us. Some of us even felt a positive discontent, and chafed against certain restrictions which were viewed in the light of a denial of human rights. These were the following: no waste paper or litter on the floors; no driving of nails into the walls; no absence from one's rooms after nine in the evening; and no company or talk after that hour. But the guardians preferred the missionary hostels on account of their better discipline and relative inexpensiveness.

Lacking robustness I stood in need of the relief provided by the missionary hostel and home life. Continuous mess life would have worn me out. It wore me out even with the interruptions. But if I had to recapitulate my education I do not think I should have tried to avoid mess life. With all its discomfort it taught me a good deal. Sheltered as I had been from the world and its rough-and-tumble, I should have seen only one side of life had I not been thrown early into this wholly different kind of existence. In it I learned endurance and became, if not easy and polished, at all events tough. I take pride in the exposure and seasoning I have undergone in mess life. I have also been the recipient of its large, though unconscious and unadorned, charity, and am grateful for it.

POLITICS AND ANTICIPATION OF WAR

In this chapter I shall sample only the collateral experiences of my student life, leaving for the next the description of my quest for knowledge. Annoyed at times by the ceaseless political chatter of my fellow-students I used to tell them airily, "I am outside Aristotle's definition of man". It was altogether an empty boast, for I could no more help absorbing politics than I could avoid breathing air. As M. Benda has said, *"Politique d'abord, veut un apotre de l'ame moderne; politique partout, peut-il constater, politique toujours, politique uniquement."*

At that time, however, to be constitutional was very much out of fashion, and the nationalist agitation in its open form had reached its lowest ebb. The years between 1910 and 1915 were pre-eminently the years of conspiratorial activities. It was in East Bengal that the underground movement had its most vigorous life and widest ramifications, and, living in Calcutta for the greater part of the year, neither my brother nor I were subjected to its continuous attraction. Nevertheless we could feel the undeclared presence of the revolutionaries, and with that also the unavowed watch of the spies. What was more significant, all unconsciously, our thoughts began to take the impress of the conspiratorial mould. Shortly after our coming to the mess Lord Hardinge made his first state entry into Delhi, the new capital. I recollected the programme in the afternoon and said to my brother, "Suppose Lord Hardinge were to be killed by a bomb." The next morning I was dismayed to find a partial confirmation of my anticipation. I was sorry for Lord Hardinge, but more afraid for myself, because I could never dismiss the likelihood of my thoughtless remark being reported to the police and the police taking action on it.

Within the next few weeks I was to receive a more personal notice of the existence of the revolutionary movement in our parts. After his return to Banagram my father was having financial anxieties and was trying to dispose of a jute press and warehouse he owned. A rich tradesman made him an offer of ten thousand rupees for the shed and the machinery. But when the transaction was on the point of being completed there was a political robbery in his house, and the man, to the best of my recollection, was killed. In the summer which followed the shed was blown away by a great storm, and the property lost nearly all its value.

More contacts with the revolutionary movement were to follow. Early in 1914 we heard that soldiers were going to be posted in the districts of East Bengal, and both Mymensingh town and Kishorganj were to receive their contingents. The troops were certainly needed, for the civil police, including its armed branch, had completely lost its morale. A man of the armed constabulary one day told me that he and his comrades knew who had committed the recent political robberies, that one early morning, while on the march in search of a party of revolutionaries, they had actually met the party but had passed on pretending not to see it, although armed with Martini-Henry rifles, because, as the man expressed it, "Nobody, not even the Inspector Babu, was ready to give his life". Thus, on coming home in the summer of 1914, I found a detachment of the 91st Punjabis stationed at Kishorganj.

A self-conscious demureness in the inhabitants added to the presence of some fifty strapping Punjabi Mussalmans warned me that the town was not normal. There were also some suspicious signs in our own family. My younger brother, who was fourteen, was seen to have acquired the habit of leaving home off and on for an hour or two and on return to be extremely unwilling to disclose where he had been. This was wholly contrary to his frank nature. My mother told me that an upper-class boy exercised quite an undue influence on him, and that this boy came at odd hours near our house and whistled, upon which my brother became very restless and eventually disappeared. As I expected, this boy promptly made his overtures to me. He called me elder brother and said that he had long been wanting to meet me in order to discuss certain questions of national welfare. I went out immediately for a walk with him, and in the course of this he lamented the decline of morals among the students. He also told me to read the works of Swami Vivekananda. I, of course, perfectly understood my role as a potential recruit and felt amused at his beating so much about the bush. But I was also annoyed because I now saw clearly where he was leading my brother.

Then came a second and a more significant warning. In accordance with the custom in the family of staging a play every summer, we were rehearsing a Tagore play that year, and one of my younger brother's class-fellows was in the cast. He came regularly for the rehearsals but one extraordinary thing about him was that he would become extremely nervous and finally fall into a fit of terror if he had to stay on after dark. He would begin almost to cry, and would not go home unless escorted back. We tried to reassure him, and then insisted on knowing what he was afraid of. At first he would say nothing, but at last one day gave the explanation that he feared he would be killed on his way home. He could not be induced to go beyond this and disclose why and by whom. We, however, clearly understood the situation. He had got mixed up with a secret society and was perhaps trying to leave it, but was being forced to remain literally at the point of the dagger or revolver.

Towards the end of the vacation the senior schoolboy asked us to dinner at what he described as a schoolboy's party. We sought our mother's permission. She saw no harm and allowed us to go, and the dinner went off well without any revelation of its true character. There were some forty boys at it, and an evident air of great cordiality, together with a good deal of *empressement* towards my elder brother and me who were the new guests. Nothing could be more natural and innocent. But as I took the dinner in the dimly lit courtyard I had a feeling that there were about me clouds that would not clear, and curtains that waved and tantalized but were never going to be lifted. So strongly was the sense of having trodden on some forbidden ground forced on us that my elder brother and I never discussed the dinner afterwards, except that one day many years later he abruptly recalled that we had been to a revolutionary banquet. The secret police also made us feel their presence in the same way. If our dear old ghosts wanted their revenge on me for my denial of them they could not have devised a more adequate vengeance. For the greater part of my life I have been compelled to live with an oppressive sensation of there being about me two worlds hidden from my eyes, spectral presences investing me closely, and bodiless evils shunning our sunlit existence yet tormenting it with their malign telekinesis.

The revolutionary movement never succeeded in sucking in either my elder brother or me, and, in my case, as I have said, the prophylactic influences were mainly two: my mother's condemnation of murder and robbery as political weapons and my knowledge of military affairs. There had been additions to this knowledge in the meanwhile. My first notions of strategy and tactics were picked up from a Bengali book, of course proscribed, of the Swadeshi days, and I was always very diligently collecting whatever military information came in my way. Uncle Anukul had given me the first part of an illustrated history of the Russo-Japanese War in English. I found in it a good account of the opening phases of the war: the landing at Chemulpo, the sinking of the *Korietz,* the last fight of the *Varyag,* the night attack on Port Arthur, and the disabling of the *Tsarevitch* and her consorts, and I became very curious to read the other parts. I saw them at a second-hand dealer's, but they were too expensive for me.

Then came the stimulus of some real wars, the Turco-Italian War and the two Balkan Wars. I followed their course with great attention. Like my father, our Press and the majority of our people were pro-Turk. I, on the contrary, though a mere boy, remained consistently anti-Turk, and the reason was, not only the anti-Muslim sentiments contracted from the Swadeshi movement, but also a rationalization of that antipathy through an interpretation of Pan-Islamism as the greatest danger facing Indian nationalism. I had imbibed this distrust of Pan-Islamism in the first instance from Uncle Anukul, but its ultimate source was an eminent nationalist thinker, Bepin Chandra Pal, who was always warning us of this danger, and of whose writings Uncle Anukul was an assiduous reader. Accordingly, I wanted Turkey, the cradle and forge of the Pan-Islamic movement, to be crippled, and was very much disappointed when the Turk, instead of being ejected, lock, stock, and barrel, from Constantinople succeeded in stabilizing a defence line at Tchataldja.

My military studies continued in mess life. Its depressing first days were partly brightened for me by a study of Napoleon's Italian campaign from a popular biography in English. It was indeed an experience to follow the splendid sweep of the campaign from Montenotte to Rivoli and make inwardly sonant the *tambourinage* of the French names against the *Paukenwirbel* of the Austrian: La Harpe, Augereau, Massena, Cervoni, and Serurier against Beaulieu, Quosdanovitch, Alvintzy, and Wurmser. I put off until my return to Banagram the application of the larger lessons of the reading, and for the time being set out to reconnoitre Fort William with ideas gathered from the siege of Mantua. The result, however, was the opposite of what I had wanted it to be. As I was approaching the Calcutta Gate after walking over the glacis from the Plassey Gate, I suddenly caught sight of a large number of turbans moving rapidly along the sunken roadway. The *pugrees* presently emerged into full view as cavalrymen. A whole regiment of Indian cavalry was coming out of the fort and proceeding towards Eden Garden Road at a moderate trot. Its English officers were also in turban. I was transfixed with an overpowering admiration, for I had never before seen any large body of troops in massed formation. The only military display regularly held in Calcutta was the Proclamation Parade on New Year's Day, but I consistently avoided it because, at it as before warships, Indians were reported to be whipped. Incidentally, these assaults on Indians at military pageants seem to have been an established tradition of British rule. In the galleries of the Victoria Memorial I have seen a picture of the reception of Sikh guns in Calcutta, showing a trooper with raised sabre charging a group of cowering Indians, both men and women, and very near them is placed another group representing the most eminent Indians of Calcutta of those days–Rajah Sir Radhakanto Deb, Prasanno Kumar Tagore, and Rustomji Cowasjee–all looking very haughty and defiant; perhaps apprehensive of their turn with the trooper. But in that accidental encounter of mine with the cavalry regiment there was no accompaniment of whipping, and I was haunted for months by the vision I had seen.

The summer vacation of 1913 was spent by me at Banagram. It was one of the pleasantest vacations of my life, although disturbed for a while by a most unpleasant interlude of cholera and deaths from cholera all around our house. My mother took stringent precautions regarding water, and we were really not afraid of the disease. What made us more uncomfortable was the unusual howling of the jackals at daytime, traditionally one of the worst of evil omens, and the weird incantations of a mullah who, having been entrusted with the task of warding off cholera from the house, discharged his duties every night with fearful yells. But the epidemic passed away with the coming of the rains, and I devoted the rest of the vacation to an absorbed study of the Russo-Japanese War. Then my elder brother and I returned to Calcutta.

This time we went to our old estate by boat, and this boat journey stands out as one of the most charming among my many charming boat journeys. We were passing for the greater part of the way through a country, which, judging by pictures, could be compared to the Norfolk Broads. Off and on I came out of the cabin and stood with my hands on the mast, gazing at the silvery waters and the green fields and plantations, and dreaming of a submarine of my own design, a vessel very much bigger and more elaborate than any submarine whose picture

I had seen. The most up-to-date submarines I had seen illustrated so far were the British D-class boats. Even they looked like mere mechanized canoes, whereas mine was to be at least as big as a destroyer, with a roomy conning-tower and watertight gun-turrets. Actually, the mental picture I had formed was an anticipation of the very much later *Surcouf,* the French submarine. As I was trying to visualize the imaginary boat's submergence and surfacing in a broad stretch of water about a quarter of a mile in front of me, there rose from its grassy edge two large cranes, flying one behind the other with wing movements so spacious and at the same time so uniform that they created the illusion of a whole flock in flight. At sunset we reached a little shining lake, or more properly what is called a *beel* in Bengali, at the southern end of which we were to moor. My father had often spoken to me of the beauty of this lake, and he had not exaggerated. I thought it would not be a bad idea to build a house by its side and live there for the rest of my life. On my expatiating on this theme to the boatman he came forward with the information that the mosquitoes of the lake were the carriers of elephantiasis. I cast an involuntary and startled look at my legs and dropped the bright new idea. It was getting dark, and the sound of temple bells was floating to us from the village. The evening worship had begun in the Kali temple established and endowed by my ancestor Kirtinarayan. We had to walk about three-quarters of a mile to reach the estate from the lake, and all the way that abstracted pensiveness which is induced by temple bells at dusk–*l' Angelus du soir hindou*–was snapped in me only by the recurring thoughts of the submarine.

WAR AND POLITICS

The outbreak of the war in 1914 found me in the hostel of the Oxford Mission with Father Carlos Edward Prior as our superintendent. Father Prior's school was Harrow, university

Cambridge, college Jesus, and Tripos mathematical. He read the New Testament in Greek, was learning Bengali and could speak it tolerably well, kept a violin in his drawer, and actually played a little brass flageolet. He must have been quite young at the time, but he was very tall and bony, wore a beard, had deep vertical wrinkles between his eyebrows, and therefore gave an impression of being older than he was. He went about bare-footed and slept on a bare bed, and communicated these two habits to me. Although extremely serious in serious matters, he had a very lively sense of humour and would often surprise us by cracking jokes of a subtly idiomatic and literary flavour in Bengali. Among Bengali writers I was delighted to find him enjoying Prabhat Mukherji best. Mukherji wrote short stories rather in the vein of O. Henry, and had none of that sentimental didacticism which is the bane of most of our novelists. Father Prior was then engaged in reading Tagore's reminiscences, and he at times sent for me to translate the more difficult passages for him. On his part he retold to us in Bengali the stories of Brer Rabbit. The cause of the uproarious enjoyment with which we listened to him was not less the manner of the retelling in Bengali than the stories themselves.

Father Prior's kindness to me was undemonstrative but continuous. More especially was it shown where I really needed external help. He was always seeing to it that I had enough exercise and took me out for long walks into the countryside around Calcutta. He also made me play games. One day I told him that I wanted to learn Latin. He replied that he would not mind my learning Latin when I was two inches taller, but for the moment I must come and play. Another time, when I was engaged in reading about naval range-finders in the *Encyclopaedia Britannica,* he came into my room, unceremoniously shut the book, and taking me by the arm dragged me out. "But, father," I protested, "I am reading about range-finders." "There will be time enough to do that," he retorted, "but if you read when you ought to play I won't let you have the *Encyclopaedia* at all."

Furthermore, perhaps observing my awkwardness, Father Prior tried to give me more self-assurance and defended me. One day he took some of his boys, including my brother and me, to the Mission's country centre at Behala. We went first to the hut of the Sisters, and when one of them came in my brother and I got up, bowed, and said, "Good afternoon." The Sister just acknowledged the salutation and, looking at Father Prior, observed in an undertone, "They seem to be impertinent." "Oh no," replied Father Prior in the same undertone, "only, they don't know." The Sister was very cordial for the rest of the visit. Later in the afternoon Father Prior and I were sitting in Father Douglas's hut. I believe I had rather annoyed Father Douglas, first, by being fidgety during the church service; secondly, by trying to strum a piano; and, lastly, by replying airily when Father Douglas asked me whether I knew Bengali or English better, "Of course, Bengali." So, when he noticed Father Prior sitting squeezed against me, he said almost in a whisper, "Come over here, instead of sitting by that awkward boy." Father Prior made a slight movement towards Father Douglas's side but added very quickly, "But he's not awkward." I am surprised myself at the distinctness with which I caught both the interchanges, for I could not then wholly follow English as spoken by Englishmen. But I suppose deaf persons are not the only people who have an uncanny sharpness of ear for things said for and against them.

It was not long before political trouble, which with us always had the added shade of racial antagonism, began in the hostel. One day, shortly after our coming, I noticed a great excitement among the students and was informed that Father Prior had made a remark which was an insult to the entire Indian nation. The young men were as worked up as a flock of rooks and said that they were not going to take it lying down.

At last it was decided that when in the evening Father Prior came to say good-night everybody was to shut the door against him. My brother regarded the whole affair as extremely childish and said he was not going to make a fool of himself. Just before dinnertime one of the organizers of the boycott walked into our room and tried to talk my brother out of his dissent. In spite of being junior to my brother, he argued his case with confidence, a confidence derived partly from his strength of character and partly, perhaps, from a consciousness of good looks and a good academic record. But my brother also showed himself equally able to maintain his ground. Although appealed to in the name of country, nation, and finally personal self-respect, he would not change his mind. That evening at dinner both he and I were treated by our fellow-boarders to a sustained but indirect trouncing of the whole tribe of toadies, sycophants, and yes-men.

The war caught me unawares. The Irish troubles had put me off the scent, and I was following that trial to the neglect of the Austro-Serbian dispute. But I was not taken intellectually unprepared. Exactly a year before I had read about the German General Staff and admired the imposing figures of the German generals, made more impressive still by their spiked helmets, cloaks, and high boots. Furthermore, my military knowledge had been increased by some readings on the American Civil War, about which I had first learnt from a popular biography of Garfield, *Log Cabin to White House,* and also from the biographies of Lincoln and Grant in the same series. The description of Garfield zigzagging away from the disastrous field of Chickamauga made an ineffaceable impression on me, and pondering over the incident I wondered whether I should be allowed, like Garfield, to complete my education and serve in a war—our war of independence—as a professor, or be drawn into it as a student, which I feared might in actual fact be the case. Even apart from its personal moral, the American Civil War interested me both politically and militarily. I was such a partisan of the North that even Lee and Stonewall Jackson left me cold. Of the Federal military leaders I liked Grant and Sherman best, and among Grant's battles Vicksburg was my favourite. McClellan, on the other hand, I positively disliked. My sympathy for the North was reinforced by the American novelist Winston Churchill's story *The Crisis,* which I read just before the outbreak of the war.

Thus it happened that in August 1914 I was able to surprise my acquaintances by chattering about the German General Staff, General Brialmont and his fortifications, artillery and aeroplanes. To no one did this showing-off of mine give greater pleasure than to an aged uncle, Mr. Das, who was a retired magistrate and the father of the cousin who owned the *Encyclopaedia Britannica.* He was delighted and annoyed at the same time by being told that I had gathered all this information from his son's set of the *Encyclopaedia Britannica,* because it was he who had bought the work for his eldest son, giving his second son a set of Nelson's *Encylopaedia* at the same time, lest there might be any misunderstanding between the brothers. In the presence of his second son, who was of my age, he declared–he was a man who piqued himself on being outspoken–that he was glad to find someone making use of the books, although those for whom they were intended were not. But both my cousins generously conceded the credit to me and were even proud that one at least of the same blood was able to tackle the bulky volumes.

India was as eager in 1914 as she showed herself in 1940 to gloat over the Allied reverses and glory in the German victories, though the expression of the malice on the first occasion was less open, less bold, and less strident. One afternoon, immediately after the declaration of war by Great Britain, a fellow-boarder shouted with glee from the second-floor veranda to us below that the British "battleship" *Amphion* had been sunk and the Russian port of Libau bombarded. I, being of the Allied persuasion, got extremely angry but had to swallow all this vicarious bragging. The next few days were bleak even on a sympathetic appraisement of the Allied resistance. I gathered from the communiques that the B.E.F. was fighting back quite successfully, but one day, trying to locate on a map Cambrai on which it had been reported to have fallen back, I was startled to discover what a headlong retreat the affair was becoming. That single discovery taught me for all time to take all military communiques at my valuation and not at their writers'. But the cheering news of the battle of the Marne followed presently. Even in India it was realized that the battle was one of the turning points of the war, and, having immediately after the victory gone to see my uncle with regained assurance, I found him turning the tables on his second son, whose sympathies were on the wrong side and who during the preceding weeks had been boasting of the feats of von Kluck, pronouncing the name a *l'anglaise*, thus making it even more sonorous than it was. Reinforced by me, my uncle (who from now on began to call me "philosopher") was able to tear off a few feathers from von Kluck's cap.

I cannot recollect that the *Emden* caused much panic among the Bengalis of Calcutta, although I came across a good deal of malicious pleasure at the discomfiture of British naval power, and also heard of the flight of the Marwari merchants to the inaccessible safety of their homes in Rajputana. At the end of September I left Calcutta for Kishorganj fully expecting Antwerp to hold out, for I had read that the fortifications of Bucharest and Antwerp, both by General Brialmont, were the best in Europe. In the course of the journey, however, I was to receive a terrible shock, though not over Antwerp. As I was getting down from the steamer at Narayanganj, a newsboy jumped on the deck across the paddle-box and put a copy of *The Statesman* in my hand. I read with horror of the sinking of the three armoured cruisers, *Aboukir, Cressy, Hogue,* one after another, apparently by the same U-boat. I had not expected the British navy to give such a poor account of itself.

At Kishorganj I found my father wholly unperturbed and confident of an ultimate Allied victory. I also heard the grotesque report of a German aeroplane engaged in observations near Kishorganj and betraying its presence by its searchlight. The searchlight was, of course, Venus appearing as the evening star. As chance would have it, in Calcutta also I had actually seen and heard a number of people discussing the evening star as a German aircraft. One evening just before my coming away, I noticed a group of men standing at the junction of Amherst Street and Corrie's Church Lane excitedly pointing to the western sky. Coming nearer I heard them speaking of German aircraft and, looking along the lane which at this point connected Amherst Street with Harrison Road, I could see Venus shining with more than its usual brilliance. Therefore I was not very much surprised by what I heard in very much less sophisticated Kishorganj. But I must say I was almost taken aback by the repetition of the same story in Calcutta in September 1939.

Coming back to Calcutta I plunged into a deeper spell of military studies. I passed from military history to the technical aspect of warfare and tried to learn the elements of gunnery and aviation. My note-books began to fill up with drawings of guns and aeroplanes, and I am sure had my room by any chance been searched by the police I should have been in trouble. My special interest at this time was the breech mechanism of guns, and the only breech I failed to master was that of the Nordenfelt automatic, over a diagram of which I pored for weeks before throwing up the sponge. Not only did I try to understand how the different types of breeches worked, I also boldly pronounced on their merits, and ended by declaring my preference for the breech of the Krupp field-gun. I did not exactly dislike the British interrupted-screw breech but had no pronounced liking for it either. The breech of the famous French Seventy-five I positively hated, notwithstanding its efficiency.

It was very much later in life that I discovered the true reason for my likes and dislikes among breech-blocks, and came to see that they had nothing to do with the question of mechanical efficiency. It was only an abstract aesthetic prepossession which was influencing me. I liked the Krupp breech because, having seen it in illustrations, not diagrams, in the open position, I was struck by its clean-cut appearance, which appealed to my innate preference for clear and well-disposed form. Perhaps if I had seen the breech in the closed position with the slot for the cartridge projecting to the left I should have held a different opinion. The English breech was to my thinking solid, very neatly adapted to its purpose, and artistic in the quiet and unassertive English manner, but it did not possess that keen edge of concinnity and elegance which cuts instantaneously into an inexperienced sensuous perception. The French block repelled me on account of its eccentricity to the bore, which I unconsciously resented as an aesthetic outrage. Its simple and rigorous logic should normally have contributed to abstract beauty, but the actual effect was the opposite.

The aesthetic predisposition which so queerly governed my judgements on gun breeches, and of which I first became conscious after reading Mr. Roger Fry, is certainly a property of my innermost being, for throughout my life it has been alert on the entire perimeter of my contacts with things and ideas outside of me, and been admitting or repelling them according to its own selectivity. It has made me lean towards certain kinds of furniture and interiors; it has made me prefer Florentine painting to Baroque, and stood in the way of my admiring as he should be admired even so great a master as Rembrandt; it has made me like Mozart better than Beethoven, place Hardy's

Return of the Native above his *Far from the Madding Crowd* in spite of my unbounded admiration for the latter book; it has at times induced me not to think less of Turgenev than of Tolstoy or Dostoevsky; and, to crown it all, it has made me partial to French prose even when I am perfectly conscious of the profundity of the English.

Along with my military studies I was also following the war from day to day. In December came the news of the battle of the Falklands. As I was reading the news, Father Prior looked over my shoulder and said, "Good news this morning, Nirad." "Yes, Father," I replied briefly but gladly. I also followed the course of the two battles of Ypres, and the other battles in which the Indian Corps took part. But after the "race to the sea" both the Western Front and the Russian Front ceased to interest me. My imagination was stirred by the Dardanelles project. I was instinctively an "Easterner", and thought that victory could most quickly be won by a thrust up the Balkans. Napoleon's Italian campaign had certainly influenced me in this way of thinking.

Even though the naval attack had failed before I started for Kishorganj to spend the summer vacation there, I left Calcutta with the highest of hopes for the campaign. The presence of the *Queen Elizabeth* gave me confidence. So did the appointment of Sir Ian Hamilton. I had heard of the fifteen-inch guns of the new battleship and seen a picture of Sir Ian, besides knowing a little of his record in the Boer War. Sir Ian's handsome face and figure, set off by the picturesque Highland costume, inclined me all in his favour. I could not, however, follow the campaign at Kishorganj, because when there I never read any newspapers. But I thought of it day after day and even dreamt of it. I pondered over what I should have done had I been the commander-in-chief of the expedition and had no manner of doubt that I should have dictated a peace in Vienna.

There is only one other experience of the First World War that I shall set down in this book. At the end of 1914 I began to notice in the Eden Gardens and on the Maidan the presence of British soldiers of a new and very attractive type, who not only wore a more pleasant shade of khaki, but were also very much younger and more refined looking than the old Regulars. I also saw in Father Prior's room postcards with photographs of young soldiers of the same type. Of course, they represented the best of the youthful generation of England of those days, which had been drawn upon for the Territorials and Kitchener's New Army, but as in Calcutta we never saw really young Englishmen, these boyish soldiers, seen either in the flesh or in photographs, made an immense appeal to me. Their usually solemn expression suggested a dreamy unworldliness which I had not expected on European faces, and I did not associate this quality with the idea of death. I had no suspicion then that these young men, whom it was so natural and so easy to idealize, were to contribute their share to the decline of English greatness by dying in their thousands on the dull battlefields of France. I learned afterwards that there was one man who had been disquieted by this fear, had tried to prevent the senseless slaughter, but had failed. Appalled by the blood toll that was extorted he set his face against a repetition of the sacrifice in a second war. This time he succeeded, although at the price of being misunderstood by a stupid section of his countrymen and slandered by malicious allies. But even so he could not prevent the turning of a second great victory into a second great defeat.

I must now revert to politics. Malice was having its day with us. In its simple form it was an unashamed gloating on the torture and suffering of small and weak nations whose only crime was to have been defended by the rulers of India. The sophisticated form of the malice let itself go in ready sneers and voluble lectures, in the best Hindu style, on the bankruptcy of European civilization, its spiritual poverty, and its moral iniquity. This repulsive exhibition of vanity and self-righteous-ness roused Tagore to indignant protest, and he put it in one of the noblest poems he ever wrote, the poem bearing the number thirty-seven in his *Valaka*. He rebuked the indifference and shoddiness of spirit, and the moral insensitiveness posing as moral elevation, which could listen from afar to the raging tempest of death and, with perfect assurance of safety, triumph in mean fault-finding.

By the end of 1915 open political agitation was showing signs of a revival, and a little later it was to grow into the Home Rule Movement led by Mrs. Besant. But it was still not this, but the revolutionary movement which was being felt by us as the most assertive political force in the country. I could observe its unseen influence playing on all the boarders as soon as I came to the Oxford Mission hostel. Some of them were whispered to be revolutionaries, or anarchists as we called them in those days, some were alleged to be spies. One young man was specially singled out as a spy and cursed in an undertone whenever he appeared at the door of his room. The charge of espionage against him rested mainly on the fact that he was the brother of a murdered police officer.

It was towards the end of 1914 that the famous Mussalmanpara bomb outrage took place. For us its special sensation lay in the circumstance that the young man put on trial for this attack was no other than the fellow-boarder who had come to persuade my brother to shut the door against Father Prior. The bomb was aimed at one of the most efficient and therefore best hated Bengali officers of the political police, who ultimately was run down by the inexorable vendetta on one of the main streets of Calcutta. On this occasion, however, the bomb missed him, and our fellow-boarder was found lying unconscious in a very severely wounded condition in one of the lanes close by. The defence tried to make out that he had found himself by accident at the door of the inspector when the bomb was thrown, and had been wounded by the explosion. The story sounded improbable even to us who wanted the case against him to fail. But the young man was acquitted, thanks largely to the evidence of one of the Fathers of the Oxford Mission who was cited as defence witness. Certain rooms of the hostel were searched after the outrage, and it was only the influence of the missionaries which averted a general search and the arrest of several other boarders. Father Prior said to me in a tone of relief the day after the search, "I'm glad, Nirad, I did not get any acid for you." He had promised to procure for me some sulphuric acid, whose sale was controlled under the Explosive Act, when I had told him that my electrical experiments were being held up for want of some acid to make a battery.

In the next few months the tempo of the revolutionary activities quickened further, and we could plainly see that the police were failing to cope with it. But the counterstroke did not take long in coming. The Defence of India Act, almost the last important political measure of Lord Hardinge, at last succeeded in seizing the revolutionary movement by the throat. With it a new fear entered our lives. The ever-present likelihood of our getting unwittingly mixed up with revolutionary activities or being pounced upon by the police unawares and detained without trial immensely strengthened the earlier sensation of having two unseen malevolent worlds about us. Quite a large number of young men among my friends, acquaintances, and relations were interned, and a larger number found their names on the black list of the police. The fate of a fellow-boarder in the Oxford Mission hostel was particularly tragic. He was detained for some time, and ultimately committed suicide to spare his family police persecution on his account.

My brother and I were able to avoid coming to harm in this queer world of revolutionary activities and police persecution.

But their shadow fell immediately and fatally on a little contraption of military associations which my younger brother and I had made. In one of the vacations I had shown this brother of mine how to make a heliograph instrument. Our first model was very crude, being made of bamboo. But when I came home for the next vacation I was delighted to find that in the meanwhile my brother had made a more elaborate and accurate instrument with which we could signal to a distance of about a mile. As we were experimenting with the instrument on the outskirts of the town, a private of the 16th Rajputs, who had replaced the 91st at Kishorganj, felt greatly interested and coming forward showed us how to signal in the morse code. Later he became very friendly with my brother. But when I was at home for yet another vacation and was one day sitting with my father in his office, in walked the sepoy. He looked very grave and even frightened, and told my father that his havildar (sergeant) had reported against him for helping Bengali school-boys engaged in making bombs and ammunition. He explained his connexion with the heliograph instrument and requested my father to destroy it there and then, for, he argued, if by any chance the complaint was followed up and the heliograph instrument found in our house, both he and the boys would be in for trouble. My father told me to bring the instrument to him and when I had done so broke it before my eyes.

At the beginning of 1916 Lord Hardinge was due to leave India. We appreciated his last kick, as we called the Defence of India Act, and speculated on his successor. I personally felt that the situation called for a Viceroy of real genius, and I often remarked to my friends, "I wish they would send out Winston Churchill." I knew that Mr. Churchill was out of office, and had an unbounded admiration for him even then. The admiration rested partly on what little I knew of his work at the Admiralty, more on his association with the Sidney Street affair, and, above all, on the impression made on me by a picture in the

Illustrated London News showing him talking to Lord Fisher. It was the bust of Napoleon on Mr. Churchill's desk which inclined me most in his favour. I did not know then how unpractical it was to expect an English politician of the first rank to come out to India, but even now I think there was something in my boyish idea. A man of genius sent out by England to India would have responded adequately to the challenge of the situation, irrespective of his political views. A Churchill would have taken instantaneous measure of the realities and either gone forward to meet the nationalist movement half-way in good time, or broken it for ever. But India had no Viceroy of genius after Lord Curzon. Hardinge, Reading, and Willingdon were clever men, who succeeded in stealing a few marches on the nationalists. They may be compared to very experienced old foxes, who from time to time add to the fox tribe's record of neat dodges in its eternally losing contest with the tribe of hounds. But they were not the grand animals to scatter the pack with a roar and a rush. Not for a single moment between 1905 and 1945 did the British Government in India succeed in wresting the initiative from the nationalists, although at quite a number of junctures that could easily have been done.

I have to add that the announcement of Lord Chelmsford's appointment as Viceroy came to me as an anticlimax after all my expectations. An utterly obscure person, I thought, a mere Governor of a minor province in Australia. His family name seemed familiar for I had heard of an English barrister called Thesiger. Could the new Viceroy be anybody related to that Thesiger, I wondered. Of course, I soon learned that he was.

POLITICS FADES AND COMES BACK

Towards the middle of 1916 certain new interests began to push away politics and the war from the foreground of my consciousness, and though the great events of the next two years, both inside and outside India, stirred some old chords, they did so as if only with the dampers falling instantaneously. The diversion began with a family event, the marriage of my sister. Marriages may be personal events in the West, with us they are family events, and if anybody denies that there can be drama and romance in such marriages he should come and see for himself what the demoniac energy and meddlesomeness of third parties can make of the union of passive firsts and seconds. Here is literally a case of *tertius gaudens,* but the other two are compelled to share the joy.

The tremendous excitement over my sister's wedding had its natural reaction in a spell of low spirits lasting some months. But towards the end of the year another adventure befell us. My father decided to send the whole family to Calcutta to live there for the time being, while he himself remained behind at Kishorganj to carry on his profession. The reason was my younger brother's political scrapes. He was getting more and more involved in revolutionary activities. I had suspected this all along. He had come to meet my brother and me at the railway station when we were coming home for my sister's wedding, and while walking over the sands of the Brahmaputra with me he suddenly began to talk about the growth of revolutionary activities in our parts. I made some brusque and contemptuous remarks in reply, never suspecting that he could have any personal feeling about this matter. He surprised me, however, by remarking very quietly and yet firmly, "But surely there can be no constructive work without the preliminary destruction of obstacles." I was startled, for although only two years older than he I looked upon him as a mere child and never expected any kind of formed opinions in him, and, far less, of course, any standing up to my confident airing of views, I being the acknowledged doctrinaire of the family. I scanned him from head to foot and made a mental note that I must clear up this matter after reaching home. What I learned there made me really anxious. I was told that one day a dagger and some other equally dubious articles had been found in his drawer by my father, and he had been given a whipping. But in the bustle and excitement of my sister's wedding I forgot this affair, and for the time being the same excitement also kept my brother engaged and out of mischief.

When I went back to Calcutta everything seemed to be right, but apparently after our coming away my brother reverted to his political activities. When my father came down to Calcutta at the end of the year he told me that the senior officer of the Intelligence Branch at Kishorganj had spoken very seriously to him and advised him to remove my brother from the town and from the influence of his revolutionary companions. The officer, my father added, had been very sympathetic and had said that if he could help it he would not bring the family under a cloud and harm the prospects of the other boys by arresting my younger brother, but that he expected my father in his turn to co-operate with him and try to wean the boy from his revolutionary proclivities. My father had agreed.

The family came to Calcutta in January 1917, and for a whole year we kept so close a watch on the young revolution-ary that there was not a single minute in the whole twenty-four hours when he was not under surveillance. One day, however, he unaccountably disappeared and did not turn up again till after three or four hours. My elder brother suspected that he had gone to meet some old associate of his who had come from Kishorganj, and our suspicions were deepened when on his return he refused to disclose where he had been. My mother gave him a number of chances to make a confession, and only when he remained obstinately silent, decided that he should be given a whipping. As my father was not present the unpleasant task of punishing the boy fell to my elder brother. My mother and I held him down, and my brother began. At first the boy resisted, but he was held down too firmly to be able to move. It was like whipping a chained dog, and as weal after weal appeared on his back, he began first to moan, then to slobber and twist, and at last sank on the floor exhausted. My mother, who had seen the whole business through without flinching, had him cleansed and washed, put him to bed, and walked away with the same firmness she had shown during the whipping. The boy lay as if in a swoon for something like four hours, and then slept well into the next day. My mother never again referred to the incident, and I had not the stomach to ask her.

After that I do not think my younger brother again thought of revolutionary activities, and by 1918 it was evident that he had been completely weaned. But his own reform was not the end of the story for him. In the summer of 1919, having gone to visit him in the hostel of the Oxford Mission where he was living, I found his room locked. I waited but he was not back even by the time the hostel gate was closed for the night. I went home in great anxiety, and spoke to my elder brother. We went to his hostel again in the morning to find his room still locked. At about nine o'clock, however, we saw him coming in. He said that he had been taken to the headquarters of the Special Branch to be examined and photographed there and been kept in detention for twenty-four hours.

More trouble was in store for him in later life. After completing his medical education in Calcutta he wanted to go to Europe, and he was very keen on going to the Pasteur Institute in Paris for advanced training in bacteriology. But he could not obtain a passport, for the police would not give him a clean bill. His dossier had got mixed up with that of a more active revolutionary with a similar name, and all kinds of sensational revolutionary crimes, like robbery and shooting, were laid at his door. My brother was, however, a man of determination. He was resolved to go, and he went in the end.

One day he received a wholly unexpected offer to be taken on as the doctor of a ship whose medical officer had died suddenly, and he sailed the very next day. He could do so without a passport, because no passports were required for mere voyages. But on reaching New York he took out a regular passport from the British Consulate there, and he completed his medical education at Vienna and Tubingen. This brother of mine is now one of the leading physicians of Calcutta. He is happy in this position, and perhaps happier still in the recollection of his feat of outwitting the police.

I appeared at my B.A. examination in 1918, and after that accompanied the family to Kishorganj. This vacation was remarkable for two things: first, for a very successful performance of one of Tagore's allegorical plays by us the brothers and sisters; and, secondly, for the total collapse in an earthquake of the house in which we were living. One of the unlooked-for participants in the play was my college friend Pankaj Siddhanta. One morning, when I was sitting on the steps of the front door before the others were up, I saw a young man coming towards me. He was followed by a coolie with a suitcase on his head. So little was the visitor expected that it took me a little time to convince myself that the person who looked so much like Pankaj Siddhanta was Pankaj himself. He came up and said in his most natural manner, which always showed an admixture of self-confidence with diffidence, "I thought I might as well pay you a visit." That he should have been able to make his way from Calcutta to Kishorganj with all the changes from train to steamer, steamer to train, and train to train was a marvel; but if anybody could be expected to accomplish it, it was Pankaj, for he was a genius both in bungling and bungling through.

My acquaintance with him dated from 1914, when both of us became boarders in the hostel of the Oxford Mission, but the acquaintance was not made in a conventional manner. One morning, when I was reading in my room, I saw a young man standing at the door, smiling hesitantly. He saw that I was taking notice of him and walked in, saying, "You are a first-year student, so am I. May I take a look round your room?" I did not have to say "Yes" for him to begin handling whatever objects on the table or on the shelves took his fancy. "Ah," he said, taking up a bottle of Burroughs Wellcome's Hazeline Snow, "I see you use cosmetics. May I put some of it on my face?" Then he made a liberal use of the cream. I was too delighted to be brought into contact with such a character to object, and after he was gone only hoped that he would come again. He did so very shortly, and gave an even better exhibition of his unconventionality. Carrying out a more searching examination of my belongings, he discovered a pot of jam and asked me what it was. I said briefly that it was jam. He asked again, "What is jam?" I replied that it was something to eat. "With rice?" he inquired. "No, no," I explained, "it is eaten either with bread or even by itself." "By itself? Then may I have a little of it?" He helped himself, and after that asked if he could take a spoonful or two more. I had no objection. Then he noticed another bottle on one of the shelves. It was a bottle of German mineral water which I was being made to take at the time. "Is that also something which can be taken?" "Yes," I replied, "but it is a medicinal water which is very unpleasant to take." Pankaj looked closely at me and did not believe me. He thought I did not want him to take this water because he had already eaten up so much of my jam, and was trying to put him off with a fib. So he said, "I think I shall try some of this also." He was allowed to, and soon got a demonstration of my truthfulness, although the cost was mine, for he made the room very messy. Last of all, he took another spoonful of the jam in order to get rid of the taste of the mineral water in his mouth, and went out.

Pankaj always did his best to live up to the initial prestige he had acquired in my eyes. But there were few other young men with whom I became more intimate or whom I respected as much. For with all his oddity, Pankaj was dreadfully earnest in the pursuit of intellectual truth. He read and talked about the most recondite things, and once, when he was in the fourth-year class, went for a lecture of Mrs. Naidu's in which she had gushed with her usual sentimentality and superficiality about Indian civilization. Pankaj put his opinion of Mrs. Naidu's lecture in a review and got it published in the college magazine. The students were furious. They printed and circulated a broadsheet with a devastating lampoon on Pankaj. As there were references in the review to some highly specialized historical studies on ancient India, of which, not being a student of history, Pankaj was not expected to have any knowledge, and as also my intimacy with him was well known, I became an object of secondary suspicion to the students. But Pankaj took it all with the same smiling and shy unconcern as he showed towards everything said for or against him.

So I was very glad to have Pankaj at Kishorganj and took him in. Within a few minutes he produced an additional proof of his resourcefulness. He opened his suitcase, took out a book, and tossing it over to me said, "Here's something I have been reading in the train." It was Amiel's *Journal Intime* in Mrs. Humphry Ward's translation. Pankaj explained that he had borrowed it from the Bengali assistant station-master of Tangi Junction, whose acquaintance he had made while waiting for his train on the lonely platform of that half-wild place. Whatever remarkable things Tangi might have seen in its later history–I believe it came to possess a very large airfield in the Second World War– the meeting on its platform between a potential lender of Amiel's journal in the person of the assistant station-master and a potential borrower in the person of Pankaj and the offhand completion of the transaction must be reckoned as the most queerly memorable event.

As interested as ever in his surroundings, Pankaj soon discovered a flowered kimono in the house and promptly decided that this was the garment in which he would show to his best advantage at Kishorganj. He played his part in the kimono and went about in it until he became an object of amused inquisitiveness in the neighbourhood. But he was also becoming the object of a more dangerous inquisitiveness. The political police noticed the presence of an unrelated young man in our house and began to make inquiries of my father, who felt some anxiety because the police were quite equal to putting Pankaj under arrest, for their code forbade their taking at its purely social value the purposeless visit of one young man to other young men. My father asked me to convey a warning to Pankaj, which I did, but he did not take the matter very seriously. He even accompanied us when we went on a short visit to our village, which was on the black-list of the police for conspiratorial activities. As chance would have it, or there may have been something other than chance in it, the very morning after our arrival the police inspector of our area rode into the courtyard of our Banagram house. Standing on the south varanda of the Hut under the Bakul Tree I watched the dismounting of the ominous khaki-clad figure. My old uncle received him and, leading him to the hut, introduced my brother and me to him. The inspector happened to know my father very well and professed to be very pleased to make the acquaintance of his friend's bright sons. He talked quite naturally and affably, but we who had been taught to look upon every police officer, even though a close relative, as a spy and a potential prosecutor, answered him with the utmost circumspection. While this game of conversational chess was going on Pankaj burst into the hut, gleefully shouting the news he had just read in the papers that Mrs. Besant had been released. I tried to retrieve the situation by replying very coolly, "Oh, she has been?" But we looked at the police inspector, the police inspector looked at us, then he looked very deliberately and, as it seemed to us, very "professionally" at Pankaj, and for the next quarter of an hour or so the conversation dragged on with the most uncomfortable self-consciousness on the part of all of us.

On our return to Kishorganj my father sent for Pankaj and told him that in the meanwhile the officer in charge of the Intelligence Branch had definitely recommended Pankaj's departure from the town. Pankaj promised to go, but he put off his going from day to day. At last my brother and I decided to take the matter in hand. One morning, after Pankaj had got up, I called two of my younger brothers and told them that Pankaj Babu was going away that night and they had better pack his things up. Poor Pankaj could not say no, but he remarked deprecatingly that there was no hurry about packing. But my brothers, taking the hint from me, went on quietly packing up Pankaj's suitcase. Word went round that Pankaj Babu was leaving by the night train, and when he went out on his afternoon visit to the friends he had made in the town they asked him if that was so. Pankaj shot an angry glance at us and said, "Ask them, they know best." But at last the entry of a hackney carriage into our yard after dinner made him throw up the sponge and dress. He was escorted to the station by the three of us brothers, and put into the train. We did not leave the station until the train had got into motion for fear of Pankaj coming back to us like a cat taken out of the house in a sack and cast off. Our oriental standards of hospitality had withered sadly under the shadow of police persecution.

Some weeks later my elder brother and the brother next to me left for Calcutta. I remained behind waiting for the news of my examination. It was at this time that an earthquake brought down our house. On 9th July, at about four in the afternoon, I was reading in bed, and the book was *The Woman in White*. My mother was chatting with a neighbour on the veranda, and my unmarried sister was with her. I could not follow their conversation, for it was reaching me only as a low hum. All of a sudden the bed under me began to quiver violently. I at first thought that I had unconsciously been shaking my legs and communicating the vibration to the bed, but looking above I saw the walls swaying in and out. My immediate impulse was to go under the heavy bed and take shelter there, but resisting it I jumped down on the floor, which I felt creeping under me. I no longer asked myself any questions but seemed to have assumed as a matter of course that I was going through an earthquake. I stood with my face towards the inner door and saw my mother rushing in through it, with my sister clinging to her and shrieking. She was coming in to take out my youngest brother, who was in the next room down with fever. I shouted and waved to her to go out, but, later, she told me that she had neither seen nor heard me. As soon as I saw my mother going out again with my brother in her arms and my sister still clinging to her, I turned round and ran out by the front door. I was just able to reach the edge of the road, which was about three yards from the western end of the house, when I found that I could walk no longer. It was becoming difficult even to remain standing. So I tried to balance myself with outstretched arms and spread-out legs. While I was in this unsteady posture an utterly new kind of scene began to sink into my consciousness wholly of its own sharpness. There was a low all-pervading rumble, but it seemed to be part of a vast preternatural and unconquerable silence by which that familiar and reassuring source of sound, the human voice, had been wholly stifled. Men were running about, but everything was unreal and trancelike, although intolerably distinct. The earth was quivering without interruption, but its progress towards destruction appeared to be agonizingly slow. I saw the north wall of our house coming down, and could note every stage of its descent from the roof level to the ground as if the collapse were being demonstrated from a very slow-moving cinema projector. I also saw the blocks of fallen masonry roll across the lawn like croquet balls, but just at that moment I fell down and became unconscious for some moments. It was only because the roll was north and south and I was standing a little to the west of the house that I was not crushed by the masonry, which was carried fifty feet from the house in a northerly direction.

Regaining consciousness, I ran round the ruins to the back of the house to find out what had happened to my mother and the others. They were crouching against the bamboo screen but were safe and unhurt. The corrugated-iron roof of the veranda had become embedded in the ground and, acting as a containing wall, prevented the debris from reaching them. But the rose bushes had been crushed. The visiting lady implored me to find out what had happened to her children, and I also suddenly recollected the book which had been in my hand before the earthquake. I distinctly remembered having gone out with it, but running back to the place where I had fallen down I could not find it. Then I thought it might have dropped from my hand and been buried under the house. Actually, even in that catastrophe, somebody had had the presence of mind to steal it. I had to pursue the loss of the book, because it was not mine but belonged to the public library. One of my brothers retrieved it from a house in the neighbourhood a year later.

I found the neighbour's children jumping about and shouting in boisterous high spirits. They were very young, and were in great glee at the wonderful sight they had seen, and had not been frightened at all, because their house, being made of bamboo, had come to no harm and, as they said, had only been curtseying. I ran back and gave the news to their mother. By that time my father had also arrived from the court. He had only one shoe on, his other foot was in its sock, for he had been resting his leg when the earthquake began, and never even remembering his shoe he had run to the house, crying, "It has come down." He was so relieved to find the family safe that he almost cried and, carrying the younger children one by one to the office hut, which was still standing, he put them down on the big bed, covered them up with whatever sheets or other clothes he could lay his hands on, and patted each of them, repeating all the while, "Go to sleep, go to sleep."

The sequel to the earthquake was great discomfort for the family for some months, which I shall not and need not describe. The only other thing which remains to be said in this chapter is that politics, despite all its reminders, remained in a state of suspended animation with me during this period. But it reasserted all its old hold with the coming of the passive resistance movement led by Mahatma Gandhi and its suppression in the summer of 1919.

CHAPTER IV

INITIATION INTO SCHOLARSHIP

THIS CHAPTER has certainly been presumptuously titled, for I never became a scholar. But every true scholar will forgive me, for he knows it as well as I do that the greater part of his *metier* is the capacity for experiencing the emotion of scholarship. Without this there is no genuine scholarship but only juggling with books for the sake of making money in a small way or a career of sorts. When, as a student, I read in one of Lord Morley's essays Mark Pattison's saying that the product of study was not the book but the man, I was awakened to a new understanding of the nature of learning. It made me conscious of the interrelatedness of personality and scholarship, and if today I have anything to add it is only the complementary proposition that scholarship itself is the product of personal temperament and what it brings to personality is only temperament returned to temperament in the form of an embodied activity.

I believe I possessed, and perhaps still possess, this temperament. Otherwise I should not have had even as a young student those strong emotions about scholarship in all its aspects which I always experienced. For instance, I should not have been impelled so involuntarily to give my reverence to the great medievalists–Stubbs, Round, Vinogradoff, Maitland in England; Quicherat, Fustel de Coulanges, Monod, Luchaire, Camille Juilian in France; Waitz in Germany. I should not have felt that fascination for palaeography, diplomatics, and textual criticism which even without being able to account for it I always felt. I should not have thought that the editing of one text with elegant finality would be a creditable achievement for a decade's hard work. The contribution of a volume or two to a collection like the great *Acta Sanctorum* of the Bollandists, or the *Rolls Series,* or the *Corpus Inscriptionum Latinarum* would not have appeared to me as the very summit of ambition and happiness. I should not have pondered for months whether to give my projected collection the form of a *corpus* or a *regesta.* I should not have longed to be a student of the Ecole des Chartes or of the Ecole Pratique des Hautes Etudes. And, finally, I should not have swallowed complete sets of the *English Historical Review* and of the *Revue Critique* as others swallow light novels, without being a specialist in any of the subjects treated in these periodicals or even intending to become one. It was scholarship in itself which interested me, and I felt irresistibly attracted by the history and methodology of every branch of learning.

It was only after I had experienced all these emotions and put for ever behind me the opportunity for making a success of my academic career that I really became aware of what I had set my heart on. In 1921 I read for the first time Anatole France's *Sylvestre Bonnard,* and in the book I recognized my ideal self mellowed and matured by age. I remember to have read somewhere, probably in Brousson's malicious reminiscences, that in later life Anatole France spoke slightingly of his first literary success. Perhaps the crowning by the Academy gave him a distaste for the book. But he was unfair, whatever the reason for his dislike. There is more in the story of the old scholar than its pleasantly sentimental atmosphere, just as there is in *Thais* more than the unpleasantly sentimental, though more fashionable, theme of a prostitute's redemption. *Sylvestre Bonnard* is the expression in literary art of the emotion of scholarship. I was capable of this emotion although I was not able to become the scholar I wanted to be. This chapter relates the story of the failure, but at the same time of the growth of the scholarly temperament in me.

FROM GROPING TO CERTAINTY

When I passed out of school the goal of the next stage of my educational progress had already become fixed. People had told me, and I had decided in my mind, that I was going to be a professor. Of course, I knew also that whether I could be one would depend on my academic record. But that in its turn depended less on chance and circumstances than on my own efforts. So far there was certainty, which was a fact exceptional in my case, for among us, the Bengali gentry, a boy went from school to university as a matter of course and selected his vocation, or, what was more common, had it selected for him, quite casually at the end of his academic career. Even my brother did not have his future so definitely chalked out before him as I had mine.

Beyond this point, however, everything was vague. I did not know what I should be a professor in, although I was pretending to have a greater liking for history than for any other subject. So, for my intermediate course (which in Calcutta University came between the school course and the university course proper and was really a higher secondary stage), I took up history, Sanskrit, and chemistry as optional subjects besides English and Bengali, which were compulsory. But during the two years of this course I fell finally in love with history, and the influences contributory to it were one or two men and a number of books read and unread.

One of my teachers of history was Mr. Bipin Gupta, an established writer in Bengali and a man highly regarded for his learning as well as for his style. He was a small and dark man with sharp features, set off by a moustache of military suggestion and large piercing eyes. He was very quiet and deliberate

in his speech and movements, and his wit and irony and
lightness of touch, which were such pronounced qualities of
his writings, could not even be suspected in his lecture-room
manner. He could paralyse into immobile silence a whole
crowd of turbulent freshers by a mere glance of his eyes. He
taught us Greek and Roman history, and one day he mentioned
Bury and Sir Arthur Evans incidentally but with such an
indefinable intensity of expression that these two men became
almost heroes to me. I never made Mr. Gupta's personal
acquaintance, but in the class in his extremely detached manner
he seemed to make an unmentioned favourite of me. My
respect for him made me respect history.

The other man who influenced me on the side of history
was a greater stranger personally, and it will be with surprise
that his name will be heard from me. He was Professor T. R.
Glover. He came to Calcutta early in 1915, and lectured in
Overtoun Hall, the hall of the Y.M.C.A. I was taken to his
lectures for the first day by Father Prior and felt so interested
that I went by myself afterwards. I could not understand the
lectures properly, not only because Professor Glover's subject
and exposition were above me, but also because at the time I
could not wholly follow English as spoken by Englishmen.
None the less the impression he made on me was profound. He
left implanted in me an ineradicable interest in early Christianity and the Roman Empire.

As for the books, the most decisive influence on me was
certainly the *Constitutional History* of Stubbs, with Green's
Short History of the English People and Mommsen's *History
of Rome* following at some remove. I hardly know what made
me read Stubbs week after week, month after month, when I
could not understand three-quarters of him. It was not accounted for by the craze for constitutional history and law
which prevailed in our midst. Educated Indians with their
newly acquired sense of politics took to these subjects as ducks

take to water, and only too many of them would have liked above everything else to have been, if not Jeffersons, at least Sieyeses. The respective merits of federal and unitary constitutions, the pros and cons of separating the judiciary from the executive, and similar questions were discussed among us with a thoroughness which would have bludgeoned into stupor persons with no natural inclination towards them. I also had an innate dislike for purely legal and morphological political speculation and avoided it. Yet I stuck to Stubbs.

The immediate occasion for my taking him up was simple. I was reading about feudalism in England in the class, and the lecturer was giving me an account which struck me as oversimplified. Tout's text-book, which we read, did not go very much deeper. So, looking for a more detailed account, I found Stubbs's work, about which I had already heard, in the college library and immediately borrowed the first volume. Given the knowledge of medieval institutions I possessed and the immaturity of my mental powers, I should have been driven away by Stubbs after breaking my teeth on him, and if I was not, even after breaking my teeth, it was to be explained only by the taste of the emotion of scholarship I found in the book.

The attraction of Green and Mommsen for me was due to the literary quality of their histories. I borrowed Green from the public library at Kishorganj. Mommsen was given to me by Father Prior from the large library of his mission. At that age, however, Green's charm was more obvious to me than Mommsen's. Green appeared to have a Keats-like delicacy and provided a complete contrast to the erudite massiveness I felt in Mommsen. With me Mommsen became a real favourite only a year or two later, although even on first acquaintance he was able to transmit his Caesarism to me, so that, asked in my intermediate examination to justify or condemn Caesar's assumption of dictatorship, I wrote magniloquently, "If Caesar was false to the constitution, he was true to Rome," forgetting that this was the shoddy plea for every shoddy coup d'etat.

Now comes the more curious part of the story. A small number of books, which even yet I have not seen and about which I had only read, stirred my imagination so deeply in my early college days that they may be reckoned as very powerful influences on my intellectual growth. The first two of them were Beloch's *Griechische Geschichte* and Busolt's work with the same title. I had learnt their names from the article on Greek history in the *Encyclopaedia Britannica*. Both the books, and more particularly Busolt's work, seemed to me to be the very model of what every historical work should be. I gathered that Busolt had given the source of every fact stated by him, discussed all the evidence and every view on every point in dispute or doubt, and provided a complete critical apparatus. That, to my thinking, was the perfection of historical writing. I did not think any the worse of Busolt because he had covered only a fragmentary section of Greek history. No serious student could do more. I raved so continuously about Busolt and Beloch to my friends that one of them, a student senior to me who regarded me with great affection, always greeted me with *"Geskiske, Geskiske"*

A third book was Bernheim's *Lehrbuch der historischen Methode und der Geschichtsphilosophie,* about which I had come to know from Professor Shotwell's article in the *Encyclopaedia Britannica.* The description of the book given in the bibliography appended to that article made me feel that no student of history could afford not to read it, and I thought I should learn German only for the sake of reading this work. There were two other books mentioned in the same bibliography which also seemed very alluring. These two, however, I read at a later stage of my scholastic career. They were, first, *Introduction aux etudes historiques,* by Langlois and

Seignobos, and, secondly, *Manuel de bibliographie historique,* by Langlois.

Although I should not have been able to read these books even if I had come across them at the time, yet I was always on the look-out for them only for the sake of obtaining the satisfaction of a visual acquaintance. I liked, and still like, to contemplate the appearance, feel the texture, and weigh the mass of the books which I cannot read. I like even to smell them. So, half with a desire to show off and half in sincere eagerness to set my eyes on the books, I forgot common sense so far as to write down the titles of Busolt's and Bernheim's books on a slip of paper and send down my younger brother, a school student, to the Alimdad Public Library at Kishorganj to look for them.

Apart from these highly specialized interests I also acquired more general intellectual tastes. The compulsion of our humanistic culture of the nineteenth century was still strong. It was almost the last proddings of this compulsion which made my brother, when he had just entered the degree class of Calcutta University in 1914, buy Comte's *Positivism,* Mill's works, and some of Huxley's essays. My brother professed at times to be a rationalist, at others an agnostic. He spoke highly of all these men. At his instance I opened Comte, but was so thoroughly frightened by what I saw inside that I never read him, then or afterwards, although a little later Lord Morley and Frederic Harrison became great favourites with me. Mill and Huxley, on the other hand, I greatly liked. It was from one of Mill's essays that I first learned of Alfred de Vigny and his three masterly stories of the grandeur and servitude of military life. The chastening beauty of a story like *Laurette ou le cachet rouge* destroyed in me all taste for such obvious and overdone anti-war propaganda as Remarque's, which became so fashionable in the intellectually and aesthetically debilitated inter war years. Through Huxley I acquired that interest in evolutionary biology which I have still retained.

Although I never made a study of the positivist system, I believe it was the influence of positivism absorbed by our culture that led all of us to feel so great an interest in universal knowledge and made us conscious that there were different types of knowledge. Some of my college fellows, my brother, and I frequently discussed the relative merits of the encyclopaedic or polymathic mind and the mind of the specialist. Someone would ask, "Who were the most encyclopaedic minds at the end respectively of the seventeenth, eighteenth, and nineteenth centuries?" Another would reply, "Leibnitz, Goethe, but hardly anyone at the end of the nineteenth century because of the growth of specialization." Those of us who were interested at all in the question almost without exception declared for the encyclopaedic type. "Synthesis" was our magic word. This tendency was reinforced in us not only by our belief that the Hindu outlook on life was "synthetic", but also by the presence in our midst of a figure of fabulous learning. He was Professor Brajendranath Seal, who in our time held the George V Chair in Philosophy in Calcutta University. Legend had it that he knew every subject equally well. Although his literary output was small everybody stood in profound awe of it, particularly as exemplified in his New Essays in Criticism. In actual fact, too, he was very learned. I, however, did not like him, or rather I disliked his style and manner, which I found intolerably ponderous and even uncouth. Thus, as soon as I had gained a little scholastic confidence, I began very irreverently to call him Elephant Seal, for physically, too, he was very large.

But even without being able to share the prevailing admiration for Professor Seal, I was in complete sympathy with the type of learned man he was. I also wanted to be an epitome of universal knowledge, and perhaps there was in my lack of enthusiasm for him a not very creditable element, a streak of jealousy. I could not, of course, be jealous of him as he was, but I did not relish at all the stories which were always being told to us of him as a youthful prodigy of learning. I had this feeling of retrospective rivalry for every established scholar of my young days, and the scholar and linguist, Harinath De, who was another legendary figure among us but who had died in 1910 or 1911, was another object of my callow envy.

For all that, I could not hide from myself that to be something like them was in my estimation to be something very great indeed, and my leanings towards encyclopaedic knowledge were disclosing themselves in every intellectual activity I undertook. In the first place, what I was primarily interested in even as a boy was the meaning and purpose of existence, and since existence had many facets my intellectual interests also became many-sided. Even without my being aware of its deep springs, my appetite for information and explanation became as varied as my mental dentition became versatile. I could pass from physics to Sanskrit literature or from novels to astronomy with an agility which seemed like volatility to those who did not know me well. On account of this I came to be called "Jack of all trades, master of none" by those who did not like me and my ways. To them I appeared like a squid or octopus of the world of knowledge. But they forgot that even a squid was not all tentacles and suckers, and my intellectual nucleus was certainly more solid than the body of the unlovely cephalopod.

Secondly, I was always very anxious to ascertain the position of any subject I was studying in the whole field of knowledge. I was not less interested in the question of its descent, filiation, and affliations than in itself. Thus I was perpetually probing round a particular subject in order to discover its limits, and most often discovered that it had none, for it appeared to be shading off on all sides into kindred subjects and disciplines, so that as a specific subject it seemed to possess no self-sufficiency. Perhaps I was unconsciously influenced in my attitude towards knowledge by my fondness for systematic zoology or taxonomy, of which I had already picked up a rudimentary notion in the zoological galleries of the Indian Museum. These gave me a demonstration in advance of the proposition I learned later from evolutionary biology that no particular form of life could be marked off from other forms in an absolutely clean-cut manner. At all events, my attitude towards knowledge was similar to my attitude towards the animal world. Knowledge no less than animals appeared to me to be divided into varieties, races, species, genera, families, orders and so forth, and all this variety seemed to be cemented together by an unbreakable living chain.

On account of this pronounced bias of mind I could not limit myself to the subject or portion of a subject set for me for the time being, but would immediately get busy with examining its bearings. I took the cue in this matter from my brother, who was a more thorough practitioner of the method. When studying the two plays of Shakespeare set for his B.A. examination he consulted every edition available in Calcutta, including the Variorum Edition of Furness, and read whatever criticism, contemporary or old, he could lay his hands on. He followed the same method with Milton, and read not only Mark Pattison and Raleigh but also the monumental biography by Masson. He was always collecting for himself, and also bringing to me, the tidings of all that had been said or written about any novel, poem or play, and from this information the conviction grew on me that not even the shortest lyric stood in cold isolation. Nothing with a place in literary history could remain incognito in our company.

Appropriately enough, the eleventh edition of the *Encyclopaedia Britannica* continued to be my mainstay in this absorbing exploration of the interrelatedness of all knowledge, and from it, in addition to acquiring the notion of correlation, I also acquired the bibliographical flair. I always read the bibliographical notes given at the end of the articles very carefully, and came to realize that before one could begin the study of any subject the essential preliminary was a knowledge of the most important books on it. What was even more valuable, I discovered that while certain books were indispensable for the study of a subject, at the same time each one of them very definitely dated, that is to say, instead of possessing an absolute value it constituted a particular landmark in the development of the subject and represented the state of knowledge or a substantial advance at a particular point of time. In other words, I acquired the sense of the relativity of knowledge. I also acquired the capacity to compile bibliographies of the subjects I was interested in, and make them not only representative of the best knowledge on it but also indicative of its historical development. This power enabled me to air an amused superciliousness towards those fellow-students who tried to hide the names of books they were reading from me. This secretiveness was a failing very common among our good students. It was after coming to Calcutta that I found ordinary schoolboys crediting the so-called "good boys" with quite a discreditable fund of jealousy. The attribution was not unjust. There was a student in our hostel who used to borrow books from my brother. Other students told me that he was very particular about keeping secret the names of the books he read. With a contemptuous toss of the chin I observed: "Does he think it takes more than five minutes to find out the names of all the books worth reading on any subject?"

It was bibliographical nose which gave me this confidence. I was as keen about mapping the world of knowledge as about studying any particular subject. Perhaps in the whole course of my life I have learnt nothing but the cartography of learning. In some ways this was inevitable. All unknown to me, even during the first two years of my gropings in the field of scholarship, an internal contradiction was crystallizing within me. On the one hand I was irresistibly drawn towards wide views, sweeping generalizations, and comprehension of wholes which were continually expanding into bigger and vaguer wholes; on the other I was beginning to feel the attraction of specialized scholarship and its methods. How this duality within my intellectual being came in the way of my academic success I shall have to relate presently.

It was only in the two years following my intermediate examination, which I passed in 1916, that I really understood the nature and methods of historical scholarship, and 1917 stands out as the decisive year in this process. But although I had entered a better college and passed into a more clearly perceived academic environment, it was not my university which contributed to the result. I shall not affect Gibbon's airy contempt for his alma mater and say, "To the University of Calcutta I acknowledge no obligation; and she will as cheerfully renounce me for a son, as I am willing to disclaim her for a mother." There were a number of professors, although not half a dozen in all, whose lectures I liked. Still, even they did not attract me strongly enough to become influences in any sense in the growth of my mind. As for the rest I paid no attention whatever to what they said and sat on one of the back-benches, either reading a book of my choice, or scribbling, or thinking my own thoughts. Speaking of later years, Calcutta University has had no occasion to claim me or even remember me, and I have had almost as little reason to recall it.

It was another institution, the Imperial Library, to which I owe nearly all my higher education. In it I came to realize the truth of Carlyle's saying, which I had read in one of the leaflets of the Everyman's Library, that "the true university of these

days is a collection of books." My brother introduced me to
the library. He had begun to go to it soon after his admission
to the B.A. class, but as the lowest age for admission to it was
eighteen I could not accompany him then. He promised to take
me later, and for two years, through his descriptions, the
Imperial Library was built up in my imagination as a place of
pilgrimage. The first visit, when it occurred, about the middle
of 1916, was no disappointment. The library was in the well-
known Metcalfe Hall, built by the citizens of Calcutta in
grateful remembrance of Sir Charles Metcalfe's liberal attitude
towards the Press in India. It was not a very large building, but
it was in the classical style, with Corinthian capitals for its
pillars, and stood gracefully conspicuous, opposite some ugly
wharves on the Hooghly River. The interior, two-storied, had
an air of lofty spaciousness, which was heightened by the
silence and, still more, by the whispered questions and answers. As I entered the large vestibule on the ground-floor the
staircase struck me as one of the handsomest things of its kind
I had ever seen. The reading room impressed me even more
deeply. It was large and high, had very tall windows, and,
within, there stood almost as tall open shelves along the walls.
These were not less than ten feet high, and in order to reach the
books on the upper shelves we had to use ladders. I had never
before seen so many books in such compact formation. The
collection in the reading-room, which was meant for reference
only, consisted of nearly four thousand volumes, and the whole
library at that date had something like or over a quarter of a
million. It was Lord Curzon who had made the library a State
institution, building it up round the nucleus provided by the
very unsatisfactory Calcutta Public library, and as its first
librarian, he had brought out a specialist from the British
Museum. Appropriately enough, there were some handsome
cases in the reading-room containing large and well-bound
folios and quartos given to the library by Lord Curzon. I

trembled from excitement when my brother took me round the reading-room shelves, pointing out to me what each contained. I could hardly take down a volume and hold it in my hand, and noticing this my brother smiled. The smell of the preservative on the leather and cloth of the books was also an excitant. The first work I took down was the library edition of Bury's *History of Greece.*

For some months after this first visit I went only occasionally to the library. But from April 1917 began a series of uninterrupted, regular, and almost daily visits which continued for some years. Neither the sun nor the rain could hold me back, and I did not use the public transport. I had my umbrella and my legs. In the three months of the summer vacation of 1917 I read every nineteenth-century and early twentieth-century classic of history, and made myself perfectly familiar with the history of historical writing. In this study Lord Acton and Dr. Gooch were my principal guides. For Lord Acton I developed a veneration which was almost idolatry, and as a personal loyalty this veneration is equalled in me only by my affection for Charlotte Bronte. I read through all the works of Lord Acton, including his letters. I also read everything published about him, and I do not think the account Lord Acton gave one night at Cannes of his projected history of freedom gave a greater thrill to Lord Bryce who listened to it, than Lord Bryce's account in his Contemporary Biography gave to me. I was shocked by Strachey's sneer about Lord Acton in his *Eminent Victorians,* and, in spite of my admiration for Strachey's brilliance, considered the remark very ill-natured and shallow.

All this reading of historical literature, together with my incursions into anthropology, which I began to study about the same time, left me, even at the end of the first three months, confirmed in the habit of thinking historically. I understood for the first time Professor Shotwell's remark in the article he had

contributed to the *Encyclopaedia Britannica* that the nineteenth century was the century of historical thought and that
the eleventh edition of this great work was itself an illustration
of the historical method. I discovered that nothing was either
complete or intelligible at one particular point of time without
a reference to its past, that is to say, its duration or history. In
the last few decades there has certainly been seen in Europe,
or at all events in England, a decline in historical knowledge,
accompanied by a pronounced recoil from the historical
attitude. This is a retrograde phenomenon, for if there is
anything which distinguishes man from the other animals it is
memory or consciousness of duration, and I cannot understand
how the European man, after having attained the high degree
of historical consciousness which he did in the nineteenth
century, can have stepped back from it to the uncultured man's
bondage to the present and the still more uncultured man's
bondage to the eschatology of political dogma. Yet what the
European man is displaying more often than not today is an
utter lack of the historical sense. I sometimes seek the solution
of the puzzle in that Spenglerian vision, the dreadful and tragic
Untergang des Abendlandes, the untimely decline of the
European peoples on their home continent, brought about by
an internal strife as insensate, as inescapable, and as suicidal as
that of the Greek cities. I ask myself: Are we witnessing a
whole society's senile decay of memory?

Besides the historical attitude, I also acquired during
these months an unshakable faith in historical integrity. When
most of my fellow-students and teachers appeared to think that
history existed only for the sake of exalting Indian nationalism,
I with all my love for my country came to regard a lapse from
historical rectitude as even more condemnable than a lapse
from moral conduct. Yet it was not my carefully fostered
moral sense but my intellect alone which led me to uphold
historical integrity with such unwavering determination. I

understood and sympathized with Lord Acton's exhortation to students of history not to debase the moral currency or to lower the standard of rectitude, but to try others by the final maxim that governs their own lives, and to suffer no man and no cause to escape the undying penalty which history has the power to inflict on wrong. My moral being adhered fanatically to this doctrine, but not my intellectual being. What I sought for and respected as a young student in historical investigation and writing was scientific truth, a truth whose claim on man in my opinion at the time transcended even that of morality.

It was a shock to my notion of historical integrity which provoked me to write my first original essay on an historical subject or, for that matter, on any subject, and, curiously enough, the provocation was given by a professor of mine whom I greatly admired and liked. Dr. Kalidas Nag, now a well-known figure in our academic circles, was then a young man and the youngest teacher of history in the Scottish Church College. He taught us ancient Indian history and was able to transmit to us his vigorous enthusiasm for his subject. He kept in touch with scholars of established reputation in this field, and brought to us the stimulating breath of the world of research. But one day towards the end of my term he unpremeditatedly let himself go in a manner which made me feel that he had a serious flaw in his scholarly constitution whose existence I had not suspected.

He did so before a member of the Calcutta University Commission presided over by Sir Michael Sadler, and the member was no less a person than Professor Ramsay Muir. The Calcutta University Commission came to visit our college at the end of 1917, and among the visitors two struck me forcibly by their appearance. One of them was Sir Michael, whose benign face I noticed particularly. The other man whose name I learned on subsequent enquiry had a severer but very intellectual countenance, and he was Professor Ramsay Muir.

One day early in January, when Professor Nag was lecturing to us, he suddenly walked into the class and quietly sat down on one of the back benches to listen to the lecture. Professor Nag, who was lecturing in his usual manner, immediately took to his wings and delivered a tremendous patriotic harangue, in which he compared the blood-thirstiness of Europeans with the tolerance and pacifism of the Hindus. Everything from the Sicilian Vespers to the Inquisition was dragged quite unnecessarily into this homily, and Professor Nag smilingly looked from side to side, obviously enjoying himself greatly. I felt angry and ashamed, and after the class went home in a boiling rage, and within a few minutes wrote down the draft of the last paragraph of the essay. Then at leisure I expanded it into a full-length composition. As the secretary of the College Historical Society had been asking me for a long time for a paper I offered it to him. He gladly accepted it, and it was read at a meeting of the society presided over by Dr. Nag himself. Dr. Nag, as enthusiastic about scholarly attainment as he had shown himself over patriotic duty, and, unconscious of the origin of the paper, praised it with a generous gusto which wholly disconcerted me. Pankaj Siddhanta, who knew how I had come to write it, however, displayed his usual indiscretion and told Professor Nag, when he was speaking well of the essay, that it had been directed against him. Professor Nag was very much surprised. But he could not understand what provocation he could have given me, and fortunately Pankaj had no time to enlighten him further. This information, apparently, made no difference to Professor Nag's opinion of me and my essay, for he went on urging me to print it in the college magazine. At that age, however, nothing frightened me more than the idea of appearing in print. I was quite determined not to make my debut in the realm of print with what I considered to be an immature essay, and I had a valid excuse for Professor Nag, for the paper had got temporarily lost under the debris of

our Kishorganj house, when it came down in the severe
earthquake I have spoken about. The paper was salvaged, and
my younger brothers scribbled their childish handwriting on its
back. It seems, however, to possess a knack for getting lost.
It was lost twice in later years, and after the second disappearance, which lasted two years, it was found again only in
1948. This recovery gives me the opportunity for reproducing
it. Of course it was written in English, the English of my
twentieth year.

A YOUTHFUL TESTAMENT

"The Objective Method in History

[Being an essay written by the author in January 1918,
when he was an undergraduate.]

"The subject of this paper may form a chapter either in a
manual or a history of historiography, and we who are
innocent of worrying about historical methods can justly ask
what kind of new acquaintance to expect from a very sounding
announcement.

"Everyone will have observed that the word 'history'
bears a double meaning. In the first place, it means the record
of events and phenomena which have happened in the world;
secondly, the events and phenomena themselves. So we make
a difference between history that is written and the history that
has taken place. The writing of history we call historiography.
I do not know if all of us have thought of how history is written.
That process has two stages. The first stage is to find our
original authorities, to examine and to criticize them and their
evidence. The second part of the work is the actual writing of
history. When all the facts are discovered the presentation of
the historical development depends upon the attitude of the
writer. It is here that the objective method touches the writing
of history, though it is not without some influence even on the

criticism and valuation of authorities. The attitude of the historian presupposes some philosophy of history. It is by its light that an author interprets events, gives his work a dominant tone or colour. When we have reached the question of attitude we are in a region where every navigator must make his own chart. The objective method is a chart which has guided many through dangerous shoals and rocks.

"If we choose to survey the historical literature of the world we can come across books which are cool in tone, impartial in statement, reserved in judgement. After reading them one cannot say that the author belonged to a certain party or nation, that he had a party to serve or a cause to defend. In ancient historiography Thucydides is the familiar example of historical reserve. Other books there are on which are cast the brand shadows of their writers. These works are probably partisan in origin and patriotic in motive. Throughout they vibrate with the passions and the antipathies of the author. The great among the writers of such books no doubt have a conscience which makes them present facts as they happened whereas their imitators forget, to say the best of them, the facts when the spirit of party is roused, but all of them come with prepossessions and opinions in whose light they see the past. Tacitus was an ardent lover of the Republic, and for more than a thousand years he has kept the world in ignorance that Imperial Rome was not the sink of vices of the whole world, nor the emperors all of them demons. Macaulay wrote to prove the superiority of the Whig cause. The works of Thiers and Lamartine were political rather than literary events. The works of these men glow with the zeal of the champion or darken with the denunciations of the hater. The author is never absent with his opinions and sympathy. The judgements of these authors are more a matter of opinion and sympathy than legitimate induction from documents. To Masson Napoleon was the ideal man, to Taine he was an Italian condottiere. Of such works we read two–Mommsen's *Roman History* and Grote's *History of Greece*. One is famous for its defence of Caesar and the other is a vindication of Athenian democracy. Such works are pre-eminently readable and possess all the charms of a pamphlet.

"The contrast of this is the objective method; it is in a word the dogma of impartiality. But this impartiality has a deeper meaning than what we understand the word to denote. To an ordinary man it means no more than justice. I may consider that I can proclaim the merits of my party, religion, or country without transgression if I am fair to the relative but inferior merits of others and do not treat a man as saint or rogue according to the side he takes. But the objective method of which I am going to speak is other than the justice of the hanging judge. There are some writers like Hallam, who, scrupulously fair though they are, are dominated by a narrowness and ponderous sententiousness in their writings. Under the clothes of the historian we discover the judge. But the objective method does not conceive of judging to be the true vocation of history, and from grounds moral as well as historical. It may be asked by what standards are we to judge bygone events and men; how are we to gauge their comparative merits and demerits? We may take our stand on the newest ideal and the most advanced position, but these ideals are a matter of historical growth. The men who with the compass of criticism in their hands', says Lord Acton, `sailed the uncharted seas of original research proposed a different view. History to be above evasion or dispute must stand on documents not on opinions. Ideas which are truths in religion and politics are forces in history. They must be respected, they must not be affirmed. By dint of a supreme reserve, by much self-control, by a timely and discreet indifference, by secrecy in the matter of the black cap history might be lifted above contention and made an accepted tribunal and the same for all.'

This impartiality is then something new. The historian must be content to state facts as they happened, or, to use a modern phrase, to show a development, without intruding his opinions and predilections into the narrative. His position is not among his fellowmen of whom he is writing. He does not share their joys or passions nor mingles in their affairs. His position is that of a spectator who stands on a balcony and watches a crowd street under him. Two words he is not expected to use, the two words 'good' and 'bad'. He can speak about anterior or posterior developments, but nothing of absolute merits. His opinions as man he must keep off as historian. The facts must speak for themselves. The position has been put very forcibly by the great French historian Fustel de Coulanges, when he said to an excited audience, 'Do not imagine you are listening to me, it is history that is speaking.' The question then is one of detachment and the task of self-elimination is exceedingly difficult, not to say impossible. Some writers have only dared to engage themselves with distant periods, where the embers, of party conflict are long extinguished.

"This objectivity is a distinct advance in the direction of the historical point of view. The fundamental idea of history is the idea of change. Institutions have evolved from certain conditions but in other conditions they may be worse than useless. It would be absurd to measure its former usefulness with notions of its present defects, and it would be idle to condemn them. History shows a development. It is probably nowhere more true to say than in the case of historical growths that necessity is the mother of invention. Human intelligence invents expedients when necessary and modifies them to meet after-conditions. Again the form of an institution may survive when its spirit is long dead and its need gone. It would be of little use to praise with Hallam the constitutionalism of certain states in the Middle Ages and to blame the tendency to despotism in others. They were developments proceeding from the nature of things and as such probably inevitable.

"To show how a thing happened is then the only aim of objective history. It has brought about great improvements in the method of history. In adopting the principles of science in details it has made itself subject to the process of scientific reasoning. Possessing no favourite view, inheriting no tradition, cherishing no legend, the objective historian can never be inclined to remove an obstacle or promote a purpose by casting ingenious doubts on ascertained facts. No facts are unwelcome to him, for he does not fear the disclosure of a skeleton, or the breaking of an idol. To him the facts and all the facts are the only things worth putting forward, and the conclusions based on them are the whole truths for which he seeks. In fact, the inauguration of the exacter methods of historical writing, or history written from documents, inscriptions and original authorities are coincident with the new views of objectivity.

"Some examples will make the attitude clear. I shall take up a topic which is of some importance in the history of Indian institutions–the caste system. It would not do to investigate it with the eyes of an orthodox Hindu or a Brahmo. Philosophical views about the morality of such things are out of place in history. We must enquire what conditions of Indian social life prompted this organization, what conceptions of life and the world defined the rules laid down for the life of an individual member. It would be fruitless to theorize about these questions. We must investigate the positive evidence of contemporary men. We must look about to find examples of such institutions in other countries. We shall not have either to blame or praise the institution. It will probably suffice to say that such conditions gave rise to it and such were the needs which it fulfilled.

"Again suppose we are enquiring about the social position of women in India. We shall surely take into account the lofty ideals as well as examples of noble womanhood in our books;

but to be absolutely truthful we must also reckon with the descriptions of, and reflexions on, women in some other books, which to our modern notions are unchivalrous, barbarous, and sometimes immoral. We must also take care not to combine together the evidence of the Vedas and the evidence of the *Mahabharata*. A comparative estimate will probably show us that these attitudes are a survival of the primeval attitude of men towards women when the latter were reckoned merely as chattels.

"If again we take the example of the French Revolution, we must draw our conclusions from facts. What shall we think of the movement if we see it through the eyes of the nobles who fled to the absolutist courts of Europe? Only as a carnival of murder and robbery. What again would a Brissot or a Saint-Just have told us? That it is a glory. Michelet and Taine will make us doubt whether any such event as the French Revolution took place, so that rational men could take such divergent views of one movement. The facts must be understood as they happened, the antecedents and the results must be taken into due account. The movement will appear as a historical change governed in its particular manifestations by particular circumstances.

"The method which I have described would probably imply that histories should be written with no object in view; it should have no theory to prove; its reasoning should be governed by all the rigidity of scientific reasoning; its aim should only be to present a development. This is writing history for history's sake, but an account of historical writings would assure us that these conceptions had only gradually gained ground in the course of the nineteenth century.

"The historical movement itself started from no objective point of view. It was in the romantic movement of the early nineteenth century as a reaction against the superficial ratio-

nalism of the eighteenth century that historical thinking had its
birth. It was also a national movement in Germany. In their
reaction from French ideas the Germans grew into national
consciousness and learned to see their past. They discovered
that institutions had a historical growth. The men of the
historical school of jurisprudence, Eichhorn and Savigny, no
less than the first great German historian of the nineteenth
century, Niebuhr, were nationalists and conservatives. This
return to the past gave birth to historical thinking in Germany
and the national enthusiasm succeeded in producing a monumental collection of the sources of German history.

"Ranke was the first great German to study history for the
sake of history. There is a story of how he began writing history
in that spirit. He, as he himself said, was struck by the difference
in the portraiture of Louis XI by Scott in *Quentin Durward* and
by his original authority Philippe de Commynes, and resolved
always to stick to his authority and never to swerve from the
truth.

"In his first book, published in 1824, he wrote that it was
the purpose of the author to relate events as they actually
happened. 'The office of judging the past,' he further said, 'and
of instructing the future has been attributed to history; but his
volume made no attempt to perform such a lofty task. The
historian must approach his subject without pre-suppositions
and write history for its own sake.' With this conception he
wrote a history of the Popes and a history of the Reformation
in Germany. When a zealous divine who also wrote histories
claimed him as a comrade he gave this answer: 'You are in the
first place a Christian, but I am in the first place an historian.
There is a gulf betwixt us.'

"He was attacked by men of parts and merits of other
schools who would continue the traditions of the hanging
judge. But there was one school in Germany which produced

great histories but in quite a different spirit. Its inspiration came from the glowing heart of Germany and the German nation. It preached German unity. Some men of this school saw in the Hohenzollerns their salvation and made history the mouthpiece of their spirit. At first three D's, Dahlmann, Duncker, and Droysen, guided this school. Droysen sung the paean of the Greek monarchies at the expense of the Greek democracies. This creed of nationalism did even affect the school of Ranke. Of his three great pupils, Waitz wrote on German institutions. So he was safe from the fervour of nationalism. Giesebrecht, one of the calmest and soundest of historians, wrote his *Deutsche Kaiserzeit,* i.e., the history of the German Empire, during the chequered years of hope and fear for the Germans between Olmutz and Sedan to show what their country once had been. When the Empire was a reality he doubted whether it was worth his while to continue his book. The Prussian School even seduced the youngest and best of Ranke's pupils, von Sybel. Sybel has produced massive and erudite histories of the French Revolution and Prussian policy, but they are not marked by the soberness and objectivity of his master. Treitschke frankly declared that he wrote for the German nation and made it his object to teach Germans to love their fatherland. Even Mommsen, whom we do not include in this school, speaks contemptuously of objectivity and says, 'Those who have lived through historical events as I have, begin to see that history is neither written nor made without love or hate.' As their purpose was fulfilled much of the aggressiveness passed away and sounder tradition of scholarship prevailed in Germany.

"The historical movement in France too sprang from the romantic movement. But there it took a liberal bent. Thierry and Michelet were liberals, but they were first of all romanticists. Thiers and Mignet came to Paris to overthrow the Bourbons and began to write history as the most effective of pamphleteering. The accounts of two themes, the Revolution and Napoleon, will show how historical writing has been influenced by the political vicissitudes of the country. Thiers and Mignet were followed by Lamartine who saw the first Revolution through the haze of that of '48. The Second Empire produced a reaction in favour of Napoleon, while its opponents attacked him violently. Lanfrey attacked Napoleon with a bitterness only surpassed by Taine. The horrors of the Commune turned Taine to the first Revolution and he applied his entomologist's method to thunder against the great upheaval. Even Aulard who professes, 'I have tried so far as in me lay to write a historical book, not to advance a theory. I should wish my work to be considered as an example of the historical method applied to the study of a period disfigured by passion and by legend . . .' may have been to some extent influenced by the movement in favour of the First Republic on the establishment of the Third.

"I have not mentioned Guizot, who had a far more judicial mind than his contemporaries, Thiers and Michelet, nor have I spoken of de Toqueville, who was no less fair because he was of a conservative temper. They, with Sorel, a later historian, represent a class of historians who combine a breadth of view and soberness of judgement with a mastery of the most rigorous of historical methods.

"Of Aulard and Fustel de Coulanges I have already quoted some sayings. The latter's theory of the Roman origin of the Merovingian institutions is, I think, the conviction of the scholar rather than of the patriot and indeed he blamed the German historians of institutions for wanting to nationalize every great institution.

"In England the Whig and the Tory parties supplied historians. Mitford's *History of Greece* was a Tory attack on Greek democracy. Alison made it his philosophy of history to demonstrate the danger of changes. Grote's history was a reply to Mitford. Arnold even approved of a little party spirit in historical books. But the work of Connop Thirwall was characterized by all the qualities of the objective historian, though it failed to be popular because of the brilliance of its rival, Grote's book. Exacter schools too were growing up in the universities. Bishop Stubbs is an example of a combination of technical power with a historical mind. He was a high-church man and a Tory, but he used to boast that no one could tell by reading his books to what party he belonged. A good example is Creighton, who has trodden over the treacherous ashes of sixteenth-century history with perfect equanimity.

"It is impossible not to admire the self-restraint of these men in the cause of knowledge. To eliminate oneself completely requires a tremendous exercise of intellectual and moral power. Yet they have been attacked in the name of morality. Is their objectivity moral indifference? Is there anything dangerous in such writings? Is it the true purpose of history 'to maintain morals as the sole criterion of men and things?' What should be our attitude to immoral men and things? What, for example, should we think of the heroes of '93 or, rather, of the Borgias? Ages of moral aspiration have set up ideals of morality before mankind which demand the highest respect. Yet would it be fair to judge them as we would judge one of ourselves? In my opinion the attitude would be more with Seignobos when he says, 'having adopted the tone of a scientific treatise I have had no occasion for a display of personal feelings,' rather than with Creighton when he says, 'Who am I that I should condemn them? Surely they knew not what they did.' The difficulty is largely solved by holding morality to be something dynamic, though it is less true for three hundred years than for three thousand. These opinions would presuppose a very great widening of the field of history, and this widening has taken place through various ways.

"In the first place, we have been taken back by thousands of years by the successive discoveries of Egyptian, Babylonian, and Agean history. Historical writing is no longer confined to the events of Europe alone. Research has been busy with Indian, Chinese, and other histories. Secondly, we have ceased to write histories of kings and battles, even of States. The historical method is applied to all spheres of human activity. Though there are some who even now advocate that the doings of States are alone the legitimate matter for histories, the *Kulturgeschichte* has gained its recognition. Thirdly, the scientific movements have been extended to the study of man, his religion, and society. Anthropology, sociology, economics, political science are now sciences. Religious dogmatism is shattered when we apply the scientific method to the Greek and the Hindu religions as well as to the Buddhist and the Christian.

"All these causes have extended the field of history in time and broadened its conception. Historical thought has received a great stimulus from the theory of evolution, for the theory is only a firm grasp of the historical principle. Its scope has become vast and its methods more accurate and complex, and a great change of attitude has been necessarily the result. Who would think of judging the world by standards either Indian or European? It must take its stand on broader human grounds. When all is changing no one attitude would serve as a measure of progress. In this infinitely complex and infinitely vast mass of ever-changing things nothing supplies us with a safe anchorage save the objective method. Such a conception of history cannot think of being partial or impartial. It shows a development and lays bare its causes. To it the epic of the *Cid* and *Ramayana* are primitive examples of poetry, the philosophy of Vedanta and of Henri Bergson efforts of the human mind to find a solution of life, the Reformation a transition from one stage of development to another through economic, political, and religious causes. It has no special liking for things Indian or European. It has grasped the unity of history in time as well as in subject-matter. The hero of this history is man in all his developments and in every climate. The conclusions of such history are independent of the views of morality, religion, or politics that the writer happened to hold.

"The value of such a history would depend upon the opinions of men about the use and scope of history. Many opinions can be gathered about the question whether history is a bundle of case laws or whether it is a school of patriotism. But the objective method does not share these views. I do not wish to detract from the merits of books written from other points of view. Though I would not have the apotheosis of Henry from any but Froude, though I would not endure the antifrancophilism of Sybel from a man without Sybel's erudition, these men have earned the gratitude of historical science and paid the price of their fame in the archives of Paris and Simancas. Yet objectivity as we now understand it rises above national fortunes and religious differences. It is something higher and more permanent. When nations will perish and kingdoms crumble history may remain, for its fortunes are independent of national interests."

ACADEMIC FAILURE

I was over-ambitious as an undergraduate. Thus it happened that I did not think too well of the essay. But reading it thirty years later as I would read an essay by a son or a pupil, I can give it its measure of praise. Apart from what powers of reading, imitation, assimilation, and expression (despite the natural immaturity of an undergraduate) it displayed, it demonstrated my capacity to formulate for myself, independently of personal example or guidance, an attitude towards life which on the one hand did not grow out of the system of values I had acquired earlier in life, and on the other was in complete opposition to the prevailing super-nationalistic ideas and emotions. I could be independent even of those whom I was accepting as my masters. Perhaps it has not escaped the alert reader that in the essay there are other borrowings of ideas and even phrases from Lord Acton besides those acknowledged, but at the same time this must also have been apparent, that my conception of the nature and purpose of history was not Lord Acton's, although his emphasis on the ethical function of history should have appealed to me on account of the predominantly ethical *Weltanschauung* of my early life. In formulating my conception of history, I was moving away, in relation to my past life, from the ethical standpoint to an amoral intellectual creed, and in relation to my countrymen and contemporaries I was erecting a barrier of intellectual isolation which was to become more and more impenetrable with years. The essay was the manifesto of a revolution within me, completed on the subconscious plane, a revolution leaping out in full panoply like Athene from the head of Zeus, which made me take an intellectual view of existence in a society which was completely anti-intellectual. Perhaps, if I had had to rewrite the essay even two years after, it would not have been written in the same words. But its content and drift would not have been different. The creed adumbrated in the youthful testament remained my single article of faith for more than twenty-five years, and the discovery I have made since has not involved any repudiation of the early faith. It has only added something and that addition is this: the objective pursuit of historical truth which, for me, means the truth regarding the meaning and purpose of existence, not only of individual human beings or even of nations, but of the universe, is inseparable from the pursuit of morality, for it gives men a true understanding of the nature of Good and the nature of Evil, a surer grasp of the principles which should regulate personal and national conduct, and a sorely needed confidence in living and dying, both as individuals and as nations.

I did well in my B.A. examination. I got my honours in history and was placed first in order of merit in the first class. The news came in a telegram when I was at Kishorganj, but so little was the result expected that I made my father telegraph back to my brother in Calcutta for confirmation. I came to learn afterwards that it had come as a surprise to my fellow-students also. One of them told me that he had indeed noticed the extent of my reading but was not sure it was not too desultory. A less charitable contemporary remarked with a sneer that I must have crammed a lot. On the whole, however, my fellow-students were pleased at the success of a dark horse, for it was the success of a student of average merit who had entered into competition with nobody and trodden on no corns.

My parents, brothers, and friends were, of course, greatly elated, and I recall with particular pleasure the letter I received from my uncle, Mr. Das, congratulating his "philosopher". But no indication of the collective sentiments of my native town, nor of my old school, reached me. The family's coming back to Kishorganj had not, in my case, restored the links broken in 1910. I was, however, to be given proof of the impression I had made on the town in very curious circumstances some months later. In the winter following my success I was coming to Kishorganj, and my train was steaming slowly into a small station in the eastern part of Dacca district. The strangeness and the loneliness of the place were exaggerated beyond measure by the silence of the midnight, the darkness all around, the chirping of the crickets, and the hissing of an engine. A second train was standing on the other line, and the illuminated windows of its coaches were the only spots of light in the whole scene. As my train came to a standstill I heard a buzz of conversation in the carriage across the line, and was utterly surprised to hear myself discussed. A group of passengers in the compartment opposite were having a chat, and one of them was saying, ". . . that little doll of a son of Upendra Chaudhuri, just think what he has done, stood first ...." The speaker and the listeners were all strangers to me, but they must have come from Kishorganj. It was a droll and at the same time uncanny coincidence for me to be eavesdropping on this conversation.

Speaking of my own feelings, as I had never before achieved any kind of academic distinction, this result naturally gave me satisfaction. But I do not think I made too much of it. I had my ideals and standards against which I judged myself and was not easily swayed by external judgements, favourable or unfavourable. Even so the result gave me confidence. I thought that my way of life, a way of life which had appeared to be very unsocial, unbalanced, and wayward in its onesided pursuit of intellectual interests, had been justified. I also thought that, having partially made good, I could with greater propriety ask for more facilities by way of books. So I went back to Calcutta to study for my M.A. degree (which in our university was a regular course of post-graduate study with a stiff examination at the end of two years) with a sense of exhilaration and adventure. It was an added exhilaration to learn that the French Revolution had for the first time been included among the special subjects in our curriculum. I had always wanted to make a study of European history and, more especially, of European history since the French Revolution. As my essay must have shown, I knew something of the rise and development of the scientific study of the subject. I had already read Aulard and heard even of Mathiez. There was also a deeper urge. Although at times the idea of becoming an Orientalist allured me, I could never get over the feeling, wholly spontaneous in me but opposed to current opinion, that to confine myself solely to Indian studies at this stage would be a great mistake, that if I did so I should in the first instance be cut off from world currents and become parochial and, next, make no progress beyond the second-rate in scholarly technique. I had already picked up a notion of the difference between the "note of the centre" and the "provincial note" from Matthew Arnold, and wanted to be trained only in the best and hardest of schools and tested by the highest of standards.

The first expression of my new adventurousness was an ambitious programme of book-buying. Reading on equally bold lines followed. It did not mean the same breaking of new ground and tilling of virgin soil as it had done in the two previous years, but if there was less pioneer work there was also the counterpoise of more thorough exploitation. The subjects were interesting, the new ones specially so, and these included not only the French Revolution, but also the history of the ancient East–the Aegean, Asia Minor, Egypt, Babylonia and Assyria, and Persia. For some months Egyptology haunted me as if I were being ridden by the spirits of the imperious old kings driven from their mummies. Besides the usual text-books I read Breasted's translation of the ancient Egyptian inscriptions and even detected one error in his chronology. I read the reports of the Egyptian Exploration Fund and looked at the reproductions of the Egyptian papyri. I even went for Lepsius's gigantic *Denkmaler aus Agypten und Athiopien.* The book was in the university library, but when I wanted to read it the library assistant roundly declared that he knew nothing of any such book. It was only when I identified it for him by referring to its size and its special case that a look of scandalized astonishment came over his face, and he cried, "Oh, that book! It is not issued to students." I was able, however, through the intercession of Dr. Banerji, who taught us the subject, to consult it. As I was turning over the leaves of the huge folios, the peons or attendants of the library looked at me with amazement. The head peon vividly defined the magnitude of my undertaking by observing to the others, "The Babu wants to read the Elephant!" The same process was repeated with Assyriology. I tried to learn cuneiform, and as the next best thing to do read whatever English translations were available to me of the Assyrian inscriptions.

Here I must say a few words about two of my teachers, one of whom was the most brilliant lecturer I heard in my college days, and the other the most painstaking and helpful. Both belonged to a type which was rare among our teachers. Our lecturers at their best were crammers in the best sense of the word, and at their worst were the worst conceivable crammers. They had a wholly artificial conception of the subjects they taught, regarding them only as conventional academic disciplines. Perhaps in the case of history this was better than what has taken its place: the Clio of the Bazaars, that impudent baggage from the harem of the nationalist movement, which in my time was just showing its painted odalisque's face at the window but has now invaded our universities. The *Hausfrau* was preferable to the strumpet. Still the conventionalized subject was not the real subject—the subject as a living and growing thing, never remaining the same from year to year, exasperating by reason of its contradictions and changefulness, but vitalizing through its creative surge and swirl.

Dr. R. C. Majumdar, who taught us ancient Indian history, brought to us this sense of the living quality of his subject. Dr. Nag had also suggested something like this. But while in those days Dr. Nag was still an apprentice in research, Dr. Majumdar was a practitioner and had already made his mark. His lectures gave me the sense of watching the process of the writing of ancient Indian history, and not merely the experience of reading it. To my great regret he left us to join

Dacca University, whose Vice-Chancellor he ultimately became.

The other teacher was Mr. Y. J. Taraporewallah. He taught us the newly introduced subject of the French Revolution. He had just returned from Cambridge, and brought to us a taste of the tutorial system of Cambridge and Oxford. While he gave us a bird's-eye view of the whole subject without referring to his authorities, I soon discovered that he was very laboriously and conscientiously keeping himself abreast of the latest books on his subject, mostly French, and ordering them both for himself and for the university library. He had mastered the perspective of Revolutionary studies and was ready to communicate his knowledge of this perspective to any student who was receptive enough. He told me to read the last volume of Lavisse's great history of France, written by Carre, Sagnac, and Lavisse himself, as the basic account of the preliminaries of the revolution. I saw Lavisse's *Histoire Contemporaine,* covering the revolutionary period in two volumes, in his hands as soon as it was published. At the time, Mr. Taraporewallah felt a human, and not merely a lecturer's, interest in the Revolution. While making us aware of the difference between the attitude of a Madelin and of a Jaures, he, I believe, rather leaned to Jaures.

He was the only one of my professors with whom I became personally intimate. But I am afraid I tried him sorely, for when I went to visit anyone in those days I did not know how to take leave gracefully after a reasonable time, and prolonged my stay unconscionably, all the while feeling the awkwardness of my hosts in addition to my own. Mr. Taraporewallah knew, however, that I was socially very inexperienced, and was always kind to me. He encouraged me to keep up the acquaintance even after I had left university, and when he finally left Calcutta in 1924 he presented me with a number of French books on the Revolution, among which was a complete act of Chuquet's history of the Revolutionary wars.

The great adventure came to nothing. I failed to pass my M.A. examination. I sat for three papers, and on the morning of the fourth day told my mother that I was unprepared, had done badly so far, and was not going up for the rest of the examination. She was taken aback, but, as a mother, felt more pity than anger. I have now discovered the main reason for my failure: it was sheer lack of vitality. My health had not been good since my B.A. examination and had been causing anxiety to my parents. My strength was not equal to sustaining even the routine of studies called for by an examination, and I had been attempting, or rather prospecting for too much. Even the giant's energy of Mommsen could not balance his output in synthesis against his output in analysis. The *Roman History* remains the parergon of the most inspired and inspiring lumberjack and quarryman of historiography. My insane ambition was to combine Mabillon, Muratori, and Tillenont with Gibbon. The idea of a gigantic corpus piling itself up in annual volumes throughout a life-time, a single-handed *Monumenta* of Indian history rivalling the corporate *Monumenta Germaniae Historica,* and the idea of a stupendous synthesis written on a grand scale over decades and revised on an equally grand scale over succeeding decades obsessed me at the same time. If the synthesis was not to be absolutely like Eduard Meyer's *Geschichte des Altertums,* the least that it had to be was Stern's *Geschichte Europas seit den Wiener Vertragen von* 1815, and I was in too great a hurry to turn out such a work. No wonder I crashed.

Besides, my reading had been too diffuse and haphazard. Not that I was not conscious of the dangers lurking in my goings-on. I had read Todd's *Student's Manual* and Professor Blackie's *Guide,* both enjoining thoroughness, in my school days. Later, Gibbon s *Autobiography* became a great favourite with me. Thus there was nothing wrong with my understanding of the nature of systematic and fruitful study. I could draw up plans which, if executed with steadfastness, would have given me not only success at examinations, but also a solid grounding in the subjects I was having to learn. But I never commanded the will-power to carry out my own deliberate projects. Frightened or tired out by the too exacting programme I was always taking the virtuous resolution to put through, I gave myself up to my immediate impulses and read only what I was momentarily interested in, and the more I read about it the more interested and bogged in its details did I become for the time being. Thus, although I came to acquire a deep knowledge of certain aspects of certain subjects very unusual in a student of my age, taking it all in all, I did not succeed in having an even grounding in any subject.

Lastly, I disliked and even despised examinations when they were not immediate realities, and got worried about them when they approached. I had appeared at my matriculation examination without any preparation whatever and came through entirely on the strength of my general attainments. I was better prepared for the next examination, but not so well as to be able to escape some weeks of exhausting mental torture. This torture became so unbearable before my B.A. examination, at which I unexpectedly did so well, that on its eve I ran up and down a ladder quite a number of times, recklessly inviting a fall and the consequent breaking of a limb or two in order to have a valid excuse for not going up. The last quarter before my M.A. examination was altogether a period of black, unrelieved misery. To turn over the pages of my unread text-books was only to realize the utter futility of trying even to cram them. Seeking relief, I turned to the making of cardboard boxes in my room and the jotting down of my ideas about the organization of a national army for India.

After the actual failure, however, I did not try to palliate it. I wrote to my father, as I had told my mother, that I was to blame, for I had really neglected my studies. My father answered with his usual magnanimity. Mr. Taraporewallah also tried to console and reassure me in a most sympathetic letter, after coming to know of what had happened. There was no reason as yet for taking it as my final failure in the academic field. But so it turned out to be.

BOOK IV

INTO THE WORLD

PREFATORY NOTE

THE STORY of my apprenticeship to life has been told. I have now to describe my entry into the world. Even in the best of circumstances we modern Indians could not expect this event to be exhilarating. Hindu society does not teach its youth to face life bravely. The phrase "courage of life" is unintelligible to a Hindu, who accepts the first wail of birth as the leitmotiv of existence and manages quite successfully to lead a mock-turtle's life during the whole of it. When I was young I had my share of reading of the didactic poems which warned us that the day of reckoning for all our childish joys and laughter was at hand. We saw the elders, both men and women, sitting head in hand, contemplating not only their own woes, which they thought were present, but also the woes of their children which they anticipated. Old Hinduism sat smoking his hookah all the while, ready to swallow the world in a bored yawn, and as if he, the greatest Old Man of the Sea any voyager through life can ever encounter, was not enough by himself, he had at his side the nightmare of middle-class unemployment. All of us were led inexorably to believe that only some extraordinary and unpredictable stroke of luck could secure for us, not good employment, but even a meagre livelihood.

If that was what the fittest of us were permitted to expect, I with my inconclusive and inadequate apprenticeship could count on nothing. As a matter of fact, I justified the worst shakings of head of our wise ones. I entered the world in 1921, and for sixteen years after that suffered such poverty, want, and humiliation as I cannot wish even an enemy, if I had any, to be punished with. The worst of it was that there was nothing heroic or ennobling in this suffering. All of it was dull, degrading and feeble and, appropriately enough, if in carrying on this struggle I at last found a vocation, that happened more through a sort of natural selection than any conscious or well-directed effort of my own.

What I experienced in my private life was, however, better than what I saw on the public plane. In our national life the period of my manhood, except for one or two short interludes, was devoid of colour and charged with tedium. Thus it could hardly be called duration. In those years time seemed to have become spatialized, transformed into a lagoon which could still break into ripples, but which nonetheless was dead, because completely cut off from all living currents. Yet even in its stagnancy the thing was not immune from an evil metamorphosis. Those who kept their eyes fixed only on the watery surface did not detect this morbid change. They found it still capable of glimmering under the sun and the moon, and failed to perceive how low the water was falling. But those who were alert could detect at the edges, first a dark line, then a ring, after that a ribbon, next a belt, and, lastly, broad patches of black, and wake up with a start to the realization that the wretched thing was drying and converting itself into a mud-flat, something worse than even its sickly self.

That is why I am inclined to call this period of our national life the years of decadence. As far back as 1922 I received a warning from Mr. Middleton Murry's book *The Problem of Style* not to employ the word "decadence" too readily and lightly. I was taught to redouble this caution by Remy de Gourmont, to whom Mr. Murry had referred his readers. So I do not make use of the word without weighing every shade of its meaning. What I am speaking about is true decadence, for during these years everything about us was decaying, literally everything ranging from our spiritual and moral ideals to our material culture, and nothing really live or organic arose to take their place. I have never even read about such a process as I have used through: it was unadulterated decadence.

My passage or, to be more accurate, my wading through this stagnant pool, in the course of which I got more duckings than breathing spaces, was relieved by a number of intellectual and spiritual renovations. These came one after another, so that I can compare them to the phenomenon of moulting in birds, and the parallel is heightened by the fact that in my case also, as in the case of certain ducks, a phase of dull, embrowned eclipse came between two moultings. These phases were periods of almost unrelieved boredom and depression for me, but fortunately I was always able to grow a new set of feathers. It is these moultings taken in their totality that constitute the acquisitions of my later life, although I have to add this also, that in the pride of my new plumage I often went astray and had more than one feather plucked off. I was also often shot at, but was never winged.

CHAPTER I

MAN AND LIFE IN CALCUTTA

LIFE IN Calcutta was the symbol and epitome of our national history, a true reflection of the creative effort in our modern existence as well as of its self-destructive duality. To live in Calcutta was to be reminded at every turn of the cultural history and achievements of modern India and to be aware of every significant activity of the present. The memories of the past were kept alive by the unending series of anniversary meetings which were a feature of the cultural life of Calcutta in my young days, and there was nothing that a student in Calcutta was more fond of than attending public meetings and listening to speeches. In addition there were physical remind-ers—statues and tablets. The former were always garlanded on the anniversary days. Therefore by merely taking note of the garlanding days and the garlanded statues a man could con-struct a calendar of saints for modern India. In their contem-porary existence the citizens showed an extreme avidity for new sensations, and their equally extreme anxiety to avoid boredom at any cost made them alert to notice any novelty and enthusiastic to discuss it. There was something in Bengali Calcutta of the Athenian eagerness to say or hear something new. On account of the presence of this psychological neces-sity, life in Calcutta resembled the process of fermentation. It could mature into a rich, colourful, and full blooded product when the persons living this life were capable of it.

On the other hand it could also turn into vinegar, and since the vinous analogy is being drawn a significant contrast should also be emphasized. The oddest thing about Calcutta was that the native human stock did not seem to be capable of taking the best advantage of the soil. With a small number of exceptions the men who made Calcutta the cradle of modern Indian culture were provincials brought up in the city. The supporters and adherents of this culture were even more decisively so. It was as if the red Pinot which makes the great wines of Burgundy had to be imported into the Cote-d'Or from Normandy.

THE PHARISEES : NATIVE AND FOREIGN

From this springs the paradox that the true natives of the city were extremely proud of it and also of themselves, and at the same time disposed to reject every reforming movement which originated in it. Let me deal with the pride first. Initially it was something worse than pride. In an old Bengali book from which I have learnt much about Calcutta society in the early nineteenth century occurs a passage which indicates that the gentry of Calcutta were given to the exhibition of a snobbery towards men from the country which bordered on the outrageous. The prevalence of this rudeness is referred to by the author in his preface, and he adduces it as his reason for writing the book. As he says: "The citizens do not welcome the intervention of a villager in their conversation even when he makes a very proper and just remark. They exclaim, 'You are only a rustic newly come to Calcutta and ignorant of its ways and therefore this discussion is none of your business,' which abashes and aggrieves the villager. It is for this reason that I am embarking on the composition of this book, so that reading it, or having it read to themselves, all newcomers might be able easily to understand the customs and manners of this city and quickly acquire skill in conversation." The state of manners revealed by this explanation would have provoked class-war in these days, but in those it only invoked humble discipleship. Even a hundred years later the people of Calcutta had not

wholly shed this arrogance. When I first came to the city I
could still hear the doggerel:

> "He's no man–the Bengali of the East;
> The Orissan's worse, for he is a beast;
> None have tails, but it's wonderful to see
> How these creatures swing from tree to tree."

With the steady influx of ever greater numbers from East
Bengal, this aggressive snobbery began to pass away, for it was
not safe to sharpen one's wits on the humourless easterner
without overwhelming numerical superiority. In private,
however, the natives of Calcutta continued for a long time to
use the contemptuous epithet "Bangal" for us and sometimes
prefixed the adjective "bl–y" to it.

Even when not uncivil they were amazingly parochial.
The world beyond the Hooghly River and the Mahratta Ditch
was a wilderness to them. Whenever an outsider told the name
of his district to a man of Calcutta the usual question put to him,
as it was put to me also, was, "At which station do you get into
train–Howrah or Sealdah?" If you said "Sealdah", you would
be duly identified as a "Bangal", if "Howrah" as a "Rehro" or
as an "Eater of bran". The sound adjective was the contemptuous epithet for the Bengali from the westernmost districts of
Bengal and the third the even more contemptuous description
of the Hindustani.

Yet, extraordinary to relate, this self-conceit was most
assertive precisely among those who had never accepted the
great movements of national revival and reformation which
had originated in Calcutta. The natives of the city were as a rule
extremely conservative. In the narrow lanes of Calcutta were
to be found, surviving and spinning out an unnatural existence,
rituals and beliefs, practices and superstitions, which by the
beginning of the twentieth century had disappeared even in the
backwaters of East Bengal. The people of Calcutta wor-

shipped the "Goddess of No Prosperity" together with the
Goddess of Prosperity; they worshipped the Goddess of Skin
Disease and of Cholera; the Goddess of Smallpox was one of
their major deities. Their menfolk were extremely afraid of
going into the water closet with their hair let down, and they
always tied its ends in a knot before going in, because they
believed the W.C.s to be the favourite haunts of evil spirits who
would possess them unless their hair was up.

Moreover, that tiresome nuisance, purity mania, which
marks most elderly women in Bengal, reached proportions in
Calcutta which I have seen nowhere else. In Mymensingh the
utmost length to which the women would go was to wash their
quilts and other bedclothes every morning, or walk with a pot
of cowdung solution, sprinkling the ground before them with
the solution in order to purify the path of their advance from
one place to another. But in Calcutta the purity fiends went to
the extreme of completely divesting themselves of clothes
when doing any household work. They were mortally afraid
of coming in contact with specks of cooked rice or other
particles of waste food and spreading the resulting contamina-
tion through the *sari*. This garment, being made of cotton, was
regarded like all cotton garments as the most dangerous
conductor of impurity. If the end or even one-tenth of the end
of a *sari* touched waste food the whole fifteen to eighteen feet
of its length became polluted. The human body on the other
hand was assumed to be a non-conductor, it was contaminated
only in those parts which were actually smeared with waste
food. Therefore the best prophylaxis against impurity was to
confront all impure things with partial and even complete
nudity. I have seen this spectacle without any effort on my part,
for the elderly women do not really care who or how many bear
witness to their devotion to purity. The demonstration is
always more embarrassing to the beholder than to the beheld.

Given this general background of thought, it was not surprising that the natives of Calcutta should have been hostile to the reforming movements. The sternest denouncers of Rammohun Roy or Tagore, for instance, were the gentry of Calcutta. But while opposed to all kinds of reform, they were most opposed to religious reform and the emancipation of women. Thus it happened that the Brahmo Samaj, which had abolished the purdah, was their particular *bete noire*. Brahmo women were looked upon as legitimate prey, and the budding city rake would say with a jaunty and leering swagger, "I've made love to Brahmo ladies," which ordinarily amounted only to some eyeing and ogling from a safe distance, for in another aspect of their character the ladies in question had with these people the formidable reputation of being regular cats.

This insensibility, and in most cases also the hostility, of the people of Calcutta to the greatest glories of their city have always puzzled me. According to the Greek saying, the first requisite to happiness is that a man should be born in a famous city. The natives of Calcutta did not appear to stand in need of a second. This was extraordinary. But in one sense these men had their place in the scheme of things. Our great reformers made use of Calcutta as the fulcrum on which to shake and lift our society. They struck the flint that was Calcutta to produce the spark of new life. Would anything less hard or less solid have served their purpose? On this score the natives of Calcutta deserve the gratitude of all modern Indians.

I shall also say a few words about the other sect of the Pharisees of Calcutta, the so-called European, but, correctly speaking, the British part of the urban community. They normally ignored the new culture of modern India, but when brought into accidental contact with it, showed even greater hostility than did the native Bengali. To these men the Bengalis who were trying to understand and assimilate European civilization were Baboos. I never came in touch with English social life in Calcutta. The days after my first coming to Calcutta were the days of racial privileges in India, and certain parts of the Eden Gardens were roped off from us. Certain other amenities were also reserved, and even where there were no express reservations we were not politely treated. My invariable rule was never to go near any of these places to invite rebuffs. But there were many amongst us who tried to sneak into them with the help of a suit of English clothes and created a clamour when they were insulted. There were others who took a peculiarly wrong-headed pleasure in hanging about these places in order to freshen their sense of injury and replenish their self-pity. But I acted on the instincts and impulses of the healthy aborigine, and in this I was influenced by the example of my parents who never went into any kind of society in which they were not treated as equals. I entertained no ambition whatever of hobnobbing with the English in India. As long as I lived in Calcutta I wore no article of English clothing and had none. In general, I disliked and despised the local English. To my mind they alone justified the gibe that the English were a nation of shopkeepers.

Even now I see no reason to retract this poor opinion. If we Indians marked down the Englishman (as we saw him in rare mutual contacts), his own people ought to enter his name in their black books, for he has made a very substantial contribution to the downfall of the British Empire in India. From his land and nation the Englishman brought many fine qualities for his work and business in this country, but his residence among us seemed to engender in him certain very offensive attributes which were as pronounced as the over-powering smell of our wild red dog *(cyon cyon dukhunensis)*, and which did untold harm to Britain's relations with India. These are matters of history. I refer to them only because my personal testimony would go a long way towards supporting the consensus of opinion among my countrymen about the

Englishman in India in the days of his power. But I do not share the opinion of my countrymen regarding the Englishmen who have remained in India after the disappearance of the Indian Empire of Great Britain. Their conduct today fills me with vicarious shame, for they are showing themselves as the same men now by their self-interested and ingratiating niceness towards us as they showed themselves in the past by their arrogant and power-intoxicated snobbery.

But at one time of my life I had an opportunity for seeing a side of English life in Calcutta which was not coloured by the prejudices of the local English against us and our prejudices against them. I saw it in the 'thirties in the concert hall of the Calcutta Symphony Orchestra. I went there in the Bengali dress, and though not stared at certainly looked conspicuous in that evening-dressed crowd. Of course, even there I had to maintain my aloofness. I do not remember to have been addressed or even greeted there by other persons except on two occasions, once by Mr. P. I. Griffiths, who at one time was the leader of the European Party in the Central Legislature, and on the second occasion by Dr. Bake, the Dutch musicologist, and his wife. But even that insulated contact helped me to form a juster conception of English life in Calcutta and I came to see that there was an amenity in it whose existence I had not suspected before, and indeed could not, by merely seeing Englishmen in the streets and shops and hearing about their doings and behaviour in their offices. In the concert hall foyer even their sipping of whisky did not look uncultured. Since I was theoretically quite familiar with the best type of English social life—memoirs and biographies were my favourite reading—I was not overwhelmed by what I saw. But my less sophisticated Indian friends whom I occasionally persuaded to accompany me to the concerts were generally disarmed in their nationalism by the spectacle of graciousness they saw, and at times even scandalized out of it by the charming *decollete* of the ladies.

The British Empire in India has perished without my ever coming into intimate personal contact with Englishmen, with the exception of less than half a dozen whom I have known more or less well. I do not regret it, for with all the Anglicism of my spirit I should have felt a total stranger in the English society of Calcutta and would have been humiliated by the demonstration.

THE SONS OF CALCUTTA

The Bengalis native to Calcutta fell perceptibly into three classes: the upper and the wealthy, the lower-middle, and the intermediate, whose members rose or fell to the two other classes wholly on the strength (or weakness) of their monetary position. In recent times a class of new rich people have sprung up, who have all the repellent characteristics of this class and can be clearly distinguished from the older rich (and the new poor) of the city. But in the first years of the twentieth century the rich of Calcutta were a fairly homogeneous set. By that time they had outgrown their caterpillarish new-rich stage of the late eighteenth and early nineteenth century and become images with all the mellowed attributes of wealth.

To begin with, they possessed a very distinctive physical appearance which marked them out for special notice among all other Bengalis and even more conspicuously from the Bengalis of East Bengal. These features were developed in the first instance by very careful selective breeding and, after that, they were favoured by the easy and comfortable life of the whole class. In trying to give an idea of this physical type, perhaps I could do no better than begin with the women, although this would necessitate a preliminary reference to an older type of Bengali beauty.

The traditional type of female beauty, accepted as the ideal all over rural Bengal, was derived from the iconography of Mahayana Buddhism and Puranic Hinduism. By this criterion a Bengali beauty was likened to a goddess, which meant that she had an oval face, wide at the forehead and pointed at the chin, long and rather narrow eyes with a perceptible slant, thin but fully modelled lips, and a complexion pronouncedly yellow with no tinge of rose, rather like beaten pure gold. Even now one can pick out Bengali girls who are exactly true to this type.

But the Calcutta type was different. It was rounder, fleshier, and rosier. Faces of this cast are very common in the Bengali drawing of the nineteenth century known as the *pats* of Kalighat, on which the well-known and fashionable contemporary Bengali painter, Mr. Jamini Roy, has based his linear technique. Nothing in the English tradition of the charming in women resembled these faces and figures, not even the bare-bosomed beauties of the Restoration, but the heavier French beauties at the court of Louis XIV offered quite close parallels to the Calcutta type. The contours of these women were distinguished by an almost cloying abundance of curves, large curves enclosing small curves, one curve melting into another, so that it was impossible to determine the origins or ends of these lines. These women harmonized with no furniture of the Western type, but were most successfully camouflaged by a bed of highly piled mattresses covered with a snow-white sheet and amply provided with bolsters. In such surroundings theirs was a protective configuration.

Since at least one-half of every mother's son is woman, the men of Calcutta also tended to approximate to this type. In any case, among the natives of the city, bones and bony effects were considered to be very unbecoming in a man. To have such an appearance was, in their eyes, equivalent to being Chuars, a tribe of low-caste and wild men of the western borders of

Bengal whose tribal name came ultimately to mean any ruffianly fellow. Whenever a Bengali of Calcutta saw a young man with rounded limbs, a round face, and large liquid eyes, he cried out in ecstasy, "A prince!" or "The scion of a noble house!" A fair complexion was an asset to a man; it was not, however, a *sine qua non* as in a woman with pretensions to beauty; but neither man nor woman could advance the slightest claim to physical attractiveness without sleekness.

Of course, every individual in this class did not breed true to type, but it was really surprising to see how many did. The less wealthy were a more mixed lot. Still, they too were more plump and chubby than could be presupposed from their less adequate means of nourishing their fatty tissues. The Bengalis of Calcutta, irrespective of wealth, took great care of their body, and more particularly of their hair and skin. The afternoon toilet of the women was a most elaborate affair, and, whether married or unmarried, a young girl would feel extremely humiliated not to appear at her best in the evenings. These men and women presented a very striking and pleasing contrast to the generally untidy and scraggy persons from East Bengal, and this was noted with ungrudging admiration by the lesser Bengali. When I first came to Calcutta the purdah used to be very strictly observed there, but whenever an East Bengal man found an opportunity to spy he breathed a rather wistful sigh.

In appearance and manner the people of Calcutta were placid and quiet. They were soft-spoken and generally courteous. That earned for them a bad reputation among the immigrants or sojourners from East Bengal. They said that the people of Calcutta had honey on their lips and poison in their hearts. I used to remonstrate that it was after all not so very bad to have honey somewhere, even if not everywhere, since we of East Bengal had poison both in our hearts and on our lips. This argument never convinced my fellow East Bengalis, for what they were mortally afraid of in the man of Calcutta was that the polished and plausible fellow would cheat them of money or wheedle them into some imprudent course by the power of his glib tongue.

The natives of Calcutta had also a very quick sense of humour. The slightest suggestion of the comic in any person or situation never escaped them, and no sly dig was lost on them. They would be ready with their laugh or come forward pat with a counterthrust. In this too they differed from us East Bengal men. To joke with the latter is always dangerous, almost as dangerous as playing with fire. There is no knowing how they will react. Therefore the Calcutta man's sense of humour, too, discredited him in the eyes of the easterner, who attributed his rival's easy smiles and careless banter to incorrigible frivolity and light-headedness. I, however, found the westerner's easier manners very agreeable, and if I have any criticism to make of his wit it is only this: that it was not very wide in range, for it was identified too often with the perpetration of a salacious innuendo.

The real shortcoming of the true native of Calcutta, as I saw it, was a pronounced lack of magnanimity and passion. His urbanity had no charity in it. After the departure of a person with whom he had talked with impeccable politeness he would make a malicious remark which revealed all the smallness of his heart. Even the greatest sons of Calcutta, some of whom were the greatest of modern Indians, were not free from this unlovable trait. But the lack of charity was shown most blatantly in the conduct of the aristocracy of Calcutta towards those whom they did not consider their equals. They would not be exactly rude, but would stare and remain silent as if they were in the presence of some strange animal. This was worse than being rude, it was being reptilian, and if the man so treated was of a sensitive nature he came away with unforgiving wrath

in his heart and with the resolve to hit the serpent on the head
if ever he found it at a disadvantage.

Even of one another, the members of the Bengali aristocracy of Calcutta spoke with amazing malice, although accompanied by every mark of outward cordiality. The people of
Calcutta in general, if all that they said was meant to be taken
seriously, seemed to entertain very odd notions about the role
of the servants in relation to the women of the family. The
reproach which came very readily to their lips when they were
angry with a certain person was that he was not the son of his
reputed father but of a servant or groom. I have read a letter
published in a Bengali newspaper of 1831, in which the
correspondent related that in a very respected household the
master and the sons came out of the zenana in the evening and
the servants went in. The motive of this particular letter was
unexceptionable. It was written in the interest of "female
education", for the writer attributed the looseness in question
to the prevailing ignorance and to the narrowness of those
who, instead of giving a good education to their womenfolk,
kept them confined to the kitchen. But I have also read another
letter of a slightly later date, which was plain blackmail. It
purported to be an eye-witness's account from a maidservant
of the misconduct of her mistress with a manservant, and the
amazing part of the communication was that the incident was
attributed to an actual Calcutta family mentioned by name. The
restrictions on the vernacular Press imposed by the English
Government and the laws of libel ultimately eliminated these
crude scandals from the newspapers. But the whispering
campaign went on for a long time. I have myself heard a number
of stories of this kind. One of them was that a certain well-
known person of north-eastern Calcutta, after whom the
Calcutta Corporation has named a thoroughfare, was actually
the son of his father's syce. Another was that a certain
notability of the last quarter of the nineteenth century was only

too ready to oblige an amorous English lieutenant-governor with a widowed sister. An acquaintance of mine even offered to produce an eyewitness to the misbehaviour of an eminent contemporary for whom he had no love, and at the time the offer was made to me, the alleged misbehaviour was at least fifty years old! This queer scandal-mongering formed the undertone of social gossip in Calcutta.

With this proneness to take the worst view of human motives and character there went an obstinate disbelief in high purpose, both exemplified in such favourite quips as "Every fellow is a thief, although I am the only one to be caught". Of this side of their nature the natives of Calcutta were perfectly conscious. In fits of self-abasement, of which too they were capable, they admitted that, compared with the Bengali from East Bengal, they lacked "sincerity", by which they really meant idealism. But in normal moods they were more disposed to me than proud of their realism. Tagore has referred to the contrast in one of his short stories written in 1892. He makes the hero of the story say: "We were from the country, and have not learnt to scoff at everything with the precocious levity of the boys of Calcutta, and therefore our faith was unshakable. The patrons of our association delivered speeches, and we begged for subscriptions from door to door, caring neither for the midday sun nor for meals, distributed handbills in the streets, arranged chairs and benches for the meetings, and rolling up our shirt-sleeves got ready to fight it out with anybody who said a word against our leaders. The city boys duly noted these characteristics and ragged us as East Bengal fools." On account of this absence of idealism and respect for causes the Bengalis of Calcutta, taken as a collective mass, could be moved to action only through their gross worldliness or what was its counterpart in them, a frothy sentimentality. During the years of my stay in Calcutta the sentimentality rather tended to gain the upper hand, but even in his most self-abandoned moments the true native of Calcutta was never worked up to such a pitch of emotional disturbance as to be wholly forgetful of his personal safety and interest.

Such shallow worldliness could not, of course, exist at all without finding some visible expression somewhere, and it did in the faces of the men and women of Calcutta. In spite of their sleekness, smooth outlines, and quick responsiveness to the humorous, these faces were extraordinarily hard, and the hardness was further accentuated by the universal habit of chewing the *pan* or betel-leaf. A small bulge was always to be seen under one of the cheeks of the men and women of Calcutta, appearing now under the right cheek and now under the left, and on account of this perpetual grinding exercise the jaws acquired a strength and prominence which was quite unexpected in visages otherwise so placid, self-satisfied, and devoid of features denoting strength of character. The eyes more particularly, when not lit up by some giddy fancy or humorous conceit, were expressionless. It was in response that these faces showed themselves at the greatest disadvantage. Many of them were fruitless in features and proportions, and should normally have pleased by reason of their symmetry, but a thin and hard enamel appeared to have vitrified all quality of being live in them. These countenances looked like cloisonne vases. Even haughtiness, which sat most easily on them, was not present in a majority of cases.

THE MANSIONS

The houses in which these people lived could be divided, like themselves, into three classes, the higher, the lower, and the intermediate. The intermediate is a very important category in Bengali society, which is divisible in the first instance into two classes, the gentlefolk and those who are not gentlefolk. There is even now no easy passage from the one to the other. But among those who are admitted to be gentlefolk or, as we say in Bengali, *Bhadra Lok*–a class based equally on occupation and on birth, there is complete elasticity in spite of the infinite gradation of wealth and standard of living which are to be found within the order and which often range from extreme poverty to extreme luxury. The intermediate group constitutes the bridge of this continuous transition. It is the middle-class within the middle-class, without which the influential and stable Bengali *Bhadra Lok* could not have maintained the health, hold, and power of their order. It is curious to note how the social fact found recognition in the sphere of transport. The railway companies in India, which began with their activities in Bengal, felt compelled, in contradistinction to the practice all over the world, to provide an "intermediate" or "inter" class between the first and second on the one hand and the third on the other.

But their medial position makes any description of the houses and ways of the intermediate social class unnecessary. Both can be reconstructed in imagination by bringing together in varying proportions a number of features from the two extreme wings. On the other hand, the houses and ways of life of the wealthy in Calcutta, and in no less degree those of the poor, presented very strongly marked characteristics, which to an observer unaffiliated to either seemed to possess, each in its way, a physical power to clutch and grip. The great mansions of Calcutta, leaving out of the reckoning some half a dozen which looked like modest imitations of Buckingham Palace, were inconspicuous from the outside. They hardly even presented a front. In most cases they lay ensconced in the familiar mass of shabby brickwork, distinguishable only by their larger proportions and more extensive dimensions, like a pyramid among mastabas.

The front entrance, as usual, was unimpressive. Even where there was a generous porch, the entrance was often no better than a mere gap between two suites of rooms, giving access to very ordinary passages and to a large quadrangle, which too was very ordinary and drab in appearance except for a hall with high arches at one end, used as the worship hall. But following one of the corridors one would come upon a door which led into a handsome entrance hall, the real entrance hall, either paved with marble or parqueted, with a flight of wide stairs in veined marble or wood covered with the usual carpet. The walls would be papered or richly painted. At the corners there would be jardinieres and tall vases of Chinese design but not always of genuine Chinese manufacture, and on or near the newel post there would be at least one bronze nude holding an electric lamp. The most ambitious *piece* in these houses was always the drawing-room. These rooms were immense, hardly ever less than fifty feet by twenty-five feet, and in some cases very much bigger. In the older houses they were built, not as drawing-rooms, but for the exhibition of *nautch* or Indian ballet dance. During the latter part of the nineteenth century, however, nearly all of them were converted into drawing-rooms in the European style. In these rooms, too, there were echoes of Buckingham Palace, for with their rugs and carpets, wall and ceiling decorations, screens, mirrors, chandeliers, vases, statuettes, and carved mahogany or gilt Louis Quinze furniture they looked like copies of one or other of the drawing-rooms of the Palace. But the general effect, though patently imitative, was never crude or tawdry. It was in very few instances, indeed, that these rooms revealed any personal taste or even idiosyncrasy, but all were dignified and respectable. Some had pictures, usually heavily framed oil paintings, and mostly family portraits. When they dated from the early nineteenth century or before they showed considerable mastery of technique.

Very few of the houses had a regular dining-room matching the drawing-room, but some had a second sitting-room furnished in the Indian style, with carpets covered with a snow-white sheet and strewn with pillows, cushions, and bolsters. But these rooms also had some European furniture–console tables with marble tops, chandeliers and wall brackets, Venetian mirrors, overmantels without mantelpieces, and a number of divans and pouffes at the corners. The piano, most often an upright and only rarely a grand, would be in either of the two rooms.

No gracious or brilliant hostess presided over these rooms, and they never hummed with conversation–either sapient or frivolous or even flirtatious. The aristocracy of Calcutta was not given to an animated or enterprising social life, and even where it was social in a lackadaisical fashion there was no place for women in the drawing-rooms. They kept themselves within the zenana, which comprised a second quadrangle behind the main one in front, and there they had unisexual small talk of their own. The outer rooms were reserved for the master of the house and his friends, but even they for the most part would only loll and lounge in them, enjoying an easy and luxurious gregariousness, and displaying some adumbration of sociability only in languid card parties. The rich of Calcutta, when they were inclined that way, kept their high spirits for their garden houses or houses of ill-fame. In my time even the garden houses were growing respectable, although they had not wholly outlived their saturnalian or satyric reputation dating from the nineteenth century.

Thus these big houses were preternaturally silent. The silence was not disturbed even by the young people, in whom these homes, though not as abundantly provided as those of the less wealth, were not lacking. *The jeunesse doree* of Calcutta showed a tendency to get out of hand when away from home, but in their houses they were as a rule quiet. Even the depraved preferred an obstinately silent viciousness to a rowdy and obstreperous viciousness. What was true of the *jeunesse doree*

was truer of the *enfance doree*. The children of the wealthy in
Calcutta appeared to be unendowed even with boyish playful-
ness. They were extremely solemn, and whenever they made
their public appearance they looked like exact, though diminu-
tive, replicas of their elders. Occasionally, passing before these
houses, one would see at the gate, among the liveried servants
and door-keepers carrying swords or muskets, who stood
admiringly contemplating him, a handsome little boy in a fine
crinkled *dhoti* and a starched shirt, or a silk suit, or even in kilt
complete with sporran and plaid. He would stand still, staring
at the crowds in the street with wide uncomprehending eyes.
The older boys usually kept indoors. They always had a large
room to themselves, generously furnished as a school-room,
in which they sat with their tutors, listening with quiet gravity
to the lessons but never giving any indication that they were
taking in anything. Most often they looked more unintelligent
than they really were. Of course, they never went out of their
houses, even for a distance of one hundred yards, except in
their carriages, which were landaus or broughams, and, later,
in big limousines or sports cars.

I have never seen the zenana of any of these houses, and
thus have no means of describing them from direct observation. But I can imagine them as a suite of bedrooms, fitted up
in a very eclectic style, rather cluttered up, but lacking nothing
in the Indian manner, and latterly in the European as well, that
could conduce to laziness. They were never on the same plane
of luxury and stateliness as the outer rooms. This part of the
houses invariably had a very large establishment of abigails
who were an incorrigibly fussy, raucous, and intriguing set. It
was rather a surprise that their placid mistresses were able to
endure them. But among themselves the women of Calcutta,
irrespective of class, are very loquacious, and that may have
supplied the connecting link.

One other feature of these houses must also be mentioned. The larger of them had a back-garden, forming a third quadrangle behind the second or zenana quadrangle. These gardens never received the care which was usually bestowed on the gardens of the surburban villas of the same owners, nor did they have the *magnolia grandiflora* with which of all flowers the Calcutta aristocracy was *engoue,* but they had a homely and in some cases a subtle appeal. Tagore in his reminiscences has described the back-garden of his ancestral Calcutta house. "It would be too much," he writes, "to claim for the garden at the back of our house the status of a garden. Its mainstay was one pomeloe, one round plum, and one Otaheite apple tree, with a row of coconut palms. At the centre was a round platform of brickwork, in whose cracks grass and a variety of wild creepers had planted the intruding banner of their usurpation. Among flower plants, only such as never died of neglect, continued to discharge an un-aggrieved duty to the best of their power, without bringing any accusation against the gardener .... I do not believe that the Garden of Eden of the First Man, Adam, was any the better laid out than this garden of ours, for it was like him unapparelled–it had not smothered itself under a load of display. For man, the exigency of display is ever on the increase. It began on the day he tasted the fruit of knowledge and will go on augmenting until the fruit is digested. The back-garden of our house was my Garden of Eden, and that was enough." Not every well-to-do person in Calcutta had the boy Tagore's sensibility. That was why they never frequented these gardens and these remained as exclusive preserves for the women and young people of the family, who ordinarily went into them when in search of sour fruits. But if they had, they might have found in them that leisure for introductions to themselves which they never had elsewhere, not even in their large and silent drawing-rooms.

THE HUMAN HIVES

To pass from these mansions to typical middle-class houses was to pass apparently into dwellings of a different species altogether. At first sight, it was the dissimilarity between the mud-walled and tiled *bustees* of the working-class and the brick-built houses of the gentlefolk which struck the observer as an un-bridgeable hiatus, both in its visual and its sociological aspect. But internally examined, a typical middle-class house was as far removed from the great mansions as they themselves were from working-class tenements. Perhaps the difference was greater, for its measure is not fully given even by confronting the peacock with the crow, which becomes all the more surprising when one considers the social and mental solidarity of the whole gentlefolk class. This leads me to define the difference between the grub and the butterfly of the same insect, rather than as the difference between two species of animals.

The middle-class house was small, sometimes even as small as twenty-five feet square. The interior showed only two colours, the grey of the cemented floors and the white of the walls and the ceilings. If any patterns were to be seen anywhere they were only pencilled scribblings by the children and marks of a deep burnt sienna tint from betel-stained fingers. After taking betel the men and women of Calcutta were given to wiping their soiled fingers on the nearest wall. There was also an impression of bareness, for these households possessed only a minimum of furniture. Most often there were only an almirah or two and a number of wooden beds, and these latter too were mere frame-works of lath on four weak legs. Those whose means permitted added some tables and chairs, and the rear was brought up by immense piles of bedding and rolls of mats and a vast assortment of earthen pots and pitchers, empty tins of all sizes and shapes, bottles and jars, and sacks for the storeroom, and iron, brass, and earthen pots and pans for the kitchen.

None of these houses had proper living-rooms. In some instances one outer room on the ground-floor, provided either with a bed, or a table with some chairs, or both, was set apart as a reception-room for visitors. If the servant lived in the house instead of going away at night to his *bustee* he usually slept in this room, and during the day his rolled-up bed and mat would occupy a part of the floor near one of the walls. The rest of the habitable rooms were bedrooms. Their typical assignment was – one to the master and mistress and the younger children, one to the grown-up girls and the widowed mother, and one to the older boys. But when a joint family lived in the same house, as often was the case, the married brothers with their young children took one each of the best rooms, and the indifferent ones were occupied by the rest of the family, the widowed mother and the marriageable girls, the older boys, and the dependants. The rooms which were not fit to sleep in, and there always were a number of them on the ground-floor of every house, were used as kitchen, store-room, and lumber-room.

In very few houses were there separate dining-rooms. The meals were taken in the kitchen, or in any odd strip of superfluous space, or even in bedrooms. In joint families past their prime the taking of meals in bedrooms was quite common, because those brothers or cousins who earned more money than the others were not willing to raise their contribution to the common household fund and yet were not ready to forgo the luxuries to which they thought their better means entitled them. So they had the standard common meal requisitioned upstairs, added to it sweets and other delicacies bought with their own money, and ate the food in the privacy of their bedrooms with their own children. Even in families which were not joint the master often took his meals privately, for as the earning member of the family he felt that he had a right to specialities which he could not and would not share with his children and wife.

The visitors, all in the case of women, and relatives in the case of men, made straight for the bedrooms, sat on the beds there and chatted. Sometimes even the intimate friends of the master of the family would come into the bedrooms. The other visitors were kept at a distance. In those houses which had no outer parlour the master often went out to talk with callers on the footpath or lane, and occasionally even carried on a shouted conversation from an upper-story window. Many of the houses had a strip of open veranda in front, which was called a *ro'k*. The elders and the young men sat cross-legged on them in the mornings and evenings, either reading their newspaper and discussing it or merely gossiping. At night beggars, vagrants. and other waifs and strays slept there. Sometimes even wandering goats appropriated them.

It must not be imagined from this description that these interiors presented a chaotic appearance. On the contrary, they were always extremely tidy. The mistress or the mistresses never permitted the slightest displacement of any object from its place. It was in no wise unusual, when a family had lived in a house for a long time, to find a bottle or a book or a bundle remaining in its place on a ledge or rack out of reach of the children for twenty years. In fact, tidiness was the forte of these interiors and inelegance the foible. Every touch of added orderliness seemed to lay an extra coat of housewifely plainness on them.

A typical bedroom would have two beds occupying half or one-third of its space, of which at least one would be a carved fourposter received by the occupant of the room at the time of his marriage as a wedding present from his father-in-law. If the second bed had legs shorter than those of the fourposter, it would be raised by putting one or two bricks under each of the legs. Along one wall would be a long row of trunks, sometimes on the ground and sometimes on a bench. Most often a second tier of trunks would be placed on top of the first tier, and on the second tier of trunks there would be piled all the spare bedding and bedclothes appertaining to the room, so that in order to get at the contents of a trunk of the lower row the trunk resting on it, together with the bedclothes on the top, would in every case have to be taken down. The mistresses of these houses thought nothing of lifting and lowering fully loaded trunks. Another section of the wall would have one or more clothes-horses pushed against it, and at the end of a blind alley formed by the narrow space left between the lower ends of the beds and the wall opposite them there would be, where the householder could afford it, a chest of drawers or a dressing-table.

In this manner all the sides of the wall would be neatly and fully occupied, and in the most conspicuous position there would be a glazed almirah, about five and a half feet high, four feet wide, and over eighteen inches in depth, containing an overcrowded array of china, wax, and celluloid dolls, toys, and gew-gaws of every kind. In certain respects the women of Calcutta were like bower birds. They could never resist gaudy trifles. At the time of their marriage they were presented with dolls and similar toys, which they brought with them with their trousseau, which in fact formed a part of their trousseau, and from year to year they went on adding to their collection. They were always buying new trifles for themselves, for example, doll's house furniture, and seizing, over and above, the toys of the children, who in the ordinary course were not allowed to play with them. They put the whole lot in the glass-fronted cupboards in their bedrooms, to be admired by other women and even by the men.

Anything in the nature of pictures in these rooms, if within the lower reaches of the walls, was sure to be calendars with brightly coloured pictures or small photographs. The bigger framed pictures, where there were any, were hung high, above the doors and windows, and in order to be seen without the discomfort of kinking the neck they were inclined at an angle of about forty-five degrees towards the floor. These were mostly coloured pictures of the gods and goddesses, very alluringly amatory if of Krishna and Radha, and if of Kali very minatory and blood-curdling, in spite of her nudity. There usually would also be another picture, a large photographic enlargement, which stood out from the rest by reason of its more prominent position as well as by having a jasmine garland hanging in a half loop from the two upper corners of its frame. It would be the portrait of the departed father or mother.

If the keynote of the large mansions was repose, that of these houses was bustle, not confused scuttling about or noise, but a methodical organization of movement and sound which created the impression of a running machine. The metabolism of these homes was quick. The mistress, the other women, and the young girls were to be seen in purposive motion from upstairs to downstairs and again from downstairs to upstairs: now putting off their *saris* and chemises to wrap only a red loom-made towel round the waist in order to bathe, do some washing, or perform some other connected task, for which immemorial custom and inexorable taboo required a clearing of the decks; now getting back into their *saris* and chemises; now rushing into the kitchen to stir or turn some dish; now setting down the pan on the floor and running to the storeroom to bring a fresh supply of oil or *ghee;* now soaping the dirty linen with energetic jerks of the forearms; and, after that, wringing it with supple twists of the wrists; in a word, seeing the household tasks through with precision and celerity and at the same time scattering all around them the charms of their throbbing fullness.

The flagstone under the tap, called the Foot of the Tap in Bengali, was in one sense the heart of the machine, surpassing even the kitchen in importance. It was almost like an altar, corresponding to the hearth of the colder countries. To this place every domestic task found its way, because every task either began or ended with a washing up of human beings as well as inanimate objects. The women would not enter the kitchen without an early-morning bath, sometimes under the tap, at others with water taken from the cistern adjoining the tap and poured over the head from a mug. These cisterns, built of brick and cement-plastered, were to be found in every house, and they received their water from the tap through a split bamboo or a tin pipe, which formed a sort of umbilical cord between the city's water supply and the domestic stock of water. If we had had Vestal Virgins we would have employed them, not to tend the fire, but the cistern.

Above everything else, the Foot of the Tap symbolized release from work. To it everybody rushed to clinch the conclusion of domestic tasks. Once the hands and feet were washed there, a human being could relax. The maid-servant scrubbing utensils under the tap and taking the water she needed through a long piece of rag which she always tied round the tap's spout in order to prevent the water from splashing on her, looked forward to the moment when she would whisk away the rag and, washing her arms up to the elbows and the legs up to the knees, also wash her hands of the back-breaking task. The master went there after his return from the office, the mistress almost every half-hour, the others when they were let off.

The domestic bustle produced continuous and consistent sound effects. In the kitchen there was a succession of bubbling, fizzling, hissing, and crackling sounds. It was punctuated intermittently by a metallic sound like that of the triangle in an orchestra, which was produced when the energetically manipulated iron or brass ladies and turners struck against the pots and pans. The scrubbing of the utensils gave out a low abrasive sound, which became gritty at times and set the teeth on edge, but was generally smooth like the process of lens grinding. When clothes were being washed the sound was now like that of bass drums and now like that of castanets, depending on the volume of the washing undertaken. Dominating every other sound was the sound of falling water. The day began with the sound of the old water rushing out through the hole at the bottom of the cistern, followed by the patter of the new water falling on its floor. A whole gamut of watery sounds continued throughout the day, and sometimes into the night when the tap was left open.

The only time of the day when there was relaxation and quiet, and even stillness, in these houses was between the end of the midday meal of the women at about one o'clock and four o'clock in the afternoon. It was the time when the hawkers of dress fabrics–chintzes, muslins, organdies, and silks; of laces, ribbons, hairpins, and combs; of toilet goods, glass bangles, toys, and, as we used to say in those days in Bengali, all the "heart-stealing goods", contributed by their cries more to the stillness of the noontide than to the noises of the great city. This was the time they chose to tempt Eve, knowing very well that Adam would be safely away in his office. The women crowded into the narrow entrance passage to make their purchases, and while the hawker displayed his goods, lectured and protested, they haggled. When not engaged with the hawkers the women spread themselves and their long and moist hair on the cool floor of their bedrooms, usually with the baby at the breast and a novel in hand. But very soon the novel dropped from the hand, and, though the baby stuck fast, making ceaseless sucking movements of its lips and cheeks, the mother slept on unmindful. She woke up only when the maid-servant rattled the knocker on the front door or water began to fall again from the tap after the midday cut-off. The nights on the other hand were not very peaceful, for the babies had a habit of waking up and crying from hour to hour as our common myna does at night.

Twice a day these houses gave out characteristic exhalations. These were nothing but the smoke from the cooking ovens, which were mere things of half a dozen bricks, some mud, and a gridiron for each. These ovens had no flues, burnt coke of a very bad quality, and were kindled with cow-dung cakes soaked in kerosene, and generated a kind of smoke whose grey density had to be breathed in order to be believed possible. This thick and strongly smelling mixture of gaseous products rose from the oven in a solid column, and met the ceiling like a water-spout. Deflected therefrom, it came down and made its way out through the doors and windows in whirling clouds. Then progressively diluting itself with the air it floated in blue wisps until it pervaded every nook and cranny of the house. There was no means of resisting it, no means of escaping from it or of blowing the rooms free of it. The wind bloweth where it listeth. So did this smoke, wind's junior partner, in Calcutta. I had to breathe this smoke for thirty-two years and know what it is. But the true native of Calcutta appeared to have his lungs enamelled against its corrosive contact. He did not mind it at all.

These houses had sprung up like mushrooms on account of the absurd value that was set in Calcutta on the possession of a house. No true son of the city would willingly marry into or give in marriage to a family which did not live in a house owned by itself. To do so was to the native of Calcutta equivalent to losing caste by marrying gypsies and their like. I was once insulted in the most atrocious manner by an old virago of a washerwoman, not a mere washerwoman by caste, but a real, practising washerwoman, because I was living in rented apartments whereas she had a brick-built house of sorts of her own. I also knew a barber, a very dignified barber he was, who owned a house in a very respectable locality and showed no alacrity to set his razor to the chin of anybody whose house did not cover something like an acre of roof-space. The natives of Calcutta were resolved to disprove the biblical saying and have, not only houses to lay their heads in, but also a Permanent Settlement in housing supplementing the Permanent Settlement in land tenure.

After they had provided houses for themselves the natives went in for house property, which, next to gilt-edged securities, was their favourite investment. They let these houses to those who did not possess houses of their own. These tenants were mostly people whom the true native of Calcutta regarded only as resident aliens. But there were also true but poor natives who did own houses. Their standing in the eyes of their fellow-natives and of their own was mud. They could never console themselves for this deprivation, nor formulate a philosophy of life independent of house property in Calcutta. Thus they were always saving every pice they could by scrimping and screwing, until they had saved enough to die as a houseowner. But even those who lived in rented houses disdained to live in flats. They would live only in independent, self-contained houses. But as it was impossible to combine independence, spaciousness, and economy, the typical middle-class house in Calcutta, in spite of being the proud citizen's castle, looked a mean castle in every instance.

LIFE IN CALCUTTA

Public life in Calcutta cried without, it uttered its voice in the streets. Whatever public activity was on for the time being became visible to the eye in the outward form of processions, open-air meetings, and other demonstrations, or could be detected in the behaviour of the concourses on the thoroughfares of the Bengali quarters, which became charged with something tense and electrical. The inhabitants of Calcutta were always prone to be a little *frondeur*. Any public excitement brought them out in the streets. A mere glance at the pavements was enough to show whether something was up or not.

Private life on the other hand was drearily monotonous. The old Bengali book about Calcutta to which I have already referred describes the daily life of the gentry of Calcutta and shows how early in the history of the city its pattern had become fixed. It describes the ways of the different classes of gentlefolk and begins with those who in spite of being wealthy still continued in business or profession. According to the book, they got up in the morning and met and talked with all classes of callers. Then came, in succession, the oil massage, bath, daily worship, meal, and a short rest. After resting, the personages put on wonderful dresses, stepped into splendid carriages or palanquins, and went to their places of work, where they stayed as long as they considered necessary. Returning home, they changed clothes, washed, and purified themselves from the previous contact with the foreign dress by touching Ganges water. Then followed a second worship and light refreshments, after which in the evening there was another reception in the outer parlour, attended by a very large number of visitors, some of whom came on business, some merely to pay their respects. Occasionally, at this time, the dignitaries went out to pay their own calls.

Of the intermediate class, the book says that their life was generally similar, although there was in it less of patronage and parlour gossip and more of work. The poor gentlefolk, according to the book, followed a similar routine, but, of course, with still less cultivation of social life, less ample meals, and an infinitely greater amount of labour. In addition, they had to trudge a good deal, and pay court and play the "yes man" to their patrons and employers, without which they could not hope to keep their jobs.

After describing the daily life of these three classes, the book goes on to consider the ways of the "extraordinary fortunate", who, as the writer puts it, lived by God's grace on the interest of their accumulated wealth or on their landed property, or in plain words ate the bread of idleness. Their life also followed the same pattern, except that they stayed at home during the day and slept, only glancing at their affairs in the afternoon.

When I read the book for the first time in the early 'thirties I was astonished to realize how much of the pattern of life fixed more than a hundred years ago had survived in the current life of the natives of the city. There was, of course, less personal worship and no recollection at all of the original reason for the elaborate change of clothing and washing in the afternoon. Nobody realized that it was a legacy from those days when the wearing of any foreign dress (Islamic in that age) was an act of ceremonial impurity. Also, the number of those who did not have to earn a living and could live in utter idleness, dawdling and sleeping through life, had increased. But the succession of daily activities in the different strata of the gentlefolk class had not altered at all. The morning gossip, the midday spell of business or siesta, the afternoon relaxation, and the evening court, had all come down unmodified.

Underlying all these activities, from getting up to going to bed again, there were two motives, or rather two urges: first, the desire for worldly success, and, secondly, satisfaction of the gregarious instinct. The desire for worldly success was of the most easily intelligible type, mere search for livelihood in the case of the poor and insatiable greed for more and ever more money in the case of those who had been emancipated from the fear of starvation. But the gregarious propensities of the natives of Calcutta were of a more complex character and require a somewhat lengthy analysis.

There was very little social life among the Bengalis of Calcutta, as understood even in the more frivolous connotation of the words "society" and "monde". No afternoon or evening parties, no dinners, no at-homes, and, of course, no dances, enlivened their existence. The heaviest social exertion in this sense that they could or would undergo was to pay formal calls. But there was something to offset this deficiency. What the native of the city lacked in sociability he made up in gregariousness. No better connoisseur of company was to be found anywhere in the world, and no one else was more dependent on the contiguity of his fellows with the same incomprehension of his obligations towards them. The man of Calcutta found the company he needed so badly and continuously readily assembled, without any effort on his part, in his office, or in his bar-library, or in his college, which were no less places for endless idle gossip than for work. In fact, an admixture of business and gossip furnished the connecting link between the activities which constituted the pursuit of money and those that constituted the pursuit of idleness. No one who has lived among Indians can have failed to have been struck by their infinite capacity to lengthen out the business of the day, at times from the early morning to midnight, and he may have been terrified by this *outre* devotion to self-interest. But all of it is not a boring excess of avarice. Quite an appreciable proportion of this assiduity in business is only a pretext for remaining in the company of fellow-men and chatting with them as long as possible. Thus, if an Indian's love of money or his conviction of the sanctity of self-interest converts all his conversation into shop-talk, it is his gregarious propensity which makes the shop-talk so interminable. What is applicable to Indian society as a whole, I found equally or more applicable to the Bengali society of Calcutta.

But the true expression of its gregariousness was disinterested. Perhaps gregariousness was the only disinterested thing in Calcutta society. Outside working hours the true native would always be roving in search of company, and his very striving for it often defeated its purpose. Every able-bodied person after his return from office and a hurried wash and tea rushed out of his house with the intention of meeting his friends, and these friends being on the same errand it occasionally happened that everybody missed everybody else. The more usual practice, however, was to avoid these misadventures by having fixed rendezvous or, as they were called in Bengali, *addas*. Each *adda* had its fixed adherents, who would begin to drop in one by one from about half-past five in the afternoon till in about an hour's time the attendance was full. These gathering-places were most often the outer parlour of one of the wealthier members of the group, but at times also an office after office hours, and, more rarely, a tea-shop. It was not obligatory for the host to be present, although he generally was, but invariably he was the least conspicuous individual in the company. The visitors had the freedom of the house, and ordered the host's servants about just as they pleased.

No refreshments were served and none were expected, but a cup or two of tea was always to be had, and this collective tea was prepared by a servant at one end of the veranda or some other corner of the outer house. In a typical Calcutta household tea was no affair of the women of the family. Like the master's English clothes, it fell within the jurisdiction of the servants of the outer house. As a general rule, these meeting-places were located in the quarter in which the greater majority of the frequenters lived. But it was not at all unusual to find a man travelling five or six miles by tram in order to join his company. This happened when a family living in a rented house moved from one quarter to another. A man was far less ready to join a new *adda* than he was to shift to a new house in a new quarter. Sometimes many years passed before a man would think of changing his company in order to avoid the long daily journey.

The people of Calcutta being facile in speech, these congregations at times became garrulous and even voluble. But in their characteristic form they were unexpectedly quiet. In fact, the real art of gregariousness in Calcutta lay in being in company and at the same time making the fact outwardly immaterial. In sharp contrast to the demoniac energy shown in rushing to the rendezvous, the languor of the actual proceedings was startling. The briskness of his steps and the eagerness on his face would vanish as soon as a man passed the door of the assembly-room. He would hardly even nod recognition to his friends, and in his turn would not be nodded to by them. He would sit down quietly in his accustomed place and look extremely contented. If there was conversation it was so leisurely a verbal exchange that nobody could discover a thread in the half-drawled relay of words. Indeed, few cared for it, and most often even half-drawled words were not forthcoming but only hems and grunts. Besides, nobody took the trouble of looking into the eyes of anybody else, even if he spoke to him. The laconic remarks and exclamations resembled bubbles in still waters which indicate the presence of fish. For the greater part of the time the company remained silent, contemplating the ceiling or any section of the wall which presented itself conveniently to the eyes, and smiling beatifically. The winter evenings were even more luxurious. Then the company would cover themselves up from head to foot in their shawls and lie back on the pillows and bolsters, quivering their legs or waggling their toes. Even literary people, that talkative crowd, came to acquire these habits. After about two hours of this relaxation the company would rise one by one, and no trace of the previous leisureliness would be observable in their movements as they ran for the tram or bus and jumped into it.

I did not understand this behaviour until in 1922 I read for the first time McDougall's *Social Psychology,* in which I found the distinction between the social and the gregarious instinct clearly drawn and properly emphasized. Reinforcing my critical armoury from the book, I began to call the gregarious natives of Calcutta Galton's Oxen, that is to say, the oxen of Damaraland in Africa. Individually these animals hardly appear even to be conscious of one another, but if separated from the herd they display extreme signs of distress and do not rest until they have regained it and buried themselves in it. That is also how every native of Calcutta feels and acts. There is nothing he dreads more than isolation, and his complaint against every place other than Calcutta is that it has no "society". The abject dependence of these people on the company of their usual friends and acquaintances makes the more wealthy of them take at their own expense a whole party of cronies with them when they have their annual outing to the hills, the seaside, or some other holiday resort. Those who cannot afford the luxury entreat their friends to come to the same place and share expenses.

The strong herd instinct of the natives of Calcutta has virtually killed family life. There is no custom among them of a man sitting with his wife and children in the evening. It is hardly possible even to find them at home at any hour of the day suitable for calls, because their days are divided into three major outings–the morning wandering in search of casual gossip, the midday stay in office, and the systematized cultivation of company in the evenings. Even when at home, no man of Calcutta, in fact no Bengali, considers it good form to speak on any subject but domestic problems and difficulties with the members of the family, and the usual tone of this conversation too is acrimonious. In the joint families brothers take very little notice of one another, and when they do they directly and ostensibly address their remarks to common friends. Fathers show no familiarity to grown-up sons, and sons avoid the fathers even more conscientiously. Husbands and wives possibly have more to say to each other, but, this intercommunication takes place in such inaccessible places and at such impossible hours that third parties have no means of judging its quality. Therefore conjugal interchanges too do not disturb the atmosphere of detachment which marks the outward aspect of family life.

But if family life in Calcutta was asphyxiated by the herd instinct, collective life was poisoned. The herd loyalty of the inhabitants of Calcutta manifested itself even more strongly as violent hostility to the other fellow's set than as attachment to one's own set. Following the English example, constant experiments were being made in the co-operative management of social, educational, cultural, civic, business, and political affairs, but these attempts were also failing as constantly. It is not in the nature of any Bengali, or for that matter of any Indian, to work by means of committees and councils, and this method, when it is not a mere make-believe, is only a disguised and therefore very useful means of exercising autocratic personal authority. It does nothing but provide openings for the spirit of faction.

The Bengalis, and more especially the Bengalis of Calcutta, were and still remain, some of the finest virtuosi of factiousness. There is hardly any branch of it which they do not practise, and hardly any activity into which it has not wormed its way. Municipalities, universities, learned societies, political parties, public offices, business concerns, clubs, and even schools are rent by cliques, and are always splitting up like protozoa. To be in the ruling clique means a temporary monopoly of all the advantages that these institutions offer, and to be outside it is to be deprived for the time being of all opportunities, rights, facilities, in a corresponding measure. One may not be able to consult even an indispensable old book or manuscript to carry out a piece of research. The latest consequence of this factiousness, now that political power has come into the hands of these clique-ridden creatures, is going to be chronic political instability. The stasis of Plato and the *asabiya* of Ibn Khaldun were as milk and water compared with this distilled spirit of factiousness.

Public opinion in Calcutta has never been hostile to the growth and existence of cliques. The reason is historical. Factiousness in a general form is prevalent all over rural Bengal, and has been so for centuries. It spread to Calcutta with the very foundation of the city, and the old Bengali book to which I have referred treats it as a social fact of long standing with firm roots. One remarkable feature of its urban growth was the conscious effort to widen the field of its operation. It was extended to every sphere of collective activity by successively bringing within its ambit social life, religious movements, civic affairs, political agitation, and, finally, the formation of ministries.

Here I cannot reproduce in its entirety the account of the factions of Calcutta given in the old Bengali book, but the kernel of all that the author has to say is contained in one sentence, couched in the quaint Bengali of those days: "The honour of the leadership of a party is steeped in nectar, many desire it, and when more than one person covet the same thing there is bound to be disunity." In its essence the factiousness of the people of Calcutta could not bear a materialistic interpretation. Its object was the satisfaction of a pride, not of an interest.

Thus it happens that barring the platitudes of the average person and the sincere indignation of the crank, nothing opposes the growth of factions. For one thing, these have always been looked upon as the salt of social existence, and, which is more important, as the only means of transacting public business within self-governing institutions. On this point too I can cite some evidence from the early nineteenth century, which interprets factions as a salutary moral influence. A well-known newspaper of those days, giving the news of the formation of a new clique in 1833 under the headline "New Clique in Social Life", welcomed the event effusively. It professed to be overjoyed by the announcement because, in its view, the growth of the city's population called for a corresponding increase in the number of cliques. The paper recalled the early history of factions in Calcutta and pointed out that originally the city possessed only two cliques, but that with its expansion and progress a corresponding multiplication of cliques had taken place, so that at the time of writing there were quite a number of cliques in Calcutta, all of which had come into existence through the fission of the two old trees and could very properly be described as their grafts or branches. In conclusion the newspaper observed that the circumstances of the times demanded an even greater increase in the number of cliques, since it was not possible to maintain social discipline without an adequate number of them. As the paper put it, the more numerous the cliques, the greater the social welfare. The argument at this point becomes too subtle for ordinary intelligence, but it would seem that what the editor had in mind was something like a balance of power among the cliques. This idea, however queer it may seem to the heretic, has historical importance, for existing in the subconscious rather than the conscious mind of the inhabitants of Calcutta, it has made a substantial contribution to the permanence of factiousness in the city. There certainly exists in Calcutta a sneaking affection for cliques, a sort of thieves' brotherhood among the cliques. Having watched the civic and political dissensions in the city over something like twenty years I can personally testify that in Calcutta no faction, however powerful during its spell of power, ever thinks of knocking a rival faction on the head and putting it out of the way forever. It does not do so even if it has the enemy completely in its power, and the only explanation that seems tenable is–Dog does not eat dog.

In this chapter I have not described the life of a very important element in the Bengali society of Calcutta. It is the Anglicized Bengali element, mostly consisting of barristers and their families, living in old Ballygunje or the Chowringhee quarter. The reason is that it is now definitely a thing of the past, although even between 1910 and 1920 it was influential and active. The Anglicism of the men and women of this class has been supplanted today by a cheaper and less efficient Anglicism, which appreciates neither the traits and values which the older generation tried to assimilate from the West nor the older generation's painstaking finesse in imitation. If a situation could be imagined in which Indians taught to read and write English of the received standard had wholly discarded that form of the language for Basic English (which can be easily imagined today), that would furnish a parallel to the transition from the Anglicism of the Bengali of the late nineteenth century and early twentieth century to the Anglicism of the Bengali of today.

The older type could always be distinguished from the normal run of Bengalis, and were invariably called Sahibs instead of Babus. Their wives too were addressed as Memsahibs. They lived in aristocratic segregation, brought about in the first instance by the orthodox of the ordinary Bengali, who considered them to have lost caste, and secondly by their own contempt for those whom they looked upon as the unredeemed rank and file of Bengali society. Naturally, they were both admired and disliked, and if they had earned the dislike by their snobbery, they also deserved the esteem on account of their scrupulous adherence to the ideals and standards they had chosen for themselves and their conscientious practice of them.

There were no set of people better posted about the appropriate times and occasions for the different kinds of English clothes, and a wrong tie or hat was likely to give rise to more trouble among them than in the best English society. They called one of their streets Mayfair, and shunned all streets with Indian names. Store Road, to their thinking, was preferable to Kalighat Road, although the one had derived its name from a grocery and the other led to the temple of the great goddess Kali herself, the patron deity of Calcutta. They preferred the European cuisine, although in its actual presentation by the Muslim *bawarchis* or cooks it was modified by the Mogul tradition. Their homes were provided with the usual drawing-rooms, dining-rooms, and studies. Altogether, on entering one of these houses it was not impossible to imagine that it was the residence of an English gentleman.

But there is no justification for being conscious only of their weak points, which were but the faults of their qualities. They had made their choice for the West, and lived in the light of their convictions. Most of them had a high literary culture,

well-developed political sense, and awareness of social and
political duties. Nearly all of them were good speakers, and
would have turned out to be honest and capable ministers. In
family life, despite the fact that some affected the ways of the
fast and more fell a prey to drink, the general tone was of
Victorian respectability, strict discharge of family obligations,
and steadiness. I use the adjective Victorian in a commenda-
tory sense, as I feel it should be. Are not the post-Victorians
a decidedly poorer lot than the Victorians? At all events, such
is the case in Bengal. That is why I take the view that many
virtues and still many more graces have passed away from
Bengali life with the disappearance of the older order of
Anglicized Bengalis. I never had the opportunity of coming in
direct personal contact with them. Even so I miss them.

Now that I have brought to a close my account of Calcutta
I am seized with a qualm. In order to explain it I have to refer
again to the old Bengali book on Calcutta. In it the expounder
of the life of the city feels doubtful whether he ought to
enlighten and educate the provincial. He says—and the opinions of this character in the book seem to reflect the views of
the author—that the provincial after settling down in Calcutta,
being received by its society in a friendly spirit, and being
enabled through his stay in it to make a fortune, usually repaid
the debt by spreading malicious tales and calumnies about it.
I wonder if I have been guilty of the same ungrateful meanness
towards the great city, and this heart-searching is all the
stronger in me because today it has been wholly conquered by
the despised provincial. From about 1920 began a process
which has re-shaped the outward aspect and the inward nature
of Calcutta. When I left it in 1942 it was not what it was in
1910, and I hear that what it is today is utterly different even
from what it was in 1942. These reports give me a notion that
a pathological megalopolitanism has taken possession of the
place. Therefore, if I have been unkind to it, it is unkindness to
the dead. The Calcutta I knew is no more: *Fuimus Troes, fuit
Ilium.*

CHAPTER II

NEW POLITICS

WHEN AFTER spending nearly five years in a sort of retreat I resumed social life in 1921, and began to cast about for lost scents and trials, I distinctly felt that the world around me had changed in the meanwhile. The changes were negative as well as positive. Certain qualities and things, dominant in the old order in which I was born and brought up, had disappeared or were disappearing. Certain other things, previously absent, were entering or holding the field. There was no aspect of our existence in which the voids and the intrusions were not crying aloud for notice. Yet the inexplicable thing was that nobody seemed to be aware of them. Even I did not perceive them in a manner more direct than that in which a blind man feels the atmosphere when he is taken from an ordinary living-room into a room in the basement. It was only after years of conscious analysis of the social transformation we were going through that I came to discover the true nature of the four years lying between 1917 and 1922–came to see that they constituted the initial stage of an undetected metastasis in our society. I shall begin my description of this transformation with an account of the new trends in our politics.

DISTURBED TONALITY

During the war we Indians were looking forward to a great advance in self-government at its end. In those days we called our political demand and goal Home Rule, and I was given to declaring off and on that if disappointed in my expectations I would emigrate from India. There was no doubt that this much-aired resolve was prompted by a cue taken subconsciously from Irish history. But in the absence of a hospitable United States, the promised land to which my exodus was to lead me took concrete shape in my mind as Tanganyika, then the scene of scattered fighting between the Germans and the forces of the British Empire. I do not know how I came to believe that after the expulsion of the Germans that part of Africa would be handed over to us for colonization. But the fantastic illusion did take hold of me, and it was fostered by a lecture given to the students of my college, Scottish Church College, by a wounded officer who had lost an arm in the fighting in Tanganyika and was spending his leave in India. He described the country to us and remarked casually that, although he did not know for certain, India might get Tanganyika. Thus the vision of a large estate, horses and livestock, a ranch house, and a pretty wife to match definitely obtained a lodgement in my brain.

But neither my friends nor even I were so foolish as to brush aside the possibility that so far from getting Tanganyika we might not have any advance in self-government even in our own country. Therefore we earnestly debated the question of "sanctions". On this point we had already arrived at a degree of certainty which amounted to cocksureness: to our thinking, there was only one thing to apply–passive resistance; and only one thing to get done as a prerequisite–transform the middle-class nationalist movement into a mass nationalist movement. Already, by 1915, the man who was to bring in the masses and conduct the passive resistance campaign had become identified to us as Mr. (not yet Mahatma) Gandhi. Although all the old leaders, and more especially Tilak, were still living and active, our eyes were fixed on Gandhi as the coming man.

But even then certain particulars about his character, ideas, and methods had reached me which jarred with the notion I had formed of him from the usual eulogistic accounts in the Press. A young nephew of mine, who had been sent to

Tagore's famous school at Santiniketan, had to be brought back because he was feeling more and more unhappy there. This boy told me that servants had been dispensed with in the hostels of the school at the instance, as he put it, of "Gandhi and his gang". A whole troupe of scantily clad cranks, he said, had descended on Santiniketan and, pouring all sorts of queer suggestions into the ears of Gurudev (or Master, as Tagore was called by the inmates of his *Ashram*), had got him to agree to make the students work in the kitchen and scullery. Even more scandalous suggestions had been put forward, the boy added, among which was the idea of making the students do the work of sweepers(!), but Tagore had not thought it advisable to go so far. My nephew spoke angrily and contemptuously of the "goings on of Gandhi and his gang" and of the mischief done by them, and his report instilled into my mind some doubts about the conventional conception of Mahatma Gandhi. Can he be a faddist, a man with a bee in his bonnet, a fanatical rough-rider of hobbies out for naive tilts at social standards and civilization? I asked myself, and I could not wholly resist the formation in my mind of an alternative image challenging the accepted one–the image of a crude thaumaturge wandering with a following of Orphic mountebanks, the coryphaeus of a pack of dancing dervishes or half-naked fakirs, for whom rational and civilized men could not feel anything but derision and contempt. But although the jarring note came early enough into my mind, as early as 1913 to be precise, it was effaced quickly because it was neither sustained nor sounded afresh by any reports besides those given to me by my nephew. Thus my old notion of Mahatma Gandhi prevailed. In fact, it was confirmed by the favourable account which my younger brother brought to me after hearing him at the time of the 1917 session of the Indian National Congress in Calcutta.

The Montagu-Chelmsford report on constitutional advance and the report of the Rowlatt Commission on revolutionary activities gave us intimation of what we could expect after the war, and very shortly there came more positive indications through two measures: the new Government of India Bill introduced in Parliament and the Rowlatt Bill in the Indian legislature. Political India was swept by the fury of disappointment and disillusionment. The 1917 declaration had made us pitch our expectations too high, which was rather different from pitching our demands too high, as we invariably did. Yet I do not think that the inadequacies of Mr. Montagu's bill would have made us so angry without the other measure. I have already spoken of the fear and hatred we felt for the Defence of India Act, and now the arbitrary powers created by that Act were going to be incorporated in the ordinary law of the country. The Rowlatt Bill provoked us all the more because we took it as the symbol of a mean and malicious ingratitude to India. Nationalist India was always prone to make a virtue and a bargaining piece of any abandonment or even suspension by it of its negative attitude, and it regarded the gesture of co-operation made by the Congress shortly after the outbreak of the war as being in itself a great service to the British people. In addition, interested but not very intelligent propaganda had created a legend of India's contribution, to the Allied war effort which bore no relation to the real contribution, substantial as that reality was. Thus the indignation in India over British ingratitude was both genuine and widespread. It appeared to most of us that the British people with their usual perfidy and Machiavellism were treating India as if she were one of the defeated enemy countries and applying the formula *vae victis* to her. Accordingly, the philosophy with which a doubting and cynical people would probably have taken the cautious measuring-out of self-government in the 1919 bill evaporated under the heat generated by the repressive bill which was its counterpart.

On the British side there may have been reasons for introducing the Rowlatt Bill which were more matter of fact and less malevolent, but we put the worst possible interpretation on the conduct of our rulers and were quite sincere in doing so. Therefore we saw no reason to abate our fierce opposition to the Rowlatt Bill. On the other hand, the obstinate tenacity with which the Government of India pursued it showed that it was actuated by an equally uncharitable interpretation of Indian intentions and motives. I still believe that a compromise over the Rowlatt Bill was desirable and possible. But in this matter Sir William Vincent, who was conducting the bill through the legislature, seems to have acted as the representative of the British element, both civil and military, of the Government of India, the whole weight of whose enormous power and influence was thrown on the side of the measure. I cannot explain the unstatesmanly obduracy of these men except on the supposition that they not only looked upon the Rowlatt Bill as their revenge for the nervous worry the Indian revolutionaries had caused them during the war, a worry which was referred to by the Mesopotamia Commission but which the Commission did not consider wholly justified, but were also determined to make the passage of the bill the test of their position and prestige in post-war India. In any case, when the long and bitter debate in the Legislative Council revealed to us that no give and take on this measure was possible, all of us were driven to the conviction that the only redress open to us was to fight it with passive resistance. We whole-heartedly approved of Mahatma Gandhi's resolve to launch passive resistance.

But the actual application of our most powerful political weapon brought me two severe shocks. The first of these was caused by the immediate degeneration of passive resistance into mob violence. I had never thought that a method of which we had thoughts so highly and on which we had based all our hopes would so easily drift towards murder, arson, and looting. I read the news from the Punjab and Gujarat with distress and anxiety. No outbursts of violence occurred in Calcutta but there were scenes of unruliness and disorder. To my great disgust I saw bands of ragged street urchins throwing mud and dust at the tram-cars. This was my first experience of a form of rebellion against British rule which was to become typical of the city. Just as the Parisian mob went for the pavements when seized with revolutionary excitement, the Calcutta mob went for the tram-cars, which to them seemed to have become symbolic of British rule. But whereas the Parisians tore up the streets with defensive intentions the Calcutta mob preferred the offensive. In the last phase anything from nitric acid to bombs was thrown at the tram-cars. Compared with this development the beginnings in 1919 were humble. But even so they made me furious.

In addition to the account of the disturbances in India, I also read the news of the riots in Egypt, and on account of my interest in Egyptian archaeology I was particularly disquieted by the reports of the attacks on the archaeological service. I came to learn that the rioters had spared only Flinders Petrie and his excavations because he had never employed the lash against his workmen. Pondering over all these events at home and abroad I wondered whether settled and orderly government was not coming to an inglorious end everywhere.

This thought was all the more persistent because beyond the disturbed oriental countries I saw something which was infinitely more disturbing. Oriental fury, I knew, would be controlled in the end because it was inherently feeble and ineffective. But Europe was a different proposition, and Europe was becoming a living furnace of revolutions. The more I tried to avoid thinking of the meteoric personalities and flaming names of the post-war revolutionary movement in Europe—the Lenins, the Trotskys, the Bela Kuns, the Rosa

Luxemburgs, the Karl Liebknechts–the more they forced me to take note of them. I had not yet read Ernst Toller's *Masses and Man,* but I could sense the spirit which was to inspire the writing of that book. Both for personal and public reasons I was yearning for quiet, repose, and serenity at that time, and the fear of having to wait for them in vain made me sick.

The second and the more serious shock came from the severity of the repression in India. With my respect for discipline and love of order I saw nothing wrong in the resolute suppression of anarchy. But as information trickled out from the Punjab I, like the rest of my countrymen, was horrified and infuriated by the disproportionate severity of the punishment and, which was more, by the gratuitous display of vindictiveness and racial arrogance that accompanied the restoration of order in the Punjab. It became a torture for us to think of Amritsar even before General Dyer described his action there with indiscreet bravado. One evening, while we were seated at meal in our hostel, a young man suddenly recalled that the Punjab leaders were to receive their sentences that day. All of us started as if we had been touched with a red-hot iron, and for a moment or two we could not eat. I did not meet or hear a single Indian in those days who did not share the indignation which made Tagore renounce his knighthood, although many of my acquaintances were also distressed by the excesses of the passive-resistance movement.

In the whole course of my life there have been three periods during which I fully shared the passions of the nationalist movement: first, during the anti-partition or Swadeshi days; secondly, in the months following the suppression of the passive-resistance movement in 1919; and, thirdly, during the civil disobedience of 1930-1. But while the first and the last of these three periods had their exultations as well as their sufferings, the middle period was a spell of uncompensated anguish which could only hurt. Many of the men who today are in positions of power in India through the abdication of Britain became permanently warped and corroded in their outlook through that suffering. In those months I could not think of British rule in India or even of British power in the world except as the Hebrew Prophets thought of Assyria and Babylon. I wished I could write like Nahum: "Thy shepherds slumber, O King of Assyria; thy nobles shall dwell in the dust; thy people is scattered upon the mountains, and no man gathereth them. There is no healing of thy bruise; thy wound is grievous; all that hear the bruit of thee shall clap the hands over thee; for upon whom hath not thy wickedness passed continually?"

It was while I was in this mood that one day I came upon two reviews in the *Times Literary Supplement* which brought me great comfort. I would give particulars of them even at the risk of drawing upon myself Pascal's terse judgement that *"Peu de chose nous console parce que peu de chose nous afflige"*. One of the two reviews was a very appreciative notice of the English translation of a Bengali novel by the two daughters of the wellknown Indian journalist Mr. Ramananda Chatterjee. I am not wholly sure of the accuracy of my recollection on this point, but I think it was in this review that I read the observation that there were at least two languages in the British Empire which possessed first-class literatures, and they were English and Bengali. I felt grateful to Santa and Sita Chatterjee for vindicating Indian talent at a moment of unparalleled national humiliation, although I had not thought much of their story when it was originally coming out as a serial.

The other review dealt with one of the greatest books of our times, Spengler's *Untergang des Abendlandes,* in its German edition. I had come upon the review quite accidentally in the library of the Presidency College, but I read it with spell-bound interest. There has been no second occasion in my life when the reading of a mere review became so exultant an experience for me as the reading of the review of Spengler's book was. The thesis of the book, summarized by the reviewer, agreed even more closely with my mood than with the mood of a war-weary and disillusioned Europe. At last I thought I had got an answer to my agonized questionings. The pride and power of Europe which had inflicted such injury and humiliation and which yet appeared so triumphant and irresistible was going to be fought by something infinitely more potent than our will and capacity; it was to be crushed by history in its inexorable sweep. There was to be no healing of that bruise.

Very soon, however, I was to have another of my unexpected intellectual and emotional rebounds. When the special session of the Congress was held in Calcutta in September 1920, I was too distracted by my academic failure to take much notice of its proceedings. After that I left Calcutta for Kishorganj and, during the next few months, remained wholly occupied with my elder brother's marriage. When the excitement of that event was over, the Congress had definitely accepted non-co-operation, but I found myself not only out of sympathy with the ideas, aims, and methods of the movement, but also violently opposed to them.

I was at Kishorganj when the new form of agitation began and did not see much commotion, for it always took a little time for the wash of any political movement to reach our small and rather sleepy place. None the less even the reports which enthusiastic would-be non-co-operators were bringing to me of wonderful things happening elsewhere annoyed me. I remained in a state of continuous irritation and was having ceaseless arguments in a bad-tempered vein. But in spite of my antagonism to non-co-operation I was still capable of being worked up through appeals to my old political loyalties, as a small incident which took place at Kishorganj at the time was to show. There was a boy of about twelve, the son of a lawyer living quite close to our house, who and whose misdeeds were notorious throughout the town. "Lord of Beasts", one of the names of Siva, was his real name, but thanks to his none too godly reputation in the neighbourhood it Had become reduced to simple Beast, and his tricks passed under the name of *beastly antics*. Now, one afternoon I heard that Beast and some of his myrmidons, of whom there were not a few, had been rounded up by the police, taken to the police station, and given a cruel beating there. I was furious, for I assumed as a matter of course that poor Beast, carried away by a sudden fit of patriotic mischief-making, had shouted *Vande Mataram* or some such slogan at the police inspector and suffered on that account.

I spoke to my father about the incident. He did not give much countenance to my excitement, which rather made me feel that with age my father was losing some of his old spirit. Then I carried my indignation to a friend of my elder brother, who had become a teacher in one of the schools of the town. He responded quickly enough, but not in the manner expected by me. "Don't, don't, please, Nirad," he cried eagerly, and implored me not to speak about the incident to anybody else, and then he told me the whole Rabelaisian truth.

What Beast had done was as wicked as it was character-istic of him. With a number of his companions he had climbed a tree just behind the unenclosed latrine of the police inspector's house, found him there, carefully watched the whole proceed-ings, and delivered a running commentary, punctuated by such shouts as "Sir, do something before you blow your trumpet", and "Sir, hold, hold, you have worked hard enough, now rest and beat your drum." As long as Nature was on the side of Beast the unfortunate police inspector had to endure all this, but no sooner was he released than he rushed out, and ordered his constables to round up Beast and his party, which was done with the result I have mentioned.

The recollection of misplaced emotion did nothing to lessen my dislike for the non-co-operation movement, although I was glad to find that my town had not tried to make capital out of Beast's escapade. At a place politically more advanced than Kishorganj and in the hands of more enterprising political workers the incident would have acquired a different aspect and old Beast become a hero. For, as I never failed to notice, our nationalism had the marvellous knack of catching and riding any reputable horse that came its way instead of trudging on its cloven hoofs. In justice to Beast as to my town I must also say, and I say it all the more gladly because I myself had to give him a beating one day for playing one of his pranks on me, that he never pretended to be a greater saint than he was. He grew up into an honest man and is now dead.

I went back to Calcutta in the summer of 1921 and found the city in the grip of a *fronde*, which made me very angry. As the temperature of the agitation rose, so did my temper, and I did not become quite normal until, early in 1922, the Chauri-Chaura outrage prompted Mahatma Gandhi to call off the movement. But the story of my relations with Gandhian politics was not to end with my disapproval of non-co-operation. During the civil disobedience movement of 1930 I veered round to a passionate approval of Mahatma Gandhi's methods and became an almost idolatrous worshipper of his personality. In all these changes of mood and affiliations between 1921 and 1930 I was governed wholly by blind impulses. I did not understand the reasons for my moods, nor the nature of Gandhism, and I do not think that there was better understanding of the tremendous phenomenon of Gandhian politics anywhere else. In 1920, I, an obscure and immature student, was not the only man to have doubts about the Gandhian way. Almost all the old leaders of the nationalist movement were sceptical and worried. Tilak was doubtful, so were C. R. Das, Pandit Malaviya, and an impressive array of personalities from all parts of India. But Tilak died, C. R. Das was won over, and Bepin Chandra Pal, who had the courage to criticize the new method publicly, had to make his exit from nationalist politics. The victory of Gandhism, which was the victory of a new kind of nationalism over all the previous forms of rational nationalism preached and practised in modern India, forced the men of all the old schools not only into silence but into incomprehension. On the other hand the followers of Gandhism could not provide greater enlightenment. They became incapable of understanding their creed by the mere fact of its victory and their belief in it. The saying *credo ut intelligam* was not to be, and could not be, their motto.

It was in the late 'thirties that, after my final emancipation from the Gandhian ideology, and after much reflection on the nature and history of Indian nationalism, that I became capable of placing Gandhism in its historical setting. As a result, what I have arrived at today is dispassionate comprehension replacing the old admiration and the older condemnation. But I cannot make my conclusions accessible to the reader without taking him over some of the ground I have traversed. I hope the account I am going to give of Indian nationalism in all its varied aspects will not only furnish a clue to my own political oscillations but also serve the larger purpose of making Indian nationalism intelligible to the world.

OUR BASIC NATIONALISM

Those who think that nationalism in India is a phenomenon of recent growth are mistaken; if they also think that it is wholly importation from the West, as I often find that they do, they are rather more in error; and those others who assert that the first and second world wars opened the flood-gates of nationalism in India are, of course, the victims of that specific form of want of culture which has it source in the common man's bondage to the present. Anybody who cares for it can find in history release from all the three errors.

It is indeed perfectly true that a particular brand of nationalism came to us from the West and for many decades powerfully influenced the native stream of nationalism. At first the two pursued roughly parallel courses. Then they intermingled and interacted. In the third phase the spirit of the older nationalism nearly swamped the spirit of the new, although the new made the old infinitely more effective than it had been at any time of its history. In its final shape our nationalism had hardly anything Western about it beyond its foreign vocabulary and partly foreign technique of operation.

The first description of the old Indian or Hindu nationalism that I have come across is to be found in Alberuni's *India,* written more than nine hundred years ago. This great Islamic scholar, *clarum et venerabile nomen,* whose aim was to compile an accurate historical record of the religion, literature, sciences, laws, and customs of the Hindus for the information of his co-religionists, had necessarily to make his acquaintance with the Hindus and in the process of this intercourse became acutely aware of all the facets of their group consciousness, which means almost the same thing as nationalism. To begin with, I shall reproduce what he says about its internal aspect.

"The Hindus," writes Alberuni, "believe that there is no country but theirs, no nation like theirs, no kings like theirs, no region like theirs, no science like theirs. They are haughty, foolishly vain, self-conceited, and stolid. They are by nature niggardly in communicating that which they know, and they take the greatest possible care to withold it from men of another caste among their own people, still much more, of course, from any foreigner."

All this was, of course, very natural in the members of a closed society based on the tie of blood; and a people so egocentric internally could not but be violently xenophobic externally. Alberuni describes this side of Hindu nationalism as well. He says, "There is very little disputing about theological topics among themselves [the Hindus]; at the utmost, they fight with words, but they will never stake their soul, or body, or their property on religious controversy. On the contrary, all their fanaticism is directed against those who do not belong to them–against all foreigners. They call them *mlechchha*, i.e. impure, and forbid having any connexion with them."

Then Alberuni details the well-known devices through which Hindu society maintains its exclusiveness, such as prohibition of inter-marriage and commensality, and he notes particularly that the Hindu neither reclaim a fellow-Hindu who has become polluted nor receive any foreigner who inclines to their religion. This, Alberuni adds, renders any connexion with the Hindus impossible and constitutes the widest gulf between them and foreigners.

Alberuni traces back the Hindu hostility to the people of the Middle East to the rivalry between Buddhism and Zoroastrianism, and says that this old enmity was intensified by the coming of Islam. I am unable to check the historical accuracy of what Alberuni says about the pre-Islamic period, but his account of the subsequent developments is perfectly correct. Alberuni relates that the repugnance of the Hindus against foreigners increased more and more when the Muslims began to make their inroads into the country. According to him, the raids into the interior of India carried out by Muhammad ibn Qasim, the Arab conqueror of Sind, planted a deeply rooted hatred in the Hindu heart for the Muslim, and this was further heightened by the raids of Sultan Mahmud of Ghazna, Alberuni's contemporary. Sultan Mahmud's expeditions, says Alberuni, scattered the Hindus in all directions like atoms of dust, and the dispersed remnants cherished the most inveterate aversion towards all Muslims. Alberuni concludes this topic with the remark that the Hindus had fled to places beyond the reach of Muslim arms, and there the antagonism between them and all foreigners was receiving more and more nourishment both from political and religious sources.

I was shocked when I read Alberuni's account of Hindu xenophobia for the first time, for I had been nurtured in the myth of Hindu tolerance and catholicity. But subsequent reading and inquiry has convinced me that Alberuni was substantially right. The hatred of the Hindu is directed against all men who are not fellow-Hindus or, theoretically, blood-kins, although he does not hate rival dogmas. The antagonism of all proselytising religions, on the other hand, is for unorthodox dogma and not for men as such.

I shall now go forward by about two hundred years and quote a Sanskrit book written towards the end of the twelfth century in order to illustrate what complexion Hindu nationalism bore at the moment of the final Muslim conquest of India. It is the book to which I referred when writing about Hindu colour prejudice–the historical poem dealing with Prithviraj the Chauhan. The preface of this book contains a lamentation over Muslim depredations on and around the sacred lake of Pushkar near Ajmere, and the lament is punctuated by a liberal abuse of the Muslims. Its artistic scheme must have been tremendously effective with Hindu listeners. The first half of each quatrain recalled some legendary association of the lake, some image firmly fixed, almost fossilized, in the Hindu consciousness, and then like a knell came a sharp reference to some Muslim sacrilege; Pushkar, once the abode of Brahma, is now swept by a great fear–the fear of Muslims; Brahma bathed there after concluding his great sacrifice, now unclean foreigners remove in its waters the fatigue of demolishing sacred buildings; once the lake was the repository of the tears of joy of Vishnu, now a bin for the waste of the vile foreigner's meals; once warmed up by the fire of the eyes of the eleven Rudras, now steaming with the hot tears of the imprisoned

Brahmins; heavenly courtesans were forbidden to enter its waters, and if the Queen of Heaven bathed in it even that was not considered quite proper, and now the lake has become the wallowing pool of abominable foreign women (the commentator explains–of Turki women) during their periods; once it provided water for the gods, now it has to supply the same water to barbarians who cut the throats of their horses after a tiring desert journey and drink the blood of their mounts to quench thirst; so on and so forth. The last allusion was a most interesting reference to a custom prevalent among the Central Asian nomads, to which Marco Polo also refers. This typically Hindu explosion of emotion, an emanation of minds held in mortmain by the past and left quick for the present and the future only by a great hatred, must have worked up contemporary Hindus to an orgy of self-pity.

This lament provides the incidental demonstration, observed in other instances also, that the growth of self-pity is always accompanied by a decline of intelligence. The poor poet could not understand why the Muslims were victorious and the Hindus defeated; he attributed the defeat to mythical causes. In the Kali Yuga, the current age and the age of sin, he said, the Brahmins having ceased performing sacrifices, Indra, the sovereign god, was being deprived of his share of oblations and becoming weak. Secondly, the mobility of Kartikeya, the warrior god, was being reduced on account of the weakness of his mount–the peacock; this weakness in its turn was due to the scarcity of rainwater. Kartikeya's peacock drank only water from the sky, but rain was not being produced in adequate quantities on account of the decline of sacrifices. Thirdly, the Solar dynasty, which in a former age had been enlivened by Vishnu incarnating himself in it as Rama, had been weakened through the incarnation of Vishnu as Buddha, and since Vishnu as an ascetic had taken the deer as friend, the elephants (i.e. the Muslims) had invaded Pushkara. The hint in this passage that some Hindus regarded Buddhism with its doctrine of non-violence as a cause of the decline of their martial spirit is interesting. Still, this rigmarole is enough to show how amply the Hindus of the twelfth century deserved to go down before the virile and living Muslims.

The Arab and the Hindu writers whom I have quoted enable us in combination to form a rough idea of the development of Hindu national feeling over nearly four hundred years. The latest researches show that the Muslim conquest of northern India was not as sudden as it formerly appeared to be. Hindu India kept up a sort of hammer and anvil conflict along the frontiers, which although not as ably and as resolutely carried on as the struggle of the Eastern Roman Empire against the Arab and the Turk, did in actual fact obstruct the complete conquest of India for centuries. The Muslims beat against that resistance like sea waves against a dyke, and after wearing it out at last broke through and flooded the country in one great rush. Till that crisis, the Hindus never abandoned the struggle. But there was also another side to the matter. Although struggling, the Hindus seem never to have been very hopeful. They were perpetually haunted by a premonition of defeat, and had more fear of the invincibility of the Muslims than confidence in their own powers. When a Hindu king defeated a Muslim army he at times assumed or was given titles which revealed the Hindu awe of Muslim arms. One of these successful kings was given the title of "Resister of the Irresistible" by his suzerain when he repulsed an Arab army which, after ravaging western India, was trying to enter the Deccan. Hindu nationalism was born in the course of this losing struggle, to the accompaniment of a growing sense of defeat. Evolved in frustration, it adapted itself more fully to frustration after the completion of the Muslim conquest, and remained for ever an anodyne for frustration and defeat, and a weapon of the defeated. The gloom of the nether world trailed in its wake and never left it.

Although Hindu nationalism did not set in its mould all at once, it began to reveal its specific qualities from the very first days of Muslim rule. Different animals behave differently when threatened with aggression. In the face of irresistible encroachment on their independence wild animals and true primitives retreat, trying to break off contact with the enemy. Alfred de Vigny has very finely embodied this idea in his poem on the death of a wolf, in the lines on the fight of the she-wolf with her cubs after the hunters had mortally wounded her mate:

> *"Mais son devoir etait de les sauver, afin*
> *De pouvoir leur apprendre a bien souffrir la faim,*
> *A ne jamais entrer dans le pacte des villes*
> *Que l'homme a fait avec les animaux serviles*
> *Qui chassent devant lui, pour avoir le coucher,*
> *Les premiers possesseurs du bois et du rocher."*

The Boers did that in South Africa in the face of English encroachments. Some Hindus also did the same thing after the Muslim conquest of the north Indian plain. They retired into the hills, the jungles, or the desert. But the greater majority reacted in the manner of the civilized man who is also degenerate. Over the whole of the Indo-Gangetic plain they tried to make the best of both worlds and, strange to say, succeeded in a very large measure, thanks to an ambidextrous incapacity which they seem to have very quickly developed–the incapacity to risk the skin and tame the heart. The Muslim rulers of India, so long as they remained strong themselves, had no Hindu rebellion to fear; on the other hand they could reckon on being able to enlist any number of Hindu helpers, provided they were ready to offer a commensurate material reward. They could employ the Hindus to carry on their administration, sometimes even to command their armies and supply them with armed men, and often to advise them as to the best means of bringing other Hindus under subjection. They could secure orthodox pundits to write their panegyrics in the best fulsome style, and even to compose erotic treatises for them. In getting all these kinds of service from the Hindus the Muslim princes encountered no difficulty whatever.

But beyond these things a line was drawn and Hinduism cried: *"Ils ne passeront pas!"* One of the greatest of the Bengali novelists of the twentieth century, Sarat Chandra Chatterji, has summed up the underlying principle of Hindu behaviour in a neat, if cynical, epigram. He makes a woman who had a low-caste paramour boast that although she had lived twenty years with him she had not for a single day allowed him to enter her kitchen.

Throughout the period of Muslim rule Hindu society as a whole, and more especially Hindu lawgivers, went on tightening the rules against intermarriage and commensality. New rules were introduced to control fraternization with the foreigner and the cultivation of his manners. Although it was not forbidden to work for the foreign ruler or wear his dress when worldly interests required these, the foreign costume had to be discarded in the outer house and the wearer to purify himself by touching Ganges water before he could go into the inner house. A Hindu who transgressed these rules and affected Islamism beyond the permissible limits was without the slightest compunction put outside the pale. It is not perhaps widely known that the great Indian poet Tagore himself belonged to a section of Bengali Brahmins who were semi-outcastes. No orthodox Brahmin of Bengal entered into marriage with the Tagores till recently. The crime of the Tagores was that at some unspecified date their ancestors, or at least one of them, had approached too close to certain Islamic emanations; tradition has it that they had inhaled the smell of the famous Islamic dish–*pillau*.

In the sphere of emotions and ideas no Hindu was expected to give the allegiance of his heart to the Muslim, and no Hindu did. The more thoroughgoing his external and interested servility, the more complete was also his emotional disaffection. The Muslim ruler could count on the loyalty of his Hindu servants and vassal princes as a class only as long as he had power and could reward and punish them; the moment he lost his power he also lost the loyalty. The Hindu clung desperately to his disloyalty, because he looked upon it as his expiation for the service he was giving to the foreign conqueror against what he called his convictions. On this disaffection rested his hope of heaven as on the service of the Muslim depended his worldly advancement. Therefore the initial hatred noted by Alberuni, with which the Hindu began his life of political subjection, went on swelling in volume during the whole period of Muslim rule. There was no fear of its atrophy from any lack of external expression. The passivity which the Hindu mode of life and the Hindu outlook generate, makes the Hindu more or less independent of action in his emotional satisfactions. On the other hand, being incapable of action, he considers it all the more his duty to nurse his hatred in secret and take care of it as a priceless heirloom from his free ancestors.

Thus Hindu nationalism during Muslim rule flourished on a plane where neither the military nor the political power of the conqueror could attack it. On its part this nationalism saw no necessity to go out of its way to challenge the foreigner's power where it was at its strongest and while it remained strong. There was certainly a subconscious feeling in the Hindu's mind that his earthworm's patience would wear out and outlast the strength of his conqueror and that his day would come in due course, without there being any occasion for risking life, worldly possessions, and ease in premature revolt. The time did come. As soon as Muslim political power weakened in India at the end of the seventeenth century and beginning of the eighteenth, Hindu nationalism rose in a flood to the political plane. The Maratha formula *"Hindu-pad padshahi"*–the imperial status of the Hindus–summed up a pan-Hindu aspiration. The Hindu exultantly stamped on the head of the exhausted enemy.

By the end of the eighteenth century Muslim political power had vanished. Then a new problem arose–whom could the Hindus hate now? I believe that among human beings, taken both individually and collectively, there always is to be found, due partly to the presence of some physiological and psychological peculiarities and partly to some critical experience in the life of the individual and the group in question, some innate predisposition towards one or the other of a pair of mental attributes correlated as opposites, for example, love and hatred, orderliness and confusion, the constructive bent and the destructive bent. I have accepted this idea from M. Julien Benda, as must have been obvious to my readers. I do not ask them to share it with me, but at all events this certainly is true, that any persistent habit of hating makes hatred an imperative emotional necessity without which the hate-addict cannot live. The hatred assumes a life of its own independent of its object, and when one object disappears it seeks, and if necessary invents, another. La Roche-foucauld has said: "It is possible to come across women who have had no love affair, but it is very rare to find a woman who has only one." In the same way there may be individuals and human groups who have never experienced a great hatred, but one who has once hated will never live without hating.

For this reason a spiritual crisis threatened the Hindus at the end of Muslim rule, but it was averted by the establishment of British power. Almost instantaneously the hatred formerly felt for the Muslim was transferred to the English, as today with the disappearance of British rule the undying hatred has again fastened itself on the Muslim. Furthermore, after the downfall of the Muslim empire the hate not only continued but was aggravated. In the age which followed, that of British rule, the continuing stream of Hindu hatred was joined by the newly created stream of Muslim hatred, for the Muslims had in the meanwhile become fellow-slaves with their former subjects. They combined with the Hindus in hating the English, and since the quality of an emotion increases with its quantity, or in other words, since all collective emotions are intensified in proportion as they are shared by greater numbers of men, the combined Hindu-Muslim hatred which came to possess the souls of Indians during British rule was even more venomous than the previously existing purely Hindu hatred.

I have never read a more impressive testimony to the emergence of this revivified hatred than the introduction to an English translation of the well-known historical work in the Persian language composed by the Muslim historian Ghulam Hussain Khan Tabatabai, which bears the title *Siyar-ul-Mutaakhkhirin*. The introduction and the translation to which I refer are by a Creole named Raymond, who had adopted the Muslim name of Haji Mustapha and adopted the Muslim mode of living. The original work was completed in 1781 and the translation in 1786. Mustapha is speaking of the Indian attitude to the newly established rule of the English:

"The general turn of the English individuals in India," he writes, "seems to be a thorough contempt for the Indians (as a national body). It is taken to be no better than a dead stock that may be worked upon without much consideration, and at pleasure. But beware! that national body is only motionless, but neither insensible nor dead. There runs throughout our author's narrative a subterranean vein of national resentment, which emits vapours now and then, and which his occasional encomiums of the English can neither conceal nor even palliate; yet he [Ghulam Husain Khan] is himself but a voice that has spoken among a million others who could speak, but are silent. Nor have signs of this national sullenness been wanting these sixteen years. Living myself in the centre of Moorshidabad, wearing an Hindostany dress, and making a practice in the evening to walk the streets with only a servant, either to listen to, or mix with, any company I meet with either there or in the marketplace, I necessarily get a variety of information, which is out of the power, and always out of the way, of any other European...."

Then Mustapha *alias* Raymond gives a number of instances of the common people's extraordinary excitement and exultation at the news of English reverses, for example, at the news of the flight of Warren Hastings from Benares at the time of Chait Singh's insurrection. These examples also indicate the limitless possibilities for mischief these situations possessed unless checked in time, by showing to what a high pitch the hopes of the populace rose at even the most trifling defeats for the English. After giving these examples Mustapha draws his moral even more pointedly:

"The reader accustomed to read accounts of India these twenty or thirty years past," he continues, "will possibly wonder at my warning him against the disaffection of a nation. which by all accounts seems to be the tamest, and most pusillanimous set of men, on the face of the earth, and the most incapable of any manly action.

"The Indians have been a more dangerous nation than they seem to be now. They may be in a slumber; but they may awake, and they deserve to have a more watchful eye than the English Government seems to think."

Mustapha was not wrong. The only material point which he failed to bring out was that as long as the English remained strong they had nothing to fear from Indian nationalism, but everything as soon as they grew weak for one reason or another.

During the whole course of the nineteenth century there never was a moment, not even in the heyday of English power and prestige, when this underground nationalism was not a live force. Once of course it burst into an eruption, in the Mutiny. But even in quiet and normal times it bubbled and simmered underneath the usual contentment of Indians with English rule, their implicit dependence on it, and their sincere praise of it. Occasionally, in the form of seditious scurrility, it came to the notice of the English rulers and prompted restrictions on the liberty of the vernacular Press. It bore the same relation to the liberal nationalism which educated Indians were learning from the West as the popular superstitions of Hinduism bore to the reforming and revivalist movements in the field of religion. The indigenous nationalism, which was a combination of atavistic and xenophobic impulses, formed a stratum parallel to the new nationalism, and the two, although not influencing or permeating each other to   begin with, were in any case inseparable in space and time. In our family there was very little encouragement for the older and the retrograde form of nationalism. If our parents referred to it at all, or made use of its concepts and vocabulary, it was always in joke. But we came to know of it and partly to absorb if from our surroundings—our school-fellows, neighbours, acquaintances, and even teachers.

There were many characteristic forms of its outward expression. Uncomplimentary comparisons of Englishmen to monkeys and other despised or malevolent animals, an example of which I have already given, and the stories about and reflections on their fair complexion, of which too I have given an example and some indication, were two very common forms. To give only a few additional examples, the others were: defacing the pictures of the Mogul emperors and English Governors-General in our text-books and pummelling them; writing abusive epithets like "forger" or "thief" below the portraits of Clive and Warren Hastings; declaring that the English language was only a borrowing from Bengali; believing and telling others, as our teachers also did, that all that the history books taught were lies; writing of the Black Hole as a tragedy and of the battle of Chillianwallah as a draw in examination papers, convinced all the while that the first was a myth and the second a defeat for the English; telling one another that there was not one chaste woman in the whole of the British Isles; slyly suggesting that the alleged ground of the resignation of Lord Curzon was only eyewash and the real ground was, not disagreement over the position of the Supply Member, but (repeated in a voice stiller and smaller than that of conscience) an affair between the bachelor Lord Kitchener and Lady Curzon. I give only a small selection, but even this will indicate the scope and character of the whispering campaign. Its object was to take revenge for the English domination of India by representing the English people as a corrupt, degenerate, and decaying race whose apparently supreme position in the world was due to their amazing talent in cunning, deceit, and chicanery.

We learned all this and a good deal more and got familiarized with the notion that the English were the greatest robbers and plunderers that ever disfigured the face of the earth. In our boyhood one of the highly recommended patriotic songs which we sang taught us:

> "For many a day, O Brethren!
> Stands despoiled a Heaven;
> The Demons, donning robbers' garb,
> The godly country freely carve;
> Of pearls they made the ocean poor,
> Stole the jewel Kohinoor."
>   etc.

Another very popular song was:

> "Gold and gems that none could weigh
> The wizard race did spirit away;
> How they stole could none descry,
> Such a spell did blind our eye.
>
> From Haughty Isle in legions vast
> Locusts come, devouring fast
> All the corn in all our land,
> To the people leave but sand.
>
> In subject Ind from day to day
> Men grow thin and pine away,
> Starved of food and worn by thought,
> By toil and hunger overwrought."

etc.

Those who speak of the recent intensification of Indian nationalism will, I feel sure, be prompted to reconsider their conclusions if they note that these songs were composed in the last quarter of the nineteenth century and learnt by us even before the Swadeshi movement of 1905. Talking of our conception of the English people as robbers, there is no belief more interesting than that which is widely held in India about the *pietra dura* work in the Taj Mahal and other Mogul buildings. Most Indians believe that the original inlaid pieces were diamonds, rubies, emeralds, sapphires, and similar precious stones, but that they were stolen by the English, who substituted coloured glass for them.

These themes propagated over years with a thoroughness unrivalled even by the Nazi propaganda service made a profound impression on all Indians, and all the more so because it was spontaneous propaganda; propaganda of the people, by the people, for the people. It implanted a fierce hatred of the Englishman in the hearts of all Indians and created an insatiable yearning for self-pity. In the scale of this sense of injury no harm that an Indian could do to an Englishman, not even assassination, appeared commensurate. Only colossal massacres of hordes of the foreign oppressor, conjured up by the imagination, held out any prospect, worth considering, of assuaging this thirst for revenge. On this point I have my personal testimony to offer. Even though all my life I have tried to maintain balance and sanity in my love of my country, I too have often been rocked by these tremors of passion. They have seized me all of a sudden, and seized me even when I was quite grown up. One day in 1931 I had gone to a concert in Calcutta with an English friend. We had bought tickets for one of the upper galleries. Below me were thronged in tiers and rows Englishmen and Englishwomen in their graceful evening dress, and I could see hardly one Indian. As I listened to the Meistersinger Overture and the Jupiter Symphony one violent thought kept recurring like the ticking of a clock in my mind, worked up as it was to a state of heated and excited imagination; it was the thought of dropping a bomb on the crowd below and killing the whole lot. On my way home I told this to my English friend. He only remarked, "How interesting!"

But I do not think he had any suspicion of how interesting it really was. Nor did I have till many years later. Other Indians certainly do not have even an inkling of the secret. When they think of their patriotism they feel that all the highest dictates of reason and morality impel them to give their best love to their country. They are incapable of perceiving that after the conscious explanation has been given there can still be a question to ask and answer. Yet to them also can be put the question which Dante in the twenty-sixth canto of the *Paradiso* makes St. John put to him:

> "... *Per intelletto umano*
> *e per autoritadi a lui concorde*
> *de' tuoi amori a Dio guarda il sovrano.*
> *Ma di' ancor se tu senti altre corde*
> *tirarti verso Lui, si che tu suone*

con quanti denti questo amor ti morde."
("On the ground of human reason and of the authorities in harmony with it, the highest of all thy loves looks to God; but say further if thou feelest other cords draw thee to Him, so that thou mayest name all the teeth by which this love bites thee."– Translation by John D. Sinclair.)

What are all the teeth with which his love for his country bites an Indian? His answer, were he capable of giving one, would contain no suggestion of the mystical realization of charity and love revealed in Dante's answer. It would describe no ascent from the plane of perverse or mundane love to the plane of just or divine love, but disclose a descent from the level even of worldly love to the underworld of hate. The teeth with which the love of his country bites the Indian are not the teeth of any human being, nor of any other mammal: not even of that fear-inspiring antediluvian felid–the sabre-toothed tiger, for no creature which has ever sucked the warm milk of its mother's breast can have teeth of such cold and petrified ferocity. They are the teeth of reptiles: the venom-injecting fangs of the krait, the low-lying and insidious cousin of the comparatively decent cobra; or, better still, the horrible fossil-ized teeth of the Mesozoic monster, Tyrannosaurus. There is no redemption for man except in charity, and lacking it the Indian cannot hope to have his sight restored to him as Dante had his through the grace of Beatrice after his confession of faith.

THE CHALLENGE OF BRITISH RULE

The creators of modern Indian culture were all born and brought up in an environment which was permeated with the spirit of this nationalism. Thus they could never be expected to face the fact of British rule in India without a violent predisposition against it. Yet the extraordinary part of the matter was that not one of them allowed his judgement to fall a victim to his emotions. The very first and supreme example of this intellectual integrity was set by the pioneer of modern Indian culture, who in his early life had been swayed by all the passion of the retrograde form of nationalism. This was Rammohun Roy, the religious reformer, who was equally a pathfinder in politics. Although a Brahmin and a Sanskrit scholar, he was also a profound student of the Arabic and Persian languages and Islamic theology. This doublesided study had the immediate effect of adding to his Hindu dislike of the foreigner the Muslim antagonism to the English as their supplanters. But in later life Rammohun abjured this hatred and came to formulate for himself and others a new conception of nationalism based on views about political independence which were as novel in his age as they have become familiar today.

The most authentic and explicit account that I have read of this transformation in Rammohun Roy is to be found in the journal of the travels in India of the young French scientist, Victor Jacquemont, whose letters from this country are better known than the journal. I came upon the passage in the magnificent quarto volumes (published in Paris in 1841) presented to the Imperial Library, Calcutta, by Lord Curzon, and bearing on the fly-leaf an inscription in his florid handwriting. As I had never seen this valuable contemporary account reproduced or even referred to in any book on Rammohun Roy, I translated it into English, and the editor of the well-known Indian magazine, *The Modern Review,* published it in his paper (June 1926, pp. 689-92). I shall reproduce a part of it to illustrate Rammohun's conception of nationalism. Jacquemont had a meeting and a long conversation with Rammohun Roy on Sunday, 21 June 1829, and in his journal under the date 25 June, he incorporated an account of both. Among other things Jacquemont noted down:

"Rammohun Roy has surprised me by the accuracy and range of his knowledge of the various States of Europe. Formerly, when he was a young man, he himself told me, this Europe, the mistress of his native land, was odious to him; in the blind patriotism of youth he detested the English and all that came from them. Since that time he had learnt more about the benefits which have followed upon the establishment of the British power, and has come to regard it as beneficial to India."

Then comes the most important passage in Jacquemont's account, which reproduces the kernel of Rammohon's argument:

"National independence is not an absolute good; the object, the goal, so to say, of society is to secure the happiness of the greatest possible number, and when, left to itself, a nation cannot attain this object, when it does not contain within itself the principles of future progress, it is better for it that it should be guided by the example and even by the authority of a conquering people who are more civilized."

This apparently unnatural advocacy of foreign domination was based on a dialectical examination of the possibility of achieving absolute independence in human society. As Jacquemont goes on to relate:

"The metaphysical intellect of Rammohun Roy did not let go this opportunity playing upon the words 'dependence' and 'independence'. 'When we have to depend,' he said to me, 'by the very conditions of our existence on all things and all beings in nature, is not this fiery love of national independence a chimera? In society individuals are constantly driven by their weakness to seek help from their neighbours, especially if the neighbours happen to be stronger than they; why, then, should a nation have the absurd pride of not depending upon another?

Conquest is very rarely an evil when the conquering people are more civilized than the conquered, because the former bring to the latter the benefits of civilization. India requires many more years of English domination so that she may not have many things to lose while she is reclaiming her political independence'."

Coming from a Europe where the tide of nationalism was at its full, Victor Jacquemont was perfectly conscious that his European readers would be scandalized by these opinions of Rammohun Roy, more especially because it was to be expected from Rammohun's knowledge of European ways and European thought that he should have become a convert to European nationalism. So Jacquemont commented:

"The sincerity of such language in the mouth of a Hindu whose thorough knowledge of the culture of Europe warrants us in assuming that he has sentiments and feelings resembling ours, might seem to be doubtful. But I have not found it so; for brought up though I have been in a country of faith in absolute liberty, in national independence at any cost, and subjected as I have been from my childhood to the opinions of those among whom I have lived, I have yet learnt from solitary reflection that this faith is more noble and generous than useful."

Rammohun Roy was regarded by his contemporaries as something of a "Medizing" Hindu, an advocate of foreign–that is to say, both Islamic and English–ways, opinions, and modes of thought. Therefore, in him, views like those recorded in Jacquemont's journal were not wholly unexpected. A more remarkable fact is a similar transformation, at the end of the nineteenth century, in the life of Swami Vivekananda, the preacher of new Hinduism. In a speech in Calcutta after his return from a tour of the West he said:

"No one ever landed on English soil with more hatred in his heart for a race than I did for the English. On this platform are present English friends who can bear witness to this fact; but the more I lived among them and saw how the machine was working—the English national life—and mixed with them, I found what the heart-beat of the nation was, and the more I loved them."

He went on to say that his work in England had been more satisfactory than his work in the United States because of the peculiar traits of the English character. Among these he singled out "the immense practicality and vitality" (the words are his) of the race. "They are a nation of heroes, they are the true Kshatriyas," he declared. After observing that their education fostered the habit of emotional reserve and that imagination was to be found among them in a lesser measure than among certain other nations on account of this habit, Swami Vivekananda immediately corrected himself by asking the question "Who knows the well-springs of the English heart?" He went on to say: "But with all this heroic superstructure, behind this covering of the fighter, there is a spring of deep feeling in the English heart. If you once know how to reach it to get there, if you have personal contact and mix with him he will open his heart, he is your friend for ever, he is your servant." Vivekananda attributed the misunderstandings between Englishmen and Indians to ignorance. "As the philosophy, our national philosophy, of the Vedanta," he observed, "has summarized all misfortune, all misery, as coming from one cause, ignorance, herein also we must understand that the difficulties that arise between us and the English people are mostly due to that ignorance: we do not know them, they do not know us." He was perfectly right. In the two centuries of British rule Indians never came to know Englishmen properly and Englishmen never knew Indians properly, and today the acquaintance has been broken off without ever being really made.

A man of the intellectual calibre of Vivekananda could not utter platitudes about the effect of British rule in India. He could as little repeat the commonplaces of the conventional upholder of British rule as the commonplaces of the conventional nationalist. I shall indicate only a bare few of the points he makes on this subject in order to give an idea of the originality of his mind. On one occasion he said that two branches of the same human stock had settled in two widely separated lands, and worked out in different circumstances and environments the problems of life, each in its particular way. They were the ancient Greeks and the ancient Hindus. But now they were meeting–the ancient Hindu was meeting the ancient Greek on Indian soil as a result of the English conquest of India, , because European civilization was Greek in everything. "Slowly and silently," declared Vivekananda, "the leaven has come. the broadening out, the life-giving; and the revivalist movement that we see all around us has been worked out by these forces together. A broader and more generous conception of life is before us."

On another occasion he said that the genius of the English race had linked the nations of the world as never before through maritime enterprise, so much so that the English roads were no longer content like the Roman roads to pass over land alone, but ploughing the deep ran from ocean to ocean; and through this achievement the English genius had provided the routes along which Hindu spirituality could go out to conquer the world. This is the only reference to the stupendous fact of English sea-power, and to its significance in history, that I have come across in any Indian writer. The average Indian is an incorrigible "land-lubber" in thought and shows no comprehension of thalassocracy.

Vivekananda added that just as in a bygone age the great Greek conqueror Alexander had united the four corners of the world and given Indian spirituality an opening to rush out to the outside world, another opportunity had come to it—out of English enterprise.

On various other occasions Vivekananda declared that one of the great blessings of British rule in India was that the days of exclusive privilege and exclusive claims were gone for ever from the soil of India. "Had it not been for the power of the Anglo-Saxons," he said, "we should not have met here today [he was speaking at a public meeting] to discuss, as we are doing today, the influence of our Indian spiritual thought."

He was ready to do equal justice to Muslim rule. He said: "Even to Muhammadan rule we owe that great blessing, the destruction of exclusive privilege. That rule was, after all, not all bad; nothing is all bad, nothing is all good. The Muhammadan conquest of India came as salvation to the downtrodden, to the poor. That is why one-fifth of our people have become Muhammadans. It was not the sword that did it all, it would be the height of madness to think that it was all the work of sword or fire."

About Vivekananda I have only to add that all the speeches and essays from which I have quoted were delivered or written in English, and in summing up his views I have used only his language.

Between Rammohun Roy and Vivekananda stands Bankim Chandra Chatterji, the creator of Hindu nationalism. He too gave the same message. He embodied his final views of British rule in India in his novel *Ananda Math*. Not satisfied with leaving the moral implied in the course of the narrative and even enunciating it in the speeches of the characters, Chatterji, who knew his readers, set it down formally in the preface, in the form of three cut-and-dried propositions; and not satisfied even with that, he reproduced in the preface to the second edition of the novel a critical estimate written in English and published in an Indian periodical (*The Liberal,* 8 April 1882), and gave his approval to the interpretation offered by the critic. Thus Chatterji's views as expressed in *Ananda Math* can be taken as views deliberately formulated and explicitly put on record by him.

The critic whom Chatterji quoted summed up the issue presented in the novel thus: "The leading idea of the plot is this: Should the national mind feel justified in harbouring violent thoughts against the British Government? Or to present the question in another form, is the establishment of English supremacy providential in any sense? Or, to put it in a still more final and conclusive form, with what purpose and with what immediate end in view did Providence send the British to this country?"

Quoting the author's preface, the critic said that the immediate object was to put an end to Muslim tyranny and anarchy in Bengal. But there was also a larger purpose. This the critic defined by quoting one of the very last speeches in the book. In order to understand this speech it is necessary to bear in mind the dramatic situation at the end of the novel, and the antecedents of that situation. Both may be summed up in a few words: Towards the end of Muslim rule in Bengal and the beginning of the British an ascetic, inspired and driven by a fiery patriotism and directed by a mysterious preceptor, organizes a religious order of rebels and revolutionaries and rises in revolt with the object of restoring Hindu rule; he wins against the Muslims but is finally defeated by the troops of the East India Company; as he is walking on the battlefield at night among the dead and wounded of both sides, his mysterious teacher appears to him and tells him to give up the struggle. When the ascetic expresses unwillingness the preceptor tries to persuade him with the following argument:

"It is so written that the English should first rule over the country before there could be a revival of the Aryan faith. Harken unto the counsels of Providence. The faith of the Aryas consists not in the worship of three hundred and thirty million gods and goddesses; as a matter of fact that is a popular degradation of religion—that which has brought about the death of the true Arya faith, the so-called Hinduism of the *Mlechchhas.* True Hinduism is grounded on knowledge and not on works. Knowledge is of two kinds–external and internal. The internal knowledge constitutes the chief part of Hinduism. But international knowledge cannot grow unless there is a development of the external knowledge. The spiritual cannot be known unless you know the material External knowledge has for a long time disappeared from the country, and with it has vanished the Arya faith. To bring about a revival, we should first of all disseminate physical or external knowledge. Now there is none to teach that; we ourselves cannot teach it. We must needs get it from other countries. The English are profound masters of physical knowledge, and they are apt teachers too. Let us make them kings. English education will give our men a knowledge of physical science, and this will enable them to grapple with the problems of their inner nature. Thus the chief obstacles to the dissemination of Arya faith will be removed, and true religion will sparkle into life spontaneously and of its own accord. The British Government shall remain indestructible so long as the Hindus do not once more become great in knowledge, virtue, and power. Hence, O Wise Man, refrain from fighting and follow me."

[This translation is that of the critic.]

Then the critic offers his own comment: "This passage embodies the most recent and the most enlightened views of the educated Hindus, and happening as it does in a novel powerfully conceived and wisely executed, it will influence the whole race for good. The author's dictum we heartily accept as it is one which already forms the creed of English education. We may state it in this form: India is bound to accept the scientific method of the West and apply it to the elucidation of all truth. This idea, beautifully expressed, forms a silver thread as it were and runs through the tissue of the whole work."

But it was not a conclusion at which Bankin Chandra Chatterji had arrived without pain. This pain is manifest in the last speeches of the militant and fiery ascetic who wants to carry on the fight in spite of his preceptor's exhortations, and we may be sure that the feelings of the ascetic are also those of Chatterji in certain moods. The ascetic declares: "I do not seek knowledge, I shall continue in the task to which I have set myself." His teacher replies that the task has been accomplished by the establishment of British rule and the only thing that remains to be done is to abandon fighting, allow the peasant to till the land, to let the corn grow and prosperity revive. The ascetic burst out: "I shall make the motherland put forth corn by drenching her with the blood of the enemy." The preceptor resumes: "Who is the enemy? The English are friends, there is no one who can fight the English and win in the end." The ascetic still declares that if he lacked strength, he could at least die fighting. "In ignorance?" retorts the preceptor, and leads the ascetic away. The anguish of the author's mind at this denouement is shown by the last comment: "Farewell came and led away Inauguration." Yet to Bankim Chandra Chatterji it was, however agonizing, only the submission of illusion to truth.

Contemporary and later readers argued, although nobody had the courage to put down the opinion in black and white, that the apparent argument of the book was not its real argument, that Chatterji was concerned really to initiate his countrymen in the doctrine and technique of revolutionary insurrection, and had introduced the peroration about British rule only as an afterthought, as a plea of good faith in case the English rulers took it into their head to persecute him for preaching sedition. I have always noticed that my countrymen are more disposed to attribute the worst cowardice, deception, and chicanery to their greatest teachers than believe that they could in any circumstances truthfully speak well of Englishmen and English rule. But I cannot as readily assume a total absence of moral courage in them. Therefore I always take it that they had the courage of their conviction, and meant what they said, and saw no reason when concerned with discovering the truth to scrutinize whether their opinions went against the interests of the foreign ruler or against the cherished superstitions of their countrymen.

These great figures of our moral and intellectual life of the nineteenth century were not lesser patriots than their tortuous latter day interpreters. All of them, from Rammohun Roy to Vivekananda, were fiery lovers of their country, and the vision they had of its free future made the utopias of contemporary Indians appear like magazine pictures placed by the side of Cinquecento paintings; and after their clarion voice the contemporaries sound like tin pipes squeaking film tunes. But these great men were determined that they would not burke the fundamental issue in nineteenth-century India, the issue of Indo-British relationship, and that on this issue they would discover and preach the truth. They did not burke the issue, and they spoke the truth. They could do so because they considered themselves the equals of the European, as fit to give in their measure as to receive in the measure of the European.

They looked upon Indo-British relationship as a barter in ideas and values and not as beggary or robbery. Conscious of the worth of their national heritage, of their own capacity for effort, and believing that nothing war beyond effort, just as nothing was to be had without effort, they could contemplate even the Purgatory without flinching; they felt no urge to deceive themselves and to prove themselves weaklings and bankrupts by falling back on envy and rancour. Theirs was a manly nature. They saw no virtue in a whining parade of frustration.

It necessarily followed that the nationalism preached by the men who held this view of British rule in India should have no affection for the remnants of the former ruling class, Muslim or Hindu, or for the movements that had for their object the reinstatement of those survivals. This misplaced and perverse sympathy was the accompaniment of the rancorous and atavistic nationalism about which I have written. But the creators of our new nationalism felt that even if the older order triumphed over the English, which they never regarded as a practical possibility, the victory would simply mean a retrogression to the past. That the principles and passions which actuated the older order held no promise for the future, did not themselves look towards the future, was an unshakable conviction with our new nationalists. Rammohun Roy did indeed go to England as the envoy of the King of Delhi to plead the King's cause, but his purpose, in so far as he represented the King, was not the restoration of Mogul sovereignty, but only some increase in the personal income of an emperor without an empire. His real mission was to press the abolition of the Suttee and place some views of his own on the governance of India before the British Government and Parliament at the time of the renewal of the Company's charter.

This attitude of opposition to the ancient regime, the creators of the new Indian nationalism consistently maintained throughout the nineteenth century, and during every conflict between the English and an indigenous Power–Muslim, Maratha, or Sikh. Above all, they maintained it at the time of the Mutiny of 1857, which provides the surest test for finding out whether a particular manifestation of Indian nationalism belongs to the old or the new type. The Swadeshi movement of 1905 was mainly an assertion of the nationalism of the new Hindu school but it also contributed materially to a revivification of the fossilized nationalism. Therefore with the Swadeshi movement also began a fantastic glorification of the Mutiny, which finally created the legend that it was the precursor of the nationalist movement of this century and the first war of Indian independence. The most ambitious statement of this thesis is to be found in the work *The Indian War of Independence,* purporting to be a history of the Mutiny, written by Vinayak Damodar Savarkar, who, to begin with, figured in a notable political trial and also in a case before the Court of Arbitration at The Hague as a dangerous revolutionary, next spent nearly twenty-five years in prison, then became the President of the Hindu Mahasabha, after that was tried for complicity in the murder of Mahatma Gandhi, and, lastly, upon being acquitted of that charge has been detained without trial under the special powers exercised by the present Government of our country in passable imitation of the previous regime.

I have watched the growth of the legend of the Mutiny in my own life. When I was a boy I first heard and then read many stories about the Mutiny which had taken shape in the previous forty years under the mild and life-giving sun of peace and security. The heroes and heroines of these tales were Nana Sahib (believed in my childhood to be still living and in hiding somewhere), Tantia Topi (the invincible Indian general), the Rani of Jhansi (with her famous cry "I shall never give up my

Jhansi"), and Kunwar Singh of Bihar, to mention only a few. I particularly remember a sensational and lurid, and of course distorted, account of the siege of Lucknow in a book in Bengali called *The River of Blood.*

But none of the creators of modern Indian nationalism encouraged the legend of the Mutiny. Bankim Chandra Chatterji had then passed out of the newly created Calcutta University and been offered an administrative post. When he went to accept it, an English official asked him if he did not think that British rule in India was coming to an end. Chatterji only replied that he would not have come at all if he believed that to be possible. Now, it must not be assumed that this was the only possible answer to the question. During the last war hundreds of thousands of my countrymen literally gate-crashed for Government jobs without giving the British nation, and with it the British Government in India, even a month's expectation of life at certain junctures. The intelligentsia of my country have always had the faith–which certainly is justified by the secular changes in our political existence–that they are indispensable as mercenaries to everybody who rules India. Thus they have seen no harm, on the contrary much merit, in offering their services wherever money was going, even when the opportunity to their own thinking was only an off-chance of pelf. In fact, the more fleeting the opportunity the stronger have they felt their bargaining position to be. Thus Chatterji had to possess an unusual degree of moral stamina to give the answer he actually gave.

THREE POSITIVE DOCTRINES

British rule in India was a case of conscience with our nineteenth-century thinkers. They dealt with it courageously, with the help of casuistry in the sense accepted in ethics. But on this particular issue they were taken to be casuists in the popular sense. I do not think, however, that they really expected to be taken otherwise. Mahatma Gandhi did not preach any heresy at all on this point. He only admonished his countrymen to bear no hatred to the British people, after declaring their rule in India to be satanic. Perhaps knowing the futility of trying to gain popular acceptance for their view of British rule, the creators of modern Indian nationalism never emphasized the purely corrective aspect of their political doctrine. All of them, as also Mahatma Gandhi, adopted a positive method, that is to say, they endeavoured to neutralize the natural reversionism of the popular brand of nationalism by infusing positive values into it. In the course of this effort three different systems of nationalist doctrines were put before the people of India one after another. The first of them was the liberal, the second new Hindu, and the third Gandhian. The first two components in this trilogy of nationalism stood in far closer relationship to each other than to the third, and taken together formed one thesis facing the Gandhian counter-thesis. Nevertheless, the Gandhian system followed the other two quite naturally. The emergence of all three was caused by the same historical logic as that which governed the actual sequence of their appearance. I shall presently let this teleological cat out of the bag, but by way of preliminary exploration have to examine the nature of the first two doctrines of modern Indian nationalism.

In spite of being conceived of as alternative or rival doctrines, these two forms of Indian nationalism were not more antithetical to each other than were nineteenth-century Liberalism and Conservatism in England, or the liberal nationalism of France and Italy and the conservative nationalism of Germany in the first half of the nineteenth century on the continent of Europe. In other words, they were the obverse and reverse of the same movement. Both recognized the same values, although in differing proportions. The liberal form of Indian nationalism thought less of the Hindu past than of the

Occidental present, the new Hindu form approached these sources contrariwise. This did not, however, prevent their having two elements in common, and having in common precisely those two elements which were the two definitely novel ones to be introduced into the traditional Indian nationalism by the new nationalism of nineteenth-century India. These were, first historical consciousness and, secondly, political consciousness. Both these qualities call for a few words of explanation because Gandhism involved a repudiation of both.

The reconstruction of the history of ancient India by Europe, Orientalists and their interpretation of the civilization of ancient Hindu India exerted a powerful influence on modern Indian nationalism, which would not have been what it became but for these researches. In the eighteenth century, on the eve of the establishment of British rule, the Hindus had no recollection of their real past, nor any idea of the true character of the classical Sanskritic civilization. Their Hinduism was a broken-up and simplified version of the Hinduism of ancient India. It was unorganized in space and unsupported in time. Its quality was neutral where it was not purely negative. Accordingly, it could never put its followers on a footing of equality with the Muslims or the English, both of whom had rich and vigorous historical traditions behind them. Although nationalism in a crude form can flourish on myths, it cannot inspire practical effort in a civilized society, nor convince civilized rivals, without becoming historical. More especially, when the opponents of a people seeking national reassertion happen to be strong, it can never secure the acceptance of its case without a genuine historical basis, which must also be admitted to be genuine by its rivals and peers. This has been proved in the instances of Nazi Germany and Japan, and may be proved again in the case of Soviet Russia. Thus, historically, European oriental research rendered a service to Indian and Asiatic nationalism which no native could ever have given. At one stroke it put the Indian nationalist on a par with his English ruler. The resuscitation of their past fired the imagination of the Hindus and made them conscious of a heritage of their very own which they could pit not only against the Muslims' but also against that of the far more powerful and virile English. Psychologically, the Indian people crossed the line which divides primitive peoples from civilized peoples. They could now be said to belong to the same species as the *Homo sapiens historicus* of Europe.

The old rancorous form of Indian nationalism saw at once the value of history as a political weapon, and was quick in seizing the facts of history and employing them in its own way, that is to say, to promote its retrograde purpose. At the end of nearly a century of unceasing effort this distortion, in combination with the general decline of education among the Indian intelligentsia, has succeeded in bringing about a significant transformation of the newly created historical traditions. In so far as these traditions have a place in the consciousness of a man of average education in India, they have become myths, mere stimulants of xenophobia on the one hand and national egotism on the other. But in the late nineteenth century the higher leadership in Indian politics was more intelligent and better educated than it has been recently, and therefore the historical extravagances of the retrograde school of nationalism, although not without their adherents, could not discolour with their turbidity the main stream of nationalist thought. I have not read one great preacher of Indian nationalism down to the second decade of the present century whose historical assumptions were not substantially tenable as pure and simple historical propositions.

Political consciousness has to be considered next: the older form of nationalism had none, if by political consciousness is understood the capacity to make a distinction between various types of political institutions and governments, and the added capacity to make a deliberate choice among these forms. The only kind of internal government the older nationalism was familiar with and could understand was absolute personal rule, and the only kind of political change it could conceive was limited to the possibility of changing the autocrat's personality through the replacement of one foreign monarch by another foreigner or a native, or the replacement of a native monarch by another native or a foreigner. It was Rammohun Roy who first made Indians conscious of the character of political institutions. The obvious indication of the influence of Bentham on Roy in the extract from Jacquemont could not have been missed by the reader. But it was not utilitarianism alone which he cultivated. He was equally familiar with all the forms of liberalism, both English and Continental, of the early decades of the nineteenth century. The story runs that on his voyage to England in 1830 he broke his leg while hurrying up to the deck of his ship at the Cape in order to greet the tricolour flag which he was seeing for the first time on a French vessel coming into harbour. Perhaps Roy was not wholly free from the weakness of ostentation, but his knowledge at all events was real, the tradition he established lasted for something like a century.

The coming of Gandhism was accompanied by an almost instantaneous disappearance of these two qualities from the nationalist movement. Nothing could be more inevitable, for there was causation as well as coincidence in this particular concatenation of events. To take the middle class intelligentsia first, the members of this social order had already begun to feel their newly acquired historical consciousness, which is to be carefully distinguished from its spurious imitation—devotion to historical myths, as a burden. At one time of my life there was nothing which came as a greater surprise to me, a student of history, than the disparagement of history by educated Indians of my class. In our schools and colleges history was supposed to be the last resort of the dullard endowed with a good rote-memory. In general conversation about the better-educated person, making a use of the authority of Longfellow which would have shocked Longfellow had he come to know of it, declared airily, "Let the dead past bury its dead." The less educated sneered on his own authority at the foolishness of those who tried to memorize the name of Akbar's grandfather without caring about his own. All this denigration of history was the natural expression of the resentment of the Hindu at being forced to learn history against his traditional disposition to ignore it.

Political consciousness was not, like history, felt actually as a burden, but it too was wearing thin, because it had never taken any deep roots. For all his preoccupation with politics, the middle class Indian never developed any real political aptitude. He never showed any understanding of representative government, nor any capacity to work it, as he certainly would and could have done, had he possessed either, in the sphere of municipal administration. His interest in democratic government, where it was not an indulgence in his favourite intellectual pastime of logic-chopping and the equally favourite practical pastime of bossing cliques, sprang only from his eagerness to find the most effective dissolvent of British power in India, and he soon discovered that the slogan of democracy was such a dissolvent as his rulers could least counteract. Our political consciousness never penetrated deeper than this and was never able to create among the general mass of the people any strong or widespread desire for internal political freedom and democratic freedom. Accordingly, there is hardly any occasion for surprise if today an overwhelming majority of the people of India are perfectly content with an oligarchical one-party dictatorship which respects political freedom and personal liberty even less than the regime which it has replaced.

Thus it happened that by the time British power in India was nearing the point of exhaustion, its potential successors were getting tired of historical and political consciousness. The masses of India did not stand in need of a relapse at all, for they had all along remained staunchly unhistorical and unpolitical. I wonder at times why the behaviourists, when challenged about their theories, do not come to India, where they would have found their paradise. No other group of human beings has succeeded to the same degree as have the masses of India in eliminating the mind in its all-important function of retaining the consciousness of duration. The common man in India lives in the everpresent and is governed solely by reflexes. But with that perverse duality which I have again and again singled out as a characteristic of our external behaviour, he has combined his unconsciousness of duration with a paralysing bondage to the past, and done this in a manner which could only make his unconsciousness of the past bear the worst possible consequences for him. I do not know of any nation besides my own which is held so relentlessly in the clutches of the past and is yet so incapable of contemplating and understanding it, and, consequently, profiting by its lessons.

If historical consciousness was non-existent among the masses of India, political consciousness took a very characteristic form, that of being entirely negative. For centuries the political creed of the Indian peasant and the Indian worker has consisted of one single article: never to trust the professions, the motives, and the doings of their rulers. This distrust of the State and the ruling order is virtually ineradicable. In the last two years I have received plenty of confirmation that it persists even after the transfer of political power to Indians. If anything, the suspicion has become intensified. Of course, the masses of India will maintain every ward appearance of siding with the ruling order as long as they believe it to be powerful, out of fear of its unlimited capacity to do harm. But as to help, they know better than to look for it to the State or any set of rulers: on that score, after Fate, they rely on their lone selves.

This very brief indication of the political psychology of the masses of India should serve to explain the disappearance, upon the emergence of Gandhism, of the historical and political consciousness on which the two previous forms of modern Indian nationalism were based. For years we had been wanting and expecting the masses to enter the nationalist movement. They were at last entering it under the leadership of Mahatma Gandhi. But it would have been utterly futile, although we were guilty of the futility, to expect them to enter politics on any terms but their own. Among these terms there could be no question of the recognition of so exotic a refinement as historical consciousness. Even politics *qua* politics could not claim inclusion. It had to be transformed into something intelligible to the masses of India, affiliated with something which ran in the blood.

This, even in approximate analysis, could only be morality, but the quest could not end there. In the ultimate analysis, something far simpler had to be discovered, for although the only idealistic principle comprehensible to the masses was morality, their morality was not and could not be the morality of the ancient Greeks, the morality of modern Europeans, or even the morality of the ancient Hindus. Before the common man of India could accept any principle, sophistication and reason had to be eliminated from it uncompromisingly. In other words, before politics could become capable of rousing the masses of India to any kind of idealistic effort it had to become identified with the intuitive, timeless, and humble morality of the masses, that morality which had survived the clash of religions in India only by being pulverized into something as amorphous and uncohering and at the same time as irresistible and pervasive as the dust of the Indo-Gangetic plain. This was the thing which constituted the lowest and simplest common factor between Indians of all classes, which as I have said was shared alike by the Muslim peasant of Kishorganj and the Hindu peasant of Kalikutch, to which even highly educated Indians surrender themselves when worn out by the exhausting struggle between their always inadequate vitality and the massive inertia of their society.

Mahatma Gandhi brought about this simplification and transformation of the nationalism of his country and by so doing was able to convert it into a mass movement. He did something more as well, he was able to strengthen the humble principle by laying on it two cloaks, one of native and the other of foreign manufacture, which immensely enhanced its prestige both at home and abroad. The native cloak was that of the traditional, self-mortifying, and beggarly asceticism of India without which idealism is never recognized as such by Indians, and the foreign vestment was borrowed from Christian pacifism, appealing and dangerous at the same time to all natures possessing a delicate moral sensibility. But whatever the character of the transformation it was only through it that Gandhi was able to give to Indian nationalism a backing of sheer numbers which it had never had before. There came into being a conscripted army of nationalism which in spite of its low training proved itself more efficient than the old Regulars.

Nothing, however, could be more of a mistake than to suppose that Mahatma Gandhi was carrying out this transmutation consciously. If anyone among our political leaders could be expected to remain wholly unaware of the novel and better adaptation of the means of the nationalist movement to its ends, that person was Mahatma Gandhi. If he said that he was applying a certain political method on account of its intrinsic moral excellence he was to be believed implicitly. No one was capable of greater literalism in such matters, unless it were St. Francis, to whom in a short appraisal I once compared Mahatma Gandhi. Therefore it would be a lack of penetration amounting to ineptitude to speak, not only of Machiavellism, but even of conscious reasoning in connexion with Mahatma Gandhi's activities. This remarkable man was the most perfect representative of the masses of India, taken of course in their state of grace. In the long history of their existence these masses have had many prophets to preach their ethos and voice their idealistic aspirations but none who so completely was their very own. Mahatma Gandhi remained theirs even after birth and education had done everything to bring about a separation. Neither his station in life nor his English education succeeded in making him understand the things of the intellect and civilization. He remained profoundly uneducated in the intellectual sense and lived in utter nakedness of spirit till his death. At last in India the Masses and the Man had become one.

But the very simplification which gave to Gandhism its victory over the two older forms of modern Indian nationalism also contained the seed of its inevitable downfall. The history of the Franciscan Order in Europe has shown that any over-simplification of moral principles involves a serious risk of degeneration. Apart from this general weakness Gandhism had two special flaws in its composition. In the first place, even after the best had been said about it, it still remained the morality of the *servus,* very pure and lofty certainly, none the less bearing in all its manifestations the unmistakable stamp of its lowly origin. Only the noble slave could have propounded this doctrine, a slave who was too weak, too modest.and meek, and too passive to break his chains, but was capable of making them immaterial in an ecstatic contemplation of his hypostasis of goodness and right. Those other men—strong, courageous, and creative, who never flag in their toil to carry forward mankind, the world, and the universe because they are sustained by the urge of life and an intuitive prevision of the future they are bringing to birth, who are symbolized for me by the young horsemen of the Parthenon–would not only have rejected this servile morality as unacceptable, but also deprecated it out of a feeling that it was alien and opposed to the law of life. This contention is not invalidated by the wide recognition of Gandhism in the West, for in the European ethos too there has always been a strand derived from the servile morality of the early Christian. In addition to being influenced by this legacy of history, European society has for one thing been democratized so far in recent years as to allow its proletarian and thus servile elements quite a disproportionate share in the formulation of its ideals, and, next, has been so severely tried, overwrought, and drained of vitality that in its moments of weariness it cannot resist the appeal of a servile morality promising it an easy release from pain or, at all events, an anodyne.

It was this servile complexion of Gandhism which created the dangerous possibility of its being rejected by the very people for whom it was intended. In certain circumstances it could be expected that even the creative, free, and forward-looking man would have moods of tenderness for this humble morality. Even when finding himself incapable of being inspired by it, he could hardly have withheld his compassion from such a pitiful figure of virtue, gentle, emaciated, mole-grey, knocking with a shrinking diffidence at his door. But the unconverted, and therefore the unredeemed, *servus* could never experience any such feeling. He was capable only of mocking at, smiting, and spitting upon it. Driven by his fleshy lusts and pride of brutality, as he most often is, a slave understands the overseer's whip far better than the virtue, the purity, and the saintliness of his fellow-slave, and of course he respects the whip very much more.

Secondly, Gandhism in its rejection of civilization and reason was in one sense a descent towards the old rancorous and atavistic form of Indian nationalism. In this respect the three successive versions of modern Indian nationalism do form a descending series. The liberal form was farthest away from the rancorous. The new Hindu form, in spite of its high intellectual standards, was in certain of its aspects a concession to atavism and was actually taken by the atavists to be so in its entire drift and scope. Gandhism took another step towards the retrograde correlative of all the three forms of modern Indian nationalism through its rejection of reason and civilization. Of course, the doctrine as preached by Mahatma Gandhi himself made no distinction between the sophistication of the ancient Hindu and that of the modern European; furthermore, although preaching a doctrine of pure negation, Mahatma Gandhi sought to take the sting out of the negation by enjoining love in all circumstances: still it did not lie in his power, once he had cut his teaching adrift to go among the multitudes, to prevent its discriminatory exploitation by the atavistic horde. One little incident, very insignificant in itself, opened my eyes to the risk at the very inception of the non-co-operation movement. One day, early in 1921, I had gone to bathe in a public tank at Kishorganj. Among the crowd in the water was an old Brahmin, washing his sacred thread and muttering his *mantras*. A small group near him was discussing the new movements, and I joined in. Suddenly the wizened old creature looked at me out of a pair of gleaming eyes and said in a voice that was piercing in its exultation and raucous in its fanaticism, "He's come to re-establish Hinduism." Mahatma Gandhi, had he heard the old man, would have shuddered at this reference to himself.

It was open to everybody to accept Mahatma Gandhi in his own way. In the end Gandhism in politics and in practice came to stand for every little else but a congealed mass of atavistic aspirations and prejudices. I would not have recorded this opinion so categorically had it not been forced on me by more than twenty-five years of observation. In truth, in the sphere of politics, the people of India, taken in the mass and including the intelligentsia, never accepted Gandhism as Mahatma Gandhi understood it: they accepted only their own version of Gandhism and made it serve their own ends. When it went against their inclinations and interests, which always were retrograde, they rejected it—their own basic morality—as completely as they rejected the civilization of the West and of ancient India. Towards the end of his life, Mahatma Gandhi seemed to have become suddenly aware of this fact, of the repudiation by his countrymen of the only thing for which he cared—his vision of truth and right. That disillusionment made him wish for death, which came with merciful swiftness from the pistol—the sacred weapon of Indian nationalism—of a Hindu fanatic. I speak of merciful swiftness because if he had lived he would have suffered tortures infinitely more cruel and excruciating than death. For the real assassin at large was not a single individual, nor a group of conspirators, nor even a reactionary minority of his people, it was an entire geographical environment, a society, a tradition acting in unison, and arrayed as a colossal, nescient murderous force against his principles and teachings.

Although in the competition between the three forms of modern Indian nationalism the victory went in the first round to new Hinduism, and in the second to Gandhism, what triumphed in the end was that far older thing, the atavistic nationalism of the Hindu. In other words, everything else capitulated to the ghastly Indo-Gangetic plain and its degenerate inhabitants, old Sycorax and her Calibanic brood. All the three modern and idealistic forms of Indian nationalism lay dead at their feet. There was thus a stern historical logic terrifying and chastening at the same time in the coincidence between the victory of the movement which Mahatma Gandhi had led and his own death. The Good that he was perished at the hands of the Evil he had helped to triumph.

I certainly had no perception of all this when in 1921 I felt an instinctive dislike for the non-co-operation movement. But it is not wholly impossible that there was lurking, in the subconscious depths of my mind and the minds of all our older nationalist leaders, the fear of the monstrous abortion that was taking shape in the womb of the future.

CHAPTER III

VANISHING LANDMARKS

THERE ARE two good reasons for which I have given precedence to politics over other things in describing what I have called an unperceived revolution, in our contemporary existence. In the first place, our new politics furnished the best illustration of that transition from positive and rational values to the negative and the sub-rational which to my thinking constituted the essence of the revolution I am speaking about. Secondly, a complete dominance by politics of all other activities went hand in hand with the same revolution. This second fact was by itself of the deepest significance, for never before had I seen such an unchallenged supremacy of politics. Incorrigibly political as we always had been, still politics with us had so far been only the *primus inter pares,* one of a triad, and it had never before been able to push religion (taken with morality) and literature out of the mind of an educated Bengali. Thus in its new dominance politics was bringing two negations into our existence—the first, its own; and the second created by the expulsion of all other pursuits and interests.

DEATH OF MORAL CONSCIOUSNESS

The first casualty was the moral awareness created by Brahmoism and new Hinduism. I do not mean by this that our society became at one stroke as dishonest, self-seeking, venal, mercenary, and insensitive to all considerations not only of probity, but also of appearances, in its pettifogging pursuit of money as it now is. But what had happened was not less, but more, dangerous and ominous, for it was insidious in its workings. People were getting used to leading the uncriticized life, which Plato has described as a life not worth living. The Nomos of a community, however seemingly well established, cannot be maintained in its health and strength without unceasing criticism, which in its turn has its springs in moral awareness. Both the criticism and the awareness seemed to have passed out of our existence altogether. So our Nomos decayed inevitably, although imperceptibly, and what has now come about through the ampler opportunities for dishonest money-making provided by the war and the subsequent acquisition of political power is only the collapse of the worn-out facade.

I shall try to bring home the reality of the earlier moral consciousness by giving one or two instances of the manner in which it acted as an inhibitory brake on certain means of making money or even a living. I used to know scores of people who would not take up law or business because these pursuits sometimes involved a slight stretching of the conscience, or would not accept Government service from patriotic objections. Next, I met people who would never solicit a superior officer for employment for their sons or relatives. I have heard high placed Bengali Government officials warning their sons that they must not expect any exercise of personal influence in their favour. Lastly, in spite of the universal prevalence of corruption, neither the bribe-taker nor his money was respected. One day I heard my father speak with crushing contempt of a neighbour who had slyly boasted to him of the "perquisites" of his son-in-law. Today it almost brings tears to one's eyes to recall those old days when men refused employment for the sake of convictions, did not betray both the Government and their convictions while in service, were ashamed of jobbery and nepotism, and thought poorly of ill-gotten gains.

A very striking revelation of the shifting of the wind came to me about 1929, as I was listening to a colloquy between my elder brother and a young woman of his acquaintance, who was a graduate of Calcutta University. My brother was speaking of a man who had embezzled a very large sum of money, a matter of some hundreds of thousands, and was drawing satisfaction from his conviction and a stiff sentence of some years of imprisonment. The young lady replied to him in a tone of quiet triumph, "But he has kept his money." This answer relieved me completely from a sense of guilt I was having in connexion with this lady. There was a coarseness of expression in her face which repelled me so much that I could not reconcile myself even to being polite to her. I was not without qualms of conscience on this score. But after that incident I gave absolution to myself, because I had at last been shown that the surprising coarseness on her young face was really a reflection of the corruption of her soul. Unfortunately this particular kind of corruption is oozing out on the face of our womenfolk commonly enough to induce a species of sex-nausea different from that preached by the old moralists and now analysed by modern psychopathologists. But the still more unfortunate fact is that the men who suffer from this nausea are often too afraid of their wives to admit the disease.

I am not going to recount the sorry tale of this decline of morals in our society. I am no satirist, and even if I were one I should have to be one with an abnormally keen appetite for satire to be capable of relishing so putrid a fare. I am intolerably sickened by the spectacle which has become so common in India today of bands of men, respectable in outward appearance but low adventurers at heart, going about sniffing on the trail of jobs which are sinecures, contracts which are mere assignments on the public revenues, orders which never insist on value for money, and similar openings for profit without effort, for the spectacle only reminds me of our scavenging birds and animals wandering about in search of offal and filth. Therefore I want to shut my eyes on this exhibition of contemporary morals, the salon of the once rejected and the now accepted. Still I cannot leave the subject without making an attempt to understand why we should have come to this pass, and when I make the effort I also make the discovery that the degradation was almost inherent in the nature of things.

Brahmoism and new Hinduism had brought a previously unperceived value into our life–the ethical value. Hindu society, or if I am not to be so sweeping, that part of Hindu society in which moral conduct was regulated solely by tradition, had no consciousness of moral problems. It was indeed in all things too superstitious, but in spite of that had not erected an altar to morality even as the Unknown God. As most of us understood and practised morality, it had not emerged out of religion, and moral commandments formed only a fraction of the formidable array of taboos which regulated every aspect of a Hindu's life. For him, were he true to his religion, eating chicken was not less of a crime than cheating, immodestly assaulting a girl not more reprehensible than looking on the face of the wife of a younger brother, a fatal accident to a cow not less calamitous than knocking down a man by rash driving. If irresponsible homicide entangled one in the paraphernalia of civil justice, irresponsible bovicide enmeshed one in the net of priestly retribution.

I shall give a recent example. A certain citizen of a small town of east Mymensingh, a contractor and thus a helper of the Allied cause during the war, had the misfortune of having his cow strangled by means of the rope with which she was tied. The incident took place towards the end of 1944, and the expiation the contractor had to make was severe. To begin with, he had to go into sackcloth, drink half a glass of bovine urine, and fast for one day. For the next three days he had to live and sleep in the open on the spot where the cow had died, and also to abstain from eating anything but plain rice unseasoned even with salt. This rice, too, he had to beg from his neighbours, and while begging he had to ask for his alms bellowing like an ox, for during these days he was not permitted to speak like a man. Furthermore, all the time he had to wear a rope round his neck. At the end of three days a most elaborate atonement ceremony was performed. He was sprinkled all over with cow's urine, all the Brahmins of the locality were fed, and the priests amply rewarded. He could do no more, in fact, he would not have been asked by society and the sacerdotal order to do more, if instead of his cow his mother had been strangled, or for that matter he had strangled her with his own hands. But as chance would have it, for the contractor, even this was not the end of the matter. It was the cold season, and as a result of the exposure undergone, he got fever and became delirious. In his delirium he called aloud for his cow, and for a day or two it seemed that he would join her. But the malady took a sudden, unexpected turn for the better, and the supreme atonement which squares up all accounts was almost miraculously averted.

These expiations for the death of cows are not rare, or in any wise exceptional, occurrences. The young nephew of mine, of whom I have spoken, was an eye-witness of the expiation I have just described, and it made a profound impression on him. Some time after this incident there was a violent thunderstorm in his town. It was a dark evening, and a big tamarind tree which stood behind the main hut of my sister's house came down with a crash and smashed one corner of it. Without heeding the danger in which she herself and her children found themselves, my sister immediately thought of the cow and her calf in the cow-shed, for she remembered that the shed was ramshackle. By a curious coincidence, almost as soon as she thought of it, another smaller tree came down on the cow-shed, and in fright the calf and the cow began to bellow piteously. My sister was extremely distressed, for my brother-in-law was away, and there was not a second man in the house except a rather stupid servant who could not be depended upon to do anything to any purpose. Then, realizing the extent of the crisis and remembering the consequences for his father of the death of a cow, my young nephew (twelve years old, four feet two inches in height, and forty-two pounds in weight) rushed out to the rescue of the cow like Napoleon on the bridge at Arcola. He found the cow-shed wrecked, but was able to bring back the cow and her calf to safety on the bedroom veranda. When a few days later my brother-in-law returned home and heard the whole story, he thanked the gods that so great a calamity had been averted and he praised his son for a brave boy. There is a proverb in Bengali to the effect that the fortunate man is he who loses his wife, but the luckless man loses his livestock.

Besides telling me these stories, my nephew, who is staying with me during the writing of this autobiography, is also serving as witness to the truth of my recollections and early impressions. I am checking all my assertions against his experiences, and in order to test my theory of the Hindu attitude towards morality, I asked him one day what *wrong* was. Without a moment's hesitation he replied that it was *sin*. Then I asked him how men could make amends for any wrong done by them. He replied, "By expiation." "What is expiation?" I finally inquired, and got the expected, in fact, the inevitable reply, "Eating something." What he had in mind was of course the eating of cowdung, which forms an indispensable part of most Hindu expiatory rites.

In my student days I heard many of my more serious and orthodox college-fellows putting in a strong defence of this intermingling in Hinduism of morality, religion, and social customs. Instead of being a thing to be abashed about, this, they declared, was the peculiar mark and glory of Hinduism, because Hinduism refused to cut up life into fragments, label one bit morality and another religion, and make an artificial distinction between things which could not be distinguished; the supreme virtue of Hinduism was that it considered life to be a unitary spiritual experience. All this was competently and plausibly put, and in unfolding the point of view the respective merits of the "analytical" and "synthetical" outlooks on life were canvassed. These were the arguments of new Hinduism. Yet I was not convinced. I had then just begun to read anthropology, and Frazer's *Golden Bough* was weaving its spell round me. I replied that if an undifferentiated promiscuity of values was a merit in a Hindu of India it could not be something else in a Veddah of Ceylon or an Arunta of Australia. The more I read and learned, the more I came to prize differentiation and complexity. I implicitly believe that culture is indeed the faculty of making distinctions.

I think there is even in the highest and most characteristic teaching of Hinduisms (apart from the layer on layer of infinitely varied primitiveness which constitutes its buried foundation), something impelling a Hindu towards the simpler in preference to the more complex, towards the unemerged in preference to the emergent, and towards the general in preference to the particular. According to some of the noblest teaching of Hinduism, the manifested universe is an illusion, the ultimate reality attributeless, and man's supreme happiness lies in putting an end to the cycle of births and deaths, or, in other words, in eliminating precisely those particular forms possessing sensible attributes which confer qualities and values on reality, and clothe it with attractiveness for us. With such a philosophical background it is not surprising that a Hindu should tend to ignore distinctions. To me, however, Hinduism appears to be swimming against the current. Although its penchant for the undifferentiated and attributeless is undoubtedly due to its anxiety to bite on the rock of truth and reality lying underneath the flux of changes, I would still say that in actual fact it is retrograde and out of sympathy with reality. For I believe in change and hold all reality to be a process, a process which is justifying itself, as well as making itself more significant, by becoming more particular and differentiated and by endowing itself with ever more new values. To ignore these particularities is to miss the meaning of the entire cosmic evolution.

I am not intimidated by the argument, or even by the possibility, that what I perceive as particular and differentiated manifestations may be nothing more than the shape or pattern my perceptive faculties are imposing on an undifferentiated reality. If all that I perceive is only subjective and nothing better, it is this subjective world alone for which I care, and I would not waste tear over the so-called real universe. But I really do not believe that the manifested and perceived world is an illusion or rather is more of an illusion than the so-called reality admitted by hair-splitting, and now atom-splitting, intellection. Without being a student of philosophy I have come to feel and believe that reality and our knowledge of it march hand in hand; also that knowledge cannot be born without some reality behind it, nor reality exist without our knowledge being largely commensurate with it. To give one or two concrete instances, musical sounds are no less real to me than the vibrations which impinge on my ears as sound, nor colours more illusory than the light waves which create the impression of colour in my eyes. I go even farther and say that my perception of right and wrong is not a whit less valid than my perception of solidity, fluidity, and gaseousness.

I am digressing. But the point I wish to make is this: that historically and for practical purposes Hinduism was being nothing but primitive and conservative in its conscious or unconscious refusal to separate morality from religion, and that when it formulated its larger philosophy of life it took a line which could not foster true ethical development. For morality is only one of the last differentiated manifestations of the undifferentiated primordial creative motive power, and if one dismissed the material world as illusion he could not make the moral and spiritual world more real. The teachers of revived Hinduism who put the Hindu incapacity for making distinctions between the various aspects of life to its credit account were to my mind only making a virtue of necessity. In the sphere of morals, Hinduism has not progressed very much beyond its primitive beginnings, nor been able to brush aside the red herring of philosophical doctrine across its track. Hindu ethics has remained immature.

The ethical immaturity of Hinduism is apparent in another direction also: in its failure to develop a high sense of personal moral responsibility. If a course of conduct–for example, the taking of bribes or not giving value for money in the public services or serving an organization or person from purely mercenary motives, disregarding one's moral convictions all the time–is sanctioned or condoned by habit or custom no Hindu, however highly cultured intellectually, will search his conscience on his own initiative and from a sense of individual duty. The doctrine of *Karma* has certainly dulled the Hindu's conscience by entrusting the ship of morality to a sort of gyropilot. I do not, of course, mean that this doctrine is identical with determinism. It is not, for it never rules out free will. But it spreads out cause and effect too far apart and, what is more serious, breaks the chain of causality by putting cause and effect on two sides of the dissolution of personality and memory. Consequently it reduces causation to something very much like fate. Moreover, moral sensibility and moral life cannot be developed on the basis of the idea of retribution alone. It must be endowed with value as an independent experience in itself. It is curious that Hinduism, which has with such insistence fostered the idea of spiritual life being a self-contained and self-sufficient activity to be prized for its own sake, has never extended the same idea to the moral sphere.

But the most serious handicap from which Hindu ethics suffers is to be found in the universal and ineradicable assumption that the gods are venal. Whether among the Hindus corruption in the temporal order has given rise to the idea of corruptibility of the divine order, or belief in the corruptibility of the divine order has induced men to imitate the gods, is a nice and perhaps insoluble question. But whichever way causation may have flowed the effect has been the same. The Hindu pantheon is as corrupt as the Indian administration. The indulgences bought from Rome which so scandalized Luther were as nothing compared with the indulgences which through the instrumentality of our priestly class we could buy from our gods. Although at times the bribe expected varied in amount according to the gradation of the offence or nature of the favour sought, the more general rule was that you could pay according to your means without regard to what you expected the gods to do. The divinities were merciful and compassionate and did not exact heavy bribes when the means were denied. They were also socialistic and gave to every man according to his need and took from him according to his capacity. A poor peasant could get moral remission for an offering worth five annas and a quarter (the lowest traditional amount), while Hindu millionaires and profiteers were expected to erect temples and *dharamsalas*.

The only man who got nothing but got punished into the bargain was the man who refused the god his bribe. In our young days we heard and read the story of a merchant called Chand who refused to worship the goddess of snakes because, as he proudly declared, having worshipped the great Siva he would not bow down his head before a wench of a pseudo-goddess. He was cruelly and terribly punished for this impiety and in the end coerced. This is a very famous Bengali legend and was very popular in my district, where a number of manuscripts of the work in which it occurs have been found. People around us who heard the story were extremely edified by it and saw nothing wrong in the persecution of Chand. But we considered his ordeals very unjust, unnatural, and almost blasphemous. Although enraptured by the story, for it is one of the most beautiful we have, we rejected the moral, and loathed the snake goddess all the more on account of her vindictiveness and malice.

The idea of the corruptibility of the gods is so widespread and firmly rooted in Hinduism that no Hindu could have understood, far less propounded, the Platonic thesis on this subject. He would have been puzzled, if not scandalized, by everything Plato has said about it: that the worst heresy, and morally the most pernicious, is that which believes in the venality of the gods and in the possibility of bribing divine justice; that the man who holds this opinion may be fairly singled out and characterized as of all impious men the wickedest and the most impious; that no man should concede to anyone, and every man disprove to the utmost of his power, the notion that the gods are appeased by the wicked and take gifts. All these contentions, and even more the blazing indignation with which Plato put them forward, would have been wholly unintelligible to the Hindu mind. Yet Hinduism is perhaps of all religions the one which furnishes the best illustration of the truth and justice of the Platonic indictment and argument.

The development of moral consciousness among the Hindus had an initial disadvantage to fight against. It lay in the fact that the greater majority of its popular gods were economic or utilitarian gods demanding nothing higher than a commercial honesty. This in itself was unsatisfactory, and when even from this level the god stooped to venality the atmosphere in the temple naturally approached that obtaining in an Indian police station or the black market, and morality received its worst blow from what is popularly believed to be its patron and protector.

Thus I am not surprised when I see today that not only the moral gymnastics but also the moral awareness of the Brahmos and the new Hindus has become an object of ridicule, and the Hindu has again become as dead to moral issues as he traditionally was. The influence of Christian-European morality has been waning during the last thirty or forty years as decisively as English political power. Now it has disappeared, or at all events is rapidly disappearing.

Still, time may not have pronounced its last verdict on this question, and in the scale of human history a cause lost in India may not turn out to be what we understand by the phrase "lost cause". Both the ridiculed Brahmos and the outmoded new Hindus saw deeper and clearer than their sleeker descendants. The first knew the Hindu weakness for making large promises and smooth excuses and told us never to make any promise but only to say, "I shall try", while Swami Vivekananda, the most powerful preacher of new Hinduism, familiar with the suicidal facility in cleverness of the Hindu, taught us that "Nothing great was ever achieved by cleverness." These are the days of infinite cleverness and large promises in India. The smooth excuses are making their inevitable appearance. Perhaps when we shall have got sick of them and of the cleverness which will be as unwearied in their invention as the spider in the spinning of his web, we shall recall the interlude in our history in which we forgot our oily cleverness for once to become moral. But even that hour of remembrance has to be waited for, because it will not come without full expiation.

DEATH OF THE OLD ANTITHESIS AND SYNTHESIS

Two other things, constituting very special features of the culture of modern India, had disappeared even more completely. Morality may have its ups and downs among men, it has its ups and downs, but in any event its horoscope is cast for eternity, and therefore in the end it manages to have the last laugh of every dog who thinks too much of his day. But the case is wholly different with things less sempiternal, activities and concepts which work within a particular framework of time and place. They may be strong and fertilizing in their season, none the less their life is tied to the life of movements out of which they are born. The antithesis between Hindu liberalism and Hindu conservatism was one of the most striking outward signs of life in our nineteenth– and early twentieth-century culture. The concept of synthesis, aiming at a fusion of the values of the East and the West, was the basic formula of that culture. We cannot conceive of modern Indian culture without them and their creative action and reaction. But both were products of the particular urges and circumstances of a particular age. Accordingly, if they are now things of the past, I cannot cherish the same hope of their resuscitation as I do of the resurgence of morality even among us. I can only record the circumstances of their extinction and pronounce an *oraison funebre*.

I have already said that Hindu conservatism scored a decisive victory over Hindu liberalism in the first decade of this century and that politics made a powerful contribution to that victory. Hindu liberalism did not, however, yield the palm to its antagonist. It continued the fight, and for some years its indefatigable exponent was the Bengali magazine *Prabasi*, on whose staff I worked in later life. But in 1913 the cause received a more powerful reinforcement in a new monthly magazine called *Savuj Patra,* brought out by the well-known literary critic, Mr. Pramatha Chaudhuri, with the collaboration of Tagore. No beleaguered garrison has ever made more spirited sorties than were made by this periodical on behalf of the lost cause of Hindu liberalism. A howl of discomfiture arose from the conservatives, who found their old and stodgy methods quite ineffective against the brilliant skirmishing of Tagore and his lieutenants. My brother, of course, at once subscribed to the magazine, and the whole family became enthusiastic Savuj-Patrites. As a counterblast the conservatives, led in this instance by Mr. C. R. Das, the leading nationalist politician, and Mr. Bepin Chandra Pal, the leading theoretician of nationalism, undertook the publication of a new type of conservative magazine, which they called *Narayan.* The names of the two magazines give a fair idea of their respective standpoints, for *Savuj Patra* means green leaf, whereas *Narayan* is one of the many names of the god Vishnu, and is applied more specifically to the fossilized ammonite worshipped by all Hindus as the god's visible symbol. But the magazines could not avert, nor as I am inclined to think even delay, the utter extinction of both the schools of thought within a few years, although they shed a last gleam of light on their passing away. The *ave atque vale* of Hindu liberalism was pronounced by Tagore in his famous speech entitled "By Authority", delivered at the beginning of 1917. As chance would have it, the same year also saw the publication of the only expression in art ever given to Hindu liberalism, in a set of lithographs after drawings by Gaganendranath Tagore, the unappreciated master of the new Indian school of painting who is to be placed above his famous brother, Abanindranath Tagore. The cartoons would not suffer by comparison with those of Daumier. In the speech Tagore denounced the authoritarianism of Hindu orthodoxy no less trenchantly than he trounced the authoritarianism of the British rulers of India.

Both, he declared, were of a piece. The speech put the conservative nationalists in an unenviable quandary. They could not do without the powerful aid Tagore was bringing to the nationalist movement, yet they could not approve of his heresy in social and religious matters. With that noble utterance Hindu liberalism passed away for ever. Its rival also died about the same time, but without leaving a valedictory message comparable in any way to that of its compeer and antagonist. The two magazines eked out an ebbing life for some years yet.

The conflict of Hindu liberalism with Hindu conservatism was a product of the formula of synthesis, inasmuch as the difference of views between them was only over the ratio to be observed in drawing upon the two sources of modern Indian culture, namely, ancient Indian civilization and European civilization; not even the ultra-conservative demanded the exclusion of the influence of Europe. Thus the controversy could not peter out unless decline had previously overtaken the very formula which was giving rise to it. That was exactly what had happened. The concept of synthesis had for some time been obsolescent in our cultural life as a creative formula. Soon it was to become wholly obsolete, although even today it is trotted out by speakers and writers in desperate need of cliches.

The reasons for the decay of the concept of synthesis, a concept which in its day sustained a genuine and brilliant cultural effort, are well worth inquiring into. In my young days I was a staunch believer in the concept, and therefore its complete ineffectiveness in inspiring or moulding any of our contemporary cultural efforts has always puzzled me, and goaded me into pursuing a sustained investigation. In its course I have at last made some discoveries in regard to the nature of the phenomenon we used to call synthesis, which go some way towards explaining the decline. I shall set forth what I have discovered before indicating the reason for the decline.

This preliminary exposition is all the more necessary because in this matter my countrymen in general are running like horses in their blinkers; they are in the hands of a force too strong for their thinking powers: therefore most of them are totally ignorant of their loss of faith in the synthesis as also of their incapacity to carry it on.

There is perhaps even more sentimentalizing and cant on the subject of the synthesis than on the common heritage of the Hindu and the Indian Muslim. The adoption of foreign ideas and institutions by an indigenous population vastly outnumbering the incoming and politically dominant foreigners, even when whole-hearted and enthusiastic, is bound to result in some admixture. As La Rochefoucauld has said: *"L'accent du pays ou l'on est ne demeure dans l'esprit et dans le coeur,"* and what was true of French provincialism in the *Grand Siecle* of French civilization can be true also of all provincialism in the *Grand Siecle* of European expansion. Even the most Westernized of Indians is likely to have traits of thought, habits of emotion, and modes of expression which will unmistakably mark him as a man of India. This aspect of the synthesis hardly needs stressing, it is something which is inherent in the nature of things, but at the same time it is also a thing in which the indigenous element is inert and negative.

Next, we have to take into account two artificial aspects of the synthesis, the patriotic and the aesthetic. The patriotic Indian often advertises his Indianness without having any acquaintance whatever with anything worthwhile in the Indian tradition. Many Hindus from the Punjab speak of the greatness of Hindu culture and religion without being able to read not only Sanskrit but even Hindi. In the days when I was a clerk in the Military Accounts Department I used very often to be admonished to read Sanskrit by my Bengali colleagues who had observed with disapprobation my fondness for

English and French literature, but whose knowledge of Sanskrit did not extend to a knowledge of even the Nagari script.

The aesthetic aspect of the belief in synthesis is less crude but to my thinking more unpleasant. It is the product of the revulsion of some of our most sensitive minds from the banality of our Westernization, and the greatest exponent of the aesthetically inspired synthesis was Tagore. If a field had to be ploughed or trees planted at Tagore' agricultural institution, the bullocks were first felicitated and the saplings appeased by the chanting of Vedic hymns, while young men and young women exhibiting varying shades of archaism in their dress and deportment went through diverse bodily movements assumed to be Indian. These antics seemed to comfort Ṭagore for the essentially utilitarian activities he was having to sponsor. Ultimately, the fashion took on, and the first ocean-going ship to be launched in India glided down the slipway to the accompaniment of Vedic hymns. Whether it did so with any confidence in Varuna's ability to save it from any faults of design there might have been in it or even with any faith in Varuna himself, is a question which did not arise at all on this occasion, and it never does on any occasion. But these meaningless and at the same time characteristic airs and graces overwhelm Indophil Westerners, and the prestige of these foreigners with Indians in its turn induces the native to think better and better of these affectations and fall more and more in love with them.

Nevertheless, after every allowance has been made for the dross in the amalgam, there still remains a solid core within the so-called synthesis. There are, however, two things about it which call for very special notice. In the first place, the Indian element in the synthesis, instead of being part and parcel of the life of Indians in the nineteenth century, was coming to them across many centuries as a thing to be recognized and received anew. Thus, when nineteenth-century Indians began to adopt the modes of thought of ancient Hindu India, they turned to something with which their living contact had long since been broken, and which consequently was external to them. In other words, they were being as imitative when copying ancient Indian ways as they were in copying the Western.

My second point, and that to my thinking is the more important one, is that the orientalism which became one of the two elements in the modern Indian synthesis, was not the native and traditional Sanskrit learning, but the new learning about the East created by the European orientalists. This fact conditioned the nature of the Sanskritic element in the synthesis. Externally viewed, modern Indian culture was based on a fusion of two independent and unconnected cultures, the European and ancient Indian. But in reality, before the synthesis was undertaken in India by Indians, the ancient Indian element had become subtly transformed by being passed through the filter of European thought and scholarship. A preliminary synthesis, if I may say so, had already been brought about by the great European orientalists for the Indian reformers to improve upon. On the whole, it would not be wrong to say that the orientalism of modern Indians was only a product of the wider movement in favour of oriental civilizations which had sprung up in the West, or, to put the matter more incisively, it was a reflection of occidental orientalism. The validity of this opinion is strengthened by the fact that most modern Indians cannot and do not read Sanskrit, and make their acquaintance with Hindu traditions and values entirely through English.

There did indeed exist a truly native Sanskrit learning. But it existed wholly as a retrograde influence, and did not form part of the new culture of modern India. Thus nothing could be more natural than the apparent paradox that while the orientalism of Europe became an integral part of modern Indian culture the traditional Sanskrit learning remained wholly outside it. This upshot was implicit in the nature of the old learning, about which I must say a few more words, following up the comparison which I have already made between our traditional Sanskrit learning and medieval Latin learning. The traditional Sanskrit learning lacked the sense and consciousness of history even more completely than did Latin learning of the Middle Ages. Medieval Latin learning had grown according to the needs and capacity of the very much more simple European society which had emerged out of Graeco-Roman society. It existed, not to make classical antiquity intelligible or accessible, but to reinforce medieval concepts. It was easily contained within the limits of the spirit of the age and widened only in step with the slow broadening out of that spirit.   In all these respects the Sanskrit learning of the traditional school was similar to medieval Latin learning. But in one respect there was a vital and essential difference. Medieval Latin learning, however unhistorical, was not static. That learning was not, in the age of Thomas Aquinas, what it had been at the time of Alcuin. There was growth, and natural growth, because during the Middle Ages European civilization was winding itself up and becoming more complex. But during the period of Muhammadan rule Hindu society was winding down and becoming simpler.   In actual fact, during these centuries, Hindu society was partly fossilizing and partly rebarbarizing itself, and the spirit of Sanskrit learning was also thoroughly adapting itself to the process. Thus it progressively became wholly incapable of sustaining creative thought. The strongest point of the pundits was their philological competence, which the new orientalists could not rival. Therefore they were profitably exploited by the moderns as philological assistants. For any other purpose suited to the times both their knowledge, which in many cases was great, and their style, which was ponderous, were useless.

No one saw this point more clearly than Bankim Chandra Chatterji, the preacher of Hindu conservatism. In the preface to his own edition of the *Gita* he wrote that those Bengalis who were educated on Western lines could no more understand the arguments of the pundits even when translated into modern Bengali than the pundits could understand the arguments of Western thinkers even when translated into their own language. In both cases, Chatterji said, a translation of the language could not be accepted as the equivalent of a translation of ideas. It was this fact that made Chatterji lay down the paradoxical and startling principle that it was the purpose of his commentary to explain the philosophy of the *Gita* to his own countrymen according to the methods of Western scholarship and with the help of Western ideas. He followed the same method in his interpretation of the life of Krishna and his expositions of the Hindu view of culture as a religious discipline. In the course of these expositions he not only referred to Matthew Arnold as an advocate of a special kind of culture, but also drew extensively on that classic of anthropology, Tylor's *Primitive Culture,* then newly published. The feud between the old and the new Sankritists persist till this day. No one can understand the true character of the Sanskritic, which is the same thing as the Hindu element in the new Indian culture, without taking into account and making allowance for this feud.

Having sufficiently cleared the decks I think I can now fire my final broadside of heterodoxy, and put on record my definite conclusion that the so-called synthesis was not a synthesis at all but only imitation of a vigorous and re-creative order. Briefly, what we had accomplished in the nineteenth century was not the creation of a new culture through the fusion of two independent elements, but simply the assimilation of two influences, complementary and contrasted, both coming from the West, but one the native product of Europe and the other its cultured harvest.

This process of imitation is still going on. But its character has changed. What formerly was a positive, selective, and assimilative process has become passive and unconscious absorption. This change in the quality of the process is due in the first instance to the decline of vitality, intelligence, and education among Indians–a retrograde phenomenon whose nature and aetiology I should like to see examined–but it is also due to the wholly novel character of the influences which are now coming from the West. Whereas the European influences of a bygone age were influences emanating from the higher centres of European culture, the intellect and the spirit, the new influences are much more elemental. Their impact is being felt for the most part on our economic life and on the basic technique of living. This more comprehensive and fiercer impact began to be felt immediately after the end of the First World War, and has continued since. At times the incursion has resembled the poltergeist's shower of stones into a sleeping household, so utterly unrelated to any existing social and cultural trends in the country have these influences been, but most often it has been as incessant–I am driven to that inescapable imagery again–as the rain of dust on the Indo-Gangetic plain. This deposit is gradually but inexorably altering the superficial aspect and inward nature of human life in India. Indian society has become more Westernized in the last twenty years than it had been in the previous one hundred and twenty years of British rule. It is being Westernized in a manner which would have been incomprehensible to an Indian of the nineteenth century, as it is incomprehensible at the present moment to a cultured contemporary European. No Indian of the now closed epoch of synthesis would have recognized the new Westernization because it is so inert and indiscriminate, the contemporary European cannot recognize it because it is so debased. And this leads me to my last point. The passing away of the concept of synthesis was a necessary corollary to the transformation in the character of the Westernization. So long as our imitation remained a rational, deliberate, and controlled activity we could retain the illusion of a process resembling fusion. But as soon as our imitation became on the one hand involuntary and compulsive, and on the other too comprehensive and rapid for our selective and assimilative capacities, we ceased to think of it as a synthesis. Consequently we also lost faith in the concept of synthesis. May the dead idea rest in peace, unexhumed by ghoulish cliche-hunters.

I am able to cite a personal testimony dating from the early 'twenties which will illustrate how this thesis of mine regarding the synthesis sprang from actual experience. When I went out into the world in 1921 I became distinctly aware that the European influences which were coming into our country at that time were totally different from those which I had felt earlier in life. This perception was so sharp that it led me within the next few years to question the soundness of two current notions, one held by European writers of a certain way of thinking, that the nationalist movement in India was really the product of a clash of civilizations, and the other held by almost all educated Indians, including myself, that modern Indian civilization was a synthesis of the values of the East and the West. Thenceforth I denied the existence no less of the conflict than of the synthesis. I put these newly formed views of mine into print in a review of Lord Ronaldshay's book, *The Heart of Aryavarta.* The article was written in November 1925, and appeared in the well-known daily paper of Calcutta, *The Statesman,* in the following January. I shall quote one or two extracts from that article which bear upon the present argument.

I began by summarizing Lord Ronaldshay's point of view. "In his interesting researches into the causes of Indian unrest," I wrote, "Lord Ronaldshay makes the discovery that the heart of Aryavarta still belongs to Vedanta philosophy, and that herein lies the explanation of its revolt against the domination of a nation which represents a stream of culture alien and unacceptable to its distinctive modes of thought, the political discontent in India being no more than the byproduct of a clash of civilizations."

Then I took note of the affiliations of the idea. "The theory of an eternal conflict, secular and spiritual, between the two antithetical civilizations–so it is said–of the East and the West," I continued, "is of course not new. It has been accepted as a working hypothesis by most historians and political thinkers for the last fifty years, in their ruminations over the relations of Europe and Asia, and under its influenrce the intermittent warfare between the peoples living on the borders of the two continents has been welded into a unified drama whose first act was played out on the plain of Marathon and the last act is yet to come. Lord Ronaldshay has affiliated the Indian nationalist movement with this tremendous historical phenomenon."

Yet I raised the question: "Is this picture of India as a battlefield of rival civilizations true?" The rest of the article was devoted to an attempt to answer the question. I cannot reproduce the whole argument here, but I shall cite the passage which contained the kernel of what I had to say. I wrote: "The undercurrent towards more and more complete Europeaniza-tion is stronger than Europeans and Indians alike choose to admit. While the English thinker sees the vision of warring civilizations, and the Bengali poet dreams of a glorious future for his countrymen, who, he confidently prophesies, will establish the brotherhood of men, and will, by sheer force of genius, reconcile 'the tiger and the ox', the European and

Indian, that is, the real cultural role of the Bengalis seems to be much less ambitious. It is to assimilate, by slow degrees, the ways of Europe, till at last civilization, in India becomes the provincial edition of the civilization of Europe, palely reflecting like the moon its borrowed light from the great sun beyond."

This conclusion was arrived at by me when I was only about half as old as I am today, but on the whole it was not a bad shot at the future. In any case, a contemporaneous testimony is there that one man had perceived something new in the air and had taken the risk of drawing a definite conclusion from what he had felt.

While all the important landmarks of our intellectual and spiritual life were vanishing gradually, there was one landmark, the most important one on the horizon of my individual and personal existence, which disappeared with a crash, at one stroke. It was my career. From the age of twelve, and for ten years, I had thought of nothing else but university teaching as my vocation, and now it was passing beyond my reach, for no one could become a university lecturer or even tutor without a Master's degree. The obstacle was not my first failure. After that it was taken as a matter of course that I should appear at the next M.A. examination. But as months went by I found my physical and mental strength progressively becoming inadequate for it. My lassitude, not noticed immediately on account of the bustle of my brother's wedding and the diversion of attention caused by it, became all too palpable when it was over. I was in a state of continual worry, trying to keep up the appearance of study, yet finding myself incapable of concentrating on it. At last, being unable to endure the torture any longer, I went up to my father and told him briefly but decidedly that I was not going up for the examination again and would accept whatever employment I could secure. My father must have been anticipating some such announcement from me, for he only said "All right." That afternoon I had a long and peaceful walk by the river. A great burden was lifted from my mind. But this respite was short-lived. It was quickly followed by a new kind of mental strain. To begin with, there was my father's coldly indifferent attitude towards me, àn attitude maintained so consistently that it hurt me more than even any angry and continuous abuse would have done. Obviously, he had cast out with a resolute exercise of the will all the ambitions he had formed on my behalf, and if any wounds were left in his mind by the operation he was not the man to make a display of them.

Within a few weeks I left for Calcutta and, arriving there, asked my friends and well-wishers to be on the look-out for some suitable employment for me. It was no easy matter, however, to decide or discover what was suitable, and to secure it was more difficult still. I was exactly like one of those thousands of fellow-graduates turned out by Calcutta University who, so to say, were nondescript in the employment market. At the end of their university career all of them found themselves untrained and unfitted for any particular vocation and were ready, in return for a fixed monthly salary, however small, to work in any situation without taking the least account of their personal tastes and aptitudes.

Fortunately, although I had to drift far from a scholastic career in accepting employment, I did not have to wait long for it, nor did I have to resort to that degrading canvassing which is the lot of almost everybody who seeks employment in India. A cousin of mine, who was in the Military Accounts Department of the Government of India, was able to get me appointed to the post of a clerk in his office. That happened in August 1921, barely three months after I had begun to look for employment. The salary given to me was double that of an ordinary clerk, and it was more than what I should have started on as a young lecturer or tutor in a college. The prospects too were good so far as money went, and that was demonstrated to me within a few months by a temporary promotion to a more important post, which doubled my salary. There was plenty of goodwill and opportunities for me in my new office, and I had only to work hard and make use of them in order to ensure for myself a prosperous and stable career in the service of the Government.

For the first few months I had the most proper feelings and sentiments about my new opportunities. I was fully conscious of my good luck and grateful for the easy escape I had had from the dilemma created for me by my academic failure. I was also pleased with my income, for it gave me a sense of self-respect. There was nothing which I had contemplated with greater dread than the likelihood of my remaining dependent on my father for an indefinite period of time. I was earning enough for my present needs, and as regards the future, that also was assured, provided I did not grudge steady work. In fact, if getting settled in life were the only consideration, I had made a far better start in the Military Accounts Department than I should have in a university.

But very soon it became disconcertingly clear to me that the kind of life the Military Accounts Department offered was impossible. I had no taste whatever for the routine work I was required to perform, and very quickly I acquired a positive dislike for it. No lure of promotion or of a better salary could put me in a frame of mind to carry on my clerical duties industriously. I began to neglect them to the detriment of my prospects. My cousin and my superior officer, all of whom had taken very kindly to me and were doing all that they could to advance my interests, remonstrated. But it was useless to argue with me. I remained wholly unreconciled to the Military Accounts Department and resolved to leave it as soon as I could. In the meanwhile, I went on neglecting my work and not only losing the good reputation I had earned for myself in the first few months, but also putting my friends in the office in a very awkward position.

No one could have gone on like this without having to pay for it, and if I was not made to do so by being turned out of my job, I had to make up in mental distress. It was of two kinds: first, the distress arising out of the aversion I felt for my work, and, secondly, the distress caused by my consciousness of my neglect of duty. Only one of two things could put an end to it— either conscientious work in my post or its immediate relinquishment. But as I did not possess the strength to have recourse to any one of these two remedies, the only result was that the double-edged suffering turned inwards and corroded me. There never was a time in my life when I was so passively and weakly pessimistic. I thought continuously of death, as if death ever helped a weak creature to find release from the punishment he was gratuitously bringing on himself through his own folly. Thus, instead of death, what came to me was a sort of moral and intellectual valetudinarianism. I led a life of extreme anaemia and feebleness. Yet the most extraordinary part of this feebleness was that if it made me incapable of effort, it did nothing to blunt the nerve of pain. The more complete the paralysis of my will and capacity for work, the more sensitive and quick did I become in suffering. The only image I can call up to convey a concrete impression of my mental state is a conceit from spiritualism, in which I do not believe. It was as if the spirit of a man lying dead on the wayside had taken a perch on a withered branch nearby and were crying bitterly as it contemplated the inert body for which it still felt a passionate and agonizing love. Yet it was neither absinthe, nor lust, nor disease, nor remorse for some hideous suppressed crime, nor unrequited love which had brought me to this pass. My low spirits were absolute. There seemed to be no cure for them.

CHAPTER IV

AN ESSAY ON THE COURSE OF
INDIAN HISTORY

For a very simple reason an autobiography cannot have the same definite and logical ending as it is always possible to give to a biography. Thus most autobiographies are brought to a close by their authors at points arbitrarily chosen by themselves. This could also have been done by me, but considering that this book is, as I must again remind my readers, more of a national than personal history, I feel I ought to round it off with something more substantial and conclusive than an indication of the settling down of a dark mood. I have also a feeling that many things in what I have written so far must have been unintelligible to the reader because I have not set down the working hypothesis on which they rest. I shall state the hypothesis now. It is nothing more nor less than a view of the course of Indian history, and I offer an essay embodying it.

I am afraid that on this subject the gulf between my assumptions and those of my countrymen in general is very wide. The seemingly odd views I have put forward are not merely an attempt to lay a crazy pavement in the well-ordered and conventional garden of Indian beliefs and eschatology, but are rather like those cracks in the plaster of a wall which indicate uncementable fissures which rend a building from the cornic to the foundation. So far as Indian history is concerned, the difference between my theory and that of my countrymen is almost like the difference between the Copernican and the pre-Copernican view regarding the earth: mine centres round a sun, that of my countrymen is egocentric. But that is not all, the differences ramify into regions farther and farther afield, until they bring within the scope of the unending conflict not only current events and past history, but, transcending India, the entire universe, the cosmic process, and ultimately even the last conundrum of all–is knowledge possible? As I see the matter, the generalizations of my countrymen are unconscious or subconscious, while I flatter myself that I have arrived at mine after laborious and deliberate inquiry. In any case, they are consciously held and I am fully aware of their implications. I know they are leading me away from my country and my people.

Research, objectivity, and intellectual honesty are obligatory on a generalizer. But Indian history makes his task relatively easy. For the most part Indian history does not even need the generalizer, it presents its own synthesis. The structure and form of Indian history is so clear and self-articulated that only the grossest kind of prepossession can hide it. With a little will-power to get rid of this obstacle to vision, and some respect for the material provided by the sources, the generalizer of Indian history can say as the French historian Fustel de Coulanges once did: "No applause for me, please; it is not I whom you hear speaking to you; it is history which is speaking through my mouth."

Indian history is like Himalayan geography. It is vast without being complicated. Not that there is not abundance and detail, and to spare. There is and indeed so much of it that among them many specialists find themselves in the predicament of an ant setting out to explore the arabesque on the facade of a mosque. From that vantage point one does not really expect to get a perspective of the whole. But take a few steps backward for a more human or birdlike *coup d'oeil* and there is the design, almost as symmetrical in its arrangements as a figure of geometry.

Again, the shape is so implicit in the material itself, so free from ambiguity in its external and internal affiliations, so firmly fixed in the relationship of the parts to the whole, that those well-known gaps in our present knowledge of Indian history do not really affect it. Future discoveries of facts can hardly disturb, far less invalidate, the broad lines of the already revealed pattern. Rather, with the exception of the earliest period of Indian history, which must still be regarded as pre-historic and proto-historic, they are more likely to fill in the details and throw the outline into clearer relief. The design even as it is, despite the faintness of the smaller details, can actually promote the quest of data. Just as the Periodic Law has stimulated the discovery of new elements in chemistry and mathematical astronomy that of new planets, the groundplan of Indian history can fruitfully canalize our search for new facts.

Besides, I have lived through contemporary events in a manner which has developed my understanding of the history of our country by sharpening my sensibility to it. In my student days I used to be specialty drawn towards those periods of history in which some great empire or nation, or at all events the power and glory of a great state, was passing away. I was induced to anguished fascination by these periods, and the earliest experience I had of this feeling was when I read about the final defeat of Athens at the hands of Sparta. I seemed to hear within me the clang of the pickaxes with which the long walls to the Peiraeus were being demolished, and was over-whelmed by a sense of desolation which men have when they see familiar landmarks suddenly disappearing or witness the unexpected *bouleversement* of the purpose they had assumed to be inherent in the unfolding of their existences. I do not know how I came to acquire through the mere reading of text-books that feeling of oneness with Athens which Pericles voices in Thucydides, but I did feel that the downfall of Athens was a monstrous and unnatural deflection of the purpose which had become manifest through Marathon and Salamis. If that was to be the end, why was the Persian war fought at all?

This surprisingly strong emotional reaction to the defeat of Athens had its source in the mood to which we had been brought by the reading of the *Ramayana* and the *Mahabharata*. There are no books more tragic in their conclusions than these great epics. In reading them we found from the very beginning Good being assailed and Righteousness defied in the most perplexing and what seemed to us the most unnecessary manner; we saw them struggling against cruel odds and in dire peril at every turn; we went through intolerable suspense; yet we were sustained by the faith that Good and Right would inevitably triumph, indeed we saw them triumph; but at that very moment victory turned to mockery and its results to Dead Sea fruit. In the *Ramayana* Rama after fighting a dreary war to rescue Sita banishes her himself. In the *Mahabharata* Krishna is killed, Arjuna's invincible arm fails him, and in the last scene we see all the Pandavas picking their way on foot across the Himalayas in a blinding snowstorm, and all of them except the eldest falling dead one after another on that *via dolorosa*. The reading of these episodes created within me the palpitating apprehension of a great disaster lurking within a great victory, of fulfilment being sardonically challenged by emptiness. The defeat of Athens dismayed me all the more because in it I saw for the first time the descent from the plane of myth to that of history, of that perverse fate which I had seen working in our epics. Even the last comfort that it might only be the device of a moral allegory was denied me. All human achievements began to stand before my eyes with unpredictable and undeserved doom hanging over them. Anguish, pity, and passion beyond measure began to enter into my contemplation of the great things done by man.

After Athens I had to read about the passing away of many empires—the break-up of the empire of the Mauryas, Guptas, and the Moguls in India; the disintegration of the Egyptian Empire created by the warrior kings of the XVIII and XIX Dynasties; the passing away of the Babylonian and Assyrian Empires; the unfulfilled promise of the Alexandrine Empire; and, above all, the decline and fall of Rome. The spectacle of the decay of the Roman Empire held me spellbound, and I followed the process phase by phase from the beginning of the troubles at the end of the epoch of the Antonines to the lingering end in Asia Minor and Constantinople. I was elated by the reconquest of Italy and Africa on behalf of the Eastern Empire by Belisarius and Narses. I was dazed by the onslaught of the Islamic hordes, when I was expecting the Empire and Heraclius to enjoy a well-earned rest after their hard-fought war with the Sassanian kingdom. The disappearance of the Roman Empire was not simply the death of an empire but the death of a world order and of a universal civilization. I could well understand why the people of the Middle Ages were never able to breathe morally, intellectually, and politically without the idea of Rome, and I also understood their reverent efforts to continue the Roman tradition. The alternative to it was vacuum.

All this reading made me extremely susceptible to the odour of decay in a civilization or political order and prompted me to sniff the atmosphere of contemporary India with an air of uneasy exploration as soon as I was old enough to try to understand and estimate the activities around me. At first I could not understand what was happening or what I was so vaguely anxious about. I had only a feeling of being vibrated across and not along the grain. I used to say in those days that nothing that I was seeing happening in my country or the world was pleasant or welcome to me. Then gradually and slowly I woke up to the fact that I was witnessing the decay of a social order. The symptoms indicated, not simply the decline of the British Empire in India (which in those days would really have been welcomed by me), but of the civilization of modern India, that is to say, the civilization created by Indians in the nineteenth century under the impact of Western influences. The more I tried to discountenance the idea the more did it force itself on me.

At last the student of the decline of empires and civilizations was having to experience the decay he had sought to understand. A collateral experience was added by the disappearance of the Austro-Hungarian Empire, the Hohenzollern Empire, the Czarist Empire, the relapse of China into anarchy, and in the wake of all these far-reaching developments have come at last the end of Japanese and German power and the disappearance of the British Empire in India. Without possessing the courage and robustness to watch a sick human being I was consumed by the morbid curiosity to watch a sick and dying civilization or political order. My curiosity has had its fill. What and how many crashes in human affairs and, worse still, what a creeping paralysis in the lives of nations have I seen and am seeing! In the world there must still be some nations like the Americans for whom the days even now ring an unceasing carillon, but for me and for many others in India they have for years only been sounding a knell.

With the consciousness of decay and destruction all around me I have at last gained an understanding of the history of my country as I never could expect to have without this personal tribulation. Not only have the achievements of our civilization in ancient and modern times become inexpressibly dearer to me, I am able also to see the mistakes committed and the wrong turns taken by my people with a disconcerting clarity of perception. I am very much like a man at the end of his days who strikes a balance-sheet of his life and ponders over how he would have relived it without those mistakes which have ruined it, and whose clairvoyance goes on increasing as it becomes more useless. With the help of personal experience I too am able now to analyse and understand better the process of our national evolution, the course of our history. It has been made incandescent by the heat of contemporary ruin.

I am setting down all this with the sole object of making it clear to the reader that to the interpretation of Indian history I am offering I have brought something more than mere reading. I have lived a part of the history of my country and my people in my own life and that has put me in sympathy with the entire process, so that my conception of Indian history is no longer purely external. I do not need to discover India by reading books, mostly in English by Englishmen, as only too many of my contemporaries have to. I have not uprooted myself from the native soil by sojourn in a foreign country or by foreign schooling; I have only to look within myself and contemplate my life to discover India; my intellect has indeed at last emancipated itself from my country, but taking stock of all the rest I can say without the least suggestion of arrogance: *l'Inde, c'est moi.*

The self-revealed form of Indian history shows a ternary sequence. In simpler terms, it divides chronologically into three cycles, each of which stands clean-cut and indivisible against what precedes and follows it.   Each possesses an internal cohesion which resists all attempts at an alternative grouping or classification. Of course, each of these cycles is also divisible into segments. But the segments fit organically into the pattern made by the whole. Even the marginal phases leave no room for doubt as to the cycle to which they naturally belong.

In regard to these cycles it is unnecessary to repeat the truism of historiography that they are inter-related. In India, as elsewhere, each successive cycle springs out of the preceding one. In one respect the relationship is even closer. In the two later cycles of Indian history are to be found survivals, from the preceding cycle or cycles, of social and cultural elements which undergo no, or at all events very little, evolutionary transformation and continue to exist as parallel forms unintegrated with the main structure and stream of each cycle. None the less, in spite of the bodily transfer of elements from cycle to cycle, it is the distinctness of the cycles and not their similarity which strikes the eye most in India. Each of these cycles has, in addition to its distinctive complexion and atmosphere, an independent cultural and social origin and nature. The civilization and life of these cycles cannot be classified as variants of the same civilization. The dominant civilization of each cycle constitutes a separate species of civilization. Thus Indian history is fundamentally discontinuous.

This process shows a strong resemblance to certain aspects of biological evolution when one considers the type of civilization which holds the Indian stage for the time being. In the first place the succession of cultures and societies is comparable (with due recognition of the difference in time scale) to the succession of what palaeontologists call dominant types of life in the different geological epochs. There is nothing more impressive in the history of the earth than the spectacle of successive groups of animals holding the world in fee and throwing into the shade all the older competing groups. In each age a new animal ruling class appears: the trilobites in the very early Palaeozoic, the fishes in the Devonian, the amphibians in the late Palaeozoic, the reptiles in the Mesozoic, the birds and mammals in the Cainozoic, and so on. The rise of each dominant group does not necessarily lead to the extinction of the older types, although the more highly specialized ones which have got into a biological blind alley usually have to succumb. A roughly similar panorama is unfolded by Indian history. Three different social-cultural complexes appear in succession and dominate the scene. Certain specimens of the previous dominant type die out, but a majority survive to form subsidiary and subordinate strata. The whole forms, as in the biological series, a conglomeration of social and cultural strands differing in kind and at different stages of development in the scale of human evolution considered as a whole. But there is no doubt as to which is the dominant type and which is setting the tone. Just as the continuance of invertebrate forms of life does not make Mesozoic times any the less the age of reptiles, or just as the existence side by side of molluscae, reptiles, birds, and mammals does not make the Cainozoic age any the less the age of birds and mammals, so the continuance into a succeeding epoch of the social and cultural forms of a previous age does not make the age in which these survivals occur a whit less distinct and individual in its dominant character.

There is also a similarity between the qualitative aspects of both the processes, the biological and the historical. Like the dominant animal type in each geological epoch, the dominant social-cultural type of each historical cycle in India arose from a human group which, to begin with, was less specialized than the type which it superseded but contained a much higher potentiality for evolving. Owing to this fact it not only became the dominant form of its age but dominated it on a new level with new attributes. When compared with the supplanted type the supplanting civilization, like the supplanting animal group, displayed in each case higher vitality and higher achievement at the moment of contact. The result was unmistakable. Each new dominance led to a fresh outburst of social and cultural activity.

The first of the three historical cycles of Indian history is by far the longest. Its beginnings cannot be dated. It is simply seen with all its basic attributes more or less fixed when towards the commencement of the third century B.C. historical records properly so-called begin to reveal the sequence of events in Indian history. But even then the light is fitful. The close of the cycle can, however, be definitely fixed. It comes to an end with catastrophic suddenness towards the end of the twelfth century A.D.

Beginning at this point the second cycle of Indian history continued to the middle of the eighteenth century. By way of greater exactness two token dates may be assigned to the commencement and close of this cycle. They are A.D. 1192, when Muhammad of Ghur defeated Prithviraj the Chauhan, and A.D. 1757, the year of Plassey. A period of five hundred and sixty-five years lies between the two dates.

The third cycle, which began towards the middle of the eighteenth century, is, to my thinking, still continuing and is likely to continue for some unpredictable length of time. Outwardly this cycle came to an end on 15 August 1947, with the termination of British rule. I prefer, however, to look upon the present phase in India as a transitional epoch, as one of those phases of oscillation which are observable in each cycle of Indian history when the dominant civilization and the dominant ethnic element pass through a moulting time and renovate themselves. The meaning of this apparently cryptic statement will be explained latter.

Perhaps another distinct cycle is to be placed before all the three just mentioned. But although its existence appears probable it lies below the horizon of historical knowledge and still falls within the competence only of Indian pre-history and proto-history. Even archaeology, which has revealed its existence, has not been able to do much for it as yet. Its relationship to what followed is at best obscure, nor is its origin and course very much better illuminated. For the present, then, we have to note the sequence of only three cycles.

Each of these can be clearly labelled. In the conventional textbooks of Indian history they are called the Hindu, the Muhammadan, and the British period of Indian history, and on this point convention has been right while its clever critics have been wrong. By applying the criterion of cultural character it is certainly justifiable to call the first cycle Hindu, the second Islamic, and the third European. By the ethnic test the first is Indo-Aryan, the second Indo-Turkish, and the third Indo-British. I employ these terms not in the strictly racial connotation but only to give a rough indication of the national character. These two criteria of differentiation may be supplemented by the linguistic. In the first cycle India used Sanskrit (with the Prakrits), in the second Persian (with the new Indian vernaculars), and in the third English (with the modern Indian languages).

This mere labelling should serve to give some indication of the causes which have brought about the triple division of Indian history, and looking more closely for them we see either one foreign influence or another not only as the cause of the cyclical structure but also as the primary and the only motive force of Indian history. The cycles of Indian history are really the periods of India's successive affiliations with some of the greatest movements in world history, and the cyclical changes have taken place only when one affiliation has yielded place to another. In other words, India has been drawn into or annexed by certain extra-Indian historical movements to become one of the areas of their operation, and in course of time Indian versions have been created of civilizations and social orders which are in their origin and character foreign, or at all events which range over areas very much larger than India. The greatest paradox connected with India is that for a country geographically so well marked from the rest of the world and so self-contained, its history is inextricably interwoven with the strands of universal history.

Future research may disclose that even in the proto-historic age the civilization which flourished in India, the remains of which have been found at Mohenjo-Daro and Harappa, was only a cousin of the civilization of Sumeria. But leaving that age aside, there is no doubt that in all the three subsequent cycles of Indian history, whatever civilization or social order arose and flourished in India was the product of extra-Indian historical movements. The Hindu and Sanskritic civilization and social order were the products of the Aryan movement, that dimly revealed *Volkerwanderung* which appears to have brought about one of the most far-reaching and fruitful revolutions in the unfolding of human civilization. It is, of course, true that in that cycle the Hindus had no recollection of their foreign origin and regarded themselves as autochthons. But in spite of this lapse of racial memory the Hindu civilization was only one of the three members of that triad of civilizations constituted by the Greeks and Romans, the Iranians, and the Hindus themselves. The Greeks, instead of fighting the savages to the north–the Cimmerians, Scythians, or whatever they were called–came into conflict with their civilized cousins to the east. This clash took place in the full view of history. In India there is no historical memory of any such conflict, but Hindu traditions are full of reminiscences of a legendary conflict between cousins, between the *Suras,* or gods, and the *Asuras,* or no-gods, which seem to indicate a family quarrel with the Iranians.

In the historical epoch from the sixth century B.C. onwards Hindu India is found to be in successive contact with the Persian Empire, the Hellenistic kingdoms, and the Roman Empire, showing a continuous interchange of influences. What was more, the population of India had its blood renewed by successive foreign invasions, that of the Scythians, Kushans, Huns, and perhaps also Parthians, and these foreigners showed themselves to be some of the most vigorous of the elements which upheld the Hindu (including the Buddhist) civilization and social order. Although looked upon as *Mlechchhas,* or unclean foreigners, by the Hindus when they first came into the country, they quickly assimilated themselves to Hindu society and contributed to the vitality and vigour of the Hindu order.

In the next cycle Indian history becomes even more clearly the part of a larger history. India was drawn and absorbed into a bigger society occupying a much more extended habitat. She became part of the Islamic world which occupied the entire Near and Middle East, North Africa, and virtually the whole of southern Asia. There are historians who regard the Islamic period of Indian history as if it were an independent entity and Indian in its essence, with only an Islamic veneer. This view is certainly wrong. Throughout the period of their domination the Muslims of India regarded themselves as part and parcel of the Islamic world and always took particular care to maintain their affiliation with the parent society. After the catastrophe of the Mongol invasions, which appeared to give a mortal blow to Islamic civilization in central Asia and Persia, India became for the time being the refuge of Muslim scholars and theologians: the blessed Dar-ul-Islam.

With the foundation of the Mogul Empire India became even more closely a component of the Islamic order. The Mogul Empire was an integral part of the comparatively stable political system which came into being in the Islamic world after the passing away of the immediate effects of the Mongol invasions. After the shattering calamity for Islam which the Mongol irruption had shown itself to be, no Muslim had perhaps hoped that Islamic society would rear its head again. But not only did it survive: its political power and splendour was revived in a manner that must have appeared providential. This achievement was due to three dynasties—the Ottoman, the Safavid, and the Chaghatai or Timurid. A new political equilibrium was reached through the abandonment as much of the extreme of universalism of the Caliphate as of the extreme of separatism which accompanied its decline. Instead of the precarious and unmanageable universal state and the equally precarious and more ephemeral dynastic states without geographical or economic logic, the political organization of Islam henceforward stood on a new basis: it reverted to the older pre-Islamic and the more stable pattern; it articulated itself in three major parts, each of which corresponded in its geographical limits to the habitats of the ancient empires into whose heritage the Islamic peoples had stepped in; the Ottoman dynasty ruled in the area once held by the Eastern Roman Empire, the Safavids revived the Sassanian Empire, the Timurids reigned in India.

The restoration of the older scheme of Oriental empires, in its more cohesive Islamic version, gave a new stability to Muslim politics. As is well known, the three new empires occasionally clashed. At one juncture the conflict between the Ottoman and the Safavid states became acute enough to remind one of the wars between the Byzantine and the Sassanian Empire. Selim and Ismail appeared like reincarnations of Heraclius and Chosroes. But these collisions occurred only in the formative periods, or when one or other of the units showed signs of being weak, locally or over a more extended area. Otherwise, while all the three remained sound and strong there was mutual respect and co-operation, reinforced by the sense of oneness of the Islamic Commonwealth, compelling though intangible. Through this balance of power, the major political triad of Islam gave for two hundred years a steadiness to the political life of the Islamic people which they had not known since the days of the early Abbasids.

The close integration of Muslim India to the bigger Islamic world is to be expected from the very nature of the Islamic conquest of India. Islam did not conquer India in the course of those elemental upheavals which created it. The conquest of India was the projection of a different aspect of Islam. Chronologically it belongs to the later phase of Islamic expansion, in which the Islamic world added two new wings to itself, one in the west in Asia Minor and the Balkans, and the other in the east in India. Both these acquisitions were made at the expense of age-old regimes, the Byzantine and the Hindu, which had remained outside the Islamic world as created by the first surge of Islamic expansion but were at the same time in unbroken geographical contact with it, the first in a state of active, and the second passive, hostility. After remaining independent during the first four hundred years of the history of Islam both were drawn into its perimeter in the course of the next four hundred years or so.

Qualitatively, the conquest of India was the extension of an already formed society, brought about by what may be described as its normal or average expansive energy. The conquest of India by Islam bears no resemblance to its conquest of Persia. That conquest was part of the process of becoming for Islam. Arabia and Persia together made Islam, but the conquest of India took place only when the Islamic order was fully grown and fully self-conscious. This conquest contributed nothing to modify Islam. In other words, India was a colonial empire of Islam.

In the third cycle, which in my opinion is continuing, the connexion of India with the Islamic world has been severed, but a new affiliation with still wider geographical and cultural boundaries has been created. India has merged in the stream of European expansion, and forms part of those portions of the world which constitute a greater Europe, which, as I see it, will ultimately come to mean the whole world. Although more specifically, during the third cycle, India has been a unit of the British Empire only, she does not on that account become less closely attached to the wider European world, of which the

British Empire or Commonwealth is only a unit. The withdrawal of British power from India does not necessarily involve the severance of the Western affiliation.

There are three things about this affiliation of India with universal history which call for special emphasis. First, in each cycle India has been drawn into or influenced by the historical movement which is the most important and significant of its age. When India became Hindu and Sanskritic Aryan expansion was certainly the most powerful force in human affairs over the Eurasiatic world. So was Islam in the days in which India was annexed by the Islamic order. On Europe as a force in modern times it really is not necessary to expatiate.

Secondly, each of the affiliations appears to be the only possible one at the particular moment in which it was established. It is difficult to see what alternative social and cultural groups could supplant the preceding ones in the succession of historical cycles in India. If the Hindu order was to yield place to a new one, it could do so only to the Islamic. Not only was the latter the only competing social and cultural organization on the frontiers of India, not only did it occupy the geographical arena from which external elements had always made their inroads into India, it was also the only social and cultural complex at that particular moment of time which possessed the requisite vitality and maturity. The Chinese world was too old to go about on a conquering mission. The European was too far away and incubating. Again, the Islamic order in India could be supplanted by no other social-cultural system than the European. When the European order dethroned the Islamic in India, it was the only living order in the world, the rest were gliding shades.

Thirdly, each affiliation has brought India into relationship with a system which was wider than the system with which it was previously affiliated, so that Indian history is seen evolving in three broadening stages of relationship with universal history. At each of these stages the geographical limits and the cultural and social affiliations of the historical phenomena with which one has to deal were widened, so that taken in this sequence the course of Indian history is seen as an expanding spiral. The ambit within which Indian history unfolds itself in each cycle is broader than that of the preceding cycle. This process covers the entire historical period in India.

Such associations with universal history could neither come into existence nor continue without bringing to bear on the smaller field of history powerful influences from the larger. What we discover in actual fact is something even more fundamental. To consider cultural history first, there has never been any civilization in India which has not had a foreign origin, has not had foreign inspiration behind it, and has not been created substantially by incoming foreign ethnic elements. Leaving aside again the earliest times, thorough investigation into which is more likely to confirm than disprove the thesis of foreign origin, we can classify the successive cultural cycles in India as Indo-Aryan, Indo-Islamic, and Indo-European. The second element in these compound terms is really the substantive element, the first only the qualifying prefix. Some may dismiss this distinction as illusory, saying that an Indian edition of, say, Islamic culture was no more different from a form of culture essentially Indian though with a tincture of Islamic traits than in a keyboard instrument G (sharp) was from A (flat). We are not dealing here, however, with what can be reduced to only a cultural "enharmonic". In practice we have very little difficulty in determining which is the principal and positive element and which secondary. The civilization of modern Egypt, for instance, is certainly Islamic or Arabic with European patches, but the civilization of South America is Latin and not American-Indian. When I speak of Indian civilization being foreign I have, with certain qualifications, the status of modern South America in mind.

I should make it absolutely plain at this point that there is as yet very inadequate realization of the fact that civilizations in the successive historical cycles in India are foreign importations, and even when there is some realization the derivation is hotly contested. In regard to the Hindu cycle the more patriotic view considers all those elements of civilization which the Hindus share with foreign peoples as borrowings from India, while the more intelligent and scholarly view assumes that the Hindu or Sanskritic civilization is very largely the result of a fusion between the incoming Aryan elements and the older Dravidian, believed to be native or indigenous, in which the more civilized Dravidian was the main ingredient or, at all events, the more decisive influence.

Since we know nothing about the ideas and institutions or even the material civilization of these so-called Dravidians, more especially in Aryavarta or the land of the Aryas, the home territory of Hindu civilization, to my thinking, this theory that Hindu civilization was largely moulded by the example or influence of the supposedly higher Dravidian culture appears like begging the question. This is nothing more than an interesting idea which at this moment we have no means whatever of proving. On the other hand, there are certain broad facts, which are well-established and which go towards supporting the hypothesis that Hindu civilization in India in all its essential features is a variant of the very much larger civilization which the speakers of the Indo-European group of languages created over vast tracts of the Eurasiatic continent.

First, there is a language whose extra-Indian origin cannot be questioned. In India Sanskrit is popularly regarded as the language of the gods and for many centuries Hindu philologists and lexicographers have made a clear distinction between

Sanskrit and Sanskritic words and truly native words. This distinction has been accepted by modern Indian philologists. Secondly, there is a basic mythology, together with a natural theology, which is common to all civilizations with an Aryan linguistic basis. Thirdly, there are certain ethical and intellectual proclivities, such as preoccupation with truth, goodness, and beauty, embodied in such precepts as "Know thyself", which are common to all Aryans. Fourthly, there is an analogous social organization, mainly crystallizing round a division of human activities into three kinds of functions, the sacerdotal and intellectual, the warlike and political, and the economic.

Apart from these external features there is one psychological fact to be taken into account. In carrying out an inquiry into the group-consciousness of the ancient Hindus, there is nothing more striking than the persistent emphasis in all their sacred books, from the Vedas to the Dharmasutras and Dharmasastras, on the distinction between the *Arya* or Āryan and the Anarya or non-Aryan. Without giving as much as a hint in these books or other books that they had ever had any notion of not being natives of the country the Hindus always advertised their sense of being an aristocracy living among hostile and inferior aliens, being always in danger of being swamped by them, and being always under the necessity of defending their society, faith and culture against these enemies. In this matter the ancient Hindu reminds one of the modern White, more especially the Boer, in South Africa. The Hindu notion of a hostile internal proletariat was stronger than even the Hindu notion of foreigners as *Mlechchhas*. Although accompanied by a lapse of memory in regard to origins, this ineradicable notion could hardly have come into existence unless Hindu society and civilization had been the creation of foreigners coming into India with the basic elements of that society and civilization already fixed on their broad lines, or had the

Hindu civilization been largely shaped by indigenous elements. I believe in the more or less independent and unadulterated evolution of Hindu culture, though in emphasizing the independent and materially Aryan character of Hindu civilization I do not imply that there was not a civilization already flourishing or decaying in India when the Aryans came in. There may have been. But whether it can be called Dravidian or not is a different question, and whatever its character it too might have been of foreign origin.

The foreign affiliation of the Islamic cycle of Indian history has been discounted on the same ground of fusion with a preexisting order. The Hindu, as the member of a closed society based on birth and blood, has great difficulty in understanding the nature of an open society which can expand itself through proselytization and conversion. Thus he derisively exclaims that the Indian Muslim is no Muslim at all but a convert, totally failing to realize that even in Arabia the Muslim is a convert. Nevertheless, since everything in Islam from religious dogmas to legal institutions is obviously of foreign origin, and since Islam has succeeded in establishing in India a society parallel to and competing with Hindu society, Hindu scholarship cannot absolutely deny the foreign character of the civilization of the Islamic cycle; what it does is to discount it with the help of the phenomenon of a cultural heritage common to the Indian Muslim and Hindu. It points to the ethnic relationship of the two, their common language, the intermingling of Islamic and Hindu strands in the culture of Muhammadan India, in the literature and the arts which arose as a result, and also to the mutual influence which Hindu and Muslim religious and philosophical thought exercised on each other. In this synthesis they see the norm of the civilization of India in the Islamic cycle. In reality, the so-called common heritage was hardly deeper than a veneer to begin with and found to be extremely fragile in the event. The relative quickness with which its hold weakened on the people of India leads one to conclude that it had some inherent weakness. So it had. The common heritage was not a homogeneous product. Even a superficial analysis shows it to have been formed of three superimposed layers corresponding and related to the three strata of society–the ruling order, the middle-classes, and the masses. Both externally and intrinsically, these three layers differed from one another. They did not grow in identical or analogous surroundings, nor did they stand on the same footing considered as cultures. Secondly, they were all more or less unstable, though in varying degrees. Perhaps the points here made would become clearer if the layers are considered separately.

The culture which flourished in the Muslim courts of India and which was mainly based on Islamic elements (although modified by Hindu influences in certain respects), was the first of the three layers of the common heritage. It was also the most unstable. The reason for this was that it depended too much on the accident of personality. With a liberal eclectic like Akbar its nurture and existence was assured. But it withered when an Aurangzib succeeded him. The most constant quantity in the Islamic state was the body of theologians whose influence was ever on the side of Islamic purism. It was a very courageous or a very liberal Islamic monarch who was able to withstand their pressure. The cultural trends of Islamic courts therefore oscillated from pole to pole, from wide-armed receptivity to non-Islamic influences to an absolute rejection of them. This fluctuation is observed not only in India but in the Caliphate too. Thus the common heritage in India never had the chance of evolving uninterruptedly within the Islamic ruling order, nor did it take deep root. The risks of eclecticism in an Islamic prince are well illustrated by the fate of Dara, son of Shah Jahan and brother of Aurangzib.

We have next to consider the second layer–that is to say, the eclectic culture of the Hindu middle-class. Its instability was due to the motive of expediency on which it was founded. The Hindu middle-class wore Muslim clothes, learned Persian, and generally affected Muslim ways because all this suited their interest. They wanted to establish themselves in the good graces of the ruling order, they wanted positions in the administrative system and they aimed at social prestige by imitating the ways of the dominant Power. The continuance of the Islamic elements in the culture of the Hindu middle-class accordingly depended on the continued existence of Muslim rule. It was thus obvious that as soon as the one disappeared the *raison d'etre* for the other would disappear too.

Last of all comes the culture of the masses. The combination of Hindu and Muslim ingredients was more stable in this stratum than in the other two, because it sprang from more organic bonds of unity. Not only were the Hindu and Muslim masses of India closely related ethnically, they were also on a level of culture which was fairly uniform and which in its essentials was a folk civilization almost wholly devoid of self-consciousness. In the contact of diverse cultures the absence of self-consciousness always favours assimilation and absorption. This was also the case with the common heritage of the Hindu and Muslim masses of India. It was dependent on the absence of sophistication, and in this lay its greatest weakness. As long as the Hindu masses of India remained the adherents of a primitive kind of Hinduism created by the break-up of the ancient Indian civilization, and the Muslim masses remained a horde of semi-Islamized converts, all was likely to go well with the common heritage. But were either of the two wings to rise to a higher plane, they were sure to move in opposite directions. In that event the Hindus would become more Hinduized and the Muslims more Islamic. This was what actually happened. As a result of the resuscitation of the Hindu past, the nineteenth century witnessed a progressive de-Islamization of the non-Muslims of India and together with it a tremendous revival of Hindu traditions. On the Muslim side there was a continuous attempt to complete the Islamization of the Muslims of India, both qualitatively and quantitatively. The proselytizing zeal of the Muslim priestly order was not satisfied with the existing state of affairs. Its steady object was an increasing reclamation of the semi-Islamized converts who had remained lax and latitudinarian in their religious tenets. The process inevitably tended towards a waning loyalty to the common heritage. The common heritage was a pleasant *modus vivendi* for the Hindus and Muslims in certain conditions. But it could do nothing, nor did it do anything, either to modify the group-consciousness of the members of the two societies or to make them forget that they were antithetical in all matters except a few inessentials.

It is relatively easy to establish the foreign character of Indo-Islamic culture, but a similar attempt to represent the civilization of modern India as equally foreign has to face many apparently solid objections. In the first place it was created by Indians, and mostly by Bengali Hindus, without any extensive participation in its creation on the part of the English rulers. Secondly, it was consciously based on the idea of a synthesis of Western and Indian elements. Therefore the demonstration of its foreign character must be based on evidence of a different order and, to begin with, on that of philology.

There is nothing more striking about the process of cultural successions in India than its accompaniment by a succession of linguistic cycles. Each new cultural cycle in India has as its complement and basis a new language which becomes the common language for the whole of India. This language is invariably the language of the dominant political element and is imposed on the rest of the population. In the first or Hindu cycle of Indian history this was Sanskrit, "the refined or modified language", which stood in antithesis to Prakrit, "the natural or unmodified language". In the second cycle, Persian took the place of Sanskrit. The French Orientalist, Anquetil Du Perron, who brought the Avesta to the knowledge of Europe, has a very interesting passage in one of his books published towards the end of the eighteenth century on the common language of India. He says:

"La plus generalement repandue, en quelque sorte la langue universelle dans l'Inde (je le dis depuis mon retour en 1762), est le *Persan moderne*. Il n'y a pas de Princes avec lesquels on ne puisse traiter par le mowen de cette langue, parlee ou ecrite. S'ils ne la savent-pas euxmemes, ils-ont des Ministres ou des Secretaires qui l'ecrivent: elle a cours meme aux maldives et a la Cote de l'Est."

In the next cycle English came to occupy an exactly similar position in India and dethroned Persian as easily as Persian had dethroned Sanskrit.

This is not, however, the whole of the linguistic revolution which takes place at every transition from one foreign affiliation to another in Indian history; the foreign influence works its way even into the body of the native languages. When one foreign domination has succeeded another the people of India have not given up their own vernaculars; they have continued to use them for all purposes except formal, public, or pan-Indian exchange of ideas. But even in private they have used a form of their vernaculars which had a very large number of foreign words. A revolution has inevitably been seen in the vocabulary of politics, intellectual life, and culture, in a word, of higher life. Thus in each succeeding cycle the abstract nouns have overwhelmingly been foreign, replacing the abstract nouns of the previously dominant language even when the new foreign words contained no new meaning nor any extension of the old meaning.

Of this trend a few examples may be taken. In northern India the word "Badshah", which is of Persian origin, was more easily understood than the Sanskritic "Samrat"; "Vazir" was more popular than "Mantri"; "fauj" (meaning army) preferred to "sena", "mahim" (campaign) to "abhijana", "siyasat" (politics) to "rajaniti", "talim" (education) to "siksha", "imtihan" (examination) to "pariksha", "khatra" (danger) to "vipad", "shadi" (marriage) to "vivaha", "dunia" (world) to "prithivi", "larai" (fight) to "yuddha", "tarakki" (progress) to "unnati", and so on and so forth. In fact, Urdu or Hindustani, which becomes more Persianized as it becomes more serious, has been formed solely by the internal linguistic revolution of which I am speaking. It is Hindi with a dominant and cultured Persian and Arabic minority.

The British cycle of Indian history too has developed a language which corresponds to Urdu and constitutes the natural spoken language of all educated modern Indians. It is one Indian vernacular or another with an English dominant and cultured minority. Sometimes it is curious to observe how closely the vogue of these foreign words resembles fashions in dress. They appear to be adopted without any compelling necessity. For instance, as I walk along the streets of Delhi, I am often accosted by workmen, labourers, hawkers, artisans, and the like, and asked, *"Sa'ab, time keya hai?"* ("Sir, what is the time?"). For these men there is not the slightest reason for employing the word "time" because there are good Sanskritic and Persian equivalents of the word which have been in use in the country for hundreds of years. In the same way everybody employs "room", "market", "garden", "shoe", "bed", "wife", "father", "son", "marriage", "danger", and similar words of workaday status without there being any obvious reason for preferring these words to their Indian equivalents. But for the most part the foreign words are the words in which a modern Indian expresses his cultural concepts. Not only does he prefer to use a mixed vocabulary in his private conversation, he would be utterly deprived of expression if he were debarred from the use of this vocabulary. It is doubtful whether in that contingency he would be articulate even in the kitchen or bedroom, for even as a small boy in the backwaters of Kishorganj I had to use the words "loaf", "toast", "stove", "frying-pan", "saucepan", "ceiling", "shoe", "powder", and "overcoat".

There is yet a third aspect of the linguistic revolution. While an educated Indian of these days speaks in private, and naturally, only in a mixed language, he is not as yet permitted to write it. No Indo-English equivalent of the Indo-Persian Urdu has as yet made its appearance as a written language, although we may expect its emergence with the disappearance of British rule in India just as Urdu made its appearance with the decline of Mogul power which brought in its train the decline of Persian–the pure language of the politically dominant element. In India bastard languages are the offspring of political interregnums. In the meanwhile, in writing, modern Indians have been using vernaculars which have been modified both semantically and syntactically by English. In the first place, current words have assumed meanings which they never bore formerly. Secondly, new words have been coined which are Indian only in appearance, whereas in reality they are only the etymological Indian equivalents of English words and become intelligible in the Indian languages only when referred back to their foreign originals. Sometimes collocations are used which are mere literal translations of English phrases, and have no idiomatic associations in themselves. The syntax of all modern Indian languages has also been profoundly affected by English, so that with their changed construction and new vocabulary the Indian languages of today are hardly intelligible to those who are familiar only with the older and purer forms.

Even I find very great difficulty in understanding current Bengali prose although I have read almost every kind of Bengali from Chandidas's (in the most archaic form) to Tagore's (in the latest and the most stilted form), and have been a writer in modern Bengali for over twenty years.

The linguistic basis of modern Indian culture, which is made up of a combination of English, a denatured written vernacular, and a mixed colloquial language, is the first proof of the essentially foreign character of modern Indian culture. The second proof is to be found in the almost exclusively exotic forms of modern Indian literature, art, thought, and moral and spiritual activity. Literary expression in prose is itself a creation of British rule in India. So far as I am aware, no Indian language had any prose literature before the end of the eighteenth century, and some had to wait for it till about the middle of the nineteenth century. The hybrid Urdu had a form of prose current from older times, but this prose was confined to certain outlying parts of the country and exercised no general influence on the culture of northern India, whose prose expression at the time was confined wholly to Persian. Within prose, all literary forms–the novel, essay, short-story, history, biography, were taken over from English. Poetry, though pre-existing, became almost unrecognizable in its new forms. An Indian who was familiar only with the older kind of poetry could not understand the new poetry, while the exponents of the new poetry became totally dead to the older poetical appeal. This alienation between the old and the new was to be observed not only in literature but in every field of intellectual and artistic activity, and even in the moral and religious. Sunday meetings and Sunday schools, congregational prayers, the liturgy, the hymn-singing, and the routine of spiritual exercise which the reformed monotheistic Hinduism popularized were, of course, wholly copied from the ritual of Christianity. What is even more striking is that even the Hindu counter-reformation took over Western modes of religious discipline and propagation. The monastic order founded by Swami Vivekananda had little in common with the pre-existing forms of Hindu monasticism and far more closely approximated to the Christian missionary societies and religious orders.

Conclusive as this antithesis between the old India and the new should be as proof of the foreign-ness of modern Indian civilization, something even more so is to be found in another characteristic displayed by it, and that is its discontinuous evolution. The successive phases of the literature, art, philosophy, and political thought of modern India do not develop out of one another and show no organic connexion. As soon as certain art or thought forms have been acclimatized in India after being adopted through the sheer impulse of imitation, and when they may be expected to lead to the creation of forms which could go on developing from their internal motive force, they are seen to be utterly disrupted and then replaced by quite new forms. It is as if a marching column were being perpetually broken up by flank attacks. A few examples will perhaps make this statement clearer. In Bengali poetry, for instance, the first modern forms were based on Shakespeare and Milton. But Tagore's showed clear signs of breaking away from both the original foreign and the derived Bengali model, and shaping itself after Shelley, Tennyson, and Swinburne. The latest phase of Bengali poetry has seen a disintegration even of the Tagorean tradition by poets who swear by T. S. Eliot, Ezra Pound, Auden, and the like. In art we have seen, successively, imitations of the European academic styles, of Mogul miniatures, of Chinese and Japanese paintings, and, last of all, of the French impressionists and post-impressionists. In political thought Rousseau, Mill and Mazzini have suffered a complete eclipse from the shadow (or the shades!) of Marx. Even the quarrels of the Trotskyites and the Stalinites are being imported with what appears to be quite unnecessary receptivity.

There are many Indians today who, tired by this endless leap-frogging and not eager to reduce culture to the level of fashions, give the widest possible berth to the handiwork of modern Indian writers and painters and live only on the fare provided by the Western masters of these imitators. In truth too, in the cultural creations of modern India, there is only too much which cannot be described as anything better than European cultural forms crudely simplified in order to be brought within the comprehension and artistic capacity of insufficiently educated Indians. For them even the normal Hollywood film has to be stepped down to an Indian level. This dilution is observable in every sphere of cultural activity. But those who can enjoy the originals usually dispense with the copies.

Another, and to my mind the most decisive, indication of the essentially foreign character of the culture of modern India is the attitude of the general body of Indians as much towards it as to its creators and exponents. By far the greater majority of Indians rejected the idea of a synthesis of the civilizations of the East and the West on which this new culture was based even when the synthesis was a living historical force. Today the concept stands wholly discredited. What Indians in the mass want is nationalism, which does not, however, preclude a wholesale and uncritical acceptance, or to be more accurate crude imitation, of Western habits of living and economic technique. This is not as consistent as it might sound, for the concept of nationalism has been working against the concept of synthesis on the conscious plane while the absorption of the Western trends has been taking place on the unconscious and the subconscious. Thus nothing that was achieved or created by means of the highest kind of intellectual, ethical, or spiritual effort of which Indians were capable in the nineteenth century retains any appeal today, and the new Hinduism of Bankim

Chandra Chatterji and Swami Vivekananda has become as alien to modern Indians as Brahmoism.

And even in the best days of the new culture of modern India its unpopularity was transferred to its preachers. Rammohun Roy and Tagore, more especially, were underrated, ridiculed, slandered, and even persecuted in a manner wholly undeserved and unexpected, and this treatment provoked a reaction in the form of an alienation of these two great men from their countrymen. Jacquemont records that Rammohun Roy was a man who always spoke, acted, and in fact lived on the defensive, and he attributes this uneasy behaviour to Ramohun's being attacked so frequently. Tagore on his part was provoked by the attitude of his countrymen to the exhibition of some asperity, and throughout his writing from all periods of his life occur unkind observations about his countrymen, some of which are so bitterly uncharitable that they make even sympathizers with Tagore wince.

Strange to say, there are suggestions of this estrangement even in the leaders of the Hindu counter-reformation. Despite being a Hindu conservative, and not a liberal like Roy or Tagore, Bankim Chandra Chatterji too could not escape disillusionment, and the literary tradition of Bengal has it that he occasionally voiced resentment at not being understood and properly assessed by his own people. Swami Vivekananda, the preacher of new Hinduism, was also conscious of a gulf between himself and the mass of Indians. He normally repressed this feeling, and showed himself as a supporter of the national traditions. But in a fugitive passage in his writings, very wistful in its involuntary slip from the consciously held theory, he seemed to give his case away. "Can you make a European society with India's religion?" he asked, and he answered, "I believe it is possible and must be."

The greatest paradox in this hostility of the general mass of Indians towards the things of the West is that, nearly all our great men of the nineteenth century were not able to gain any recognition from their countrymen nor exert any influence over them until they were recognized in the West. Vivekananda records: "I travelled twelve years all over India, finding no way to work for my countrymen, and that was why I went to America." His countrymen welcomed him back as a great Hindu only when the Parliament of Religions at Chicago had given him an unexpectedly favourable reception. This is also true of Rammohun Roy, Tagore, and Gandhi, and if today Bankim Chandra Chatterji is not as highly rated in his country as Tagore or Gandhi it is largely because he received less European recognition than they. Tagore was looked upon almost as an illiterate person before he received the Nobel Prize. In my matriculation paper in Bengali I was asked to rewrite a passage from him in "chaste and elegant Bengali". This happened in 1914, one year after the award of the Prize, when the backwash of that sensational recognition had not yet penetrated the academic sanctuary.

It is this perversity which makes most great Indians feel like strangers in their land. Jacquemont wrote of Rammohun Roy: "He has known this pain of isolation. He has grown in a region of ideas and feelings which is higher than the world in which his countrymen live; he lives alone; and though perhaps the consciousness of the good he is accomplishing affords him a perpetual source of satisfaction, sadness and melancholy mark his grave countenance." This is true of all of them, a group of alienated, Dantean figures, in death sleeping far away from their ungrateful country.

I wonder if I have been able to make the argument convincing. I am conscious that I have talked rather round the subject than on it, but a real demonstration would require a book, and this is only a short essay. I hope, however, that I have been able at all events to make clear what I mean when I say that the culture of each cycle of Indian history has had a foreign origin and foreign affiliations. I shall now pass on to politics.

Here the thesis can be enunciated even more emphatically than in the case of culture: No great political concept has ever governed political life in India which has not been created by foreigners, and none but foreigners have ever been able to establish and maintain stable political regimes in this country. A partial demonstration of this proposition is being attempted with the Hindu cycle of Indian history. Throughout the historical period of that cycle, roundly extending from 500 B.C. to A.D. 1200, we are confronted by the spectacle of an immense number of dynastic states, rising, disappearing and struggling with one another, at times establishing some sort of an empire through the establishment of the suzerainty of one of the dynastic states over the others, and at times reduced to such disintegration that no coherent picture or unbroken sequence of these states can be established. They are seen rolling down the flanks of the more solidly established Hindu society like loose boulders.

The only parallel to this state of affairs that I can find is in the Islamic world after the decline of the Caliphate. In that epoch the political life of Islam, which in the earliest age had been dominated by a universal state, went on disintegrating till it became the sum-total of a vast number of dynastic states, rising, falling, expanding, shrinking, each in its allotted span of time and section of territory. The process of the emergence of small dynastic states by secession and succession, of their progress towards some sort of an empire by virtue of naked power, and their decline into something less than even a dynastic chieftainship, began in the Islamic world with the secession of Spain from the Caliphate of Baghdad at the very beginning of the Abbasid period. It gained fresh momentum at the death of Al-Mamun, when the Tahirids in Khurasan, the Saffarids in Sejstan, the Tulunids in Egypt and Syria, and the Samanids in Transoxiana and Persia (not to speak of the Idrisids in Morocco and the Aghlabids in Ifriqiah who broke off from the Caliphate during the height of Abbasid power) asserted their virtual independence. This trend went on gaining strength till the political organization of Islam was deprived for some centuries of all stability.

By the end of the tenth century a state of affairs was reached in which not a single constituent of the Islamic political structure—territory, ethnic group, military power, dynasty—remained constant for any length of time. Everything resolved into shifting sand which the winds might blow into chance patterns, but which fundamentally remained incohesive. In the end, the Islamic ecumenical order, considered from the political point of view, was shattered into fragments. The primeval and basic political welter common to all oriental countries was reached. The state became loose down to the last divisible cell, and sovereignty was reduced to the lowest denomination of political power; there was degeneration combined with negation.

One unifying force, however, played on this world, but it was a wild and elemental force: it was the kingdom-hunting urge of men of the soldier-of-fortune type. The emergence of these men was a distinctive feature of Islamic power-politics, which took a pronouncedly individualistic turn. In its highest and most powerful manifestation the individual was a conquistador, in its average a *condottiere,* and if the type of the individual was the soldier of fortune, the type of power, even if not naked in all its aspects, was at least non-traditional. By means of it even a bandit could insult a caliph. The most significant of the individuals, the men who brought about the most sweeping transformations and put in train the most revolutionary developments, were all newcomers to power. They were the *nouveaux riches,* the parvenus, of power. Some of them even suggest the anthropologist's head-hunter. The association of ideas would not be basically unjust, for the crown-hunt as it revealed itself in the Islamic world may justly and correctly be regarded as a sublimation of the more primitive self-assertive urge.

Yaqub ibn-al Lavth al-Saffar, Mahmud of Ghazna, Muizz-ud-din Muhammad bin Sam of Ghur, Timur, Babur–are all examples of this type. Islamic society continued to shoot up these rocket-like personalities even down to the eighteenth century, and two of the last but of the very greatest were Nadir Shah and Ahmad Shah Abdali. In this aspect, too, the Hindu political order of the period from 500 B.C. to A.D. 1200 resembled the Islamic order in the particular phase we are now considering. It produced men–the Pushyamitras, the Satakarnis, the Kanishkas, Samudraguptas, Harshas and a host of others who in a timeless Valhalla would rub friendly shoulders with the Mahmuds and Timurs and Nadirs. Even Asoka belonged to this type in his early life, and the one relatively small provincial conquest he made resulted, according to his own statement, in the slaughter of one hundred thousand men, the death through disease and other causes of many times that number, and the deportation of one hundred and fifty thousand men. Probably the timely conversion to Buddhism of this Hindu king saved him from being classed with Assur-nasir-pal and Nebuchadnezzar.

This remarkable similarity between the course and structure of Hindu politics in historical times and the course and structure of Islamic politics at the time of the decline of the Caliphate and before the re-establishment of stability by the Ottoman, the Safavid, and Mogul dynasties, **leads** one to wonder whether the cause of the instability (combined with the occasional appearance of powerful and large kingdoms) can in both cases be the same. To my mind, there is no doubt that this is so. In the case of Hindu political history our knowledge is confined to the later part, the earlier part is legendary and indefinite. But in regard to the Muslims the whole process is known, and we find from it that the peculiar instability in Islamic politics which we are here considering was the result of the decline of the original political vigour of Islam. Its early political vigour has two tremendous achievements to its credit: first, the expansion of Islam and the creation of an Islamic universal state; and, secondly, the protection of the newborn Islamic society when it was in a process of becoming in a hostile world. But in two hundred years this early energy, the energy of the Arab and a combination of the Arab and the Persian, was exhausted and the Islamic world was swept for the time being by a more predatory form of political energy.

As I see the matter under the influence of the Islamic analogy, in India in the political sphere and in the historical age of the Hindu cycle, a comparable picture was unfolding itself. Hindu society was witnessing the play of a predatory political energy, following the decay of the original political energy which was contributed by the incoming foreign Aryan, who in his political and martial role came to be known as the *Kshattriya*. Kshattriya energy was able to accomplish the colonization of India but was apparently exhausted before it could achieve anything further; and what took its place was a pseudo-Kshattriya energy constituted by three elements: first, the remnants and passing revivals of the old Kshattriya energy; secondly, the aboriginals and other primitive elements of the Indian population who assumed Kshattriyahood; and, thirdly, foreigners coming into India and giving themselves the status of a Kshattriya on the strength of their military prowess. I do not say that these pseudo-Kshattriyas were barbarians; they were no more so than were the Saljuq monarchs, or Mahmud of Ghazna, or Babur, or even Timur. But they could not, by reason of their being the exhausted remnants of the old ruling order or barbarians newly received into the civilized order, create great and lasting political structures.

The analogy becomes more striking still if, together with the political activities, we consider also the political concepts. In the Islamic world we see the hold of one great political concept, arising from the creation and sway of the Islamic universal state, the historic Caliphate, and constituting a theoretical embodiment of the idea of such a state. Islamic political thought was never able to put forward an alternative concept. The theory of a pan-Islamic state was formulated with precision only after the historic Caliphate had decayed beyond any hope of revival. Most nations have evolved politically from the smaller to the larger entity, from the city or tribe to the empire. With the Islamic peoples, however, the order of evolution was reversed. They began with a *de facto* universal state and stepped down to the competition of the disintegrated constituents. But in the field of theory the concept of a single *imperium* for all the Islamic peoples was systematized only when the disintegration of the universal Islamic state had begun. Although Al-Mawardi, the first systematizer, may have intended his exposition to be a practical aid to the power and prestige of the later Abbasids, smarting under Buwayhid tutelage, as things turned out, the theory of Caliphate was only a retrospective and idealistic formulation of the grammar of a vanished reality. But its splendour hovered ever afterwards about the Islamic world, at times spurring the predatory kings to vigorous efforts towards restoring the great *imperium*, at others mocking the actuality of political chaos.

A similar phenomenon is observable in the Hindu cycle of Indian history. The concept of a single pan-Hindu *imperium*, brought into being by the martial energy of the Kshattriya, symbolized by the *Asvamedha,* or horse sacrifice, and resulting in the establishment of a *Dharmarajya,* or Kingdom of Righteousness, was formulated in the early age of Kshattriya power, and Indian political thought created no second political concept for Hindu society considered as a whole. In the historical age we find one Hindu king after another striving to establish his suzerainty, instigated by this concept. Like the Muslim potentates they at times succeeded partially. But for most of the time, the striving resulted only in a fierce civil war among the pseudo-Kshattriyas. The whole of the historical age of the Hindu cycle ran its course without there being created in India a political order properly so-called. Thus it is not surprising that the collective memory of Indians has lost all recollection of the political structures of the historic Hindu cycle. They were, too ephemeral to obtain a lodgment in historical memory. The Muslim conquest only completed the oblivion.

The first political order in India to bring into existence a continuous tradition was established by the Muslim conquerors of India, and it had as its centre the Sultanate of Delhi. Both the leadership and the rank and file of the conquerors were overwhelmingly Turkish, a people noted for political and military ability in the Islamic world. Even when the central authority at Delhi fell into decay, the presence of these Muslim colonists as a ruling order throughout the length and breadth of northern India, and their religious and cultural and social cohesion kept alive the sense of there being a strong and unifying political element in the country, and this feeling, in its turn, sustained the consciousness of continuity and stability in political life. Even when the provincial governors declared themselves independent and set up kingdoms which acknowledged no practical allegiance to Delhi, as they did for instance in Bengal and Gujarat during the Turco-Afghan epoch, they did not undermine the idea of a continuing political order, because, being Muslims and foreigners, they were taken collectively and considered as a single political entity quite distinct from the general mass of the people. When there was no strong central kingdom there still was a strong and homogeneous ruling class. Owing to this fact there was no sense in the country that political power was being sucked in, as by a quicksand, by the larger social soil lying underneath the state, and was having to be thrown out again and again by the same soil in ever diluted strength.

Still, the earlier Muslim rulers were not wholly successful. To begin with, the Muslim conquest of India had taken place when the Islamic world was politically disrupted by the weakness of the Caliphate and the usurpations of the ambitious crown-hunters. *Imarat al-Istila,* or "Amirate by seizure", was an insoluble dilemma for the Islamic theologians, jurists, and political thinkers of this period. To this pre-existing confusion the Mongol irruption brought a further and calamitous addition. The Islamic world, passing through its own times of trouble, could not be expected to bring into being in India a stable political tradition when it did not possess such a thing itself. This achievement was reserved for the Chaghatai or Mogul dynasty. The emperors of that line for the first time established the idea of a common *imperium* for India and made the people of the country look upon such an *imperium,* realized in fact, as an indispensable condition of social existence. Thus it happens that not only the political memories but also the political institutions and habits of contemporary India run back to the reign of Akbar. Nothing in the field of Indian politics can be understood unless traced back continuously to that epoch. Summed up in its bare essentials, the political history of India shows the Aryan, the Turk, the Turko-Mongol *cum* Persian as the only creators of political concepts and political orders in India up to the end of the seventeenth century, and after that the Anglo-Saxon takes their place. The rest have been only sterile imitators when they have either been given opportunities to exercise political functions by the decline of a particular foreign ruling order, or have in their incompetent vanity and xenophobia sought to exercise them. In these intervals there have been seen in India only a futile pursuit of the political concepts of the preceding foreign rulers, inefficient manipulation of the political machinery left by them and, above all, an egregious aping of their arrogance and airs.

Thus the course of Indian history is seen as a process in which three far-reaching movements of world history–the Aryan expansion, the Islamic expansion, and the European expansion – have forced or worked their way into the country and introduced new ethnic elements, new languages, new cultures, new social organizations, and new political concepts and institutions. The mind no less than the blood of the human group living in India has been renovated by them, and all creative effort by this group has been made possible only through these renovations. But the same process has also brought into being a foil to its achievement by depositing an internal proletariat which is incapable of utilizing the present and is always in bondage to the past.

At intervals in Indian history there occur phases which have the appearance of being periods of national freedom and resurgence. In reality, these are only the periods in which the internal proletariat finds an opportunity to rise to the surface. There is no true national resurgence in India because there are no true nationals. What passes as the autochthon of India is only a pseudo-autochthon. No doubt he always stands in opposition to the dominant order, the dominant outlook of mind, and the dominant civilization, but he is only the fossilized remnant of a former dominant order. In a majority of cases he fails to present any determinate character even in fossilization.

I shall cite one or two examples from contemporaneous developments in order to give a touch of concreteness to the argument. In northern India people find it impossible to define the status which India has attained to after the winding-up of British rule without employing either of two foreign words: the English word "independence" and, more frequently, the Persian "azadi". The dress in which the present Prime Minister of India is seen on formal occasions is not a reversion from the English dress he used to put on in his younger days to a Hindu mode: it is a relic of Islamic rule. If the English suit is to be discarded on the ground of its association with political subjection the *sherwani* and the *pajama* have no stronger claims on us. In fact, the disappearance of British rule in India has, in its immediate effects, provided a most interesting demonstration of the Islamization of India and of the Hindu.

Even the maniacal hatred of the Muslim which is sweeping over Hindu India today has not emancipated the Hindu from his Islamic ways. The fierce maenads from the divided Punjab who even in buses mutter imprecations against Muslims have no idea of the true character of their *shalwar* and *kurta*. On the contrary they appear to be inordinately proud of them. Of course, they have every right to their pride, for not Solomon in all his glory was arrayed like one of these, and it is doubtful even if those iridescent creatures of wild nature, the mandrills and the macaws, are none the less, this dress is as Islamic as the *shariat,* and a symbol of the thoroughness with which the Hindu of north-western India sold his body and soul to the Muslim conqueror. The still more surprising fact is that the vogue of the *shalwar* is spreading. Even Bengali women are getting into it, oblivious of the meagre proportions, which do not show to advantage in a garment which at times requires twelve yards of material and when hung up to dry covers at least five feet of the line, and oblivious of the further consideration that one of the most positive tests of Hinduism and

Islamism in the women of northern India used to be the absence or presence of sewn nether garments.

It is in relatively few instances that the withdrawal of British power is leading back Indians to Hindu forms in cultural or even daily life. The movements towards greater Sanskritization of the Hindi language is perhaps one of them. But the truth is that the internal proletariat of India has neither the vitality nor the will-power to go back to any older form deliberately. What it displays is only what is exposed by circumstances extraneous to itself. Thus it happens that what one sees in India today is an immense expanse of debased Europeanization, mottled here and there with Hindu or Muslim traits. For example, even in the most rabid anti-British days excited nationalist crowds did not go for the European dress as such. They attacked only its finer details; they snatched away ties, trampled on hats, pulled out the shirt and made its ends hang over the trousers. Indianized so far, the European dress was left alone. In actual fact, many of the nationalists preferred and prefer to be in a basic (if not base) English dress consisting of a pair of trousers and a sleeveless shirt. The popularity of this dress is increasing even in Bengal, where till recently one had to apologize if seen in the European dress in society. Nowadays the European dress is neither frowned upon nor jeered at, provided it is not too well-cut, nor too complete, nor too clean.

In the same way, in India, during the last twenty years or so, an amazing "mensal" arrogance has been growing. Ever greater numbers of the middle-class are beginning to take their meals on any available kind of table covered with rubber-cloth, sometimes even a writing-table, and eat off brass plates placed on them, helping themselves with ladles. Those who are taking to these new table-manners look down on those who still eat in the old Indian fashion, squatting on the floor, with such incredible snobbery that if it were possible for the tables to absorb even a part of the pride of their owners they would become as resonant and capricious as violins. These are only two aspects of a vast but easy assimilation of European ways. In almost all Indophil Westerners this exhibition induces a deep distress, and they try to persuade themselves and us that what they see is only a crude varnish and the underlying reality is some solid timber. They provide us with various grades of intellectual and spiritual sandpaper to scrape off our unattractive outer finish. We also diligently rub ourselves with them. But what we actually accomplish by the persistent employment of the abrasive is an attenuation of our substance, for we are not solid timber varnished or veneered: we are only plywood.

The *pastiche* which is of the very stuff of our being gains all the greater significance because it is unaccompanied by the possession: of any positive selfhood, or, for that matter, even any striving after it. This statement will sound odd in view of the fanatical group-consciousness which is prevalent in India today. But all this rich and varied group-consciousness is not the consciousness of being something, but the consciousness of not being something else. A Hindu is not a Mussalman; a Mussalman is not a Hindu, a Sikh is neither Hindu nor Mussalman, and so on and so forth. The true definition of a Hindu in contemporary India is that he is a non-Muslim, and that of a Muslim that he is a non-Hindu. If the Hindu were assured the satisfaction of being something inimical to the Muslim and distinct he would not care if everything from the Vedas down to the sacred thread went to the refuse heap. On his part, the Muslim would be ready to forget all about even the *shariat* if he had the assurance of not being merged in the Hindu. Most of the Hindus who nowadays are leaving their ancestral homes and virtually ruining themselves for ever, because these homes have fallen within Pakistan, are unfamiliar even with the *Ramayana* and the *Mahabharata*, and the Muslims of the same category are ignorant even of the *ibadat*, the so-called five pillars or five elementary duties of the Muslim. The fanaticism lies not in conviction but in the hatred felt for the not-self. This group-consciousness is an expression, to apply the diagnosis of M. Benda, of the will of man to establish himself in the real existence. This will is identical with the will to seize some temporal advantage and to feel one's distinctness from everybody else, a will which seeks a double satisfaction, the satisfaction of an interest as well as the satisfaction of a pride.

The explanation of all the aspects of the behaviour of the internal proletariat, including its negation, lies, of course, in the manner of its creation. As the process is cyclical and continuous we have to postulate the existence of the internal proletariat at a given point of time in order to analyse it. Let us then consider the composition of the internal proletariat at the height of vigour of one of the cycles of foreign political and cultural domination of India. At this given moment the internal proletariat is divisible into three classes like the Mendelian hybrid. The first group is constituted by pure recessives, the unadaptive remnants of an old dominant order which are incapable not only of acquiring new values but also of any further development of the old. They are not even good preservers, for they cannot keep the old values healthy and undistorted. In their custody the old values undergo partly petrifaction and partly degeneration. The second class is comprised by the pure dominants who, rising from the most adaptive part of the proletariat, join the new order. The character and functions of this class do not stand in need of explanation. The third group is by far the largest and it is composed of what may be called false dominants, who breed both recessives and dominants according to circumstances. The character and behaviour of this group depend entirely on the power and energy of the foreign dominant order. If that remains strong the ponderous mass of the pseudo-dominants behaves in one way, and if not in quite another.

Now let us see what happens when the dominant foreign order of one cycle decays. By the very process of its decay it adds a new stratum to the recessive elements pre-existing in the internal proletariat, and the newest recessives also show themselves to be most virulent of the retrograde influences. This is best illustrated by the attitude of the Indian Muslims (consisting of one-time colonists and indigenous converts) from the end of the eighteenth century to the end of the nineteenth. The loss of political power did not bring in its wake the moral acquiescence of the Indian Muslim in British rule. In a military report on the attitude of Oudh Muslims towards British rule submitted in the late 'seventies of the last century, they were described as being in a state of "impotent disaffection". The whole Muslim community in India may be said to have remained in a state of "impotent disaffection" long after it had relinquished all hope of reviving and re-establishing its political power. Their defeat at the hands of the British left the Muslims in a wilderness, dazed and staggering, but irreconcilable. The remnants of the Hindu dominant order displayed similar characteristics during Muslim rule.

What happens in the next phase is connected with the fortunes of the great mass of the false dominants. With the disappearance of the dominant power they begin partly to breed recessives, but for the most part they run wild. Thus, periodically, the greater portion of the internal proletariat of India is rebarbarized, and this rebarbarization is very important for the propagation of the culture of the next dominant order. The indigenous converts to the new dominant order come wholly from the false dominants of the older, who have run wild in the meanwhile.

This part of the process is best illustrated by the role of the Bengali middle-class in building up the culture of modern India. Bengal, even in the great days of Indo-Aryan and Indo-Muslim civilization, was an outlying region, the Balkans of India; it relapsed into cultural colourlessness very quickly, once at the end of Hindu rule, and for a second time at the end of the Muhamadan. The first relapse has given to Bengal its large Muslim population and has been responsible for the partition of the province in our days; the second relapse made the Bengali the earliest and most successful agent of the Europeanization of India in the best sense of the term. The Hindu intelligentsia of Bengal having been rebarbarized most thoroughly were best able to accept the new values promptly. The process is similar to that of restoring the fertility of land by allowing it to lie fallow. Without this running wild of a great portion of the internal proletariat, the cyclical emergence of civilizations and political orders in India under foreign influence and leadership would have been more difficult.

Thus in the course of history the internal proletariat of India is being perpetually reinforced by the same foreign motive power which is keeping the country within the orbit of civilization. But with its enlargement the proletariat is undergoing a twofold change. In the first place it is becoming more heterogeneous and, consequently, more rancorous. As each dominant foreign influence passes away, there appears within the internal proletariat a new retrograde and atavistic element, which, while it is ready to unite with the older retrograde elements in the common hostility to the dominant power, is fundamentally irreconcilable with them. Peace is maintained among these pariahs of the internal proletariat, or from another point of view its Brahmins, by the dominant power, primarily by means of its strength, and indirectly by the hatred which it inspires. But as soon as the dominant power disappears the inherent disharmony of the internal proletariat comes into play.

Its heterogeneous components snarl at one another and fly at one another's throat like jackals and hyenas after the departure of the tiger. This disgusting squabble lasts until the king of the jungle reappears, bringing with him peace.

Secondly, every additional cycle of Indian history brings about an alteration of the ratio between the rancorous and atavistic part of the internal proletariat and that other part which is capable of rebarbarization, to the disadvantage of the second part. Fossils possessing only the venom of living things gain on those who retain potentiality for growth, even though for no other end than the acceptance and imitation of the values and ways of the dominant civilization of the day. While civilization has been decaying and reviving cyclically in India, within the internal proletariat, the number of those who can be reclaimed to civilized life has been decreasing from cycle to cycle. Although India has never yet been betrayed by the greatest and strongest historical movements, the field of their operation is becoming increasingly barren.

The interplay of the foreign element and the internal proletariat has given to the course of Indian history the form of a struggle, and the continuity of the struggle is the fact which invests the foreign affiliations of Indian society and civilization with their special importance and meaning. In one sense the emphasis on foreign affiliations is pointless, for there have been few civilizations whose origins cannot be traced to a source lying outside the geographical limits of the region in which they have come to maturity, and there are few nations which can be called pure autochthons. Foreign affiliation in this form is universal. But in speaking of the foreign affiliations of Indian civilization I do not have this commonplace in mind. The foreign influences in Indian history are exceptional in their character, and are also exceptional in their operation and results. These exceptional and significant features may be summarized under the following heads: first, three of the greatest historical movements have forced their way into India in successive ages and created three different types of civilization; secondly, the civilizations have remained essentially foreign even at the highest point of their development within India and have ceased to be living as soon as they have been cut off from the source and been assimilated by the previously existing population; thirdly, the civilizations have always been in conflict with the greater portion of the local population; and, lastly, neither political order nor civilization has come into being in India when a powerful external force has not been in possession of the country. I do not know of any other country exhibiting these features in its history. The normal course is for foreign influences, whether cultural or ethnic, to fuse with the pre-existing elements, unfold as a synthesis, and then decay for ever. The regular ebb and flow, the ever-present conflict, and the inevitable involvement in the greatest movements of history appear to be unique to India.

This struggle which is one of the constants of Indian history, has the outward appearance of being a conflict between a foreign aristocracy and an internal proletariat; but in reality the internal proletariat is a passive element, the active opponent of the foreign aristocracy is the country and its climate. There are many geographical regions in the world which are utterly incapable of developing a high civilization, but there is perhaps not one other which so irresistibly draws civilizations to it, and strangles them as irresistibly as does the Indo-Gangetic plain. It is the Vampire of geography, which sucks out all creative energy and leaves its victims as listless shadows. The high mean temperature, together with its immense daily range of rise and fall, hardly allows the body to attend to anything more fruitful than the daily adaptation to the weather. The unbroken flatness of the plain finds its counterpart in dullness of the mind, monotony of experience, and narrowness of interests. With this climate and physiography is combined a diet which is so highly adapted to the environment that it is as fatal to creative energy as the other two. Starch seasoned with spices is the typical food of the Indo-Gangetic plain, and it is capable of nurturing no other forms of human activity or outlook on life than what possesses its own insipidity.

This terrible *milieu* has told on all the foreign immigrants into India. Platitudinous as this statement has become, it is still the inescapable truth. I do not know what air-conditioning and artificial regulation of temperature may do for the future, but so far no foreigner in India—Aryan, Turk, or Anglo–Saxon–has been able to escape the consequences of living in the Indo-Gangetic plain. His energy has been drained, his vitality sapped, and his will and idealism enfeebled. Thus, in the last resort, the perpetuation of the foreigner's rule and cultural function in India has been dependent on continuous reinforcement from the home territory. As long as the peoples or the civilizations which have come into India have remained vigorous in the homelands and have been able to reinforce the colonial wing, all has gone well with political regimes and cultures in India. But both have fallen into decay as soon as the source has become weak or exhausted. In this process the internal proletariat has played a passive part. It has only risen to the surface like scum in stagnant waters. There is not a single example in Indian history of the internal proletariat's success in overthrowing a foreign Power by means of its own strength and efforts. Nor would anyone expect it to do so, for the geographical environment works more continuously on the internal proletariat than on the foreigner. When one group of foreigners is exhausted by it there is another to take its place. But the internal proletariat is not replenished by new stock. Its debilitation has neither been healed nor interrupted. Thus at every given point of time the degeneracy of the proletariat is greater than the degeneracy of the foreign ruler.

I shall illustrate the process of decline of the foreigner's political power in India with the example of the downfall of the Mogul Empire. Influenced by the doctrines and emotional predispositions of nationalism modern historians often isolate the Islamic cycle of Indian history from its pan-Islamic setting and regard it as a self-contained national unit. This artificial restriction of the field of view has confused the search for the causes of the decline of the Mogul Empire, leading historians to exaggerate secondary factors or represent symptoms as causes. Cliches about the intolerance of Aurangzib exhaust their usefulness as soon as they have drawn attention to the immediate occasion of the revolts of the Rajputs and the Marathas, which were the first symptoms of the decline of Mogul power in India. They become irrelevant beyond that point. There were other Muslim monarchs of India who were not less intolerant of Hinduism than Aurangzib. None of the founders of Muslim power in India with the exception of Akbar–Sultan Mahmud, Muizzud-din Muhammad bin Sam, Qutb-ud-din Aibak, Alauddin Khalji, were noted for any particular affection for the Hindus. Nor was an Islamic society brought into being from the shores of the Atlantic to the banks of the Oxus by adopting the principle of perfect equality between the conqueror and the unconverted conquered. If an empire is founded as well as destroyed by intolerance, then intolerance ceases to have any causal significance for any part of the process.

The fact of the matter is that the harmful effect of an intolerant policy is dependent entirely upon the ratio of power between the parties concerned. The intolerance of the Red Indian by the American European has created no worse troubles for the United States than has the tolerance of the East Indian by the Englishman for Great Britain. It is the pursuit of a strong policy when the requisite strength is absent which is harmful. But even then tolerance and intolerance are factors of minor importance. No amount of tolerance can save an empire which has lost its vitality. Intolerance at the worst can but hasten its decline.

Again, the attribution of the decline of the Mogul Empire to the uprising of the Hindu element, Maratha or Rajput, certainly rests on wrong assumptions: one wrong assumption regarding the real basis of Muslim political power in India; and another in respect of the attitude of the Hindus to Muslim rule. Tolerance or no tolerance, the Hindus of India were never reconciled to Muslim rule and were never prepared to accept it as anything but an unavoidable and necessary evil to be endured only as long as the hated and unclean foreigner had the strength to maintain his domination. The Rajputs were in perpetual revolt, and if the Maratha revolt came towards the end of the Mogul Empire it was contemporaneous with the attempt of the Moguls to bring the Deccan completely under their rule, and it could not be put down only because the empire had lost its strength. Aurangzib's son, Bahadur Shah, certainly had an opportunity to crush the Marathas finally, but he did not make use of the opportunity. By that time the empire had ceased to receive new administrators and soldiers from Iran and Turkestan, and the resident Muslims were too degenerate. In the ultimate analysis Muslim rule in India never rested on anything but its own strength. It was created, renovated, and maintained at every stage primarily by the innate vitality of Islamic society, and it perished only when that source ran dry.

This will become evident, almost self-evident, if we consider the decline of the Mogul Empire in India in its larger framework. What was in decay in the eighteenth century was not a single Muslim state, but a whole family of them. Along with the Mogul state in India, its cousins outside and children within were all in a state of confirmed decline or congenital feebleness. The   strength of all the three dynastic empires which constituted the political triad of later Islamic history was ebbing away. The greatness of the Ottoman Empire began to pass away not long after its apogee under Suleyman the Magnificent, the power of the Safavids disappeared before the first quarter of the eighteenth century was completed and the ineffectiveness of the Mogul Empire became patent with the death of Bahadur Shah I in 1712. The political exhaustion was pan-Islamic.

There is, besides, the final outcome to consider. The Muslim in India was supplanted, not by the internal proletariat, but by the Englishman. The entry of the European into the country was quiet and disguised, so much so that writing towards the end of the eighteenth century, the French orientalist, Anquetil Du Perron, put forward the thesis that a revival of the political power of the indigenous elements was taking place in India. Yet this European writer should have been the last person to lose sight of the larger background of the English conquest of India, which was only one of the aspects of the secular struggle of the European peoples with the Muslims. The struggle had begun with the very emergence of Islam, but the new Europe which was rising out of the ruins of the Roman Empire did not become involved in it until the Arabs came to Spain. After that the conflict continued through Tours, the Crusades, the expulsion of the Moors from Spain, the siege of Malta, Lepanto, and the two sieges of Vienna, and perhaps it is still continuing. By the eighteenth century, however, Europe had definitely gained the upper hand and forced the Islamic world to the defensive. In this phase, Austria and Russia delivered the attack on the land side, while the maritime power of the western European countries enabled them to take the Islamic world in the rear in India and the Indian Archipelago. This aspect of the colonial expansion of the European peoples was overlooked by contemporaries and is still overlooked. But it was the force generated by this tremendous historical phenomenon which was taking India in its stride in the eighteenth century. The revolt of the internal proletariat against Muslim rule was only the ass's kicking of the sick lion.

After what has been written so far I do not think my readers are waiting for me to set down in so many words my diagnosis of the present moment of our history. They must be assuming that it is something like what follows: that the third cycle of Indian history with its affiliation to Great Britain has come to an end; that the British people, weakened by circumstances which neither originated nor developed in India, have had to relax their hold on India and the internal proletariat has risen to fill the void; and that the waning of the British power with its complement of the self-assertion of the proletariat is the subject of this book. They must be wondering also whether I am looking to any particular nation of the present-day world to set in motion the forces which will establish a fourth foreign affiliation for India, and, not seeing any obvious signs of any country getting ready to do so, they may doubt whether my generalizations about what has happened in the past are likely to remain valid for the future.

My readers would be partly right in attributing these views to me and in raising the question of the future, but I shall surprise them by adding that I do not regard the present juncture of our history at all as the true end of the third cycle, in which India is affiliated to Europe. As I see it, it is a period of oscillation within the third cycle, in which the foreign Power concerned is passing through its times of trouble and of moulting. Such oscillations in any particular foreign Power's hold on India, qualitatively very similar to the true end of a cycle but quantitatively not so thoroughgoing and decisive, are common in Indian history, and they create the illusion of an Indian autarchy.

In the Hindu cycle there were quite a number of such interludes, and in the next cycle the period lying between the invasion of Timur and the invasion of Babur was certainly such a phase. In the same manner, today, the power of Europe in India appears to be passing through a period of eclipse owing to the existence of an internal crisis in the evolution of the European world. Old Europe has been weakened by the internecine wars of its national states, just as the Greek city states were weakened by their internecine feuds. The European peoples are, however, reorganizing themselves on a broader geographical basis round the Atlantic under the leadership of the United States, which already occupies the position of leader in the new Europe which has come into being across the Atlantic. This far-reaching reorganization of Europe is now going on, but it is still not complete. Therefore old Europe is yet in the throes of a crisis, and this crisis cannot but affect its relations with the rest of the world. The ebb-tide of European power in Asia which we are seeing today is one aspect of the altered relationship.

But this unsettled state of affairs cannot continue indefinitely. As soon as Europe has recreated and renovated itself there is likely to be a reassertion of the old domination, perhaps in a more intensive and extensive form. Great Britain's place in this renovated Europe is not a material consideration for India. The foreign affiliation of the third cycle of Indian history must be regarded, in any correct view of it, as being European rather than merely British, and as such not necessarily involved in the national vicissitudes of the English people. The European affiliation of India is not bound to keep company with British decline. At this moment, however, it is not necessary to postulate a British decline. Britain may secure an important and honoured place in the reorganized and greater Europe, which is clearly going to have an Anglo-Saxon leadership constituted by a fraternal association of the British Commonwealth and the United States. Working within the emerging polity of the larger Europe, the Anglo-Saxon can be expected to lay claim to a special association with India on historical grounds. In plain words I expect either the United States singly or a combination of the United States and the British Commonwealth to re-establish and rejuvenate the foreign domination of India.

What fruit this reimposition of foreign rule will bear in the field of culture and politics is a question on which it is possible only to speculate. But history furnishes us with some guidance. Three distinct civilizations and three distinct political orders have been created in the past in India through foreign affiliations. But there has been a difference, a qualitative difference, between the creations in the cultural sphere and the achievements in the political. In the field of culture there has been a decrease in quality from cycle to cycle, while in the field of politics there has been an increase. Of the three historical civilizations that have arisen so far in India–the Indo-Aryan, the Indo-Islamic, and the Indo-European–by far the most original and massive was the first. The creations of the second cycle, though magnificent, were on a lower plane, while the culture of the third phase has proved to be the least solid and individual of the three. The civilization of ancient India did not stand in the main line of the cultural evolution of mankind. It was a collateral specimen. None the less, it was a great civilization, taking its place in its own right by the side of the greatest civilizations known to history. The civilization of the next cycle stood on a lower plane; it was a branch and variety of the Islamic civilization, though it was a rich branch which Islam could not afford to do without, and without reckoning which the cultural record of Islam would have been poorer. The civilization of the third cycle stands on an altogether lower level. It is purely imitative, though some of it is very fine imitation. Here the question has been, not of making an Indian contribution to European civilization, but of creating an Indian version of European civilization in our own interest, for our private use, and in order to keep ourselves within the pale.of civilized life. From cycle to cycle the cultural worth and individuality of India has been decreasing.

The political organization of India, on the contrary, has been becoming stronger, more unified, and more perfect from cycle to cycle. Hindu political capacity could not accomplish much beyond the colonization of India and the imposition of a sort of generic unity in the country's linguistic, cultural and social forms. In addition, it left behind the idea of a pan-Hindu political order, but such attempts as it made to realize this ideal in practice left no mark on the traditions and habits of the people of India. The Muslims carried the unfinished political task very much farther. Although they also could not finally unify India, they left the idea of an all-India political order firmly fixed in the collective consciousness and the habit of obeying a central authority better established than it was before they came. In the third cycle another long step forward was taken, and although even the Englishman was not able to complete the task, India under his domination attained a level of political organization which was the highest in her long history. Thus, while in the cultural sphere India has been running down from cycle to cycle, beginning with creation and ending in imitation, in the political sphere she has been winding up from inchoateness to organization.

At the root of both lies the ethnic factor. The civilization of the first historical cycle of India was the most original and massive because it was the creation of foreigners who had settled down in the country in large numbers and virtually swamped the older population. The cultural creations of the next cycle were the work of a smaller number of foreigners, helped by indigenous converts and reinforced from time to time by immigrants from the home territory of Islamic civilization. The civilization of the third age was the handiwork almost wholly of the indigenous elements. Thus, with the progressive dilution of the foreign element, there has also been a dilution of the quality of the culture. But the political evolution of India has not been affected by this ethnic dilution. It has been influenced by the ethnic factor in a different manner. The political capacity of each successive foreign element in India has been higher than that of its predecessor. The Turk had greater political ability than the Hindu, and the Anglo-Saxon greater than the Turk. The qualitative gain in the political field in each cycle of Indian history is attributable to this cause.

Projecting the past into the future it is permissible to anticipate that we shall be more imitative in the cultural field and more organized in the political. I am not saddened by the first possibility. Although I do believe that individual Indians will be born who will be capable of making notable contributions to the world civilization of the future, collectively, we shall never again achieve anything like the greatness and individuality of the Hindu civilization. That civilization is dead for ever, and cannot be resuscitated, and to hope to create a second civilization of the same order is for us today a superannuated piece of folly. It is too late to be ambitious.

The question with us is only the question of remaining within the orbit of civilized life. We Hindus boast that while all other ancient nations and civilizations have passed away, we and our civilization still survive. This is a perverse boast, inasmuch as our survival is only a mummified continuity, and to be thus extant is, to quote Sir Thomas Browne, only a fallacy in duration. But we may and should cherish the more natural and legitimate ambition of escaping the doom of petrifaction that hangs over everything that lives, the doom of passing from the stage of becoming to that of mere being that has overtaken the greater part of the universe and even organic nature. If the history of the universe shows anything it shows reality as a process, a process which is always casting up and casting off, carrying forward and leaving behind. As it forges on, the process is always leaving behind as mere being the greater portion of what it is begetting. Most things, most creatures, and most nations have thus been inexorably left behind, but through a miracle of history we in India have escaped the doom. We have been drawn thrice into the stream of life of becoming, of civilization, and rescued from petrifaction, though in the normal course of history we should have become dead. Today the doom is again knocking at our door, the hand of the mummy is beckoning to us, and we have only to surrender ourselves to the hour to become an archaeological site. At this moment of our history the instinct of life impels me to look abroad, for it is only through a renewed affiliation with the countries which stand in the mainstream of human evolution that we can hope to live. The choice before us is of revolving round ourselves to die, or of revolving round a sun in order to live.

I have laid my cards on the table. Some will be angered by my views, some will cavalierly brush them aside, but the greater majority of my countrymen will not even perceive that there is anything to object to or to endorse–they will ignore me. I cannot control any of these reactions, but for myself I can say that nobody could be more conscious than I am of the pitfalls which lie in the path of the man who wants to discover the truth about contemporary India. The imagination and even the reason of modern Indians are dominated by a vast and strange body of myths. The word myth is used here as the synonym of the German term *Mythos* or *Mythus,* which has been defined in a German dictionary as "a symbolic idea with life-renewing force", and explained by a German writer in the following words: "Myth is the word and the vision which tells about the *Volk* and God, about what has really happened." I am indebted for these definitions to Dr. Stirk's essay in the book *The*

German Mind and Outlook, and I should like to quote his own language in order to indicate the mental state of the victim of myths. Dr. Stirk says: "The German with whom one was talking would go off at a tangent; his eyes would shine and take on a far-away look; and in superior and often chiding tones he would utter such words and phrases as 'Aber, der Fuhrer!', or 'Der Hitler weiss am besten!'; or he would rave about 'deutsche Niebelungentreue,' or 'das Reich der Deutschen', or 'die Stimme des Blutes', or 'Blut und Boden'." There are Indian equivalents for each of these formulae. The only difference between the myth-mad German and the myth-mad Indian is that the fit has no lucid moments in the Indian, and he is more messianic than historical.

If this is the main obstacle to vision on our side of the fence, an incessant drizzle of praise with the same obscuring effect on truth is beating down on us from a wholly unexpected occidental, and more especially English, monsoon. I never had any idea that Englishmen could be so fulsome, having been more used to seeing them giving demonstrations, sometimes unnecessary demonstrations, of their famous national reserve. After the publication of the English translation of the *Gitanjali* there was a proposal to confer a degree of doctorate of Oxford on Tagore. Upon this Lord Curzon as Chancellor sought information from Sir Denison Ross, the Orientalist, whether Tagore was up to the mark, and with a disarmingly naive expression of John Bull's disbelief in the merits of foreigners completed the query by throwing out a hint himself that Tagore was not. Today Indians of far lesser calibre are being advertised by a class of fawning Englishmen as some of the greatest men of the modern world. The yahoos of the past have become the houyhnhnms of the present.

I may be asked what harm is there in burying the hatchet and letting bygones be bygones in the interest of a better future.

I shall reply that there is distinct harm, because in the circumstances which exist today this friendliness can only foster a
repulsive growth of opportunism and hypocrisy. Neither the
Englishman nor the Indian has yet earned the right to forget the
past. Bad blood is let out only when one brave man meets
another brave man in a clean fight. It is not neutralized by an
understanding of expediency. A Botha or a Smuts could shake
hands with a Milner because the Boer had fought the Englishman and the Englishman had fought the Boer. As between
Indians and Englishmen this purification by fire has not taken
place. When I remember how until even ten years ago all those
Englishmen who had anything to do with us or our country, as
a rule, denied every capability and every quality in us, and when
I set the interested superciliousness of yesterday against the
interested complaisance of today, I blush for the English
character, and my shame is not lessened by the manner of the
flattery. It is being ladled out to us with an intellectual
incompetence and vulgarity of language, a combination of
poor knowledge, poorer logic, and the poorest conceivable
English–that marks the men without elevation of character
who are its purveyors also as an unutterable *canaille ecrivante
et parlante*. Let me also make it clear that I disapprove equally
of the conduct of those Indians who, after crediting the
Englishman with every form of falsehood, deceit, and treachery till yesterday, and regarding him literally as Satan, have
today suddenly become aware of his virtues. Altogether, I feel
an unconquerable revulsion from this new friendliness. For me
its visual complement is a collection of faces so greasily made
up that as the lips open to utter the inane and yet leering
civilities thick drops of greenish oil seem to roll out of them.
My notion of what is proper and honest between Englishmen
and Indians today is clear-cut and decisive. I feel that the only
course of conduct permissible to either side in their political

and public relations at the present moment is an honourable taciturnity. The rest must be left to the healing powers of Time.

Thus, taken between the native obscurant and the foreign, India is becoming a *terra incognita;* she is being annexed to that vast stretch of the Eurasiatic continent, already including in it the Soviet Union and China, which is barred to truth, and out of which only partisan voices can reach the outside world. But throughout my life I have tried to remain free from the influence of the myths to which my countrymen have succumbed, realizing what a suicidal thing it is for a nation to have a false view of its history and consequently of its future. Even if I had not been warned on this score by my reading of history, I have been warned by the awful spectacle of the ruin the Germans and the Japanese have brought on themselves through their adherence to myths.

Therefore, having set myself to find the truth about my country, I have not spared myself either the toil of investigation or the check of criticism. The thesis of this book has been taking shape in my mind for over twenty years. At various times during this period I felt inclined or tempted to set it down in writing. But I always refrained, not caring to put forward conclusions of whose soundness I was not fully convinced. Besides, I was not willing to publish anything which could be read as an indictment of my people so long as I entertained the slightest hope of being disproved by them. At last, in May 1947, I began work on the book, and I did so only when the conviction was forced on me that unless I acted promptly the demonstration of my thesis was likely to precede its enunciation. But even then I had no suspicion that such a confirmation of the main idea of the book would be provided as has been during the two years over which for want of leisure the writing of the book had to be spread. There are many passages in the book which will read like reflections after the event whereas actually they were written in anticipation. In no case have these passages been retouched.(1)

Those who will read the book will, I hope, take into account the toil and the criticism which have gone to its making. The conclusions embodied in it are not the first half-baked ideas that came into my mind. Nor are they to be put to the sole proof of the daily flux of events, which when not correlated over a fairly long period of time is, on account of the refraction it generates, more of a hindrance than a help in grasping large historical perspectives. Therefore, if I have tried to arrive at conclusions which will remain valid for all time, I have also taken a very large field and body of reference from which to draw these conclusions. I have read the history of my country, a history of some three thousand years, and tried to connect it with what is known of the entire history of mankind. I have also observed the events and phenomena around me in my own life. I have meditated over what I have read and what I have observed, formulated conclusions and rejected them, until those that survived became irresistible. I believe they now stand clear of subjective and passing clouds and embody a more or less sound view of Indian history, which can be left with some confidence to be tested by time.

From the personal standpoint, this historical thesis has emancipated me from a malaise that has haunted me throughout my life. During the years of my education I was becoming a stranger to my environment and organizing my intellectual and moral life along an independent nexus; in the next ten years I was oppressed by a feeling of antagonism to the environment;

---

(1) Two more years have intervened between the completion of the book and its publication, making the explanation given in the text still more necessary. – N.C.C.

and in the last phase I became hostile to it. When I was young and immature, I was led by this maladjustment to strike a Byronic attitude. I thought I was born to be misunderstood and rebellious. I have been cured of this habit of posturing. Today I nurse no grievance, because I have at last unravelled the genesis and growth of my maladjustment. The process was simply this: that while I was being carried along by the momentum of our history, most of my countrymen were being dragged backwards by its inertia. We had been travelling in opposite directions, and are still doing so. I can now see both the motions as from an independent point in space. I have found liberation from a nightmare.

This is something–this emancipation. These are indeed the days of emancipation for *all* in India. But there is an essential difference between the emancipation of one man and that of the rest of the four hundred million. They are freedmen, I am a free man, and though I do not know why I should have been singled out for so great a gift of grace, I am grateful to the God of Life and Creation for it. Yet this is not the whole story. I should be guilty of the blackest ingratitude to life if I were to say that on the eve of my exit from the universe as a conscient being I am only resigned to it. For long years I thought that the best which that thinking reed, man, could do was to go on maintaining an unyielding defiance to the universe. I subscribed to a creed of intellectual Promethenism and repeated in the words of one of the greatest of my masters, and in despair and pain:

"The entire universe does not have to take up arms in order to crush man; a whiff of vapour, a drop of water is enough to kill him. But when the universe crushes man, he is still greater than that by which he is killed. For he knows that he dies and is also aware of the advantage which the universe has over him; the universe knows nothing of all this."

But in the last five or six years, through another miracle, I have been enabled to put an end to this duality and found peace in a new form of monism. I have come to see that I and the universe are inseparable, because I am only a particle of the universe and remain so in every manifestation of my exist-ence—intellectual, moral, and spiritual, as well as physical. Thus on the one hand I have been disenthralled by knowledge. On the other I have believed in order to understand, and have been rewarded with joy. I have found that to sit by the rivers of Babylon is not necessarily to weep in Hebraic sorrow. Today, borne on a great flood of faith, hope, and joy in the midst of infinite degradation, I feel that I shall be content to be nothing for ever after death in the ecstasy of having lived and been alive for a moment. I have made the discovery that the last act is glorious however squalid the play may be in all the rest.

POSTSCRIPT

Certain passages in this final chapter may require some elucidation:

P. 564.– The Dravidian theory referred to was already popular in my college days, long before the discovery of the pre-historic culture of the Indus basin. Its motives were largely emotional. At first it was preached by the Hindu liberals who wanted to counteract the Aryanism of the Hindu conserva-tives. Later the patriotic eagerness to discount all foreign influences on India gained wider currency for it. The now fashionable theory of the derivation of certain elements of the Hindu civilization from the Harappa culture is only an applica-tion of the older concept to a new set of facts. Most of the speculation on this subject appears to be distressingly lacking in scholarly caution.

P. 598.– The passage "... not seeing any obvious signs", etc., was written before the momentum of Russian expansionism had become as evident in Asia as it is today, but I always felt that the future of India was involved in the American-Soviet conflict. It is my conviction, however, that in Asia as elsewhere it will be America which will win in the end. The paragraphs following this passage were written even before the conclusion of the Brussels Treaty.

P. 606.– The China referred to is Kuomintang China. The passage reflects my view that democratic professions can be made to serve untruth as readily as Communism, and that this confidence trick by the oligarchs (in the Platonic sense) of Asia is the most insidious trap that lies in the path of the Western democracies.

I would further add that the precise meaning of the Arabic word *asabiya* (p. 461) is in some doubt, and also that no English translation of Tagore's *Valaka* (p. 370) exists, although there is a French translation by Kalidas Nag and Pierre-Jean Jouve. But I have been told that the poem to which I refer was published in an English translation in *The Times* in 1916.

N.C.C.

THE CONTINENT OF CIRCE

NIRAD C. CHAUDHURI

THIS BOOK, the result of a life-time's effort to understand the nature of things Indian, describes the human situation in India after independence. Applying the historical method, the author sees no staticity in it, but discovers a continuing, dynamic, and even explosive process, within which history and geography have worked to create dissimilar communities and endless conflicts. The account is therefore a 'motion-picture', which links events as recent as Nehru's death with those as far off as the Aryan migrations in a coherent, though shifting, perspective, and which also reveals that the grip of their established traditions on all the communities has not relaxed.

The human groups dealt with are the Aboriginals, Hindus with their Anglicized variety, Muslims, Eurasians, and Indian Christians. The main feature of the book is the imaginative interpretation of the Hindu personality based on original sources. The author puts forward the revolutionary thesis that the Hindus are really Europeans in India, corrupted and denatured by the tropical environment. The geographical setting, whose stupefying essence pervades the book, exerts its baleful influences on all the incoming peoples, for which reason the author has called India the Continent of Circe.